Welcome to your *Kaplan NCLEX-PN® Course*. Use the guidelines below as you prepare for your class and during ongoing preparation for the examination.

## Kaptest.com Students

Before the first class, complete the following:

❑ You will receive an email with instructions to set up your password. If you do not receive one, go to www.kaptest.com, click "Log In," then select "Forgot your password?"

❑ Complete the user profile on the home page. Read and accept the enrollment agreement.

❑ Review the technical requirements to assure trouble-free access to the online resources.

❑ Go to the course syllabus by clicking on the link under the heading "My Courses."

❑ Prior to class, read chapters 1 to 9 in the *NCLEX-PN® Content Review Guide*.

❑ Prior to class, review any client need areas identified as weaknesses by viewing the Online Content Lectures found in Phase One of your syllabus. Follow this *NCLEX-PN® Content Review Guide* as you view the videos.

❑ If you have additional questions regarding your Kaplan NCLEX-PN® program, first sign in to your student homepage and select "Help."

## Students: https://nursing.kaplan.com

Before the first class, complete the following:

❑ Your resources are located on the Kaplan/Institutional Testing website, at https://nursing.kaplan.com. Use the same user name and password you used during school. If you cannot remember your user name and password, contact 1-877-572-8457.

❑ Click on the NCLEX-PN® Prep link on your homepage to access the Kaplan NCLEX-PN® resources.

❑ Prior to class, review any client need areas identified as weaknesses by viewing the Online Content Lectures found in Phase One of your syllabus. Follow this *NCLEX-PN® Content Review Guide* as you view the videos.

❑ Follow this *NCLEX-PN® Content Review Guide*.

# NCLEX-PN®
# Content Review Guide

THIRD EDITION

Published by Kaplan Publishing, a division of Kaplan, Inc.
395 Hudson Street
New York, NY 10014

Printed in the United States of America

10 9 8 7 6 5 4 3 2 1

ISBN: 978-1-62523-246-5 | Item Number: RN5052F

**Barbara J. Irwin, M.S.N., R.N.**
*Executive Director of Nursing*

**Barbara Arnoldussen, M.B.A., R.N.**

**Judith A. Burckhardt, Ph.D., R.N.**

**Barbara Dobish, M.S.N., R.N.**

**Cindy Finesilver, M.S.N., R.N.**

**Pamela Gardner, M.S.N., R.N.**

**Ellen Mahoney, C.S., D.N.S., R.N.**

**Marlene Redemske, M.S.N., M.A., R.N.**

Welcome! By joining our program, you've taken an important step toward passing the National Council Licensure Examination for Practical Nurses (NCLEX-PN®).

Our many years of experience indicate that your success on the NCLEX-PN® examination is keyed to two specific factors: your educational background and your exam preparation. It is the amount and intensity of study you devote to our course that will earn you the greatest benefit from the materials. The best results come to those who actively participate in test preparation. We are your coaches. We'll show you how the NCLEX-PN® examination works, what you do and don't need to know, and the smartest way to take the NCLEX-PN® examination. We'll help you analyze your practice performance and show you where you need to make improvements. We will give you all the help, advice, and encouragement we can, but only you can do the work. Get to know all the benefits the Kaplan® Review for the NCLEX-PN® examination has to offer so you can make the most of your study time.

If you have any questions, please ask your Kaplan faculty or nursing school faculty. The more you know, the better your chances for success on the NCLEX-PN® examination.

After you complete your course and take the NCLEX-PN® examination, please tell us how you did. Kaplan's Research and Curriculum Development Team works hard to ensure that your course materials reflect the latest subtle changes in the NCLEX-PN® examination and that our lessons employ the most effective and innovative teaching methods. In order to evolve and improve, we need your help. Please take a few moments to share your thoughts on how the course helped you by completing the end-of-course survey. Thank you in advance for choosing Kaplan for your studies.

KAPLAN
395 Hudson Street
New York, NY 10014
Attn: NCLEX Curriculum

Or send us an email at:
NCLEX-Expert@Kaplan.com
customer.care@kaplan.com (kaptest.com)

Our best wishes for an interesting and satisfying nursing career.

*NCLEX is a trademark of N.C.S.B.N., Inc.

*Please note: All Kaplan lectures, web content, and printed and electronic media are the property of Kaplan Nursing and are copyrighted under law.*

# Contents

**Chapter 1**  **The NCLEX-PN® Examination**

➤ Unit 1: The NCLEX-PN® Examination . . . . . . . . . . . . . . . . . . . . . . . . . . . . . . . . . . . . . . 3
➤ Unit 2: Guide for Test-Takers Repeating the NCLEX-PN® Examination . . . . . . . . . . . . 7

**Chapter 2**  **Kaplan's Review for the NCLEX-PN® Examination**

➤ Unit 1: Kaplan's Course Materials . . . . . . . . . . . . . . . . . . . . . . . . . . . . . . . . . . . . . . . . 19
➤ Unit 2: How to Use Kaplan's NCLEX-PN® Review Course . . . . . . . . . . . . . . . . . . . . . . 21
➤ Unit 3: User's Guide for Online Assets—kaptest.com . . . . . . . . . . . . . . . . . . . . . . . . 29
➤ Unit 4: User's Guide for Online Assets—https://nursing.kaplan.com . . . . . . . . . . . . 37
➤ Unit 5: Kaplan's Decision Tree . . . . . . . . . . . . . . . . . . . . . . . . . . . . . . . . . . . . . . . . . . . 43

**Chapter 3**  **Safe and Effective Care Environment**

➤ Unit 1: Coordination of Care . . . . . . . . . . . . . . . . . . . . . . . . . . . . . . . . . . . . . . . . . . . . 47
➤ Unit 2: Safety and Infection Control . . . . . . . . . . . . . . . . . . . . . . . . . . . . . . . . . . . . . . 67

**Chapter 4**  **Health Promotion and Maintenance**

➤ Unit 1: Growth and Development . . . . . . . . . . . . . . . . . . . . . . . . . . . . . . . . . . . . . . . . 93
➤ Unit 2: Childbearing—Normal . . . . . . . . . . . . . . . . . . . . . . . . . . . . . . . . . . . . . . . . . . 111
➤ Unit 3: Childbearing—Maternal Complications . . . . . . . . . . . . . . . . . . . . . . . . . . . . 127
➤ Unit 4: Childbearing—Neonatal Normal . . . . . . . . . . . . . . . . . . . . . . . . . . . . . . . . . . 141
➤ Unit 5: Neonatal Complications . . . . . . . . . . . . . . . . . . . . . . . . . . . . . . . . . . . . . . . . . 147
➤ Unit 6: Reproduction . . . . . . . . . . . . . . . . . . . . . . . . . . . . . . . . . . . . . . . . . . . . . . . . . 153
➤ Unit 7: Prevention and Early Detection of Disease . . . . . . . . . . . . . . . . . . . . . . . . . . 159

**Chapter 5**  **Physiological Integrity 1: Basic Care and Comfort**

➤ Unit 1: Mobility and Immobility . . . . . . . . . . . . . . . . . . . . . . . . . . . . . . . . . . . . . . . . . 185
➤ Unit 2: Conditions Limiting Mobility . . . . . . . . . . . . . . . . . . . . . . . . . . . . . . . . . . . . . 193
➤ Unit 3: Interventions to Promote Comfort . . . . . . . . . . . . . . . . . . . . . . . . . . . . . . . . . 213
➤ Unit 4: Musculoskeletal Trauma . . . . . . . . . . . . . . . . . . . . . . . . . . . . . . . . . . . . . . . . 217
➤ Unit 5: Rest and Sleep Disturbances . . . . . . . . . . . . . . . . . . . . . . . . . . . . . . . . . . . . . 227
➤ Unit 6: Nutrition . . . . . . . . . . . . . . . . . . . . . . . . . . . . . . . . . . . . . . . . . . . . . . . . . . . . . 235
➤ Unit 7: Elimination . . . . . . . . . . . . . . . . . . . . . . . . . . . . . . . . . . . . . . . . . . . . . . . . . . . 253

**Chapter 6**  **Psychosocial Integrity**

➤ Unit 1: Coping and Adaptation . . . . . . . . . . . . . . . . . . . . . . . . . . . . . . . . . . . . . . . . . 271
➤ Unit 2: Psychosocial Adaptation . . . . . . . . . . . . . . . . . . . . . . . . . . . . . . . . . . . . . . . . 291
➤ Unit 3: Psychopathology . . . . . . . . . . . . . . . . . . . . . . . . . . . . . . . . . . . . . . . . . . . . . . 295
➤ Unit 4: Chemical Dependency . . . . . . . . . . . . . . . . . . . . . . . . . . . . . . . . . . . . . . . . . . 307
➤ Unit 5: Abuse and Neglect . . . . . . . . . . . . . . . . . . . . . . . . . . . . . . . . . . . . . . . . . . . . . 313

**Chapter 7**    **Physiological Integrity 2: Physiological Adaptation**

➤ Unit 1: Medical Emergencies ...................................................319

➤ Unit 2: Fluid and Electrolyte Imbalances .....................................345

➤ Unit 3: Alterations in Body Systems ...........................................357

➤ Unit 4: Cancer ....................................................................371

**Chapter 8**    **Physiological Integrity 3: Reduction of Risk Potential**

➤ Unit 1: Sensory and Perceptual Alterations ..................................383

➤ Unit 2: Alterations in Body Systems ...........................................401

➤ Unit 3: Perioperative Care .....................................................433

➤ Unit 4: Diagnostic Tests ........................................................439

➤ Unit 5: Therapeutic Procedures ...............................................449

**Chapter 9**    **Physiological Integrity 4: Pharmacological and Parenteral Therapies**

➤ Unit 1: Blood Component Therapy .............................................465

➤ Unit 2: Intravenous Therapy ...................................................467

➤ Unit 3: Medications .............................................................471

➤ Unit 4: Side Effects of Medications ...........................................553

**Index** ...................................................................................559

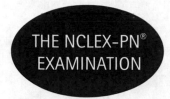

THE NCLEX–PN®
EXAMINATION

**Chapter 1**

The NCLEX-PN® Examination


Guide for Test-Takers
Repeating the
NCLEX-PN® Examination

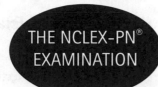
THE NCLEX–PN®
EXAMINATION

Have you talked to LPN/LVNs about their experiences taking the NCLEX–PN® examination? If so, they probably told you it was unlike any nursing test they had ever taken. How can that be? Let's talk about the NCLEX–PN® examination.

The NCLEX–PN® examination stands for *National Council Licensure Examination for Practical Nurses* and is prepared by the National Council of State Boards of Nursing (NCSBN). The purpose of the exam is to determine if you are safe to begin practice as an entry-level practical/vocational nurse. The NCLEX–PN® examination is a test of minimum competency and is based on the required knowledge and behavior for the entry-level practice of practical/vocational nursing. This exam tests not only your knowledge, but also your ability to make decisions.

The NCLEX–PN® examination is a computer adaptive test, which means each test is assembled interactively based on the accuracy of the candidate's responses to the questions. This ensures that the question you are answering will not be "too hard" or "too easy" for your skill level. The first question will be near the level of minimum competency. If you answer the question correctly, the next question will be slightly more difficult. If you miss the question, the next question will be slightly easier. As you answer questions, the computer is able to calculate your level of competence, as well as select questions that represent all areas of practical/vocational nursing as defined by the NCLEX–PN® test plan.

## Taking the Exam

You have a maximum of 5 hours to complete the exam, which includes the beginning tutorial, a break reminder after the first two hours of testing, a break reminder after an additional 90 minutes of testing, and any additional breaks you may take.

There is no time limit for each question. The NCLEX–PN® examination is a variable-length adaptive test, which means that your test will be anywhere from 85 questions to 205 questions. Twenty-five of the questions are experimental items, which are not scored. Your test will end when the computer has determined your ability and you have taken at least 85 questions, or when you have reached the maximum testing time of 5 hours, or when you have answered 205 questions.

# Facts about the NCLEX-PN® Examination

## The purpose of the exam

1. To determine if you are a safe and effective practical/vocational nurse
2. To safeguard the public
3. To test for minimum competency to practice practical/vocational nursing

## The test content

4. Based on the knowledge and activities of an entry-level practical/vocational nurse
5. Written by nursing faculty and clinical specialists
6. Majority of questions are self-contained, multiple-choice questions with 4 possible answer choices
7. Some questions may ask you to select all answers that apply, fill-in-the-blank, select hot spots, use charts/exhibits, listen to sounds, and/or identify pictures.
8. Some questions may ask you to use the mouse to identify a location on a graphic or drag and drop answers from an unordered answer column to an ordered answer column.
9. Based on integrated nursing content, *not* on the medical model of medical, surgical, obstetrics, pediatrics, and psychiatric nursing
10. Includes 25 experimental questions being tested for future exams; these questions do not count.

## Administration of the CAT

11. The CAT (Computer Adaptive Test) adapts to your knowledge, skills, and ability level.
12. The question sequence is determined interactively.
13. The computer selects questions based on the item difficulty and the test plan.
14. You individually schedule a date and time to take the exam at a testing center.
15. You sit at an individual computer station.

## Taking the exam

16. Computer knowledge is not required to take this exam.
17. You use a mouse to highlight and lock in your answer.
18. You receive instructions and a practice exercise before beginning the exam.
19. Any necessary background information appears on the screen with the question.
20. The computer selects the initial question near the level of passing.
21. The computer selects the next question on the basis of your response to the first question.

22. If your answer is correct, the next question is slightly more difficult.
23. If your answer is incorrect, the next question is slightly easier.
24. Questions are selected to precisely measure your ability in each area of the test plan.

## Timing

25. There is no time limit for each individual question.
26. You will answer a minimum of 85 questions to a maximum of 205 questions.
27. The maximum time for the exam is 5 hours, including the practice exercise and all breaks.
28. A pop-up window appears offering an optional 10-minute break after 2 hours and 3.5 hours of testing.

## The exam will end

29. When the computer has determined your ability, or
30. When a maximum of 5 hours of testing is reached, or
31. When a maximum of 205 questions have been answered.

## Scoring

32. It is a pass/fail exam.
33. There is no penalty for guessing.
34. The 25 experimental questions are not counted.

## Concerns

35. You cannot change answers after you select NEXT. Questions are selected by the computer according to the accuracy of your previous responses.
36. You cannot go back to a previous question.
37. You cannot skip a question. You must answer the question to go on.

## Advantages

38. Testing is available year-round, 15 hours a day, 6 days a week, in 5-hour time slots.
39. Results are released by the individual State Board; time will vary by State Board.
40. If you fail, your state will determine when you can re-test.

## Registration

Registration information is available from your State Board of Nursing or your nursing school senior advisor. To obtain the address and phone number of an individual State Board of Nursing, contact:

**National Council of State Boards of Nursing**
**111 E. Wacker Drive, Suite 2900**
**Chicago, IL 60601-4277**
**www.ncsbn.org**

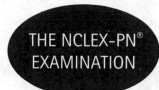
## GUIDE FOR TEST-TAKERS REPEATING THE NCLEX-PN® EXAMINATION

Some people may never have to read this section, but it's a certainty that others will. The most important advice we can give to repeat test-takers is *don't despair*. There is hope. We can get you through the NCLEX-PN® examination.

### YOU ARE NOT ALONE

Think about that awful day when the big brown envelope arrived. You just couldn't believe it. You had to tell family, friends, your supervisor, and coworkers that you didn't pass. When this happens, each unsuccessful candidate feels like he or she is the only person that has failed the exam.

### SHOULD YOU TEST AGAIN?

Absolutely! You completed your nursing education to become a practical/vocational nurse. The initial response of many unsuccessful candidates is to declare, "I'm never going back! That was the worst experience of my life! What do I do now?" When you first received your results, you went through a period of grieving—the same stages that you learned about in nursing school. Three to four weeks later, you find that you want to begin preparing to retake the exam.

### HOW TO INTERPRET UNSUCCESSFUL TEST RESULTS

Most unsuccessful candidates on the NCLEX-PN® examination will usually say, "I almost passed." Some of you did almost pass, and some of you weren't very close. If you fail the exam, you will receive a Candidate Performance Report from National Council. In this report, you will be told how many questions you answered on the exam. The more questions you answered, the closer you came to passing. The only way you will continue to get questions after you answer the first 85 is if you are answering questions close to the level of difficulty needed to pass the exam. If you are answering questions far above the level needed to pass or far below the level needed to pass, your exam will end at 85 questions.

Figure 1 shows a representation of what happens when a candidate fails in 85 questions. This student does not come close to passing. In 85 questions, this student demonstrates an inability to consistently answer questions correctly at or above the level of difficulty needed to pass the exam. This usually indicates a lack of nursing knowledge, considerable difficulties with taking a standardized test, or a deficiency in critical thinking skills.

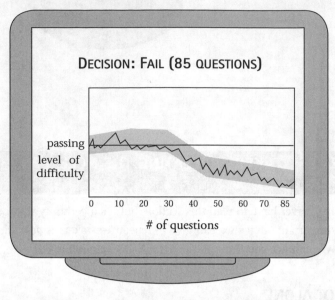

**Figure 1**

Figure 2 shows what happens when a candidate takes all 205 questions and fails. This candidate "almost passed." If the last question is below the level of difficulty needed to pass, the candidate fails.

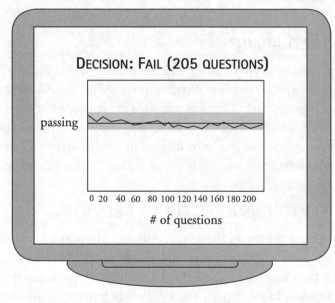

**Figure 2**

If the last question is above the level of difficulty needed to pass, the candidate passes. If you took a test longer than 85 questions and failed, you were probably familiar with most of the content you saw on the exam, but you may have had difficulty using critical thinking skills or taking standardized tests.

The information contained on the Candidate Performance Report helps you identify your strengths and weaknesses on this particular NCLEX-PN® examination. This knowledge will help you identify where to concentrate your study when you prepare to retake the exam.

Contact NCLEX-expert@kaplan.com for assistance with your continued preparation.

## PREPARATION FOR THE EXAMINATION

**I saw nursing topics that were not familiar to me.**

Review the Candidate Performance Report and identify the client need areas where you were "below passing." Review your Kaplan test results and identify client need areas where your scores were below the benchmark score. Review content using the content videos and your NCLEX-PN® Content Review Guide beginning with your weakest content areas and progressing to your stronger content areas.

**I saw medications that were not familiar to me.**

It is difficult to memorize individual medications. Organize your study of medications based on the classification system. The pharmacology section in your NCLEX-PN® Content Review Guide is organized according to medication classifications. You will need to memorize the generic and trade names of medications in each classification. As you read topics in your guide, if a medication is mentioned, look it up so you understand its use in the context of what it is used for.

**I prepared for the exam just like I prepared for tests in nursing school.**

The purpose of the NCLEX-PN® examination is to test critical thinking and clinical judgment needed to safely care for clients in all health care settings. Passing-level questions on NCLEX-PN® are written at the application and analysis level. If you prepare for NCLEX-PN® by answering knowledge and comprehension questions, you are not using the type of thinking required. The Decision Tree has been designed to act as a framework or guide to approach application and analysis level questions.

**I memorized facts without understanding the principles of client care.**

If you memorize facts about a disease process, that may not help you answer the questions on NCLEX-PN®. NCLEX-PN® tests the candidate's ability to prioritize, provide safe and effective nursing care, and evaluate the client's response to care. Understanding, not memorization, allows you to approach, analyze and determine the best clinical judgment for each question.

## THE NCLEX-PN® EXAMINATION

**I was not sure about the type of questions I would see on NCLEX-PN®.**

Go to www.ncsbn.org and review the candidate information about the alternate-format item questions and the test plan for the exam. When you take Kaplan nursing tests, the questions are written at the level of difficulty needed to pass NCLEX-PN®. The NCLEX-PN® examination is testing your ability to critically think in complex client care situations.

**I did not understand Computer Adaptive Testing (CAT).**

Review the candidate information on www.ncsbn.org about computer adaptive testing. When taking the NCLEX-PN® examination, the next question depends on only 2 things: first, whether you answered the previous question correctly or incorrectly, and second, the area of the test plan from which the next question must come to maintain the percentages in each area.

**I thought I would complete the exam with the minimum amount of questions.**
It is possible to pass or fail the test with the minimum or maximum amount
of questions or anywhere in between the minimum or maximum number. The
computer will continue to give you questions as long as you are at or above the
passing line. You need to prepare to take the maximum number of questions.
Better to be prepared for longer and be short than the reverse. If you are getting
questions, you are still in the game. *Stay focused!*

**I began to lose my concentration when the computer continued to give me
questions.**
If you lose your concentration, you need to recognize it and regain your ability
to concentrate. Take a mental break while sitting at the computer or leave the
computer station for a short time. Our longer tests allow you to get in mental
shape for a longer test. Follow the guidelines given for each test.

## TEST-TAKING ISSUES

**I had difficulty identifying what the questions were asking.**

Take your time and read each question and its answer choices. Do not try to
answer a question without identifying the topic. Remember, you cannot answer
the question until you are clear about what you are being asked.

**I did not carefully consider each answer choice.**
NCLEX questions are written so that more than one answer might *seem* correct.
It is important to consider each answer choice very carefully before selecting
your final answer.

**I did not eliminate answers when I considered the answer choices.**
Eliminate answers you know are incorrect. If you are not sure about an answer,
keep it under consideration.

**I am not good at selecting answers that require me to establish priorities of
care.**
When you are answering questions, think about answers that provide for client
safety or reduce the risk of injury. Is assessment or implementation the best and
most important action for the nurse to take? Does Maslow's hierarchy or the
ABCs apply?

**I answered the questions based on my "real world" experiences.**
The NCLEX-PN® exam is based on "ivory-tower nursing." When you answer a
question, think about what the author of a nursing textbook would do. Do not
consider what you do at work or what you see others doing.

**When I thought two answer choices seemed correct, I did not know how to
choose the correct one.**
Read the question and then each answer choice. Think about priorities: client
safety, Maslow, and the ABCs. There is only one best answer. If you can do only
one thing and walk away, what will the outcome be for your client?

**I began to believe I would not pass.**

When you feel this coming on, you need to take a break and do some positive thinking. As long as the computer is still asking you questions, you are still in the running. Tell yourself you are doing okay. Repeat positive thinking statements. Refocus your brain on each question.

## EVALUATE YOUR CAT EXPERIENCE

Some students attribute their failure to the CAT experience. Comments we have heard include:

*"I didn't like answering questions on the computer."*

*"I looked up every time the door opened."*

*"I should have taken a snack. I got so hungry!"*

*"After two and a half hours I didn't care what I answered. I just wanted the computer to shut off!"*

*"I didn't expect to be there for 4 hours!"*

*"I should have rescheduled my test, but I just wanted to get it over with!"*

*"I found the background noise distracting."*

Do any of these comments sound familiar? It is important for you to take charge of your CAT experience. Here's how:

- Choose a familiar testing site.
- Select the time of day that you test your best. (Are you a morning or afternoon person?)
- Accept the earplugs when offered!
- Take a snack and a drink for your break.
- Take a break if you become distracted or fatigued during the test.
- Contact the proctors at the test site if something bothers you during the test.
- Plan on testing for 5 hours. If you get out early, it's a pleasant surprise.
- Say to yourself every day, "I will be successful."

After determining why you failed, the next step is to establish a plan of action for your next test. Remember, you should prepare differently this time. Consider the following when setting up your new plan of study:

## YOU'VE SEEN THE TEST

You may wish that you didn't have to walk back into the testing center again, but if you want to be a practical nurse, you must go back. But this time you have an advantage over a first time test taker: you've seen the test! You know exactly what you are preparing for, and there are no unknowns. The computer will remember what questions you took before, and you will not be given any of the same questions. But the content of the question, the style of the question, and the kinds of answer choices will not change. You will not be surprised this time.

## STUDY BOTH CONTENT AND TEST QUESTIONS

By the time you retest, you will be out of nursing school for 3–6 months or longer. Remember that old saying, "What you are not learning, you are forgetting"? Because this exam is based on nursing as it is practiced in the United States, you must remember all you can about nursing theory and use sound clinical judgment to select the correct answers.

You must also master exam-style test questions. It is essential that you be able to correctly identify what each question is asking. You will not predict answers. You will think about each and every answer choice to decide if it answers the reworded question. To master test questions, you must practice answering them. We recommend you answer hundreds of exam-style test questions, especially at the application level of difficulty.

## KNOW ALL OF THE WORDS AND THEIR MEANINGS

Some students who have to learn a great deal of material in a short period of time have trouble learning the extensive vocabulary of the discipline. For example, difficulty with terminology is a problem for many good students who study history. They enjoy the concepts but find it hard to memorize all of the names and dates that allow them to do well on history tests. If you are one of those students who have trouble memorizing terms, you may find it useful to review a list of the terminology you must know to pass the NCLEX-PN® examination.

## PRACTICE TEST-TAKING STRATEGIES

There is no substitute for mastering the nursing content. This knowledge, combined with test-taking strategies, will help you select a greater number of correct answers. For many students, the strategies mean the difference between a passing test and a failing test. Using strategies effectively can also determine whether you take a short test (85 questions) or a longer test (up to 205 questions).

## TEST-TAKING STRATEGIES THAT DON'T WORK ON THE NCLEX-PN® EXAMINATION

Whether you realize it or not, you developed a set of test-taking strategies in nursing school to answer teacher-generated test questions that are written at the knowledge/comprehension level of difficulty. These strategies include:

- "Cramming" hundreds of facts about disease processes and nursing care.

- Recognizing and recalling facts rather than understanding the pathophysiology and the needs of a client with an illness.

- Knowing who wrote the question and what is important to that instructor.

- Predicting answers based on what you remember or who wrote the test question.

- Selecting the response that is a different length compared to the other choices.

- Selecting the answer choice that is grammatically correct.

- When in doubt, choosing answer choice C.

These strategies will not work because the NCLEX-PN® examination tests your ability to make safe, competent decisions.

## SUCCESSFUL TEST-TAKERS OF THE NCLEX-PN® EXAMINATION:

- Have a good understanding of nursing content.

- Have the ability to tackle each test question with a lot of confidence because they assume that they can figure out the right answer.

- Don't give up if they are unsure of the answer. They are not afraid to think about the question and the possible choices in order to select the correct answer.

- Possess the know-how to correctly identify the question.

- Stay focused on the question.

- Know how to pace themselves throughout the test.

## UNSUCCESSFUL TEST-TAKERS OF THE NCLEX-PN® EXAMINATION:

- Assume that they either know or don't know the answer to the question.

- Memorize facts to answer questions by recall or recognition.

- Read the question, read the answers, read the question, and pick an answer.

- Choose answer choices based on a hunch or a feeling instead of thinking critically.

- Answer questions based on personal experience rather than nursing theory.

- Give up too soon because they aren't willing to think hard about questions and answers.

- Don't stay focused on the question.

- Take the test too quickly or too slowly.

Work to become a successful test-taker!

## PREPARE TO RETAKE THE NCLEX-PN® EXAMINATION

1. **Evaluate your content knowledge.**

   The National Council's Diagnostic Profile is organized according to the Categories of Client Needs. It is important that you have a comprehensive understanding of the concept of Client Needs.

2. **Think about your strong and weak areas.**

   You will note that the Kaplan Readiness Test results and the National Council's Diagnostic Profile are organized according to the Categories of Client Needs. In which areas did you do well? In which areas do you need more study?

3. **Plan a study schedule.**

   Plan your study time to include all nursing content but emphasize areas identified as weaknesses on your diagnostic profile from the National Council. Preparation for retaking the NCLEX-PN® examination should include a minimum of 4-6 weeks of concentrated study. Establish specific daily goals and reward yourself when you accomplish them. Don't let yourself fall behind.

4. **Begin studying.**

   At first you may find it difficult to review the nursing content. You may find yourself saying, "I know this already." You may find yourself remembering the questions that were on your NCLEX-PN® examination. **FORGET THEM!** You will not see any of the same questions when you retest. Focus your energy on understanding the nursing content.

5. **Read the assigned pages in *the NCLEX-PN® Content Review Guide*.**

   Begin with your areas of weakness and work toward your areas of strength. If you don't understand a word or have a question about a topic, look it up in your nursing course books. Include these notes in your *NCLEX-PN® Content Review Guide*.

6. **Watch the content videos.**

   Videos of essential nursing content that map to the *NCLEX-PN® Content Review Guide* are available on your home page. Watch the content in the areas identified as weaknesses on your Candidate Performance Report. Take notes in the *NCLEX-PN® Content Review Guide* as you watch the content videos. Be aware that the RN scope of practice is discussed in the content videos; while much of the content is applicable to the PN/VN scope of practice, some of it is not. Think about the PN/VN scope of practice as defined by your state board of nursing as you are reviewing the content.

7. **Review the Decision Tree.**

    Kaplan developed the Decision Tree to provide you with the critical thinking framework and clinical judgment required to successfully answer passing-level questions on the NCLEX-PN® examination. Make the commitment to use the Decision Tree when practicing questions in preparation for the NCLEX-PN® examination and when taking the actual exam.

8. **Review Kaplan's Test-Taking Workshop.**

    These strategies are not a substitute for knowledge of nursing content but will provide you with tools to utilize your nursing knowledge and answer application-level questions correctly.

9. **Review the class lessons when they are available on the website.**

    The questions reviewed are exam-style and of varying levels of difficulty. The discussion of the explanations to the questions does three things: First, it gives you the correct answer; second, it reviews the knowledge and thought process that leads to the correct answer; third, it points out the wrong thinking behind the incorrect answer choices. If you have difficulty with a question, stop the recording and ask yourself why you missed the question. Did the question concern nursing knowledge you didn't know? Did you misread the question? Did you make an assumption or base your answer on what you have seen in the "real world" instead of "ivory tower" nursing? Was it a test-taking problem?

    If there is content that you don't understand or don't remember, look it up.

10. **After you finish, go back and review your notes.**

    Do you have a complete understanding of the content areas? If not, more study is needed.

11. **Practice with the Qbank.**

    Build your confidence by using the Decision Tree to answer Qbank questions. You determine the content and select the number of questions contained in each test (85 questions). Build your Qbank test from all 8 client need areas. This will enable you to consistently review essential nursing content. Begin with areas of the test plan that most challenge you and then work your way through to your strengths. To make the most of your Qbank experience, only answer questions using 'timed test.' Typically, students who use 'tutor mode' answer more questions correctly because they view explanations prior to selecting answers. This does not, however, give you accurate feedback about how you are answering questions.

12. **Be confident!**

    Don't schedule to retake the NCLEX-PN® examination until you have allowed yourself sufficient time to prepare for the exam. Then walk into the exam knowing that you are prepared and ready to pass. Take charge of your environment. Arrange the computer keyboard and light for comfort. View the exam like a marathon and ration your energy and effort. Be prepared to answer all 205 questions. If you lose your concentration, raise your hand and take a short break. Comprehensive preparation and a positive attitude are the ingredients for success on the NCLEX-PN® examination.

## Content of the NCLEX-PN® Examination

| CLIENT NEEDS | PERCENTAGE OF ITEMS FROM EACH CATEGORY/SUBCATEGORY |
|---|---|
| **Safe and Effective Care Environment** | |
| Coordinated Care | 16–22% |
| Safety and Infection Control | 10–16% |
| **Health Promotion and Maintenance** | 7–13% |
| **Psychosocial Integrity** | 8–14% |
| **Physiological Integrity** | |
| Basic Care and Comfort | 7–13% |
| Pharmacological Therapies | 11–17% |
| Reduction of Risk Potential | 10–16% |
| Physiological Adaptation | 7–13% |

KAPLAN'S
REVIEW FOR THE
NCLEX-PN®
EXAMINATION

## Chapter 2

Kaplan's Course Materials


How to Use Kaplan's
NCLEX-PN® Review Course


User's Guides


Kaplan's Decision Tree

You have chosen the best review to prepare for the NCLEX-PN® examination. It is important that you take advantage of all the resources found in Kaplan's Review course to ensure your success on the NCLEX-PN® examination. Familiarize yourself with all of the material so you can prepare a study plan that fits into your schedule. Since most students test within 8 weeks of graduation, Kaplan has designed several schedules for you to choose from. Before looking at the schedules, let's talk about resources.

## MATERIALS FOR KAPLAN'S NCLEX-PN® REVIEW COURSE

### The *NCLEX-PN® Content Review Guide*
- Review frequently tested, minimum-competency nursing content
- Read content sections before class or study session

### Class Lessons
- Learn how to apply your nursing knowledge to answer questions similar to those on the actual exam
- Discuss critical thinking and clinical judgment specific to the NCLEX-PN® examination
- Review questions using Kaplan's Decision Tree to ensure success on the NCLEX-PN® examination

### Online Assets
- 24-hour, 7-day-a-week access during your enrollment period
- Audio/video streaming of essential nursing content; audio streaming of class questions

### Orientation to Kaplan's NCLEX-PN® Review Course
- Learn about Kaplan's NCLEX-PN® Review Course
- Explains how to use online assets

### Class Questions
- Guided review of questions using Kaplan's Decision Tree; includes explanations of correct and incorrect responses
- Master critical thinking by repeating and/or reviewing the questions at your own pace.

## Nursing Content

- Take notes as you review nursing content essential for success on the NCLEX-PN® examination. Please note that the audio/video streaming of essential nursing content is produced to the RN scope of practice and you should consider this when watching the content videos.
- Review the content as often as required.

## Decision Tree

- Kaplan's critical thinking framework based on clinical nursing judgment
- Enables candidates to correctly answer application/analysis questions utilizing critical thinking

## Test Taking Workshop

- Learn how to think your way through the types of questions you will see on the NCLEX-PN® examination
- Establish a way to approach application- and analysis-level questions

## Kaplan's Strategy Seminar for the NCLEX-PN® examination

- Learn what you need to know about the NCLEX-PN® examination

## Qbank

- 1,000+ test questions
- Create customized practice tests
- Receive immediate on-screen feedback
- Review detailed explanations of right and wrong answers

Welcome to Kaplan NCLEX Prep! This is the recommended study plan for utilizing the Kaplan NCLEX Prep resources. These resources are designed to give you plenty of realistic practice for success on Test Day. As you begin your preparation, please keep in mind that preparing for the NCLEX-PN® is a marathon, not a sprint! It is important to not rush your studies, but also not to procrastinate.

Whether you take the Kaplan NCLEX-PN® Review online or in a traditional classroom setting, Kaplan's NCLEX-PN® Review course offers you many resources to ensure your success on the exam. These resources include the *NCLEX-PN® Content Review Guide*, review of questions, and online study center. While you are utilizing the Kaplan NCLEX Prep resources, it is important that you follow these steps: analyze, review/remediate, think, study, and then continue practicing. Remediation is the key to your success on the NCLEX-PN®.

## PHASE 1: PRIOR TO YOUR KAPLAN NCLEX REVIEW COURSE

Complete the following resources on your student homepage.

**\*\*Please note:** *Directions in italics apply only to Institutional students that are enrolled in the Kaplan Institutional program via their school and access their NCLEX resources via their Kaplan Institutional homepage.*

**Date**
**Completed**

| | |
|---|---|
| | Download and read the *NCLEX-PN® Content Review Guide* eBook. It can be downloaded to any computer or eReader device. |
| | Watch the **Online Content Lectures/***PN Review of Essential Nursing Content* videos. |
| | Download the **Classroom Posters.** These will be referenced in the Review Course. |

## PHASE 2: ATTEND YOUR KAPLAN NCLEX REVIEW COURSE

Kaplan's review course consists of four 3.5-hour sessions led by one of our expert nurse educators. Your review will concentrate on helping you answer passing-level NCLEX questions by utilizing your clinical judgment skills in order to ensure success on Test Day. While the structure of the lectures is not content-focused, you will receive high-yield content tips while reviewing NCLEX-style questions in class.

| 1. Orientation/Decision Tree/Coordinated Care |
| 2. Coordinated Care/Safety/Infection Control/HPM/BCC |
| 3. BCC/Psychosocial/Physiologic Adaptation/Reduction of Risk |
| 4. Reduction of Risk/Pharmacology/Roadmap for Future Study |

## PHASE 3: AFTER ATTENDING THE KAPLAN NCLEX REVIEW COURSE

**Date Completed**

| | |
|---|---|
| | Qbank—Take one 85-question Qbank test each day and review/remediate, following the steps below. |
| | Take the **PN Readiness Test** and review/remediate. |
| | ** *Institutional students will be proctored by the school on a date/time scheduled by school faculty. The test will be scheduled in the Green Integrated Testing box.* |
| | Take **Qbank Sample Tests 1 and 2** and review/remediate, following the steps below. (Space these out in Phase 3 between other Qbank tests). |
| | Take **four 50-question Qbank Tests** back-to-back approximately 1 week prior to your NCLEX Test Day. Set aside time to take the test in one sitting, and treat it as a mock NCLEX. This will be 200 questions (205 max questions are allowed on NCLEX) and may take several hours to complete. Take the test in a quiet, controlled, distraction-free environment to simulate Test Day. Review/remediate. |

As you are completing tests, look at your **Analysis** page to see how you performed on the test. Aim for scores of 65 percent or higher on Qbank tests and 75 percent or higher on the PN Readiness Test. (*Institutional students: your school may require higher on any of these resources.*) Use the test analysis to identify your lowest client need categories. Ask yourself the following and assess how you are thinking:

1.  Did I change any answers? Which way? Right to wrong, or wrong to right?

2.  Did I take enough time on each question or did I take too much time on each question?

3.  Did I lose concentration, and if so, is there a pattern? Did I need to take a break?

After analyzing the test, **review/remediate** all questions. Ask yourself the following:

1.  Did I not know the content of the question?

2.  For questions I got wrong, why did the author of this question choose one answer, and why did I choose another?

3.  Did I use the Decision Tree?

4.  Am I seeing improvement as I progress from test to test?

5.  Am I assessing how I am thinking?

6.  Did I take a break at the best time for myself?

Use the **Online Content Lectures**/*PN Review of Essential Nursing Content* videos and your *NCLEX-PN® Content Review Guide* eBook to fill in any knowledge gaps, working from your content need area of greatest weakness toward your area of greatest strength.

You should complete all Qbank questions and the PN Readiness Test and review/remediate all questions before you take the NCLEX. The day before your test, rest your mind and exercise your body. You are embarking upon the final step towards beginning your exciting new career as a nurse!

## Additional Resources

The **Decision Tree** and *Review Class Sessions/PN Class Questions* videos revisit information covered in the Review Course. Also available is a **Test-Taking Workshop** (this workshop references RN, but is applicable to your PN studies.) Additional guidance on formulating your study plan leading up to your NCLEX Test Date can be found in Chapter 2 of the *NCLEX-PN® Content Review Guide* eBook. You can also email NCLEX-Expert@kaplan.com for NCLEX- or content-specific questions, or for additional prep advice/guidance.

### STUDY SCHEDULE

It is important that you plan a schedule that allows you time to answer all the questions. Kaplan Nursing designed several schedules for you to choose from based on your scheduled test date.

Select the schedule that allows you to complete all of Kaplan's questions prior to your test date. Stick closely to your schedule, because delaying test dates can negatively affect your outcome on the NCLEX-PN® examination. (See research at https://www.ncsbn.org/delaystudy2006.pdf.) If your scheduled test date is not included in the following, adjust your schedule accordingly.

## TESTING TWO WEEKS AFTER THE END OF CLASS?

The following are approximate time frames for completion and review of each question set or test. Use the times to plan your study schedule.

### Week 1 after end of class

Readiness Test: 100 questions (2 hrs)

　　Review every question (4-6 hrs)

Qbank: Six 85-question tests (1.7 hrs each test)

　　　Review every question before taking the next test (3-5 hrs each test)

### Week 2 after end of class

Sample tests: 50 questions (1 hr)

　　Review every question (2-3 hrs)

Qbank: Five 85-question tests (1.7 hrs each test)

　　　Review every question before taking the next test (3-5 hrs each test)

Do not study the day before your test. Use your body, and rest your mind.

## TESTING THREE WEEKS AFTER THE END OF CLASS?

The following are approximate time frames for completion and review of each question set or test. Use the times to plan your study schedule.

### Week 1 after end of class

Qbank: Four 85-question tests (1.7 hrs each test)

   Review every question before taking the next test (3-5 hrs each test)

### Week 2 after end of class

Qbank: Four 85-question tests (1.7 hrs each test)

   Review every question before taking the next test (3-5 hrs each test)

### Week 3 after end of class

Sample tests: 50 questions (1 hr)

   Review every question (2-3 hrs)

Qbank: Four 85-question tests (1.7 hrs each test)

   Review every question before taking the next test (3-5 hrs each test)

Do not study the day before your test. Use your body, and rest your mind.

## TESTING FIVE WEEKS AFTER THE END OF CLASS?

The following are approximate time frames for completion and review of each question set or test. Use the times to plan your study schedule.

### Week 1 after the end of class

Qbank: Four 85-question tests (1.7 hrs each test)

 Review every question before taking the next test (3-5 hrs each test)

### Week 2 after end of class

Qbank: Two 85-question tests (1.7 hrs each test)

 Review every question before taking the next test (3-5 hrs each test)

### Week 3 after end of class

Qbank: Two 85-question tests (1.7 hrs each test)

 Review every question before taking the next test (3-5 hrs each test)

### Week 4 after end of class

Qbank: Two 85-question tests (1.7 hrs each test)

 Review every question before taking the next test (3-5 hrs each test)

### Week 5 after end of class

Sample tests: 50 questions (1 hr)

 Review every question (2-3 hrs)

Qbank: Two 85-question tests (1.7 hrs each test)

 Review every question before taking the next test (3-5 hrs each test)

Do not study the day before your test. Use your body, and rest your mind.

## REVIEWING QUESTIONS

It is important you review the rationales to all the questions you answered, even the questions you answered correctly. Why is this important? If you missed questions, you want to learn from your mistakes. If you answered questions correctly, you want to know why, so you can use the same thinking to successfully answer more questions.

If you incorrectly answer a question, it is important for you to determine why you missed the question. Consider the following:

1. **Did you miss the question because you did not know the content?**

    If so, look up the content immediately. Rather than trying to memorize the content, try to understand the concepts. Do not make a list of missed topics with the intent of looking the topics up "later." If you have to look up a list of topics, you will be trying to master a large quantity of data. Cramming did not work in nursing school, and it will not work now.

2. **Did you miss the question because you did not correctly identify the topic of the question?**

    You know you have misidentified the topic if you are reading the rationale and it is about a topic you did not consider. Look carefully at the stem of the question and the answers to determine the topic. Refer to the Decision Tree.

3. **Did you miss the question even though you correctly identified the topic?**

    Use all the steps of the Decision Tree. Many times students will choose the second best answer because they did not recognize the patterns found in the answer choices. Another reason candidates answer questions incorrectly is because they do not thoughtfully consider each answer choice. Slow down and THINK!

KAPLAN'S REVIEW FOR THE NCLEX-PN® EXAMINATION

# User's Guide for Online Assets–kaptest.com

These User's Guides will answer many of the questions you may have about using Kaplan's online resources. The online resources include the online review of class questions and content and the Qbank.

## QUESTIONS

If you have questions about your username/password, www.kaptest.com, how to access your online assets, or any technical issues, call 1-800-KAP-TEST (1-800-527-8378) or email customer.care@kaplan.com. If you have questions about the content, please email NCLEX-Expert@kaplan.com. To ensure a prompt response, include the QID number (the ID number of the question) you are referring to.

## KAPLAN'S ONLINE RESOURCES

All students enrolled in a Kaplan NCLEX-PN® Review Course have online resources. The Online Study Center is included in your enrollment and allows you to review and reinforce course content at your convenience. Your online access begins as soon as you have paid in full.

Once you receive your login information, go to **www.kaptest.com** and click on "Log In." This will take you to a login screen. Log in using your email and password.

KAPLAN
TEST PREP

1-800-KAP-TEST     Sign in

Search by keyword or class code

**Sign In**

Email Address:

Password:

☐ Remember me

Sign In

Forgot Your Password?

Your privacy is very important to us

If you have forgotten your password, you can retrieve it by going to www.kaptest.com. Click on the "Log in" button and on the next screen, click "Forgot Your Password?" From there, follow the onscreen instructions to reset your password.

Please check all mailboxes in your email account. Some emails may get delivered to your bulk mailbox or end up in your spam folder rather than your inbox.

Your Course Syllabus looks like this:

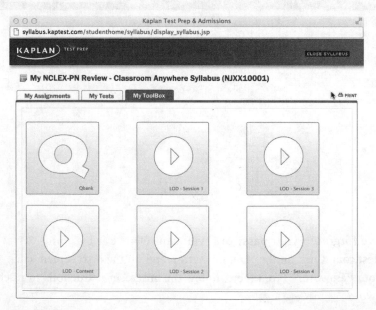

The tabs at the top of the screen are labeled "My Assignments," "My Tests," and "My Toolbox."

## My Assignments

The "My Assignments" tab contains your class schedule and assigned reading for each class. It also contains links to important information about the NCLEX-PN® examination.

## My Toolbox

Clicking on the "My Toolbox" tab allows you to access the Qbank, Lessons on Demand (LOD content) for essential nursing content, and a review of class questions (LOD Sessions 1–4).

# Using Qbank

## The Splash Page

Qbank contains more than 1,000 exam-style questions written at the knowledge, comprehension, application, and analysis levels of difficulty. You formulate your own tests by selecting areas of the NCLEX-PN® test plan, the number of questions on each test, and whether you want to answer questions in testing or tutorial mode.

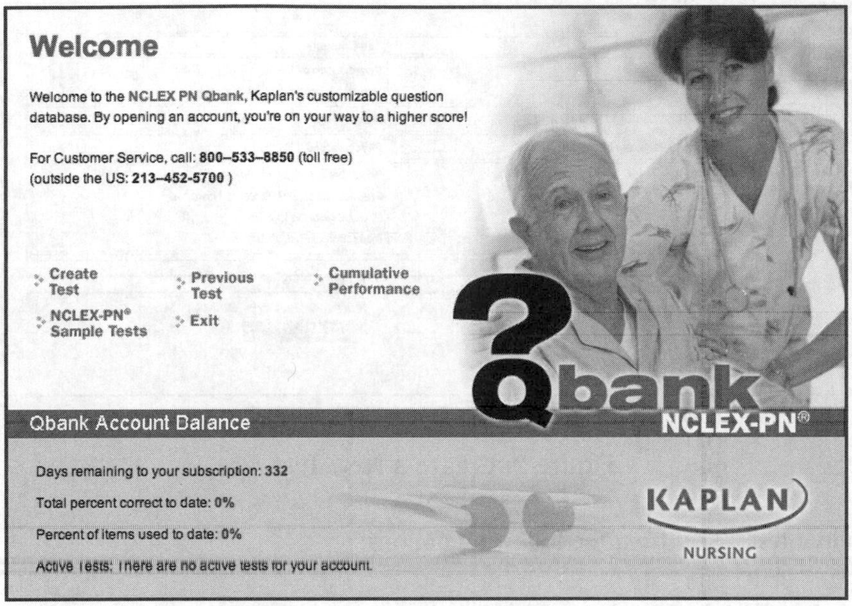

**Welcome**

Welcome to the NCLEX PN Qbank, Kaplan's customizable question database. By opening an account, you're on your way to a higher score!

For Customer Service, call: **800–533–8850** (toll free)
(outside the US: **213–452–5700** )

- **Create Test**
- **Previous Test**
- **Cumulative Performance**
- **NCLEX-PN® Sample Tests**
- **Exit**

**Qbank Account Balance**

Days remaining to your subscription: 332

Total percent correct to date: 0%

Percent of items used to date: 0%

Active Tests: There are no active tests for your account.

**Figure 1. Splash Screen**

The splash page presents you with a list of options:

> **Create a test:** Clicking on this allows you to put new tests together.

> **Previous test:** This feature allows you to finish suspended tests and review completed tests.

> **Cumulative performance:** This indicates how you are performing in all areas of the test plan.

> **NCLEX-PN® Sample tests:** Two 50-question tests based on the NCLEX-PN® test plan are provided for your review.

## Create a New Test

This page enables you to build your tests.

**Figure 2. Create a New Test**

To build a test, select from the following options:

- **Test Style:**

    Choose a *timed test* when you want to practice testing under exam-like conditions. The program will determine the amount of testing time based on the number of questions selected. When the test is complete, your results are displayed and you can then review the questions. In timed mode, you cannot review the explanations until you answer all the questions.

    If you select *tutor mode,* the test is not timed and you are able to view the explanations after answering each question. Your results are displayed at the end of the test.

- **Question Reuse Mode:**

    Select questions from unused questions, questions you have answered incorrectly, or from all items in the test pool.

- **Test Content:**

    Select content from the NCLEX-PN® examination blueprint.

    If you check "Select All Test Content," the test will include questions from all areas of the test plan.

If you check the "Main Category," questions are selected from Safe and Effective Care, Health Promotion and Maintenance, Psychosocial Integrity, and Physiological Integrity.

If you check the "Subcategories," your questions will only come from selected subcategories. This enables you to target your studies.

- **Number of Available Questions:**

    Click the "See how many questions are available" button to find out how many questions are available to you. The questions contained in the Sample Tests are not included in the "Number of Available Questions."

- **Create Test:**

    Enter the number of questions in the test. Choose from 85 questions. After selecting the number of questions, click the CREATE TEST button to begin your testing experience.

## The Testing Screen

After creating a test, the testing experience begins. The testing screen consists of 3 parts:

1) the question is displayed at the top of the screen,

2) the answer choices are below the stem of the question, and

3) the toolbar is at the bottom of the screen.

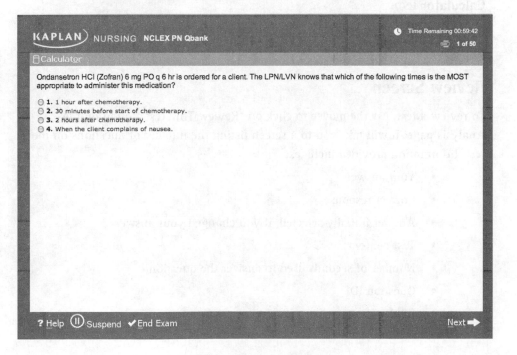

**Figure 3. Testing Screen**

The item number you are currently answering appears in the upper-right corner of the screen. The time remaining in the test (if you are in timed mode) is located in the upper-right corner. You should always be aware of the time remaining because you will not receive any warning before time expires.

### Selecting an Answer

Each answer choice is preceded by a radio button.

- *To select an answer*, use the mouse to click on the radio button preceding the answer. If you are satisfied with your answer, click NEXT. Your answer will be entered and the next question appears.
- *To de-select the answer*, simply click on another radio button.

### The Toolbar

Three icons appear on the bottom of the tool bar: NEXT, SUSPEND, and END TEST.

- Click on NEXT to enter your answer.
- Click on SUSPEND to suspend the test. To resume the test, click on PREVIOUS TESTS found on the splash page or on the left margin of the screen.
- END EXAM will end the test and allow you to review your performance analysis.
- HELP will provide directions for the screen.

### Calculator Icon

Click on the CALCULATOR icon to use the drop-down calculator. Click on the "X" in the upper right corner of the calculator to make the calculator disappear.

## Review Screen

To review a test, use the mouse to click on "Review This Test" found on the Analysis page. It will take you to a screen listing the number of questions on the test. Information provided includes:

- Your answer
- Correct response
- Answer initially selected, if you changed your answer
- Test content
- Number of seconds used to answer the question
- Question ID
- Explanation

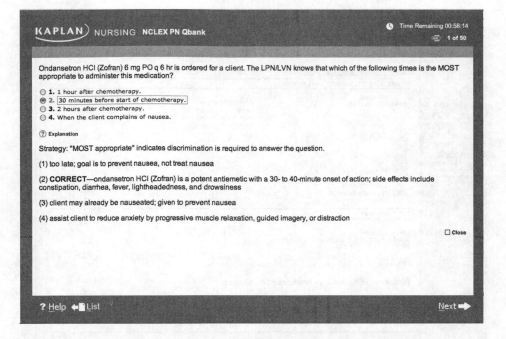

**Figure 4. Review Screen—Question Detail**

There are 3 icons on the toolbar located at the bottom of the Review screen.
Next allows you to view the next question and explanation on the test. List takes you
back to the review page. Help takes you to a NCLEX-PN® Qbank information page.

## Cumulative Performance

The Cumulative Performance page gives you a raw percentage in each area of
the NCLEX-PN® examination blueprint. Try to achieve 60% correct on all of your
tests. Again, reviewing *all* questions will ensure success on Test Day.

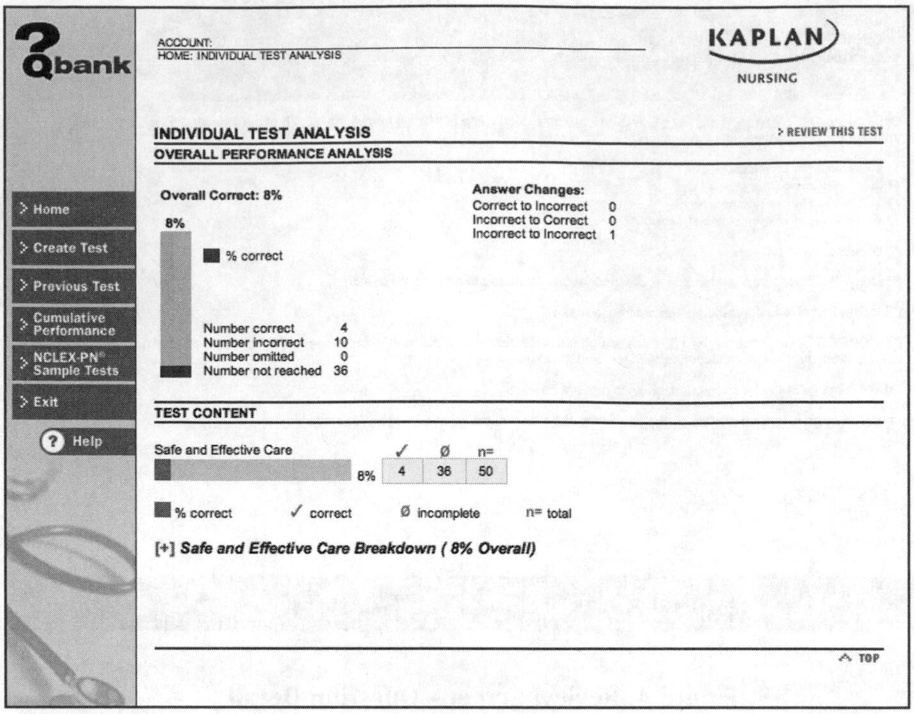

**Figure 5. Cumulative Performance**

## FREE–REPEAT GUARANTEE

If you are a graduate of an ACEN-accredited PN/VN nursing program taking the exam for the first time within six months of graduation and do not pass the NCLEX-PN® exam, you are eligible to receive either a 100% tuition refund OR a free 3-month repeat of your enrollment. (Refund does not include shipping or installment billing fees).

To claim the guarantee, you must meet the following eligibility criteria:

- Attend all class sessions live, live online or online. Up to two live class sessions can be made up online as directed by Kaplan.
- Take the Kaplan Readiness Test from your online account.
- Answer at least 900 questions on your Online Question Bank before your exam date.

To qualify for the 100% tuition refund, you must not access the Online Study Center resources after the date of your NCLEX-PN® exam. If you choose to repeat the program, you will not be eligible for the money back option. You must call 1-800-KAP-TEST within 20 days of the date of your NCLEX-PN® exam to select the repeat or money back option and for further instructions.

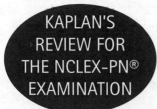
# User's Guide for Online Assets–https://nursing.kaplan.com

All students enrolled in a Kaplan NCLEX-PN® Integrated Testing courses have online resources. The Online Study Center is included in your Integrated Testing program and allows you to review and reinforce course content at your convenience. Your online access to the Kaplan NCLEX-PN® online resources begins according to your school policy.

Once you receive your login information, go to https://nursing.kaplan.com and log in using the username and password given to you. If you have forgotten your username and password, contact integrated.support@kaplan.com or call 1-877-572-8457.

**Please check all mailboxes in your email account. Some emails may get delivered to your bulk mailbox or end up in your spam folder rather than your inbox.**

To access the Kaplan online NCLEX-PN® Prep website, click on the NCLEX-PN® Prep link at the top of the home page.

Your Course Syllabus looks like this:

| NCLEX-PN ® Prep | | Back | Homepage |
|---|---|---|---|
| **NCLEX-PN ® Qbank** | | | |
| Qbank | | | Go |
| Qbank Sample Tests | | | Go |
| **NCLEX-PN ® Review** | | | |
| PN Decision Tree | | | Go |
| PN Class Questions - Lesson 1 | | | Go |
| PN Class Questions - Lesson 2 | | | Go |
| PN Class Questions - Lesson 3 | | | Go |
| PN Class Questions - Lesson 4 | | | Go |
| PN Review of Essential Nursing Content | | | Go |

- The Qbank Sample Tests contain two 50-question tests.
- The Decision Tree link contains a video and explanation of the Kaplan Decision Tree.
- The PN Class Questions-Lessons 1–4 contain explanations of the NCLEX-PN® examination preparation class questions.
- The Review of Essential Nursing Content contains video lectures of the *NCLEX-PN® Content Review Guide*.

**Qbank**

Qbank contains more than 1,000 exam-style questions written at the knowledge, comprehension, application and analysis levels of difficulty. You formulate your own tests by selecting areas of the NCLEX-PN® test plan and the number of questions on each test.

Clicking on "GO" next to Qbank allows you to access the Qbank questions.

**KAPLAN NURSING**

CHANGE PASSWORD  HELP  LOG OUT

Home  Integrated Testing  Focused Review Tests  NCLEX ® Prep  Essential Nursing Skills  Test Results

NCLEX-PN® Prep> PN Qbank > Create a New Test          Back    Homepage

**PN QBANK Navigation**

> Create Test
> Previous Tests
> Cumulative Performance
> NCLEX-PN® Prep Sample Tests

**Question Reuse Mode**

○ Unused Only    ○ Unused + Incorrect    ○ Incorrect Only    ○ All Items

**Test Content**

☐ Select all Test Content

| Main Category | | Sub Categories | |
|---|---|---|---|
| Safe and effective care environment | ☐ | Coordinated care | ☐ |
| | | Safety and infection control | ☐ |
| Health promotion and maintenance | ☐ | Health promotion & maint | ☐ |
| Psychosocial integrity | ☐ | Psychosocial integrity | ☐ |
| | | Basic care and comfort | ☐ |
| Physiological integrity | ☐ | Pharmacological therapies | ☐ |
| | | Reduction of risk potential | ☐ |
| | | Physiological adaptation | ☐ |

Available Questions: [    ]

**Create Test**

Number of Questions (85 max): [    ]

Create Test

# Create a New Test

This page presents you with a list of options:

**Create a test:** Allows you to put new tests together

**Previous tests:** Allows you to finish suspended tests and review completed tests

**Cumulative performance:** Indicates how you are performing in all areas of the test plan

**Sample tests:** Provides two 50-question tests based on the NCLEX test plan for your review

- **Test Style:**

    Choose *timed mode* when you want to practice testing under exam-like conditions. The program will determine the amount of testing time based on the number of questions selected. When the test is complete, your results are displayed and you can then review the questions. In the timed mode, you cannot review the explanations until you answer all the questions. To ensure success on Test Day, answer 95% of Qbank questions in timed mode.

    In *tutor mode* the test is not timed and you are able to view the explanations after answering each question. Your results are displayed at the end of the test. Use tutor mode only to become familiar with how Qbank works. After you have become familiar with Qbank, create all tests to timed mode.

- **Question Reuse Mode:**

    Select questions from unused questions, questions you have answered incorrectly, or from all items in the test pool.

- **Test Content:**

    Select content from the NCLEX-PN® examination blueprint. If you check "Select All Test Content," questions are selected from all areas of the test plan.

    If you check "Main Category," questions are selected from Safe and Effective Care, Health Promotion and Maintenance, Psychosocial Integrity, and Physiological Integrity. If you check "Subcategories," questions will come only from selected subcategories. This enables you to target your studies.

- **Available Questions:**

    Based on your selections, the number of questions available will calculate automatically. The questions contained in the Sample Tests are not included in the "Number of Available Questions."

- **Create Test:**

    Select the number of questions in the test, choosing from 5 to 50 questions. After selecting the number of questions, click Create Test to begin your testing experience.

## The Testing Screen

After creating a test, the testing experience begins. The testing screen consists of 3 parts:

*1*) the question is displayed at the top of the screen,

*2*) the answer choices are below the stem of the question, and

*3*) the toolbar is at the bottom of the screen.

The item number you are currently answering appears in the upper-right corner of the screen. The time remaining on the test (if you are in timed mode) is located in the upper-right corner. Always be aware of the time remaining because you will not receive any warning before time expires.

### Selecting an Answer

Each answer choice is preceded by a radio button.

- *To select an answer*, use the mouse to click on the radio button preceding the answer. If you are satisfied with your answer, click Next. Your answer will be entered and the next question appears.

- *To de-select an answer*, simply click on another radio button.

## The Toolbar

Three icons appear on the bottom of the tool bar: NEXT, SUSPEND, and END TEST.

- Click on NEXT to enter your answer.
- Click on SUSPEND to suspend the test. To resume the test, click on previous tests located on the splash page or on the left margin of the screen.
- END TEST will end the test and allow you to review your performance analysis.
- HELP will provide directions for the screen.

## Review Screen

To review, use the mouse to click on REVIEW found on the Analysis page. It will take you to a screen listing the number of questions on the test. Information provided includes:

- Your answer
- Correct response
- Client needs
- Client needs category
- Number of seconds used to answer the question
- Question ID
- Explanation (to view the question and explanation)

**NCLEX-PN Prep> Review Results**

[Analyze This Test] [Back] [Homepage]

| Test Type: | NCLEX-PN Prep | Test Name: | Qbank (Oct 9 2009 8:23AM) |
|---|---|---|---|

Review Results

| Q# | Correct? | Seconds Used | ClientNeeds | ClientNeedCategory | Q.ID | Explanation |
|---|---|---|---|---|---|---|
| 1 | ✓ | 71 | Physiological integrity | Physiological adaptation | n000445 | View Explanation |
| 2 | ✓ | 24 | Safe and effective care environment | Coordinated care | n000838 | View Explanation |
| 3 | ✓ | 37 | Psychosocial integrity | Psychosocial integrity | n000575 | View Explanation |
| 4 | ✗ | 23 | Physiological integrity | Reduction of risk potential | n000151 | View Explanation |
| 5 | ✓ | 72 | Psychosocial integrity | Psychosocial integrity | n000588 | View Explanation |

There are 2 icons on the toolbar located at the bottom of the Review screen. BACK TO RESULTS takes you back to the REVIEW RESULTS page. NEXT allows you to view the next question and explanation on the test.

# Cumulative Performance

The Cumulative Performance page gives you a raw percentage in each area of the NCLEX-PN® examination blueprint. Try to achieve 60% correct on all of your tests. Again, reviewing all questions will ensure success on Test Day.

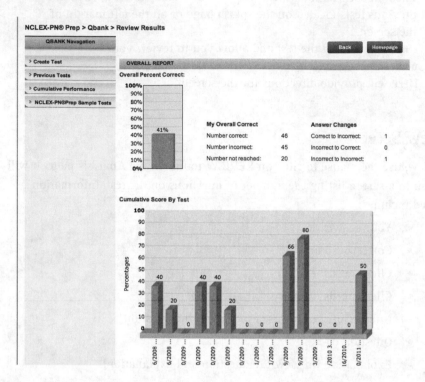

Kaplan has developed the Kaplan Decision Tree®—a critical thinking framework specifically for passing questions on the NCLEX-PN® examination. It is important to master the Decision Tree and use it consistently when answering higher-level test questions.

## Kaplan Decision Tree® for Answering Application/Analysis Questions

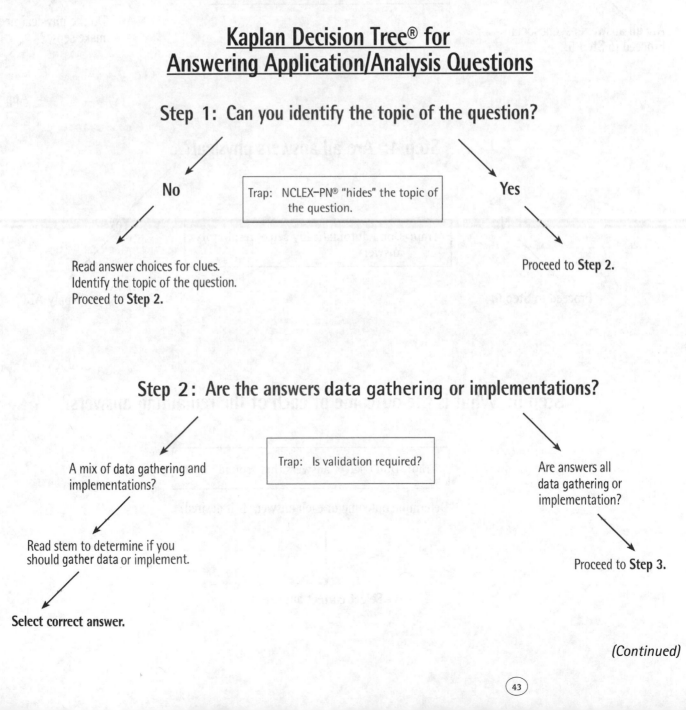

### Step 1: Can you identify the topic of the question?

**No**

Trap: NCLEX–PN® "hides" the topic of the question.

**Yes**

Read answer choices for clues.
Identify the topic of the question.
Proceed to **Step 2.**

Proceed to **Step 2.**

### Step 2: Are the answers data gathering or implementations?

A mix of data gathering and implementations?

Trap: Is validation required?

Are answers all data gathering or implementation?

Read stem to determine if you should gather data or implement.

Proceed to **Step 3.**

**Select correct answer.**

*(Continued)*

## Step 3: Does Maslow apply?

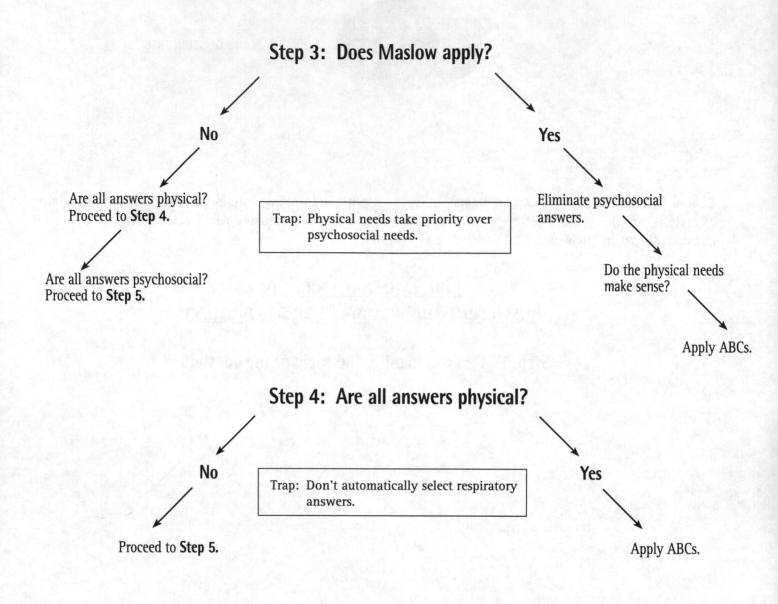

**No**

Are all answers physical?
Proceed to **Step 4.**

Are all answers psychosocial?
Proceed to **Step 5.**

Trap: Physical needs take priority over
psychosocial needs.

**Yes**

Eliminate psychosocial
answers.

Do the physical needs
make sense?

Apply ABCs.

## Step 4: Are all answers physical?

**No**

Trap: Don't automatically select respiratory
answers.

Proceed to **Step 5.**

**Yes**

Apply ABCs.

## Step 5: What is the outcome of each of the remaining answers?

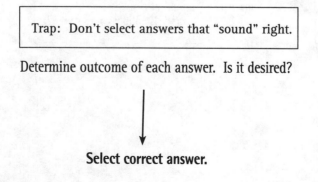

Trap: Don't select answers that "sound" right.

Determine outcome of each answer. Is it desired?

**Select correct answer.**

SAFE and
EFFECTIVE CARE
ENVIRONMENT

**Chapter 3**

Coordination of Care

Safety and Infection Control

## NURSE/CLIENT RELATIONSHIP

**A.** Professionalism

    1. Specific knowledge and skills—foundation of nursing science

    2. Person-centered

    3. Autonomy and accountability—adheres to standards of practice and is responsible for care given

    4. Nurse practice act

    5. Ethical standards
       a. Respect for human dignity—give respectful service regardless of client's personal characteristics
       b. Confidentiality—does not discuss condition with anyone not involved with care
       c. Competence—has knowledge and skills to provide care
       d. Advocacy—protects client from incompetent or unethical practice
       e. Research—participates in process of scientific inquiry
       f. Promotion of public health—committed to local and global goals for health of community

**B.** Therapeutic nature of the nurse/client relationship

    1. Professional
       a. Client-centered
       b. Responsible
       c. Goal-oriented
       d. Ethical

    2. Characterized by genuineness

    3. Nurse acts as a role model

    4. Nurse copes with own feelings

    5. Protected relationship—nurse or client (client) cannot be forced to reveal communication between them unless person who would benefit from relationship agrees to reveal it

## CLIENT'S BILL OF RIGHTS

**A.** Privacy

1. Right to be left alone without unwarranted or uninvited publicity

2. Right to make personal choices without interference (e.g., contraception, abortion, right to refuse treatment)

3. Right to have personal information kept confidential and distributed only to authorized personnel (consider the Health Insurance Portability and Accountability Act—HIPPA)
   a. Violated when confidential information revealed to unauthorized person(s), or unauthorized personnel directly or indirectly observes client without permission
   b. Authorized personnel—people involved in diagnosis and treatment (related to care of client)
   c. Health care team can't use data, photographs, videotapes, research data without explicit permission of client
   d. Be cautious about release of information on the phone (difficult to identify caller accurately)
   e. Necessary to obtain client's permission to release information to family members or close friends
   f. For employees, can only verify employment and comply with a legal investigation

**B.** Respectful care

**C.** Current information

**D.** Informed consent

1. Requirements
   a. Capacity—age (adult), competence (can make choices and understand consequences)
   b. Voluntary—freedom of choice without force, fraud, deceit, duress, coercion
   c. Information must be given in understandable form (lay terminology)
   d. Cannot sign informed consent if client has been drinking alcohol or has been premedicated
   e. Informed consent may not be required in emergency situations.

2. Minors who can provide own consent for treatment
   a. Married minors
   b. Over a specific age (e.g., 12) for STDs, HIV testing, AIDS treatment, drug and alcohol treatment
   c. Emancipated and mature minors
   d. Minors seeking birth control services
   e. Minors seeking outclient psychiatric services or inclient voluntary admissions to a psychiatric facility
   f. Pregnant minor
      1) Can sign consent for themselves and the fetus
      2) After delivery
         a) The mother retains right to provide consent for infant

b) Mother cannot give own consent unless she fits into one of other exemptions

3. Includes
   a. Explanation of treatment and expected results
   b. Anticipated risks and discomforts
   c. Potential benefits
   d. Possible alternatives
   e. Answers to questions
   f. Statements that consent can be withdrawn at any time

4. Legal responsibility
   a. Rests with individual who will perform treatment
   b. When nurse witnesses a signature, it means that there is reason to believe that the client is informed about upcoming treatment

E. Confidentiality

1. Right to privacy of records

2. Information used only for purpose of diagnosis and treatment

3. Not released to others without permission; verify identity of person asking for information

F. Refusal of treatment

1. Self-determination act—federal law requiring health care facilities to provide written information to adult clients about their rights to make health care decisions

2. Aggressive treatment
   a. Extraordinary support measures used to maintain individual's physiologic processes
   b. May be withheld to avoid prolonging life without dignity
   c. Supportive care is provided to promote comfort and reduce suffering

3. Advanced directives
   a. Living wills
      1) Legal document signed by competent individual indicates treatment or life-saving measures (e.g., surgery, CPR, antibiotics, dialysis, respirator, tube feedings) to be used if individual's ability to make decisions is lost due to a terminal illness or a permanently unconscious state.
      2) Indicates who is authorized to make health care decisions if individual becomes incapacitated
      3) Legally binding in most states
   b. Durable power of attorney
      1) Permits a competent adult to appoint surrogate or proxy in the event that the adult becomes incompetent
      2) Health care provider must follow decisions stated in documents
      3) In most states proxy can perform all legal actions needed to fulfill adult's wishes

G. Reasonable response to a request for services

H. Right to know hospital/clinic regulations

## RESTRAINTS

A. Restraints

1. Omnibus Budget Reconciliation Act provides clients with the right to be free from physical and chemical restraints imposed for the purpose of discipline or convenience and not required to treat medical symptoms

2. Mechanical restraint
   a. Needed to meet the client's therapeutic needs or ensure safety
   b. Least restrictive type of restraint to meet needs
   c. Accurate and thorough documentation needed

3. Chemical restraint
   a. Psychotropic drugs cannot be used to control behavior
   b. Can be used only for diagnoses-related conditions
   c. Inappropriate use causes deep sedation, agitation, combativeness

4. Informed consent is needed to use restraints

5. If client is unable to consent to use of restraints, then consent of proxy must be obtained after full disclosure of risks and benefits

6. Restraint of client without informed consent or sufficient justification is false imprisonment

B. Nursing considerations

1. Observe and document need for restraints (risk for falls, risk of injury to others, potential for removal of IV lines or other equipment)

2. Consider and document use of alternative measures

3. Health care provider's order is required specifying duration and circumstances under which restraints should be used

4. Cannot order restraints to be used PRN

5. Monitor client closely, periodically observe for continued need for restraints, document

6. Remove for skin care and range of motion exercises

7. Use alternative measures prior to use of restraints (reorientation, family involvement, frequent assistance with toileting)

## ADVOCACY

A. Nurse as client advocate should

1. Actively support clients' rights

2. Defend clients' participation in decisions affecting them

3. Safeguard clients' autonomy and independence

4. Provide clients with information about needs and available options so that clients can make informed decisions about health care

5. Communicate clients' needs to interdisciplinary team (RN, PT, dietician, social worker, psychologist)

## LEGAL ISSUES

**A.** Negligence—unintentional failure of individual to perform an act that a reasonable person would or would not perform in similar circumstances; can be act of omission or commission

**B.** Malpractice—professional negligence involving misconduct or lack of skill in carrying out professional responsibilities

   1. Required elements
      a. Duty—legal relationship between nurse and client
      b. Breach of duty
      c. Causation—nurse conduct causes injury
      d. Injury

**C.** Invasion of privacy—release of information to an unauthorized person without the client's consent

**D.** Assault—intentional threat to cause harm or offensive contact; battery—intentional touching without consent

**E.** False imprisonment

   1. Client is denied discharge from a health care facility
   2. Client is denied discharge after signing an against medical advice (AMA) document
   3. Client is placed in restraints without appropriate medical need

**F.** Laws

   1. Rules of conduct established and enforced by authority
   2. Reflect public policy
   3. Indicates what society views as good and bad, right and wrong behavior

**G.** Accountability

   1. Nurse is responsible for using reasonable care in practicing nursing
   2. To remain competent, nurse needs to participate in lifelong learning programs

**H.** State laws

   1. Nurse practice acts—define "reasonable care" in each state; scope of nursing practice, roles, rules, educational requirements
   2. Good Samaritan laws—limit the liability of professionals in emergency situations
   3. Tarasoff Act—duty to warn of threatened suicide or harm to others
   4. Licensure requirements—differ slightly in LPN/LVN requirements among states

## COORDINATED CARE

**A.** Health care focuses on individual client needs along the health continuum (wellness to illness)

**B.** Managed care

　1. Goal is reduced health care costs

　2. Focuses on client outcomes and maintenance of quality

　3. Uses an interdisciplinary approach

　4. Emphasizes costs; approval needed for diagnostic tests

　5. Critical pathways (care maps) used as foundations for activities and guide services that clients receive for specific health conditions

**C.** Continuous quality improvement (CQI; previously called quality assurance)

　1. Prevention-focused approach provides basis for managing risk

　2. Involves organized incident reporting

　3. Managed by team of 5–10 people

　4. Process
　　a. Senior management establishes policy
　　b. Coordinator provides for process and management health care team training
　　c. Team, headed by a team leader, evaluates and improves the process

**D.** Risk management

　1. Planned program of loss prevention and liability control

　2. Problem-focused

　3. Identifies, evaluates, develops plan, and takes corrective action against potential risks that would injure clients, staff, visitors

　4. Focuses on noncompliance, informed consent, right to refuse treatment

**E.** Collaborative practice team

　1. Consists of clinical experts: nursing, medicine, physical therapy, social work

　2. Determines expected outcomes

　3. Determines appropriate interventions with a specified time frame

　4. Involves specific client diagnoses that are high-volume (frequently seen), high-cost, high-risk (frequently develop complications)

**F.** For coordinated care to be successful, need

　1. Support from health care providers, nurses, administrators

　2. Qualified nurse managers

　3. Collaborative practice teams

　4. Quality management system

5. All professionals are equal members of the team (one discipline doesn't determine interventions for another discipline)

6. Members agree on final draft of critical pathways, take ownership of client outcomes, accept responsibility and accountability for interventions and client outcomes

G. Critical pathways

1. Reduce complications

2. Reduce cost

3. Increase collaboration

4. Improve quality of care

5. Provide direction for care

6. Orient staff to expected outcomes for each day

7. If outcomes not achieved, case manager is notified and situation is analyzed to determine how to modify critical path

8. Alteration in time frame or interventions is a "variance"

9. All variances are tracked to note trends

10. Variance—change in established plan that includes more, different, or fewer services to client to achieve desired outcome

11. Interventions presented in modality groups (medications, nursing activities)

12. Include
   a. Specific medical diagnoses
   b. Expected length of stay
   c. Client identification data
   d. Appropriate time frames (days, hours, minutes, visits) for interventions
   e. Clinical outcomes
   f. Client outcomes

H. Variances

1. Deviations from specific plans (individual receives more, less, or different services)

2. Information is included in a database and is used to evaluated services provided

3. Continuous quality improvement (CQI) strategies are used to monitor variances

I. Case manager—usually has advanced degree and considerable experience

1. Doesn't provide direct client care

2. Supervises care provided by licensed and unlicensed personnel

3. Coordinates, communicates, collaborates, solves problems

4. Facilitates client care for a group of clients (10–15)

5. Follows client through the system from admission to discharge

6. Notes "variances" from expected progress

**J.** Case management

1. Identifies, coordinates, monitors implementation of services needed to achieve desired outcomes within specified period of time

2. Involves principles of CQI

3. Promotes professional practice

## DELEGATION

**A.** Responsibility and authority for performing a task (function, activity, decision) is transferred to another individual who accepts that responsibility and authority

**B.** Depending on state Nurse Practice Acts, PNs may delegate tasks to nursing assistive personnel (NAP) (NAP includes the nursing providers excluding RNs and PNs, such as UAP, NAs, CNAs, etc.)

**C.** Delegator remains accountable for task

**D.** Delegatee is accountable to delegator for responsibilities assumed

**E.** Licensed individual asking another to perform a task that is one of his/her responsibilities

**F.** Definitions

1. Responsibility—obligation to accomplish a task

2. Accountability—accept ownership for results or lack of results

**G.** In delegation, responsibility is transferred; in accountability, it is shared

**H.** Guidelines

1. Can delegate only those tasks for which you are responsible

2. Responsibility is determined by

   a. Nurse practice acts (defines scope of nursing practice)

   b. Standards of care (established by organization)

   c. Job description (defined by organization)

   d. Policy statement (from organization)

3. Must transfer authority (the right to act) along with the responsibility to act

4. Empowers delegatee to accomplish task

**I.** Steps for delegation

1. Define task to be delegated

   a. Can delegate only work for which you have responsibility and authority

   b. Delegate what you know best so you can provide guidance and feedback

      1) Routine tasks

      2) Tasks you don't have time to accomplish

      3) Tasks with lower priority

    2. Determine who should receive delegated task

    3. Identify what the task involves, determine its complexity

    4. Match task to individual by observing individual skills and abilities

       a. Evaluate capacity of individual to perform task

       b. Consider availability, willingness to assume responsibility

    5. Provide clear communication about your expectations regarding the task, answer questions

**J.** To delegate

    1. Assume face-to-face position

    2. Establish eye contact

    3. Describe task using "I" statements

    4. Provide what, when, where, how of the task to be delegated

    5. State if delegatee needs to provide written or verbal report after the task is completed

    6. If written report is needed, inform delegatee where to put the report (e.g., table, chart, form)

    7. Identify what changes or incidents need to be brought to delegator's attention (e.g., "If client's BP is greater than 140/90, let me know immediately.")

    8. Provide reason for task, give incentive for accepting responsibility and authority

    9. Tell delegatee how and how often task will be evaluated

   10. Describe expected outcome and timeline for completion of task

**K.** Identify constraints for completing task and risks

**L.** Identify variables that would change authority and responsibility (e.g., "Feed client if coherent and awake; if client is confused, do not feed and notify me immediately.")

**M.** Obtain feedback from delegatee to make sure he/she understands task to be performed and your expectations; ask for questions, give additional information

**N.** Reach mutual agreement on task

**O.** Monitor performance and results according to established goals

**P.** Give constructive feedback to delegatee

**Q.** Confirm that delegated tasks are performed as agreed

**R.** Delegator must remain accessible during performance of task

**S.** Levels of delegation (in ascending order)

    1. Gather information for delegatee so you can decide what needs to be done

    2. List alternate courses of action and allow delegatee to choose course of action

    3. Have delegatee perform part of task and obtain approval before proceeding with the rest of the task

4. Have delegatee outline entire course of action for the task and approve it before proceeding

5. Allow delegatee to perform entire task using any preferred methods and report only results

**T.** Rule for determining delegatee—delegate to lowest person on hierarchy who has the required skills and abilities and who is allowed to do the task legally and according to the organization

**U.** Obstacles to delegation

1. Nonsupportive environment—rigid organizational culture, lack of resources (limited personnel)

2. Insecure delegator

3. Fear of competition

4. Fear of liability

5. Fear of loss of control

6. Fear of overburdening others

7. Fear of decreased personal job satisfaction

8. Unwilling delegatee

9. Fear of failure

10. Inexperience

**V.** Ineffective delegaton

1. Underdelegation

   a. Doesn't transfer full authority

   b. Takes back responsibility

   c. Fails to equip or direct delegatee

   d. Questions competence of delegatee

2. Reverse delegation—lower person on hierarchy delegates to person higher on hierarchy

3. Overdelegation—delegator loses control of the situation by delegating too much authority and responsibility to delegatee

**W.** Rights of delegation

1. Right task

2. Right person (knowledge, skills, abilities)

3. Right time (not in a crisis)

4. Right information

5. Right supervision (is task being performed correctly?)

6. Right follow-up

**X.** Delegation empowers others, builds trust, enhances communication and leadership skills, develops teamwork, increases productivity

**Y.** Failure to delegate and supervise properly can result in liability; need to consider delegatee's competence and qualifications

**Z.** Delegator has responsibility to make sure persons under his or her supervision perform consistently with established standards of nursing practice

## CARE TEAMS

A. Staff mixes—combination of registered nurses (RNs), licensed practical or vocational nurses (LPN/LVNs), nursing assistive personnel (NAP), and support staff combined to complement, not substitute for, professional staff

1. RN
   a. Performs most assessments
   b. Admits new clients
   c. Discharges clients
   d. Cares for complex clients
   e. Retains care of clients with diagnoses unique to the unit (particularly in situations of "pulled" or reassigned nurses)
   f. Performs client and family teaching about new diagnoses, diagnostic tests, medications, skills for self-care, and discharge/home care

2. LPN/LVN
   a. Assist with implementation of defined plan of care
   b. Perform procedures according to protocol
   c. Differentiate normal from abnormal; report data to RN
   d. Care for physiologically stable clients with predictable conditions
   e. Has knowledge of asepsis and dressing changes
   f. Ability to administer medications varies with educational background and state nurse practice act

3. Nursing assistive personnel (NAPs)
   a. Assist with direct client care activities (bathing, transferring, ambulating, feeding, toileting, obtaining vital signs, height, weight, intake and output, housekeeping, transporting, stocking supplies)
   b. Includes nurses aides, assistants, technicians, orderlies, nurse extenders
   c. Scope of nursing practice is limited

B. Hierarchy or chain of command

1. Organizational hierarchy—designed to promote smooth functioning within a large and complex organization

2. Hierarchy—employees are ranked according to their degrees of authority within an organization

3. Chain of command—emphasis on vertical relationships (e.g., nurse reports to nurse manager who reports to nursing supervisor, etc.)

4. Nurse reports variances, problems, and concerns to next person with authority in direct line in their area

## CRITICAL THINKING

A. Involves creativity, problem-solving, decision-making

B. Nursing responsibilities

1. Observe

2. Decide what data are important

3. Validate and organize data

4. Look for patterns and relationships

5. State problem

6. Transfer knowledge from one situation to another

7. Decide on criteria for evaluation

8. Apply knowledge

9. Evaluate according to criteria established

## DECISION MAKING

A. Purposeful and goal-directed; nurse identifies and selects options and alternatives

B. Types of decision making

1. Prescriptive

   a. Involves routine decisions with objective information

   b. Options are known and predictable

   c. Decisions made according to standard procedures or analytical tools

2. Behavioral

   a. Involves the nonroutine and unstructured information

   b. Options are unknown or unpredictable

   c. Decisions made by obtaining more data, using past experiences, using creative approach

3. Satisficing

   a. Solution minimally meets objectives

   b. Expedient; use when time is an issue

4. Optimizing

   a. Goal is to select ideal solution

   b. Best decision comes from this process but is the most time consuming

C. Phases

1. Define objectives

2. Generate options

3. Analyze options
   a. Identify advantages and disadvantages
   b. Rank options
4. Select option that will successfully meet the defined objective
5. Implement the selected option
6. Evaluate the outcome

## PROBLEM SOLVING

**A.** Focus is trying to solve immediate problems; includes decision making

**B.** Methods

1. Trial and error
   a. Repeated attempts at different solutions until it is identified that one solution works best
   b. Used by inexperienced staff

2. Experimentation
   a. Study problem using trial periods or pilot projects to determine best outcome
   b. Will have greater probability of achieving best outcome if sufficient time devoted to the process

3. Purposeful inaction
   a. Do-nothing approach
   b. Use when problem is judged to be insignificant or outside a person's control

**C.** Steps

1. Define the problem
2. Gather data
3. Analyze data
4. Develop solutions
5. Select and implement a solution
6. Evaluate the results

## DOCUMENTATION

**A.** Purpose

1. Promotes communication
2. Maintains a legal record
3. Meets requirements of regulatory agencies
4. Required for third-party reimbursement

**B.** Characteristics of good documentation

1. Legible
2. Accurate

3. Timely

4. Thorough

5. Well organized and concise (follow chronological order of events)

6. Confidential

7. Proper grammar and spelling

8. Authorized abbreviations

C. Documenting changes in client conditions

1. Data Collection

a. Client's vital signs, symptoms, behaviors, complaints, responses to treatments (PRN meds, dietary changes, I and O)

b. Information from family members or significant other

2. Notify RN or health care provider if client's physiological status and functional abilities change significantly

3. Notify family or significant other about changes in client's condition and plan of care

a. Nature of change

b. Why changes were made

c. Actions undertaken to provide needed care for client

d. Help family to take active part in client's care and management

e. Follow policy for privacy and confidentiality

5. Document in timely manner

a. Date and time

b. Nursing data collection

c. Name of RN or health care provider informed

d. Date, time, method (e.g., telephone)

e. Information provided about client

f. Actions taken (revisions in plan of care)

g. Information given and to whom (client, name of family, significant other)

h. Responses by client and family members or significant other

6. Considerations

a. If an error is made in charting, use a single line through the error and doc your initials, date, and time—do not erase, white out, or scratch out an error

b. Do not chart for anyone else

c. Keep your electronic access private

d. Do not leave your electronic chart open when you are not in attendance

## INCIDENT REPORTS

A. Definition

1. Agency record of unusual occurrence or accident and physical response

2. Accurate and comprehensive report on any unexpected or unplanned occurrence that affects or could potentially affect a client, family member, or staff person

**B.** Purpose

    1. Documentation and follow-up

    2. Used to analyze the severity, frequency, and cause of occurrences

    3. Analysis is the basis for intervention

**C.** Charting

    1. Don't include a reference to the incident report

    2. Don't use words such as "error" or "inappropriate"

    3. Don't include inflammatory words or judgmental statements

    4. If there are adverse reactions to incident, chart follow-up note updating client's status

    5. Documentation of client's reactions should be included as status changes and should be continued until client returns to original status

**D.** Sequence

    1. Person discovers and reports actual or potential risk

    2. Risk manager receives report within 24 hours

    3. Investigation of incident is conducted

    4. Referring health care provider and risk management committee consult together

**E.** Risk manager

    1. Clarifies misinformation for client and family

    2. Explains what happened to client and family

    3. Client is referred to appropriate resources

    4. Care is provided free of charge

    5. All records, incident reports, follow-up actions taken are filed in a central location

**F.** Common situations that require an incident report

    1. Medication errors—omitted medication, wrong medication, wrong dosage, wrong route

    2. Complications from diagnostic or treatment procedures (e.g., blood sample stick, biopsy, x-ray, LP, invasive procedure, bronchoscopy, thoracentesis)

    3. Incorrect sponge count in surgery

    4. Failure to report change in client's condition

    5. Falls

    6. Client is burned

    7. Break in aseptic technique

    8. Medical—legal incident

        a. Client or family refuses treatment as ordered and refuses to sign consent

        b. Client or family voices dissatisfaction with care and situation cannot be or has not been resolved

## CHANGE OF SHIFT REPORT

**A.** Regularly scheduled, structured exchange of information

**B.** Focuses on anticipated needs of individual clients in next 24 hours

**C.** Enables health care workers to
1. Organize work for specified time period
2. Communicate concerns
3. Provide continuity of care or consistent follow-through

**D.** Included
1. Client's status
2. Current care plan
3. Responses to current care
4. Things needing further attention

**E.** Reporting nurse describes
1. Actual or potential client needs
2. How these needs were addressed during previous shift by nursing and interdisciplinary team
3. Information about laboratory studies, diagnostic tests, treatments, and nursing activities anticipated during next shift
4. Reporting nurse must legally communicate all facts relevant to continuity of care of assigned clients
5. Information must be pertinent, current, and accurate

**F.** Change-of-shift reports should not contain
1. Information already known by the oncoming shift
2. Descriptions of routines (AM or PM care)
3. Rumors or gossip
4. Opinions or value judgements (about client's lifestyle)
5. Client information that does not relate to health condition, needs, or treatments (e.g., idiosyncrasies)

**G.** To give change-of-shift report
1. Gather data to be discussed (flow sheets, work sheets, Kardex, progress notes, chart)
2. Avoid copying data in order to prevent errors and reduce time required
3. Use outline to organize report
4. Provide in logical, uniform manner

**H.** To deliver change-of-shift report, include
1. Client information
   a. Name, room, and bed number
   b. Note if off the unit (recovery room, diagnostic test, etc.)
2. Medical plan
   a. Admitting diagnosis
   b. Attending health care provider
   c. Major diagnostic or surgical procedures with dates
   d. Health care provider's orders that have been discontinued or affect next shift

   e. IV solutions, flow rates, when current bag is scheduled to be completed, amount of solution remaining to be infused

   f. Medications

   g. Response to treatment (expected and untoward effects)

   h. Client's emotional response to condition

   i. Use of and response to PRN meds

   j. Completion of special procedures

  3. Nursing plan

   a. Personalized nursing approaches

   b. Special equipment, supplies, or pacing of activities

   c. Response to diet

   d. Behavioral response to treatment and health status (e.g., denial, frustration)

   e. Nursing data collection (e.g., vital signs, I and O, activity level)

   f. New concerns

   g. Changing client needs

   h. Client outcomes

   i. Interdisciplinary plans

   j. Referrals

   k. Teaching plans

   l. Discharge plans

**I.** Nurse receiving report should learn

 1. Individual client's symptoms

 2. Discomforts

 3. What has been done

 4. What remains to be done

 5. How client has responded to treatments and activities so changes can be made to meet client needs

**J.** Types of change-of-shift reports

 1. Face-to-face

   a. Reporting nurse answers questions from oncoming staff

   b. Provides flexibility to report to a number of different oncoming staff

   c. Provides flexibility in pacing and sequencing of report

   d. Nurses listen to report only on their clients

 2. Taped

   a. Less time-consuming because of lack of interruptions

   b. Nurse is frequently more systematic and thorough

   c. Gives nurse more sense of control over the process

   d. Reporting nurse can perform nursing activities while next shift is listening to report

   e. Reporting nurse returns to clarify information, answer questions, update information that changed since report was recorded

**K.** Method of service delivery and change-of-shift reports

 1. Functional method

   a. RN of previous shift reports to RN of oncoming shift

   b. Other staff may attend report or be given report according to assignments from RN

2. Team nursing method
   a. All members of oncoming shift attend report
   b. Reduces amount of time and communication needed to make changes in nursing care for client

3. Primary nursing method
   a. RN assigned to direct care of individual clients reports to RN assigned to direct care of same individual clients

4. Case management method
   a. Scheduled structured discussions with nursing team and interdisciplinary team in addition to change-of-shift reports

## CULTURAL NORMS

A. Cultural norms—group of individuals' values and beliefs that strongly influence individual's actions and behaviors

B. Values—personal preferences, commitments, motivations, patterns of using resources, objects, people, or events that have special meaning and influence individual's choices, behaviors, actions

C. Beliefs

1. Basic assumptions or personal convictions that the individual thinks are factual or takes for granted

2. Used to determine values

3. Handed down from generation to generation

4. Include cultural traditions

## ETHICS

A. Definition

1. Principles of right and wrong, good and bad

2. Governs our relationship with others

3. Used to identify solutions to problems arising from conflicts

4. Based on personal beliefs and cultural values that guide decision-making and determine conduct

5. As cultural diversity increases, need to understand ethical principles increases

B. ANA Code of Ethics—decision-making framework for solving ethical problems

1. Nurse provides care with respect for human dignity and uniqueness of individual without consideration of social or economic status, personal attributes, or nature of health problems

2. Nurse safeguards the client's right to privacy

3. Nurse acts to safeguard client and public when health care and safety are at risk from incompetent, unethical, or illegal practice of an individual

4. Nurse assumes responsibility and accountability for own individual actions and judgments

5. Nurse maintains competence in nursing

6. Nurse uses informed judgment, competence, and qualifications in accepting responsibilities and delegating nursing activities to others

7. Nurse participates in activities contributing to the development of the profession's body of knowledge

8. Nurse participates in profession's efforts to implement and improve standards of care

9. Nurse participates in profession's efforts to establish and maintain conditions of employment conducive to high-quality nursing care

10. Nurse participates in profession's efforts to protect the public from misinformation and misrepresentation and to maintain the integrity of nursing

11. Nurse collaborates with members of the health professions and others to promote community and national efforts to meet the health care needs of the public

C. Ethical principles of nursing

1. Autonomy—support of client's independence to make decisions and take action for themselves

2. Beneficence—duty to help others by doing what is best for them; for refusal of care, autonomy overrides beneficence

3. Nonmaleficence—"do no harm"; act with empathy toward client and staff without resentment or malice; violated by acts performed in bad faith or with ill will, or when making false accusations about client or employee

4. Justice—use available resources fairly and reasonably

5. Veracity—communicate truthfully and accurately

6. Confidentiality—safeguard the client's privacy

7. Fidelity—following through on what the nurse says will be done; carefully attending to the details of the client's care

D. Ethical reasoning process

1. Recognize a moral issue

2. Analyze facts and identify the dilemma

3. Decide on possible alternative actions

4. Select specific action

5. Evaluate the effectiveness of the action

E. Behaviors for handling complaints

1. Use active listening without interrupting or arguing

2. Don't get defensive

3.  Ask person what is expected for solution to problem

4.  Explain what you can and cannot do to solve the problem

5.  Agree on specific steps that will be taken and determine a timeline

## INFECTIONS AND INFECTION CONTROL

**A.** Data Collection

   1.  Local (focal point)—heat, redness, pain/tenderness, swelling, possible drainage (bloody, serous, purulent), abscess (localized collection of pus), cellulitis (involving cellular and connective tissue)

   2.  Systemic (generalized)—fever, malaise, weakness

   3.  White blood cell count (WBC)—normally 5,000–10,000/mm$^3$; increase indicates the presence of disease or injury; differential of 30–40% lymphocytes; increased number of immature neutrophils ("shift to left")

   4.  Erythrocyte sedimentation rate (ESR)—elevations greater than 15–20 mm/h indicate the presence of inflammation

   5.  Cultures of suspected infectious site
      a.  Should be obtained before onset of antibiotic therapy
      b.  Specimens must be carefully collected and identified
      c.  Preliminary results in 24 hrs; final results in 72 hrs

   6.  Highly sensitive C-reactive protein (hsCRP)–marker of inflammation

**B.** Diagnose

   1.  Inflammation—immediate, short-term, nonspecific response to the side effects of injury, i.e., physical irritants (trauma/foreign body) or chemical irritants (strong acids/alkalies) or invasion by microorganisms

   2.  Communicable diseases—caused by pathogenic microorganisms and transmitted by direct contact, droplet spread, contaminated articles, or through carriers (see Table 1)

   3.  Hospital-Acquired Infections (HAI)—nearly 2 million (5%) hospital clients acquire an infection in the hospital; most often caused by *Staphylococcus aureus*

**C.** Plan/Implementation

   1.  Treatment of infection or infectious disease with appropriate antibiotic medication

   2.  Standard Precautions (barrier)—used with all clients
      a.  Primary strategy for noscomial infection control

Table 1

| COMMON COMMUNICABLE DISEASES OF CHILDHOOD | | |
|---|---|---|
| NAME/ INCUBATION | TRANSMISSION/CLINICAL PICTURE | NURSING CONSIDERATIONS |
| Chickenpox (Varicella) 13-17 days | Prodromal: slight fever, malaise, anorexia<br>Rash is pruritic, begins as macule, then papule, and then vesicle with successive crops of all three stages present at any one time; lymphadenopathy; elevated temperature<br>Transmission: spread by direct contact, airborne, contaminated object | Isolation until all vesicles are crusted; communicable from 2 days before rash<br>Avoid use of aspirin due to association with Reye's syndrome; use Tylenol<br>Topical application of calamine lotion or baking soda baths<br>Airborne and contact precautions in hospital |
| Diphtheria 2-5 days | Prodromal: resembles common cold<br>Low-grade fever, hoarseness, malaise, pharyngeal lymphadenitis; characteristic white/gray pharyngeal membrane<br>Transmission: direct contact with a carrier, infected client contaminated articles | Contact and droplet precautions until two successive negative nose and throat cultures are obtained<br>Complete bedrest; watch for signs of respiratory distress and obstruction; provide for humidification, suctioning, and tracheostomy as needed; severe cases can lead to sepsis and death<br>Administer antitoxin therapy |
| Pertussis (Whooping Cough) 5-21 days, usually 10 | Prodromal: upper respiratory infection for 1-2 weeks<br>Severe cough with high-pitched "whooping" sound, especially at night, lasts 4-6 weeks; vomiting<br>Transmission: direct contact, droplet, contaminated articles | Hospitalization for infants; bedrest and hydration<br>Complications: pneumonia, weight loss, dehydration, hemorrhage, hernia, airway obstruction<br>Maintain high humidity and restful environment; suction; oxygen<br>Administer erthromycin and pertussis immune globulin |
| Rubella (German Measles) 14-21 days | Prodromal: none in children, low fever and sore throat in adolescent<br>Maculopapular rash appears first on face and then on rest of the body<br>Symptoms subside first day after rash<br>Transmission: droplet spread and contaminated articles | Contact precautions<br>Isolate child from potentially pregnant women<br>Comfort measures; antipyretics and analgesics<br>Rare complications include arthritis and encephalitis<br>Droplet precautions<br>Risk of fetal deformity |
| Rubeola 10-20 days | Prodromal: fever and malaise followed by cough and Koplik's spots on buccal mucosa<br>Erythematous maculopapular rash with face first affected; turns brown after 3 days when symptoms subside<br>Transmission: direct contact with droplets | Isolate until 5th day; maintain bedrest during first 3-4 days<br>Institute airborne and seizure precautions<br>Antipyretics, dim lights; humidifier for room<br>Keep skin clean and maintain hydration |
| Scarlet fever 2-4 days | Prodromal: high fever with vomiting, chills, malaise, followed by enlarged tonsils covered with exudate, strawberry tongue<br>Rash: red tiny lesions that become generalized and then desquamate; rash appears within 24 hours<br>Transmission: droplet spread or contaminated articles<br>Group A beta-hemolytic streptococci | Droplet precautions for 24 hours after start of antibiotics<br>Ensure compliance with oral antibiotic therapy<br>Bedrest during febrile phase<br>Analgesics for sore throat<br>Encourage fluids, soft diet<br>Administer penicillin or erythromycin |
| Mononucleosis 4-6 weeks | Malaise, fever, enlarged lymph nodes, sore throat, flulike aches, low-grade temperature<br>Highest incidence 15-30 years old<br>Transmission: direct contact with oral secretions, unknown | Advise family members to avoid contact with saliva (cups, silverware) for about 3 months<br>Treatment is rest and good nutrition; strenuous exercise is to be avoided to prevent spleen rupture<br>Complications include encephalitis and spleen rupture |
| Tonsillitis (streptococcal) | Fever, white exudate on tonsils<br>Positive culture GpA strep | Antibiotics<br>Teach parents serious potential complications: rheumatic fever, glomerulonephritis |
| Mumps 14-21 days | Malaise, headache, fever, parotid gland swelling<br>Transmission: direct contact with saliva, droplet | Isolation before and after appearance of swelling<br>Soft, bland diet<br>Complications: deafness, meningitis, encephalitis, sterility |

b. Most important way to reduce transmission of pathogens

c. Standard precautions apply to contact with blood, body fluids, nonintact skin and mucous membranes from all clients

d. Handwashing
   1) Done immediately on contact with blood or bodily fluids
   2) Wash hands before putting on or taking off gloves, between client contacts, between procedures or tasks with same client, immediately after exposure to blood or bodily fluids

e. Gloves
   1) Use clean, nonsterile when touching blood, body fluids, secretions, excretions, contaminated articles
   2) Put on gloves just before touching mucous membranes or nonintact skin, for touching blood, body fluids, secretions, contaminated items, or if gloves torn or heavily soiled
   3) Change gloves between tasks/procedures
   4) Remove gloves promptly after use, before touching items and environmental surfaces

f. Masks, eye protection, face shield (Personal Protective Equipment)
   1) Used to protect mucous membranes of eyes, nose, mouth during procedures and client care activities likely to generate splashes or sprays of blood, bodily fluids, or excretions

g. Gowns (Personal Protective Equipment)
   1) Use clean, nonsterile gowns to protect skin and prevent soiling of clothing during procedures and client care activities likely to generate splashes and sprays of blood, bodily fluids, or excretions
   2) Should remove promptly, and wash hands after leaving client's environment

h. Environmental control
   1) Do not need to use special dishes, glasses, eating utensils; can use either reusable or disposable
   2) Don't recap used sharps, or bend, break, or remove used needles
   3) Don't manipulate used needle with two hands; use a one-handed scoop technique
   4  Place used sharps in a puncture-resistant container
   5) Use mouthpieces, resuscitation bags, or other devices for mouth-to-mouth resuscitation

i. Client placement
   1) Private room if client has poor hygiene habits, contaminates the environment, or can't assist in maintaining infection control precautions (e.g., infants, children, altered mental status client)
   2) When cohorting (sharing room) consider the epidemiology and mode of transmission of the infecting organism

j. Transport
   1) Use barriers (e.g., mask, impervious dressings)
   2) Notify personnel of impending arrival and precautions needed
   3) Inform client of ways to assist in prevention of transmission

3. Transmission-based precautions apply to clients with documented or suspected infections with highly transmissible or epidemiologically important pathogens; prevent spread of pathogenic organisms
   a. Airborne precautions
      1) Used with pathogens smaller than 5 microns that are transmitted by airborne route; droplets or dust particles that remain suspended in the air
      2) Private room with monitored negative air pressure with 6–12 air changes per hour (airborne infection isolation room)
      3) Keep door closed and client in room; susceptible persons should not enter room or wear N-95 HEPA filter
      4) Can cohort or place client with another client with the same organism, but no other organism
      5) Place mask on client if being transported
      6) Tuberculosis – wear fit-test respirator mask
      7) Example of disease in category: measles (rubeola), *M. tuberculosis*, varicella (chicken pox), disseminated zoster (shingles)
   b. Droplet precautions
      1) Used with pathogens transmitted by infectious droplets
      2) Involves contact of conjunctiva or mucous membranes of nose or mouth; happens during coughing, sneezing, talking, or during procedures such as suctioning or bronchoscopy
      3) Private room or with client with same infection but no other infection; wear mask if in close contact
      4) Maintain spatial separation of three feet between infected client and vistors or other clients
      5) Door may remain open
      6) Place mask on client if being transported
      7) Example of disease in category: diphtheria, group A streptococcus pneumonia, pneumonia or meningitis caused by *N. meningitidis* or *H. influenzae* type B, rubella, mumps, pertussis
   c. Contact precautions
      1) Needed with client care activities that require physical skin-to-skin contact (e.g., turn clients, bathe clients), or occurs between two clients (e.g., hand contact), or occurs by contact with contaminated inanimate objects in client's environment
      2) Private room or with client with same infection but no other infection
      3) Clean, nonsterile gloves for contact with clients or potentially contaminated areas
      4) Change gloves after client contact with fecal material or wound drainage
      5) Remove gloves before leaving client's environment and wash hands with antimicrobial agent
      6) Wear gown when entering room if clothing will have contact with client, environment surfaces, or if client is incontinent, has diarrhea, an ileostomy, colostomy, or wound drainage
      7) Remove gown before leaving room

8) Use dedicated equipment or clean and disinfect between clients

9) Example of diseases in category: infection caused by multidrug-resistant organisms (e.g., MRSA and vancomycin-resistant organisms); herpes simplex; herpes zoster, *clostridium difficile*, respiratory syncytial virus, scabies, excessive wound drainage, fecal incontinence or discharge which suggests increased potential for environmental contamination, rotavirus, hepatitis type A (diapered or incontinent clients)

## TUBERCULOSIS

**A.** Data Collection

1. Progressive fatigue, nausea, anorexia, weight loss

2. Irregular menses

3. Low-grade fevers over a period of time

4. Night sweats

5. Irritability

6. Cough with mucopurulent sputum, occasionally streaked with blood; chest tightness and a dull aching chest; dyspnea

7. Diagnostic procedures
   a. Skin testing (see Table 2)
   b. Sputum smear for acid-fast bacilli, induce by respiratory therapy in AM and PM
   c. Chest x-ray routinely performed on all persons with positive PPD to detect old and new lesions; tubercules may be seen in lungs
   d. QuantiFERON-TB Gold test–results within 24 hours

**B.** Diagnose

1. Transmitted by aerosolization; bacillus multiplies in bronchi or alveoli, resulting in pneumonitis; may lie dormant for many years and be reactivated in periods of stress; may spread to other parts of body

●Table 2

| TB SKIN TESTING | |
|---|---|
| **TEST** | **NURSING CONSIDERATIONS** |
| Mantoux Test (PPD) | Given intradermally in the forearm<br>15-mm induration (hard area under the skin) = significant (positive) reaction for clients without certain risk factors<br>Read in 48-72 hours<br>Does not mean that active disease is present, but indicates exposure to TB or the presence of inactive (dormant) disease<br>Greater than 5 mm for clients with AIDS = positive reaction<br>TB infection may still be present in elderly or immunocompromised with induration less than or equal to 10 mm |
| Multiple Puncture Test (Tine) | Read test in 48-72 hours<br>Vesicle formation = positive reaction<br>Screening test only<br>Questionable or positive reactions verified by Mantoux Test |

2. Risk factors
   a. Close contact with someone who has active tuberculosis
   b. Immunocompromised
   c. IV drug abuser
   d. Persons who live in institutions
   e. Lower socioeconomic group
   f. Immigrants from countries with a high prevalence of tuberculosis (Latin American, Southeast Asia, Africa)

3. Incidence increasing in immigrant populations, poverty areas, elderly, alcoholics, drug abusers, and persons with AIDS

**C.** Plan/Implementation

1. Notification of state health department; evaluation of contacts

2. Isoniazid prophylaxis—not recommended for those individuals >35 years old who are at low risk because of increased risk of associated toxic hepatitis; persons <35 get 6–9 months therapy with isoniazid
   a. Household contacts
   b. Recent converters
   c. Persons under age 20 with positive reaction and inactive TB
   d. Susceptible health care workers
   e. Newly infected persons
   f. Significant skin test reactors with abnormal x-ray studies
   g. Significant skin test reactors up to age 35

3. Chemotherapy—to prevent development of resistant strains, two or three medications are usually administered concurrently; frequently a 6- or 9-month regimen of isoniazid and rifampin; ethambutol and streptomycin may be used initially (see page 512)

4. Isolation for 2 to 4 weeks (or three negative sputum cultures) after drug therapy is initiated; sent home before this (family already exposed)

5. Reinforce teaching
   a. Cover mouth and nose with tissue when coughing, sneezing, laughing; burn tissues
   b. Avoid excessive exposure to dust and silicone
   c. Handwashing
   d. Must take full course of medications
   e. Encourage to return to clinic for sputum smears
   f. Good nutrition

## HEPATITIS

**A.** Data Collection

1. Fatigue

2. Jaundice (icterus), yellow sclera

3. Anorexia, RUQ pain and tenderness, malaise

4. Clay-colored stools, tea-colored urine

| CLASSIFICATIONS OF HEPATITIS | | | | |
|---|---|---|---|---|
| **TYPE** | **HIGH RISK GROUP** | **INCUBATION** | **TRANSMISSION** | **NURSING CONSIDERATIONS** |
| Hepatitis A (HAV) | Young children<br>Institutions for custodial care<br>International travelers to developing countries | 15-50 days | Common in fall, early winter<br>Fecal–oral<br>Shellfish from contaminated water<br>Poor sanitation<br>Contaminated food handlers<br>Oral–anal sexual activity | Survives on hands<br>Diagnostic tests—<br>  Cultured in stool and detected in serum before onset of disease<br>Prevention–improved sanitation; Hepatitis A vaccine<br>Treated with gamma globulin early postexposure<br>No preparation of food |
| Hepatitis B (HBV) | Immigrants from areas of HBV endemicity<br>Drug addicts<br>Fetuses from infected mothers<br>Homosexually active men<br>Clients on dialysis<br>Male prisoners<br>Transfusion recipients<br>Health care workers | 48-180 days | Blood and body fluids<br>Parenteral drug abuse<br>Sexual contact<br>Hemodialysis<br>Accidental contaminated needle exposure<br>Maternal–fetal route | Diagnostic tests–<br>  Hepatitis B surface antigen, anti-HBc, anti-HBe<br>  Treatment–Hepatitis B vaccine (Heptavax-B, Recombivax HB), Hepatitis B immune globulin (HBIg) postexposure; interferon alpha-2b; lamivudir<br>Chronic carriers—frequent; potential for chronicity 5-10%<br>Complications: cirrhosis; liver cancer |
| Hepatitis C (HCV) | Persons receiving frequent blood transfusions<br>International travelers<br>Hemophilia clients | 14-180 days | Contact with blood and body fluids<br>IV drug users | May be asymptomatic<br>Complications: cirrhosis; liver cancer<br>Great potential for chronicity |
| Delta or Hepatitis D (HDV) | Drug addicts<br>Concurrent HBV infection | 14-56 days | Coinfects with Hepatitis B<br>Close personal contact<br>Parenteral transmission | Diagnostic test–HD Ag in serum |
| Hepatitis E | Persons living in under-developed countries | 15-64 days | Oral-fecal<br>Contaminated water | Resembles Hepetitis A<br>Does not become chronic<br>Usually seen in young adults<br>Seen in travelers from Asia, Africa, Mexico |
| Toxic Hepatitis | Elderly<br>Drug-induced (INH, diuretics, Tetracycline, carbon tetachloride, Tylenol, ETOH)<br>Alcohol | | Noninfectious inflammation of liver | Removal of causative substance<br>Check level of consciousness<br>Encourage fluids |

5. Pruritus: accumulation of bile salts under the skin

6. Liver function studies: elevated ALT, AST, alkaline phosphatase (ALP)

7. Prolonged PT

8. Percutaneous liver biopsy

9. Antibodies to specific virus, e.g., anti-HAV

B. Diagnose

1. Acute inflammatory disease of the liver resulting in cell damage from liver cell degeneration and necrosis

2. Potential nursing diagnoses
   a. Fatigue
   b. Physical mobility, impaired
   c. Impaired liver function
   d. Acute pain
   e. Deficient knowledge

3. Classifications (see Table 3)

C. Plan/Implementation

1. Frequent rest periods

2. Contact precautions in addition to standard precautions for clients diagnosed with hepatitis A

3. Diet low in fat, high in calories, carbohydrates and protein; no alcoholic beverages

4. For pruritus—calamine, short clean nails, antihistamines

5. Medications
   a. Vitamin K
   b. Antiviral drugs: interferon and lamivudine
   c. Post-exposure hepatitis B vaccine

6. Reinforce client and family teaching
   a. Avoid alcohol and potentially hepatotoxic prescription/OTC medications (particularly aspirin and sedatives)
   b. Balance rest and activity periods
   c. Techniques to prevent spread
   d. Cannot donate blood
   e. Note and report recurrence of signs and symptoms

## LYME DISEASE

A. Data Collection

1. Stage 1
   a. Rash (erythematous papule that develops into lesion with a clear center) develops at site of tick bite within 2 to 30 days; concentric rings develop, suggesting a bull's-eye; lesion enlarges quickly
   b. Regional lymphadenopathy
   c. Development of flulike symptoms (malaise, fever, headache, myalgia, stiff neck, arthralgia, conjunctivitis) within one to several months, lasts 7–10 days and may reoccur

2. Stage 2
   a. Develops within 1–6 months if untreated
   b. Cardiac conduction defects

    c. Neurologic disorders: facial paralysis; paralysis that is not permanent

  3. Stage 3

    a. Arthralgias, enlarged or inflamed joints occur within one to several months after the initial infection

    b. May persist for several years

**B.** Diagnose

  1. Multisystem infection transmitted to humans by tick bite

  2. Most common in summer months

**C.** Plan/Implementation

  1. Prevention

    a. Cover exposed areas when in wooded areas

    b. Check exposed areas for presence of ticks

  2. Nursing care

    a. Administer antibiotics for 3–4 weeks: doxycycline, ceftriaxone, azithromycin during stage 1

    b. Administer IV penicillin G during later stages

## SEXUALLY TRANSMITTED DISEASES (STDs)

**A.** Data Collection (see Table 4)

**B.** Diagnose—potential nursing diagnoses

  1. Health maintenance, altered

  2. Sexual patterns, altered

**C.** Plan/Implementation (see Table 4)

## AIDS

**A.** Data Collection

  1. HIV positive—presence of HIV in the blood

  2. AIDS—syndrome with CD4/TC counts below 200

  3. Opportunistic infections

    a. *Pneumocystis jiroveci* pneumonia

      1) Gradually worsening chest tightness and shortness of breath

      2) Persistent, dry, nonproductive cough, rales

      3) Dyspnea and tachypnea

      4) Low-grade/high fever

      5) Progressive hypoxemia and cyanosis

    b. *C. albicans* stomatitis or esophagitis

      1) Changes in taste sensation

      2) Difficulty swallowing

      3) Retrosternal pain

      4) White exudate and inflammation of mouth and back of throat

Table 4

| SEXUALLY TRANSMITTED DISEASES | | | | |
|---|---|---|---|---|
| TYPE | SYMPTOMS | DIAGNOSTIC TESTS | TRANSMISSION AND INCUBATION | NURSING CONSIDERATIONS |
| Syphilis | Stage 1: painless chancre disappears within 4 weeks<br>Stage 2: copper-colored rash on palms and soles; low-grade fever<br>Stage 3: cardiac and CNS dysfunction | VDRL, RPR, FTA-ABS, MHA-TP (to confirm syphilis when VDRL and RPR are positive) | Mucous membrane or skin; congenital; kissing, sexual contact<br>10-90 days | Prevention—condoms<br>Treat with penicillin G IM<br>For PCN allergy—erythromycin for 10-15 days<br>Ceftriaxone and tetracyclines (nonpregnant females)<br>Retest for cure<br>Abstinence from sexual activity until treatment complete<br>Reportable disease |
| Gonorrhea | Thick discharge from vagina or urethra<br>Frequently asymptomatic in females<br>If female has symptoms, usually has purulent discharge, dysuria, and dyspareunia (painful intercourse)<br>Symptoms in male include painful urination and a yellow-green discharge | Culture of discharge from cervix or urethra<br>Positive results for other STD diagnostic tests | Mucous membrane or skin; congenital; vaginal, orogenital, anogenital sexual activity<br>2-7 days | IM ceftriaxone 1 time and PO doxycillin BID for 1 week; azithromycin<br>IM aqueous penicillin with PO probenecid (to delay penicillin urinary excretion)<br>PO azithromycin or doxycycline is used to treat chlamydia, which coexists in 45% of cases<br>Spectinomycin if allergy to ceftriaxone<br>Monitor for complications, pelvic inflammatory disease |
| Genital Herpes (HSV-2) | Painful vesicular genital lesions<br>Difficulty voiding<br>Recurrence in times of stress, infection, menses | Direct examination of cells<br>HSV antibodies | Mucous membrane or skin; congenital<br>Virus can survive on objects such as towels<br>3-14 days | Acyclovir (not cure)<br>Emotional support<br>Sitz baths<br>Local medication<br>Client must notify sexual contacts<br>Monitor Pap smears on regular basis—increased incidence of cancer of cervix<br>Precautions about vaginal delivery |
| Chlamydia | Men—dysuria, frequent urination, watery discharge<br>Women—may be asymptomatic, thick discharge with acrid odor, pelvic pain, yellow-colored discharge; painful menses | Direct examination of cells<br>Enzyme-linked ELISA | Mucous membrane; sexual contact<br>1-3 weeks | Notification of contacts<br>May cause sterility<br>Treat with azithromycin, doxycycline, erythromycin |
| Condylomata acuminata (genital warts) | Initially single, small papillary lesion spreads into large cauliflowerlike cluster on perineum and/or vagina or penis; may be itching/burning | Direct exam<br>Biopsy<br>HPV | Majority due to human papilloma virus (HPV)<br>Mucous membrane; sexual contact; congenital<br>1-3 months | Curettage, cryotherapy with liquid nitrogen or podophyllin resin<br>Kerotolytic agents<br>Avoid intimate sexual contact until lesions are healed<br>Strong association with incidence of genital dysplasia and cervical carcinoma<br>Atypical, pigmented, or persistent warts should be biopsied<br>Notify contacts |

    c. *C. neoformans*—severe debilitating meningitis

        1) Fever, headache, blurred version

        2) Nausea and vomiting

        3) Stiff neck, mental status changes, seizures

    d. Cytomegalovirus (CMV)—significant factor in morbidity and mortality

        1) Fever, malaise

        2) Weight loss, fatigue

        3) Lymphadenopathy

        4) Retinochoroiditis characterized by inflammation and hemorrhage

        5) Visual impairment

        6) Colitis, encephalitis, pneumonitis

        7) Adrenalitis, hepatitis, disseminated infection

    e. Kaposi's sarcoma—most common malignancy

        1) Small purplish-brown, nonpainful, nonpruritic palpable lesions occurring on any part of the body

        2) Most commonly seen on the skin

        3) Diagnosed by biopsy

4. Diagnostic tests

    a. Positive HIV antibody on enzyme-linked immunosorbent assay (ELISA) and confirmed by Western blot assay or indirect immunoflourescence assay (IFA)

    b. Viral load testing, CD4 to CD8 ratio, antigen assays

    c. Radioimmunoprecipitation assay (RIPA)

    d. CBC reveals leukopenia with serious lymphopenia, anemia, thrombocytopenia

**B.** Diagnose

1. AIDS (acquired immunodeficiency syndrome)—a syndrome distinguished by serious deficits in cellular immune function associated with positive human immunodeficiency virus (HIV); evidenced clinically by development of opportunistic infections (e.g., *Pneumocystis jiroveci* pneumonia, *Candida albicans*, cytomegalovirus), enteric pathogens, and malignancies (most commonly Kaposi's sarcoma)

    a. High-risk groups

        1) Homosexual/bisexual men, especially with multiple partners

        2) Intravenous drug abusers

        3) Hemophiliacs via contaminated blood products

        4) Blood transfusion recipients prior to 1985

        5) Heterosexual partners of infected persons

        6) Children of infected women/in utero or at birth

    b. Transmission—contaminated blood or body fluids, sharing IV drug needles, sexual contact, transplacental and possibly through breast milk

    c. Time from exposure to symptom manifestation may be prolonged (10–12 years)

Table 5

| NURSING CARE OF A CLIENT WITH ACQUIRED IMMUNE DEFICIENCY SYNDROME | |
|---|---|
| **PROBLEM** | **NURSING CONSIDERATIONS** |
| Fatigue | Provide restful environment<br>Assist with personal care<br>Monitor tolerance for visitors |
| Pain | Give meds as appropriate<br>Obtain level of pain |
| Disease susceptibility | Implement infection control precautions<br>Handwashing on entering and leaving room<br>Monitor for oral infections and meningitis<br>Give antibiotics as ordered |
| Respiratory distress | Monitor vital signs, breath sounds<br>Give bronchodilators and antibiotics as ordered<br>Suction and maintain $O_2$ as ordered<br>Monitor for symptoms of secondary infections |
| Anxiety, depression | Use tact, sensitivity in gathering personal data<br>Encourage expression of feelings<br>Respect client's own limits in ability to discuss problems |
| Anorexia, diarrhea | Monitor weight<br>Encourage nutritional supplements<br>Observe hydration |

**C.** Plan/Implementation

1. Preventive measures
   a. Avoidance of IV drug use (needle-sharing)
   b. Precautions regarding sexual patterns—sex education, condoms, avoid multiple partners
   c. Use standard precautions

2. Nursing care (see Table 5)
   a. No effective cure; antiviral agents are being used to slow progression of symptoms
   b. Treatment specific to the presenting condition
      1) Kaposi's sarcoma—local radiation (palliative), single agent/combination chemotherapy
      2) Fungal infections—nystatin swish and swallow, clotrimazole oral solution, amphotericin B with/without flucytosine
      3) Viral infections—Acyclovir, Ganciclovir
   c. Contact precautions in addition to standard precautions
   d. Nutrition—high protein and calories
   e. Symptomatic relief—comfort measures
   f. Maintain confidentiality
   g. Provide support
      1) Client and family coping—identify support systems

2) Minimize social isolation—no isolation precautions are needed to enter room to talk to client, take VS, administer PO medications

3) Encourage verbalization of feelings

h. Reinforce client/family discharge teaching

1) Behaviors to prevent transmission—safe sex, not sharing toothbrushes, razors, and other potentially blood-contaminated objects

2) Measures to prevent infections—good nutrition, hygiene, rest, skin and mouth care, avoid crowds

## POISON CONTROL

**A.** Data Collection

1. Airway, breathing, circulation (ABC)—treat the client first, then the poison

2. Identify poison—amount ingested, time of ingestion; save vomitus

3. Diagnostics
   a. Urine and serum analysis
   b. Long-bone x-rays if lead deposits suspected
   c. CAT scan, EEG

**B.** Diagnose—potential nursing diagnoses

1. Injury, risk for

2. Health maintenance, altered

●Table 6

| TEACHING PREVENTION OF ACCIDENTAL POISONING IN CHILDREN | |
|---|---|
| **ACTION** | **RATIONALE** |
| Proper storage—locked cabinets | Once child can crawl, can investigate cabinets and ingest contents of bottles |
| Never take medicine in front of children | Children are interested in anything their parents take and will mimic taking medicine |
| Never leave medication in purse, on table, or on kitchen counter | Children will investigate area and ingest bottle contents |
| Never refer to medicine as candy | Increases interest in taking medicine when unsupervised |
| Leave medicines, cleaning supplies in original containers | Pill boxes, soda bottles increase attractiveness and inhibit identification of substance should poisoning occur |
| Provide activities and play materials for children | Encourages child's interest without endangering him/her |
| Teach need for supervision of small children | Small children cannot foresee potential harm and need protection |

C. Plan/Implementation

1. Prevention—most toxic ingestions are acute (see Table 6)
   a. Child-proofing—store all potentially poisonous substances in locked out-of-reach area
   b. Increased awareness of precipitating factors
      1) Growth and development characteristics—under/overestimating the capabilities of the child
      2) Changes in household routine
      3) Conditions that increase emotional tension of family members

2. Instructions for caretaker in case of suspected poison ingestion
   a. Recognize signs and symptoms of accidental poisoning—change in child's appearance/behavior; presence of unusual substances in child's mouth, hands, play area; burns, blisters and/or suspicious odor around child's mouth; open/empty containers in child's possession
   b. Initiate steps to stop exposure
   c. Call Poison Control Center first—be prepared to provide information
      1) Substance—name, time, amount, route
      2) Child—condition, age, weight
   d. Poison Control Center (PCC) will advise to begin treatment at home or to bring child to an emergency facility
   e. Syrup of Ipecac is no longer recommended for treatment at home; Any Ipecac in the home should be disposed of safely
   f. No emetic or other substance should be given at home without consultation with the PCC or health care provider
   g. Save any substance, vomitus, stool, urine
   h. Contraindications to inducing vomiting
      1) When child is in danger of aspiration—decreased level of consciousness, severe shock, seizure(s), diminished gag reflex
      2) When substance is petroleum distillate (lighter fluid, kerosene, paint remover) because of increased risk of aspiration pneumonia, or strong corrosive (acid/alkali drain cleaner), which may redamage esophagus and pharynx
   i. General considerations
      1) Water may be used to dilute the toxin; avoid giving large amounts of fluids when medication has been ingested because this may accelerate gastric emptying and speed drug absorption
      2) Milk may delay vomiting
      3) Do not attempt to neutralize a strong acid/alkali because this may cause a heat-producing reaction that can burn tissue
      4) There are only a few specific antidotes (physiologic antagonist reversing effect); there is no universal antidote

3. Emergency care in a health care facility
   a. Basic life support
      1) Respiratory—intubate if comatose, seizing, or no gag reflex; frequent blood gases
      2) Circulation
         a) IV fluids; maintain fluid and electrolyte balance

    b) Cardiac monitor—essential for comatose child and with tricyclic antidepressant or phenothiazine ingestion

  b. Gastric lavage—client is intubated and positioned head down and on left side; large oro/nasogastric tube inserted and repeated irrigations of normal saline instilled until clear; not more than 10 ml/kg

  c. Activated charcoal—absorbs compounds, forming a nonabsorbable complex; 5–10 g for each g of toxin
    1) Give within 30 minutes of ingestion and after emetic
    2) Mix with water to make a syrup; given PO or via gastric tube

4. Hasten elimination
  a. Cathartic—to speed substance through lower GI tract
  b. Diuretics—for substances eliminated by kidneys
  c. Chelation—heavy metals (e.g., mercury, lead, and arsenic) are not readily eliminated from body; progressive buildup leads to toxicity; a chelating agent binds with the heavy metal, forming a complex that can be eliminated by kidneys, peritoneal hemodialysis (e.g., deferoxamine, dimercaptrol, calcium EDTA)

5. Prevent recurrence—crisis intervention with nonjudgmental approach; acknowledge difficulty in maintaining constant supervision; explore contributory factors; reinforce education about growth and development influences as well as passive (child restraint closures) and active safety measures

## ASPIRIN (SALICYLATE) POISONING

**A.** Data Collection

1. Tinnitus, nausea, sweating, dizziness, headache

2. Change in mental status

3. Increased temperature, hyperventilation (respiratory alkalosis)

4. Later, metabolic acidosis, bleeding, and hypovolemia

**B.** Diagnose

1. Toxicity begins at doses of 150–200 mg/kg
  a. Altered acid–base balance (respiratory alkalosis) due to increased respiratory rate
  b. Increased metabolism causes greater $O_2$ consumption, $CO_2$ and heat production
  c. Metabolic acidosis results in hypokalemia, dehydration, and kidney failure
  d. May result in decreased prothrombin formation and decreased platelet aggregation, causing bleeding

**C.** Plan/Implementation

1. Induce vomiting, initiate gastric lavage with activated charcoal

2. Monitor vital signs and laboratory values

3. Maintain IV hydration and electrolyte replacement; monitor I and O, skin turgor, fontanels, urinary specific gravity

4. Reduce temperature—tepid water baths or hypothermia blankets; prone to seizures

5. Vitamin K, if needed, for bleeding disorder; guaiac of vomitus/stools

6. IV sodium bicarbonate enhances excretion

## ACETAMINOPHEN POISONING

**A.** Data Collection

1. First 2 hours, nausea and vomiting, sweating, pallor, hypothermia, slow-weak pulse

2. Followed by latent period (1–1.5 days) when symptoms abate

3. If no treatment, hepatic involvement occurs (may last up to 1 week) with RUQ pain, jaundice, confusion, stupor, coagulation abnormalities

4. Diagnostic tests—serum acetaminophen levels at least 4 hours after ingestion; liver function tests AST, ALT, and kidney function tests (creatinine, BUN)—change in renal and liver function is a late sign

**B.** Diagnose

1. Toxicity begins at 150 mg/kg

2. Major risk is severe liver damage

**C.** Plan/Implementation

1. Induce vomiting

2. *N*-Acetycysteine–specific antidote; most effective in 8–10 hours; must be given within 24 hours; given PO every 4 hours 72 hours or IV 3 doses

3. Monitor liver and kidney function

4. Maintain hydration; monitor output

## LEAD TOXICITY (PLUMBISM)

**A.** Data Collection

1. Physical symptoms
   a. Irritability
   b. Sleepiness
   c. Nausea, vomiting, abdominal pain, poor appetite
   d. Constipation
   e. Decreased activity
   f. Increased intracranial pressure (e.g., seizures and motor dysfunction)

2. Environmental sources
   a. Flaking, lead-based paint (primary source)
   b. Crumbling plaster
   c. Odor of lead-based gasoline
   d. Pottery with lead glaze
   e. Lead solder in pipes

3. Diagnostic tests
   a. Blood lead level 9 micrograms per deciliter is normal
   b. Erythrocyte protoporphyrin (EP) level
   c. CBC—anemia
   d. X-rays (long bone/GI)—may show radiopaque material, "lead lines"

**B.** Diagnose

1. Child—practice of pica (habitual and compulsive ingestion of nonfood substances); children absorb more lead than adults; paint chips taste sweet

2. Pathology—lead is slowly excreted by kidneys and GI tract; stored in inert form in long bones; chronic ingestion affects many body systems
   a. Hematological—blocks formation of hemoglobin, leading to microcytic anemia (initial sign) and increased erythrocyte protoporphyrin (EP)
   b. Renal—toxic to kidney tubules, allowing an abnormal excretion of protein, glucose, amino acids, phosphates
   c. CNS—increases membrane permeability, resulting in fluid shifts into brain tissue, cell ischemia, and destruction causing neurological and intellectual deficiencies with low-dose exposure; with high-dose exposure, intellectual delay, convulsions, and death (lead encephalopathy)

**C.** Plan/Implementation

1. Chelating agent—promotes lead excretion in urine and stool (dimercaprol, calcium disodium, EDTA), succimer; deferoxamine
   a. Maintain hydration
   b. Identify sources of lead and institute deleading procedures; involve local housing authorities as needed
   c. Reinforce instruction to parents about supervision for pica and ways to encourage other activities for the child

## HAZARDS AND HAZARDOUS WASTE

**A.** Types of hazards

1. Chemical hazards—dusts, gases, fumes, mists

2. Psychophysiologic hazards—stress associated with job demands (e.g., rotating shifts, overtime, violence in the workplace)

3. Biologic hazards—exposure to infectious agents (e.g., TB, hepatitis B)

4. Ergonomic hazards—imbalance between individual and equipment, such as repetitive actions leading to carpal tunnel syndrome (ergonomics: study of interaction of human body with use of mechanical and electrical machines)

5. Safety hazards—precautions with equipment, fire safety, electrical systems

6. Hazardous materials (e.g., explosion from stored chlorine used for private swimming pool, radioisotope accident in nuclear medicine)
   a. Exposure—presence of hazardous waste in environment
   b. OSHA (Federal Occupational Safety and Health Administration) mandates acceptable levels of exposure to chemicals
   c. Dose—amount of substance inhaled, ingested, absorbed through skin or eyes
   d. When there is a problem during transportation of chemical materials, information is provided from a central source; advises rescue and health care workers about the substance, its effect, and how to treat exposure

**B.** Hazardous materials causing immediate threat to life; client treated and then decontaminated

1. Chlorine

2. Cyanide

3. Ammonia

4. Phosgene

5. Hydrogen sulfide

6. Organophosphate insecticides

7. Nitrogen dioxide

**C.** Hazardous materials with cancer-causing potential; client decontaminated and then treated

1. Polychlorinated biphenyls

**D.** Goals

1. Decontaminate individual

2. Prevent spread of contamination

3. Clean and remove contaminated water and waste

4. Monitor personnel exposed

## ACCIDENT PREVENTION

**A.** Newborn infant

1. Don't smoke around infants, increases risk of upper respiratory tract infections

2. Don't leave infant unattended in a high place or unstrapped in a safety seat

3. Use rear-facing car safety seat

4. Make sure furniture is free of lead-based paint

5. Crib slats should be no further apart than 2 3/8"; the mattress and bumper pads should be tight-fitting

**B.** 2 months old

1. Don't hold infant while smoking or drinking hot liquid

2. Set water heater at 120–130°F; test bath water temperature with inner aspect of the wrist before immersing infant

**C.** 4 months old

1. Keep small objects and small pieces of food out of infant's reach

2. Don't use teething biscuits—they become small and can obstruct airway

3. Teach older siblings/children not to give infant small things

**D.** 6 months old

1. Child-proof the home, especially the kitchen and bathroom; remove all dangerous items or place out of reach

2. Use safety gates at bottom/top of stairs; use drawer safety latches, plug fillers

3. Keep poison control number on phone; use as needed

**E.** 9 months old

1. Use nonskid rugs, socks with nonskid strips, nonskid strips in bathtub

2. Keep wastebaskets covered or out of reach

3. Pad sharp edges of furniture

4. Never leave child unattended near water or in bathtub

5. Don't use electrical appliances near water

**F.** 1 to 3 years old

1. Don't use toys with small pieces

2. Hold child's hand when walking near the street

3. Encourage the child to sit down while eating

4. Turn pot handles toward the back of the stove

5. Use rear-facing car seat until age 2 yrs or until child reaches height and weight allowed by car safety seat manufacturer; after age 2 yrs or has outgrown rear-facing car seat, use forward-facing car seat with harness as long as possible

**G.** 3 to 6 years old

1. Use bicycle helmet; ride bicycle on right-hand side of the road or on sidewalk; make sure the bicycle is the correct size, feet should touch the ground when sitting on the bicycle seat

2. Teach child not to eat things from outside (e.g., mushrooms) until checked by parents

3. Look both ways before crossing street

4. If weight or height above forward-facing limit, use belt-positioning booster seat until seat belt fits properly

**H.** 6 to 11 years old

1. Obey traffic signals while on bike; use reflectors on bike; wear light clothing

2. When playing group sports look for teams divided by size and maturation, not by age; use protective equipment

**I.** Adolescent

1. Teach appropriate ways to deal with anger and threats

2. Teach safety for swimming and diving

3. Use car safety restraint; lap and seat belts

4. Teach hazards of drinking and driving

**J.** Adult

1. Use car safety restraint

2. Teach responsible behavior to reduce sexually transmitted diseases and alcohol-related accidents

3. Suicide prevention

4. Handgun control and safety

5. Motorcycle helmet use

6. Smoke and carbon monoxide detector use; fire extinguisher use

**K.** Elderly

1. At risk for injuries
   a. Muscle weakness
   b. Changes in balance
   c. Gait abnormalities
   d. Slowed reaction time
   e. Use of medications
   f. Chronic medical conditions (e.g., Parkinson's disease)
   g. Changes in vision, hearing, smell

2. Remove throws rugs, door thresholds; make sure floors are smooth and nonslip

3. Clear pathways of furniture

4. Use solid chairs with arm rests

5. Provide good lighting with accessible switches; use night light

6. Adapt kitchen and bathroom; use raised toilet seat, grab bars

7. Use cordless phone

8. Teach correct way to go up and down stairs; use hand rail, don't limit vision by carrying large load

9. Don't wear long gowns or robes or pants with flowing material

10. Wear study, comfortable, nonskid shoes; don't wear flimsy slippers

11. Keep pet feeding dishes out of main walkway

12. Maintain mobility through exercise and assistive devices

## DISASTER PLANNING

A. Prioritizing—greatest good for the greatest number of people

1. Resources used for clients with strongest probability of survival

2. Nurses make tough decisions about which order clients will be seen

3. Decisions are based on injuries and knowledge of probable outcomes

4. Use Airway, Breathing, Circulation, neurologic Dysfunction (ABCDs) to prioritize

B. Planning

1. Triage under usual conditions
   a. Emergent—immediate threat to life
   b. Urgent—major injuries requiring immediate treatment
   c. Nonurgent—minor injuries that do not require immediate treatment

2. Triage with mass casualties
   a. Red—unstable clients who require immediate care to save life (e.g., occluded airway, active hemorrhaging); first category seen
   b. Yellow—stable clients who can wait 30–60 minutes for treatment (e.g., moderate burn, eye injury); second category to be seen
   c. Green—stable clients who can wait longer to be treated (e.g., "walking wounded"); third category to be seen
   d. Black—unstable clients having massive injuries that will probably prove fatal (e.g., massive body trauma); last category to be treated; supportive and comfort measures provided (e.g., pain control)
   e. DOA (dead on arrival)

C. Implementation

1. Care standardized according to standing orders
   a. IV fluids
   b. Lab tests
   c. Diagnostic procedures
   d. Medications (e.g., analgesics, tetanus prophylaxis, antibiotics)

2. Specialists become "generalists"

3. Nurses may have expanded responsibilities (e.g., suturing, surgical airway)

4. Use of diagnostic procedures may be limited (e.g., CT scans) with multiple trauma

5. Use of hospital resources determined by designated disaster medical officer

6. Areas of hospital are used as needed for treatment

7. Resources are obtained to provide emotional and spiritual care to clients and families

8. Person is designated to deal with media and traffic control

9. Measures are implemented to track unidentified clients

10. Procedures for handling evidence from disaster may be implemented

11. Hospitals practice disaster drills several times a year

## BIOTERRORISM

Table 7

| BIOTERRORISM | | | |
|---|---|---|---|
| Type | Symptoms | Transmission and Incubation | Nursing Considerations |
| Anthrax Cutaneous | 1–7 days after exposure: itching with small papule or vesicle<br>2 days after lesion formation: enlarged painless lesion with necrotic center<br>7–10 days after lesion formation: black eschar forms; sloughs after 12th day | Skin contact<br>1–7 days<br>No person-to-person transmission<br>High rish: exposure to contaminated animal hides, veterinarians, personnel who handle contaminated materials, military | Standard precautions Decontamination<br>• Bag clothes in labeled, plastic bags<br>• Do not agitate clothes<br>• Instruct client to shower thoroughly with soap and water and shampoo hair<br>• Wear gloves, gown, and respiratory protection<br>• Decontaminate surfaces with bleach solution (one-part household bleach to nine-parts water)<br>• Administer oral fluoroquinolones for post-exposure prophylaxis<br>• Administer doxycycline, erythromycin, ciprofloxacin |
| Anthrax Inhalation | Initial: sore throat, mild fever, muscles aches, malaise followed by possible brief improvement<br>2–3 days later: abrupt onset of respiratory failure and shock, fever, hemorrhagic meningitis | Aerosolized spores<br>1–7 days up to 60 days<br>No person-to-person transmission | Standard precautions Ventilator support for respiratory therapy IV and PO ciprofloxacin and doxycycline |
| Botulism | Drooping eyelids, weakened jaw clench, dysphasia, blurred vision, symmetric descending weakness, 12–72 hours after exposure respiratory dysfunction; may cause death | Contaminated food 12–36 hours Aerosol inhalation 24–72 hours No person-to-person transmission | Standard precautions Contact health department and Centers for Disease Control and Prevention (CDC) if suspicion of single case Supportive care |
| Plague Bubonic | Fever, headache, general illness, painful, swollen regional lymph nodes (bubo); develops into septicemia and plague pneumonia | Infected rodent to man by infected fleas 2–8 days | Standard precautions for treatment of bubo; Droplet precautions for plague pneumonia Administer antibiotics Apply insecticides to kill fleas, control rat population |

(*continued*)

● Table 7
(Continued)

| BIOTERRORISM | | | |
|---|---|---|---|
| Type | Symptoms | Transmission and Incubation | Nursing Considerations |
| Pneumonic Plague | 2–4 days after exposure, fever, productive cough containing infectious particles, chest pain, hemoptysis, bronchopneumonia, rapid shock, and death | Aerosolized inhalation 1-3 days Person-to-person transmission occurs through large aerosol droplets | Droplet precautions until 72 hours of antibiotic therapy Place in private room or cohort with clients with same diagnosis Administer antibiotics: Streptomycin, ciprofloxacin, doxycycline Decontamination • Bag clothes in labeled, plastic bags • Do not agitate clothes • Instruct client to shower thoroughly with soap and water and shampoo hair • Wear gloves, gown, and respiratory protection • Decontaminate surfaces with bleach solution (one-part household bleach to nine-parts water) |
| Smallpox | Occur in 10–17 days; fever, myalgia synchronous onset of rash that is most prominent on face and extremities (palms and soles included), rash scabs over in 1-2 weeks | Airborne and droplet exposure, contact with skin lesions Client infectious until scabs separate (about 3 weeks) | Airborne, contact, and standard precautions place in private room with door closed, monitored negative air pressure, 6-12 air exchanges per hour Decontaminate items contaminated by infectious lesions using contact precautions; single case is considered a public health emergency If exposed, administer vaccination within 3 days of contact; vaccination does not give lifelong immunity |

*Note:* The plagues (bubonic and pneumonic) are included together.

HEALTH PROMOTION and MAINTENANCE

**Chapter 4**

Growth and Development

Childbearing—Normal

Childbearing—Maternal Complications

Childbearing—Neonatal Normal

Neonatal Complications

Reproduction

Prevention and Early Detection of Disease

## HEALTH MAINTENANCE

**A.** Data Collection

1. Factors influencing growth and development
   a. Genetic, hereditary
   b. Environmental
      1) Family, cultural
      2) Socioeconomic
      3) Living environment
   c. Gender
   d. Parental
   e. Stress
   f. Relationships and attachments
   g. Physical and emotional health (see Table 1)

2. Expected stages of play development
   a. Age characteristics
      1) Exploratory—(holding toys: age 0–1 yr)
      2) Toys as adult tools—(imitation: age 1–7 yr)
      3) Games and hobbies (age 8–12 yr)
   b. Social characteristics
      1) Solitary play—alone, but enjoys presence of others, interest centered on own activity (infancy)
      2) Parallel play—plays alongside, not with, another; characteristic of toddlers, but can occur in other age groups (toddler)
      3) Associative play—no group goal; often follows a leader (preschool)
      4) Cooperative play—organized, rules, leader/follower relationship established (school-age)

3. Physical measurements compared with expected norms
   a. Height
   b. Weight
   c. Head circumference
   d. Chest circumference

4. Screening tests
   a. Denver II—evaluates children from birth to 6 years in 4 skill areas: personal–social, fine motor, language, gross motor

1) Age adjusted for prematurity by subtracting the number of months preterm

2) Questionable value in testing children of minority/ethnic groups

b. Stanford–Binet

c. IQ related to genetic potentialities and environment; intelligence tests used to determine IQ; mental age × 100 = IQ/chronological age

Table 1

| OVERVIEW OF ERIKSON'S DEVELOPMENTAL TASKS THROUGHOUT THE LIFE SPAN | | | | |
|---|---|---|---|---|
| **AGE** | **STAGE** | **ERIKSON'S TASK** | **POSITIVE OUTCOME** | **NEGATIVE OUTCOME** |
| Birth to 1 year | Infancy | Trust vs. mistrust | Trusts self and others | Demonstrates an inability to trust; withdrawal, isolation |
| 1 year to 3 yrs | Toddler | Autonomy vs. shame and doubt | Exercises self-control and influences the environment directly | Demonstrates defiance and negativism |
| 3 to 6 yrs | Preschool | Initiative vs. guilt | Begins to evaluate own behavior; learns limits on influence in the environment | Demonstrates fearful, pessimistic behaviors; lacks self-confidence |
| 6 to 12 yrs | School-age | Industry vs. inferiority | Develops a sense of confidence; uses creative energies to influence the environment | Demonstrates feelings of inadequacy, mediocrity, and self-doubt |
| 12 to 20 yrs | Adolescence | Identity vs. role diffusion | Develops a coherent sense of self; plans for a future of work/education | Demonstrates inability to develop personal and vocational identity |
| 20 to 35 yrs | Young adulthood | Intimacy vs. isolation | Develops connections to work and intimate relationships | Demonstrates an avoidance of intimacy and vocational career commitments |
| 35 to 65 yrs | Middle adulthood | Generativity vs. stagnation | Involved with established family; expands personal creativity and productivity | Demonstrates lack of interests, commitments Preoccupation with self-centered concerns |
| 65+ yrs | Late adulthood | Integrity vs. despair | Identification of life as meaningful | Demonstrates fear of death; life lacks meaning |

**B.** Diagnose

1. Potential nursing diagnoses

   a. Knowledge deficit

   b. Decreased growth

   c. Decreased development

   d. Changes in growth and development pattern

2. Process—sequence is orderly and predictable; rate tends to be variable within (more quickly/slowly) and between (earlier/later) individuals

3. Growth—increase in size (height and weight); tends to be cyclical, more rapid *in utero*, during infancy, and adolescence

4. Development—maturation of physiological and psychosocial systems to more complex state
   a. Developmental tasks—skills and competencies associated with each developmental stage that have an effect on subsequent stages of development
   b. Developmental milestone—standard of reference to compare the child's behavior at specific ages
   c. Developmental delay(s)—variable of development that lags behind the range at a given age

5. Muscular coordination and control—proceeds in head-to-toe (cephalocaudal), trunk-to-periphery (proximodistal), gross-to-fine developmental pattern

C. Plan/Implementation

1. Establish a therapeutic relationship

2. Identify age-appropriate behavioral milestones

3. Educate caregivers on proper health care for children
   a. Pediatrician visits, immunization schedules, childhood diseases
   b. Review diet and exercise patterns

4. Observe for alterations of parenting
   a. Behavior patterns of parents and child
   b. Identify healthy relationships and unhealthy relationships, e.g., failure to thrive, indications of child abuse

5. Observe and document screening

6. Promote socialization, activity, play
   a. Promote improved social skills and decreased social isolation
   b. Provide simple activities or tasks to promote self-esteem

7. Meet basic health and safety needs (hygienic, nutritional, rest and exercise)

8. Recognize spans and ranges of normalcy

## INFANCY—BIRTH TO 12 MONTHS

A. Data Collection (see Table 2)

1. Physical growth and development (see Table 2)

2. Developmental milestones (see Table 2)

3. Attachment established during first year

B. Diagnose

1. Potential nursing diagnoses
   a. Injury, risk for
   b. Parenting, risk for altered

2. Potential problems in infancy
   a. Injury
   b. Failure to thrive
   c. Development delay

C. Plan/Implementation

1. Screen infants routinely for growth and development

2. Evaluate infant/parent relationships during feeding activities

3. Begin anticipatory guidance activities with parents

4. Select age-appropriate toys (see Table 2)

5. Introduce complementary foods
   a. Introduce only one food at a time for each two-week period
   b. Least allergenic foods are given in first half of the first year; more allergenic foods, (e.g., egg, orange juice) are offered in last half of first year; usual order: cereal, fruits, vegetables, potatoes, meat, egg, orange juice

6. Document age-appropriate social skills, social attachments, reaction to separation
   a) Phases of separation anxiety
      1) Protest—cries/screams for parents; inconsolable by others
      2) Despair—crying ends; less active; disinterested in food/play; clutches "security" object if available
      3) Denial—appears adjusted; evidences interest in environment; ignores parent when he/she returns; resigned, not contented

Table 2

| INFANT GROWTH AND DEVELOPMENT | |
|---|---|
| **1 MONTH** | **7 MONTH** |
| Head sags<br>Early crawling movements | Sits for short periods using hands for support<br>Grasps toy with hand (partially successful)<br>Fear of strangers begins to appear<br>Lability of mood (abrupt mood shifts) |
| **2 MONTH** | **8 MONTH** |
| Closing of posterior fontanelle<br>Diminished tonic neck and Moro reflexes<br>Able to turn from side to back<br>Eyes begin to follow a moving object<br>Social smile first appears | Anxiety with strangers |
| **3 MONTH** | **9 MONTH** |
| Can bring objects to mouth at will<br>Head held erect, steady<br>Binocular vision<br>Smiles in mother's presence<br>Laughs audibly | Elevates self to sitting position<br>Rudimentary imitative expression<br>Responds to parental anger<br>Expressions like "dada" may be heard |
| **4 MONTH** | **10 MONTH** |
| Appearance of thumb apposition<br>Absent tonic neck reflex<br>Evidence of pleasure in social contact<br>Drooling<br>Moro reflex absent after 3-4 mo | Crawls well<br>Pulls self to standing position with support<br>Brings hands together<br>Vocalizes one or two words |
| **5 MONTH** | **11 MONTH** |
| Birth weight usually doubled<br>Takes objects presented to him/her | Erect standing posture with support |
| **6 MONTH** | **12 MONTH** |
| Average weight gain of 4 oz per week<br>  during second 6 mo<br>Teething may begin (lower central incisors)<br>Can turn from back to stomach<br>Early ability to distinguish and recognize<br>  strangers | Birth weight usually tripled<br>Needs help while walking<br>Sits from standing position without<br>  assistance<br>Eats with fingers<br>Usually says two words in addition to<br>  "mama" and "dada" |
| AGE-APPROPRIATE TOYS | |
| Birth to 2 months | Mobiles |
| 2-4 mo | Rattles, cradle gym |
| 4-6 mo | Brightly colored toys (small enough to grasp, large enough for safety) |
| 6-9 mo | Large toys with bright colors, movable parts, and noisemakers |
| 9-12 mo | Books with large pictures, large push-pull toys, teddy bears |

## TODDLER—12 TO 36 MONTHS

**A.** Data Collection (see Table 3)

    1. Growth and development (see Table 3)

    2. Begins to establish independence

**B.** Diagnose

    1. Potential nursing diagnoses
       a. Injury, risk for
       b. Poisoning, risk for
       c. Nutrition: less than body requirements, altered

    2. Potential problems in toddlerhood
       a. Negativism
       b. Safety, abuse

**C.** Plan/Implementation

    1. Routine screening of toddler growth and development

    2. Evaluate toddler, parent reactions to separation

    3. Continue anticipatory guidance activities with parents

    4. Reinforce the desirability of stable daily routines for play, feeding and rest

    5. Select age-appropriate toys (see Table 3)

**Table 3**

| TODDLER GROWTH AND DEVELOPMENT | |
|---|---|
| **15 MONTH** | **24 MONTH** |
| Walks alone<br>Builds 2-block tower<br>Throws objects<br>Grasps spoon<br>Names commonplace objects | Early efforts at jumping<br>Builds 5- to 6-block tower<br>300-word vocabulary<br>Obeys easy commands |
| **18 MONTH** | **30 MONTH** |
| Anterior fontanelle usually closed<br>Walks backward<br>Climbs stairs<br>Scribbles<br>Builds 3-block tower<br>Oral vocabulary–10 words<br>Thumb sucking | Walks on tiptoe<br>Builds 7- to 8-block tower<br>Stands on one foot<br>Has sphincter control for toilet training |
| **AGE-APPROPRIATE TOYS** | |
| Push-pull toys | Dolls |
| Low rocking horses | Stuffed animals |

## PRESCHOOL—36 MONTHS TO 6 YEARS

**A.** Data Collection (see Table 4)

1. Growth and development (see Table 4)

2. Psychosexual development begins

**B.** Diagnose

1. Potential nursing diagnoses
   a. Injury, risk for
   b. Grieving, dysfunctional
   c. Difficulty in group situations

2. Potential problems in preschool years
   a. Fear of injury, mutilation, and punishment
   b. Safety

**C.** Plan/Implementation

1. Screen school-aged children routinely for growth and development

2. Evaluate parent/child relationships

3. Continue anticipatory guidance activities with parents

4. Reinforce the desirability of stable daily routines for play, feeding, and rest

5. Reinforce the idea of parents as role models who allow their children to make age appropriate decisions

6. Select age-appropriate toys (see Table 4)

●Table 4

| PRESCHOOL GROWTH AND DEVELOPMENT | |
|---|---|
| **3 YEARS** | **5 YEARS** |
| Copies a circle | Runs well |
| Builds bridge with 3 cubes | Jumps rope |
| Less negativistic than toddler, decreased tantrums | Dresses without help |
| Learns from experience | 2,100-word vocabulary |
| Rides tricycle | Tolerates increasing periods of separation from parents |
| Walks backward and downstairs without assistance | Beginnings of cooperative play |
| Undresses without help | Gender-specific behavior |
| 900-word vocabulary, uses sentences | Skips on alternate feet |
| May invent "imaginary" friend | Ties shoes |
| **4 YEARS** | |
| Climbs and jumps well | |
| Laces shoes | |
| Brushes teeth | |
| 1,500-word vocabulary | |
| Skips and hops on one foot | |
| Throws overhead | |
| **AGE-APPROPRIATE TOYS AND ACTIVITIES** | |
| Child imitative of adult patterns and roles. Offer playground materials, housekeeping toys, coloring books, tricycles with helmet. | |

## SCHOOL AGE—6 TO 12 YEARS

A. Data Collection (see Table 5)

1. Growth and development (see Table 5)

2. Intense period of industry and productivity

3. Begins logical patterns of thought

4. Peer relationships important

5. Likes and dislikes established

B. Diagnose

1. Potential nursing diagnoses
   a. Injury, risk for
   b. Grieving, dysfunctional
   c. Difficulty with social relationships, school
   d. Difficulty with body image, self-esteem, self-concept

Table 5

| SCHOOL-AGE GROWTH AND DEVELOPMENT | |
|---|---|
| **6 YEARS** | **9 YEARS** |
| Self-centered, show-off, rude<br>Extreme sensitivity to criticism<br>Begins losing temporary teeth<br>Appearance of first permanent teeth<br>Ties knots | Skillful manual work possible<br>Conflicts between adult authorities and peer group<br>Better behaved<br>Conflict between needs for independence and dependence<br>Likes school |
| **7 YEARS** | **10–12 YEARS** |
| Temporal perception improving<br>Increased self-reliance for basic activities<br>Team games/sports/organizations<br>Develops concept of time<br>Boys prefer playing with boys and girls with girls | Remainder of teeth (except wisdom) erupt<br>Uses telephone<br>Capable of helping<br>Increasingly responsible<br>More selective when choosing friends<br>Develops beginning of interest in opposite sex<br>Loves conversation<br>Raises pets |
| **8 YEARS** | |
| Friends sought out actively<br>Eye development generally complete<br>Movements more graceful<br>Writing replaces printing | |
| AGE-APPROPRIATE TOYS, GAMES, AND ACTIVITIES | |
| Construction toys<br>Use of tools, household and sewing tools, table games, sports | Participation in repair, building, and mechanical activities, household chores |

2. Potential problems in school-age years
   a. Enuresis: bed-wetting
   b. Encopresis: incontinence of feces
   c. Safety: injuries, head lice are common

**C.** Plan/Implementation

1. Screen school-aged children routinely for growth and development

2. Evaluate parent/child relationships

3. Continue anticipatory guidance activities with parents

4. Reinforce the desirability of stable daily routines for play, feeding, and rest

5. Reinforce the idea of parents as role models who allow their children to make age-appropriate decisions

6. Select age-appropriate toys (see Table 5)

7. Encourage physical activity

## ADOLESCENCE—12 TO 20 YEARS

**A.** Data Collection (see Table 6)

1. Growth and development (see Table 6)

2. Body image very important

3. Peer and social relationships very important

4. Identity/autonomy important

**B.** Diagnose

1. Potential nursing diagnoses
    a. Injury, risk for
    b. Self-esteem disturbance
    c. Health maintenance, altered

2. Potential problems in adolescence
    a. Adolescent pregnancy
    b. Poor self-image
    c. Safety
    d. Drug and alcohol misuse/abuse
    e. AIDS
    f. High school dropout
    g. Violence

Table 6

| ADOLESCENT GROWTH AND DEVELOPMENT | |
|---|---|
| **PHYSICAL DEVELOPMENT—PUBERTY** | **FEMALE CHANGES** |
| Attainment of sexual maturity<br>Rapid alterations in height and weight<br>Girls develop more rapidly than boys<br>Onset may be related to hypothalmic activity, which influences pituitary gland to secrete hormones affecting testes and ovaries<br>Testes and ovaries produce hormones (androgens and estrogens) that determine development of secondary sexual characteristics<br>Pimples or acne related to increased sebaceous gland activity<br>Increased sweat production<br>Weight gain proportionally greater than height gain during early stages<br>Initial problems in coordination—appearance of clumsiness related to rapid, unsynchronized growth of many systems<br>Rapid growth may cause easy fatigue<br>Preoccupation with physical appearance | Increase in pelvic diameter<br>Breast development<br>Altered nature of vaginal secretions<br>Appearance of axillary and pubic hair<br>Menarche—first menstrual period |
| | **PHYSICAL DEVELOPMENT—ADOLESCENT** |
| | More complete development of secondary sexual characteristics<br>Improved motor coordination<br>Wisdom teeth appear (ages 17-21) |
| | **PSYCHOSEXUAL DEVELOPMENT** |
| | Masturbation as expression of sexual tension<br>Sexual fantasies<br>Experimental sexual intercourse |
| | **PSYCHOSOCIAL DEVELOPMENT** |
| **MALE CHANGES** | Preoccupied with rapid body changes, what is "normal"<br>Conformity to peer pressure<br>Moody<br>Increased daydreaming<br>Increased independance<br>Moving toward a mature sexual identity |
| Increase in genital size<br>Breast swelling<br>Appearance of pubic, facial, axillary, and chest hair<br>Deepening voice<br>Production of functional sperm<br>Nocturnal emissions | |

**C.** Plan/Implementation

1. Screen the adolescent routinely for growth and development

2. Evaluate parent/child/peer relationships

3. Continue anticipatory guidance activities with parents and adolescents

4. Reinforce the desirability of stable daily routines for work and rest

5. Continue to reinforce the idea of parents and significant others as role models who allow their children to make age-appropriate decisions

6. Counsel adolescent to delay impulsive actions with long-term consequences (e.g., adolescent pregnancy, drug and alcohol misuse, AIDS, high school dropout), and the use of problem-solving skills

7. Encourage the development of educational/vocational options

8. Promote appropriate, safe approaches to resolve conflicts with peers and adults

## 20 TO 35 YEARS

**A.** Data Collection (see Table 7)

   1. Growth and development (see Table 7)

   2. Work, career important

   3. Establishes intimacy

**B.** Diagnose—potential nursing diagnoses

   1. Altered health maintenance

   2. Altered self-esteem

   3. Difficulty with relationships

   4. Potential for increased stress

**C.** Plan/Implementation

   1. Meet physical and mental health needs

   2. Evaluate relationships, especially with chosen partner

   3. Observe responses to stress

   4. Anticipatory guidance

●Table 7

| ADULTHOOD GROWTH AND DEVELOPMENT | | |
|---|---|---|
| **20 to 33 YEARS** | **33 to 40 YEARS** | **35 to 45 YEARS** |
| Decreased hero worship<br>Increased reality<br>Independent from parents<br>Possible marriage, partnership<br>Realization that everything is not black or white, some "gray" areas<br>Looks towards future, hopes for success<br>Peak intelligence, memory<br>Maximum problem-solving ability | Period of discovery, rediscovery of interests and goals<br>Increased sense of urgency<br>Life more serious<br>Major goals to accomplish<br>Plateaus at work and marriage, partnership<br>Sense of satisfaction | (There in some overlap in years)<br>Self-questioning<br>Fear of middle age and aging<br>Reappraises the past<br>Discards unrealistic goals<br>Potential changes of work, marriage, partnership<br>"Sandwich" generation—concerned with children and aging parents<br>Increased awareness of mortality<br>Potential loss of significant others |

## 35 TO 65 YEARS

A. Data Collection (see Table 8)

   1. Physical functioning (see Table 8)

   2. Cognitive functioning (see Table 8)

   3. Relationships change

   4. Work, career important

B. Diagnose—potential nursing diagnoses

   1. Decreased cognitive and physical functioning

   2. Altered family

   3. Self-care deficit

   4. Altered body image

C. Plan/Implementation

   1. Help client adjust to changes of aging

   2. Help client adjust to changing roles

   3. Anticipatory guidance

Table 8

| MIDDLE ADULTHOOD GROWTH AND DEVELOPMENT | | |
|---|---|---|
| **45 to 55 YEARS** | **48 to 60 YEARS** | **50 to 65 YEARS** |
| Graying hair, wrinkling skin | Evaluates past | Increasing physical decline |
| Pains and muscle aches | Sets new goals | Increasingly forgetful |
| Realization—future shorter time span than past | Defines value of life, self | Accepts limitations |
| Menopause | Assesses legacies—professional, personal | Modification of lifestyle |
| Decreased sensory acuity | Serenity and fulfillment | Decreased power |
| Powerful, policy makers, leaders | Balance between old and young | Retirement |
| Relates to older and younger generations | Accepts changes of aging | Less restricted time, able to choose different activities |

## 65 AND ABOVE

A. Data Collection (see Tables 9, 10)

1. Physical and cognitive functioning (see Table 9, 10)

2. Significant relationships change

3. Activities may be limited

4. Decreased sense of taste and smell

5. Financial constraints

B. Diagnose

1. Self-care deficit

2. Isolation

3. Altered relationships

4. Decreased independence

5. Family processes, altered

C. Plan/Implementation

1. Assist clients with adjusting to lifestyle changes

2. Allow client to verbalize concerns

3. Prevent isolation

4. Provide assistance as required

Table 9

| LATE ADULTHOOD | | |
|---|---|---|
| **SYSTEM** | **CHANGES** | **NURSING CARE** |
| Integumentary | Skin cells replaced more slowly | Maintain nutrition because wounds heal more slowly |
| | Thinning skin | Prevent bumps and scraps since skin is more fragile |
| | Decreased response to pain and temperature changes | Be careful when using heating pads or ice therapy; use fan or air conditioning in hot weather |
| | Decreased subcutaneous tissue | Inspect skin for breakdown, protect bony prominences, frequent change in position; provide adequate clothing for protection and to maintain body warmth |
| | Decreased lubrication and sweating | Use lotions to maintain moisture; avoid hot water, use mild soap, rinse thoroughly and pat skin dry; offer fluids to prevent heat stroke, use fans or air conditioning in hot weather |
| Neurological Vision | Use artificial tears | Wear corrective lens |
| | Dry cornea | Offer large print books |
| | Presbyopia (farsightedness) | Take time to focus |
| | Decreased tolerance to glare or changes in light | Wear tinted glasses |
| | | Turn on lights |
| | | Use night light |
| | Alterations in color perception | Green, blue, violet are harder to see than red, orange, yellow; offer bright colors |
| Hearing | Presbycusis (progressive loss of hearing and sound discrimination); increased build-up of wax | Face person, speak slowly and clearly using lower tone, ensure adequate lightening |
| | | Determine if person hears better from one side |
| | | Offer well-seasoned food, encourage client to eat; use smoke detectors |
| Taste and smell | Decreased | |
| Cardiovascular | Decreased cardiac muscle strength, reduced stroke volume, decreased cardiac output; decreased elasticity of blood vessels | Encourage regular exercise routine, maintain fluid balance, change position slowly, encourage low cholesterol diet, sit with feet and legs elevated, medication as required |
| Respiratory | Cough reflex decreased | Cut food into small pieces, eat slowly |
| | Rib cage less mobile, decreased strength of respiratory muscles, decreased vital capacity | Do not smoke, avoid smoke-filled rooms, crowds during winter, exercise, deep breathe, encourage erect posture, balance rest and activity |

*(Continued)*

● Table 9 (cont'd)

| LATE ADULTHOOD (cont'd) | | |
| --- | --- | --- |
| SYSTEM | CHANGES | NURSING CARE |
| Musculoskeletal | Calcium loss from bone (greater in females), gradual loss of muscular strength and endurance | Maintain calcium intake, regular exercise, avoid fatigue, use assistive devices when needed, ensure home environment is safe |
| Urinary | Decreased renal function, diminished bladder capacity, delayed urge to void causes frequent urination, urgency to void which contributes to incontinence; increased incidence of cystitis, skin irritation | Determine medication usage, side effects, and toxicity because medication is excreted through the kidneys; maintain adequate fluid intake, toilet frequently; observe for signs of UTI; observe men for signs of benign prostatic hypertrophy |
| Gastrointestinal | Decreased saliva production, decreased ability to chew, decreased thirst sensation, delayed emptying of the stomach and esophagus, decreased digestion, decreased absorption of nutrients, increased constipation | Encourage fluids; encourage dental care; encourage foods high in roughage, regular exercise, regular toileting; encourage nutritional intake, offer smaller meals more frequently |
| Endocrine | Decreased ability to respond to stress because of body's decreased response to adrenal and thyroid hormones; decreased response to insulin | Maintain weight and nutrition, regular exercise and check-ups |
| Reproductive Female | Decreased estrogen causes vaginal walls to shrink, thin; vaginal secretions decrease | Encourage use of vaginal lubricants; continue annual Pap smears and mammograms |
| Male | Secretion of testosterone continues but is decreased; prostate increases; decreased rate and force of ejaculation | Encourage annual prostate exams |

Table 10

| ADULTHOOD GROWTH AND DEVELOPMENT | |
|---|---|
| **65 to 80 YEARS** | **>80 YEARS** |
| Physical decline | Signs of aging very evident |
| Loss of significant others | Few significant relationships |
| Appraisal of life | Withdrawal, risk of isolation |
| Appearance of chronic diseases | Self-concern |
| Reconciliation of goals and achievements | Accepting of death, face mortality |
| Changing social roles | Increased losses |
| | Decreased abilities |

## INTELLECTUAL DELAY

**A.** Data Collection

  1. Sensory deficits (see Table 11)

  2. Physical anomalies

  3. Delayed growth and development

**B.** Diagnose

Definition: Sub-average intellectual function (IQ less than 70) with concurrent impairment in adaptive functioning; onset under the age of 18

  1. Characteristics
     a. Lack of, or destruction of, brain cells

  2. Causes
     a. Heredity
     b. Infection
     c. Fetal anoxia
     d. Cranial or chromosomal abnormalities
     e. Intracranial hemorrhage

Table 11

| INTELLECTUAL DELAY | | | | |
|---|---|---|---|---|
| CLASSIFICATION | IQ RANGE | PRESCHOOL GROWTH AND DEVELOPMENT | SCHOOL TRAINING AND EDUCATION | ADULT SOCIAL/ VOCATIONAL LEVEL |
| I. Mild | 55-70 | Slow to walk, feed self, and talk compared with other children | With special education, can learn reading and math skills for third-to-sixth grade level | Can achieve social/vocational self-maintenance<br>May need occasional psychosocial support |
| II. Moderate | 40-55 | Delays in motor development<br>Can do some self-help activities | Responds to training<br>Does not progress with reading or math skills<br>Poor communication skills | Sheltered, usually incapable of self-maintenance |
| III. Severe | 25-40 | Marked delay in development<br>May be able to help self minimally | Can profit from habit training<br>Has some understanding of speech | Dependent on others for care<br>Can conform to routine |
| IV. Profound | Under 25 | Significant delay, minimal-capacity functioning | May respond to skill training<br>Shows basic emotional responses | Incapable of self-maintenance, needs nursing care |

**C.** Plan/Implementation

1. Assist parents with adjustment

2. Provide sensory stimulation

3. Encourage socially acceptable behavior

4. Provide emotional support

## FETAL ALCOHOL SYNDROME

**A.** Data Collection

1. Thin upper lip, epicanthal folds, maxillary hypoplasia

2. Intellectual delay, motor deficiencies, microcephaly, and hearing disorders

3. Irritability during infancy and hyperactivity during childhood

4. Small for gestational age

**B.** Diagnose

1. Leading cause of intellectual delay

2. Caused by excessive alcohol ingestion

3. Preventable if mother avoids alcohol during pregnancy

**C.** Plan/Implementation

1. Prevention
   a. Instruct women to stop consuming alcohol 3 months before conception
   b. There is no safe level of alcohol consumption during pregnancy

2. Monitor infant's weight gain

3. Promote nutritional intake

## DOWN SYNDROME

**A.** Data Collection

1. Intellectual delay–IQ range from 20 to 70

2. Marked hypotonia; short stature

3. Altered physical development–epicanthal folds, low-set ears, protruding tongue, low nasal bridge

**B.** Diagnose

1. Characteristics
   a. Chromosomal abnormality involving an extra chromosome (number 21)

2. Causes
   a. Unknown
   b. Associated with maternal age greater than 35

**C.** Plan/Implementation

1. Provide stimulation—OT, PT, special education

2. Observe for signs of common physical problems: 30–40% have heart diseases; 80% have hearing loss; respiratory infections are common

3. Establish and maintain adequate nutrition, parental education, and support

## LEARNING DISABILITIES

**A.** Data Collection

1. Hyperkinesis (sometimes absent)

2. Decreased attention span, i.e., attention deficit disorder (ADD)

3. Perceptual deficits

4. Aggression/depression

**B.** Diagnose

1. Characteristics
   a. Learning and behavioral disorders that occur because of CNS malfunctioning
   b. Neuropsychological testing—reveals individual differences
   c. Average to high IQ

**C.** Plan/Implementation

1. Reduce frustration

2. Special educational intervention; small class size

3. Provide safety and security

4. Administer medications, e.g., Ritalin, Dexedrine

5. Refer to appropriate resources—special education, parent support groups

## HUMAN SEXUALITY

**A.** Data Collection

1. Physical appearance

2. Physical limitations

3. Sexual role performance problems
   a. Infertility
   b. Frigidity
   c. Impotence
   d. Premature ejaculation
   e. Inability to achieve orgasm
   f. Dyspareunia (pain with intercourse)

4. Sexual role functioning
   a. Homosexuality
   b. Bisexuality
   c. Sexual ambiguity
   d. Transsexual surgery
   e. Transvestism

**B.** Diagnose

1. Expression of person's sexual identity

2. Involves sexual relationships and self-concept

**C.** Plan/Implementation

1. Don't allow your personal beliefs to interfere with your ability to help client express concerns

2. Remain nonjudgmental

3. Acknowledge feelings may be uncomfortable

4. Provide information as needed

## PREGNANCY

A. Data Collection

1. Estimated date of confinement (EDC)
   a. Nägele's rule—count back three months from first day of last menstrual period and add seven days and one year
   b. Ultrasonography—estimates fetal age from head measurements
   c. Fundal height—measurement of fundal height from the top of symphysis pubis to the top of the fundus with a flexible, nonstretchable tape measure, used as a gross estimate of dates
      1) Above the level of symphysis—between 12 and 14 weeks
      2) At the umbilicus or 20 cm—about 20 weeks
      3) Rises about 1 cm/week until 36 weeks, after which it varies

2. Obstetric classification
   a. Gravida—the total number of pregnancies regardless of duration (includes present pregnancy); nulligravida—woman who has never been pregnant
   b. Para—number of past pregnancies that have gone beyond the period of viability (capability of the fetus to survive outside of the uterus—after 20 weeks gestation or >500 g) regardless of the number of fetuses or whether the infant was born alive or dead; primipara—woman who has completed one pregnancy with fetus that reached stage of viability
   c. Term—born from beginning of 38 to end of 42 week
   d. Abortion—any pregnancy that terminates before the period of viability

3. Characteristic findings
   a. Uterus—increases in size, at 12–14 weeks, above symphysis pubis
   b. Cervix—softens, mucus plug in canal, bluish color (Chadwick's sign)
   c. Abdomen—stretches, striae
   d. Breasts—enlarged, tender
   e. Blood volume—increases 30% and peaks at 28 weeks
   f. Cardiac output—increased by 750 ml/min
   g. Ventilation—decreased tidal volume in third trimester
   h. Digestion—decreased peristalsis and increased pressure
   i. Skin
      1) Pink or reddish streaks (striae gravidarum) on breasts, abdomen, buttocks, and/or thighs; result of fat deposits causing stretching of the skin
      2) Increased pigmentation on the face; blotchy brown areas on the forehead and cheeks (chloasma or "mask of pregnancy"); on the abdomen, dark line from the umbilicus to the symphysis pubis (linea nigra)
      3) Minute vascular spiders

       4) Umbilicus is pushed outward and by the seventh month, depression disappears, becomes a darkened area on the abdominal wall

       5) Sweat and sebaceous glands more active

  j. Urinary—frequency and stasis result from pressure

  k. Endocrine

     1) Placenta—produces estrogen, progesterone, human chorionic gonadotrophin (hCG), human placental lactogen (hPL)

     2) Pituitary—elevated estrogen and progesterone, suppressed LH, FSH, and oxytocin

     3) Weight gain—steady, consistent is ideal; based on pre-pregnancy BMI

       a) BMI less than 18.5; total weight gain range 28-40 lb

       b) BMI 18.5-24.9; total weight gain range 25-35 lb

       c) BMI 25-29.9; total weight gain 15-25 lb

       d) BMI greater than 30; weight gain total 11-20 lb

4. Diagnostic test—hCG is measured by radioimmunoassay in blood and urine; serum more sensitive, so results are more accurate and available earlier

5. Verifying pregnancy

  a. Presumptive—changes felt by woman: amenorrhea, nausea/vomiting ("morning sickness"), breast sensitivity, fatigue, lassitude, quickening (maternal perception of fetal movement occurring between 16 and 20 weeks of gestation), urinary frequency

  b. Probable—changes observed by examiner: uterine enlargement, soufflé and contractions, positive urine pregnancy tests, Hegar's sign (softening and compressibility of isthmus of uterus), Chadwick's sign

  c. Positive—definite signs of pregnancy: fetal heartbeat (8–12 weeks by Doptone and by 18–20 weeks auscultation), palpation of fetal movement, outline of fetal skeleton by sonogram or x-ray (done only if absolutely necessary late in pregnancy)

6. Fetal data collection

  a. Fetal heart rate (FHR)—a significant predictor of fetal well-being; at term 110-160 beats/min

  b. Fetal movement (FM)—a regular pattern of 10 movements in one hour twice a day is a good indicator of fetal well-being; fewer than three movements in a one-hour period should be reported

**B.** Diagnose

1. Potential nursing diagnoses

  a. Deficient knowledge

  b. Risk for ineffective role performance

  c. Risk for imbalanced nutrition: less than body requirements

  d. Risk for fetal injury

2. Fertilization—union of ovum and spermatozoa, occurs about 24 hours after ovulation; usually outer third of fallopian tube

3.  Implantation

    a.  Upper part of uterus

    b.  About one week after fertilization

4.  Early placental development

    a.  Combination of endometrium and fetal chorionic layer (maternal and embryonic parts)

    b.  Chorion produces human chorionic gonadotrophin (hCG)

    c.  Transmits nutrients from maternal bloodstream by a number of mechanisms

    d.  Transfer of oxygen from mother to fetus by diffusion

    e.  Removes waste products of fetal metabolism into mother's bloodstream from which they will be excreted

**C.**  Plan/Implementation

1.  Encourage prenatal care

2.  Manage discomforts of pregnancy (see Table 1)

Table 1

| DISCOMFORTS OF PREGNANCY | |
|---|---|
| **DATA COLLECTION FINDINGS** | **NURSING CONSIDERATIONS** |
| Nausea and vomiting (morning sickness) | May occur any time of day<br>Dry crackers on arising<br>Eat small, frequent meals<br>Avoid strong odors and greasy foods |
| Constipation, hemorrhoids | Bulk foods, fiber<br>Generous fluid intake<br>Encourage regularity, routine |
| Leg cramps | Increase calcium intake<br>Flex feet, local heat |
| Breast soreness | Well-fitting bra<br>Bra may be worn at night |
| Backache | Emphasize posture<br>Careful lifting<br>Good shoes<br>Pelvic tilt exercises |
| Heartburn | Small frequent meals<br>Antacids—avoid those containing phosphorus<br>Decrease fatty and fried foods<br>Avoid supine position after meals |
| Dizziness | Slow, deliberate movements<br>Support stockings<br>Monitor intake |
| Vertigo, lightheadedness | Vena cava or maternal hypotensive syndrome<br>Turn on left side |
| Urinary frequency | Kegel exercises<br>Decrease fluids before bed<br>Report signs of infection |

## FETAL DEVELOPMENT

A. Data Collection

1. Maternal considerations
   a. High-risk group
   b. Environment
   c. Medications, drugs, alcohol
   d. Nutrition—should be no attempt at weight reduction
   e. Age

2. Genetic considerations
   a. African Americans for sickle-cell disease, Northern European descendants of Ashkenazi Jews for Tay-Sach's disease, Mediterranean ancestry for thalassemia; couples with a history of a child with a defect; family history of a structural abnormality or systemic disease that may be hereditary; closely related parents; women over 40
   b. Chromosomal alteration—may be numeric or structural
      1) Down syndrome (trisomy 21)—increased in women over 35 years; characterized by a small, round head with flattened occiput, low-set ears, large fat pads at the nape of a short neck, protruding tongue, small mouth and high palate, epicanthal folds with slanted eyes, hypotonic muscles with hypermobility of joints, short, broad hands with inward curved little finger, transverse simian palmar crease, mental deficiencies
      2) Turner's syndrome (female with only one X)—characterized by stunted growth, fibrous streaks in ovaries, usually infertile, no intellectual impairment, occasionally perceptual problems
      3) Klinefelter's syndrome (male with extra X)—normal intelligence to mild intellectual delay, usually infertile
   c. Autosomal defects—defects occurring in any chromosome pair other than the sex chromosomes
      1) Autosomal dominant—union of normal parent with affected parent gene; the affected parent has a 50% chance of passing on the abnormal gene in each pregnancy; BRCA-1 and BRCA-2 breast cancer, Type 2 diabetes, Marfan syndrome, polycystic kidney disease
      2) Autosomal recessive—requires transmission of abnormal gene from both parents for expression of condition; cystic fibrosis, sickle cell disease
      3) Sex-linked transmission traits—trait carried on a sex chromosome (usually the X chromosome); may be dominant or recessive, but recessive is more prevalent; e.g., hemophilia, color blindness
   d. Inborn errors of metabolism—disorders of protein, fat, or carbohydrate metabolism due to absent or defective enzymes that generally follow a recessive pattern of inheritance

1) Phenylketonuria (PKU)—disorder due to autosomal recessive gene creating a deficiency in the liver enzyme phenylalanine hydroxylase, which metabolizes the amino acid phenylalanine; results in metabolites accumulation in the blood; toxic to brain cells

2) Tay-Sach's disease—autosomal recessive trait resulting from a deficiency of hexosaminidase A, resulting in apathy and regression in motor and social development and decreased vision

3) Cystic fibrosis (mucoviscidosis or fibrocystic disease of the pancreas)—an autosomal recessive trait characterized by generalized involvement of exocrine glands, resulting in altered viscosity of mucus-secreting glands throughout the body

3. Diagnostic tests

a. Alpha-fetal protein test—fetal serum protein to predict neural tube defects, threatened abortion, fetal distress

1) Done between 16 and 18 weeks

2) High incidence of false-positive results (delivered normal neonates)

3) Usual concurrent test for presence of acetylcholinesterase

b. Chorionic villus sampling—early antepartal test to diagnose fetal karyotype, sickle-cell anemia, PKU, Down syndrome, Duchenne muscular dystrophy

1) Done between 8 and 12 weeks

2) Complications include bleeding, spontaneous abortion, rupture of membranes

3) Rh-negative mother should receive Rho(D) immune globulin (IGIM) after test to prevent Rh isoimmunization

4) Ultrasound used to guide

5) Full bladder required

c. Amniocentesis—amniotic fluid is aspirated by a needle inserted through the abdominal and uterine walls

1) Done at 16 weeks to detect genetic disorder; possible after week 14

2) Done at 30 weeks to determine L/S ratio (lecithin/ sphingomyelin) to determine lung maturity

3) Prior to the procedure, the client's bladder should be emptied; ultrasonography (x-ray only if necessary) is used to avoid trauma from the needle to the placenta, fetus

4) Test results take 2 to 4 weeks

5) Complications include premature labor, infection, Rh isoimmunization, abruptio placentae, amniotic embolism

6) Monitor fetus electronically after procedure, monitor for uterine contractions; Rh-negative mother should receive Rho(D) immune globulin after procedure

7) Teach client to report decreased fetal movement, contractions, or abdominal discomfort after procedure

d.  Ultrasound—transducer on abdomen transmits sound waves that show fetal image on screen
    1)  As early as five weeks to confirm pregnancy, gestational age
    2)  Multiple purposes—to determine position, number, measurement of fetus(es) and other structures (placenta)
    3)  Client must drink fluid prior to test to have full bladder to assist in clarity of image
    4)  No known harmful effects for fetus or mother
    5)  Noninvasive

e.  Non-stress test (NST)—tocodynamometer records fetal movements, and Doppler ultrasound measures fetal heart rate to obtain fetal well-being after 28 weeks
    1)  Client should eat snacks
    2)  A reactive test (a good finding) is two or more FHR accelerations of 15 bpm lasting 15 seconds over a 20-minute interval, and return of FHR to normal baseline

f.  Contraction stress test (CST), either nipple stimulation or oxytocin stimulation—evaluates fetal response to stress of labor
    1)  Performed after 28 weeks
    2)  Woman in semi-Fowler's or side-lying position
    3)  Positive-late decelerations with at least 50% of contractions; potential risk to fetus, cesarean may be necessary
    4)  Negative result—no late decelerations with a minimum of three contractions lasting 40–60 seconds in 10-minute period
    5)  Monitor for post-test labor onset

**B.**  Diagnose—potential nursing diagnoses

1.  Knowledge deficits

2.  Lack of prenatal care

**C.**  Plan/Implementation

1.  Reinforce teaching of optimal nutrition and exercise

2.  Advise avoidance of hazards
    a.  Urinary tract infections (UTI)—lower tract characterized by urinary frequency and urgency, dysuria, and sometimes hematuria; manifested in upper tract by fever, malaise, anorexia, nausea, abdominal/back pain; confirmed by >100,000/ml bacterial colony count by clean catch urine; sometimes asymptomatic; treated with sulfa-based medications and ampicillin
    b.  TORCH test series—group of maternal systemic infections that can be transmitted across the placenta or by ascending infection (after rupture of membranes [ROM]) to the fetus; infection early in pregnancy may produce significant and devastating fetal deformities, whereas later infection may result in overwhelming active systemic disease and/or CNS involvement causing severe neurological impairment or death of newborn
        1)  Toxoplasmosis (protozoa; transplacental to fetus)—discourage eating undercooked meat and handling cat litter box

            2) Other

               a) Syphilis

               b) Varicella/shingles (transplacental to fetus or droplet to newborn)—caution susceptible woman about contact with the disease and Zoster Immune Globulin for exposure

               c) Group B beta-hemolytic streptococcus (direct or indirect to fetus during labor and delivery)—treated with penicillin

               d) Hepatitis B (transplacental and contact with secretions during delivery)—screen and immunize maternal carriers; treat newborn with HBIg

               e) Hepatitis A—need to encourage good handwashing techniques

               f) AIDS (as with hepatitis)—titers in newborn may be passive transfer of maternal antibodies or active antibody formation

            3) Rubella (transplacental)—prenatal testing required by law; caution susceptible woman about contact; vaccine is not given during pregnancy

            4) Cytomegalovirus (CMV)—transmitted in body fluids; detected by antibody/serological testing

            5) Herpes 2 (transplacental, ascending infection within 4–6 hours after ROM or contact during delivery if active lesions)—cesarean delivery if active lesions

    3. Reinforce teaching of danger signs of pregnancy

       a. Gush of fluid or bleeding from vagina

       b. Regular uterine contractions

       c. Severe headaches, visual disturbances, abdominal pain, or persistent vomiting

       d. Fever or chills

       e. Swelling in face and fingers

       f. Decrease in fetal movement

## LABOR AND DELIVERY

**A.** Data Collection

    1. Characteristic findings

       a. Onset

          1) Lightening—subjective sensation as fetus descends into pelvic inlet

             a) Primipara (occurs up to two weeks prior to delivery)

             b) Multipara (may not occur until labor begins)

          2) Softening of cervix

          3) Expulsion of mucus plug (show)

          4) Uterine contractions that are progressive and regular

       b. Cervical changes

          1) Effacement—progressive thinning and shortening of cervix (0–100%)

          2) Dilation—opening of cervix os during labor (0–10 cm)

       c. Rupture of membranes—rupture of amniotic sac (ROM)

          1) Check fetal heart tones to determine fetal distress

  2) Prolapsed cord

    a) Symptoms—premature rupture of membranes, presenting part not engaged, fetal distress, protruding cord

    b) Nursing care—call for help, push against presenting part to relieve pressure on cord, place in Trendelenburg or knee-chest position

    c) Treatment successful—fetal heart tones remain unchanged

2. Fetal monitoring

  a. Intermittent auscultation

  b. Electronic monitoring

    1) External—monitors uterine contractions and FHR

      a) Transabdominal, noninvasive

      b) Client needs to decrease extra-abdominal movements

    2) Internal—continuous data for both FHR and intrauterine pressure

      a) Membranes must be ruptured, cervix sufficiently dilated, and presenting part low

      b) Invasive procedure

  c. Results of monitoring

    1) Normal FHR 120–160; must obtain a baseline

3. Tachycardia (>160 bpm lasting longer than 10 minutes)—early sign of fetal hypoxia, associated with maternal fever, fetal anemia, fetal or maternal infection, drugs (atropine, vistaril), maternal hyperthyroidism, fetal heart failure; nonreassuring sign when associated with late decelerations, severe variable decelerations, or absence of variability

4. Bradycardia (<110 bpm lasting longer than 10 minutes)—late sign of fetal hypoxia, associated with maternal drugs (anesthetics), prolonged cord compression, fetal congenital heart block, maternal supine hypotensive syndrome; nonreasurring sign when associated with loss of variability and late decelerations

5. Variability—Beat-to-beat fluctuation; measured by EFM only

  a. Normal (6–25 bpm)—indicator of fetal well-being

  b. Absent (0–2 bpm) or decreased (3–5 bpm) may be associated with fetal sleep state, fetal prematurity, reaction to drugs (narcotics, barbiturates, tranquilizers, anesthetics), congenital anomalies, hypoxia, acidosis; if persists for more than 30 minutes, is indicator of fetal distress

  c. Increased (greater than 25 bpm)—significance unknown

6. Accelerations—15 bpm rise above baseline followed by a return; usually in response to fetal movement or contractions; indicates fetal well-being

7. Decelerations—fall below baseline lasting 15 seconds or more, followed by a return

  a. Early: onset close to beginning or before peak of contraction; most often uniform mirror image of contraction on tracing; associated with head compression, in second stage with pushing; reassuring pattern

b. Late: onset after contraction is established, usually begins at the peak of the contraction, with slow return to baseline after the contraction is complete; indicative of fetal hypoxia because of deficient placental perfusion; caused by PIH, maternal diabetes, placenta previa, abruption placentae; nonreasurring sign

c. Variable decelerations–transient U/V-shaped reduction occurring at any time during uterine contracting phase; decrease usually more than 15 bpm, lasting 15 seconds, return to baseline in less than 2 minutes from onset, indicative of cord compression, which may be relieved by change in mother's position; ominous if repetitive, prolonged, severe, or slow return to baseline, administer $O_2$, discontinue oxytocin

d. Nursing interventions for abnormal results

   1) None for early decelerations

   2) For late decelerations (at the first sign of abnormal tracing)– position mother left side-lying (if no change, move to other side, Trendelenburg or knee-chest position); administer oxygen by mask, start IV or increase flow rate, stop oxytocin if appropriate, prepare for C-section

   3) Variable decelerations change maternal position to relieve pressure on the umbilical cord

8. Factors affecting labor and delivery

a. Lie–relationship of spine of fetus to spine of mother; longitudinal (parallel), transverse (right angles), oblique (slight angle off a true transverse lie)

b. Presentation–part of fetus that presents to (enters) maternal pelvic inlet

   1) Cephalic/vertex–head (95% of labors)

   2) Breech/buttocks (3–4%)

      a) Frank (most common)–flexion of hips and extension of knees

      b) Complete–flexion of hips and knees

      c) Footing/incomplete–extension of hips and knees

   3) Shoulder (transverse lie)–rare

c. Attitude–relationship of fetal parts to each other; usually flexion of head and extremities on chest and abdomen to accommodate to shape of uterine cavity

d. Position–relationship of fetal reference point to maternal pelvis (see Figure 1); to find best location for FHR assessment, determine the location of the fetal back; weeks of gestation may alter the location, as well

   1) Expressed as standard three-letter abbreviation; e.g., LOA = left occiput anterior, indicating vertex presentation with fetal occiput on mother's left side toward the front of her pelvis (see Figure 1)

      a) LOA–left occiput anterior, most common; FHR best heard below umbilicus on mother's left side

      b) LOP–left occiput posterior

      c) ROA–right occiput anterior

      d) ROP–right occiput posterior

    e) LSA—left sacrum anterior
    f) RSA—right sacrum anterior
  2) Configuration and diameter of pelvis
  3) Distensibility of uterus

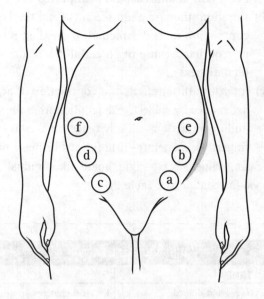

**Figure 1. Determining Position**

  e. Station—level of presenting part of fetus in relation to imaginary
     line between ischial spines (zero station) in midpelvis of mother
     (see Figure 2)
     1) −5 to −1 indicates a presenting part above zero station
        (floating); +1 to +5, a presenting part below zero station
     2) Engagement—when the presenting part is at station zero or below

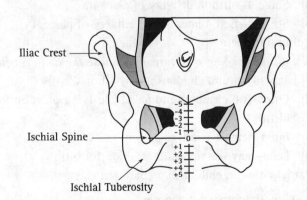

**Figure 2. Station of Presenting Part**

  f. Contractions
     1) Three phases
        a) Increment—steep crescent slope from beginning of the
           contraction until its peak
        b) Acme/peak—strongest intensity
        c) Decrement—diminishing intensity

2) Characteristics of contractions
   a) Frequency: time frame in minutes from the beginning of one contraction to the beginning of the next one or the peak of one contraction to the peak of the next; frequency less than every two minutes should be reported
   b) Duration: time frame in seconds from the beginning of a contraction to its completion; more than 90 seconds should be reported because of potential risk of uterine rupture or fetal distress
   c) Intensity: the strength of a contraction at acme; may be determined by subjective description from the woman, palpation (mild contraction—slightly tense uterus easy to indent with fingertips; moderate—firm fundus difficult to indent with fingertips; strong—rigid, board-like fundus)
g. True vs. false labor (see Table 2)

Table 2 ●

| TRUE VS. FALSE LABOR | |
|---|---|
| **TRUE** | **FALSE** |
| Cervix progressively effaced and dilated | Cervical changes do not occur |
| Contractions—regular with increasing frequency (shortened intervals), duration, and intensity | Contractions—irregular with usually no change in frequency, duration, or intensity |
| Discomfort radiates from back around the abdomen | Discomfort is usually abdominal |
| Contractions do not decrease with rest | Contractions may lessen with activity or rest |

h. Stages of labor
   1) Stage 1—beginning to complete cervical dilation (0–10 cm)
   2) Stage 2—complete dilation to birth of baby
   3) Stage 3—birth to delivery of placenta
   4) Stage 4—first 4 hours after delivery of placenta
i. Cultural influences
   *Not all members of a culture will choose the actions below.*
   1) Japan—natural childbirth, may labor silently
   2) China—stoic response to pain, side-lying position for labor and birth
   3) India—female relatives present
   4) Laos—may use squatting position for birth
j. Participation in childbirth preparation classes

**B.** Diagnose—potential nursing diagnoses

1. Potential knowledge deficits

2. Difficulty adapting and coping with stress

3. Risk of complications

4. Need for pain management

5. Labor may not progress

**C.** Plan/Implementation

1. Monitor progress—maternal
   a. First stage of labor
      1) Phase one (latent): 0–3 cm; contractions 10–30 sec long, 5–30 min apart; mild to moderate
      2) Phase two (active): 4–7 cm; contractions 40–60 sec long, 3–5 min apart; moderate to strong
      3) Phase three (transition): 8–10 cm; contractions 45–90 sec long, 1½–2 min apart; strong
   b. Second stage labor
      1) Phase 1: 0 to +2 station; contractions 2–3 min apart
      2) Phase 2: +2 to +4 station; contractions 2–2.5 min apart; increase in dark red bloody show; increased urgency to bear down
      3) Phase 3: +4 to birth; contractions 1–2 min apart; fetal head visible; increased urgency to bear down
   c. Third stage of labor
      1) Placental delivery—slight gush of blood and lengthening of umbilical cord; check for remaining fragments
   d. Fourth stage of labor: first 4 hours after delivery

2. Monitor progress—fetal
   a. During labor check FHR
   b. Manage fetal distress (see Table 3)

●Table 3

| MANAGEMENT OF FETAL DISTRESS | |
| --- | --- |
| **DATA COLLECTION FINDINGS** | **NURSING CONSIDERATIONS** |
| Irregular fetal heartbeat | Turn client onto left side<br>Give supplemental oxygen<br>Check for cord prolapse<br>Start intravenous line |
| Umbilical cord prolapse | Elevate presenting part off the cord<br>Call for help<br>Place client in Trendelenburg or knee-chest position<br>Give supplemental oxygen<br>Start intravenous line |

3. Monitor discomfort/exhaustion/pain control—support client in choice of pain control
   a. Relaxation techniques taught during pregnancy where breathing is taught as a relaxed response to contraction
   b. Low back pain—advise massage of sacral area
   c. Use different breathing techniques during different phases of labor
   d. Encourage rest between contractions

4. Keep couple informed of progress

5. Newborn care at delivery—immediate actions
   a. Establish airway
   b. Observe for Apgar score at 1 and 5 minutes
   c. Clamp umbilical cord

   d.  Maintain warmth

   e.  Place identification band on baby and mother

## POSTPARTUM

**A.**  Data Collection (see Table 4)

   1.  Physical

   2.  Cultural influences

**B.**  Diagnose—potential nursing diagnoses

   1.  Physical mobility, impaired

   2.  Parenting, risk for altered

   3.  Self-care deficit

**C.**  Plan/Implementation

   1.  If ordered, RhoGAM to mother—RhoGAM promotes lysis of fetal
       Rh-positive RBCs circulating in maternal bloodstream before
       Rh-negative mother develops her own antibodies to them

   2.  Observe lochia color and volume

   3.  Check episiotomy and perineum for signs and symptoms of infection

   4.  Observe for attachment/bonding—influenced by maternal psychosocial-
       cultural factors, infant health status, temperament, and behaviors,
       circumstances of the prenatal, intrapartal, postpartal, and neonatal
       course; evidenced initially by touching and cuddling, naming, "en face"
       positioning for direct eye contact, later by reciprocity and rhythmicity
       in maternal–infant interaction

   5.  Promote successful feeding

   6.  Nonnursing woman—suppress lactation
       a.  Mechanical methods—tight-fitting bra for 72 hours, ice packs,
           minimize breast stimulation

Table 4

| FOURTH STAGE OF LABOR | | |
|---|---|---|
| **FIRST 1–2 HOURS** | | **NURSING CONSIDERATIONS** |
| Vital signs (BP, pulse) | q 15 min | Follow protocol until stable |
| Fundus | q 15 min | Position—at the level of the umbilicus for the first 12 hours, then descends by one finger breadth each succeeding day, pelvic organ usually by day 10 |
| Lochia (color, volume) | q 15 min | Lochia (endometrial sloughing)—day 1-3 rubra (bloody with fleshy odor; may be clots); day 4-9 serosa (pink/brown with fleshy odor); day 10+ alba (yellow–white); at no time should there be a foul odor (indicates infection) |
| Urinary | Measure first void | May have urethral edema, urine retention |
| Bonding | Encourage interaction | Emphasize touch, eye contact |

7.  Nursing woman—successful lactation is dependent on infant sucking and maternal production and delivery of milk (letdown/milk ejection reflex); monitor and teach preventive measures for potential problems (see Table 5)
    a.  Nipple irritation/cracking
        1)  Nipple care—clean with warm water, no soap, and dry thoroughly; absorbent breast pads if leaking occurs; apply ice before breastfeeding; apply breast milk to nipples and areola after each feeding and air dry; apply warm compresses after each feeding and air dry
        2)  Position nipple so that infant's mouth covers a large portion of the areola and release infant's mouth from nipple by inserting finger to break suction
        3)  Rotate breastfeeding positions
    b.  Engorgement—nurse frequently (every 30 minutes to 3 hours) and long enough to empty breasts completely (evidenced by sucking without swallowing); warm shower or compresses to stimulate letdown; alternate starting breast at each feeding; mild analgesic 20 minutes before feeding and ice packs between feedings for pronounced discomfort
    c.  Plugged ducts—area of tenderness and lumpiness often associated with engorgement; may be relieved by heat and massage before feeding
    d.  Expression of breast milk—to collect milk for supplemental feedings, to relieve breast fullness or to build milk supply; may be manually expressed or pumped by a device and refrigerated for no more than 48 hours or frozen in plastic bottles (to maintain stability of all elements) in refrigerator freezer for 2 weeks and deep freezer for 2 months (do not thaw in microwave or on stove)
    e.  Medications—most drugs cross into breast milk; check with health care provider before taking any medication

●Table 5

| LACTATION PRINCIPLES | |
|---|---|
| **BREAST CARE—ANTEPARTUM AND POSTPARTUM** | **INITIATING BREAST FEEDING** |
| Soap on nipples should be avoided during bathing to prevent dryness<br>Redness or swelling can indicate infection and should always be investigated | Relaxed position of mother is essential—support dependent arm with pillow<br>Alternate which breast is offered first<br>Five minutes on each breast is sufficient at first—teach proper way to break suction<br>Most of the areola should be in infant's mouth to ensure proper sucking |

8. "Postpartum blues" (day 3–7)—normal occurrence of "roller coaster" emotions, weeping, "letdown feeling"; usually relieved with emotional support and rest/sleep; report if prolonged or later onset

9. Urinary incontinence
   a. Kegel exercises—tighten pubococcygeal muscles, hold for count of 3, then relax; do 10 times tid
   b. Avoid diuretics such as caffeine

10. Sexual activities—abstain from intercourse until episiotomy is healed and lochia has ceased (usually 3–4 weeks); may be affected by fatigue, fear of discomfort, leakage of breast milk, concern about another pregnancy; discuss couple's desire for and understanding about contraceptive methods; breast feeding does not give adequate protection; oral contraceptives should not be used during breastfeeding

## SPONTANEOUS ABORTION

**A.** Data Collection

1. Persistent uterine bleeding and cramplike pain

2. Laboratory finding—negative or weakly positive urine pregnancy test

3. Obtain history, including last menstrual period

4. Types (see Table 1)

Table 1

| CLINICAL CLASSIFICATION OF SPONTANEOUS ABORTION | | |
|---|---|---|
| **TYPE** | **DATA COLLECTION FINDINGS** | **NURSING CONSIDERATIONS** |
| Threatened | Vaginal bleeding and cramping<br>Soft uterus, cervix closed | Ultrasound for intrauterine sac, quantitative hCG<br>Decrease activity for 24-48 hours, avoid stress, no sexual intercourse for 2 weeks after bleeding stops<br>Monitor amount and character of bleeding; report clots, tissue, foul odor |
| Inevitable, if cervical dilation cannot be prevented | Persistent symptoms, hemorrhage, moderate to severe cramping<br>Cervical dilation and effacement | Monitor for hemorrhage (save and count pads) and infection; if persistent or increased symptoms, D and C<br>Emotional support for grief and loss |
| Incomplete | Persistent symptoms, expulsion of part of products of conception | Administer IV/blood, oxytocin<br>D and C or suction evacuation |
| Complete | As above, except no retained tissue | Possible methylergonovine (Methergine); no other treatment if no evidence of hemorrhage or infection |
| Missed—fetus dies *in utero* but is not expelled | May be none/some abating of above symptoms<br>Cervix is closed<br>If retained >6 weeks, increased risk of infection, DIC, and emotional distress | D and C evacuation within 4-6 weeks<br>After 12 weeks, dilate cervix with several applications of prostaglandin gel or suppositories of laminaria (dried sterilized seaweed that expands with cervical secretions) |
| Habitual—3 or more | May be incompetent cervix, infertility | Cerclage (encircling cervix with suture) |

**B.** Diagnose

1. Causes

    a. Chromosomal abnormalities

    b. Teratogenic drugs

    c. Abnormalities of female reproductive tract

2. Potential nursing diagnosis
   a. Anxiety, fear
   b. Deficient knowledge
   c. Deficient fluid volume
   d. Grieving

3. Termination of pregnancy spontaneously at any time before the fetus has attained viability

C. Plan/Implementation

1. Monitor vital signs

2. Monitor for bleeding, cramping, pain

3. Monitor hydration status and electrolyte balance

4. Administer Rho(D) immune globulin (IGIM) as needed

5. Save all tissues

6. Teach purpose of bedrest

7. Prepare client for surgical procedure if indicated (D and C, therapeutic abortion)

8. Provide emotional support for grief and loss

## ECTOPIC PREGNANCY

A. Data Collection

1. Missed period

2. Unilateral lower quadrant pain after 4–6 weeks of normal pregnancy

3. Rigid, tender abdomen

4. Referred shoulder pain can occur

5. Low hematocrit, low hCG levels in urine and blood

6. Bleeding—gradual oozing to frank bleeding

B. Diagnose

1. Pain due to implantation of egg outside of uterus

2. Potential for anxiety and grieving

3. Potentially life-threatening to mother due to hemorrhage

4. Causes
   a. Pelvic inflammatory disease (PID)
   b. Previous tubal surgery
   c. Congenital anomalies of the fallopian tubes

C. Plan/Implementation

1. Prepare for surgery

2. Monitor for shock preoperatively and postoperatively

3. Provide emotional support and expression of grief

4. Administer Rho(D) immune globulin (IGIM) to Rh-negative women

5. Discharge teaching

## HYPERTENSION IN PREGNANCY

A. Preexisting hypertension (HTN)—diagnosed and treated before the 20th week of pregnancy; requires strict medical and obstetrical management

B. Gestational Hypertension—characterized by hypertension (systolic pressure greater than 140 mm Hg and/or diastolic pressure greater than 90 mm Hg) without proteinuria after 20 weeks gestation and resolving by 12 weeks postpartum; treated with frequent evaluation of BP and protein in urine

C. Preeclampsia and Eclampsia

1. Data Collection—increased risk in African Americans, primigravida older than 35 years or younger than 17 years, multiple fetuses or history of diabetes and renal disease, family history of pregnancy-induced hypertension (PIH); prenatal screening at each visit for symptomatology

● Table 2

| CHARACTERISTICS OF PREECLAMPSIA AND ECLAMPSIA | | | | | |
|---|---|---|---|---|---|
| CONDITION | BP | PROTEINURIA | SEIZURES | HYPERREFLEXIA | OTHER |
| Mild preeclampsia | Greater than 140/90 mm Hg after 20 weeks gestation | 300 mg/L per 24 h Greater than 1+ random sample | No | No | Mild facial edema Weight gain (greater than 4.5 lb/wk) |
| Severe preeclampsia | Greater than 160/110 mm Hg | Greater than 500 mg/L per 24 h Greater than 3+ random sample | No | Yes | Headache Oliguria Blurred vision RUQ pain Thrombocytopenia HELLP (hemolysis, elevated liver enzymes, low platelet count) |
| Eclampsia | Greater than 160/110 mm Hg | Marked proteinuria | Yes | No | Same as severe preeclampsia Severe headache Renal failure Cerebral hemorrhage |

Table 3

| PREECLAMPSIA AND ECLAMPSIA TREATMENT | |
|---|---|
| **CONDITION** | **TREATMENT** |
| Mild preeclampsia | Bed rest in left lateral position<br>Monitor BP daily<br>6–8 8 oz drinks/day<br>Frequent follow up |
| Severe preeclampsia | Depends on fetal age<br>Only cure is delivery of fetus (induction of labor)<br>Control BP (hydralyzine), prevent seizures (magnesium sulfate)<br>Prevent long term morbidity and maternal mortality<br>Emotional support if delivery prior to age of viability |
| Eclampsia<br>(Medical Emergency) | Support through seizures and potential coma<br>Ensure patent airway, O2 support<br>DIC management<br>Delivery of fetus<br>Emotional support if delivery prior to age of viability<br>In cases of severe hypertension, seizures may still occur 24–48 h<br>   postpartum; monitor magnesium sulfate or hydralazine if continued<br>   postpartum |

## PLACENTA PREVIA

**A.** Data Collection

1. First- and second-trimester spotting

2. Third trimester bleeding that is sudden, profuse, *painless*

3. Ultrasonography—classified by degree of obstruction

**B.** Diagnose

1. The placenta is implanted in the lower uterine segment, usually near or over the cervical opening

2. Potential nursing diagnoses
   a. Impaired fetal gas exchange
   b. Risk for deficient fluid volume
   c. Deficient knowledge
   d. Risk for maternal injury
   e. Anxiety and fear

**C.** Plan/Implementation

1. Hospitalization initially
   a. Bedrest side-lying or Trendelenburg position for at least 72 hours
   b. Ultrasound to locate placenta
   c. No vaginal, rectal exam unless delivery would not be a problem (if becomes necessary, must be done in OR under sterile conditions)
   d. Amniocentesis for lung maturity; monitor for changes in bleeding and fetal status
   e. Daily Hgb and Hct

    f. Two units of cross-matched blood available

    g. Monitor amount of blood loss

  2. Send home if bleeding ceases and pregnancy to be maintained

    a. Limit activity

    b. No douching, enemas, coitus

    c. Monitor fetal movement

    d. NST at least every 1–2 weeks

    e. Monitor complications

  3. Delivery by cesarean if evidence of fetal maturity, excessive bleeding, active labor, other complications

## ABRUPTIO PLACENTAE–"PREMATURE SEPARATION OF PLACENTA"

**A.** Data Collection

  1. *Painful*, dark red vaginal bleeding; bleeding may be scant to profuse

  2. Abdomen (uterus) is tender, painful, tense

  3. Possible fetal distress, maternal shock

  4. Contractions

**B.** Diagnose

  1. Premature separation of the placenta

  2. Occurence increased with maternal hypertension and cocaine abuse

  3. Potential nursing diagnoses

    a. Deficient fluid volume

    b. Impaired fetal gas exchange

    c. Acute pain

    d. Anxiety and fear

**C.** Plan/Implementation

  1. Monitor maternal and fetal progress

    a. Blood loss seen may not match symptoms

    b. Could have rapid fetal distress

  2. Prepare for immediate delivery

  3. Monitor for postpartal complications

    a. Disseminated intravascular coagulation (DIC)

    b. Pulmonary emboli

    c. Infection

    d. Renal failure

## DIABETES IN THE PREGNANT WOMAN

**A.** Data Collection

1. Urine screening for ketones

2. Blood sugar levels; oral glucose tolerance test

3. Glucose tolerance test (1-h test at 24–28 weeks) for women at average risk
   a. Age 25 or older
   b. Obesity
   c. Family history of diabetes in first-degree relative
   d. Hispanic, African American, Native American, or Asian American
   e. History of abnormal glucose tolerance

4. Glycosylated hemoglobin (indicates past serum glucose levels over previous 3 months); normal is 3.5–6 %

**B.** Diagnose

1. Potential nursing diagnoses
   a. Deficient knowledge
   b. Risk for risk-prone behaviors
   c. Risk for unstable blood glucose
   d. Imbalanced nutrition; less than body requirements

2. Classification
   a. Type 1–complications more common
   b. Type 2
   c. Gestational diabetes (GDM)–increased demand for insulin during pregnancy
   d. Impaired fasting glucose tolerance

3. Diabetes increases risk for
   a. Maternal infections–UTIs, vaginal yeast infections
   b. Hypertensive states of pregnancy
   c. Hydramnios (>2,000 ml amniotic fluid) and consequent preterm labor
   d. Macrosomia (large for gestational age but may have immature organ systems)
   e. Congenital anomalies (neural tube defects)
   f. Prematurity and stillbirth
   g. Respiratory distress syndrome (RDS)
   h. Untreated ketoacidosis can cause coma and death of mother and fetus

4. Gestational diabetes
   a. Hyperglycemia after 20 weeks when insulin need accelerates
   b. Usually controlled by diet
   c. Oral hypoglycemics not used–teratogenic and increase risk of neonatal hypoglycemia
   d. Risk factors
      1) Obesity
      2) Family history of diabetes

3) History of gestational diabetes

4) Hypertension, PIH, recurrent UTIs, monilial vaginitis, polyhydramnios; previously large infant (9-lb, 4,000 g or more)

5) Previously unexplained death/anomaly or stillbirths

6) Glycosuria, proteinuria on two or more occasions

5. Testing for diabetes—at 24–28 weeks for all gravidas

   a. Screen blood glucose level 1 hour after 50 g concentrated glucose solution

   b. Glucose tolerance test; normal findings:

   FBS—less than 92 mg/dL

   1 hour—less than 180 mg/dL

   2 hours—less than 153 mg/dL

   3 hours—less than 140 mg/dL

   c. If two or more abnormal findings, significant for diabetes

   d. Glycosylated hemoglobin (HbA$_{1c}$)—measures control past three months; elevations (>6–8%) in first trimester associated with increased risk of congenital anomalies and spontaneous abortion; in the last trimester, elevations with macrosomia

**C.** Plan/Implementation

1. Reinforce need for careful monitoring throughout pregnancy, including frequent medical/nursing evaluations

2. Evaluate understanding of modifications in diet/insulin coverage

3. Reinforce client and significant other teaching

   a. Diet—eat prescribed amount of food daily at same times

   b. Home glucose monitoring

   c. Insulin—purpose, dosage, administration, action, side effects, potential change in amount needed during pregnancy as fetus grows and immediately after delivery, no oral hypoglycemics (teratogenic)

4. Assist with stress reduction

5. Fetal surveillance

## CARDIAC DISEASE

**A.** Data Collection

1. Chest pain

2. Dyspnea with exertion; dyspnea at rest; edema

3. Monitor vital signs and do EKG, as heart lesion (especially those of mitral valve) may become aggravated by pregnancy

**B.** Diagnose

1. Potential nursing diagnoses

   a. Acute pain

   b. Decreased cardiac output

    c.  Impaired fetal gas exchange

    d.  Anxiety and fear

    e.  Deficient knowledge

    f.  Activity intolerance

    g.  Maternal injury

2. Treatment of heart disease in pregnancy is determined by the functional capacity of the heart, and type of delivery will be influenced by the mother's status and the condition of the fetus

**C.** Plan/Implementation

1. Monitor maternal vital signs and fetal heart rate

2. Encourage rest and adequate nutrition during pregnancy

3. Explain importance of avoidance and early treatment of upper respiratory infections

4. Be alert for signs of heart failure

5. During labor

    a.  Monitor vital signs frequently

    b.  Place client on cardiac monitor and on external fetal monitor.

    c.  Maintain bedrest with mother in side-lying or semi-recumbent position

    d.  Administer oxygen as prescribed

    e.  Monitor for signs of pulmonary edema and heart failure

    f.  Provide emotional support

### SYPHILIS

**A.** Data Collection

1. Blood tests (VDRL)

2. Primary lesion (chancre) located on internal or external genitalia
    a.  Secondary stage may be unnoticeable

3. Previous obstetrical history of spontaneous abortion, premature births, or full-term stillbirth

4. Method of infection
    a.  Congenital
    b.  Acquired—sexually

**B.** Diagnose—potential nursing diagnoses

1. Delayed growth and development

2. Deficient knowledge

**C.** Plan/Implementation

1. Administer penicillin, which crosses placenta, thereby additionally treating fetus

## GONORRHEA

A. Data Collection

1. Positive culture of vaginal secretions

2. Purulent discharge or asymptomatic

B. Diagnose

1. Potential nursing diagnoses
   a. Risk for infection
   b. Deficient knowledge

2. May complicate pregnancy and cause sterility

C. Plan/Implementation

1. Reinforce teaching about antibiotic as ordered

2. Instill prophylactic medication into baby's eyes after delivery

## HYDATIDIFORM MOLE (GESTATIONAL TROPHOBLASTIC DISEASE)

A. Data Collection

1. Elevated hCG levels

2. Uterine size greater than expected for dates

3. No FHR

4. Minimal dark red/brown vaginal bleeding with passage of grapelike clusters

5. No fetus by ultrasound

6. Increased nausea and vomiting and associated pregnancy-induced hypertension (PIH)

B. Diagnose

1. Degenerative anomaly of chorionic villi

C. Plan/Implementation

1. Curettage to completely remove all molar tissue that can become malignant

2. Pregnancy is discouraged for 1 year

3. hCG levels are monitored for 1 year (if continue to be elevated, may require hysterectomy and chemotherapy)

4. Contraception discussed; IUD not used

5. Administer Rho(D) immune globulin (IGIM) to Rh-negative women

## PRETERM LABOR

A. Data Collection

1. Occurs between 20 and 37 weeks gestation, uterine contractions and cervical changes

2. Risk factors
   a. African American
   b. Older than 35 or younger than 17
   c. Low socioeconomic status
   d. Previous preterm labor or birth
   e. Medical disease
   f. Smoking or substance abuse
   g. Problems with pregnancy

B. Diagnose—potential nursing diagnoses

1. Acute pain

2. Risk for fetal injury

3. Deficient knowledge

C. Plan/Implementation

1. Bedrest, side-lying

2. Uterine monitoring, daily weights

3. Maintain good nutrition

4. Relaxation techniques

5. Administration of medication (e.g., terbutaline)

## INDUCTION OF LABOR

A. Data Collection

1. Mother cannot have CPD

2. Fetus must have mature vertex presentation

3. Fetus must have engaged head

4. Mother has "ripened" cervix, or it is induced to "ripen"

5. Indications
   a. Diabetes
   b. Postmaturity
   c. Pregnacy-induced hypertension
   d. Fetal jeopardy
   e. Logistical factors—(rate of rapid birth, distance from hospital)

B. Diagnose—potential nursing diagnoses

1. Risk for maternal and fetal injury

2. Deficient knowledge

**C.** Plan/Implementation

   1. RN assesses fetus continuously by external monitor

   2. Monitor BP, pulse, progress of labor of mother

   3. Prepare for amniotomy (rupture of membranes)

   4. Oxytocin

     a. Administer via infusion pump

     b. Usual contraction pattern: q 2–3 minutes, lasting for 90 seconds or less

     c. Stop infusion if fetal distress or hypertonic contractions begin (contractions that last more than 90 seconds or occur more frequently than every 2 minutes)

## CESAREAN DELIVERY

**A.** Data Collection

   1. Dystocia (abnormal or difficult labor)

   2. Previous Cesarean birth

   3. Breech presentation or CPD

   4. Fetal distress

   5. Active maternal gonorrhea or herpes type 2 infections

   6. Prolapsed umbilical cord

   7. Hypertensive states of pregnancy

   8. Placenta previa, abruptio placentae

   9. Fetal anomalies (e.g., hydrocephaly)

**B.** Diagnose

   1. Potential nursing diagnoses

     a. Anxiety

     b. Powerlessness

     c. Deficient knowledge

   2. Classification

     a. Vertical incision

       1) More blood loss

       2) Rapid delivery

     b. Low-segment transverse incision

       1) Less blood loss

       2) Vaginal birth after Cesarean (VBAC) a possibility

**C.** Plan/Implementation

   1. Obtain lab tests—type and crossmatch, urinalysis, CBC

   2. Provide routine preop care; IV fluid

3. Provide emotional support; new mother first, surgical client second

4. Administer preop medication–usually lower narcotic dose than routine preop medication

5. Place retention catheter to ensure empty bladder

6. Monitor for hemorrhage
   a. Check fundus for firmness and location; massage if boggy
   b. Check skin incision for signs of excessive bleeding
   c. Check vital signs for evidence of shock

7. Routine postop care

8. Provide comfort measures and medications to control pain

9. Splint the incision site while the client does deep breathing exercises

10. Give the mother her infant as soon as possible to promote parent/child bonding

11. Encourage ambulation

## PRECIPITIOUS DELIVERY OUTSIDE HOSPITAL SETTING

A. Data Collection

1. Determine that transport to hospital/birthing center is not possible

2. Evaluate mother's cognitive status and explain actions

B. Diagnose–potential nursing diagnoses

1. Risk for maternal and fetal injury

2. Deficient knowledge

C. Plan/Implementation

1. Remain with client

2. Prepare sterile or clean environment

3. Support infant's head; apply slight pressure to control delivery

4. Slip a nuchal cord, if present, over head

5. Rotate infant externally as head emerges

6. Deliver shoulders, trunk

7. Dry baby and place on mother's abdomen

8. Hold placenta as delivered

9. Wrap baby in blanket and put to breast

10. Check for bleeding and fundal tone

11. Arrange transport to hospital

## POSTPARTUM HEMORRHAGE

A. Data Collection

1. Boggy uterus

2. Excessive bleeding

3. Lochia regressing to a previous stage

4. History
   a. Multiparity
   b. Retained placental fragments
   c. Overdistended uterus
   d. Prolonged labor or delivery of infant

B. Diagnose—potential nursing diagnoses

1. Deficient fluid volume

2. Risk for infection

3. Risk for maternal injury

4. Impaired parenting

C. Plan/Implementation

1. Massage uterus postpartally if not firm

2. Monitor involution for early identification of problems

3. Administer oxytocin or methylcryonovine maleate as ordered
   a. Produces contractions of uterus
   b. Controls postpartum hemorrhage
   c. Potential side effects are hypertension, nausea, and vomiting

4. Monitor for signs of shock

## POSTPARTUM INFECTION

A. Data Collection

1. Temperature 100.4°F or higher on any two consecutive postpartum days exclusive of the first 24 hours; chills, tachycardia

2. Abdominal pain or severe afterpains, perineal discomfort

3. Lochia—foul odor, prolonged rubra phase, decreased or increased amount

4. Localized tenderness

5. Diagnostic tests
   a. Blood cultures, culture of lochia, urine cultures, increased erythrocyte sedimentation rate (ESR)
   b. White blood cell count—significant increase over a 6-hour time period

B. Diagnose—potential nursing diagnoses

1. Risk for infection

2. Deficient knowledge

C.  Plan/Implementation

1.  Encourage early ambulation

2.  Change peripads frequently

3.  Provide adequate nutrition and fluid intake

4.  Monitor for signs of infection

5.  Administer antibiotics if ordered

## POSTPARTUM DEPRESSION

A.  Data Collection

1.  Decrease in estrogen and progesterone may precipitate "baby blues"

2.  Occurs in first year, often by fourth week

3.  Possibly associated with changing hormone levels

4.  Sadness and crying

5.  Difficulty concentrating

B.  Diagnose—potential nursing diagnoses

1.  Insomnia

2.  Risk for self-directed violence

3.  Interrupted family processes

4.  Anxiety/disturbed thought processes

C.  Plan/Implementation

1.  Encourage verbalization of feelings and identification of concerns

2.  Observe for potential suicidal behavior

3.  Consult with medical and psychiatric staff

4.  Support groups

5.  Administer medication

6.  Assist with care of the baby

## NORMAL NEWBORN

Table 1

| NEWBORN DATA COLLECTION | | |
|---|---|---|
| **SYSTEM** | **DATA COLLECTION** | **NURSING CONSIDERATIONS** |
| Respiration/ perfusion | Rate—quiet vs. active<br>Labored—retractions, grunting<br>Color, heart rate, heart murmurs<br>Nose breather | Keep airway patent<br>Limit activities—decreases $O_2$ consumption<br>Monitor blood gases/blood pressure<br>Keep supplemental $O_2$ use limited to that required<br>Monitor for respiratory distress (increased respiratory rate, grunting, nasal flaring, intercostals retractions)<br>Prepare for possible intubation |
| Nutrition | Weight and length<br>Head circumference<br>Bottle feeding<br>Chest circumference<br>Situations that increase demand:<br>  Sepsis<br>  Ventilatory distress<br>  Stress | Monitor volume of fluid intake<br>Dipstick and specific gravity on urine<br>Caloric value of intake<br>Monitor output volume in first 24 hours |
| Heat regulation | Ability to maintain normal body temperature<br>Acidosis may develop if poor temperature regulation | Provide regular monitoring<br>Adjust environmental temperature appropriately:<br>  Body covering<br>  Warmer or isolette |
| CNS | Reflexes:<br>  Tonic neck<br>  Babinski<br>  Moro<br>  Autonomics—sucking, rooting, swallowing<br>Fontanelles—bulging or flat<br>Severe hypo- or hyperactivity<br>Activity/sleep/cry:<br>  Hyperirritable<br>  Depressed<br>Anatomical anomalies:<br>  Cranial—hydrocephalus, microcephaly<br>  Spinal<br>Paralysis/paresis:<br>  Erb's palsy<br>  Bell's palsy<br>  Lower extremities | Respond to life-threatening problems immediately:<br>  Absence of swallow reflex<br>  Bulging fontanelle<br>  Cranial nerve injuries |
| Parenting | Infant—behavior, individual differences<br>Mother/father:<br>  Pattern of touching<br>  Reciprocity of interaction<br>  Age and development level<br>  Guilt, anxiety, grief reactions<br>  Ability to interact | Report any deviations |
| Circumcision | Observe for infection, bleeding | Record first voiding after procedure<br>Apply dressing |

**A.** Data Collection (see Table 1)

1. Airway—bulb suctioning—mouth first, then nose

2. Apgar score (performed at 1 and 5 minutes of age)
   a. Scoring (see Table 2)
   b. Interpretations
      1) 0–3: poor
      2) 4–6: fair
      3) 7–10: excellent

Table 2

| APGAR SCORE | | | |
|---|---|---|---|
| | 0 | 1 | 2 |
| Heart rate | Absent | Slow (<100 bpm) | Normal (>100 bpm) |
| Respiratory effort | Absent | Slow, irregular | Good cry |
| Muscle tone | Flaccid | Some flexion | Active |
| Reflexes | No response | Weak cry | Vigorous cry |
| Color | Blue, pale | Body pink, extremities blue | Completely pink |
| TOTAL _____ | | | |

3. Measurements at term
   a. Weight—6–9-lb (2,700–4,000 g); normal five to ten percent weight loss in first few days should be regained in 1–2 weeks
   b. Length—19–21 inches (48–53 cm)
   c. Head circumference—13–14 inches (33–35 cm); 1/4 body length
   d. Chest—1 inch less than head circumference, 12–13 inches (30.5–33 cm)

4. Vital signs
   a. Temperature
      1) Rectal—not recommended as routine because of potential for rectal mucosa irritation and increased risk of perforation
      2) Axillary—97.7–99.7°F (36.5–37.6°C); thermometer should remain in place at least 3 minutes unless an electronic thermometer is used
   b. Apical rate—100 bpm (sleep); 120–160 bpm (awake); up to 180 bpm (crying); documented after auscultation for 1 full minute when infant not crying
   c. Respirations—30–60 breaths/min; primarily diaphragmatic and abdominal, synchronous with chest movements; may be short (<15 sec) periods of apnea; since neonate is an obligatory nose breather, it is important to keep nose and mouth clear
   d. Blood pressure—65/41 mm Hg in arm and calf

5. Posture
   a. Maintains fetal position for several days
   b. Resistance to extension of extremities

6. Skin—sensitive to drying
   a. Erythematous (beefy red) color for a few hours after birth; then pink or as expected for racial background; acrocyanosis (bluish discoloration of hands and feet) is normal for 24 hours
   b. Vernix caseosa—protective gray-white fatty substance of cheesy consistency covering the fetal/newborn skin; do not attempt vigorous removal
   c. Lanugo—light distribution of downy, fine hair may be over the shoulder, forehead, and cheeks; extensive amount is indicative of prematurity
   d. Milia—distended sebaceous glands appearing as tiny, white, pinpoint papules on forehead, nose, cheeks, and chin of neonate that disappear spontaneously in a few days or weeks
   e. Pigmentation
      1) Mongolian spots—bluish gray or dark nonelevated pigmentation area over the lower back and buttocks present at birth in some infants (African American, Hispanic, Asian)
      2) Birthmarks
         a) Telangiectatic nevi ("stork bites")—cluster of small, flat, red localized areas of capillary dilatation usually on eyelids, nose, nape of neck; can be blanched by the pressure of the finger; usually fade during infancy
         b) Nevus vasculosus (strawberry mark)—raised, demarcated, dark red, rough-surfaced capillary hemangioma in dermal and subdural layers; grow rapidly for several months and then begin to fade; usually disappear by 7 years of age
         c) Nevus flammeus (port wine stain)—reddish, usually flat, discoloration commonly on the face or neck; does not grow and does not fade

7. Head—may appear asymmetrical because of overriding of cranial bones during labor and delivery (molding)
   a. Fontanelles—"soft spots" at junction of cranial bones
      1) Anterior fontanel—diamond shaped 2.5–4 cm, easily felt, usually open and flat (may be moderate bulging with crying/stooling); sustained bulging occurs with increased intracranial pressure, depression with dehydration; may be slight pulsation; closes by 18 months of age
      2) Posterior—triangular 0.5–1 cm, not easily palpated; closes between 8 and 12 weeks of life
   b. Cephalhematoma—collection of blood under the periosteum of a cranial bone appearing on first and second day; does not cross suture line; disappears in weeks to months
   c. Caput succedaneum—localized soft swelling of the scalp often associated with a long and difficult birth; present at birth; overrides the suture line; fluid is reabsorbed within hours to days after delivery

    d. Face—symmetrical distribution and movement of all features; asymmetry may signify paralysis of facial cranial nerve (Bell's palsy)

    e. Eyes—eyelids may be edematous; pupils equal and react to light; absence of tears, corneal reflex, blink reflex

    f. Mouth—sucks well when stimulated; hard and soft palate intact when examined with clean-gloved finger, gag reflex, rooting reflex

    g. Ears—tops (pinnae) should be parallel with the inner and outer canthus of eyes; low-set ears are associated with chromosomal abnormalities, intellectual delay and/or internal organ abnormalities; hearing is evaluated by an arousal response to loud or moderately loud noise unaccompanied by vibration, startle reflex

8. Chest—breast enlargement lasting up to 2 weeks may occur in both males and females

9. Abdomen

    a. Cylindrical and slightly protuberant

    b. Umbilical cord—initially white and gelatinous with 2 arteries and 1 vein, shriveled and black by 2–3 days, falls off within 1–2 weeks; foul-smelling discharge is indicative of infection requiring immediate treatment to prevent septicemia

    c. First stool is black and tarry (meconium) passed within 12–24 hours; followed by thin green-brown transitional stools the third day; then 1–2 formed pale yellow to light brown stools/day with formula feeding or loose golden yellow stools with sour milk odor with every breast feeding

10. Genitourinary—urine is present in bladder at birth, but neonate may not void for 12–24 hours (may be brick-red spots on diaper from passage of uric acid crystals); thereafter usually voids pale yellow urine 6–10 times/day

    a. Female—labia relatively large and approximated; may have normal thick white discharge; a white cheese-like substance (smegma) and/or blood tinge (pseudomenstruation)

    b. Male—testes can be felt in scrotum

11. Trunk and extremities

    a. Arms and legs symmetric in shape and function

    b. Hips abduct to >60°; symmetric inguinal and buttocks creases indicating no hip dislocation

    c. Foot in straight line

12. Reflexes

    a. Rooting and sucking—turns toward any object touching/stroking cheek/mouth, opens mouth, and sucks rhythmically when finger/nipple is inserted into mouth (usually disappears by 4–7 months)

    b. Pupillary—constriction on exposure of light

    c. Palmar grasp—pressure on palm elicits grasp (fades by 3–4 months)

    d.  Plantar grasp—pressure on sole behind toes elicits flexion (lessens by 8 months)

    e.  Tonic neck—fencing position; lying on back with head turned to one side, arm and leg on that side of body will be in extension while extremities on opposite side will be flexed (disappears by 3–4 months)

    f.  Moro—elicited by sudden disturbance in the infant's immediate environment, body will stiffen, arms in tense extension followed by embrace gesture with thumb and index finger in a "c" formation (disappears after 3–4 months)

    g.  Positive-supporting—infant will stiffen legs and appear to stand when held upright

    h.  Stepping reflex—when held upright with one foot touching a flat surface, will step alternatingly (fades 4–5 months)

    i.  Babinski's sign—stroking the sole of the foot from heel upward across ball of foot will cause all toes to fan (reverts to usual adult response by 12 months)

**B.**  Diagnose—potential nursing diagnoses

  1.  Airway clearance, ineffective

  2.  Thermoregulation, ineffective

  3.  Growth and development, altered

**C.**  Plan/Implementation

  1.  Establish airway and maintain

  2.  Observe for Apgar score at 1 and 5 minutes

  3.  Clamp umbilical cord

  4.  Maintain warmth and keep exposure to environment minimal

  5.  Place identification band on baby and mother

  6.  Administer prophylactic medications
    a.  Eye prophylaxis
    b.  Administer intramuscular vitamin K—for first 3–4 days of life the neonate is unable to synthesize vitamin K, which is necessary for blood clotting and coagulation

  7.  Record first stool and urine

  8.  Weigh and measure baby

  9.  Observe and support mother–infant bond

  10.  Begin and monitor feeding schedule

    a. Before initiating first formula feeding, check for readiness (active bowel sounds, absence of abdominal distention, and lusty cry) and for absence of gagging, choking, regurgitating associated with tracheoesophageal fistula or esophageal atresia by giving a small amount of sterile water (glucose is irritating to lungs)

    b. Since colostrum is readily absorbed by the gastrointestinal and respiratory system, breastfeeding may be started immediately after birth

11. Umbilical cord care—clean cord and surrounding skin; no tub baths until cord falls off; fold diapers below to maintain dry area; report redness, drainage, foul odor

12. Care of penis

    a. Uncircumcised—do not force retraction of foreskin (complete separation of foreskin and glans penis takes from 3–5 years); parents should be told to gently test for retraction occasionally during the bath, and when it has occurred, gently clean glans with soap and water

    b. Circumcised (surgical removal of prepuce/foreskin)

        1) Ensure signed permission before procedure; provide comfort measures during and after procedure

        2) Postprocedure monitor for bleeding and voiding, apply A and D ointment or petroleum jelly (except when Plastibell is used)

        3) Teach parents to clean area with warm water squeezed over penis and dry gently; a whitish yellow exudate is normal and should not be removed; if Plastibell is used, report to pediatrician if it has not fallen off in about 8 days

## HYPERBILIRUBINEMIA

**A.** Data Collection

1. Physiologic jaundice—caused by immature hepatic function; jaundice after 24 hours, peaks at 72 hours, lasts 5 to 7 days; no treatment necessary

2. Breastmilk jaundice (early onset)—caused by poor milk intake; onset 2–3 days, peak 2–3 days; treated by frequent breastfeeding, caloric supplements

3. Breastmilk jaundice (late onset)—caused by factor in breast milk; onset 4–5 days, peak 10–15 days; treated by discontinuing breast feeding for 24 hours

4. Pathologic Jaundice (Hemolytic anemia)—caused by blood antigen incompatibility; onset first 24 hours; peak variable; treated by phototherapy, exchange transfusions

**B.** Diagnose—potential nursing diagnoses

1. Risk for injury (CNS involvement)

2. Risk for injury (effects of treatment)

**C.** Plan/Implementation

1. Monitor serum bilirubin levels (greater than or equal to 13–15 mg/dL)

2. Observe depth and extent for jaundice

3. Observe behavior of infant

4. Phototherapy
   a. Observe for side effects
   b. Patch eyes; uncover eyes every 2 hours
   c. Expose as much skin as possible; cover genitals
   d. Provide sensory stimulation
   e. Provide opportunities for bonding

5. Exchange transfusion if necessary to remove excess bilirubin

## HEMOLYTIC DISEASE OF NEWBORN (PATHOLOGIC JAUNDICE)

A. Data Collection

1. Jaundice within 24 hours of birth

2. Serum bilirubin level elevates rapidly

3. Hematocrit decreased, anemia due to hemolysis of large number of erythrocytes

4. Coombs Test—detects antibodies attached to circulating erythrocytes, performed on cord blood sample

B. Diagnose

1. Destruction of RBCs from antigen–antibody reaction

2. Baby's Rh antigens enter mother; mother produces antibody; antibodies re-enter baby and causes hemolysis and jaundice

3. Rare during first pregnancy

C. Plan/Implementation

1. Assist in early identification

2. Phototherapy with fluorescent lighting—alters nature of bilirubin to aid excretion; infant's eyes and genitals must be covered

3. Exchange transfusion, if indicated—removes bilirubin and maternal hemolytic antibodies

D. Evaluation

1. Has child been protected from eye irritation and dehydration during phototherapy?

2. Has parent/child relationship been maintained during treatments?

## HYPOGLYCEMIA

A. Data Collection

1. Blood sugar <30–35 mg/dL (normal 40–80 mg/dL)

2. Jitteriness

3. Irregular respiratory effort

4. Cyanosis

5. Weak, high-pitched cry

6. Lethargy

7. Twitching

8. Eye-rolling

9. Seizures

**B.** Diagnose—potential nursing diagnoses

1.   Deficient knowledge

2.   Risk for unstable glucose

**C.** Plan/Implementation

1.   Monitor glucose level soon after birth and repeat in 4 hours

2.   Administer glucose carefully to avoid rebound hypoglycemia

3.   Initiate feedings if infant not lethargic; determine glucose levels immediately before feeding

## NARCOTIC-ADDICTED INFANTS/ NEONATAL ABSTINENCE SYNDROME

**A.** Data Collection

1.   High-pitched cry, hyperreflexivity, decreased sleep

2.   Diaphoresis, tachypnea (greater than 60/min), restlessness

3.   Tremors, uncoordinated sucking, frequent sneezing and yawning

4.   Drug withdrawal from narcotics, barbiturates, or cocaine; may manifest as early as 12–24 hours after birth, up to 7–10 days after delivery

**B.** Diagnose—potential nursing diagnoses

1.   Risk for injury

2.   Nutrition, less than body requirements

3.   Risk for impaired parent/child attachment

**C.** Plan/Implementation

1.   Determine muscle tone, irritability, vital signs

2.   Administer phenobarbital, chlorpromazine, diazepam, paregoric as ordered

3.   Report symptoms of respiratory distress

4.   Reduce environmental stimulation (e.g., dim lights, decrease noise level)

5.   Provide adequate nutrition/fluids; provide pacifier for nonnutrive sucking

6.   Monitor mother–child interactions

7.   Wrap infant snugly, rock, and hold tightly

## CLEFT LIP AND PALATE

**A.** Data Collection

1.   Cleft lip—small or large fissure in facial process of upper lip or up to nasal septum, including anterior maxilla

2. Cleft palate—midline, bilateral, or unilateral fissures in hard and soft palate

B. Diagnose

1. Definition—congenital malformation

2. Lip is usually repaired during 1 to 3 months of age

3. Palate is usually repaired before child develops altered speech patterns, between 12 and 18 months

C. Plan/Implementation

1. Parents will have strong reaction to birth of defective infant—provide support and information

2. Determine infant's ability to suck

3. Surgical repair
   a. Preoperative
      1) Maintain adequate nutrition
      2) Feed with soft nipple, special lamb's nipple, Brechet feeder (syringe with rubber tubing), or cup
   b. Postoperative
      1) Maintain airway
         a) Observe for respiratory distress, aspiration, or blockage from edema, check ability to swallow
         b) Provide suction equipment and endotracheal tube at bedside
      2) Guard suture line
         a) Keep suture line clean and dry
         b) Use lip-protective devices, i.e., Logan bow or tape (see Figure 1)
         c) Maintain side-lying position
         d) Clean suture line with cotton-tipped swab dipped in saline, then apply thin coat of antibiotic ointment
         e) Minimize crying
         f) Use elbow restraints as needed

**Figure 1.  Logan Bar**

3) Provide nutrition
   a) Use feeding techniques to minimize trauma—usually very slow to feed
   b) Burp baby frequently during feedings
4) Facilitate parents' positive response to child
5) Provide referrals to speech therapy and orthodontists as needed

## COLD STRESS

**A.** Data Collection

1. Mottling of skin or cyanosis

2. Abnormal blood gases (metabolic acidosis), hypoxia, hypoglycemia

**B.** Diagnose

1. Infant unable to increase activity and lacks a shivering response to cold

2. Heat is produced through metabolic process

3. Oxygen consumption and energy are diverted from maintaining normal brain cell, cardiac function, and growth to thermogenesis

4. Causes
   a. Hypoxemia ($PO_2$ less than 50 torr)
   b. Intracranial hemorrhage or any CNS abnormality
   c. Hypoglycemia (less than 40 mg/dL)

**C.** Plan/Implementation

1. Place in heated environment immediately after birth; dry infant immediately

2. Maintain neutral thermal environment
   a. Double-walled or servocontrolled incubator
   b. Radiant warming panel
   c. Open bassinet with cotton blankets
   d. Place infant on mother's abdomen

3. Monitor temperature

4. Fabric-insulated cap for head

**D.** Evaluation

1. Have complications been prevented?

## NORMAL REPRODUCTION

**A.** Data Collection

   1. Knowledge of normal sexual function

   2. Prevention of illness through self-care

   3. Promotion of health through control of fertility

   4. Cultural influences

**B.** Diagnose

   1. Potential nursing diagnoses
      a. Health-seeking behaviors (reproduction)
      b. Readiness for enhanced knowledge
      c. Anxiety related to reproductive health

   2. Diagnostic tests and procedures (e.g., culdoscopy, laparoscopy)

**C.** Plan/Implementation

   1. Provide privacy

   2. Determine knowledge

   3. Teach about breast self-exam (BSE), Pap test, mammogram, testicular self-exam

   4. Instruct client in breast self-exam
      a. Examine monthly
         1) Menstruating women—1 week after onset of menstrual period
         2) Nonmenstruating women—American Cancer Society suggests a routine, such as the first day of each month
      b. Procedure
         1) Inspect breasts in mirror
         2) Examine breasts first with arms at sides, second with arms above head, and third with hands on hips
         3) Use finger pads of 3 middle fingers to palpate breasts to detect unusual growths while lying down
         4) Look for dimpling or retractions
         5) Examine nipples for discharge, changes, swelling

   5. Provide information about mammography
      a. Determine knowledge of procedure
      b. Schedule after menstrual period (less breast sensitivity)
      c. Inform client that test may cause discomfort: compresses breast between two sheets of x-ray film

6. Provide health teaching about testicular self-exam
   a. Procedure
      1) Support testes in palm of one hand and palpate between thumb and forefinger
      2) Best performed in shower when cremaster muscles are relaxed and testes are pendulous
   b. Schedule once monthly

7. Determine knowledge of birth control
   a. Factors
      1) Impact of age, developmental level
      2) Desires of both partners
      3) Capability of use
      4) Permanent or temporary
   b. Plan—teach methods of contraception (see Table 1)

8. Determine knowledge of menopause, climacteric
   a. Menstruation ceases
   b. Symptoms related to hormone changes—vasomotor instability, emotional disturbances, atrophy of genitalia, uterine prolapse
   c. Estrogen replacement therapy (ERT)—contraindicated if family history of breast or uterine cancer, hypertension, or thrombophlebitis
   d. Kegel exercises—for strengthening pubococcygeal muscles
   e. Supplemental calcium—(1 gram HS) to slow osteoporosis
   f. Regular exercise and good nutrition

## REPRODUCTIVE DISORDERS

A. Data Collection (see Table 2)

B. Diagnose—potential nursing diagnoses
   1. Sexuality patterns, altered
   2. Adjustment, impaired
   3. Family processes, altered

C. Plan/Implementation (see Table 2)

●Table 1

| METHODS OF CONTRACEPTION | |
|---|---|
| **METHOD** | **NURSING CONSIDERATIONS** |
| Oral contraceptives—"the pill" | 1. Action—inhibits the release of FSH, resulting in anovulatory menstrual cycles; close to 100% effective<br>2. Side effects—nausea and vomiting (usually occurring the first 3 months), increased susceptibility to vaginal infections<br>3. Contraindications—hypertension, thromboembolic disease, and history of circulatory disease, varicosities, or diabetes mellitus<br>4. Teaching—swallow whole at the same time each day; one missed pill should be taken as soon as remembered that day or two taken the next day; more than one missed pill requires use of another method of birth control for the rest of the cycle; consume adequate amounts of vitamin B; report severe/persistent chest pain, cough and/or shortness of breath, severe abdominal pain, dizziness, weakness and/or numbness, eye or speech problems, severe leg pain |
| Hormone injections—<br>methoxyprogesterone<br><br><br><br><br><br>MPA and estradiol | Injectable progestin that prevents ovulation for 12 weeks. Convenient because it is unrelated to coitus (requires no action at the time of intercourse) and is 99.7% effective. Injections must be given every 12 weeks. The site should not be massaged after the injection because this accelerates the absorption and decreases the effectiveness time. Menstrual irregularity, spotting, and breakthrough bleeding are common. Return to fertility is 6 to 12 months<br><br>A monthly injectable contraceptive. Similar to oral contraceptives in chemical formulation, but has the advantage of monthly rather than daily dosing. Provides effective, immediate contraception within 5 days of the last normal menstrual period (LNMP)<br>Menstrual periods less painful and with less blood loss than methoxyprogesterone<br>Return to fertility is 2 to 4 months |
| Intrauterine device (IUD) | 1. Action—presumed either to cause degeneration of the fertilized egg or render the uterine wall impervious to implantation; nearly 100% effective<br>2. Inserted by health care provider during the client's menstrual period, when the cervix is dilated<br>3. Side effects—cramping or excessive menstrual flow (for 2-3 months), infection<br>4. Teaching—check for presence of the IUD string routinely, especially after each menstrual period; report unusual cramping, late period, abnormal spotting/bleeding, abdominal pain or pain with intercourse, exposure to STDs, infection, missing/shorter/longer IUD string |
| Condom—rubber sheath applied over the penis | 1. Action—prevents the ejaculate and sperm from entering the vagina; helps prevent sexually transmitted disease; effective if properly used; OTC<br>2. Teaching—apply to erect penis with room at the tip every time before vaginal penetration; use water-based lubricant, e.g., K-Y jelly, never petroleum-based lubricant; hold rim when withdrawing the penis from the vagina; if condom breaks, partner should use contraceptive foam or cream immediately |
| Female (vaginal) condom | Allows the woman some protection from disease without relying on the male condom. The device is a polyurethane pouch inserted into the vagina, with flexible rings at both ends. The closed end with its ring functions as a diaphragm. The open end with its ring partially covers the perineum. The female condom should not be used at the same time that the male partner is using a condom. Failure rates are high with the female condom, at about 21%. Increased risk of infections. |
| Diaphragm—flexible rubber ring with a latex-covered dome inserted into the vagina, tucked behind the pubic bone, and released to cover the cervix | 1. Action—prevents the sperm from entering the cervix; highly effective if used correctly<br>2. Must be fitted by health care provider and method of inserting practiced by the client before use<br>3. Risk—urinary tract infection (UTI) and toxic shock syndrome (TSS)<br>4. Teaching—diaphragm should not be inserted more than 6 hours prior to coitus; best used in conjunction with a spermicidal gel applied to rim and inside the dome before inserting; additional spermicide is necessary if coitus is repeated; remove at least once in 24 hours to decrease risk of toxic shock syndrome; report symptoms of UTI and TSS |
| Vaginal spermicides (vaginal cream, foam, jellies) | 1. Action—interferes with the viability of sperm and prevents their entry into the cervix; OTC<br>2. Teaching—must be inserted before each act of intercourse; report symptoms of allergic reaction to the chemical |
| Subdermal implant | 1. Action—effective for 5 years; requires surgical insertion and removal<br>2. Side effects—irregular bleeding, nausea, skin changes |
| Natural family planning (rhythm method, basal body temperature, cervical mucus method) | 1. Action—periodic abstinence from intercourse during fertile period; based on the regularity of ovulation; variable effectiveness<br>2. Teaching—fertile period may be determined by a drop in basal body temperature before and a slight rise after ovulation and/or by a change in cervical mucus from thick, cloudy, and sticky during nonfertile period to more abundant, clear, thin, stretchy, and slippery as ovulation occurs |

*(continued)*

Table 1 (cont'd)

| METHODS OF CONTRACEPTION | |
|---|---|
| METHOD | NURSING CONSIDERATIONS |
| Coitus interruptus | 1. Action—man withdraws his penis before ejaculation to avoid depositing sperm into vagina; variable effectiveness |
| Sterilization | 1. Vasectomy (male)—terminates the passage of sperm through the vas deferens<br>   a. Usually done in health care provider's office under local anesthesia; permanent and 100% effective<br>   b. Teaching—postprocedure discomfort and swelling may be relieved by mild analgesic, ice packs, and scrotal support; sterility not complete until the proximal vas deferens is free of sperm (about 3 months), another method of birth control must be used until two sperm-free semen analysis; success of reversal by vasovasostomy varies from 30 to 85%<br>2. Tubal ligation (female)—fallopian tubes are tied and/or cauterized through an abdominal incision, laparoscopy, or minilaparotomy<br>   a. Teaching—usual postop care and instructions; intercourse may be resumed after bleeding ceases<br>   b. Success of reversal by reconstruction of the fallopian tubes is 40-75% |

*(Continued)*

● Table 2

| PROBLEMS OF THE REPRODUCTIVE TRACT | | |
|---|---|---|
| **DISORDER** | **DATA COLLECTION** | **NURSING CONSIDERATIONS** |
| Infertility | Inability to conceive after a year of unprotected intercourse<br>Tests include check of tubal patency, sperm analysis<br>Affects approximately 10-15% of all couples | Support and assist clients through tests<br>Allow expression of feelings and refer to support groups as needed<br>Alternatives include artificial insemination, *in vitro* fertilization, adoption |
| Simple vaginitis | Yellow discharge, itching, burning | Douche, antibiotics, sitz baths |
| Atrophic vaginitis | Occurs after menopause<br>Pale, thin, dry mucosa, itching, dyspareunia | Treated with topical estrogen cream, water-soluble vaginal lubricants, antibiotic vaginal suppositories and ointments |
| Candida albicans | Odorless, cheesy white discharge<br>Itching, inflamed vagina and perineum | Topical clotrimazole<br>Nystatin |
| Toxic shock syndrome (TSS) | Sudden-onset fever, vomiting, diarrhea, drop in systolic blood pressure, and erythematous rash on palms and soles | Early diagnosis critical to avoid involvement with other organ systems<br>Managed with antibiotics, fluid and electrolyte replacement<br>Educate about use of tampons |
| Pelvic inflammatory disease (PID) | Local infection spreads to the fallopian tubes, ovaries, and other organs<br>Malaise, fever, abdominal pain, leukocytosis, and vaginal discharge<br>Risk factors—20 years old or younger, multiple sex partners, IUD, vaginal douching, smoking, history of STDs, history of PID | Managed with antibiotics, fluid and electrolyte replacement, warm douches to increase circulation, rest<br>Can cause adhesions that produce sterility |
| Mastitis | Reddened, inflamed breast<br>Exudate from nipple<br>Fever, fatigue, leukocytosis, pain | Systemic antibiotics, warm packs to promote drainage, rest, breast support |
| Fibrocystic changes | Multiple cyst development<br>Free-moving, tender, enlarged during menstrual period and about 1 week before | Review importance and technique of breast self-exam<br>Provide frequent monitoring for changes<br>Prepare for possibility of aspiration, biopsy, or surgery<br>Diet changes and vitamin supplements<br>Benign, but associated with increased risk of breast cancer |
| Cancer of the cervix | Early—asymptomatic<br>Later—abnormal bleeding, especially postcoital<br>Risk factors—low socioeconomic status, began sexual activity or had pregnancy at a young age, multiple sexual partners | Preparation for tests, biopsy<br>Internal radiation therapy<br>Pap smear |
| Breast cancer | Small, fixed, painless lump<br>Rash, or in more advanced cases, change in color, puckering or dimpling of skin, pain and/or tenderness, nipple retraction or discharge<br>Axillary adenopathy<br>Risk factors—family history of mother, sister, or daughter developing premenopausal breast cancer, age >50, menses begins before age 12, no children or first pregnancy occurs after age 30, menopause after age 55 | Mammography screening<br>Prepare for surgery and/or radiation, chemotherapy |
| Uterine fibroids (myomas) | Low back pain, fertility problems,<br>Menorrhagia | Benign tumors of myometrium<br>Size and symptoms determine action<br>Prepare for possible hysterectomy (removal of uterus) or myomectomy (partial resection of uterus) |
| Uterine displacement/ prolapse | Weak pelvic support, sometimes after menopause<br>Pain, menstrual interruption, fertility problems<br>Urinary incontinence | Kegel exercises—isometric exercises of the muscle that controls urine flow (pubococcygeus, or PC muscle) can improve pelvic musculature support<br>Pessary—device inserted into vagina that gives support to uterus in cases of retroversion or prolapse; must be inserted and rechecked by health professional<br>Hormone replacement therapy—improves pelvic muscle tone<br>Surgical intervention—colporrhaphy (suturing fascia and musculature to support prolapsed structures) |

*(continued)*

Table 2 (cont'd)

| PROBLEMS OF THE REPRODUCTIVE TRACT | | |
|---|---|---|
| **DISORDER** | **DATA COLLECTION** | **NURSING CONSIDERATIONS** |
| Endometriosis | Found in colon, ovaries, supporting ligaments, causes inflammation and pain<br>Causes dysmenorrhea and infertility, backache<br><br>Most common in young nulliparous women | Advise client that oral contraceptives suppress endometrial buildup or that surgical removal of tissue is possible<br>Inform client that symptoms abate after childbirth and lactation |
| Endometrial cancer | Watery discharge, irregular menstrual bleeding, menorrhagia<br>Diagnosed by endometrial biopsy or curettage<br>Risk factors—age >55, postmenopausal bleeding, obesity, diabetes mellitus, hypertension, unopposed estrogen replacement therapy | Internal radiation implants:<br>  Must restrict movements; bedrest with air mattress<br>  Enema, douche, low-residue diet, ample fluids<br>  Indwelling catheter and fracture pan for elimination<br>  Visitors and professionals wear protective garments and limit exposure time<br>  Dislodged implant must be handled with special tongs and placed in lead-lined container for removal; call hospital radiation therapy specialist first<br>Hysterectomy:<br>  Subtotal—removal of fundus only<br>  Total—removal of the uterus (vagina remains intact)<br>  Total abdominal hysterectomy with bilateral salpingo-oophorectomy (TAH-BSO)—removal of uterus, fallopian tubes, and ovaries<br>  Radical—removal of lymph nodes as well as TAH-BSO<br>  Observe for hemorrhage, infection, thrombophlebitis<br>  If ovaries removed, estrogen replacement therapy (ERT) may be needed |
| Ovarian cyst | Pelvic discomfort<br>Palpable during routine exam | May do biopsy or removal to prevent necrosis<br>Monitor by sonography |
| Ovarian cancer | Family history of ovarian cancer, client history of breast, bowel, endometrial cancer, nulliparity, infertility, heavy menses, palpation of abdominal mass (late sign), diagnosis by ultrasound, CT, x-ray, IVP | Surgical removal, chemotherapy, staging of tumor after removal<br>Foster verbalization of feelings, ensure continuity of care, encourage support systems |
| Orchitis | Complication of mumps, virus, STD; may cause sterility, pain, and swelling | Prophylactic gammaglobulin if exposed to mumps virus<br>Administration of drugs specific for organism<br>Ice packs to reduce swelling, bedrest, scrotal support |
| Prostatitis | May be complication of lower UTIs<br>Acute—fever, chills, dysuria, purulent penile discharge; elevated WBC and bacteria in urine<br>Chronic—backache, urinary frequency, enlarged, firm, slightly tender prostate | Antibiotics, sitz baths<br>Increased fluid intake<br>Activities to drain the prostate |
| Benign prostatic hypertrophy (BPH) | Enlargement of the glandular and cellular tissue of the prostate, resulting in compression on the urethra and urinary retention; most often in men over 50 years old<br>Dysuria, frequency, urgency, decreased urinary stream, hesitancy, and nocturia; later symptoms may be cystitis, hydronephrosis, or urinary calculi<br>KUB, x-ray, IVP, and cystoscopy demonstrate prostate enlargement and urinary tract change | Preoperative<br>  Promote urinary drainage<br>  Assure nutrition<br>  Correct fluid and electrolyte balance<br>  Antibiotics<br>  Acid-ash diet to treat infection<br>Postoperative<br>  Assure patency of three-way Foley catheter; may have continuous irrigation with normal saline to remove clots (CBI)<br>  If traction on catheter (pulled taut and taped to abdomen or leg to prevent bleeding), keep client's leg straight<br>  Monitor drainage (reddish-pink and progress to clear)<br>  Discourage attempts to void around catheter; control/treat bladder spasms<br>  Teach bladder retraining by contracting and relaxing sphincter; instruct to avoid heavy lifting, straining at bowel movement, prolonged travel; inform about potential for impotence and discuss alternative ways of expressing sexuality |
| Prostate cancer | Urinary urgency, frequency, retention<br>Back pain or pain radiating down leg<br>Risk factors—increasing age | Hormonal and chemotherapy; surgical removal |

## HEALTH AND WELLNESS

A. Wellness—person functions at highest potential for well-being

B. Health promotion

   1. Activities that assist person to develop resources that improve quality of life

   2. Alteration of personal habits, lifestyle, environment to reduce risks and enhance health and well-being

C. Concepts

   1. Self-responsibility
      a. Individual has control over life
      b. Individual can make choices that promote health

   2. Nutritional awareness—properly balanced diet

   3. Stress reduction and management—manages stress appropriately

   4. Physical fitness—regular exercise promotes health
      a. Improves cardiovascular functioning
      b. Decreases cholesterol and LDLs
      c. Reduces weight
      d. Prevents body degeneration and osteoporosis
      e. Improves flexibility, muscle strength, endurance

D. Programs

   1. General wellness

   2. Smoking cessation

   3. Exercise/physical conditioning

   4. Weight control

   5. Stress management

   6. Nutritional awareness

   7. Work safety

## HEALTH SCREENING

A. Newborn

1. PKU (phenylketonuria)—absence of enzyme needed to metabolize essential amino acid phenylalanine; Guthrie blood test

2. Hypothyroidism—deficiency of thyroid hormones; heel-stick blood sample

3. Galactosemia—error of carbohydrate metabolism

4. Sickle-cell disease—abnormally shaped hemoglobin

5. HIV (human immunodeficiency virus)

B. Infant/child

1. Developmental screening—Denver-II

2. Carrier screening for siblings and family members of a child with cystic fibrosis

3. Cholesterol screening for children with family history of hyperlipidemia, xanthomas, sudden death, early angina, or MI (less than 50 yr men, less than 60 yr women) in siblings, parents, uncles, aunts, grandparents

4. Lead poisoning—children (6–72 months) at highest risk
   a. Live in deteriorated housing
   b. Siblings or close peer with lead poisoning
   c. Household member with hobbies (e.g., stained glass) or lead-related occupations

5. Neuroblastoma—measure VMA and HVA (catecholamine metabolities)

C. School-age

1. Hearing and vision tests at 4 yr, 5 yr, then yearly during school

2. Height, weight

3. Dental exam

4. Medical assessment

5. Psychological exams

D. Adolescent

1. Developmental screening

2. PPD

3. Sexuality
   a. Menstrual history
   b. Extent of sexual activity
   c. Contraceptive knowledge

4. Affect—symptoms of depression

5. Breast self-exam or testicular exam

6. Pelvic with pap smear—if sexually active or 18 years old, performed annually

E.  Adult/elderly

1.  Breast self-exam or testicular exam (see Table 1)

2.  Cancer screenings

    a.  Sigmoidoscopy— over 50 years old, performed every 10 years

    b.  Fecal occult blood test— over 50 years old, performed yearly

    c.  Digital rectal exam— over 40 years old, performed yearly

    d.  Pelvic exam for women—18–40 years old, performed every 3 years with Pap test

    e.  Endometrial tissue sample for women who are at risk at menopause

    f.  Mammography for women 35–39 years old once as baseline, after 40 yearly

    g.  Health counseling and cancer check-ups— over 40 years old, performed yearly

3.  Hypertension screening (see Tables 2 and 3)

4.  Diabetes screening

5.  Hearing and vision screening

●Table 1

| SELF-CARE: REPRODUCTIVE SYSTEM | | |
|---|---|---|
| **TEST** | **AGE TO BEGIN (YRS)** | **REPEAT** |
| Breast self-exam | 18–20 | Monthly |
| Papanicolaou test (Pap smear) | 18, or at least start of sexual activity | Yearly |
| Mammogram | 35-39 <br> 40 and older | Once as baseline <br> Annually |
| Testicular self-exam | 18–20 | Monthly |

●Table 2

| BLOOD PRESSURE SCREENING (mm Hg)* | | |
|---|---|---|
| **SYSTOLIC** | **DIASTOLIC** | **FOLLOW-UP RECOMMENDED** |
| <120 | <80 | Recheck in 2 years |
| 120–139 | 80–89 | Recheck in 1 year |
| 140–159 | 90–99 | Confirm within 2 months |
| 160–179 | 100–109 | Evaluate or refer to source of care within 1 month |
| 180–209 | 110–119 | Evaluate or refer to source of care within 1 week |
| ≥210 | ≥120 | Evaluate or refer to source of care immediately |

*Recommendations are for adults aged 18 and older.*

Table 3

| ERRORS IN BLOOD PRESSURE MEASUREMENT | |
|---|---|
| Inaccurately high | Cuff is too short or too narrow (e.g., using a regular blood pressure cuff on an obese arm), or the brachial artery may be positioned below the heart |
| High diastolic | Unrecognized auscultatory gap (a silent interval between systolic and diastolic pressures that may occur in hypertensive clients or because you deflated the blood pressure cuff too rapidly; immediate reinflation of the blood pressure cuff for multiple blood pressure readings (resultant venous congestion makes the Korotkoff sounds less audible); if the clients supports his or her own arm, then sustained muscular contraction can raise the diastolic blood pressure by 10% |
| Inaccurately low | Cuff is too long or too wide; the brachial artery is above the heart |
| Low systolic | Unrecognized auscultatory gap (a rapid deflation of the cuff or immediate reinflation of the cuff for multiple readings can result in venous congestion, thus making the Korotkoff sounds less audible and the pressure appear lower) |

## IMMUNITY

A. Data Collection

1. Antigen/antibody response
   a. Antigen—a foreign protein that stimulates antibody formation response
   b. Antibody—protective protein that acts as a defense mechanism

2. Active immunity
   a. Permanent
   b. Antigenic substance stimulates the individual's own antibody formations (e.g., tetanus)

3. Passive immunity
   a. Temporary
   b. Resistance acquired by introduction of antibodies from a source other than the individual (e.g., gamma globulin, breast feeding)

B. Diagnose

1. Antigen/antibody response—functions to neutralize, eliminate, or destroy substances recognized as foreign (nonself) by the body before the occurrence of potential harm to body tissues

C. Plan/Implementation

1. Recommended immunization schedule for infants and children (see Table 4) and adults (see Tables 5 and 6)

2. Contraindications to immunization
   a. Severe febrile illness
   b. Live viruses should not be given to anyone with altered immune system, e.g., undergoing chemotherapy, radiation, or with immunological deficiency
   c. Previous allergic response to a vaccine
   d. Recently acquired passive immunity, e.g., blood transfusion, immunoglobulin

**Table 4**

**Figure 1. Recommended immunization schedule for persons aged 0 through 18 years – United States, 2014.**
**(FOR THOSE WHO FALL BEHIND OR START LATE, SEE THE CATCH-UP SCHEDULE [FIGURE 2]).**
These recommendations must be read with the footnotes that follow. For those who fall behind or start late, provide catch-up vaccination at the earliest opportunity as indicated by the green bars in Figure 1. To determine minimum intervals between doses, see the catch-up schedule (Figure 2). School entry and adolescent vaccine age groups are in bold.

| Vaccine | Birth | 1 mo | 2 mos | 4 mos | 6 mos | 9 mos | 12 mos | 15 mos | 18 mos | 19–23 mos | 2-3 yrs | 4-6 yrs | 7-10 yrs | 11-12 yrs | 13–15 yrs | 16–18 yrs |
|---|---|---|---|---|---|---|---|---|---|---|---|---|---|---|---|---|
| Hepatitis B[1] (HepB) | 1st dose | ←2nd dose→ | | | ←3rd dose→ | | | | | | | | | | | |
| Rotavirus[2] (RV) RV1 (2-dose series); RV5 (3-dose series) | | | 1st dose | 2nd dose | See footnote 2 | | | | | | | | | | | |
| Diphtheria, tetanus, & acellular pertussis[3] (DTaP: <7 yrs) | | | 1st dose | 2nd dose | 3rd dose | | | ←4th dose→ | | | | 5th dose | | | | |
| Tetanus, diphtheria, & acellular pertussis[4] (Tdap: ≥7 yrs) | | | | | | | | | | | | | | (Tdap) | | |
| *Haemophilus influenzae* type b[5] (Hib) | | | 1st dose | 2nd dose | See footnote 5 | | ←3rd or 4th dose, See footnote 5→ | | | | | | | | | |
| Pneumococcal conjugate[6] (PCV13) | | | 1st dose | 2nd dose | 3rd dose | | ←4th dose→ | | | | | | | | | |
| Pneumococcal polysaccharide[6] (PPSV23) | | | | | | | | | | | | | | | | |
| Inactivated poliovirus[7] (IPV) (<18 yrs) | | | 1st dose | 2nd dose | ←3rd dose→ | | | | | | | 4th dose | | | | |
| Influenza[8] (IIV; LAIV) 2 doses for some: See footnote 8 | | | | | Annual vaccination (IIV only) | | | | | | Annual vaccination (IIV or LAIV) | | | | | |
| Measles, mumps, rubella[9] (MMR) | | | | | | | ←1st dose→ | | | | | 2nd dose | | | | |
| Varicella[10] (VAR) | | | | | | | ←1st dose→ | | | | | 2nd dose | | | | |
| Hepatitis A[11] (HepA) | | | | | | | ←2-dose series, See footnote 11→ | | | | | | | | | |
| Human papillomavirus[12] (HPV2: females only; HPV4: males and females) | | | | | | | | | | | | | | (3-dose series) | | |
| Meningococcal[13] (Hib-MenCY ≥ 6 weeks; MenACWY-D ≥9 mos; MenACWY-CRM ≥ 2 mos) | | | See footnote 13 | | | | | | | | | | | 1st dose | | Booster |

Range of recommended ages for all children | Range of recommended ages for catch-up immunization | Range of recommended ages for certain high-risk groups | Range of recommended ages during which catch-up is encouraged and for certain high-risk groups | Not routinely recommended

This schedule includes recommendations in effect as of January 1, 2014. Any dose not administered at the recommended age should be administered at a subsequent visit, when indicated and feasible. The use of a combination vaccine generally is preferred over separate injections of its equivalent component vaccines. Vaccination providers should consult the relevant Advisory Committee on Immunization Practices (ACIP) statement for detailed recommendations, available online at http://www.cdc.gov/vaccines/hcp/acip-recs/index.html. Clinically significant adverse events that follow vaccination should be reported to the Vaccine Adverse Event Reporting System (VAERS) online (http://www.vaers.hhs.gov) or by telephone (800-822-7967).Suspected cases of vaccine-preventable diseases should be reported to the state or local health department. Additional information, including precautions and contraindications for vaccination, is available from CDC online (http://www.cdc.gov/vaccines/recs/vac-admin/contraindications.htm) or by telephone (800-CDC-INFO [800-232-4636]).

This schedule is approved by the Advisory Committee on Immunization Practices (http//www.cdc.gov/vaccines/acip), the American Academy of Pediatrics (http://www.aap.org), the American Academy of Family Physicians (http://www.aafp.org), and the American College of Obstetricians and Gynecologists (http://www.acog.org).

**NOTE:** The above recommendations must be read along with the footnotes of this schedule.

## Footnotes — Recommended immunization schedule for persons aged 0 through 18 years—United States, 2014

For further guidance on the use of the vaccines mentioned below, see: http://www.cdc.gov/vaccines/hcp/acip-recs/Index.html.
For vaccine recommendations for persons 19 years of age and older, see the adult immunization schedule.

**Additional information**

- For contraindications and precautions to use of a vaccine and for additional information regarding that vaccine, vaccination providers should consult the relevant ACIP statement available online at http://www.cdc.gov/vaccines/hcp/acip-recs/index.html.
- For purposes of calculating intervals between doses, 4 weeks = 28 days. Intervals of 4 months or greater are determined by calendar months.
- Vaccine doses administered 4 days or less before the minimum interval are considered valid. Doses of any vaccine administered ≥5 days earlier than the minimum interval or minimum age should not be counted as valid doses and should be repeated as age-appropriate. The repeat dose should be spaced after the invalid dose by the recommended minimum interval. For further details, see *MMWR, General Recommendations on Immunization and Reports* / Vol. 60 / No. 2; Table 1. *Recommended and minimum ages and intervals between vaccine doses* available online at http://www.cdc.gov/mmwr/pdf/rr/rr6002.pdf.
- Information on travel vaccine requirements and recommendations is available at http://wwwnc.cdc.gov/travel/destinations/list.
- For vaccination of persons with primary and secondary immunodeficiencies, see Table 13, "*Vaccination of persons with primary and secondary immunodeficiencies*," in General Recommendations on Immunization (ACIP), available at http://www.cdc.gov/mmwr/pdf/rr/rr6002.pdf.; and American Academy of Pediatrics. Immunization in Special Clinical Circumstances, in Pickering LK, Baker CJ, Kimberlin DW, Long SS eds. *Red Book: 2012 report of the Committee on Infectious Diseases. 29th ed.* Elk Grove Village, IL: American Academy of Pediatrics.

1. **Hepatitis B (HepB) vaccine. (Minimum age: birth)**
**Routine vaccination:**
**At birth:**
- Administer monovalent HepB vaccine to all newborns before hospital discharge.
- For infants born to hepatitis B surface antigen (HBsAg)-positive mothers, administer HepB vaccine and 0.5 mL of hepatitis B immune globulin (HBIG) within 12 hours of birth. These infants should be tested for HBsAg and antibody to HBsAg (anti-HBs) 1 to 2 months after completion of the HepB series, at age 9 through 18 months (preferably at the next well-child visit).
- If mother's HBsAg status is unknown, within 12 hours of birth administer HepB vaccine regardless of birth weight. For infants weighing less than 2,000 grams, administer HBIG in addition to HepB vaccine within 12 hours of birth. Determine mother's HBsAg status as soon as possible and, if mother is HBsAg-positive, also administer HBIG for infants weighing 2,000 grams or more as soon as possible, but no later than age 7 days.

**Doses following the birth dose:**
- The second dose should be administered at age 1 or 2 months. Monovalent HepB vaccine should be used for doses administered before age 6 weeks.
- Infants who did not receive a birth dose should receive 3 doses of a HepB-containing vaccine on a schedule of 0, 1 to 2 months, and 6 months starting as soon as feasible. See Figure 2.
- Administer the second dose 1 to 2 months after the first dose (minimum interval of 4 weeks), administer the third dose at least 8 weeks after the second dose AND at least 16 weeks after the **first** dose. The final (third or fourth) dose in the HepB vaccine series should be administered no earlier than age 24 weeks.
- Administration of a total of 4 doses of HepB vaccine is permitted when a combination vaccine containing HepB is administered after the birth dose.

**Catch-up vaccination:**
- Unvaccinated persons should complete a 3-dose series.
- A 2-dose series (doses separated by at least 4 months) of adult formulation Recombivax HB is licensed for use in children aged 11 through 15 years.
- For other catch-up guidance, see Figure 2.

2. **Rotavirus (RV) vaccines. (Minimum age: 6 weeks for both RV1 [Rotarix] and RV5 [RotaTeq])**
**Routine vaccination:**
Administer a series of RV vaccine to all infants as follows:
   1. If Rotarix is used, administer a 2-dose series at 2 and 4 months of age.
   2. If RotaTeq is used, administer a 3-dose series at ages 2, 4, and 6 months.
   3. If any dose in the series was RotaTeq or vaccine product is unknown for any dose in the series, a total of 3 doses of RV vaccine should be administered.

**Catch-up vaccination:**
- The maximum age for the first dose in the series is 14 weeks, 6 days; vaccination should not be initiated for infants aged 15 weeks, 0 days or older.
- The maximum age for the final dose in the series is 8 months, 0 days.
- For other catch-up guidance, see Figure 2.

3. **Diphtheria and tetanus toxoids and acellular pertussis (DTaP) vaccine. (Minimum age: 6 weeks. Exception: DTaP-IPV [Kinrix]: 4 years)**
**Routine vaccination:**
- Administer a 5-dose series of DTaP vaccine at ages 2, 4, 6, 15 through 18 months, and 4 through 6 years. The fourth dose may be administered as early as age 12 months, provided at least 6 months have elapsed since the third dose.

**Catch-up vaccination:**
- The fifth dose of DTaP vaccine is not necessary if the fourth dose was administered at age 4 years or older.
- For other catch-up guidance, see Figure 2.

4. **Tetanus and diphtheria toxoids and acellular pertussis (Tdap) vaccine. (Minimum age: 10 years for Boostrix, 11 years for Adacel)**
**Routine vaccination:**
- Administer 1 dose of Tdap vaccine to all adolescents aged 11 through 12 years.
- Tdap may be administered regardless of the interval since the last tetanus and diphtheria toxoid-containing vaccine.
- Administer 1 dose of Tdap vaccine to pregnant adolescents during each pregnancy (preferred during 27 through 36 weeks gestation) regardless of time since prior Td or Tdap vaccination.

**Catch-up vaccination:**
- Persons aged 7 years and older who are not fully immunized with DTaP vaccine should receive Tdap vaccine as 1 (preferably the first) dose in the catch-up series; if additional doses are needed, use Td vaccine. For children 7 through 10 years who receive a dose of Tdap as part of the catch-up series, an adolescent Tdap vaccine dose at age 11 through 12 years should NOT be administered. Td should be administered instead 10 years after the Tdap dose.
- Persons aged 11 through 18 years who have not received Tdap vaccine should receive a dose followed by tetanus and diphtheria toxoids (Td) booster doses every 10 years thereafter.
- Inadvertent doses of DTaP vaccine:
  - If administered inadvertently to a child aged 7 through 10 years may count as part of the catch-up series. This dose may count as the adolescent Tdap dose, or the child can later receive a Tdap booster dose at age 11 through 12 years.
  - If administered inadvertently to an adolescent aged 11 through 18 years, the dose should be counted as the adolescent Tdap booster.
- For other catch-up guidance, see Figure 2.

5. ***Haemophilus influenzae* type b (Hib) conjugate vaccine. (Minimum age: 6 weeks for PRP-T [ACTHIB, DTaP-IPV/Hib (Pentacel) and Hib-MenCY (MenHibrix)], PRP-OMP [PedvaxHIB or COMVAX], 12 months for PRP-T [Hiberix])**
**Routine vaccination:**
- Administer a 2- or 3-dose Hib vaccine primary series and a booster dose (dose 3 or 4 depending on vaccine used in primary series) at age 12 through 15 months to complete a full Hib vaccine series.
- The primary series with ActHIB, MenHibrix, or Pentacel consists of 3 doses and should be administered at 2, 4, and 6 months of age. The primary series with PedvaxHib or COMVAX consists of 2 doses and should be administered at 2 and 4 months of age; a dose at age 6 months is not indicated.
- One booster dose (dose 3 or 4 depending on vaccine used in primary series) of any Hib vaccine should be administered at age 12 through 15 months. An exception is Hiberix vaccine. Hiberix should only be used for the booster (final) dose in children aged 12 months through 4 years who have received at least 1 prior dose of Hib-containing vaccine.

*(Continued)*

Table 4 (Cont'd) •

For further guidance on the use of the vaccines mentioned below, see: http://www.cdc.gov/vaccines/hcp/acip-recs/index.html.

**5. *Haemophilus influenzae* type b (Hib) conjugate vaccine (cont'd)**
- For recommendations on the use of MenHibrix in patients at increased risk for meningococcal disease, please refer to the meningococcal vaccine footnotes and also to *MMWR* March 22, 2013; 62(RR02);1-22, available at http://www.cdc.gov/mmwr/pdf/rr/rr6202.pdf.

**Catch-up vaccination:**
- If dose 1 was administered at ages 12 through 14 months, administer a second (final) dose at least 8 weeks after dose 1, regardless of Hib vaccine used in the primary series.
- If the first 2 doses were PRP-OMP (PedvaxHIB or COMVAX), and were administered at age 11 months or younger, the third (and final) dose should be administered at age 12 through 15 months and at least 8 weeks after the second dose.
- If the first dose was administered at age 7 through 11 months, administer the second dose at least 4 weeks later and a third (and final) dose at age 12 through 15 months or 8 weeks after second dose, whichever is later, regardless of Hib vaccine used for first dose.
- If first dose is administered at younger than 12 months of age and second dose is given between 12 through 14 months of age, a third (and final) dose should be given 8 weeks later.
- For unvaccinated children aged 15 months or older, administer only 1 dose.
- For other catch-up guidance, see Figure 2. For catch-up guidance related to MenHibrix, please see the meningococcal vaccine footnotes and also *MMWR* March 22, 2013; 62(RR02);1-22, available at http://www.cdc.gov/mmwr/pdf/rr/rr6202.pdf.

**Vaccination of persons with high-risk conditions:**
- Children aged 12 through 59 months who are at increased risk for Hib disease, including chemotherapy recipients and those with anatomic or functional asplenia (including sickle cell disease), human immunodeficiency virus (HIV) infection, immunoglobulin deficiency, or early component complement deficiency, who have received either no doses or only 1 dose of Hib vaccine before 12 months of age, should receive 2 additional doses of Hib vaccine 8 weeks apart; children who received 2 or more doses of Hib vaccine before 12 months of age should receive 1 additional dose.
- For patients younger than 5 years of age undergoing chemotherapy or radiation treatment who received a Hib vaccine dose(s) within 14 days of starting therapy or during therapy, repeat the dose(s) at least 3 months following therapy completion.
- Recipients of hematopoietic stem cell transplant (HSCT) should be revaccinated with a 3-dose regimen of Hib vaccine starting 6 to 12 months after successful transplant, regardless of vaccination history; doses should be administered at least 4 weeks apart.
- A single dose of any Hib-containing vaccine should be administered to unimmunized* children and adolescents 15 months of age and older undergoing an elective splenectomy; if possible, vaccine should be administered at least 14 days before procedure.
- Hib vaccine is not routinely recommended for patients 5 years or older. However, 1 dose of Hib vaccine should be administered to unimmunized* persons aged 5 years or older who have anatomic or functional asplenia (including sickle cell disease) and unvaccinated persons 5 through 18 years of age with human immunodeficiency virus (HIV) infection.
  *Patients who have not received a primary series and booster dose or at least 1 dose of Hib vaccine after 14 months of age are considered unimmunized.

**6. Pneumococcal vaccines. (Minimum age: 6 weeks for PCV13, 2 years for PPSV23)**
**Routine vaccination with PCV13:**
- Administer a 4-dose series of PCV13 vaccine at ages 2, 4, and 6 months and at age 12 through 15 months.
- For children aged 14 through 59 months who have received an age-appropriate series of 7-valent PCV (PCV7), administer a single supplemental dose of 13-valent PCV (PCV13).

**Catch-up vaccination with PCV13:**
- Administer 1 dose of PCV13 to all healthy children aged 24 through 59 months who are not completely vaccinated for their age.
- For other catch-up guidance, see Figure 2.

**Vaccination of persons with high-risk conditions with PCV13 and PPSV23:**
- All recommended PCV13 doses should be administered prior to PPSV23 vaccination if possible.
- For children 2 through 5 years of age with any of the following conditions: chronic heart disease (particularly cyanotic congenital heart disease and cardiac failure); chronic lung disease (including asthma if treated with high-dose oral corticosteroid therapy); diabetes mellitus; cerebrospinal fluid leak; cochlear implant; sickle cell disease and other hemoglobinopathies; anatomic or functional asplenia; HIV infection; chronic renal failure; nephrotic syndrome; diseases associated with treatment with immunosuppressive drugs or radiation therapy, including malignant neoplasms, leukemias, lymphomas, and Hodgkin disease; solid organ transplantation; or congenital immunodeficiency:
  1. Administer 1 dose of PCV13 if 3 doses of PCV (PCV7 and/or PCV13) were received previously.
  2. Administer 2 doses of PCV13 at least 8 weeks apart if fewer than 3 doses of PCV (PCV7 and/or PCV13) were received previously.

**6. Pneumococcal vaccines (cont'd)**
  3. Administer 1 supplemental dose of PCV13 if 4 doses of PCV7 or other age-appropriate complete PCV7 series was received previously.
  4. The minimum interval between doses of PCV (PCV7 or PCV13) is 8 weeks.
  5. For children with no history of PPSV23 vaccination, administer PPSV23 at least 8 weeks after the most recent dose of PCV13.
- For children aged 6 through 18 years who have cerebrospinal fluid leak; cochlear implant; sickle cell disease and other hemoglobinopathies; anatomic or functional asplenia; congenital or acquired immunodeficiencies; HIV infection; chronic renal failure; nephrotic syndrome; diseases associated with treatment with immunosuppressive drugs or radiation therapy, including malignant neoplasms, leukemias, lymphomas, and Hodgkin disease; generalized malignancy; solid organ transplantation; or multiple myeloma:
  1. If neither PCV13 nor PPSV23 has been received previously, administer 1 dose of PCV13 now and 1 dose of PPSV23 at least 8 weeks later.
  2. If PCV13 has been received previously but PPSV23 has not, administer 1 dose of PPSV23 at least 8 weeks after the most recent dose of PCV13.
  3. If PPSV23 has been received but PCV13 has not, administer 1 dose of PCV13 at least 8 weeks after the most recent dose of PPSV23.
- For children aged 6 through 18 years with chronic heart disease (particularly cyanotic congenital heart disease and cardiac failure), chronic lung disease (including asthma if treated with high-dose oral corticosteroid therapy), diabetes mellitus, alcoholism, or chronic liver disease, who have not received PPSV23, administer 1 dose of PPSV23. If PCV13 has been received previously, then PPSV23 should be administered at least 8 weeks after any prior PCV13 dose.
- A single revaccination with PPSV23 should be administered 5 years after the first dose to children with sickle cell disease or other hemoglobinopathies; anatomic or functional asplenia; congenital or acquired immunodeficiencies; HIV infection; chronic renal failure; nephrotic syndrome; diseases associated with treatment with immunosuppressive drugs or radiation therapy, including malignant neoplasms, leukemias, lymphomas, and Hodgkin disease; generalized malignancy; solid organ transplantation; or multiple myeloma.

**7. Inactivated poliovirus vaccine (IPV). (Minimum age: 6 weeks)**
**Routine vaccination:**
- Administer a 4-dose series of IPV at ages 2, 4, 6 through 18 months, and 4 through 6 years. The final dose in the series should be administered on or after the fourth birthday and at least 6 months after the previous dose.

**Catch-up vaccination:**
- In the first 6 months of life, minimum age and minimum intervals are only recommended if the person is at risk for imminent exposure to circulating poliovirus (i.e., travel to a polio-endemic region or during an outbreak).
- If 4 or more doses are administered before age 4 years, an additional dose should be administered at age 4 through 6 years and at least 6 months after the previous dose.
- A fourth dose is not necessary if the third dose was administered at age 4 years or older and at least 6 months after the previous dose.
- If both OPV and IPV were administered as part of a series, a total of 4 doses should be administered, regardless of the child's current age. IPV is not routinely recommended for U.S. residents aged 18 years or older.
- For other catch-up guidance, see Figure 2.

**8. Influenza vaccines. (Minimum age: 6 months for inactivated influenza vaccine [IIV], 2 years for live, attenuated influenza vaccine [LAIV])**
**Routine vaccination:**
- Administer influenza vaccine annually to all children beginning at age 6 months. For most healthy, nonpregnant persons aged 2 through 49 years, either LAIV or IIV may be used. However, LAIV should NOT be administered to some persons, including 1) those with asthma, 2) children 2 through 4 years who had wheezing in the past 12 months, or 3) those who have any other underlying medical conditions that predispose them to influenza complications. For all other contraindications to use of LAIV, see *MMWR* 2013; 62 (No. RR-7):1-43, available at http://www.cdc.gov/mmwr/pdf/rr/rr6207.pdf.

**For children aged 6 months through 8 years:**
- For the 2013–14 season, administer 2 doses (separated by at least 4 weeks) to children who are receiving influenza vaccine for the first time. Some children in this age group who have been vaccinated previously will also need 2 doses. For additional guidance, follow dosing guidelines in the 2013-14 ACIP influenza vaccine recommendations, *MMWR* 2013; 62 (No. RR-7):1-43, available at http://www.cdc.gov/mmwr/pdf/rr/rr6207.pdf.
- For the 2014–15 season, follow dosing guidelines in the 2014 ACIP influenza vaccine recommendations.

**For persons aged 9 years and older:**
- Administer 1 dose.

For further guidance on the use of the vaccines mentioned below, see: http://www.cdc.gov/vaccines/hcp/acip-recs/index.html.

**9. Measles, mumps, and rubella (MMR) vaccine. (Minimum age: 12 months for routine vaccination)**
**Routine vaccination:**
- Administer a 2-dose series of MMR vaccine at ages 12 through 15 months and 4 through 6 years. The second dose may be administered before age 4 years, provided at least 4 weeks have elapsed since the first dose.
- Administer 1 dose of MMR vaccine to infants aged 6 through 11 months before departure from the United States for international travel. These children should be revaccinated with 2 doses of MMR vaccine, the first at age 12 through 15 months (12 months if the child remains in an area where disease risk is high), and the second dose at least 4 weeks later.
- Administer 2 doses of MMR vaccine to children aged 12 months and older before departure from the United States for international travel. The first dose should be administered on or after age 12 months and the second dose at least 4 weeks later.

**Catch-up vaccination:**
- Ensure that all school-aged children and adolescents have had 2 doses of MMR vaccine; the minimum interval between the 2 doses is 4 weeks.

**10. Varicella (VAR) vaccine. (Minimum age: 12 months)**
**Routine vaccination:**
- Administer a 2-dose series of VAR vaccine at ages 12 through 15 months and 4 through 6 years. The second dose may be administered before age 4 years, provided at least 3 months have elapsed since the first dose. If the second dose was administered at least 4 weeks after the first dose, it can be accepted as valid.

**Catch-up vaccination:**
- Ensure that all persons aged 7 through 18 years without evidence of immunity (see *MMWR* 2007; 56 [No. RR-4], available at http://www.cdc.gov/mmwr/pdf/rr/rr5604.pdf) have 2 doses of varicella vaccine. For children aged 7 through 12 years, the recommended minimum interval between doses is 3 months (if the second dose was administered at least 4 weeks after the first dose, it can be accepted as valid); for persons aged 13 years and older, the minimum interval between doses is 4 weeks.

**11. Hepatitis A (HepA) vaccine. (Minimum age: 12 months)**
**Routine vaccination:**
- Initiate the 2-dose HepA vaccine series at 12 through 23 months; separate the 2 doses by 6 to 18 months.
- Children who have received 1 dose of HepA vaccine before age 24 months should receive a second dose 6 to 18 months after the first dose.
- For any person aged 2 years and older who has not already received the HepA vaccine series, 2 doses of HepA vaccine separated by 6 to 18 months may be administered if immunity against hepatitis A virus infection is desired.

**Catch-up vaccination:**
- The minimum interval between the two doses is 6 months.

**Special populations:**
- Administer 2 doses of HepA vaccine at least 6 months apart to previously unvaccinated persons who live in areas where vaccination programs target older children, or who are at increased risk for infection. This includes persons traveling to or working in countries that have high or intermediate endemicity of infection; men having sex with men; users of injection and non-injection illicit drugs; persons who work with HAV-infected primates or with HAV in a research laboratory; persons with clotting-factor disorders; persons with chronic liver disease; and persons who anticipate close, personal contact (e.g., household or regular babysitting) with an international adoptee during the first 60 days after arrival in the United States from a country with high or intermediate endemicity. The first dose should be administered as soon as the adoption is planned, ideally 2 or more weeks before the arrival of the adoptee.

**12. Human papillomavirus (HPV) vaccines. (Minimum age: 9 years for HPV2 [Cervarix] and HPV4 [Gardasil])**
**Routine vaccination:**
- Administer a 3-dose series of HPV vaccine on a schedule of 0, 1-2, and 6 months to all adolescents aged 11 through 12 years. Either HPV4 or HPV2 may be used for females, and only HPV4 may be used for males.
- The vaccine series may be started at age 9 years.
- Administer the second dose 1 to 2 months after the first dose (minimum interval of 4 weeks), administer the third dose 24 weeks after the first dose and 16 weeks after the second dose (minimum interval of 12 weeks).

**Catch-up vaccination:**
- Administer the vaccine series to females (either HPV2 or HPV4) and males (HPV4) at age 13 through 18 years if not previously vaccinated.
- Use recommended routine dosing intervals (see above) for vaccine series catch-up.

**13. Meningococcal conjugate vaccines. (Minimum age: 6 weeks for Hib-MenCY [MenHibrix], 9 months for MenACWY-D [Menactra], 2 months for MenACWY-CRM [Menveo])**
**Routine vaccination:**
- Administer a single dose of Menactra or Menveo vaccine at age 11 through 12 years, with a booster dose at age 16 years.
- Adolescents aged 11 through 18 years with human immunodeficiency virus (HIV) infection should receive a 2-dose primary series of Menactra or Menveo with at least 8 weeks between doses.
- For children aged 2 months through 18 years with high-risk conditions, see below.

**Catch-up vaccination:**
- Administer Menactra or Menveo vaccine at age 13 through 18 years if not previously vaccinated.
- If the first dose is administered at age 13 through 15 years, a booster dose should be administered at age 16 through 18 years with a minimum interval of at least 8 weeks between doses.
- If the first dose is administered at age 16 years or older, a booster dose is not needed.
- For other catch-up guidance, see Figure 2.

**Vaccination of persons with high-risk conditions and other persons at increased risk of disease:**
- Children with anatomic or functional asplenia (including sickle cell disease):
  1. For children younger than 19 months of age, administer a 4-dose infant series of MenHibrix or Menveo at 2, 4, 6, and 12 through 15 months of age.
  2. For children aged 19 through 23 months who have not completed a series of MenHibrix or Menveo, administer 2 primary doses of Menveo at least 3 months apart.
  3. For children aged 24 months and older who have not received a complete series of MenHibrix or Menveo or Menactra, administer 2 primary doses of either Menactra or Menveo at least 2 months apart. If Menactra is administered to a child with asplenia (including sickle cell disease), do not administer Menactra until 2 years of age and at least 4 weeks after the completion of all PCV13 doses.
- Children with persistent complement component deficiency:
  1. For children younger than 19 months of age, administer a 4-dose infant series of either MenHibrix or Menveo at 2, 4, 6, and 12 through 15 months of age.
  2. For children 7 through 23 months who have not initiated vaccination, two options exist depending on age and vaccine brand:
    a. For children who initiate vaccination with Menveo at 7 months through 23 months of age, a 2-dose series should be administered with the second dose after 12 months of age and at least 3 months after the first dose.
    b. For children who initiate vaccination with Menactra at 9 months through 23 months of age, a 2-dose series of Menactra should be administered at least 3 months apart.
    c. For children aged 24 months and older who have not received a complete series of MenHibrix, Menveo, or Menactra, administer 2 primary doses of either Menactra or Menveo at least 2 months apart.
- For children who travel to or reside in countries in which meningococcal disease is hyperendemic or epidemic, including countries in the African meningitis belt or the Hajj, administer an age-appropriate formulation and series of Menactra or Menveo for protection against serogroups A and W meningococcal disease. Prior receipt of MenHibrix is not sufficient for children traveling to the meningitis belt or the Hajj because it does not contain serogroups A or W.
- For children at risk during a community outbreak attributable to a vaccine serogroup, administer or complete an age- and formulation-appropriate series of MenHibrix, Menactra, or Menveo.
- For booster doses among persons with high-risk conditions, refer to *MMWR* 2013; 62(RR02);1-22, available at http://www.cdc.gov/mmwr/preview/mmwrhtml/rr6202a1.htm.

**Catch-up recommendations for persons with high-risk conditions:**
  1. If MenHibrix is administered to achieve protection against meningococcal disease, a complete age-appropriate series of MenHibrix should be administered.
  2. If the first dose of MenHibrix is given at or after 12 months of age, a total of 2 doses should be given at least 8 weeks apart to ensure protection against serogroups C and Y meningococcal disease.
  3. For children who initiate vaccination with Menveo at 7 months through 9 months of age, a 2-dose series should be administered with the second dose after 12 months of age and at least 3 months after the first dose.
  4. For other catch-up recommendations for these persons, refer to *MMWR* 2013; 62(RR02);1-22 available at http://www.cdc.gov/mmwr/preview/mmwrhtml/rr6202a1.htm.

**For complete information on use of meningococcal vaccines, including guidance related to vaccination of persons at increased risk of infection, see *MMWR* March 22, 2013; 62(RR02);1-22, available at http://www.cdc.gov/mmwr/pdf/rr/rr6202.pdf.**

**FIGURE 2. Catch-up immunization schedule for persons aged 4 months through 18 years who start late or who are more than 1 month behind —United States, 2014.**

The figure below provides catch-up schedules and minimum intervals between doses for children whose vaccinations have been delayed. A vaccine series does not need to be restarted, regardless of the time that has elapsed between doses. Use the section appropriate for the child's age. Always use this table in conjunction with Figure 1 and the footnotes that follow.

| Vaccine | Minimum Age for Dose 1 | Minimum Interval Between Doses | | | |
|---|---|---|---|---|---|
| | | Dose 1 to dose 2 | Dose 2 to dose 3 | Dose 3 to dose 4 | Dose 4 to dose 5 |
| **Persons aged 4 months through 6 years** | | | | | |
| Hepatitis B[1] | Birth | 4 weeks | 8 weeks and at least 16 weeks after first dose; minimum age for the final dose is 24 weeks | | |
| Rotavirus[2] | 6 weeks | 4 weeks | 4 weeks[2] | | |
| Diphtheria, tetanus, & acellular pertussis[3] | 6 weeks | 4 weeks | 4 weeks | 6 months | 6 months[3] |
| Haemophilus influenzae type b[5] | 6 weeks | 4 weeks if first dose administered at younger than age 12 months 8 weeks (as final dose) if first dose administered at age 12 through 14 months No further doses needed if first dose administered at age 15 months or older | 4 weeks[5] if current age is younger than 12 months and first dose administered at < 7 months old 8 weeks and age 12 months through 59 months (as final dose)[5] if current age is younger than 12 months and first dose administered between 7 through 11 months (regardless of Hib vaccine [PRP-T or PRP-OMP] used for first dose); OR if current age is 12 through 59 months and first dose administered at younger than age 12 months; OR first 2 doses were PRP-OMP and administered at younger than 12 months. No further doses needed if previous dose administered at age 15 months or older | 8 weeks (as final dose) This dose only necessary for children aged 12 through 59 months who received 3 (PRP-T) doses before age 12 months and started the primary series before age 7 months | |
| Pneumococcal[6] | 6 weeks | 4 weeks if first dose administered at younger than age 12 months 8 weeks (as final dose for healthy children) if first dose administered at age 12 months or older No further doses needed for healthy children if first dose administered at age 24 months or older | 4 weeks if current age is younger than 12 months 8 weeks (as final dose for healthy children) if current age is 12 months or older No further doses needed for healthy children if previous dose administered at age 24 months or older | 8 weeks (as final dose) This dose only necessary for children aged 12 through 59 months who received 3 doses before age 12 months or for children at high risk who received 3 doses at any age | |
| Inactivated poliovirus[7] | 6 weeks | 4 weeks[7] | 4 weeks[7] | 6 months[7] minimum age 4 years for final dose | |
| Meningococcal[13] | 6 weeks | 8 weeks[13] | See footnote 13 | See footnote 13 | |
| Measles, mumps, rubella[9] | 12 months | 4 weeks | | | |
| Varicella[10] | 12 months | 3 months | | | |
| Hepatitis A[11] | 12 months | 6 months | | | |
| **Persons aged 7 through 18 years** | | | | | |
| Tetanus, diphtheria; tetanus, diphtheria, & acellular pertussis[4] | 7 years[4] | 4 weeks | 4 weeks if first dose of DTaP/DT administered at younger than age 12 months 6 months if first dose of DTaP/DT administered at age 12 months or older and then no further doses needed for catch-up | 6 months if first dose of DTaP/DT administered at younger than age 12 months | |
| Human papillomavirus[12] | 9 years | Routine dosing intervals are recommended[12] | | | |
| Hepatitis A[11] | 12 months | 6 months | | | |
| Hepatitis B[1] | Birth | 4 weeks | 8 weeks (and at least 16 weeks after first dose) | | |
| Inactivated poliovirus[7] | 6 weeks | 4 weeks | 4 weeks[7] | 6 months[7] | |
| Meningococcal[13] | 6 weeks | 8 weeks[13] | | | |
| Measles, mumps, rubella[9] | 12 months | 4 weeks | | | |
| Varicella[10] | 12 months | 3 months if person is younger than age 13 years 4 weeks if person is aged 13 years or older | | | |

**NOTE:** The above recommendations must be read along with the footnotes of this schedule.

## Recommended Adult Immunization Schedule—United States - 2014

**Note: These recommendations must be read with the footnotes that follow containing number of doses, intervals between doses, and other important information.**

Figure 1. Recommended adult immunization schedule, by vaccine and age group[1]

| VACCINE ▼ AGE GROUP ► | 19-21 years | 22-26 years | 27-49 years | 50-59 years | 60-64 years | ≥ 65 years |
|---|---|---|---|---|---|---|
| Influenza[2,*] | 1 dose annually | | | | | |
| Tetanus, diphtheria, pertussis (Td/Tdap)[3,*] | Substitute 1-time dose of Tdap for Td booster; then boost with Td every 10 yrs | | | | | |
| Varicella[4,*] | 2 doses | | | | | |
| Human papillomavirus (HPV) Female[5,*] | 3 doses | 3 doses | | | | |
| Human papillomavirus (HPV) Male[5,*] | 3 doses | 3 doses | | | | |
| Zoster[6] | | | | | 1 dose | |
| Measles, mumps, rubella (MMR)[7,*] | 1 or 2 doses | | | | | |
| Pneumococcal 13-valent conjugate (PCV13)[8,*] | 1 dose | | | | | |
| Pneumococcal polysaccharide (PPSV23)[9,10] | 1 or 2 doses | | | | | 1 dose |
| Meningococcal[11,*] | 1 or more doses | | | | | |
| Hepatitis A[12,*] | 2 doses | | | | | |
| Hepatitis B[13,*] | 3 doses | | | | | |
| Haemophilus influenzae type b (Hib)[14,*] | 1 or 3 doses | | | | | |

*Covered by the Vaccine Injury Compensation Program

Legend:
- For all persons in this category who meet the age requirements and who lack documentation of vaccination or have no evidence of previous infection; zoster vaccine recommended regardless of prior episode of zoster
- Recommended if some other risk factor is present (e.g., on the basis of medical, occupational, lifestyle, or other indication)
- No recommendation

Report all clinically significant postvaccination reactions to the Vaccine Adverse Event Reporting System (VAERS). Reporting forms and instructions on filing a VAERS report are available at www.vaers.hhs.gov or by telephone, 800-822-7967.

Information on how to file a Vaccine Injury Compensation Program claim is available at www.hrsa.gov/vaccinecompensation or by telephone, 800-338-2382. To file a claim for vaccine injury, contact the U.S. Court of Federal Claims, 717 Madison Place, N.W., Washington, D.C. 20005; telephone, 202-357-6400.

Additional information about the vaccines in this schedule, extent of available data, and contraindications for vaccination is also available at www.cdc.gov/vaccines or from the CDC-INFO Contact Center at 800-CDC-INFO (800-232-4636) in English and Spanish, 8:00 a.m. - 8:00 p.m. Eastern Time, Monday - Friday, excluding holidays.

Use of trade names and commercial sources is for identification only and does not imply endorsement by the U.S. Department of Health and Human Services.

The recommendations in this schedule were approved by the Centers for Disease Control and Prevention's (CDC) Advisory Committee on Immunization Practices (ACIP), the American Academy of Family Physicians (AAFP), the American College of Physicians (ACP), American College of Obstetricians and Gynecologists (ACOG) and American College of Nurse-Midwives (ACNM).

3. Nursing care (see Tables 6 and 7)

● Table 6

| | TETANUS, DIPTHERIA AND ACELLULAR PERTUSSIS (Td/TDAP) | INFLUENZA | PNEUMOCOCCAL POLYSACCHARIDE (PPSV) | MEASLES AND MUMPS | SMALL POX |
|---|---|---|---|---|---|
| **SUMMARY OF ADOLESCENT/ADULT IMMUNIZATION RECOMMENDATIONS** | | | | | |
| **Indications** | All adults Tdap should replace a single dose of Td for adults aged < 65 years who have not previously received a Tdap dose. | Ages 19–49 for persons with medical/exposure indications Adults 50 y and older Clients with chronic conditions During influenza season for women in 2nd and 3rd trimester of pregnancy Persons traveling to foreign countries Residents of nursing homes, long-term care, assisted-living facilities | Ages 19–64 for persons with medical/exposure indications Adults 65 y and older Alaskan Natives and some Native Americans Residents of nursing homes, long-term care, assisted-living facilities | Adults born after 1957 without proof of vaccine on or after first birthday HIV-infected persons without severe immunosuppression Travelers to foreign countries Persons entering college | First responders |
| **Schedule** | Two doses 4-8 wk apart Third dose 6-12 mo Booster at 10 y intervals for life Tdap or Td vaccine used as indicated | Annually each fall | One dose Should receive at age 65 if received at least 5 y previously Administered if vaccination status unknown | One dose Two doses if in college, in health care profession, or traveling to foreign country with 2nd dose one month after 1st | One dose |
| **Contra-Indications** | Severe allergic reaction to previous dose Encephalopathy not due to another cause within 7 days of DTaP | Allergy to eggs | | Severe allergic reaction Known severe immunodeficiency | History of eczema or other skin conditions that disrupt epidermis, pregnancy or breast feeding, or women who wish to conceive 28 days after vaccination Immunosuppression, allergy to small pox vaccine receiving topical ocular steroid medication, moderate-to-severe recurrent illness, being under the age of 18, household contacts with history of eczema |
| **Comments** | Precautions: Moderate or severe illness with or without fever | | | Check pregnancy status of women Should avoid pregnancy for 30 d after vaccination Elevated temperature may be seen for 1-2 weeks Precautions: Recent receipt of antibody-containing blood product Moderate or severe illness with or without fever | Vaccinia can be transmitted from an unhealed vaccination site to other persons by close contact. Wash hands with soapy water immediately after changing bandage; place bandages in sealed plastic bag; cover site with gauze and wear long-sleeved clothing. When performing client care, keep site covered with gauze and a semipermeable dressing. |

*(continued)*

Table 6 (cont'd)

| | | | SUMMARY OF ADOLESCENT/ADULT IMMUNIZATION RECOMMENDATIONS | | | |
|---|---|---|---|---|---|---|
| | **RUBELLA** | **HEPATITIS B** | **POLIOVIRUS: IPV** | **VARICELLA** | **HEPATITIS A** | **HUMAN PAPILLOMAVIRUS VACCINE (HPV)** |
| **Indications** | Persons (especially women) without proof of vaccine on or after first birthday Health-care personnel at risk of exposure to rubella and who have contact with pregnant clients | Persons at risk to exposure to blood or blood-containing body fluids Clients and staff at institutions for developmentally disabled Hemodialysis clients Recipients of clotting-factor concentrates Household contacts and sex partners of clients with HBV Some international travelers Injecting drug users Men who have sex with men Heterosexuals with multiple sex partners or recent STD Inmates of long-term correctional facilities All unvaccinated adolescents | Travelers to countries where it is epidemic Unvaccinated adults whose children receive IPV | Persons without proof of disease or vaccination or who are seronegative Susceptible adolescents/ adults living in house holds with children Susceptible healthcare workers Susceptible family contacts of immunocompromised persons Nonpregnant women of childbearing age International travelers High risk persons: teachers of young children, day care employees, residents and staff in institutional settings, college students, inmates and staff of correctional institutions, military personnel | Travelers to countries with high incidence Men who have sex with men Injecting and illegal drug users Persons with chronic liver disease Persons with clotting factor disorders Food handlers | All females age 11/12 to 25 |
| **Schedule** | One dose | Three doses Second dose 1-2 mo after 1st Third 4-6 mo after 1st | IPV recommended Two doses at 4-8 wk intervals Third dose 2-12 mo after second **OPV no longer recommended in U.S.** | Two doses separated by 4-8 wk | Two doses separated by 6-12 mo | Three doses Second dose 2 mo after 1st Third dose 6 mo after 2nd |
| **Contra-indications** | Allergy to neomycin Pregnancy Receipt of immune globulin or blood/ blood products in previous 3-11 mo | Severe allergic reaction to vaccine | Severe allergic reaction after previous dose | Severe allergic reaction to vaccine Immunosuppressive therapy or immunodeficiency (including HIV infection) Pregnancy | Severe allergic reaction to vaccine | |
| **Comments** | Check pregnancy status of women Should avoid pregnancy for 3 mo after vaccination | Precautions: Low birth weight infant Moderate or severe illness with or without fever | Temperature elevation may be seen for 1–2 weeks Precautions: Pregnancy moderate or severe illness with or without fever | Check pregnancy status of women Should avoid pregnancy for 1 mo after vaccination Immune globulin or blood/blood product in previous 11 mo Moderate or severe illness with or without fever | Swelling and red-ness at injection site common Precaution: pregnancy | |

● Table 7

| NURSING CONSIDERATIONS FOR THE CHILD RECEIVING IMMUNIZATION | | |
|---|---|---|
| **NAME** | **ROUTE** | **NURSING CONSIDERATIONS** |
| DTaP (diphtheria, tetanus, pertussis) | IM anterior or lateral thigh (No IMs in gluteal muscle until after child is walking) | Potential side effects include fever within 24-48 hours, swelling, redness, soreness at injection site<br>More serious side effects—continuous screaming, convulsions, high fever, loss of consciousness<br>Do not administer if there is past history of serious reaction |
| MMR (measles, mumps, rubella) | SC anterior or lateral thigh | Potential side effects include rash, fever, and arthritis; may occur 10 days to 2 weeks after vaccination<br>May give DTaP, MMR, and TIPV at same time if family has history of not keeping appointments for vaccinations |
| IPV (inactivated polio) | IM | Reactions very rare |
| HB (hepatitis B) | IM vastus lateralis or deltoid | Should not be given into dorsogluteal site<br>Mild local tenderness at injection site |
| Tuberculosis test | Intradermal | May be given 4-6 year and 11-16 years if in high prevalence areas<br>Evaluated in 48-72 hours<br>PPD (purified protein derivative) 0.1 ml<br>Tine test (multiple puncture) less accurate |
| TD (tetanus/ diphtheria booster) | IM anterior or lateral thigh | Repeat every 10 years |
| Live attenuated rubella | SC anterior or lateral thigh | Give once only to women who are antibody-negative for rubella, and if pregnancy can be prevented for 3 months postvaccination |
| Live attenuated mumps | SC | Give once<br>Prevention of orchitis (and therefore sterility) in susceptible males |

## ALLERGEN RESPONSE

A. Data Collection

1. Prodromal—complains of weakness, apprehension, impending doom, dry/scratchy throat (feeling of "lump in throat"); nausea and vomiting

2. Cutaneous—generalized intense pruritus and urticaria (hives), angioedema (swelling) of lips and eyelids

3. Bronchial—increasing respiratory distress with audible wheezing, rales; diminished breath sounds heard on auscultation

4. Circulatory—hypotension and a rapid, weak, irregular pulse, dysrhythmias, shock, cardiac arrest can occur within minutes

**B.** Diagnose

1. Hypersensitivity—exaggerated or inappropriate reaction of a previously sensitized immune system resulting in a typical pathological process and tissue damage

2. Anaphylaxis—serious multiple system response (vasogenic shock) to an antigen-antibody reaction upon subsequent exposure (rarely upon first contact) to a substance (allergen) for which the person has developed a severe hypersensitivity

3. Immense amounts of histamine are rapidly dispersed throughout the circulatory system resulting in extensive vasodilation and increased capillary permeability leading to acute hypovolemia and vascular collapse; there is also severe edema of bronchial tissue resulting in pulmonary obstruction; without treatment, severe hypoxemia and ultimately death will occur

4. Common allergens—drug/chemicals (penicillin, radiopaque dyes, aspirin, bisulfates, vaccines, blood components), toxins (snake, bee, wasp, hornet), and food (berries, chocolate, eggs, shellfish, seafood, nuts)

5. Potential nursing diagnoses
   a. Skin integrity, impaired
   b. Airway clearance, ineffective

**C.** Plan/Implementation

1. Establish airway (ABC)

2. Administer aqueous epinephrine (adrenaline) 1:1,000—0.1 ml up to 0.5 ml (0.1 mg/kg body weight) SC in arm opposite to side of injection/sting; same dose may be repeated every 15–20 minutes PRN (three times with children)

3. Oxygen, suction, and life support as needed; start IV

4. Tourniquet may be applied on extremity proximal to injection of allergen to prevent further absorption.

5. Other medications may be used—diphenhydramine as antihistamine, aminophylline for severe bronchospasm, vasopressors for severe shock, corticosteroids for persistent/recurrent symptoms

6. Ask all clients about possible allergic reactions to foods, medications, insects

7. Ensure that clients remain in health setting at least 20–30 minutes after receiving injection

8. Teach client and family how to avoid the identified allergen; ensure/reinforce wearing Medic-Alert items

9. For sensitivity to insect venom, instruct the client and/or family members in the use of the emergency anaphylaxis kit (either epinephrine and syringes or automatic injector), to be kept with the person at all times

10. Hyposensitization/desensitization/immunotherapy—SC administration of gradually increasing dosages of the offending allergen

## LATEX ALLERGY

**A.** Data Collection

  1.  Urticaria, rash, lip, mouth and upper airway edema

  2.  Flushing and generalized edema

  3.  Rhinitis, conjunctivitis

  4.  Bronchospasms

  5.  Anaphylactic shock

**B.** Diagnose

  1.  Caused by repeated exposure to latex products

  2.  High risk populations
      a.  Children with spina bifida
      b.  Clients with urogenital abnormalities
      c.  Clients with spinal cord injuries
      d.  History of multiple surgeries
      e.  Health care workers

**C.** Plan/Implementation

  1.  Screen for latex sensitivity

  2.  Provide latex-safe environment

  3.  Reinforce instructions to client to avoid latex products
      a.  Gloves
      b.  Catheters
      c.  Brown ace bandages
      d.  Band-Aid dressing
      e.  Elastic pressure stocking
      f.  Balloons
      g.  Condoms
      h.  Feminine hygiene pad

  4.  Wear Medic-Alert identification

## ATOPIC ALLERGY

**A.** Data Collection

  1.  History of offending allergen, pollens (trees, grass, weeds), or environmental substances (dust, animals, feathers)

  2.  Upper respiratory symptoms—rhinorrhea (runny nose), sneezing, mucosal edema, and congestion, pharyngeal and conjunctival itching and tearing

  3.  Etiology and severity may be determined by skin testing

**B.** Diagnose

  1.  Airway clearance, ineffective

  2.  Includes hay fever, rhinitis, asthma

C. Plan/Implementation

1. Provide symptomatic relief

2. Teach client how to avoid allergies

## PHYSICAL (COLLECTION OF DATA)

A. Purpose

1. Determine client's current health status

2. Interpret physical data

3. Decide on interventions based on data obtained

B. Preparation

1. Gather equipment
   a. Ophthalmoscope
   b. Tuning fork
   c. Cotton swabs
   d. Snellen eye chart
   e. Thermometer
   f. Penlight
   g. Tongue depressor
   h. Ruler/tape measure
   i. Safety pin
   j. Balance scale
   k. Gloves
   l. Nasal speculum
   m. Vaginal speculum

2. Provide for privacy (drape) in quiet, well-lit environment

3. Explain procedure to client

4. Ask client to empty bladder

5. Drape client for privacy

6. Compare findings on one side of body with other side and compare with normal

7. Make use of teaching opportunities (dental care, eye exams, self-exams of breast or testicle)

8. Use piece of equipment for entire process, then return to equipment tray

C. Techniques used in order performed, except for the abdomen

1. Inspection (visually examined)
   a. Starts with first interaction
   b. Provide good lighting
   c. Determine
      1) Size
      2) Shape

        3) Color

        4) Texture

        5) Symmetry

        6) Position

2. Palpation (touch)
   a. Warm hands
   b. Approach slowly and proceed systematically
   c. Use fingertips for fine touch (pulses, nodes)
   d. Use dorsum of fingers for temperatures
   e. Use palm or ulnar edge of hand for vibration
   f. Use light palpation only
   g. Ballottement—push fluid-filled tissue toward palpating hand so object floats against fingertips
   h. Determines
      1) Masses
      2) Pulsation
      3) Organ size
      4) Tenderness or pain
      5) Swelling
      6) Tissue fullness and elasticity
      7) Vibration
      8) Crepitus
      9) Temperature
      10) Texture
      11) Moisture
3. Percussion (tap to produce sound and vibration)
   a. Types
      1) Direct—strike body surface with 1 or 2 fingers
      2) Indirect—strike finger or hand placed over body surface
      3) Blunt—use reflex hammer to check deep tendon reflexes; Use blunt percussion with fist to determine costovertebral angle (CVA) tenderness

b. Sounds
   1) Resonance—moderate-to-loud, low-pitched (clear, hollow) sound of moderate duration; found with air-filled tissue (normal lung)
   2) Hyperresonance—loud, booming, low-pitched sound of longer duration found with overinflated air-filled tissue (pulmonary emphysema); normal in child due to thin chest wall
   3) Tympany—loud, drumlike, high-pitched or musical sound of moderately long duration found with enclosed, air-filled structures (bowel)
   4) Dull-soft, muffled, moderate-to-high-pitched sound of short duration; found with dense, fluid-filled tissue (liver)
   5) Flat—very soft, high-pitched sound of short duration; found with very dense tissue (bone, muscle)

c. Determines
   1) Location, size, density of masses
   2) Pain in areas up to depth of 3–5 cm (1–2 inches)

d. Performed after inspection and palpation, except for the abdomen; for abdomen perform inspection, auscultation, percussion, palpation

4. Auscultation
   a. Equipment
      1) Use diaphragm of stethoscope to listen to high-pitched sounds (lung, bowel, heart); place firmly against skin surface to form tight seal (leave ring)
      2) Use bell to listen to soft, low-pitched sounds (heart murmurs); place lightly on skin surface
   b. Listen over bare skin (not through clothing); moisten body hair to prevent crackling sounds

D. Findings

1. General survey
   a. General appearance
      1) Apparent age
      2) Sex
      3) Racial and ethnic group
      4) Apparent state of health
      5) Proportionate height and weight
      6) Posture
      7) Gait, movements, range of motion
      8) Suitable clothing
      9) Hygiene
      10) Body and breath odor
      11) Skin color, condition
      12) Presence of assistive device, hearing aid, glasses
   b. General behavior
      1) Signs of distress
      2) Level of consciousness, oriented ×3, mood, speech, thought process appropriate
      3) Level of cooperation, eye contact (culture must be considered)

● Table 8

| NORMAL VITAL SIGNS | | | |
|---|---|---|---|
| **AGE** | **NORMAL RESPIRATORY RATE** | **NORMAL PULSE RATE** | **NORMAL BLOOD PRESSURE (BP)** |
| Newborn | 30-60 per minute | 120-160 beats per minute (bpm) May go to 180 when crying | 65/41 mm Hg |
| 1-4 years | 20-40 per minute | 80-140 beats per minute (bpm) | 90-99/60-65 mm Hg |
| 5-12 years | 15-25 per minute | 70-115 beats per minute (bpm) | 100-110/56-60 mm Hg |
| Adult | 12-20 per minute | 60-100 beats per minute (bpm) | less than 120/80 mm Hg |
| Factors influencing respiration: fever, anxiety, drugs, disease | | | |
| Factors influencing BP: disease, drugs, anxiety, cardiac output, peripheral resistance, arterial elasticity, blood volume, blood viscosity, age, weight, exercise | | | |
| Factors influencing pulse rate and rhythm: drug, pathology, exercise, age, gender, temperature, BP, serum electrolytes | | | |

2. Vital signs (see Table 8)
   a. Temperature (see Table 9)
      1) Infants—performed axillary
      2) Intra-auricular probe allows rapid, noninvasive reading when appropriate
      3) Tympanic membrane sensors—positioning is crucial, ear canal must be straightened
   b. Pulse (rate, rhythm)
   c. Respirations (rate, pattern, depth)
      1) Adult—costal (chest moves), regular, expiration slower than inspiration, rate 12–20 respirations/minute
      2) Neonates—diaphragmatic (abdomen moves), irregular, 30–50 respirations/minute
      3) Breathing patterns
         a) Abdominal respirations—breathing accomplished by abdominal muscles and diaphragm; may be used to increase effectiveness of ventilatory process in certain conditions
         b) Apnea—temporary cessation of breathing
         c) Cheyne-Stokes respiration—periodic breathing characterized by rhythmic waxing and waning of the depth of respirations
         d) Dyspnea—difficult, labored, or painful breathing (considered "normal" at certain times, e.g., after extreme physical exertion)
         e) Hyperpnea—abnormally deep breathing
         f) Hyperventilation—abnormally rapid, deep, and prolonged breathing
            i. Caused by central nervous system disorders, drugs that increase sensitivity of respiratory center or acute anxiety
            ii. Produces respiratory alkalosis due to reduction in $CO_2$
         g) Hypoventilation—reduced ventilatory efficiency; produces respiratory acidosis due to elevation in $CO_2$
         h) Kussmaul's respirations (air hunger)—marked increase in depth and rate

  i) Orthopnea—inability to breathe except when trunk is in an upright position

Table 9

| NORMAL BODY TEMPERATURE | | |
|---|---|---|
| METHOD USED | FAHRENHEIT | CELSIUS |
| Oral | 98.6° | 37.0° |
| Rectal | 99.6° | 37.6° |
| Axillary | 97.6° | 36.5° |
| Factors influencing reading: elderly client, faulty thermometer, dehydration, environment, infections | | |

  j) Periodic breathing—rate, depth, or tidal volume changes markedly from one interval to the next; pattern of change is periodically reproduced
  k) Cyanosis—skin appears blue because of an excessive accumulation of unoxygenated hemoglobin in the blood
  l) Stridor—harsh, high-pitched sound associated with airway obstruction near larynx
  m) Cough
    i. Normal reflex to remove foreign material from the lungs
    ii. Normally absent in newborns
 d. Blood pressure
  1) Check both arms and compare results (difference 5–10 mm Hg normal)
  2) Pulse pressure (normal 30–40 mm Hg)
  3) Cover 50% of limb from shoulder to olecranon with cuff; too narrow: abnormally high reading; too wide: abnormally low reading

3. Nutrition status
 a. Height, weight; ideal body weight, men—106 lbs for first 5 feet, then add 6 lbs/inch; women—100 for first 5 feet, then add 5 lbs/inch; add 10% for client with larger frame; subtract 10% for client with small frame

4. Skin
 a. Check for pallor on buccal mucosa or conjunctivae, cyanosis on nail beds or oral mucosa, jaundice on sclera
 b. Scars, bruises, lesions
 c. Edema (eyes, sacrum), moisture, hydration
 d. Temperature, texture, turgor (pinch skin, tented 3 seconds or less is normal), check over sternum for elderly

5. Hair
 a. Hirsutism—excess
 b. Alopecia—loss or thinning

6. Nails (indicate respiratory and nutritional status)
 a. Color

    b.  Shape, contour (normal angle of nail bed less than or equal to 160°, clubbing: nail bed angle greater than or equal to 180° due to prolonged decreased oxygenation)

    c.  Texture, thickness

    d.  Capillary refill (normal less than or equal to 3-second return of color)

7.  Head

    a.  Size, shape, symmetry

    b.  Temporal arteries

    c.  Cranial nerve function (see Table 10)

8.  Eyes

    a.  Ptosis—drooping of upper eyelid

    b.  Color of sclerae, conjunctiva

    c.  Pupils

        1)  Size, shape, equality, reactivity to light and accommodation (PERRLA)

    d.  Photophobia—light intolerance

    e.  Nystagmus—abnormal, involuntary, rapid eye movements

    f.  Strabismus—involuntary drifting of one eye out of alignment with the other eye; "lazy eye"

    g.  Corneal reflex

    h.  Visual fields (peripheral vision)

    i.  Visual acuity—Snellen chart, normal 20/20

    j.  Corneal light reflection—same position on each cornea; asymmetrical reflection—strabismus

9.  Ears

    a.  Pull pinna up and back to examine children's (3 years of age and older)

    b.  Pull pinna down and back to examine infants' and young childrens' (younger than 3 years of age) ears

    c.  Weber test—determines bone conduction; vibrating tuning fork placed in middle of forehead; normal—hear sound equally in ears

    d.  Rinne test—compares bone conduction with air conduction; vibrating tuning fork placed on mastoid process, when client no longer hears sound, positioned in front of ear canal; normal—should still be able to hear sound; air conduction greater than bone conduction by 2:1 ratio (positive Rinne test)

10.  Nose and sinuses

    a.  Septum midline

    b.  Alignment, color, discharge

    c.  Palpate and percuss sinuses

11.  Mouth and pharynx

    a.  Oral mucosa

    b.  Teeth (normal 32)

    c.  Tongue

    d.  Hard and soft palate

    e.  Uvula, midline

    f.  Tonsils

g. Gag reflex

h. Swallow

i. Taste

12. Neck

a. Range of motion of cervical spine

b. Cervical lymph nodes (normal less than or equal to 1 cm round, soft, mobile) nontender

c. Trachea position

d. Thyroid gland

e. Carotid arteries—check for bruit and thrill

f. Jugular veins

13. Thorax and lungs

a. Alignment of spine

b. Anteroposterior to transverse diameter (normal adult 1:2 to 5:7); 1:1 barrel chest

c. Respiratory excursion

d. Respirations

e. Tactile fremitus—(vibration produced when client makes sound of "99")

f. Diaphragmatic excursion—determines degree and symmetry of diaphragm movement; percuss from areas of resonance to dullness

g. Breath sounds—bilaterally equal

1) Normal

a) Vesicular—soft and low-pitched breezy sounds heard over most of peripheral lung fields

b) Bronchovesicular—medium pitched, moderately loud sounds heard over the mainstem bronchi

c) Bronchial—loud, coarse, blowing sound heard over the trachea

2) Adventitious (abnormal); caused by fluid or inflammation

a) Rales (crackles)—crackling or gurgling sounds (also known as crackles)
commonly heard on inspiration

b) Rhonchi—musical sounds or vibrations commonly heard on expiration

c) Wheezes—squeaky sounds heard during inspiration and expiration associated with narrow airways

d) Pleural friction rub—grating sound or vibration heard during inspiration and expiration

h. Vocal resonance

1) Bronchophony—say "99" and hear more clearly than normal; loud transmission of voice sounds caused by consolidation of lung

2) Egophony—say "E" and hear "A" due to distortion caused by consolidation of lung

3) Whispered pectoriloquy—hear whispered sounds clearly due to dense consolidation of lung

i. Costovertebral angle percussion—kidneys

● Table 10

| CRANIAL NERVES | | | |
|---|---|---|---|
| **#/NERVE** | **FUNCTION** | **NORMAL FINDINGS** | **NURSING CONSIDERATIONS** |
| (I) Olfactory | Sense of smell | Able to detect various odors in each nostril | Have client smell a nonirritating substance such as coffee or tobacco with eyes closed<br>Test each nostril separately |
| (II) Optic | Sense of vision | Clear (acute) vision near and distant | Snellen eye chart for far vision<br>Read newspaper for near vision<br>Ophthalmoscopic exam |
| (III) Oculomotor | Pupil constriction, raising of eyelids | Pupils equal in size and equally reactive to light | Instruct client to look up, down, inward<br>Observe for symmetry and eye opening<br>Shine penlight into eye as client stares straight ahead<br>Ask client to watch your finger as you move it toward face |
| (IV) Trochlear | Downward and inward movement of eyes | Able to move eyes down and inward | (See Oculomotor) |
| (V) Trigeminal | Motor—jaw movement<br>Sensory—sensation on the face and neck | Able to clench and relax jaw<br>Able to differentiate between various stimuli touched to the face and neck | Test with pin and wisp of cotton over each division on both sides of face<br>Ask client to open jaw, bite down, move jaw laterally against pressure<br>Stroke cornea with wisp of cotton |
| (VI) Abducens | Lateral movement of the eyes | Able to move eyes in all directions | (See Oculomotor) |
| (VII) Facial | Motor—facial muscle movement<br>Sensory—taste on the anterior two-thirds of the tongue (sweet and salty) | Able to smile, whistle, wrinkle forehead<br>Able to differentiate tastes among various agents | Observe for facial symmetry after asking client to frown, smile, raise eyebrows, close eyelids against resistance, whistle, blow<br>Place sweet, sour, bitter, and salty substances on tongue |
| (VIII) Acoustic | Sense of hearing and balance | Hearing intact<br>Balance maintained while walking | Test with watch ticking into ear, rubbing fingers together, Rinne and Weber tests<br>Test posture, standing with eyes closed<br>Otoscopic exam |
| (IX) Glossopharyngeal | Motor—pharyngeal movement and swallowing<br>Sensory—taste on posterior one-third of tongue (sour and bitter) | Gag reflex intact, able to swallow<br>Able to taste | Place sweet, sour, bitter, and salty substances on tongue<br>Note ability to swallow and handle secretions<br>Stimulate pharyngeal wall to elicit gag reflex |
| (X) Vagus | Swallowing and speaking | Able to swallow and speak with a smooth voice | Inspect soft palate—instruct to say "ah"<br>Observe uvula for midline position<br>Rate quality of voice |
| (XI) Spinal accessory | Motor—flexion and rotation of head; shrugging of shoulders | Able to flex and rotate head; able to shrug shoulders | Inspect and palpate sternocleidomastoid and trapezius muscles for size, contour, tone<br>Ask client to move head side to side against resistance and shrug shoulders against resistance |
| (XII) Hypoglossal | Motor—tongue movements | Can move tongue side to side and stick it out symmetrically and in midline | Inspect tongue in mouth<br>Ask client to stick out tongue and move it quickly side to side<br>Observe midline, symmetry, and rhythmic movement |

14. Heart Sounds (corresponds with Figure 1)
   a. Angle of Louis—manubrial sternal junction at second rib
   b. Aortic and pulmonic areas—right and left intercostal spaces alongside sternum
   c. Erbs' point—third intercostal space just to the left of the sternum
   d. Tricuspid area—fourth or fifth intercostal space to the left
   e. Mitral area—fifth intercostal space at left midclavicular line (apex of heart)
   f. Point of maximal impulse (PMI)
      1) Impulse of the left ventricle felt most strongly
      2) Adult—left fifth intercostal space in the midclavicular line
      3) Infant—lateral to left nipple
   g. $S_1$ and $S_2$
      1) $S_1$ "lubb"—closure of tricuspid and mitral valves; dull quality and low pitch; onset of ventricular systole (contraction)
      2) $S_2$ "dubb"—closure of aortic and pulmonic valves; snapping quality; onset of diastole (relaxation of atria, then ventricles)
   h. Murmurs—abnormal sounds caused by turbulence within the heart valve; turbulence within a blood vessel is called a bruit

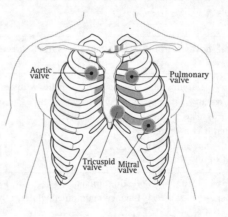

**Figure 1. Heart Sounds**

   i. Pulse deficit—difference between apical and radial rate
   j. Jugular veins—normally distend when the client lies flat, but are not visible when the client's head is raised 30–45°

15. Peripheral vascular system
   a. Pulses
      1) Radial—passes medially across the wrist; felt on radial (or thumb) side of the forearm
      2) Ulnar—passes laterally across the wrist; felt on the ulnar (little finger) side of the wrist
      3) Femoral—passes beneath the inguinal ligament (groin area) into the thigh; felt in groin area
      4) Carotid—pulsations can be felt over medial edge of sternocleidomastoid muscle in neck
      5) Pedal (dorsalis pedis: dorsal artery of the foot)—passes laterally over the foot; felt along top of foot

      6)  Posterior tibial—felt on inner side of ankle below medial malleous

      7)  Popliteal—felt in popliteal fossa, the region at the back of the knee

      8)  Temporal—felt lateral to eyes

      9)  Apical—left at fifth intercostal space at midclavicular line

16.  Breasts and axillae
   a.  Size, shape, symmetry
   b.  Gynecomastia—breast enlargement in males
   c.  Nodes—normal nonpalpable

17.  Abdomen
   a.  Knees flexed to relax muscles and provide for comfort
   b.  Inspect and auscultate, then percuss and palpate
   c.  Symmetry, contour
   d.  Umbilicus
   e.  Bowel sounds; normal high-pitched gurgles heard with the diaphragm of the stethoscope at 5–20-second intervals
       1)  Hypoactive– <3/minute
       2)  Hyperactive—loud, frequent
   f.  Aorta, renal, iliac, femoral arteries auscultated with the bell of the stethoscope
   g.  Peritoneal friction rub—grating sound varies with respirations; inflammation of liver
   h.  Liver and spleen size
   i.  Inguinal lymph nodes
   j.  Rebound tenderness—inflammation of peritoneum
   k.  Kidneys
   l.  Abdominal reflexes

18.  Neurological system
   a.  Deep tendon reflexes (DTRs)—determines sensory and motor pathways; compare bilaterally; 0 (absent) through 4+ (hyperactive) scale
   b.  Cerebellar function—coordination; point-to-point touching, rapid, alternating movements, gait
   c.  Mental status (cerebral function)
   d.  Cranial nerve function
   e.  Motor function
       1)  Strength
       2)  Tone
   f.  Sensory function
       1)  Touch, tactile localization
       2)  Pain
       3)  Pressure
       4)  Temperature
       5)  Vibration
       6)  Proprioception (position sense)
       7)  Vision
       8)  Hearing
       9)  Smell
       10)  Taste

19. Musculoskeletal system
    a. Muscle tone and strength
    b. Joint movements; crepitus-grating sound abnormal

20. Genitalia
    a. Inspect outer structures (labia, urethral meatus, vaginal introitus, anus, penis, scrotum)
    b. Note any abnormalities
        1) Hypospadias—urethral meatus located on the underside of the penile shaft
        2) Epispadias—urethral meatus located on the upper side of the penile shaft
        3) Hemorrhoids—dilated veins in the anal area

PHYSIOLOGICAL
INTEGRITY 1

[BASIC CARE AND COMFORT]

**Chapter 5**

Mobility and Immobility

Conditions Limiting Mobility

Interventions to Promote
Comfort

Musculoskeletal Trauma

Rest and Sleep Disturbances

Nutrition

Elimination

## MOBILITY

**A.** Data Collection

1. Body build, height, weight—proportioned within normal limits

2. Posture, body alignment—erect
   a. Lumbar lordosis—exaggerated concavity in the lumbar region
   b. Kyphosis—exaggerated convexity in the thoracic region
   c. Scoliosis—lateral curvature of a portion of the vertebral column

3. Gait, ambulation—smooth

4. Joints—freely movable (see Table 1)

5. Skin integrity—intact

6. Muscle tone, elasticity, strength—adequate

7. Exercise level—appropriate

8. Rest and sleep patterns—adequate

9. Sexual activity—appropriate

10. Job-related activity—acceptable

11. Developmental mobility—within normal limits

● **Table 1**

| JOINT MOVEMENTS | |
|---|---|
| **MOVEMENT** | **ACTION** |
| Flexion | Decrease angle of joint, e.g., bending elbow |
| Extension | Increase angle of joint, e.g., straightening elbow |
| Hyperextension | Excessively increase angle of joint, e.g., bending the head backward |
| Abduction | Moving bone away from midline of body |
| Adduction | Moving bone toward midline of body ("add" to body) |
| Rotation | Moving bone around its central axis |
| Dorsiflexion | Flexion of the foot toward the trunk of the body ("toes toward the nose") |
| Plantar flexion | Flexion of the foot away from the trunk of the body ("pointing the toes") |
| Inversion | Turning the foot inward at the ankle |
| Eversion | Turning the foot outward at the ankle |
| Pronation | Rotation of the forearm so that the palm of the hand turns downward |
| Supination | Rotation of the forearm so that the palm of the hand turns upward |

**B.** Diagnose

1. Activity
   a. Maintains muscle tone and posture
   b. Serves as an outlet for tension and anxiety

2. Exercise
   a. Maintains joint mobility and function
   b. Promotes muscle strength
   c. Stimulates circulation
   d. Promotes optimum ventilation
   e. Stimulates appetite
   f. Promotes elimination
   g. Enhances metabolic rate

3. Potential nursing diagnoses
   a. Impaired walking
   b. Activity intolerance
   c. Risk for falls
   d. Risk for injury

**C.** Plan/Implementation

1. Avoid injury
   a. Prevent motor vehicle accidents, use seat belts and helmets
   b. Avoid job-related accidents, follow safety procedures
   c. When engaging in contact sports, perform proper body conditioning and use protective devices
   d. For aged persons, rugs should be secure, stairways lit and clear of debris
   e. During pregnancy use bathtub grips, low-heeled shoes
   f. Assist client to sit on side of bed
      1) Place hand under knees and shoulders of client
      2) Instruct client to push elbow into bed; at the same time the nurse should lift the client's shoulders with one arm and swing the client's legs over edge of bed with the other arm
   g. Assist client to stand
      1) Face client with hands firmly grasping each side of his/her rib cage
      2) Push nurse's knee against one knee of the client
      3) Rock client forward as he/she comes to a standing position
      4) Pivot client to position him/her to sit in chair (placed on client's stronger side)
   h. Assist client out of bed
      1) If client has a weaker side, move the client toward the stronger side (easier for client to pull the weak side)
      2) Use the larger muscles of the legs to accomplish a move rather than the smaller muscles of the back
      3) Drawsheets are a better method of moving a client than sliding a client across a surface

   4) Always have an assistant standing by if there is any possibility
      of problems in completing a transfer
   i. Reinforce teaching of ADLs
      1) Observe what client can do and allow him/her to do it
      2) Encourage client to exercise muscles used for activity
      3) Start with gross functional movement before going to finer
         motions
      4) Extend period of activity as much and as fast as the client can
         tolerate
      5) Give positive feedback immediately after every accomplishment

## IMMOBILITY

**A.** Data Collection

   1. Gait, ambulation

   2. Joint movement

   3. Muscle tone

   4. Skin integrity

● Table 2

| THERAPEUTIC EXERCISES | | |
|---|---|---|
| **EXERCISE** | **DESCRIPTION** | **RATIONALE** |
| Passive range of motion | Performed by nurse without assistance from client | Retention of joint range of motion; maintenance of circulation |
| Active assistive range of motion | Performed by client with assistance of nurse | Increases motion in the joint |
| Active range of motion | Performed by client without assistance | Maintains mobility of joints and incrreses muscle strength |
| Active resistive range of motion | Performed by client against manual or mechanical resistance | Provision of resistance to increase muscle power; 5-pound bags/weights may be used |
| Isometric exercises | Performed by client; alternate contraction and relaxation of muscle without moving joint | Maintenance of muscle strength when joint immobilized |

**B.** Diagnose

   1. Activity intolerance

   2. Impaired walking

   3. Risk for Disuse Syndrome

   4. Fatigue

**C.** Plan/Implementation

   1. Therapeutic exercises (see Table 2)

   2. Prevent complication of immobility (see Table 3)

   3. Maintain specific therapeutic positions (see Table 4)

Table 3

| COMPLICATIONS OF IMMOBILITY | | |
|---|---|---|
| **COMPLICATION** | **SEQUELAE** | **NURSING CONSIDERATIONS** |
| Decubitus ulcer | Osteomyelitis<br>Tissue maceration<br>Infection | Frequently turn, provide skin care<br>Ambulate as appropriate<br>Use draw sheet when turning to avoid<br>  shearing force<br>Provide balanced diet with adequate<br>  protein, vitamins, and minerals<br>Use air mattress, flotation pads, elbow<br>  and heel pads, sheepskin<br>Assist with use of Stryker frame or<br>  Circ-O-Lectric bed |
| Sensory input changes | Confusion, disorientation | Orient frequently<br>Place clock, calendar within sight |
| Osteoporosis | Pathological fractures<br>Renal calculi | Encourage weight-bearing on long bones<br>Provide balanced diet<br>Monitor estrogen therapy, if ordered |
| Negative nitrogen balance | Anorexia, debilitation,<br>  weight loss | Give high-protein diet and small,<br>  frequent feedings |
| Hypercalcemia | Impaired bone growth | Reduce calcium in diet, encourage fluids |
| Increased cardiac workload | Tachycardia | Use trapeze to decrease Valsalva<br>  maneuver when moving in bed<br>Teach client how to move without<br>  holding breath |
| Contractures | Deformities | Frequent change of position<br>Use pillows, trochanter rolls, foot board<br>  to promote proper body alignment<br>Exercise as appropriate |
| Thrombus formation | Pulmonary emboli | Leg exercises—flexion, extension of toes<br>  for 5 minutes every hour<br>Ambulate as appropriate<br>Frequent change of position<br>Avoid using knee gatch on bed or pillows<br>  to support knee flexion<br>Use TED or elastic hose<br>Check for pain, edema, and warmth |
| Orthostatic hypotension | Weakness, faintness,<br>  dizziness | Teach client to rise from bed slowly<br>Increase activity gradually |
| Stasis of respiratory<br>  secretions | Hypostatic pneumonia | Teach client the importance of turning,<br>  coughing, and deep breathing<br>Administer postural drainage as<br>  appropriate |
| Constipation | Fecal impaction | Ambulate as appropriate<br>Increase fluid intake and fiber in diet<br>Insure privacy for use of bed pan or<br>  commode<br>Administer stool softeners, e.g., Colace |
| Urinary stasis | Urinary retention<br>Renal calculi | Have client void in normal position, if<br>  possible<br>Increase fluid intake<br>Low-calcium diet, increase acid ash<br>  residue to acidify urine and prevent<br>  formation of calcium stones |
| Boredom | Restlessness | Allow visitors, use of radio, television<br>Schedule occupational therapy |
| Depression | Insomnia<br>Restlessness | Encourage self-care<br>Start with simple, gross activity before<br>  advancing to finer motor movements<br>Increase period of activity as rapidly as<br>  client can tolerate<br>Support client with positive feedback<br>  for effort/accomplishment |

| SPECIFIC THERAPEUTIC POSITIONS | |
|---|---|
| **POSITION** | **FUNCTION** |
| Supine | Avoids hip flexion, which can compress arterial flow |
| Dorsal recumbent | Supine with knees flexed, more comfortable |
| Prone | Promotes extension of the hip joint<br>Not well tolerated by persons with respiratory or cardiovascular difficulties |
| Side lateral or side-lying | Allows drainage of oral secretions |
| Knee-chest | Provides maximal visualization of rectal area |
| Side with upper leg bent (Sim's) | Allows drainage of oral secretions<br>Decreases abdominal tension |
| Head elevated (Fowler's) | Increases venous return<br>Allows maximal lung expansion<br>High-Fowler's: 60-90°<br>Fowler's: 45-60°<br>Semi-Fowler's: 30-45°<br>Low-Fowler's: 15-30° |
| Modified Trendelenburg (feet elevated 20°, knees straight, trunk flat, and head slightly elevated) | Increases blood return to heart<br>Used for shock |
| Head elevated and knees elevated | Increases blood return to heart<br>Relieves pressure on lumbosacral area |
| Elevation of extremity | Increases venous return<br>Decreases blood volume to extremity |
| Lithotomy (Flat on back, thighs flexed, legs abducted) | Increases vaginal opening for examination |

●Table 4

## ASSISTIVE DEVICES

A. Tilt table
1. Used for weight-bearing on long bones to prevent decalcification of bones and resulting bone weakness, renal calculi
2. Stimulates circulation to lower extremities
3. Use elastic stockings to prevent postural hypotension
4. Should be done gradually; board can be tilted in 5-10° increments
5. Blood pressure should be checked during the procedure
6. If blood pressure goes down and dizziness, pallor, diaphoresis, tachycardia, or nausea occur, stop procedure

B. Crutches (see Table 5)
1. Guideline for crutch height—measure two fingers below axilla
2. client should support weight on handpiece, not on axilla—brachialas plexus may be damaged, producing "crutch palsy"
3. Crutches should be kept 8 to 10 inches out to side
4. Elbows should be flexed at 20–30° angle for correct placement of hand grips
5. Stop and rest if diaphoretic or short of breath

Table 5

| CRUTCH WALKING GAITS | | |
|---|---|---|
| GAIT | DESCRIPTION | USES |
| Four-point | Slow, safe; right crutch, left foot, left crutch, right foot | Use when weight-bearing is allowed for both legs |
| Two-point | Faster, safe; right crutch and left foot advance together; left crutch and right foot advance together | Use when weight-bearing is allowed for both legs |
| Three-point | Faster gait, safe; advance weaker leg and both crutches simultaneously; then advance good leg | Use when weight-bearing is allowed on one leg |
| Swing-to-swing-through | Fast gait but requires more strength and balance; advance both crutches followed by both legs (or one leg is held up) | Use when partial weight-bearing is allowed on both legs |

NOTE: To go up stairs: advance good leg first, followed by crutches and affected leg. To go down stairs: advance crutches with affected leg first, followed by good leg. ("Up with the good, down with the bad.")

C. Walker

1. Definition—metal frame with handgrips, four legs and an open side; used for clients who need greater stability than that provided by other ambulatory aids

2. Guidelines for use
   a. Elbows should be flexed at 20–30° angle when standing with hands on grips
   b. Lift and move walker forward 8–10 inches
   c. With partial or nonweight-bearing put weight on wrists and arms and step forward with affected leg, supporting self on arms, and follow with good leg
   d. Nurse should stand behind client, hold onto gait belt at waist as needed for balance
   e. Sit down by grasping armrest on affected side, shift weight to good leg and hand, lower self into chair
   f. Client should wear sturdy shoes

D. Cane
   1. Types
      a. Straight cane—least stable type
      b. Quad cane—has four legs, provides more stability

   2. Guideline for use
      a. Tip should have concentric rubber rings as shock absorber and to provide optimal stability
      b. Flex elbow 30° angle and hold handle; tip of cane should be 15 cm lateral to the base of the fifth toe
      c. Hold cane in hand opposite affected extremity
      d. Advance cane and affected leg
      e. Lean on cane when moving good leg
      f. To go up and down stairs, step up on good extremity, then place cane and affected extremity on step; reverse when going down ("up with the good, down with the bad")

E.  Lift (Hoyer)

    1.  Used for clients who cannot help themselves and/or are too heavy for safe lifting by others

    2.  Mechanically operated metal frame with a sling usually made of canvas straps

    3.  Lock the bed; raise the bed to promote the use of good body mechanics by the nurse

    4.  Center canvas straps under client by rolling client side to side, one under the shoulders and one under the knees

    5.  Widen base-adjusting lever and lock

    6.  Position lift base under bed and center lift arm over the canvas sling; lock lift wheels

    7.  While holding onto arm, release valve to lower arm enough to attach sling

    8.  Attach sling to overhead arm using hook facing away from client

    9.  The shorter arm of the sling goes under the client's back; client should be centered in sling

    10.  Instruct client to cross arms over chest and lock lift wheels

    11.  Close release valve and pump using long, slow, even strokes; then unlock lift wheels

    12.  One person guides lift, second person lifts legs off the bed and steadies the sling

    13.  Position wheelchair between lift base legs; lock legs and lift wheels

    14.  One person slowly releases valve to lower arm while second person guides client into wheelchair

F.  Sliding board

    1.  Place wheelchair close to bed, lock wheels, lock the bed

    2.  Remove arm rest from wheelchair

    3.  Powder the sliding board

    4.  Place one end of sliding board under client's buttocks; the other end on the surface of the wheelchair

    5.  Instruct client to push up with hands to shift buttocks, and then slide across board to wheelchair

    6.  Assist client to slide gently off the bed

G.  Adaptive devices

    1.  Buttonhook—threaded through buttonhole to assist with buttoning shirts

    2.  Extended shoe horn—can also be used to turn light switches on and off from wheelchair

3. Gel pad—placed under plate or items to prevent shifting during use

4. Foam build-ups—applied to eating utensils, pen and pencils, buttonhook

5. Velcro straps—applied to utensils, pen, and pencil to stabilize in hand

6. Long-handled reacher—assists to obtain objects from high or low location

## HERNIATED INTERVERTEBRAL DISK

**A.** Data Collection

  1. Low back pain (knifelike)

  2. Lack of muscle tone

  3. Poor posture or body mechanics

  4. Sensory changes

**B.** Diagnose

  1. Diagnostic procedures
      a. Computerized tomography
      b. Magnetic resonance imaging
      c. Myelography—encourage fluids, keep head of bed elevated 30° to reduce risk of seizures
      d. Diskogram

  2. Surgical procedures
      a. Laminectomy—excision of a portion of the lamina to expose the affected disk for removal
      b. Laminectomy with fusion—involves several disks; operation includes use of bone graft to strengthen the weakened vertebral column
      c. Minimally invasive surgery; microdiskectomy
      d. Interbody cage fusion

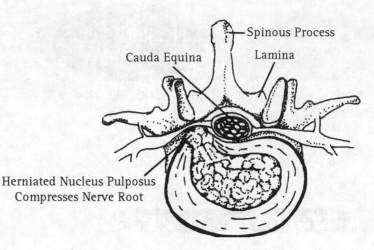

**Figure 1. Herniated Intervertebral Disk**

**C.** Plan/Implementation

1. Preoperative
   a. Apply moist heat
   b. Put client in Fowler's position with moderate hip and knee flexion
   c. Use firm mattress, bedboard, or floor for back support
   d. Isometric exercises for abdominal muscles
   e. Daily exercise program
   f. Assist with exercises initiated in physical therapy
   g. Medications—muscle relaxants, NSAIDs, analgesics
   h. Traction—separates vertebrae to relieve pressure on nerve
   i. TENS (transcutaneous electrical nerve stimulation)

2. Postoperative
   a. Maintain body alignment
   b. Log-roll every two hours with pillow between legs
   c. Calf exercises
   d. Determine sensation and circulatory status, especially of lower extremities
   e. Monitor elimination
   f. Assist with ambulation
   g. Support neck after cervical laminectomy
   h. Straight back during ambulation

3. Reinforce client teaching
   a. Exercise daily but avoid strenuous exercises
   b. Correct posture at all times
   c. Avoid prolonged sitting, standing, walking, driving
   d. Rest at intervals
   e. Use hardboard or firm mattress for bed
   f. Avoid prone position
   g. Avoid straining or lifting heavy objects

## DEVELOPMENTAL DYSPLASIA OF THE HIP (DDH)

**A.** Data Collection

1. Uneven gluteal folds and thigh creases (deeper on affected side)
   (see Figure 2)

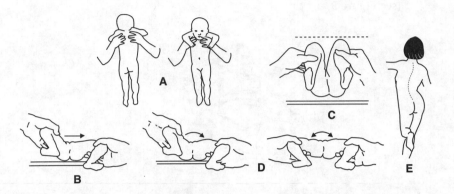

**Figure 2. Congenital Hip Dislocation**

2. Limited abduction of hip with pain

3. Ortolani's sign (seen in infants less than 4 weeks old) (see Figure 2)
   a. Place infant on back, leg flexed
   b. Click sound heard when affected hip is moved to abduction

4. Shortened limb on affected side in older infant and child

5. Delays in walking; limp, lordosis, and waddling gait with older child

**B.** Diagnose

1. Predisposition
   a. Intrauterine position (breech)
   b. Gender (female)
   c. Hormonal imbalance (estrogen)
   d. Cultural and environmental influences—some cultures carry their
      children straddled against the hip joint, causing a decreased
      incidence (Far Eastern and African); cultures that wrap infants
      tightly in blankets or strap to boards have high incidence (Navajo
      Indian)

2. Definition—acetabulum unable to hold head of femur

3. Confirmed by x-ray

4. Potential nursing diagnoses
   a. Physical mobility, impaired
   b. Body image disturbance
   c. Injury, risk for

**C.** Plan/Implementation

1. Newborn to 6 months (intervention varies with age and extent)
   a. Reduced by manipulation
   b. Splinted with proximal femur centered in the acetabulum in position of flexion
   c. Pavlik harness—worn full-time for 3–6 months until hip stable (see Figure 3)

**Figure 3. Pavlik Harness**

   d. Encourage normal growth and development by allowing child to perform appropriate activities
   e. Tell parents to move child from one room to another for environmental change
   f. Discuss modification in bathing, dressing, and diapering with parents
      1) Since harness is not to be removed, sponge bath is recommended
      2) Put undershirt under chest straps and knee sox under foot and leg pieces to prevent skin irritation
      3) Check skin areas 2–3 times a day
      4) Gently massage skin under straps daily to stimulate circulation
      5) Avoid use of lotions and powders
      6) Place diapers under straps
      7) Pad shoulder straps as needed

**Figure 4. Hip Spica Cast**

g. Tell parents to touch and hold child to express affection and reinforce security

2. 6–18 months
   a. Gradual reduction by traction (bilateral Bryant's traction)
   b. Cast for immobilization

3. Older Child
   a. Preliminary traction
   b. Open reduction
   c. Hip spica cast (see Figure 4)

## SCOLIOSIS

A. Data Collection (see Figure 5)

1. Poor posture

2. Uneven hips or scapulae

3. Kyphosis lump on back

4. Uneven waistline

5. Visualization of deformity—bend at waist 90°

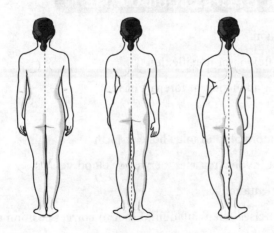

**Figure 5. Scoliosis**

B. Diagnose

1. Definition—lateral deviation of one or more vertebrae commonly accompanied by rotary motion

2. Types
   a. Functional—flexible deviation that corrects by bending
   b. Structural—permanent, hereditary deviation

3. Potential nursing diagnoses
   a. Disturbed body image
   b. Deficient knowledge
   c. Ineffective therapeutic regimen management
   d. Impaired physical mobility

**C.** Plan/Implementation

1. Exercise for functional type—teach isometric exercises to strengthen the abdominal muscles
   a. Sit-ups
   b. Pelvic tilt
   c. Push-ups with pelvic tilt

2. Electrostimulation

3. Surgery—spinal fusion with Harrington rod insertion; Dwyer instrumentation with anterior spinal fusion

4. Thoracolumbosacral orthotic (TLSO) brace
   a. Effective for 30-40 degree curves not associated with extreme deformity
   b. Underarm orthosis made of plastic custom molded to the body and shaped to correct or hold the deformity
   c. Wear for 23 hours—removed 1 hour for personal hygiene
   d. Wear protective shirt under brace
   e. Skin care to pressure areas
   f. Reinforce teaching isometric exercises to strengthen abdominal muscles

## CLUB FOOT (TALIPES EQUINOVARUS)

**A.** Data Collection

1. Plantar flexion or dorsiflexion

2. Inversion/adduction of forepart of foot

**B.** Diagnose

1. Rigid abnormality of talus bone at birth

2. Does not involve muscles, nerves, or blood vessels

**C.** Plan/Implementation

1. Foot exercises—manipulation of foot to correct position every 4 hours regularly

2. Casts and splints correct the deformity in most cases if applied early (see Figure 6); changed every few days for 1–2 weeks, then at 1–2-week intervals to accommodate infant's rapid growth

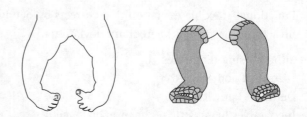

**Figure 6.  Casting of Talipes Equinovarus**

3. Surgery is usually required for older child

4. Denis-Browne—horizontal abduction bar with footplates

## JOINT DISORDERS

**A.** Data Collection (see Table 1)

**B.** Diagnose (see Table 1)
1. Risk factors
    a. Osteoarthritis
        1) Increased age
        2) Obesity
        3) Trauma to joints due to repetitive use
            a) Carpet installer
            b) Construction worker
            c) Farmer
            d) Sports injuries
    b. Rheumatoid arthritis
        1) Positive family history
    c. Gout
        1) Obesity
        2) Diuretics
        3) Family history

2. Diagnostic tests
    a. Arthrocentesis—needle puncture of a joint space to remove accumulated fluid
        1) Strict asepsis is essential to avoid infection
        2) Usually elastic bandage wrap and joint rest for 24 hours to prevent hemorrhage
    b. Arthroscopy—direct visualization of a joint by use of arthroscope
        1) Local anesthesia given
        2) Teach breathing exercises to reduce discomfort
        3) Post-test bulky pressure dressing applied

3. Potential nursing diagnoses
    a  Acute/chronic pain
    b. Impaired physical mobility
    c. Self-care deficit
    d. Disturbed body image
    e. Ineffective role performance

**C.** Plan/Implementation
1. Nursing care (see Table 1)
2. Medications:  analgesics, anti-inflammatory meds

Table 1

| JOINT DISORDERS | | | | |
|---|---|---|---|---|
| **TYPE** | **DATA** | **DIAGNOSE** | **DIAGNOSTIC TESTS** | **NURSING CONSIDERATIONS** |
| Rheumatoid arthritis Juvenile rheumatoid arthritis (JRA) | Joint pain, swelling, and limitation of movement Contracture deformities Nodules over bony prominences Ulnar deviation High fever and rheumatoid rash, particularly seen in JRA Salmon-pink macular rash on chest, thighs, and upper arms | Systemic; pannus formation Bony ankylosis Progressive Remissions and exacerbations | Rheumatoid factor (may be negative) C-reactive protein ESR, ANA Aspiration of synovial fluid X-rays | Pain management, rest, activity, exercise Weight control if obese Heat (e.g., warm tub baths; warm, moist compresses; paraffin dips) Splints for joints Analgesics, anti-inflammatory drugs Disease-modifying antirheumatic drugs Immunosuppressive drugs Antitumor necrosis drugs |
| Osteoarthritis | Joint pain, swelling, and limitation of movement Contracture deformities Joint stiffness after rest Heberden's nodes of fingers and Bouchard's nodes of hand | Nonsystemic; spur formation; closure of joint spaces Degenerative No remissions | X-rays of joints show narrowing of joint spaces | Pain management, rest, activity, exercise Weight control if obese Analgesics, anti-inflammatory drugs Heat application |
| Gout | Joint pain, swelling, limitation of movement Contracture deformities Tophi | Nonsystemic Disturbed purine metabolism Elevated uric acid in blood Tophi formation (deposits of urates in joints) Exacerbations | X-rays Blood tests—WBC, ESR, uric acid level Synovial aspiration | Pain management Diet: avoid meats rich in purines (e.g., organ meats, sardines, fish), alcohol, ketoacidosis, dehydration Analgesics—aspirin Medications for gout |

## PAGET'S DISEASE

**A.** Data Collection

1. Pain

2. Bowed legs, decreased height

3. Shortened trunk with long-appearing arms

4. Enlarged skull

5. Labored, waddling gait

6. Kyphosis

7. Pathologic fractures

**B.** Diagnose

1. Unknown etiology

2. Excessive bone resorption (loss)

3. Occurs more often in older adults

**C.** Plan/Implementation

1. Administer analgesics

2. Encourage rest

3. Prevent pathological fractures by using safety precautions

4. Administer medications: calcitonin, biphosphonates, e.g., alendronate, pamidronate

## BURSITIS

A. Data Collection

1. Pain due to inflammation

2. Decreased mobility, especially on abduction

B. Diagnose

1. Definition—inflammation of connective tissue sac between muscles, tendons, and bones, particularly affecting shoulder, elbow, and knee

2. Potential nursing diagnoses
   a. Acute/chronic pain
   b. Impaired physical mobility
   c. Self-care deficit

C. Plan/Implementation

1. Rest

2. Immobilize affected joint with pillows, splints, slings

3. Administer pain medication, muscle relaxants, steroids

4. Apply heat/cold packs to decrease swelling

5. Promote exercise (ROM)

6. Assist in performance of ADL by modifying activities relative to limitations

7. Assist with cortisone injection, draining of bursae

## OSTEOPOROSIS

A. Data Collection

1. Decreased height

2. Low back pain, especially hips and spine

3. Kyphosis

B. Diagnose

1. Reduction in bone mass with no changes in mineral composition

2. Degenerative disease characterized by generalized loss of bone density and tensile strength

3. Diagnosed by bone mineral density (BMD) T-scores—BMD T-score less than or equal to 2.5 indicates osteoporosis

4. Risk factors
   a. Age greater than 60 years
   b. Small-framed and lean body build
   c. Caucasian or Asian race
   d. Inadequate intake of calcium or vitamin D

     e. Postmenopausal

     f. Immobility

     g. History of smoking

     h. High alcohol intake

     i. Prolonged use of steroids

  5. Potential nursing diagnoses

     a. Acute/chronic pain

     b. Self-care deficit

     c. Risk for trauma

**C.** Plan/Implementation

  1. Diet high in calcium, protein, and vitamin D

  2. Teach about medications

  3. Encourage weight-bearing on the long bones (walking)

  4. ROM exercises

  5. Physiotherapy

  6. Safety precautions to prevent pathological fractures

     a. Use back brace or splint for support

     b. Use bedboards or hard mattress

  7. Administer medications: calcitonin (Miacalcin); biphosphonates, e.g., alendronate; selective receptor modulators, e.g., raloxifene; estrogen replacement therapy

## OSTEOMYELITIS

**A.** Data Collection

  1. Pain

  2. Swelling, redness, warmth on affected area

  3. Fever, leukocytosis

  4. Elevated sedimentation rate

  5. Positive culture and sensitivity

  6. X-ray of affected part

**B.** Diagnose

  1. Infection of the bone caused by *Staphylococcus aureus*, carried by the blood from a primary site of infection or from direct invasion, e.g., orthopedic procedures or fractures

  2. Risk factors

     a. Poorly nourished

     b. Elderly

     c. Obesity

     d. Impaired immune system

     e. Long-term corticosteroid therapy

3. Potential nursing diagnoses
   a. Acute pain
   b. Ineffective tissue perfusion
   c. Risk for injury
   d. Deficient knowledge

**C.** Plan/Implementation

1. Teach about risk factors for osteomyelitis; e.g. joint prosthesis

2. Medications: analgesics, antibiotics, antipyretics

3. Support affected extremity with pillows, splints to maintain proper body alignment

4. Provide cool environment and lightweight clothing

5. Avoid exercise and heat application to the affected area

6. Encourage fluid intake, monitor intake and output

7. Asepsis with wound care

8. Provide diversionary activities

9. High-protein diet with sufficient carbohydrates, vitamins, and minerals

10. Reinforce instruction about wound care and antibiotic administration

## OSTEOMALACIA

**A.** Data Collection

1. Bone pain and tenderness

2. Muscle weakness

3. Bowed legs, kyphosis

4. X-ray (porous bones)

**B.** Diagnose

1. Decalcification of bones due to inadequate intake of vitamin D, absence of exposure to sunlight, or intestinal malabsorption

2. Potential nursing diagnoses
   a. Injury, risk for
   d. Body image disturbance

**C.** Plan/Implementation

1. Administration of analgesics

2. Increase sun exposure

3. Reinforce about vitamin D foods (milk, eggs, vitamin D enriched cereals and bread products)

4. Administer vitamin D, calcium, and expose to sunlight and/or ultraviolet irradiation

5. Assist with performance of ADL to prevent pathological fractures

## SPINA BIFIDA/NEURAL TUBE DEFECTS

**A.** Data Collection (see Figure 7)

1. Dimpling at the site (spina bifida occulta)

2. Bulging, saclike lesion filled with spinal fluid and covered with a thin, atrophic, bluish, ulcerated skin (meningocele)

3. Bulging, saclike lesion filled with spinal fluid and spinal cord element (myelomeningocele)

4. Hydrocephalus increases risk

5. Paralysis of lower extremities

6. Musculoskeletal deformities—club feet, dislocated hips, kyphosis, scoliosis

7. Neurogenic bladder and bowel, prolapsed rectum

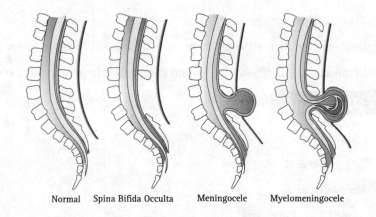

Normal    Spina Bifida Occulta    Meningocele    Myelomeningocele

**Figure 7.  Types of Spina Bifida**

**B.** Diagnose

1. Congenital anomaly of the spinal cord characterized by nonunion between the laminae of the vertebrae

2. Risk factors
   a. Maternal folic-acid deficiency
   b. Previous pregnancy affected by neural tube defect

3. Etiology
   a. Combination of unknown genetic/environmental factors
   b. Advanced maternal age
   c. High levels of alpha-fetoprotein at amniocentesis

**C.** Plan/Implementation

1. Occulta:  no treatment

2. Meningocele/myelomeningocele:  surgical repair at 24–48 hours

3. Observe for irritation, CSF leakage and signs of infection, hydrocephalus

4. Maintain optimum asepsis; cover lesion with moist sterile dressings

5. Position client on abdomen or semiprone with sandbags

6. Provide optimum skin care, especially to perineal area

7. Check for abnormal movement of extremities, absent or abnormal reflexes, incontinence, fecal impaction, flaccid paralysis of lower extremities

8. Observe for increased intracranial pressure (headache, changes in LOC, motor functions, and vital signs)

9. Observe for symptoms of meningeal irritation or meningitis

10. Provide frequent sources of stimulation appropriate for child's age level

11. Provide postoperative care—vertebral fusion or surgical repair

12. Focus postoperative observation on detecting signs of meningitis, shock, increased intracranial pressure, and respiratory difficulty

13. Foster parental bonding

14. Reinforce family teaching on how to care for child at home

15. Discuss with family referrals for PT, orthopedic procedures, bladder and bowel management

## HYDROCEPHALUS

A. Data Collection

1. Fronto-occipital circumference increases at abnormally fast rate (see Figure 8)

2. Split sutures and widened distended, tense fontanelles

3. Prominent forehead, dilated scalp veins

4. Sunset eyes, nystagmus

5. Irritability, vomiting

6. Unusual sleepiness

7. Convulsions

8. High-pitched cry

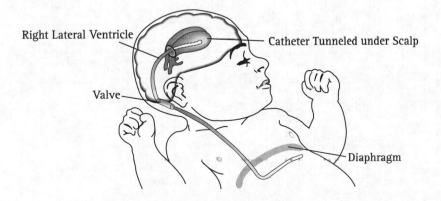

**Figure 8. Ventriculoperitoneal Shunt for Hydrocephalus**

B. Diagnose

1. Congenital or acquired condition characterized by an increase in the accumulation of CSF within the ventricular system and subsequent increase in ventricular pressure

2. Causes
   a. Neoplasm
   b. Aqueductal stenosis—stenosis/obstructions in ventricular system
   c. Spina bifida
   d. Congenital cysts/vascular malformations

3. Types
   a. Communicating—due to increased production of CSF or impaired absorption of CSF
   b. Noncommunicating—due to obstruction/blockage of CSF circulation between ventricles and subarachnoid space

C. Plan/Implementation

1. Operative management
   a. Ventriculoperitoneal shunt—connection between ventricles and peritoneal cavity (see Figure 8)
   b. Ventricular atrial shunt—connection between ventricles and right atrium
   c. Ventricular drainage—provides external drainage of fluid

2. Observation of shunt functioning

3. Observe for increased intracranial pressure and for signs of shunt infection (irritability, high pitched cry, lethargy)

4. Postoperative positioning-on unoperated side in flat position; do not hold infant with head elevated

5. Shunt needs to be modified as child grows

6. Continual testing for developmental abnormalities/intellectual delay

7. Assist with discharge planning/community referral

## NEUROMUSCULAR DISORDERS

**A.** Data Collection (see Table 2)

**B.** Diagnose (see Table 2)

Table 2 ●

| NEUROMUSCULAR DISORDERS | | |
|---|---|---|
| | **CEREBRAL PALSY** | **MUSCULAR DYSTROPHY** |
| **Data** | Athetosis, spasticity, rigidity, ataxia, atonicity; repetitive, involuntary, slow, gross movements<br>Neonate: cannot hold head up, feeble cry, inability to feed, body noticeably arched or limp<br>Infant: failure-to-thrive syndrome<br>Toddler/preschooler: intellectual delay, delayed physical development | Muscle weakness, lordosis/scoliosis, waddling gait, joint contractures<br>Stumbling and falling |
| **Analysis** | Voluntary muscles poorly controlled due to brain damage<br>Etiology: unclear<br>Predisposition: prematurity, existing prenatal brain abnormalities, trauma, anoxia, or infection at time of birth<br>Treatment: ambulation devices, surgical lengthening of heel cord to promote stability and function<br>Medications: muscle relaxants, tranquilizers, anticonvulsants baclofen intrathecal pump | Progressive muscular weakness, atrophy of voluntary muscles, no nerve effect<br>Etiology: genetic<br>Diagnostic tests:<br>  CPK (creatinine phosphokinase), abnormal electromyogram, abnormal muscle biopsy<br>Predisposition: heredity<br>Progressive/terminal<br>Treatment: intensive physical therapy, active and passive stretching and ROM<br>Light spinal braces or long leg braces may help ambulation |
| **Potential nursing diagnosis** | Nutrition: less than body requirements<br>Compromised family coping<br>Self-care deficit<br>Impaired physical mobility<br>Delayed growth and development | Self-care deficit<br>Compromised family coping<br>Body image disturbance<br>Impaired physical mobility<br>Ineffective breathing pattern<br>Impaired swallowing<br>Delayed growth and development |

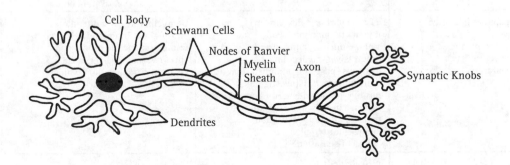

**Figure 9. Anatomy and Physiology of the Neuron**

C. Plan/Implementation

1. Cerebral palsy
   a. Assist with early diagnosis
   b. Assist with physical and occupational therapy
   c. Give referrals to appropriate agencies
   d. Provide emotional support to parents and client
   e. Assist with feeding, place food at back of mouth or on either side of tongue toward cheek, apply slight downward pressure with the spoon
   f. Never tilt head backward when feeding (leads to choking)
   g. High-calorie diet

2. Muscular dystrophy
   a. Promote safety to avoid slips and falls due to gait and movement disturbances; use braces or wheelchair
   b. Assist with diagnostic tests
   c. Client/parent education on nature of the disease
   d. Provide emotional support to child and family
   e. Discuss balance between activity and rest for the child
   f. Prevent contractures
   g. Referrals to appropriate agencies

## DISTURBED TRANSMISSION OF NERVE IMPULSES

A. Data Collection (see Table 3)

B. Diagnose (see Table 3)

Table 3

| DISORDERS OF NERVE IMPULSE TRANSMISSION | | | |
|---|---|---|---|
| | **PARKINSON'S DISEASE** | **MYASTHENIA GRAVIS** | **MULTIPLE SCLEROSIS** |
| **Data** | Tremors (pill-rolling motion), akinesia (loss of automation), rigidity, weakness<br>"Motorized" propulsive gait, slurred monotonous speech, dysphagia<br>Salivation, masklike expression, drooling<br>Constipation<br>Depression<br>Dementia | Muscular weakness produced by repeated movements soon disappears following rest<br>Diplopia, ptosis, impaired speech, dysphagia<br>Respiratory distress<br>Periods of remissions and exacerbations | Early—vision, motor sensation changes<br>Late—cognitive and bowel changes<br>Muscular incoordination, ataxia, spasticity, intention tremors, nystagmus, chewing and swallowing difficulties, impaired speech<br>Incontinence, emotional instability, sexual dysfunction |
| **Analysis** | Deficiency of dopamine; increased acetylcholine levels<br>Etiology unclear; chronic and progressive; intellect intact<br>Does not lead to paralysis | Deficiency of acetylcholine at myoneural junction<br>Etiology unclear; chronic and progressive; intellect intact<br>Diagnosis—based on administration of anticholinesterase (neostigmine); positive result evidenced by a striking increase in muscular strength 5-10 minutes after administration<br>No muscular atrophy<br>No loss of sensation | Demyelination of white matter throughout brain and spinal cord<br>Etiology unclear; chronic and progressive; intellect intact<br>Leads to paraplegia or complete paralysis |
| **Nursing diagnosis** | Self-care deficit<br>Nutrition, altered<br>Body image disturbance<br>Caregiver rule strain<br>Communication, impaired verbal<br>Impaired walking<br>Impaired swallowing | Self-care deficit<br>Airway clearance, ineffective<br>Physical mobility, impaired<br>Impaired swallowing<br>Anxiety/fear | Self-care deficit<br>Nutrition, altered<br>Urinary elimination, altered<br>Physical mobility, impaired<br>Fatigue<br>Disturbed Visual, Kinesthetic, Tactile, Sensory Perception<br>Powerlessness<br>Compromised/Disabled Family Coping |

**C.** Plan/Implementation

1. Parkinson's disease
    a. Encourage finger exercises, e.g., typing, piano-playing
    b. ROM as appropriate
    c. Reinforce teaching of client ambulation modification, refer to physical therapy
        1) Goose-stepping walk
        2) Walk with wider base
        3) Concentrate on swinging arms while walking
        4) Turn around slowly using small steps
    d. Promote family understanding of the disease
        1) Client's intellect is not impaired
        2) Sight and hearing are intact
        3) Disease is progressive but slow
        4) Does not lead to paralysis
    e. Refer for speech therapy, potential stereotactic surgery
    f. Administer dopaminergics (levodopa-carbidopa); dopamine agonists (pramipexole); anticholinergics (benztropine); antivirals (amantadine)

2. Myasthenia gravis
    a. Promote family understanding of the disease
        1) It is neither a central nervous system nor a peripheral nervous system disease
        2) There is no muscular atrophy or loss of sensation
        3) It is not hereditary
    b. Administer medications
        1) Anticholinesterases
        2) Corticosteroids
        3) Immunosuppressants
    c. Good eye care
    d. Maintain optimal mobility
    e. Provide environment that is restful and free of stress
    f. Reinforce client teaching
        1) Importance of taking medications on time; dosage depends on physiological needs and living patterns
        2) Wear Medic-Alert band
        3) Avoid factors that may precipitate myasthenia crisis, e.g., infections, emotional upsets, use of streptomycin or neomycin (they produce muscular weakness), surgery
        4) Be alert for myasthenia crisis—sudden inability to swallow, speak, or maintain a patent airway

3. Multiple sclerosis (MS)
    a. Reinforce relaxation and coordination exercises
    b. Progressive resistance exercises, ROM
    c. Warm baths and packs
    d. Administer medications–immunosuppressants; corticosteroids; antispasmodics; interferon beta-1a; monoclonal antibodies
    e. Wide-based walk, use of cane or walker

f. Use weighted bracelets and cuffs to stabilize upper extremities

g. Bladder and bowel training (care of Foley catheter if appropriate)

h. Self-help devices

i. Eye patch for diplopia

j. No tetracycline or neomycin because they increase muscle weakness with MS

k. Occupational therapy

l. Provide emotional support

m. Referrals—National Multiple Sclerosis Society

## AMYOTROPHIC LATERAL SCLEROSIS (LOU GEHRIG'S DISEASE)

**A.** Data Collection

1. Tongue fatigue, atrophy with fasciculations (brief muscle twitching)

2. Nasal quality to speech, dysarthria

3. Dysphagia, aspiration

4. Progressive muscular wasting, atrophy, spasticity, weakness
   a. Usually begins in upper extremities
   b. Distal portion affected first
   c. Fasciculations

5. Emotional lability, cognitive dysfunction

6. Respiratory insufficiency (usual cause of death)

7. No alteration in autonomic, sensory, or mental function

**B.** Diagnose

1. Progressive, degenerative disease involving the lower motor neurons of the spinal cord and cerebral cortex; the voluntary motor system is particularly involved with progressive degeneration of the corticospinal tract, leads to a mixture of spastic and atrophic changes in cranial and spinal musculature

2. No specific pattern exists—involvement may vary in different parts of the same area

3. Possible etiologies
   a. Genetic, familial
   b. Chronic (slow) viral infection
   c. Autoimmune disease
   d. Toxic, metabolic

**C.** Plan/Implementation

1. Apply principles of care of client with progressive, terminal disease

2. Treat self-care deficits symptomatically

3. Maintain adequate nutrition

4. Physical therapy

5. Adaptive home equipment

6. Provide psychosocial support

**PHYSIOLOGICAL INTEGRITY 1**

UNIT 3  **INTERVENTIONS TO PROMOTE COMFORT**

[BASIC CARE AND COMFORT]

**PAIN**

**A.** Data Collection

1. The fifth vital sign
2. History
   a. P–precipitating factors
   b. Q–quality
   c. R–region/radiation
   d. S–severity
   e. T–timing

3. Potential responses to pain (see Table 1)

●Table 1

| POTENTIAL RESPONSES TO PAIN | |
|---|---|
| **DATA COLLECTION** | **RESULT** |
| Increased BP and heart rate leads to increased blood flow to brain and muscles Rapid, irregular respirations leads to increased $O_2$ supply to brain and muscles | Enhanced alertness to threats Preoccupation with painful stimulus |
| Increased pupillary diameter leads to increased eye accommodation to light | Increased visual perception of threats |
| Increased perspiration | Removal of excess body heat |
| Increased muscle tension leads to increased neuromuscular activity | Musculoskeletal system ready for rapid motor activity and responsiveness |
| Altered GI motility leads to nausea and vomiting | Altered metabolic processes |
| Apprehension, irritability, and anxiety Verbalizes pain | Enhanced mental alertness to threats Communication of suffering and pleas for help |

**B.** Diagnose

1. Definition—"Whatever the person says it is, and it exists whenever the person says it does"

2. Types
   a. Acute—an episode of pain that lasts from a split second to about 6 months; causes decreased healing, vital sign changes, diaphoresis
   b. Chronic—an episode of pain that lasts for 6 months or longer; causes fatigue, depression, weight gain, immobility

3. Factors influencing pain experiences
   a. Individual's responses or reactions to pain are generally dependent on what is expected and accepted in his/her culture
   b. Past experiences with pain generally make the individual more sensitive to the pain experience

4. Potential nursing diagnoses
   a. Acute/chronic pain
   b. Activity intolerance
   c. Ineffective therapeutic regimen management
   d. Readiness for enhanced comfort
   e. Social isolation
   f. Imbalanced nutrition: less than body requirements

C. Plan/Implementation

1. Establish a therapeutic relationship
   a. Tell client you believe what he/she says about his/her pain experience
   b. Listen and allow client to verbalize
   c. Allow client to use own words in describing pain experience

2. Establish a 24-hour pain profile
   a. Location
      1) External
      2) Internal
      3) Both external and internal
      4) Area of body affected
   b. Character and intensity
      1) Acute/chronic
      2) Mild/severe
   c. Onset
      1) Sudden
      2) Gradual
   d. Duration
   e. Precipitating factors
   f. Identify associated manifestations, as well as alleviating or aggravating factors

3. Reinforce client teaching about pain and its relief
   a. Explain quality and location of impending pain, (e.g., before uncomfortable procedure)
   b. Help client learn to use slow, rhythmic breathing to promote relaxation
   c. Explain effects of analgesics and benefits of preventative approach
   d. Demonstrate splinting techniques that help reduce pain

4. Reduce anxiety and fears
   a. Give reassurance
   b. Offer distraction
   c. Spend time with client

5. Provide comfort measures
   a. Proper positioning
   b. Cool, well ventilated, quiet room
   c. Back rub
   d. Allow for rest

6. Administer pain medications
   a. Use preventive approach
      1) If pain is expected to occur throughout most of a 24-hour period, a regular schedule is better than prn
      2) Usually takes a smaller dose to alleviate mild pain or prevent occurrence of pain
      3) Pain relief is more complete and client spends fewer hours in pain
      4) Helps prevent addiction
   b. PCA (patient-controlled analgesia) pumps—a portable device that delivers predetermined dosage of intravenous narcotic (e.g., dose of 1 mg morphine with a lock-out interval of 5–15 minutes for a total possible dose of 5 mg per hour)
   c. Non-opioid analgesics
   d. Nonsteroidal anti-inflammatory drugs
   e. Opioids
   f. Anticonvulsants
   g. Alpha-2 adrenergics

7. Other methods of pain relief
   a. Neurectomy/sympathectomy
   b. TENS (transcutaneous electric nerve stimulation)—produces tingling, buzzing sensation in area of pain; used for chronic and acute pain

8. Complementary and alternative methods of pain control
   a. Relaxation
   b. Meditation
   c. Progressive relaxation
   d. Yoga/exercise
   e. Distraction
   f. Imagery
   g. Herbal remedies
   h. Biofeedback
   i. Acupuncture
   j. Heat/cold application
   k. Therapeutic touch; consider cultural factors
   l. Massage
   m. Hypnosis

## CONTUSIONS, SPRAINS, JOINT DISLOCATIONS

**A.** Data Collection

1. Contusions
   a. Ecchymosis
   b. Hematoma

2. Strains/sprains
   a. Pain
   b. Swelling

3. Joint dislocations
   a. Pain
   b. Deformity

**B.** Diagnose

1. Contusions—injury of soft tissue

2. Strains—muscle pull and/or tendon pull or tear

3. Sprains—torn ligament or stretched ligament

4. Dislocation—displacement of joint bones so their articulating surfaces lose all contact

**C.** Plan/Implementation

1. Contusions—treated with cold application for 24 hours followed by moist heat; apply elastic bandage

2. Strains/sprains—treated with rest and elevation of affected part; intermittent ice compresses for 24 hours, followed by heat application; apply elastic pressure bandage; minimize use

3. Dislocations—considered an orthopedic emergency; treated with immobilization and reduction, e.g., the dislocated bone is brought back to its normal position, usually under anesthesia; bandages and splints are used to keep affected part immobile until healing occurs

## FRACTURES

**A.** Data Collection

1. Swelling, pallor, ecchymosis

2. Loss of sensation to body parts

3. Deformity

4. Pain and/or acute tenderness

5. Muscle spasms

6. Loss of function, abnormal mobility

7. Crepitus (grating sound on movement of ends of broken bone)

8. Shortening of affected limb

9. Decreased or absent pulses distal to injury

10. Affected extremity colder than contralateral part

**B.** Diagnose

1. Fractures—break in continuity of bone

2. Types (see Figure 1, panels A–D)

3. Complications of fractures
   a. Fat emboli—caused after fracture of long bones when fat globules move into bloodstream; may occlude major vessels
   b. Hemorrhage
   c. Delayed union—healing of fracture is slowed; caused by infection or distraction of fractured fragments; will see increase in bone pain
   d. Malunion—improper alignment of fracture fragments; may develop with premature weight-bearing
   e. Nonunion—healing has not occurred 4–6 months after fracture; insufficient blood supply, repetitive stress on fracture site, infection, inadequate internal fixation; treated by bone grafting, internal fixation, electric bone stimulation
   f. Sepsis
   g. Compartment syndrome—high pressure within a muscle compartment of an extremity compromises circulation; pressure may be internal (bleeding) or external (casts); if left untreated neuromuscular damage occurs within 4–6 hours; limb can become useless within 24–48 hours; will see unrelenting pain out of proportion to injury and unrelieved by pain medication, decreased pulse strength, possible cyanosis, and pale cool extremity
   h. Peripheral nerve damage

A. Complete: break across entire cross-section of bone

B. Incomplete: break through portion of bone

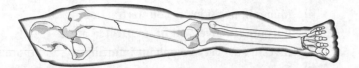

C. Closed: no external communication

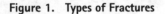

D. Open: extends through skin

**Figure 1.  Types of Fractures**

**C.** Plan/Implementation

1. Provide emergency care
   a. Immobilization before client is moved by use of splints; immobilize joint below and above fracture
   b. In an open fracture, cover the wound with sterile dressings or cleanest material available; control bleeding by direct pressure
   c. Check temperature, color, sensation, capillary refill distal to fracture
   d. Emergency room—give narcotic adequate to relieve pain (except in presence of head injury)

2. Treatment
   a. Splinting—immobilization of the affected part to prevent soft tissue from being damaged by bony fragments
   b. Internal fixation—use of metal screws, plates, nails, and pins to stabilize reduced fracture
   c. Open reduction—surgical dissection and exposure of the fracture for reduction and alignment
   d. Closed reduction—manual manipulation or traction of fracture

3. Traction (see Figures 2–6)
   a. Purposes
      1) Reduce the fracture
      2) Alleviate pain and muscle spasm
      3) Prevent or correct deformities
      4) Promote healing
   b. Types of traction
      1) Skin (Buck's extension, Russell's, pelvic traction)—
         pulling force applied to skin
      2) Skeletal (halo, Crutchfield tongs)—pulling force applied to bone
   c. Care
      1) Maintain straight alignment of ropes and pulleys
      2) Assure that weights hang free
      3) Frequently inspect skin for breakdown areas
      4) Maintain position for countertraction
      5) Encourage movement of unaffected areas
      6) Investigate every complaint immediately and thoroughly
      7) Maintain continuous pull
      8) Clean pins with half-strength peroxide or saline and sterile
         swabs 1–2 times a day, if ordered

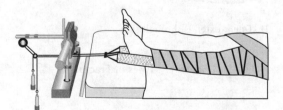

**Figure 2.  Buck's Traction**

Relieves muscular spasm of legs and back; if no fracture, may turn to either side; with fracture, turn to unaffected side. 8–20 lb used; 40 lb for scoliosis. Elevate foot of bed for countertraction. Use trapeze for moving. Place pillow beneath lower legs, not heel. Don't elevate knee gatch.

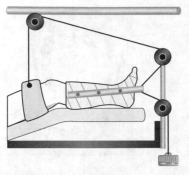

**Figure 3.  Russell's Traction**

"Pulls" contracted muscles; elevate foot of bed with shock blocks to provide countertraction; sling can be loosened for skin care; check popliteal pulse. Place pillows under lower leg. Make sure heel is off the bed. Must not turn from waist down. Lift client, not leg, to provide assistance.

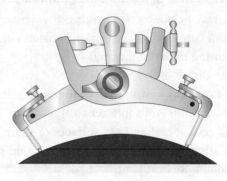

**Figure 4.  Cervical (skull tongs)**

Realigns fracture of cervical vertebrae and relieves pressure on cervical nerve; never lift weights—traction must be continuous. No pillow under the head during feeding; hard to swallow, may need suctioning.

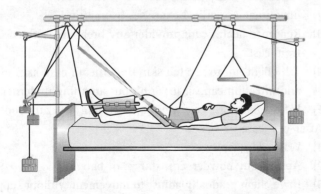

**Figure 5.  Balanced Suspension**

Realigns fractures of the femur; uses pulley to create balanced suspension by countertraction to the top of the thigh splint.  Thomas splint (positioned under anterior thigh) with Pearson attachment (supports leg from knee down) frequently used.

**Figure 6.  Halo Jacket (vest)**

Provides immobilization of cervical spine; pins are used to maintain traction; care of insertional site includes cleansing area around pins using sterile technique. If prescribed by health care provider, clean with half-strength peroxide or saline and sterile swabs 1–2 times/day.

4. Casting—provides rigid immobilization of affected body part for support and stability, may be plaster or fiberglass (lighter weight, stronger, water-resistant, porous; diminishes skin problems, does not soften when wet, thus allowing for hydrotherapy)
   a. Immediate care
      1) Avoid covering cast until dry (48 hours or longer); handle with palms, not fingertips (plaster cast)
      2) Avoid resting cast on hard surfaces or sharp edges
      3) Keep affected limb elevated above heart on soft surface until dry; don't use heat lamp
      4) Watch for danger signs, e.g., blueness or paleness, pain, numbness, or tingling sensations on affected area; if present, elevate casted area; if it persists, contact health care provider
      5) Elevate arm cast above level of heart
   b. Intermediate care
      1) When cast is dry, client should be mobilized
      2) Encourage prescribed exercises (isometrics)
      3) Report to health care provider any break in cast or foul odor from cast
      4) Tell client not to scratch skin underneath cast, skin may break and infection can set in; don't put anything underneath cast
      5) If fiberglass cast gets wet, dry with hair dryer on cool setting
   c. After-cast care
      1) Wash skin gently
      2) Apply baby powder, cornstarch, or baby oil
      3) Have client gradually adjust to movement without support of cast
      4) Inform client that swelling is common
      5) Elevate limb and apply elastic bandage
   d. Complications
      1) Impaired circulation
      2) Peripheral nerve damage
      3) Pressure necrosis

## FRACTURED HIP

**A.** Data Collection

1. Leg shortened, adducted, externally rotated

2. Pain

3. Hematoma, ecchymosis

4. Confirmed by x-rays

**B.** Diagnose

1. Commonly seen with elderly women with osteoporosis

2. Potential nursing diagnoses
   a. Impaired physical mobility
   b. Risk for peripheral neurovascular function
   c. Risk for impaired gas exchange
   d. Acute pain

**C.** Plan/Implementation

1. Total hip replacement—acetabulum, cartilage, and head of femur replaced with artificial joint (see Figure 7)

2. Abduction of affected extremity (use splints, wedge pillow, or 2 or 3 pillows between legs)

3. Turn client as ordered; keep heels off bed

4. Ice to operative site

5. Overbed trapeze to lift self onto fracture bedpan

6. Initial ambulation with walker

7. Crutch walking—three-point gait

8. Chair with arms, wheelchair, semireclining toilet seat

9. Medications—anticoagulants to prevent pulmonary embolism, antibiotics to prevent infection

10. Don't sleep on operated side

11. Don't flex hip more than 90°

12. Continuous passive motion device—used after knee replacement to prevent development of scar tissue; extends and flexes knee

13. Prevention of thromboembolism—low molecular weight heparin (LMWH) and warfarin; do not sit for prolonged periods

14. Use adaptive devices for dressing—extended handles, shoe horns

15. Report increased hip pain to health care provider instantly

16. Cleanse incision daily with mild soap and water; dry thoroughly

17. Reinforce teaching—inspect hip daily for redness, heat, drainage; if present, call health care provider immediately

18. Complications
    a. Dislocation of prosthesis
    b. Excessive wound drainage
    c. Thromboembolism
    d. Infection

19. Reinforce postoperative discharge teaching
    a. Maintain abduction
    b. Avoid stooping
    c. Do not sleep on operated side until directed to do so
    d. Flex hip only to 1/4 circle
    e. Never cross legs
    f. Avoid position of flexion during sexual activity
    g. Walking is excellent exercise; avoid overexertion
    h. In 3 months, will be able to resume ADLs, except strenuous sports

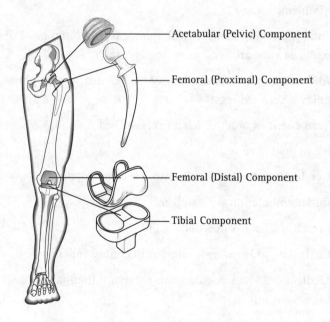

Figure 7. Total Hip and Knee Replacement

## AMPUTATION

**A.** Data Collection

   1. Trauma

   2. Peripheral vascular disease

   3. Osteogenic sarcoma

**B.** Diagnose

   1. Disarticulation—resection of an extremity through a joint

   2. Above-knee amputation (AKA)

   3. Below-knee amputation (BKA)

   4. Guillotine or open surface

   5. Closed or flap

**C.** Plan/Implementation (see Table 1)

   1. Delayed prosthesis fitting—residual limb covered with dressing and elastic bandage or residual limb sock; note if penrose drain is inserted; reapply bandages every 4–6 hours

   2. Immediate prosthesis fitting—residual limb covered with dressing and rigid plastic dressing; Penrose drain usually not inserted; rigid dressing helps prevent bleeding by compressing residual limb

   3. Phantom pain—experienced immediately postop up to 2–3 months postop; occurs more frequently in AK amputations; feeling that extremity is crushed, cramped, or twisted into abnormal position; may be intense burning or cramping
     a. Acknowledge feelings
     b. Early intensive rehabilitation
     c. Residual limb desensitization with kneading massage
     d. Distraction and activity
     e. TENS (transcutaneous electrical nerve stimulation), ultrasound, local anesthetic
     f. Beta blockers used for dull, burning sensations
     g. Anticonvulsants used for stabbing and cramping sensations
     h. Antidepressants used to improve mood and coping ability
     i. Antispasmodics for muscle spasms or cramping
     j. Complementary and alternative therapies

   4. Promotion of mobility—ROM exercises; trapeze with overhead frame; firm mattress; prone position every 3 hours for 20 to 30 minutes

Table 1

| POST–OPERATIVE AMPUTATION CARE | | |
|---|---|---|
| **TYPE OF CARE** | **DELAYED PROSTHESIS FITTING** | **IMMEDIATE PROSTHESIS FITTING** |
| Residual limb care | Observe dressings for signs of excessive bleeding; keep large tourniquet on hand to apply around residual limb in event of hemorrhage; dressings changed daily until sutures removed; wrap with elastic bandage to shape, reduce edema, and keep dressing in place; figure-eight because it prevents restriction of blood flow | Observe rigid dressing for signs of oozing; if blood stain appears, mark area and observe every 10 minutes for increase; report excessive oozing immediately to health care provider; provide cast care; guard against cast slipping off |
| Positioning | If ordered by health care provider, elevate residual limb by elevating foot of bed to hasten venous return and prevent edema. | Elevation of residual limb for 24 hours usually sufficient; rigid cast acts to control swelling |
| Turning | Turn client to prone position for short time first postop day, then 30 min 3 times daily to prevent hip contracture; have client roll from side to side | Same; rigid cast, however, acts to prevent both hip and joint contractures |
| Exercises | Have client start exercises to prevent contractures 1st or 2nd day postop, including: active range of motion, especially of remaining leg, strengthening exercises for upper extremities, hyperextension of residual limb | Exercises not as essential because rigid dressing prevents contractures; early ambulation prevents immobilization disabilities |
| Ambulation | Dangle and transfer client to wheelchair and back within 1st or 2nd day postop; crutch walking started as soon as client feels sufficiently strong | Dangle and assist client to ambulate with walker for short period 1st day; increase length of ambulation each day; in physical therapy client uses parallel bars, then crutches, then cane |
| Psychological support | Observe for signs of depression or despondency; remind depressed client that he/she will receive prosthesis when wound heals | Observe for signs of depression; clients usually less depressed if they awaken with prosthesis attached |
| Discharge | Teach residual limb care—inspect daily for abrasions, wash, expose to air, do not apply lotions, use only cotton or wool residual limb socks | Same |

## HOSPITALIZED CLIENTS

**A.** Data Collection

1. Restlessness

2. Fatigue

3. Inability to concentrate

4. Irritability

5. Depression

6. Hallucinations after extended periods of sleeplessness

**B.** Diagnose

1. Rest—basic physiological need
   a. Allows body to repair its own damaged cells
   b. Enhances removal of waste products from the body
   c. Restores tissue to maximum functional ability before another activity is begun

2. Sleep—basic physiological need, although the purpose and reason for it is unclear; possible theories include:
   a. To restore balance among different parts of the central nervous system
   b. To mediate stress, anxiety, and tension
   c. To help a person cope with daily activities

3. Causes of disturbances
   a. Stress
   b. Drugs, e.g., hypnotics, barbiturates
   c. Unfamiliar environment

4. Potential nursing diagnoses
   a. Sleep pattern disturbance
   b. Activity intolerance
   c. Injury, risk for

**C.** Plan/Implementation

1. Establish database on client's pattern of rest and sleep

2. Give care in blocks of time to allow uninterrupted periods of rest and sleep

3. Remove unpleasant odors

4. Avoid unnecessary light and noises

5. Avoid excessively warm or cool temperatures

6. Reposition client as appropriate

7. Spend time with client

8. Give unhurried backrub

9. Straighten and replace wrinkled or soiled linens

10. Give warm, nonstimulating beverages

11. Give pain medication—preferable to sleep medications, which interfere with REM stage of sleep

12. Provide diversionary and occupational activities during the day to relieve boredom and utilize nighttime for sleep

13. Listen actively to client's concerns

14. Explain treatments ahead of time

15. Give a thorough orientation to the hospital setting

## ELDERLY CLIENTS

A. Data Collection

1. Difficulty getting to sleep

2. Waking early in the morning

3. Brief periods of wakefulness during the night

B. Diagnose

1. Sleep patterns change with advancing age

2. Levels of deep sleep occur less frequently

C. Plan/Implementation

1. Establish regular schedule for sleeping, go to bed at same time and wake up at same time

2. Avoid caffeinated beverages late in the evening

3. Establish bedtime ritual
   a. Warm bath
   b. Warm milk

4. Exercise regularly

5. If unable to sleep, perform quiet activity or read

6. Bedroom should be well ventilated and humidified

7. Reduce daytime napping and inactivity

8. Evaluate for sleep apnea

9. Evaluate for nocturia

## SLEEP APNEA SYNDROME

**A.** Data Collection

1. Client snores loudly, stops breathing for 10 seconds or more, then awakens abruptly with loud snort; multiple nighttime awakenings

2. Excessive daytime sleepiness

3. Morning headache

4. Sore throat

5. Personality and behavioral changes

6. Dysrhythmias, hypertension, increased risk of stroke, myocardial infarction and heart failure

**B.** Diagnose

1. Occurs in older, overweight men, elderly, people with thick necks, smokers

2. Polysomnography (PSG)—EEG, EMG, ECG, oxygen saturation levels; diaphragmatic movement monitored during sleep

3. Types
   a. Obstructive—lack of airflow due to occlusion of pharynx
   b. Central—cessation of airflow and respiratory movements
   c. Mixed—combination of central and obstructive apnea within an episode

**C.** Plan/Implementation

1. Avoid alcohol and medications that depress upper airway

2. Weight-reduction diet and activity

3. For severe cases, if client is hypoxic and hypercapnic, will use continuous positive airway pressure (CPAP) or bilevel positive airway pressure (BIPAP) with additional oxygen

4. Position-fixing devices used to prevent tongue obstruction and subluxation of neck

5. Surgery to correct obstruction

6. Low-flow oxygen

7. Tracheostomy if life-threatening dysrhythmias are present; unplugged only during sleep

## ALZHEIMER'S DISEASE

**A.** Data Collection

1. Forgetfulness progressing to inability to recognize familiar faces, places, objects

2. Depression, paranoia, combativeness

3. Unable to formulate concepts and think abstractly

4. Impulsive behavior

5. Short attention span

6. Agitation and increase in physical activity

7. Night wandering

8. Inability to perform ADLs (unkempt appearance)

9. Dysphasia

10. Incontinence

**B.** Diagnose

1. Progressive, irreversible, degenerative neurological disease characterized by loss of cognitive function and disturbance in behavior

2. Risk factors
   a. Age
   b. Family history

3. Potential nursing diagnoses
   a. Self-care deficit
   b. Communication, impaired verbal
   c. Incontinence, total

4. Death occurs due to complications
   a. Pneumonia
   b. Malnutrition
   c. Dehydration

**C.** Plan/Implementation

1. Support cognitive function
   a. Provide calm, predictable environment and present change gradually
   b. Establish regular routine
   c. Give clear and simple explanations and repeat information
   d. Display clock and calendar
   e. Color-code objects and areas

2. Provide for safety
   a. Use night light, call light, and low bed with half-bed rails
   b. Allow smoking only with supervision
   c. Monitor medications and food intake
   d. Secure doors leading from house
   e. Gently distract and redirect during wandering behavior
   f. Avoid restraints (increases combativeness)
   g. Client should wear identification bracelet or neck chain
   h. Frequent reorientation

3. Reduce anxiety and agitation
   a. Reinforce positive self-image

    b.  Encourage to enjoy simple activities (e.g., walking, exercising, socializing)

    c.  Keep environment simple, familiar, noise-free

    d.  If client experiences catastrophic reaction (overreaction to excessive stimulation), remain calm and stay with client; provide distraction such as listening to music, rocking, stroking to quiet client

4.  Improve communication

    a.  Reduce noise and distractions

    b.  Use clear, easy-to-understand sentences

    c.  Provide lists and simple written instructions

5.  Promote independence in ADLs

    a.  Organize daily activities into short, achievable steps

    b.  Allow client to make choices when appropriate

    c.  Encourage to participate in self-care activities

6.  Provide for socialization

    a.  Encourage letters, visits (one or two persons at a time), phone calls

    b.  Provide a pet

7.  Promote good nutrition

    a.  Simple, calm environment

    b.  Offer one dish at a time to prevent playing with food

    c.  Cut food into small pieces to prevent choking

    d.  Check temperature of foods to prevent burns

    e.  Use adaptive equipment as needed for feeding self

    f.  Provide apron or smock instead of bib to respect dignity

8.  Promote balance of activity and rest

    a.  Allow client to walk in protected environment

    b.  Provide music, warm milk, back rub to encourage sleep

    c.  Discourage long naps during the day

9.  Provide teaching and support to caregivers

    a.  Refer to Alzheimer's Association, family support groups, respite care, adult day care

10.  Complementary/alternative therapy

    a.  Ginkgo biloba

    b.  Fish high in omega-3 fatty acids

    c.  1000 international units vitamin E twice daily

11.  Administer medications–cholinesterase inhibitors; NMDA-receptor antagonists; antidepressants

## THYROID DISORDERS

**A.**  Data Collection (see Table 1)

**B.**  Diagnose (see Table 1)

**C.**  Plan/Implementation

Table 1

| THYROID DISORDERS | | |
|---|---|---|
| | **MYXEDEMA/HYPOTHYROIDISM** | **GRAVES' DISEASE/HYPERTHYROIDISM** |
| **Data Collection** | Diagnostic tests: ↓ BMR (basal metabolic rate) ↓ T3 ↓ T4 ↑ TSH<br>Decreased activity level<br>Sensitivity to cold<br>Potential alteration in skin integrity<br>Decreased perception of stimuli<br>Obesity, weight gain<br>Potential for respiratory difficulty<br>Constipation<br>Alopecia<br>Bradycardia<br>Dry skin and hair<br>Decreased ability to perspire<br>Reproductive problems | Diagnostic tests: ↑ BMR ↑ T3 ↑ T4 High titer anti-thyroid antibodies<br>Hyperactivity<br>Sensitivity to heat<br>Rest and sleep deprivation<br>Increased perception of stimuli<br>Weight loss<br>Potential for respiratory difficulty<br>Diarrhea<br>Tachycardia<br>Exophthalmus<br>Frequent mood swings<br>Nervous, jittery<br>Fine, soft hair |
| **Analysis** | Hyposecretion of thyroid hormone<br>Slowed physical and mental functions | Hypersecretion of thyroid hormone<br>Accelerated physical and mental functions |
| **Predisposing factors** | Inflammation of thyroid<br>Iatrogenic–thyroidectomy, irradiation, overtreatment with antithyroids<br>Pituitary deficiencies<br>Iodine deficiency<br>Idiopathic | Thyroid-secreting tumors<br>Iatrogenic–overtreatment for hypothyroid<br>Pituitary hyperactivity<br>Severe stress, e.g., pregnancy |
| **Treatment and management** | Hormone replacement | Antithyroid drugs (SSKI methimazole, propylthiouracil)<br>Irradiation ($^{131}$I)<br>Surgery |
| **Potential nursing diagnosis** | Disturbed body image<br>Imbalanced nutrition: more than body requirements<br>Activity intolerance<br>Constipation<br>Hypothermia<br>Deficient knowledge<br>Decreased cardiac output | Activity intolerance<br>Altered body temperature<br>Social interaction, impaired<br>Imbalanced nutrition: less than body requirements<br>Hyperthermia<br>Fatigue<br>Risk for impaired tissue integrity |

1. Myxedema/hypothyroidism
   a. Pace activities
   b. Allow client extra time to think, speak, act
   c. Teaching should be done slowly and in simple terms
   d. Frequent rest periods between activities
   e. Maintain room temperature at approximately 75°F
   f. Provide client with extra clothing and bedding
   g. Restrict use of soaps and apply lanolin or creams to skin
   h. High-protein, low-calorie diet
   i. Small, frequent feedings
   j. Prevent constipation—high-fiber, high-cellulose foods
   k. Increase fluid intake
   l. Cathartics or stool softeners as ordered
   m. Explain to client that symptoms are reversible with treatment
   n. Explain to family that client's behavior is part of the condition and will change when treatment begins
   o. Administer drug replacement therapy

    p. Administer sedatives carefully–risk of respiratory depression

    q. Instruct about causes of myxedema coma (acute illness, surgery, chemotherapy, discontinuation of medication)

2. Graves' disease/hyperthyroidism

    a. Limit activities to quiet ones (e.g., reading, knitting)

    b. Provide for frequent rest periods

    c. Restrict visitors and control choice of roommates

    d. Keep room cool; advise light, cool clothing

    e. Avoid stimulants, (e.g., coffee)

    f. Accept behavior

    g. Use calm, unhurried manner when caring for client

    h. Interpret behavior to family

    i. Administer antithyroid medication, irradiation with $^{131}$I PO (short-term)

    j. Provide post-thyroidectomy care

       1) Low or semi-Fowler's position

       2) Support head, neck, and shoulders to prevent flexion or hyperextension of suture line

       3) Tracheostomy set at bedside

       4) Give fluids as tolerated

       5) Observe for complications

          a) Laryngeal nerve injury–detected by hoarseness

          b) Thyroidtoxicosis–increased temperature and increased pulse, hypertension; treatment–hypothermia blanket, $O_2$, potassium iodine, propylthiouracil (PTU), Inderal, hydrocortisone, acetaminophen; also caused by trauma, infection, palpation, RAI therapy

          c) Hemorrhage; check back of neck for bleeding

          d) Respiratory obstruction

          e) Tetany (decreased calcium from parathyroid involvement)–check Chvostek's and Trousseau's signs

       6) Analgesics, cold steam inhalations for sore throat

       7) Adjust diet to new metabolic needs

    k. Antithyroid medications–methimazole; propylthiouracil; potassium iodide (SSKI); radioactive iodine

## PARATHYROID DISORDERS

A. Data Collection (see Table 2)

B. Diagnose (see Table 2)

C. Plan/Implementation (see Table 2)

Table 2

| PARATHYROID DISORDERS | | |
|---|---|---|
| | **HYPOPARATHYROIDISM** | **HYPERPARATHYROIDISM** |
| **Data Collection** | Tetany<br>Muscular irritability (cramps, spasms)<br>Carpopedal spasm, clonic convulsions<br>Dysphagia<br>Paresthesia, laryngeal spasm<br>Anxiety, depression, irritability<br>Tachycardia<br>+ Chvostek's sign<br>+ Trousseau's sign | Fatigue, muscle weakness<br>Cardiac dysrhythmias<br>Emotional irritability<br>Renal calculi<br>Back and joint pain, pathological fractures<br>Pancreatitis, peptic ulcer |
| **Diagnose** | Decreased secretion of parathyroid hormone<br>Introgenic–post thyroidectomy<br>Hypomagnesemia<br>Diagnostic tests:<br>  Serum calcium ↓<br>  Serum phosphorus ↑<br>  ↓ parathyroid hormone (PTH)<br>  X-ray–bones appear dense | Oversecretion of parathyroid hormone<br>Benign parathyroid tumor<br>Parathyroid carcinoma<br>Neck trauma<br>Neck radiation<br>Diagnostic tests:<br>  ↑ Serum calcium<br>  ↓ Serum phosphorus<br>  X-ray–bones appear porous<br>  ↑ serum parathyroid hormone |
| **Potential nursing diagnosis** | Risk for injury<br>Deficient knowledge | Risk for injury<br>Impaired urinary elimination<br>Nutrition: less than body requirements<br>Constipation |
| **Plan/ Implementation** | Emergency treatment–calcium chloride or gluconate over 10–15 minutes<br>Calcitriol 0.5–2 mg daily for acute hypocalcemia<br>Ergocalciferol 50,000–400,000 units daily<br>Observe for tetany<br>Low-phosphorus, high-calcium diet | Relieve pain<br>Prevent formation of renal calculi increase fluid intake<br>Offer acid-ash juices (improves solubility of calcium)<br>Administer appropriate diet<br>Prevent fractures<br>Safety precautions<br>Monitor potassium levels (counteracts effect of calcium on cardiac muscles)<br>Provide postparathyroidectomy care (essentially same as for thyroidectomy)<br>IV Lasix and saline promote calcium excretion<br>IV phosphorus is used only for rapid lowering of calcium level<br>Surgery–parathyroidectomy |

PHYSIOLOGICAL
INTEGRITY 1

UNIT 6  **NUTRITION**

[BASIC CARE AND COMFORT]

## NUTRITION

**A.** Data Collection

1. Physical signs (see Table 1)

2. Laboratory values: hemoglobin, hematocrit, serum albumin

●**Table 1**

| PHYSICAL SIGNS OF ADEQUATE NUTRITIONAL STATUS | |
|---|---|
| **BODY AREA** | **NORMAL APPEARANCE** |
| Hair | Shiny, firm, intact scalp without areas of pigmentation |
| Teeth | Evenly spaced, straight, no cavities, shiny |
| Tongue | Deep red in color |
| Gums | Firm, without redness, even-colored |
| Skin | Smooth, moist, even shading |
| Nails | Firm, without ridges |
| Extremities | Full range of motion |
| Abdomen | Flat, nontender |
| Legs | Good color |
| Skeleton | No malformations |
| Weight | Normal for height |
| Posture | Erect |
| Muscles | Firm |
| GI | Good appetite and digestion |
| Vitality | Good endurance, good sleep patterns |

3. Health history

a. Chronic diseases—dietary alteration may be necessary because of disease entity, e.g., low-sodium diet for heart disease

b. Therapies—treatment modalities may alter food intake, e.g., side effects of chemotherapy and radiation therapy, such as nausea and vomiting, may cause a decrease in intake

c. Surgeries—some surgeries may alter actual intake, e.g., head and neck surgery, and/or absorption concurrent with digestion, e.g., GI surgery

d. Usual eating habits (takes 1–2 weeks for malnutrition to develop)

e.  Recent changes in appetite or food history

f.  Level of growth and development (increased needs)

**B.**  Diagnose

1.  Caloric requirement—a calorie is a measurement unit of energy; person's height and weight, as well as level of activity, determine energy need; average adult requires anywhere from 1,500 kcal to 3,000 kcal a day

2.  Fluid requirement—average fluid requirement for normal healthy adult is approximately 1,800–2,500 ml/day

3.  Nutrient requirements

a.  Carbohydrates—first substance used for energy production in starvation; only source of energy production for the brain

b.  Fats—second source of energy production used by the body in starvation; waste products are ketone bodies, which can create an acidic environment in the blood

c.  Proteins—last energy source used in starvation; depletion of protein leads to muscle wasting as well as loss of oncotic pressure in the vascular space; low albumin level in the blood indicates protein malnutrition

d.  Vitamins—organic substances found in foods; essential in small quantities for growth and for transformation of food substances into tissue

1)  Fat-soluble vitamins (see Table 2)

2)  Water-soluble vitamins (see Table 3)

3)  Minerals (see Table 4)

Table 2

| FAT-SOLUBLE VITAMINS | | | |
|---|---|---|---|
| **VITAMINS** | **FUNCTION(S)** | **PRIMARY SOURCE(S)** | **CLINICAL MANIFESTATION(S)** |
| A | Visual acuity Adaptation to light and dark | Beta-carotene Liver Egg yolk Cream, milk, margarine Yellow fruits, and orange and green leafy vegetables (carrots, squash, peaches) Butter, cheese | **D:** Night blindness, skin infection, xerophthalmia, corneal ulceration **T:** CNS changes (lethargy, headache) GI (portal hypertension) |
| D | Calcification of bones Absorption of Ca, phosphorus | Fish oils Fortified milk/dairy products, egg yolks Sunlight's irradiation of body cholesterol | **D:** Rickets, poor bone growth **T:** Hypercalcemia, renal calculi |
| E | Antioxidant Growth | Green leaf vegetables Fats, oils Liver Grains, nuts | **D:** Breakdown of red blood cells Hemolytic anemia **T:** Fatigue, headache, blurred vision, diarrhea |
| K | Blood clotting | Leafy vegetables Eggs, cheese Synthesized by intestinal bacteria | **D:** Bleeding, bruises **T:** Anemia, liver/renal damage, and intestinal bacterial infection |
| **D: DEFICIENCY  T: TOXICITY** | | | |

● Table 3

| WATER-SOLUBLE VITAMINS | | | |
|---|---|---|---|
| **VITAMINS** | **FUNCTION(S)** | **PRIMARY SOURCES** | **CLINICAL MANIFESTATION(S)** |
| Thiamine ($B_1$) | Normal growth<br>Carbohydrate<br>  metabolism | Legumes, meat<br>Enriched grains<br>Eggs, fish | **D:** Beriberi (numbness,<br>  decreased reflexes fatigue)<br>  Wernicke-Korsakoff<br>    syndrome<br>**T:** Shock |
| Riboflavin ($B_2$) | Coenzyme in protein<br>  and energy<br>  metabolism | Milk<br>Liver (organ meats) | **D:** Ariboflavinosis<br>  Tissue inflammation |
| Niacin (nicotinic acid) | Normal growth | Meat<br>Grains | **D:** Pellagra (rough, scaly skin,<br>  glossitis, decreased weight)<br>**T:** Vasodilation, flushing |
| Pyridoxine ($B_6$) | Amino acid<br>  metabolism | Corn and soy<br>Meat and liver<br>Yeast, egg yolk,<br>  sunflowers | **D:** Anemia, CNS changes<br>  (seizures)<br>  Peripheral neuropathy<br>**T:** Diminished proprioceptive<br>  sensory function |
| Folic acid | RBC formation | Liver<br>Oranges<br>Broccoli | **D:** Anemia<br>**T:** Diminished proprioceptive<br>  and sensory function |
| Cyanocobalamin ($B_{12}$) | Nerve function<br>RBC formation | Meat<br>Milk, eggs | **D:** Pernicious anemia |
| Ascorbic acid (C) | Collagen synthesis | Fruits, esp. citrus<br>Vegetables<br>Tomatoes | **D:** Scurvy (joint pain and<br>  weakness)<br>  Anemia (in infants)<br>**T:** Oxalate hypersensitivity |
| **D: DEFICIENCY   T: TOXICITY** | | | |

● Table 4

| MINERALS | | | |
|---|---|---|---|
| **MINERAL** | **PRIMARY FUNCTION(S)** | **PRIMARY SOURCE(S)** | **DEFICIENCY SYMPTOM(S)** |
| Calcium | Bone formation<br>Muscle contraction<br>Thrombus formation | Milk products<br>Green leafy vegetables<br>Eggs | Rickets<br>Porous bones<br>Tetany |
| Phosphorus | Bone formation<br>Cell permeability | Milk, eggs<br>Nuts | Rickets |
| Fluoride | Dental health | Water supply | Dental caries |
| Iodine | Thyroid hormone synthesis | Seafood<br>Iodized salt | Goiter |
| Sodium | Osmotic pressure<br>Acid-base balance<br>Nerve irritability | Table salt<br>Canned vegetables<br>Milk, cured meats<br>Processed foods | Fluid and electrolyte<br>  imbalance |
| Potassium | Water balance in cells<br>Protein synthesis<br>Heart contractility | Grains, meats<br>Vegetables | Arrhythmias<br>Fluid and electrolyte<br>  imbalance |
| Iron | Hemoglobin synthesis | Liver, oysters<br>Leafy vegetables<br>Apricots | Anemia<br>Lethargy |

Table 5 •

| FOOD GUIDELINES | | |
|---|---|---|
| **Group** | **Food Examples** | **Recommended Daily Intake** |
| Grains | Bread, cereals, cooked cereals, popcorn, pasta, rice, tortillas<br>Half of all grains should be whole grains | Children—3–5 ounce equivalents<br>Teens—5–7 ounce equivalents<br>Young adults—6–8 ounce equivalents<br>Adults—6–7 ounce equivalents<br>Older adults—5–6 ounce equivalents |
| Vegetables | Dark green vegetables (broccoli, spinach, greens, leafy vegetables), orange vegetables (carrots, pumpkin, sweet potatoes), dried beans and peas (split peas, pinto, kidney, black, soy [tofu]), starchy vegetables (corn, peas, white potatoes) | Children—1–1½ cups<br>Teens—2–3 cups<br>Young adults—2½–3 cups<br>Adults—2½–3 cups<br>Older adults—2–2½ cups |
| Fruits | Apple, bananas, strawberries, blueberries, orange, melons, dried fruits, fruit juices | Children—1–1½ cups<br>Teens—1½–2 cups<br>Young adults—2 cups<br>Adults—1½–2 cups<br>Older adults—1½–2 cups |
| Oils | Nuts, butter, margarine, cooking oils, salad dressings | Children—3–4 teaspoons<br>Teens—5–6 teaspoons<br>Young adults—6–7 teaspoons<br>Adults—5–6 teaspoons<br>Older adults—5–6 teaspoons |
| Milk | Milk, yogurt, cheese, puddings | Children—2 cups<br>Teens—3 cups<br>Young adults—3 cups<br>Adults—3 cups<br>Older adults—3 cups |
| Meat and beans | Meat, poultry, fish, dry beans, eggs, peanut butter, nuts, seeds | Children—2–4 ounce equivalents<br>Teens—5–6 ounce equivalents<br>Young adults—5½–6½ ounce equivalents<br>Adults—5–6 ounce equivalents<br>Older adults—5–5½ ounce equivalents |

**C.** Plan/Implementation

1. General diet—eat a variety of foods (see Table 5)

2. Vegetarian diet
   a. Types
      1) Vegan diet includes fruits, vegetables, nuts, beans, and seeds; excludes all sources of animal protein, fortified foods, and nutritional supplements
      2) Lactovegetarian diet includes all foods on a vegan diet, along with milk, cheese, yogurt, and other milk products as the only source of animal protein
      3) Ovovegetarian diet includes all foods on a vegan diet, along with eggs as the only source of animal protein
      4) Lactoovovegetarian diet includes all foods on a vegan diet, along with milk, cheese, yogurt, other milk products, and eggs as only sources of animal protein
      5) "Red-meat abstainers" consider themselves vegetarians and eat animal products with the exception of red meat
   b. Analysis
      1) Become vegetarians due to religion (Seventh Day Adventists), ecology, economic reasons, health reasons

2) Risk deficiency of vitamin $B_{12}$ associated with megaloblastic anemia; vitamin $B_{12}$ is found only in animal products

3) Risk toxic levels of vitamin A causing anorexia, irritability, dry skin, hair loss

   c. Plan/Implementation

1) Increase intake of legumes, beans, nuts, seeds, tofu, dark green leafy vegetable

2) Eat fortified cereals, soy beverages, and meat analogs

3) Must eat adequate amounts of protein, calcium, zinc, vitamin D, and vitamin $B_{12}$

4) During pregnancy should take supplements to meet increased nutritional needs

5) Children may experience mild anemia due to the poor availability of iron from grains and legumes; should include source of vitamin C with meals; diet should include nonmeat animal proteins such as milk, cheese, and eggs; vegan diet is unable to sustain growth needs of children

6) Vegetarian diet often causes weight loss due to elimination of meat which is a major source of fat; fat has twice the number of kilocalories per gram than carbohydrates or proteins

3. Choose My Plate—recommendations by the U.S. Department of Agriculture; includes diet choices for vegetarians and members of ethnic/cultural groups (see Figure 1)

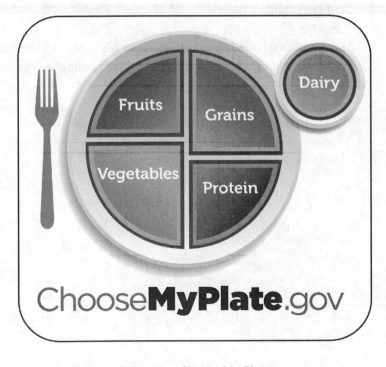

**Figure 1. Choose My Plate**

4. Common therapeutic diets (see Table 6)

5. Complementary/Alternative therapies
   a. General guidelines for herbal and dietary supplements
      1) Supplements do not compensate for an inadequate diet
      2) Recommended daily amounts (RDA) should not be exceeded due to the potential for toxicity
      3) Multivitamin-mineral products recommended for certain age or gender groups contain different amounts of some minerals
      4) Iron supplements beyond those contained in multivitamin-mineral combinations are intended for short-term or special-need (e.g., pregnancy) use and should not be taken for longer periods of time because of potential for toxicity
      5) Most adolescent and adult females consume calcium 1,000 to 1,300 mg daily
      6) Supplementing with selenium as an antioxidant and zinc to prevent colds and promote wound healing is not proven

6. Herbals used to lower cholesterol:
   a. Flax or flaxseed
      1) Decreases the absorption of other medications
      2) Nausea, vomiting, increased flatulence
      3) May decrease absorption of other medications
   b. Garlic
      1) Increases the effects of anticoagulants and antiplatelets
      2) Increases the hypoglycemic effects of insulin
      3) May stimulate labor
   c. Green tea
      1) Produces a stimulant effect when the tea contains caffeine
      2) Multiple drug interactions–anticoagulants, antiplatelets, beta blockers
   d. Soy
      1) Multiple drug interactions–estrogens, tamoxifen

## COMMON THERAPEUTIC DIETS

| CLEAR LIQUID DIET | FULL LIQUID DIET | LOW–FAT, CHOLESTEROL– RESTRICTED DIET |
|---|---|---|
| Sample meal items:<br>Gelatin dessert, popsicle, tea with lemon, ginger ale, bouillon, fruit juice without pulp | Sample meal items:<br>Milkshakes, soups, custard; all clear liquids | Sample meal items:<br>Fruit, vegetables, cereals, lean meat |
| Common medical diagnoses:<br>Postoperative; acute vomiting or diarrhea | Common medical diagnoses:<br>GI upset (diet progression after surgery) | Common medical diagnoses:<br>Atherosclerosis, cystic fibrosis (CF) |
| Purpose:<br>To maintain fluid balance | Purpose:<br>Nutrition without chewing | Purpose:<br>To reduce calories from fat and minimize cholesterol intake |
| Not allowed:<br>Fruit juices with pulp, milk | Not allowed:<br>Jam, fruit, solid foods, nuts | Not allowed:<br>Marbled meats, avocados, milk, bacon, egg yolks, butter |
| **SODIUM–RESTRICTED DIET** | **HIGH–ROUGHAGE, HIGH–FIBER DIET** | **LOW–RESIDUE DIET** |
| Sample meal items:<br>Cold baked chicken, lettuce with sliced tomatoes, applesauce | Sample meal items:<br>Cracked wheat bread, minestrone soup, apple, brussel sprouts | Sample meal items:<br>Roast lamb, buttered rice, sponge cake, "white" processed foods |
| Common medical diagnoses:<br>Heart failure, hypertension, cirrhosis | Common medical diagnoses:<br>Constipation, large bowel disorders | Common medical diagnoses:<br>Temporary GI/elimination problems (e.g., lower bowel surgery) |
| Purpose:<br>To lower body water and promote excretion | Purpose:<br>To maximize bulk in stools | Purpose:<br>To minimize intestinal activity |
| Not allowed:<br>Preserved meats, cheese, fried foods, cottage cheese, canned foods, added salt | Not allowed:<br>White bread, pies and cakes from white flour, "white" processed foods | Not allowed:<br>Whole wheat, corn, bran |
| **HIGH–PROTEIN DIET** | **RENAL DIET** | **LOW PHENYLALANINE DIET** |
| Sample meal items:<br>30 grams powdered skim milk and 1 egg in 100 ml water<br>*or*<br>Roast beef sandwich and skim milk | Sample meal items:<br>Unsalted vegetables, white rice, canned fruits, sweets | Sample meal items:<br>Fats, fruits, jams, low-phenylalanine milk |
| Common medical diagnoses:<br>Burns, infection, hyperthyroidism | Common medical diagnoses:<br>Chronic renal failure | Common medical diagnoses:<br>Phenylketonuria (PKU) |
| Purpose:<br>To re-establish anabolism to raise albumin levels | Purpose:<br>To keep protein, potassium, and sodium low | Purpose:<br>Low-protein diet to prevent brain damage from imbalance of amino acids |
| Not allowed:<br>Soft drinks, "junk" food | Not allowed:<br>Beans, cereals, citrus fruits | Not allowed:<br>Meat, eggs, beans, bread |

## CULTURAL FOOD PATTERNS

*Not all members of a culture choose to follow all dietary traditions.*

A. Orthodox Jewish

   1. Dietary laws based on Biblical and rabbinical regulations

   2. Laws pertain to selection, preparation, and service of food

   3. Laws
      a. Milk/milk products never eaten at same meal as meat (milk may not be taken until 6 hours after eating meat)
      b. Two meals contain dairy products and one meal contains meat
      c. Separate utensils are used for meat and milk dishes
      d. Meat must be kosher (drained of blood)
      e. Prohibited foods
         1) Pork
         2) Diseased animals or animals who die a natural death
         3) Birds of prey
         4) Fish without fins or scales (shellfish—oysters, crab, lobster)

B. Muslim

   1. Dietary laws based on Islamic teachings in Koran

   2. Laws
      a. Fermented fruits and vegetables prohibited
      b. Pork prohibited
      c. Alcohol prohibited
      d. Foods with special value: figs, olives, dates, honey, milk, buttermilk
      e. Follow humane process of slaughter of animals for meat

   3. 30-day period of daylight fasting required during Ramadan

C. Hispanic

   1. Basic foods:  dried beans, chili peppers, corn

   2. Use small amounts of meat and eggs

D. Puerto Rican

   1. Main type of food is viandos—starchy vegetables and fruits (plantain and green bananas)

   2. Diet includes large amounts of rice and beans

   3. Coffee main beverage

E. Native American

   1. Food has religious and social significance

   2. Diet includes meat, bread (tortillas, blue corn bread), eggs, vegetables (corn, potatoes, green beans, tomatoes), fruit

   3. Frying common method of food preparation

F. African American

   1. Minimal use of milk in diet

   2. Frequent use of leafy greens (turnips, collards, and mustard)

   3. Pork common in diet

**G.** French American

    1. Foods are strong-flavored and spicy

    2. Frequently contains seafood (crawfish)

    3. Food preparation starts with a roux made from heated oil and flour, vegetables and seafood added

**H.** Chinese

    1. Uses freshest food available; cooked at a high temperature in a wok using a small amount of fat and liquid

    2. Meat used in small amounts

    3. Eggs and soybean products used for protein

**I.** Japanese

    1. Rice is basic food

    2. Soy sauce is used for seasoning

    3. Tea is main beverage

    4. Seafood frequently used (sometimes raw fish—sushi)

**J.** Southeast Asian

    1. Rice is basic food, eaten in separate rice bowl

    2. Soups frequently used

    3. Fresh fruits and vegetables frequently part of diet

    4. Stir-frying in wok is common method of food preparation

**K.** Italian

    1. Bread and pasta are basic foods

    2. Cheese frequently used in cooking

    3. Food seasoned with spices, wine, garlic, herbs, olive oil

**L.** Greek

    1. Bread is served with every meal

    2. Cheese (feta) frequently used for cooking

    3. Lamb and fish frequently used

    4. Eggs used in main dish, but not breakfast food

    5. Fruit used for dessert

## PREMATURE INFANTS

**A.** Data Collection

    1. Body composition—premature infant has more water, less protein and fat per pound than full-term infant

    2. Poor temperature control due to little subcutaneous fat

3. Bones are poorly calcified

4. Sucking reflexes are poor

5. Gastrointestinal and renal function are poor

6. Prone to infection

7. Immature development of lungs

**B.** Diagnose

1. Less than 2,500 g and less than 37 weeks gestation

2. Nutritional requirements
   a. 100–200 cal/kg/day
   b. Higher sodium, calcium, and protein requirements than full-term infant

**C.** Plan/Implementation

1. Feeding
   a. Parenteral nutrition—usually required until oral feedings can be established
   b. Gavage feedings—usually given because of poor sucking coordination
   c. Soft (preemie) nipples are usually effective for very small infants

2. Supplements
   a. Vitamins A, C, D, and iron are usually given orally
   b. Occasionally, vitamin E is needed to prevent oxidation of RBCs
   c. Long-chain fats are not well tolerated; medium-chain triglycerides (MCTs) are often used
   d. Glucose is often substituted for lactose in premature formulas because of its passive absorption in GI tract
   e. Vitamin K prophylaxis to prevent clotting problems

## FULL-TERM INFANTS

**A.** Data Collection

1. Energy requirements are high; 120 cal/kg/day

2. Rooting and sucking reflexes are well developed

3. Six to eight wet diapers per day and at least 1 stool daily

**B.** Diagnose

1. Weighs more than 2,500 g and greater than 37 weeks' gestation

**C.** Plan/Implementation

1. Breast feeding
   a. Human milk is ideal food; recommended for first 6 to 12 months of life
   b. Colostrum is secreted at first
      1) Clear and colorless

   2) Contains protective antibodies

   3) High in protein and minerals

  c. Milk is secreted after day 2 to 4

   1) Milky white appearance

   2) Contains more fat and lactose than colostrum

 2. Formula feeding

  a. Formula is cow's milk modified to resemble human milk more closely

   1. Diluted to reduce protein content

   2. Sugar is added to increase carbohydrate content

   3. Home preparation from evaporated milk is most economical

   4. Formula is necessary for first 12 months of life; then, unmodified cow's milk is acceptable

   5. If problems with diarrhea, change formula to prevent profound dehydration

  b. Feeding technique

   1. Child should be cradled when fed

   2. Child should be regulator of milk volume

 3. Introduction to solid foods (see Table 7)

  a. Introduce only one at a time for each two-week period

  b. Least allergenic foods are given in first half of the first year; more allergenic foods (e.g., egg, orange juice) are offered in last half of first year; usual order: cereal, fruit, vegetables, potatoes, meat, egg, orange juice

  c. No honey should be given during first year due to high risk of botulism

● Table 7

| INTRODUCTION TO SOLID FOODS | |
|---|---|
| **AGE** | **FOOD** |
| 1-4 months | Liquid vitamins only—A, D, C, fluoride (if indicated) |
| 4-5 months | Cereal—usually rice is first; strained fruit |
| 5-6 months | Strained vegetables; strained meat |
| 7-9 months | Chopped meat; hard breads and "finger foods"; potato baked, mashed |

## TODDLERS

**A.** Data Collection

 1. Six to eight teeth have erupted

 2. Begins to use large muscles and bones

**B.** Diagnose

 1. 12 to 36 months

C. Plan/Implementation

1. Allow choice of foods from food pyramid to prevent struggle over eating

2. Needs fewer calories in diet but more protein and calcium than infant

## PRESCHOOLER AND SCHOOL-AGE

A. Data Collection

1. Growth rate slows

2. Protein and calcium needs remain high

B. Diagnose

1. Growth rate is gradual until adolescence; then spurts occur

C. Plan/Implementation

1. Nutritional intake (see Table 8)

Table 8

| NUTRIENT INTAKE FOR CHILDREN | |
|---|---|
| FOOD | SERVINGS |
| Fruits and vegetables | 4–8 |
|   Vitamin C type | 1–2 |
|   Vitamin A type | 1–2 |
|   Fruit type | 1–2 |
|   Other vegetables | 1–2 |
| Cereals (bread, etc.) | 4 |
| Fats and carbohydrates | To meet caloric needs |
| Meats (proteins, peanuts, eggs) | 3 |
| Milk (cheese, yogurt) | 2–3 |

## ADOLESCENT NUTRITION

A. Data Collection

1. Rapid growth spurts occur

2. Acne develops

B. Diagnose

1. Caloric, calcium, and protein needs are high

2. Females experience menstrual losses of iron; require increased intake

3. Mineral and vitamin needs are high because of rapid tissue growth

**C.** Plan/Implementation

    1. High-calorie, high-protein diet

    2. High intake of iron for menstruating adolescents

    3. High minerals and vitamins in diet

## ADULT AND ELDERLY POPULATION

**A.** Data Collection

    1. Balanced diet continues to be important

    2. Calorie limitation with decreasing physical activity

    3. Declining ability to chew and changing taste perception can cause impaired nutrition in the elderly

**B.** Diagnose

    1. With increased age, reduction in calories needed, improved food quality

    2. Need same level of minerals and vitamins as in early adulthood

**C.** Plan/Implementation

    1. Goal is to decrease calories but to ensure food consumed is high in minerals and vitamins

    2. Prevent osteoporosis in postmenopausal women

    3. Complementary/Alternative Therapy

        a. To reduce all-cause mortality, older adults should consume oral protein and energy supplements

## NUTRITION DURING PREGNANCY AND LACTATION

**A.** Data Collection

    1. Pre-pregnancy weight

    2. Maternal age

    3. Labs: hemoglobin and hematocrit

    4. Pre-existing health problems

**B.** Diagnose

    1. Age and parity of mother varies

    2. Preconception nutrition influences overall requirements

    3. Individual needs vary; recommended weight gain is 24–28 pounds

    4. Folic acid needed to prevent neural tube defects and megaloblastic and macrocytic anemia

**C.** Plan/Implementation

    1. Diet plan for pregnancy and lactation (see Table 9)

    2. High-risk pregnancies

      a. Adolescence

        1) Must meet own nutritional requirements (high protein and calcium)

        2) Tendency to deliver low-birthweight babies

Table 9

| DIET PLAN FOR PREGNANCY AND LACTATION | | |
|---|---|---|
| **FOOD** | **PREGNANCY** | **LACTATION** |
| Protein (meat, 1 egg, cheese) | 3 servings | 4 servings |
| Vegetable—yellow or green (includes vitamin C foods) | 5 servings | 5-6 servings |
| Bread and cereal (whole grain or enriched) | 5 servings | 5 servings |
| Milk products (cheese, ice cream, milk, cottage cheese) | 4 cups | 5 cups |
| Calories over maintenance | +300/day | +500/day |
| Folic acid | 400 mcg | 280 mcg |

      b. Diabetes

        1) Glucose levels must be monitored closely

        2) Prevent postmature deliveries

        3) C-section may be necessary because mother may not be able to handle the glucose requirements of labor

      c. Sickle cell—stress of labor and pregnancy must be considered in relation to oxygenation capabilities of these mothers; C-section is usually indicated

      d. Cardiac—myocardial stress specifically related to delivery may require decreased activity, as well as C-section, to decrease demand on heart

## ENTERAL NUTRITION

**A.** Alternative feeding (required because of inability to use gastrointestinal route)

**B.** Liquid food delivered to the stomach, distal duodenum, or proximal jejunum via a nasogastric, percutaneous endoscopic gastrostomy (PEG), or percutaneous endoscopic jejunostomy (PEJ) tube

**C.** Conditions requiring enteral feeding (see Table 10)

● Table 10

| CONDITIONS REQUIRING ENTERAL FEEDING | |
|---|---|
| **CONDITION** | **CAUSE** |
| Preoperative need for nutritional support | Inadequate intake preoperatively, resulting in poor nutritional state |
| Gastrointestinal problems | Fistula, short-bowel syndrome, Crohn's disease, ulcerative colitis, nonspecific maldigestion or malabsorption |
| Side effects of oncology therapy | Radiation, chemotherapy |
| Alcoholism, chronic depression, eating disorders | Chronic illness, psychiatric, or neurological disorder |
| Head and neck disorders or surgery | Disease or trauma |

**D.** Complications of enteral feeding (see Table 11)

● Table 11

| COMPLICATIONS OF ENTERAL FEEDINGS | |
|---|---|
| **COMPLICATION** | **NURSING CONSIDERATIONS** |
| Mechanical<br>Tube displacement | Replace tube |
| Aspiration | Elevate head of bed, check residual before feeding |
| Gastrointestinal<br>Cramping, vomiting, diarrhea | Decrease feeding rate<br>Change formula to more isotonic<br>Administer at room temperature |
| Metabolic<br>Hyperglycemia | Monitor glucose, serum osmolality<br>  Monitor glucose, give insulin if needed<br>Reduce infusion rate |
| Dehydration | Flush tube with water according to hospital policy |
| Formula–drug interactions | Check compatability<br>Flush tubing prior to and after medication |

## PARENTERAL NUTRITION

**A.** Data Collection

　　1. Conditions requiring enteral feeding (see Table 10)

**B.** Diagnose

　　1. Method of supplying nutrients to the body by the intravenous route
　　　(see Figure 2)

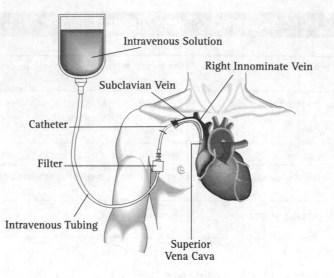

**Figure 2.  Parenteral Nutrition (PN)**

2. Types of solutions
   a. PN—amino acid-dextrose formulas; 2–3 liters of solution given over 24 h; 500 ml of 10% fat emulsions (Intralipid) given with PN over 6 h 1–3 times/week; fine bacterial filter used
   b. TNA (Total Nutrient Admixture)—amino acid-dextrose-lipid, "3-in-1" formula; 1-liter solution given over 24 h; no bacterial filter used
   c. Lipids—provides fatty acids

3. Methods of administration
   a. Peripheral—used to supplement oral intake; should not administer dextrose concentrations above 10% due to irritation of vessel walls; usually used for less than 2 weeks
   b. Central—catheter inserted into subclavian vein
      1) Peripherally inserted catheters (PICC)—catheter threaded through central vein; dextrose solution ≥10% basilic or cephalic vein to superior vena cava; usually ≤4 weeks
      2) Percutaneous central catheters through subclavian vein
      3) Triple lumen central catheter often used; distal lumen (16-gauge) used to infuse or draw blood samples, middle lumen (18-gauge) used for PN infusion, proximal lumen (18-gauge) used to infuse or draw blood and administer medications
      4) If single lumen catheter used, cannot use to administer medications (may be incompatible) or give blood (RBCs coat catheter lumen); medications and blood must be given through peripheral IV line, not piggyback to the PN IV line
   c. Atrial
      1) Right atrial catheters—Hickman/Biovac and Groshong
      2) Subcutaneous port—Huber needle used to access port through skin

**C.** Plan/Implementation

1. Initial rate of infusion 50 ml/h and gradually increased (100–125 ml/h) as client's fluid and electrolyte tolerance permits

2. Infuse solution by pump at constant rate to prevent abrupt change in infusion rate
   a. Increased rate results in hyperosmolar state (headache, nausea, fever, chills, malaise)
   b. Slowed rate results in "rebound" hypoglycemia caused by delayed pancreatic reaction to change in insulin requirements; do not discontinue suddenly

3. Client must be carefully monitored for signs of complications; infection and hyperglycemia are common (see Table 12)

Table 12

| COMPLICATIONS OF PN | |
|---|---|
| **COMPLICATION** | **NURSING CONSIDERATIONS** |
| Infection/Sepsis | Maintain closed intravenous systems with filter<br>No blood drawn or medications given through PN line<br>Dry sterile occlusive dressing applied to site |
| Pneumothorax because of line placement | PN to be started only after chest x-ray validates correct placement<br>Monitor breath sounds and for presence of shortness of breath |
| Hyperglycemia<br>Hyperosmolar coma | Monitor glucose level and serum osmolality<br>Administer insulin according to sliding scale insulin |
| Hypoglycemia | Hang 10% dextrose solution if PN discontinued suddenly |
| Fluid overload | Monitor breath sounds, weight and peripheral perfusion<br>Do not "catch up" if PN behind |
| Air embolism | Monitor for respiratory distress<br>Valsalva maneuver during tubing and cap change |

4. Change IV tubing and filter every 24 hours

5. Keep solutions refrigerated until needed; allow to warm to room temperature before use

6. If new solution unavailable, use 10% dextrose and water solution until available

7. Monitor daily weight, glucose, temperatures, intake and output; three times a week check BUN, electrolytes (calcium, magnesium); check CBC, platelets, prothrombin time, liver function studies (AST, ALT), prealbumin, serum albumin once a week

8. Do not increase flow rate if PN behind scheduled administration time

9. Discontinuation
   a. Gradually tapered to allow client to adjust to decreased levels of glucose

b.  After discontinued, isotonic glucose solution administered to prevent rebound hypoglycemia (weakness, faintness, diaphoresis, shakiness, confusion, tachycardia)

## URINARY ELIMINATION

**A.** Data Collection

    1. Characteristics of urine

        a. Color—yellow

        b. Consistency—clear, transparent

        c. Specific gravity—1.010–1.030

        d. pH—4.5–8.0

        e. 24-hour production—1,000–2,000 mL (approximately 1 mL/Kg/hr)

    2. Serum changes

        a. BUN (normal 10–20 mg/dL)

        b. Creatinine (normal 0.7–1.4 mg/dL)

**B.** Diagnose

    1. Potential nursing diagnoses

        a. Urinary elimination, altered

        b. Fluid volume deficit, risk for

    2. Definitions

        a. Anuria—total urinary output <100 mL/24 hours

        b. Oliguria—total urinary output 100–400 mL/24 hours

        c. Polyuria—total urinary output >2000 mL/24 hours

        d. Dysuria—painful or difficult voiding

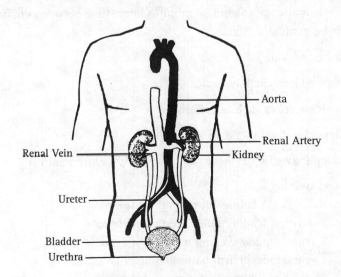

**Figure 1. Urinary System**

3. Predisposing factors
   a. Bedrest
   b. Tumors
   c. Prostatic hypertrophy, anticholinergic medications
   d. Decreased bladder tone—previous use of indwelling catheter, childbirth
   e. Cancer
   f. Neurogenic—CVA, spinal injuries
   g. Calculi
   h. Stress
   i. Urinary tract infection

**C.** Plan/Implementation

1. Hydration—adequate intake 1,500–2,000 mL/day

2. Voiding habits
   a. Know client's pattern
   b. Provide time and privacy

3. Reinforce Kegel exercises—strengthen muscles of pelvic floor; tighten pelvic muscles for count of 3, then relax for count of 3; perform lying down, sitting and standing for total of 45

4. Reinforce bladder retraining
   a. Triggering techniques—stroking medial aspect of thigh, pinching area above groin, pulling pubic hair, providing digital anal stimulation (used with upper motor neuron problem); Valsava and Credé maneuvers (used with lower motor neuron problem)
   b. Intermittent catheterization every 2–3 hours after attempting to void and Valsalva or Credé maneuver; if volume is less than 150 mL, time interval is increased to 3–4 hours, then 4–6 hours; never more than 8 hours
   c. Toileting schedule—first thing in AM, before and after meals, before and after physical activity, bedtime
   d. Bladder training—drink a measured amount of fluid every 2 hours, then attempt to void 30 minutes later; time between voiding should be gradually increased

5. Catheterization

6. Respond immediately to call

7. Avoid diuretics such as caffeine

8. Encourage fluid intake to 2,000 mL

9. Clamp indwelling catheters intermittently before removal

10. Toilet training
    a. Never begin before 18th month of life
    b. 2–3 years: bladder reflex control achieved
    c. 3 years: regular voiding habits established
    d. 4 years: independent bathroom activity
    e. 5 years: nighttime control expected

11. Enuresis—bedwetting in a child over 4 years old
    a. Usually have small bladder capacity
    b. More common in males
    c. Tend to be deep sleepers

## BOWEL ELIMINATION

A. Data Collection

1. Abdomen nontender and symmetrical

2. High-pitched gurgles indicate normal peristalsis

3. Stool light to dark brown in color

4. Negative guaiac for occult blood

5. Negative for fat, mucus, pus, pathogens

B. Diagnose—potential nursing diagnoses

1. Bowel incontinence

2. Constipation

3. Perceived constipation

4. Risk for constipation

5. Diarrhea

C. Plan/Implementation

1. Promote normal elimination
   a. Encourage client to respond to urge to defecate
   b. Provide facilities, privacy, and allow sufficient time
   c. Fluids—encourage adequate intake; 8 or more glasses of fluid daily
   d. Foods—encourage fiber, fruits, vegetables, grains
   e. Activity—encourage exercise and ambulation to maintain muscle tone
   f. Emotional state—teach client that stress affects autonomic nervous system, which controls peristalsis
   g. Positioning
      1) For ambulatory client—teach that optimal posture is with feet flat on floor, hips and knees flexed
      2) For bedrest client—place in Fowler's position on bedpan

## CONGENITAL MALFORMATIONS OF THE URINARY TRACT

**A.** Data Collection (see Table 1)

**B.** Diagnose (see Table 1)

**C.** Plan/Implementation (see Table 1)

● Table 1

| CONGENITAL MALFORMATIONS OF THE URINARY TRACT | | |
|---|---|---|
| **DATA COLLECTION FINDINGS** | **ANALYSIS** | **NURSING CONSIDERATIONS** |
| Epispadias | Urethral opening on dorsal surface of the penis | Surgical correction<br>No circumcision—foreskin used in surgical repair |
| Hypospadias | Male urethral opening on the ventral surface of penis, or female urethral opening in vagina | Surgical reconstruction<br>No circumcision—foreskin used in surgical repair |
| Bladder exstrophy | Posterior and lateral surfaces of the bladder are exposed | Reconstructive surgery to close bladder and abdominal wall |

## RENAL AND URETERAL CALCULI (CRYSTALLIZATION)

**A.** Data Collection

1. Pain—(renal colic)—depends on location of stone (flank pain with renal calculi, radiating pain with ureter or bladder stones; pain often severe

2. Diaphoresis

3. Nausea and vomiting

4. Fever, chills, and hematuria

5. Hematuria, WBCs and bacteria in urine

**B.** Diagnose

1. Nephrolithiasis—kidney stones; urolithiasis—urinary stones

2. Causes
   a. Obstruction and urinary stasis
   b. Hypercalcemia, dehydration, immobility

3. Diagnostic tests—intravenous pyelogram, renal ultrasound, CT scan, cystoscopy, x-rays of kidneys, ureter, and bladder (KUB)

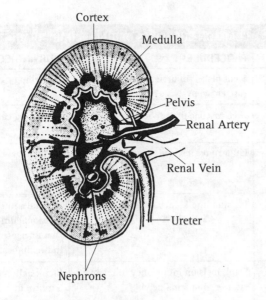

**Figure 2. Kidney**

C. Plan/Implementation

1. Monitor I and O and temperature

2. Avoid overhydration or underhydration to decrease pain when passing stone

3. Strain urine and check pH of urine

4. Monitor temperature

5. Analgesics

6. Diet for prevention of stones—most stones contain calcium, phosphorus, and/or oxalate
   a. Low in calcium—avoid milk, cheeses, dairy products
   b. Low in sodium—sodium increases calcium in urine
   c. Low in oxalates to prevent increased calcium absorption (avoid: spinach, cola, tea, chocolate)
   d. Avoid vitamin D-enriched foods (increases calcium absorption)
   e. Decrease purine sources—organ meats
   f. To make urine alkaline, restrict citrus fruits, milk, potatoes
   g. To acidify urine increase consumption of eggs, fish, cranberries

7. Drug therapy
   a. Antibiotics (broad spectrum)
   b. Thiazide diuretics, orthophosphate, sodium cellulose phosphase—decrease calcium reabsorption
   c. Allopurinol and vitamin $B_6$ (pyridoxine)—decrease oxalic acid levels
   d. Allopurinol—decrease uric acid levels

8. Surgery (see Table 2)

| COMMON SURGERIES OF THE URINARY TRACT | | |
|---|---|---|
| NAME | PROCEDURE | NURSING CONSIDERATIONS |
| Stenting | Stent placed in ureter during ureteroscopy | Indwelling catheter may be placed |
| Retrograde ureteroscopy | Ureteroscope used to remove stone | Indwelling catheter may be placed |
| Percutaneous ureterolithotomy or nephrolithotomy | Lithotripter inserted through skin | Ureterostomy tube may be left in place |
| Nephrolithotomy | Incision into kidney to remove stones | Ureteral catheter<br>Incisional drain<br>Don't irrigate nephrostomy tube<br>Indwelling catheter |
| Pyelolithotomy | Flank incision into kidney to remove stones from renal pelvis | Incisional drain<br>Surgical dressing<br>Ureteral catheter |
| Ureterolithotomy | Incision into ureter to remove stones | Do not irrigate ureteral catheter<br>Check incisional drain<br>Check surgical dressing |
| Nephrectomy | Removal of kidney due to tumor, infection, anomalies | Penrose drain<br>Indwelling catheter<br>Surgical dressing<br>Check urine output closely<br>"Last resort" intervention |
| Nephrostomy | Flank incision and insertion of nephrostomy tube into renal pelvis | Penrose drain<br>Surgical dressing |

8. Mechanical intervention (cystoscopy with catheter insertion)

9. Extracorporeal shock-wave lithotripsy
   a. Strain urine following procedure
   b. Voided parts of stones sent to lab for analysis
   c. Encourage to increase fluid intake to facilitate passage of broken stones
   d. Teach to report fever, decreased urinary output, pain
   e. Hematuria expected but should clear in 24 hours

## CYSTITIS

A. Data Collection

   1. Urgency, frequency

   2. Burning on urination

B. Diagnose

   1. Inflammation of bladder

   2. Predisposing factors
      a. Females more prone
      b. Catheterization, instrumentation

**C.** Plan/Implementation

1. Obtain clean-catch midstream urine specimen for urinalysis, urine culture, colony count, and possibly Gram stain

2. Force fluids 3,000 mL/day

3. Cranberry juice or other urinary acidifiers

4. Culture and sensitivity (C and S)

5. Medications: antibiotics, urinary tract analgesics (e.g., phenazopyridine)

6. Encourage females to void before and after intercourse

7. Clean properly after defecation (wipe front to back)

8. Void every 2 to 3 hours

## PYELONEPHRITIS

**A.** Data Collection

1. Chills, fever

2. Malaise

3. Flank pain

4. Urinary frequency, dysuria

5. CVA tenderness from scarring

**B.** Diagnose

1. Definition—inflammation of kidney caused by bacterial infection

2. Predisposing factors
   a. Urinary tract infection
   b. Pregnancy
   c. Tumor
   d. Urinary obstruction
   e. Usually caused by *E. coli*

3. Diagnostic tests—urinalysis (RBCs, bacteria, leukocyte casts)

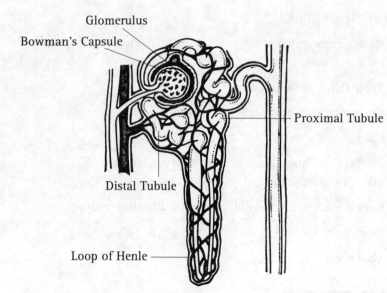

**Figure 3.  Nephron**

**C.**  Plan/Implementation

1.  Bedrest during acute phase

2.  Antibiotic therapy, antiseptics, analgesics

3.  Encourage fluid intake 3000 ml/day

## GLOMERULONEPHRITIS

**A.**  Data Collection

1.  Fever, chills

2.  Hematuria, red cell casts, proteinuria, urine dark-colored

3.  Weakness, pallor

4.  Dyspnea, weight gain, lung rales, fluid overload

5.  Anorexia, nausea, vomiting (uremia)

6.  Generalized and/or facial and periorbital edema

7.  Moderate-to-severe hypertension

8.  Headache, decreased level of consciousness, confusion

9.  Abdominal or flank pain

10.  Oliguria with fixed specific gravity (indicates impending renal failure)

11.  Antistreptolysin-O titers, decreased serum complement levels, renal biopsy

**B.**  Diagnose

1.  Damage to glomerulus caused by an immunological reaction that results in proliferative and inflammatory changes within the glomerular structure

2. Acute glomerulonephritis (most common) usually caused by beta-hemolytic streptococcal infection elsewhere in the body (URI, skin infection); *Chlamydia, pneumococcal, mycoplasma,* or *klebsiella* pneumonia; autoimmune disease e.g., SLE; *streptococcal* infection elsewhere in the body

3. Occurs 10 days after a skin or throat infection

C.  Plan/Implementation

1. Administer medications to eliminate infection; alter immune balance to alleviate inflammation; treat volume overload and hypertension
   a.  Antibiotics
   b.  Corticosteroids
   c.  Antihypertensives
   d.  Immunosuppressive agents
   e.  Diuretics

2. Restrict sodium intake; restrict water if oliguric

3. Daily weights, monitor I and O

4. Bedrest

5. High-calorie, low-protein diet

6. Dialysis or plasma electrophoreses if renal failure develops (antibody removal)

## PROSTATIC HYPERTROPHY/BENIGN PROSTATIC HYPERPLASIA

A.  Data Collection

1. Hesitancy (dribbling, weak urinary stream)

2. Frequency, urgency, dysuria, nocturia

3. Hematuria before or after voiding

4. Retention

B.  Diagnose

1. Enlargement of the prostate gland; causes urinary flow obstruction, possible infection

2. Benign hypertrophy, increase in size with age (over 50)

3. BUN and creatinine

4. Prostate-specific antigen (PSA)–normal is less than 4 mg/mL; may be increased in prostatitis, prostatic hypertrophy, prostate cancer

5. Trans-abdominal or trans-rectal ultrasound

6. Prostate biopsy

C.  Plan/Implementation

1. Conservative—urinary antiseptics and follow-up

2. Administer medications
   a. 5-alpha reductase inhibitors
   b. Alpha-blocking agents

3. Suprapubic cystostomy—opening into bladder, drainage via catheter through abdominal wall (temporary measure to divert urine)
   a. Covered with sterile dressing
   b. Connected to sterile closed drainage system
   c. To test ability to void, clamp catheter for 4 hours, have client void, unclamp catheter and measure residual urine; if residual is less than 100 ml on 2 occasions (morning and evening), catheter is removed
   d. After removal of catheter, sterile dressing placed over site

4. Prostatectomy
   a. Transurethral (TURP)
   b. Suprapubic resection (through bladder)
   c. Retropubic resection (through abdomen)

5. Observe for shock and hemorrhage—check dressing and drainage: urine may be reddish-pink initially, monitor continuous bladder irrigation (CBI); monitor vital signs

6. Monitor intake and output after catheter removed; expect dribbling and urinary leakage around wound

7. Avoid long periods of sitting and strenuous activity until danger of bleeding is over

8. Complementary and alternative therapies
   a. Saw palmetto
   b. Lycopene

9. Avoid consumption of large amounts of fluids, caffeine

10. Avoid anticholinergic, antihistamine, and decongestant medications

## URINARY DIVERSIONS

**A.** Data Collection

  1.  Bladder tumors requiring cystectomy

  2.  Birth defects

  3.  Strictures and trauma to ureters and urethra

  4.  Neurogenic bladder

  5.  Interstitial cystitis

**B.** Diagnose

  1.  Types (see Table 3 and Figure 4)

●Table 3

| URINARY DIVERSIONS | | |
| --- | --- | --- |
| **NAME** | **PROCEDURE** | **NURSING CONSIDERATIONS** |
| Nephrostomy | Flank incision and insertion of nephrostomy tube into renal pelvis | Penrose drain<br>Surgical dressing |
| Ureterosigmoidostomy | Ureters detached from bladder and anastomosed to sigmoid colon | Urine and stool are evacuated through anus<br>Encourage voiding via rectum every 2-4 h; no enemas or cathartics<br>Monitor complications—fluid and electrolyte imbalance, pyelonephritis, obstruction |
| Cutaneous ureterostomy | Single or double-barreled stoma, formed from ureter(s) excised from bladder and brought out through the skin into the abdominal wall | Stoma usually constructed on right side of abdomen below waist<br>Extensive nursing intervention required for alteration in body image |
| Ileal conduit | Portion of terminal ileum is used as a conduit; ureters are replanted into ileal segment; distal end is brought out through skin and forms a stoma | Most common urinary diversion<br>Check for obstruction (occurs at the anastomosis)<br>Postop mucus threads normal |
| Koch pouch Continent ileal conduit | Ureters are transplanted to an isolated segment of ileum (pouch) with a one-way value; urine is drained by a catheter | Urine collects in pouch until drained by catheter<br>Valve prevents leakage of urine<br>Drainage of urine by catheter is under control of client<br>Pouch must be drained at regular intervals |

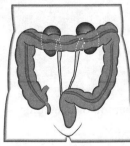
Ureterosigmoidostomy

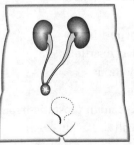
Cutaneous Ureterostomy

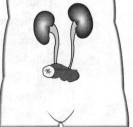
Ileal Conduit

**Figure 4. Types of Urinary Diversions**

**C.** Plan/Implementation (see Table 3)

## ACUTE KIDNEY DISORDERS

A. Data Collection

1. Oliguric phase of acute kidney injury (AKI)
   a. Urinary output less than 0.5 mL/Kg/hr
   b. Nausea, vomiting
   c. Irritability, drowsiness, confusion, coma
   d. Restlessness, twitching, seizures
   e. Increased serum $K^+$, BUN, creatinine
   f. Increased $Ca^+$, $Na^+$, pH
   g. Anemia
   h. Pulmonary edema, CHF
   i. Hypertension
   j. Albuminuria

2. Diuretic or recovery phase of acute kidney injury
   a. Urinary output 4–5 liter/day
   b. Increased serum BUN
   c. $Na^+$ and $K^+$ loss in urine
   d. Increased mental and physical activity

3. Chronic
   a. Anemia
   b. Acidosis
   c. Azotemia
   d. Fluid retention
   e. Urinary output alterations

B. Diagnose

1. Causes of acute kidney injury
   a. Prerenal
      1) Circulating volume depletion
      2) Vascular obstruction
      3) Vascular resistance
   b. Acute kidney injury (see Table 4)
      1) Acute tubular necrosis (ATN)
         a) Nephrotoxic drugs
         b) Transfusion reaction
      2) Trauma
      3) Glomerulonephritis
      4) Severe muscle exertion
      5) Genetic conditions
   c. Postrenal failure
      1) Obstruction–benign prostatic hyperplasia, tumors, renal or urinary calculi

2. Causes of chronic kidney injury
   a. Hypertension
   b. Diabetes mellitus
   c. Lupus erythematosus
   d. Sickle cell disease
   e. Chronic glomerulonephritis
   f. Repeated pyelonephritis
   g. Polycystic kidney disease
   h. Nephrotoxins

● Table 4

| ACUTE KIDNEY INJURY | |
|---|---|
| **LOW-OUTPUT STAGE** | **HIGH-OUTPUT STAGE** |
| Limit fluids | Fluids as needed to replace output |
| Diet adjustment | Diet adjustment |
| Specific medications as needed, e.g., Kayexalate for high potassium | Replacement for potassium |
| Treatment: dialysis (hemodialysis or peritoneal dialysis) | Treatment: dialysis (hemodialysis or peritoneal dialysis) |

**C.** Plan/Implementation

1. Dialysis (see Tables 5 and 6)

2. Monitor potassium levels; sodium polystyrene sulfonate (orally or retention enema) for elevated levels

3. Daily weight, I and O

4. Diet
   a. Oliguric phase—limit fluids; restriction of protein, potassium, and sodium
   b. After diuretic phase—high carbohydrate diet; restriction of protein, potassium, and sodium
   c. Chronic failure—regulate protein intake, fluid intake to balance fluid losses, some restriction of sodium and potassium, vitamin supplements; more protein allowed with dialysis

Table 5

| HEMODIALYSIS AND PERITONEAL DIALYSIS | | |
|---|---|---|
| | **HEMODIALYSIS** | **PERITONEAL DIALYSIS** |
| Circulatory access | Subclavian catheter<br>AV fistula, AV graft | Catheter in peritoneal cavity<br>(Tenckoff, Gore-Tex) |
| Dialysis bath | Electrolyte solution similar to that of normal plasma | Similar to hemodialysis |
| Dialyzer | Artificial kidney machine with semipermeable membrane | Peritoneum is dialyzing membrane |
| Procedure | Blood shunted through dialyzer for 3-5 h 2 to 3 times/wk | Weigh client before and after dialysis<br>Repeated cycles can be continuous<br>Catheter is cleansed and attached to line leading to peritoneal cavity<br>Dialysate infused into peritoneal cavity to prescribed volume<br>Dialysate is then drained from abdomen after prescribed amount of time |
| Complications | Hemorrhage<br>Hepatitis<br>Nausea and vomiting<br>Disequilibrium syndrome<br>Muscle cramps<br>Air embolism<br>Sepsis | Protein loss<br>Peritonitis<br>  Cloudy outflow, bleeding<br>  Fever<br>  Abdominal tenderness, lower back problems<br>  Nausea and vomiting<br>  Exit site infection |
| Nursing considerations | Check "thrill" and bruit every 8 h<br>Don't use extremity for BP or to obtain blood specimens<br>Monitor BP, apical pulse, temperature, respirations, breath sounds, weight<br>Monitor for hemorrhage during dialysis and 1 h after procedure | Constipation may cause problems with infusion and outflow; high-fiber diet, stool softener<br>If problems with outflow, reposition client (supine or low-Fowler's, side to side)<br>Monitor BP, apical pulse, temperature, respirations, breath sounds, weight<br>Clean catheter insertion site and apply sterile dressing |

● Table 6

| PERITONEAL DIALYSIS | |
|---|---|
| **TYPES** | **NURSING CONSIDERATIONS** |
| Continuous ambulatory (CAPD) | Client performs self-dialysis 7 days/wk for 24 h/day<br>Dialysate warmed (use heating pad), infused, dwell time 4-8 h<br>Tubing and bag disconnected or rolled up and worn under clothing<br>After dwell time, fluid drained back into bag and process repeated |
| Automated | Uses machine with warming chamber for dialysate infusion, dwell, and outflow<br>Times and volumes preset; 30-minute exchanges (10 minutes for infusion, 10 min for dwell, 10 min for outflow) for 8-10 h |
| Intermittent | 4 days a week for 10 h/day<br>Can be automated or manual |
| Continuous | Automated machine used at night<br>Final exchange is left in place during the next day and then drained that night |

5. Monitor IV fluids

6. Use of diuretics controversial

7. Aluminum hydroxide used for elevated phosphate levels

8. Bedrest during acute phase

9. Good skin care

10. Monitor for infection; antibiotics if needed

11. Renal transplant

    a. Donor selection: cadaver, identical twin, tissue match, histocompatible

    b. Preop: client education

        1) Explain surgical procedure and follow-up care to client

        2) Show client where the donated kidney will be located (iliac fossa anterior to iliac crest)

        3) Use of immunosuppressive drugs (e.g., prednisone, imuran, cyclosporine) (see page 527)

        4) Need for infection prevention (gingival disease and cavities)

    c. Postop

        1) Monitor vital signs, intake and output—expect scant urine production for several weeks postop

        2) Daily weight

        3) Vascular access care—may need hemodialysis until transplanted kidney functions well (2–3 weeks for kidney from cadaver)

        4) Psychological support for donor and recipient

5) Monitor for complications
   a) Hemorrhage
   b) Shock
   c) Rejection–acute (days to months; decreased urine output, increased BUN and creatinine, fever, tenderness and swelling over graft site); chronic (months to years; gradual decrease in renal function, proteinuria, gradual increase in BUN and creatinine)
   d) Infection
   e) Pulmonary complications
   f) Side effects of immunosuppressive and steroid medications

PSYCHOSOCIAL
INTEGRITY

## Chapter 6

Coping and Adaptation

Psychosocial Adaptation

Psychopathology

Chemical Dependency

Abuse and Neglect

## MENTAL HEALTH CONCEPTS

**A.** Data Collection

1. Appearance, behavior, or mood
   a. Well groomed, relaxed
   b. Self-confident, self-accepting

2. Speech, thought content, and thought process
   a. Clear, coherent
   b. Reality-based

3. Sensorium
   a. Oriented to person, place, and time
   b. Good memory
   c. Ability to abstract

4. Insight and judgment—accurate self-perception and awareness

5. Family relationships and work habits
   a. Satisfying interpersonal relationships
   b. Ability to trust
   c. Ability to cope effectively with stress
   d. Environmental mastery

6. Level of growth and development

**B.** Diagnose

1. Potential support systems or stressors
   a. Religious organizations or community support
   b. Family
   c. Socioeconomic resources
   d. Education
   e. Cultural norms

2. Potential risk factors
   a. Family history of mental illness
   b. Medical history—imbalances can cause symptoms resembling emotional illness

3. Satisfaction of basic human needs in order of importance (Maslow) (see Figure 1)

a. Physical—oxygen, water, food, sleep, sex
b. Safety—physical, security, order
c. Love and belonging—affection, companionship, identification
d. Esteem and recognition—status, success, prestige
e. Self-actualization—self-fulfillment, creativity

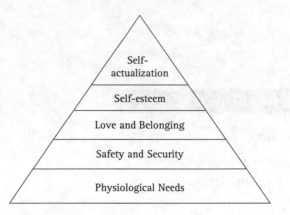

**Figure 1. Maslow Hierarchy of Needs**

4. Potential nursing diagnoses
   a. Social interaction, impaired
   b. Anxiety
   c. Individual coping, ineffective
   d. Self-esteem disturbance

Table 1

| THERAPEUTIC RESPONSES | | |
|---|---|---|
| **RESPONSE** | **GOAL/PURPOSE** | **EXAMPLES** |
| Using silence (nonverbal) | Allows client time to think and reflect; conveys acceptance <br> Allows client to take lead in conversation | Use proper nonverbal communication, remain seated, maintain eye contact, sit quietly and wait |
| Using general leads or broad openings | Encourages client to talk <br> Indicates interest in client <br> Allows client to choose subject <br> Sets tone for depressed client | "What would you like to talk about? Then what? Go on. . ." <br> "What brought you to the hospital?" <br> "What can you tell me about your family?" |
| Clarification | Encourages recall and details of particular experience <br> Encourages description of feelings <br> Seeks clarification, pinpoints specifics <br> Makes sure nurse understands client | "Give me an example." <br> "Tell me more." <br> "And how do you feel when you're angry?" <br> "Who are 'they'?" |
| Reflecting | Paraphrases what client says <br> Reflects what client says, especially feelings conveyed | "It sounds like you're feeling angry." <br> "In other words, you really felt abandoned." <br> "I hear you saying it was hard to come to the hospital." |

**C.** Plan/Implementation

1. Therapeutic communication—listening to and understanding client while promoting clarification and insight (see Tables 1, 2, and 3)

   a. Goals

      1) To understand client's message (verbal and nonverbal)
      2) To facilitate verbalization of feelings
      3) To communicate understanding and acceptance
      4) To identify problems, goals, and objectives

   b. Guidelines

      1) Nonverbal communication constitutes two-thirds of all communication and gives the most accurate reflection of attitude; key point of psychiatric interventions is say nothing, listen

         a) Physical appearance, body movement, posture, gesture, facial expression
         b) Contact—eye contact, physical distance maintained, ability to touch and be touched

      2) The person's feelings and what is verbalized may be incongruent, e.g., client denies feeling sad but appears morose

      3) Implied messages are as important to understand as overt behavior, e.g., continual interruptions may represent loneliness or fear

● Table 2

| RESPONSES TO AVOID IN THERAPEUTIC COMMUNICATION | |
| --- | --- |
| **RESPONSE** | **EXAMPLES** |
| Closed-ended questions that can be answered by a "yes" or "no" or other monosyllabic responses; prevents sharing; puts pressure on client | "How many children do you have?"<br>"Who do you live with?"<br>"Are you feeling better today?" |
| Advice-giving—encourages dependency, may not be right for a particular client | "Why don't you. . . ?"<br>"You really should cut your hair and wear makeup." |
| Responding to questions that are related to one's qualifications or personal life in an embarrassed or concrete way; keep conversation client-centered | "Yes, I am highly qualified."<br>"You know nurses are not permitted to go out with their clients." |
| Arguing or responding in a hostile way | "If you do not take your medication, there is really nothing we can do to help you." |
| Reassuring—client benefits more by exploring own ideas and feelings | "You will start feeling much better any day."<br>"Don't worry, your health care providers will do everything necessary for your care." |
| "Why" questions—can imply disapproval and client may become defensive | "Why didn't you take your medication?" |
| Judgmental responses—evaluate client from nurse's values | "You were wrong to do that. "<br>"Don't you think your being unfaithful has destroyed your marriage?" |

Table 3

| TREATMENT MODALITIES FOR MENTAL ILLNESS | | |
|---|---|---|
| **TYPE** | **ASSUMPTIONS** | **FOCUS OF TREATMENT** |
| Biological | Emotional problem is an illness<br>Cause may be inherited or chemical in origin | Medications, ECT |
| Psychoanalytical (individual) | Anxiety results when there is conflict between the id, ego, and superego parts of the personality<br>Defense mechanisms form to ward off anxiety | The therapist helps the client to become aware of unconscious thoughts and feelings; understand anxiety and defenses |
| Milieu therapy | Providing a therapeutic environment will help increase client's awareness of feelings, increase sense of responsibility, and help him/her return to his/her community | Positive physical and social environment<br>Structured groups and activities<br>One-on-one intervention<br>May be token program, open wards, self-medication |
| Group therapy | Relationship with others will be recreated among group members and can be worked through; members can also directly help one another | Members meet regularly with a leader to form a stable group<br>Members learn new ways to cope with stress and develop insight into their behavior with others |
| Family therapy | The problem is a family problem, not an individual one<br>Sick families lack a sense of "I" in each member<br>The tendency is to focus on sick member's behavior as the source of trouble<br>The sick member's symptom serves a function in the family | Therapist treats the whole family<br>Helps members to each develop their own sense of identity<br>Points out function of sick member to the rest of the family |
| Activity therapy | Important group interactions occur when group members work on a task together or share in recreation | Organized group activities created to promote socialization, increase self-esteem |
| Play therapy | Children express themselves more easily in play than in verbal communication<br>Choice of colors, toys, and interaction with toys is revealing as reflection of child's situation in the family | Provide materials and toys to facilitate interaction with child, observe play, and help child to resolve problems through play |
| Behavioral therapy and behavior modification | Psychological problems are the result of learning<br>Deficiencies can be corrected through learning | Operant conditioning—use of rewards to reinforce positive behavior; becomes more important than external reinforcement<br>Desensitization—used to treat phobias; client slowly adjusts to threatening objects |

## ANXIETY

**A.** Data Collection

   1. Cardiovascular

     a. Increased pulse, blood pressure, and respiration

     b. Palpitations, chest discomfort/pain

     c. Perspiration, flushing, and heat sensations

     d. Cold hands and feet

     e. Headache

   2. Gastrointestinal

     a. Nausea, vomiting, and diarrhea

     b. Belching, heartburn, cramps

3. Musculoskeletal
   a. Increased muscle tension and tendon reflexes
   b. Increased generalized fatigue
   c. Tremors, jerking of limbs
   d. Unsteady voice

4. Intellectual
   a. Poor comprehension—may be unable to follow directions
   b. Poor concentration, selective inattention
   c. Focus on detail
   d. Impaired problem solving
   e. Unable to communicate
      1) Thoughts may become random, distorted, disconnected with impaired logic
      2) Rapid, high-pitched speech

5. Social and emotional
   a. Feelings of helplessness and hopelessness
   b. Feelings of increased threat, dread, horror, anger, and rage
   c. Use of defense mechanisms and more primitive coping behaviors
      1) Shouting, arguing, hitting, kicking
      2) Crying, rocking, curling up, and withdrawal

**B.** Diagnose

1. Definition—feeling of dread or fear in the absence of an external threat or disproportionate to the nature of the threat

2. Predisposing conditions
   a. Prolonged unmet needs of dependency, security, love, and attention
   b. Stress threatening security or self-esteem
   c. Unacceptable thoughts or feelings surfacing to consciousness, e.g., rage, erotic impulses, flashbacks

3. Levels of anxiety
   a. Mild—high degree of alertness, mild uneasiness
   b. Moderate—heart pounds, skin cold and clammy, poor comprehension
   c. Severe—symptoms of moderate anxiety plus hallucinations, delusions
   d. Panic—symptoms of severe anxiety plus inability to see and hear, inability to function; may regress to less appropriate behaviors

4. Ego defense mechanisms—methods, usually unconscious, of managing anxiety by keeping it from awareness; may be adaptive or maladaptive
   a. Denial—failure to acknowledge an intolerable thought, feeling, experience, or reality, e.g., an alcoholic who says he does not have a drinking problem
   b. Displacement—redirection of emotions or feelings to a subject that is more acceptable or less threatening, e.g., yelling at the dog when angry with the boss
   c. Projection—attributing to others one's unacceptable feelings, impulses, thoughts, or wishes, e.g., saying someone you are angry with dislikes you

d. Undoing—an attempt to erase an unacceptable act, thought, feeling, or desire, e.g., apologizing excessively; obsessive compulsive behavior

e. Compensation—an attempt to overcome a real or imagined shortcoming, e.g., a small person excels in sports

f. Symbolization—a less threatening object or idea is used to represent another, e.g., dreams, phobias

g. Substitution—replacing desired, impractical, or unobtainable object with one that is acceptable or attainable, e.g., marrying someone who looks like previous significant other

h. Introjection—a form of identification in which there is a symbolic taking into oneself the characteristics of another, e.g., blaming oneself when angry with another

i. Repression—unacceptable thoughts kept from awareness, e.g., inability to remember a traumatic event

j. Reaction formation—expressing attitude directly opposite to unconscious wish or fear, e.g., being excessively kind to a person who is actually disliked

Table 4

| NURSING INTERVENTIONS IN ANXIETY | |
|---|---|
| **GENERAL PRINCIPLES** | **NURSING CONSIDERATIONS** |
| Determine level of anxiety | Look at body language, speech patterns, facial expressions, defense mechanisms, and behavior used<br>Distinguish levels of anxiety |
| Keep environmental stresses/ stimulation low when anxiety is high | First action<br>Need to intervene with severe or panic level<br>Brief orientation to unit or procedures<br>Written information to read later, when anxiety is lower<br>Pleasant, attractive, uncluttered environment<br>Provide privacy if presence of other clients is overstimulating<br>Provide physical care if necessary<br>Avoid offering several alternatives or decisions when anxiety is high |
| Assist client to cope with anxiety more effectively | Acknowledge anxious behavior; reflect and clarify<br>Always remain with client who is moderately or severely anxious<br>Assist client to clarify own thoughts and feelings<br>Encourage measures to reduce anxiety, e.g., exercise, activities, talking with friends, hobbies<br>Assist client to recognize his/her strengths and capabilities realistically<br>Provide therapy to develop more effective coping and interpersonal skills, e.g., individual, group<br>May need to administer antianxiety medications |
| Maintain accepting and helpful attitude toward client | Use an unhurried approach<br>Acknowledge client's distress and concerns about problem<br>Encourage clarification of feelings and thoughts<br>Evaluate and manage own anxiety while working with client<br>Recognize the value of defense mechanisms and realize that client is attempting to make the anxiety tolerable in the best way possible<br>Acknowledge defense but provide reality, e.g., "You do not see that you have a problem with alcohol but your blood level is high."<br>Do not attempt to remove a defense mechanism at any time |

k. Regression—return to an earlier developmental phase in the face of stress, e.g., bedwetting, baby-talk

l. Dissociation—detachment of painful emotional experience from consciousness, e.g., sleepwalking

m. Suppression—consciously putting a disturbing thought or incident out of awareness, e.g., deciding not to deal with something unpleasant until next day

n. Sublimation—substituting constructive activity for strong impulses that are not acceptable

5. Potential nursing diagnoses

a. Individual coping, ineffective

b. Anxiety

● Table 5

| ANXIETY DISORDERS | | |
|---|---|---|
| **TYPE** | **DATA** | **NURSING CONSIDERATIONS** |
| Phobia | Apprehension, anxiety, helplessness when confronted with phobic situation or feared object<br>Examples of specific fears:<br>Acrophobia—heights<br>Claustrophobia—closed areas<br>Agoraphobia—open spaces | Avoid confrontation and humiliation<br>Do not focus on getting client to stop being afraid<br>Systematic desensitization<br>Relaxation techniques<br>General anxiety measures (see Table 4)<br>May be managed with antidepressants |
| Obsessive-compulsive disorder (OCD) | Obsession—repetitive, uncontrollable thoughts<br>Compulsion—repetitive, uncontrollable acts, e.g., rituals, rigidity, inflexibility | Accept ritualistic behavior<br>Structure environment<br>Provide for physical needs<br>Offer alternative activities, especially ones using hands<br>Guide decisions, minimize choices<br>Encourage socialization<br>Group therapy<br>Managed with clomipramine (Anafranil), SSRIs<br>Stimulus–response prevention |
| Conversion hysteria | Physical symptoms with no organic basis, unconscious behavior—could include blindness, paralysis, convulsions without loss of consciousness, stocking and glove anesthesia, "la belle indifference" | Diagnostic evaluation<br>Discuss feelings rather than symptoms<br>Promote therapeutic relationship with client<br>Avoid secondary gain |

C. Plan/Implementation

1. Goals

a. Decrease anxiety

b. Recognize anxiety, e.g., restlessness

c. Identify precipitants of anxiety

d. Establish more effective coping mechanisms

e. Increase self-esteem

2. Institute measures to decrease anxiety (see Table 4)

3. Provide nursing care for anxiety disorders (see Table 5)

4. Administer antianxiety medications as ordered (see pages 474–475)

5. Use realistic, measurable objectives to evaluate effectiveness

## CRISIS INTERVENTION

**A.** Data Collection (see Table 6)

1. Stages of crisis
   a. Denial
   b. Increased tension, anxiety
   c. Disorganization, inability to function
   d. Attempts to escape the problem, pretends problem doesn't exist, blames others
   e. Attempts to reorganize
   f. General reorganization

2. Precipitating factors
   a. Developmental stages
      1) Birth, adolescence
      2) Midlife, retirement
   b. Situational factors
      1) Natural disasters
      2) Financial loss
   c. Threats to self-concept
      1) Loss of job
      2) Failure at school
      3) Onset of serious illness

**B.** Diagnose (see Table 6)

1. Characteristics
   a. Temporary state of disequilibrium precipitated by an event
   b. Self-limiting—usually 4–6 weeks
   c. Crisis can promote growth and new behaviors

2. Potential nursing diagnoses
   a. Individual coping, ineffective
   b. Powerlessness
   c. Grieving, dysfunctional

**C.** Plan/Implementation (see Table 6)

1. Goal-directed, focus on the here and now

2. Focus on client's immediate problems

3. Explore nurse's and client's understanding of the problem
   a. Define the event (client may truly not know what has precipitated the crisis)
   b. Confirm nurse's perception by reviewing with client
   c. Identify the factors that are affecting problem-solving
   d. Evaluate how realistically client sees the problems or concerns

4. Help client become aware of feelings and validate them
   a. Acknowledge feelings (e.g., "This must be a painful situation for you.")
   b. Avoid blaming client for problems and concerns
   c. Avoid blaming others, as this prevents insight

●Table 6

| SITUATIONAL CRISES | | |
|---|---|---|
| | **GRIEVING CLIENT** | **DYING CLIENT** | **RAPE TRAUMA** |

| | GRIEVING CLIENT | DYING CLIENT | RAPE TRAUMA |
|---|---|---|---|
| **Data Collection Findings** | Stages of grief<br>  a. Shock and disbelief<br>  b. Awareness of the pain of loss<br>  c. Restitution<br>Acute grief period 4-8 wks<br>Usual resolution within 1 yr<br>Long-term resolution over time | Stages of dying<br>  a. Denial<br>  b. Anger<br>  c. Bargaining<br>  d. Depression<br>  e. Acceptance | Stages of crisis<br>  a. Acute reaction lasts 3-4 wk<br>  b. Reorganization is long-term<br>Common responses to rape<br>  a. Self-blame, embarrassment<br>  b. Phobias, fear of violence, death, injury<br>  c. Anxiety, insomnia<br>  d. Wish to escape, move, relocate<br>  e. Psychosomatic disturbances |
| **Diagnose** | Potential problems<br>  a. Family of deceased or separated<br>    – Guilt<br>    – Anger<br>    – Anxiety<br>  b. Client undergoing surgery or loss of body part<br>    – Anger<br>    – Withdrawal<br>    – Guilt<br>    – Anxiety<br>    – Loss of role | Potential problems<br>  a. Avoidance behavior<br>  b. Inability to express feelings when in denial<br>  c. Feelings of guilt<br>  d. Withdrawal<br>  e. Lonely, frightened<br>  f. Anxiety of client and family | Potential problems<br>  a. Fears, panic reactions, generalized anxiety<br>  b. Guilt<br>  c. Inability to cope<br>Current crisis may reactivate old unresolved trauma<br>Follow emergency room protocol: may include clothing, hair samples, NPO<br>Be alert for potential internal injuries, e.g., hemorrhage |
| **Intervention** | Apply crisis theory<br>Focus on the here and now<br>Provide support to family when loved one dies<br>Provide family privacy<br>Encourage verbalization of feelings<br>Facilitate expressions of anger and rage<br>Emphasize strengths<br>Increase ability to cope<br>Support adjustment to illness, loss of body part | Apply crisis theory<br>Support staff having feelings of loss<br>Keep communication open<br>Allow expression of feelings<br>Focus on the here and now<br>Let client know he/she is not alone<br>Provide comforting environment<br>Be attentive to need for privacy<br>Provide physically comforting care, e.g., back rubs<br>Give sense of control and dignity<br>Respect client's wishes | Apply crisis theory<br>Focus on the here and now<br>Write out treatments and appointments for client, as anxiety causes forgetfulness<br>Record all information in chart<br>Give client referrals for legal assistance, supportive psychotherapy, and rape crisis center<br>Follow up regularly until client is improved |

    d. Encourage ventilation with nurse to relieve anxiety

    e. Tell client he will feel better, but it may take 1 or 2 months

5. Develop a plan

    a. Encourage client to make as many arrangements as possible (avoid dependence)

    b. Write out information, since comprehension is impaired (e.g., referrals)

    c. Maximize client's situational supports

6. Find new coping skills and manage feelings

    a. Focus on strengths and present coping skills

    b. Encourage client to form new coping skills and social outlets, reaching out to others

    c. Facilitate future planning

1) Ask client "What would you like to do?", "Where would you like to go from here?"
2) Give referrals when needed, family counseling, vocational counseling

## POST-TRAUMATIC STRESS DISORDER (PTSD)

**A.** Data Collection

1. Exposure to a traumatic event (e.g., combat, rape, murder, fire, other catastrophe)

2. Response to trauma causes intense fear or horror

3. Recurrent or distressing recollections of event (images, thoughts, feelings)

4. Distressing dreams or nightmares

5. Acting or feeling like the trauma is recurring (flashbacks)

6. Hypervigilance and exaggerated startle response

7. Irritability or outbursts of anger

8. Avoidance or numbing

**B.** Diagnose

1. Duration of symptoms is at least one month

2. Syndrome can emerge months to years after traumazing event

3. Biological changes due to impact of stressor and excessive arousal of sympathetic nevous system

**C.** Plan/Implementation

1. Help client integrate the traumatic experience
   a. Encourage client to talk about painful stored memories
      1) Have client recall images of traumatic event with as much detail as possible (called flooding); will be done by staff with high level of expertise
      2) Use empathic responses to the expressed distress (e.g., "That must have been hard for you.")
      3) Remain nonjudgmental about client's shameful or horrific experience
      4) Allow client to grieve over losses
   b. Assist client to challenge existing ideas about event and substitute more realistic thoughts and expectations
      1) Point out irrational thinking to the client
      2) Help client recognize the limits of his/her control over the stressful event

2. Assist client with emotional regulation
   a. Help client label his/her feelings and find ways to express them safely

   b.  Reinforce stress management techniques

   c.  Involve client in anger management program

   1)  Recognize anger as normal feeling

   2)  Encourage time-out or other ways of walking away from problematic situations involving anger

   3)  Maintain nonintrusive communication techniques

   a) Speak in first person

   b) Move away from object (person) of anger

   c) Cognitive restructuring (e.g., using thoughts like "This person cannot make me lose control")

   d.  Develop a schedule of regular physical activity with client (e.g., walking, running, weightlifting)

   e.  Use empowering strategies such as keeping a journal of disturbed thoughts and feelings in response to flashbacks, nightmares, or other problems

   f.  Reduce sleep disturbances

   1)  Regular bedtime

   2)  Use bed for sleeping and lovemaking exclusively; no TV or reading

   3)  Do not lie in bed sleepless for more than half an hour; get up and move around and then come back to bed

3.  Enhance the client's support systems

   a.  Refer to self-help group

   b.  Include family and friends in psychoeducational activities

   c.  Explore opportunities for socialization

## DEPRESSION

**A.**  Data Collection

1.  Possible changes in self-esteem/self-confidence

   a.  Low self-esteem

   b.  Self-deprecation

   c.  Feelings of helplessness/hopelessness

   d.  Obsessive thoughts and fears

   e.  Ruminations and worries

   f.  Sense of doom, failure

   g.  Regressed behavior—immature, demanding, whines for help

2.  Possible changes in self-care

   a.  Unkempt, depressed appearance

   b.  Multiple reports of physical discomfort

   c.  Prone to injury, accidents, and infections

   d.  Lack of energy

   e.  Changes in usual sleep pattern

   1)  Insomnia

   2)  Feels unrested after night's sleep

   f.  Weight loss, poor appetite, weight gain

   g.  Constipation

      h.  Amenorrhea

      i.  Lack of sexual desire

  3.  Possible changes in cognitive/mental functioning

      a.  Decreased attention span and concentration

      b.  Slowed speech, thought processes, and motor activity

      c.  Impaired reality testing (psychotic depression)

      d.  Withdrawn

      e.  Ambivalent and indecisive behavior

      f.  Agitation and psychomotor restlessness

      g.  Suicidal ideation

  4.  Suicide/homicide potential

      a.  Has plan and means to carry out plan; actual date established (anniversary, birthdate, etc.)

      b.  Identifies others who may become involved in the plan

**B.**  Diagnose

  1.  Psychodynamics

      a.  Depression—response to real or imagined loss

      b.  Anger and aggression toward self results from feelings of guilt about negative or ambivalent feelings

      c.  Introjection occurs (incorporation of a loved or hated object or person into one's own ego)

  2.  Types of depression—determined by onset and severity of symptoms

      a.  Major depression

      b.  Dysthymic disorder

      c.  Bipolar disorder

  3.  Potential nursing diagnoses

      a.  Self-care deficit

      b.  Self-esteem disturbance

      c.  Individual coping, ineffective

      d.  Social interaction, impaired

      e.  Violence:  self-directed, risk for

      f.  Powerlessness

      g.  Hopelessness

**C.**  Plan/Implementation

  1.  Be alert for signs of self-destructive behavior

      a.  Report all behavior changes to the team, especially increased energy or agitation

      b.  In psychotic depression, observe for any signs that voices are commanding client to harm self (e.g., question the client, "What are the voices saying to you?")

  2.  Meet physical needs

      a.  Promote nutrition

          1)  Provide pleasant surroundings and companionship during meals

          2)  Give more frequent feedings, favorite foods because of decreased appetite

    b.  Medicate for constipation PRN and encourage fluids

    c.  Promote rest

        1)  Medicate for insomnia PRN and watch while client swallows pill

        2)  Provide a quiet sleeping arrangement; stay with client if necessary; check on client periodically

    d.  Promote self-care as much as possible

3.  Decrease anxiety and indecisiveness

    a.  Administer antianxiety medications

    b.  Listen to and explore feelings

        1)  Avoid pep talks; don't disagree with self-deprecation because client will not believe it

        2)  Avoid excessive cheeriness and promise of a bright future

        3)  Keep encouragement brief; client cannot incorporate compliments

    c.  Avoid presenting choices, as client feels too inadequate to make decisions

    d.  Be brief and simple, avoid long explanations because of decreased attentiveness and poor concentration

        1)  Give a brief orientation

        2)  Use simple language and repeat when necessary

    e.  Provide a structured, written schedule

4.  Support self-esteem

    a.  Provide a warm, supportive environment

    b.  Be patient while client is slowed down and cannot think quickly; demonstrate acceptance to promote client self-acceptance

    c.  Provide consistent daily care

        1)  One-to-one nursing coverage is ideal

        2)  Be consistent and predictable—keep all appointments and make few staff changes (they may be seen as a rejection)

        3)  Anticipate staff feelings of ineffectiveness as part of caring for depressed clients and continue a positive approach

    d.  Give tasks to relieve guilt and increase self-esteem

        1)  Avoid tasks at which the client will fail

        2)  Give simple tasks that require minimal concentration

5.  Help decrease social withdrawal

    a.  Pursue the client who avoids contact because of fear of rejection

        1)  Sit with client during long quiet times

        2)  Point out when client stays alone excessively

        3)  Touch to promote acceptance (note: do *not* touch the psychotic client, as this may be seen as intrusion); be aware of cultural acceptance of touch

    b.  Introduce to others when ready

6.  Help with anger and fear of losing control

    a.  Channel anger into acceptable outlets (e.g., sports, carpentry)

    b.  Encourage expressions of anger—small expressions initially; client may become suicidal if anger is expressed before able to do so safely

7. Encourage coping
   a. Imply confidence in client's capabilities
      1) Don't make client dependent
      2) Discuss excessive demands
   b. Give assistance when needed, but work together

8. Administer antidepressant medications
   a. Caution client about side effects and time required for medication to become effective
   b. Observe for suicidal tendency as depression lifts, usually at 10 days to 2 weeks after start of medication

9. Assist with electroconvulsive therapy (ECT)—convulsions similar to grand mal seizures are induced to treat depression
   a. Preparation of client (see Table 7)
   b. Procedure
      1) Anesthetist gives short-acting intravenous anesthesia and muscle-relaxing drug, e.g., succinylcholine (Anectine)
      2) Keep oxygen and suction on hand
      3) Position client in supine position with arms at sides during convulsion
   c. Side effects and complications
      1) Confusion and memory loss for recent events
      2) Transient headaches, muscle soreness, drowsiness
   d. Postprocedure care
      1) Orient client; client will not remember treatment
      2) Take blood pressure, respirations
      3) Stay with client during period of confusion
      4) Signs of diminished depression appear after 6–12 treatments

10. Alternative/Complementary therapies
    a. Phototherapy
       1) First-line treatment for season affective disorders (SAD)
       2) Minimum 2,500 lux of light 30 minutes a day
    b. St. John's wort
       1) Herbal preparation
       2) Do not take if major depression, pregnancy, or in children younger than 2 years
       3) Do not take with amphetamines, MAOIs, SSRIs, levodopa, and 5-HT
       4) Avoid tyramine-containing foods
       5) Contraindicated in pregnancy and during lactation
    c. Exercise
       1) 30 minutes at least 5 times per week

**NURSING CONSIDERATIONS FOR ELECTROCONVULSIVE THERAPY (ECT)** ● Table 7

1. Prepare client by explaining procedure and telling client about potential temporary memory loss and confusion
2. Informed consent, physical exam, labwork
3. NPO after midnight for an early morning procedure
4. Have client void before ECT
5. Remove dentures, glasses, jewelry
6. Give muscle relaxant and short-acting barbiturate anesthetic to induce brief general anesthesia
7. Given Atropine 30 min before treatment to decrease secretions
8. Have oxygen and suction on hand
9. After procedure, take vital signs, orient client
10. Observe client's reaction and stay with him
11. Observe for sudden improvement and indications of suicidal threats after ECT treatment

## SUICIDE

A. Data Collection

  1. Symptoms same as in depression

  2. Behavioral clues of impending suicide (see Table 8)

Table 8 ●

**BEHAVIORAL CLUES OF IMPENDING SUICIDE**

1. Any sudden change in client's behavior
2. Becomes energetic after period of severe depression
3. Improved mood 10-14 days after taking antidepressant may mean suicidal plans made
4. Finalizes business or personal affairs
5. Gives away valuable possessions or pets
6. Withdraws from social activities and plans
7. Appears emotionally upset
8. Presence of weapons, razors, pills (means)
9. Has death plan
10. Leaves a note
11. Makes direct or indirect statements (e.g., "I may not be around then.")

B. Diagnose

  1. Predisposing factors

    a. Male over 50 years old

    b. Age range 15–19 years old

    c. Clients with poor social attachments; isolation

    d. Clients with previous attempts

    e. Clients with personality disorders

    f. Psychotic individuals with command hallucinations to kill themselves

    g. Overwhelming precipitating events

      1) Terminal or degenerative disease, e.g., cancer, kidney disease

      2) Death or loss of loved one through divorce or separation

      3) Financial loss, job loss, school failure

2. Understanding self-destructive behavior
   a. Attempts to cope fail, leaving the client with low self-esteem and feelings of hopelessness and helplessness
   b. Client feels guilty and overwhelmed in response to precipitating event and may see suicide as relief
   c. Ambivalence about suicide may lead to cry for help or attention
   d. Aggression and rage turned toward self (introjection) or into an attempt to punish others
   e. Most common as depression is lifting
      1) 10–14 days after antidepressant medication begun
      2) New signs of energy or improvement

3. Potential nursing diagnoses
   a. Violence: self-directed, risk for

C. Plan/Implementation

1. Implement measures for depression

2. Be alert for signs of self-destructive behavior (see Table 8)

3. Remove all potentially dangerous items

4. Provide strong therapeutic relationship to increase client self-worth
   a. Establish authoritative and credible matter-of-fact manner to increase confidence
   b. Place on one-to-one observation and stay with client to help control self-destructive impulses
   c. Let the client know that the nurse will assist in seeking every possible resource to ease troubles
   d. Relieve client's feelings of embarrassment (e.g., "I see you are upset. You are wise to seek help.")

5. Discuss all behavior with team members
   a. Note indirect clues as cry for help (e.g., presence of pills)
   b. Observe for sudden increased energy level as indication of possible impending suicide attempt
   c. Note increase in anxiety, insomnia

6. Give client a sense of control other than through suicide
   a. Assist with problem-solving and decision-making
   b. Develop and use a suicidal contract
   c. Avoid excess support, as this encourages dependency and eventual feelings of abandonment

7. Provide family therapy where indicated
   a. Avoid taking client's side as family is not direct cause of suicidal urge
   b. Look for scapegoating or acting out of family destructiveness

8. Intervene quickly and calmly during actual attempts
   a. Remove the harmful objects from the client (e.g., razor, ropes) without inflicting harm on self and/or client
   b. Stay by the client's side and reassure the client that you are there to help

    c. Avoid judgmental remarks or interpretations (e.g., "Why did you do this?")

  9. Contract with client

    a. "No suicide," "no harm," or "no self-injury" contracts are made between psychiatric health care professionals and clients who are admitted to a psychiatric unit with depression and/or suicide ideation or self-injurious acting-out

    b. Clients agree to contact staff if they have an impulse to be self-destructive

    c. Client is asked to abide by the signed contract

    d. Client is periodically reminded of the contract

    e. Limit-setting lets client know that self-destructive acts are not permitted

## SITUATIONAL ROLE CHANGES

**A.** Data Collection

  1. Death of spouse/significant other

  2. Divorce/separation

  3. Personal illness/injury

  4. Marriage

  5. Job loss

  6. Retirement

  7. Pregnancy/new baby

  8. Job change/relocation

  9. "Empty nest"/child leaving home

  10. Graduation from high school/college/tech school

  11. Spouse beginning or ending full-time employment

**B.** Diagnose

  1. Coping strategies—specific skills or actions consciously used to manage effects of stress

  2. Reactions to change can be positive, negative, neutral

  3. Reactions determined by

    a. Client's learned behaviors to cope with change

    b. Significance of event

    c. Client's physical and emotional state at time of change

    d. Client's control over change

    e. Number of changes over lifetime

    f. Positive or negative resolution to previous changes

**C.** Plan/Implementation

1. Place changes in time line; rank from least to most severe

2. Discuss resolution to previous changes; determine what was helpful in the past

3. Use learned coping strategies
   a. Establish and maintain a routine
   b. Limit or avoid changes
   c. Designate time to focus on adaptation to change
   d. Use time efficiently
   e. Change environment to reduce stress
   f. Regular exercise
   g. Humor
   h. Good nutrition
   i. Rest/sleep
   j. Relaxation techniques
   k. Utilize support system
   l. Work on increasing self-esteem
   m. Pray/meditate
   n. Some cultures use rituals

## STRESS

**A.** Data Collection

1. Headache
2. Sleep problems, fatigue, irritability
3. Restlessness, rapid speech and movement
4. GI upset
5. Tachycardia, palpitations, hot flashes
6. Frequent urination, dry mouth
7. Crying
8. Use of alcohol or drugs
9. Withdrawal from friends and family

**B.** Diagnose

1. Stressors
   a. Family
   b. Job
   c. Environment
   d. Lifestyle
   e. Body image changes
   f. Situation role change

**C.** Plan/Implementation

1. Determine what client sees as stressful

2. Identify how stressful these items are to client

3. Determine how client has coped with stressors in the past

4. Provide support—encourage family visits, listen to client's concerns, involve pastoral and social services

5. Provide control—maintain client independence; allow client to make choice concerning timing and sequencing of activities

6. Provide information—answer questions, provide information about procedures, events

7. Recognize client feelings—acknowledge anger

8. Support client's own coping strategies

9. Interventions
   a. Biofeedback—use of electrical instruments to identify somatic changes (e.g., muscle activity, skin surface activity)
   b. Progressive muscle relaxation—tensing then relaxing major muscle groups in sequential steps
   c. Meditation—conscious removal of thoughts filling mind, or filling mind with only one thought
   d. Guided imagery—thinking about peaceful scene involving total relaxation

## BURNOUT

A. Data Collection

1. Emotional or physical exhaustion

2. Depersonalization, inability to become involved with others

3. Decreased effectiveness

4. Stress-related behavior becomes persistent problem

5. Usual coping strategies ineffective

6. Person feels overwhelmed, helpless

7. At risk for physical or mental illness

B. Diagnose

1. Process in which the person disengages from his/her work in response to stress

2. Sources of stress may be in environment, self, or in interactions

3. Determined by the person's ability to adapt

C. Plan/Implementation

1. Provide social support

2. Begin counseling

3. Utilize employee assistance programs

## SUPPORT SYSTEMS

**A.** Data Collection

1. Family—role of each member (authority figure, peacemaker)

2. Spouse/significant other

3. Friends

4. Coworkers

5. Groups, clubs, organizations

6. Pet or inanimate object (security blanket)

**B.** Diagnose

1. Culture and socioeconomic status influence support systems

2. Social network defines client's self-image and sense of belonging

**C.** Plan/Implementation

1. Determine developmental stage (adolescence, early adulthood, late adulthood) to plan utilization of support systems

2. Enlist support persons who have been effective in previous, similar, stressful situations

## SUDDEN INFANT DEATH SYNDROME (SIDS)

**A.** Data Collection

1. Occurs during first year of life, peaks at two to four months

2. Occurs between midnight and 9 AM

3. Increased incidence in winter, peaks in January

**B.** Diagnose

1. Thought to be brainstem abnormality in neurologic regulation of cardiorespiratory control

2. Third leading cause of death in children from one week to one year of age

3. Higher incidence of SIDS
   a. Infants with documented apparent life-threatening events (ALTEs)
   b. Siblings of infant with SIDS
   c. Preterm infants who have pathological apnea
   d. Preterm infants, especially with low birth weight
   e. Black infants
   f. Multiple births
   g. Infants of addicted mothers
   h. Infants who sleep on abdomen

**C.** Plan/Implementation

1. Home apnea monitor

2. Place all healthy infants in supine position to sleep

3. Support parents, family

4. Referral to Sudden Infant Death Foundation

## COUNSELING TECHNIQUES

**A.** Techniques

1. Confrontation—call attention to discrepancies between what the client says (verbal communication) and what the client does (nonverbal communication)

2. Contracting—establish expected behaviors and goals as well as rules and consequences with client that structure nurse/client interactions

3. Focusing—create order, guidelines, and priorities by assisting the client in identifying problems and establishing their relative importance

4. Interpreting—explore with the client possible explanations for feelings

5. Making connections—help the client connect seemingly isolated phenomena by filling in blanks and establishing relationships

6. Modeling—exemplify through actions and verbalizations the behaviors that the client is working toward

7. Providing feedback—give the client constructive information about how the nurse perceives and hears him/her

8. Reframing—look at the issue through a different perspective by using different examples and descriptions

9. Stating observations—describe what is happening in the nurse/client relationship that might have relevance to other things happening in client's life

10. Summarizing—give feedback to client about the general substance of the interview or interpersonal exchange before ending

**B.** Implementation

1. These techniques aid the nurse in promoting change and growth in clients

2. Nurse should demonstrate behaviors of
   a. Congruence or genuineness
   b. Empathy (the ability to see things from the client's perspective)
   c. Positive regard or respect

## RELIGIOUS AND SPIRITUAL INFLUENCES ON HEALTH

**A.** Data Collection

1. Wears amulets, charms, clothing, jewelry

2. Carries a talisman (object that has supernatural powers)

3. Makes noise to scare off evil entities

4. Drinks/ingests potions, tonics, or foods

5. Performs or refrains from performing activity at certain times

6. Method of disposal of objects that come into contact with person

7. Performs religious ceremony (e.g., baptism)

8. Avoids doing actions that are harmful to others

9. Avoids behaviors that are not socially sanctioned

10. Emotional investment related to aspects of mind or soul, distinct from body

11. Reflects individual values, beliefs, ethical choices

**B.** Diagnose

1. Religion provides explanation for illness and misfortune

2. Religion can prevent illness and misfortune

3. Client's spiritual beliefs affect all aspects of life, relationships, sense of right and wrong

4. Religion is the basis for health care behaviors and decisions

5. Religion is a basic human need that must be satisfied for individual's well-being

**C.** Plan/Implementation

1. Seek assistance from persons knowledgeable about client's religious practices

2. Be aware of your own spirituality and beliefs

3. Be respectful and sensitive to client's religious beliefs

4. Do not impose your own religious beliefs on client or believe that if client finds religion, this will spiritually enrich client

5. Observe client's verbal and nonverbal behavior; may indicate spiritual distress

6. Examples
   a. Roman Catholic—sacrament of the sick
   b. Buddhist—believe in healing through faith
   c. Christian Science—practice spiritual healing
   d. Church of Jesus Christ of Latter Day Saints—anoint with oil, pray, lay on hands
   e. Hinduism—faith healing

    f.  Islam—use herbal remedies and faith healing

    g.  Jehovah's Witness—mental and spiritual healing

    h.  Judaism—prays for sick

    i.  Mennonite—prayer and anointing with oil

    j.  Seventh-Day Adventist—anointing with oil and prayer

    k.  Unitarian/Universalist—use of science to facilitate healing

## BIPOLAR DISORDER

**A.** Data Collection

1. Disoriented, incoherent
2. Delusions of grandeur
3. Flight of ideas, easily distractable
4. Inappropriate dress; excessive makeup and jewelry
5. Lacks inhibitions
6. Uses sarcastic, profane, and abusive language
7. Quick-tempered, agitated
8. Talks excessively, jokes, dances, sings; hyperactive
9. Can't stop moving to eat, easily stimulated by environment
10. Decreased appetite
11. Weight loss
12. Insomnia
13. Regressed behavior
14. Sexually indiscreet, hypersexual

**B.** Diagnose

1. Psychodynamics
   a. Bipolar disorder is an affective disorder
   b. Reality contact is less disturbed than in schizophrenia
   c. Elation or grandiosity can be a defense against underlying depression or feelings of low self-esteem
   d. Testing, manipulative behavior results from poor self-esteem

2. Predisposing factors
   a. Hereditary—genetic
   b. Biochemical

3. Problems
   a. Easily stimulated by surroundings
      1) Hyperactive and anxious
      2) Unable to meet physical needs
   b. Aggressive and hostile due to poor self-esteem
   c. Denial
   d. Testing, manipulative, demanding, disruptive, intrusive behavior
   e. Superficial social relationships

4. Potential nursing diagnoses
    a. Thought processes, altered
    b. Self-care deficit
    c. Violence: self-directed or directed at others, risk for
    d. Social interaction, impaired
    e. Self-esteem disturbance

C. Plan/Implementation

1. Institute measures to deal with hyperactivity/agitation
    a. Simplify the environment and decrease environmental stimuli
        1) Assign to a single room away from activity
        2) Keep noise level low
        3) Soft lighting
    b. Limit people
        1) Anticipate situations that will provoke or overstimulate client, e.g., activities, competitive situations
        2) Remove to quiet areas
    c. Distract and redirect energy
        1) Choose activities for brief attention span, e.g., chores, walks
        2) Choose physical activities using large movements until acute mania subsides, e.g., dance
        3) Provide writing materials for busy work when acute mania subsides, e.g., political suggestions, plans

2. Provide external controls
    a. Assign one staff person to provide controls
    b. Do not encourage client when telling jokes or performing, e.g., avoid laughing
    c. Accompany client to room when hyperactivity is escalating
    d. Guard vigilantly against suicide as elation subsides and mood evens out

3. Institute measures to deal with manipulativeness
    a. Set limits, e.g., limit phone calls when excessive
        1) Set firm consistent times for meetings—client often late and unaware of time
        2) Refuse unreasonable demands, e.g., asks for date with the nurse
        3) Explain restrictions on behavior and reasons so client does not feel rejected
    b. Communicate using a firm, unambivalent consistent approach
        1) Use staff consistency in enforcing rules
        2) Remain nonjudgmental, e.g., when client disrobes say, "I cannot allow you to undress here."
        3) Never threaten or make comparisons to others, as it increases hostility and poor coping
    c. Avoid long, complicated discussions
        1) Use short sentences with specific straightforward responses
        2) Avoid giving advice when solicited, e.g., "I notice you want me to take responsibility for your life."

4. Meet physical needs
   a. Meet nutritional needs
      1) Encourage fluids; offer water every hour because client will not take the time to drink
      2) Give high-calorie finger foods and drinks to be carried while moving, e.g., cupcakes, sandwiches
      3) Serve meals on tray in client's room when too stimulated
   b. Encourage rest
      1) Sedate PRN
      2) Encourage short naps
   c. Supervise bathing routines when client plays with water or is too distracted to clean self

5. Administer medications

6. Help decrease denial and increase client's awareness of feelings
   a. Encourage expression of real feelings through reflecting
   b. Help client acknowledge the need for help when denying it, e.g., "You say you don't need love, but most people need love. It's okay to feel that."
   c. Function as a role model for client by communicating feelings openly
   d. Help client recognize demanding behavior, e.g., "You seem to want others to notice you."
   e. Encourage client to recognize needs of others
   f. Have client verbalize needs directly, e.g., wishes for attention

## SCHIZOPHRENIA

A. Data Collection

1. Withdrawal from relationships and from the world
   a. Neologisms, rhyming so that others can't understand communication
   b. Concrete thinking
   c. Social ineptitude—aloof and fails to encourage interpersonal relationships, ambivalence toward others

2. Inappropriate or flat effect

3. Hypochondriasis and/or depersonalization

4. Suspiciousness—sees world as a hostile, threatening place

5. Poor reality testing
   a. Hallucinations—false sensory perceptions in the absence of an external stimulus; may be auditory, visual, olfactory, or tactile
   b. Delusions—persistent false beliefs, e.g., client may believe stomach is missing
      1) Grandeur—belief that one is special, e.g., a monarch
      2) Persecutory—belief that one is victim of a plot
      3) Ideas of reference—belief that environmental events are directed toward the self, e.g., client sees people talking and believes they are discussing the client

6. Loose associations

7. Short attention span, decreased ability to comprehend stimuli

8. Regression

9. Inability to meet basic survival needs
   a. Unable to feed oneself (poor nutritional habits)
   b. Poor personal hygiene
   c. Inappropriate dress for the weather/environment

**B.** Diagnose

1. Specific types of schizophrenia (see Table 1)

Table 1

| SCHIZOPHRENIA | |
|---|---|
| TYPE | PRESENTING SYMPTOMS |
| Disorganized | Inappropriate behavior such as silly laughing and regression, transient hallucinations |
| Catatonic | Sudden-onset mutism, bizarre mannerisms, remains in stereotyped position with waxy flexibility; may have dangerous periods of agitation and explosivity |
| Paranoid | Late onset in life, characterized by suspicion and ideas of persecution and delusions |
| Undifferentiated | General symptoms of schizophrenia<br>Symptoms of more than one type of schizophrenia |
| Residual | No longer exhibits overt symptoms |

2. Potential nursing diagnoses
   a. Disturbed thought processes
   b. Disturbed sensory perception
   c. Self-care deficit
   d. Violence: directed toward self or others, risk for
   e. Social isolation

**C.** Plan/Implementation (see Tables 2 and 3)

1. Maintain client safety
   a. Protect from altered thought processes
      1) Decrease sensory stimuli, remove from areas of tension
      2) Validate reality, do not argue
      3) Recognize that client is experiencing hallucination
      4) Do not argue with client
      5) Respond to feeling or tone of hallucination or delusion
      6) Be alert to hallucinations that command client to harm self or others
   b. Protect from erratic and inappropriate behavior
      1) Communicate in calm, authoritative tone
      2) Address client by name
      3) Observe client for early signs of escalating behavior
   c. Administer antipsychotic medications

2. Meet physical needs of severely regressed clients
   a. Poor basic hygiene—may have to be washed initially
   b. Poor nutritional habits—may have to be fed
      1) Ask client to pick up fork; if unable to make decision, then feeding is necessary
      2) When ready, encourage client to eat in dining room with others
   c. May be nonverbal initially; do not force into groups

● Table 2

| NURSING CARE OF CLIENT WHO ACTS WITHDRAWN | |
|---|---|
| **Problem** | **Interventions** |
| Lack of trust and feeling of safety and security | Keep interactions brief, especially orientation<br>Structure environment<br>Be consistent and reliable; notify client of anticipated schedule changes<br>Decrease physical contact<br>Eye contact during greeting<br>Maintain attentiveness with head slightly leaning toward client and nonintrusive attitude<br>Allow physical distance<br>Accept client's behavior, e.g., silence; maintain matter-of-fact attitude toward behavior |
| Hallucinations | Maintain accepting attitude<br>Do not argue with client about reality of hallucinations<br>Comment on feeling, tone of hallucination, e.g., "That must be frightening to you."<br>Encourage diversional activities, e.g., playing cards, especially activities in which client can gain a sense of mastery, e.g., artwork<br>Encourage discussions of reality-based interests |
| Lack of attention to personal needs, e.g., nutrition, hygiene | Determine adequacy of hydration, nutrition<br>Structure routine for bathing, mealtime<br>Offer encouragement or assistance if necessary, e.g., sit with client or feed client if appropriate<br>Decrease environmental stimuli at mealtime, e.g., suggest early dinner before dining room crowds<br>Positioning and skin care for catatonic client |

3. Establish a therapeutic relationship—engage in individual therapy
   a. Institute measures to promote trust
      1) Same as general withdrawal from reality (see Table 2)
      2) Be consistent and reliable in keeping all scheduled appointments
      3) Avoid direct questions (client may feel threatened)
      4) Accept client's indifference, e.g., failure to smile or greet nurse, and avoidance behavior, e.g., hostility or sarcasm
      5) Discuss all staff changes, especially vacations and absences
   b. Encourage client's affect by verbalizing what you observe, e.g., "You seem to think that I don't want to stay." Use client's name in a calm, authorative tone
   c. Tolerate silences—may have to sit through long silences with client who is too anxious to speak (catatonic)
   d. Accept regression as a normal part of treatment when new stresses are encountered

1) With delusional regression, respond to associated feeling, not to the delusion, e.g., client claims he has no heart, nursing response: "You must feel empty."
2) Help pinpoint source of regression, e.g., anxiety about discharge

Table 3

| NURSING CARE OF A CLIENT WHO ACTS SUSPICIOUS | |
|---|---|
| **Problem** | **Interventions** |
| Mistrust and feeling of rejection | Keep appointments with clients<br>Clear, consistent communication<br>Allow client physical distance and keep door open when interviewing<br>Genuineness and honesty in interactions<br>Recognize testing behavior and show persistence of interest in client |
| Delusions | Allow client to verbalize the delusion in a limited way<br>Do not argue with client or try to convince that delusions are not real<br>Point out feeling tone of delusion<br>Provide activities to divert attention from delusions<br>Solitary activities best at first and then may progress to noncompetitive games or activities<br>Do not reinforce delusions by validating them<br>Focus on potential real concerns of client |

4. Engage in family therapy—especially when client is returning to family; understand the problem involves the family; establish a "family client" in need of support

5. Engage in socialization or activity group therapy according to client's ability
   a. Accept nonverbal behavior initially
   b. If client cannot tolerate group, do not force or embarrass
   c. Act as a social role model for client

6. Provide simple activities or tasks to promote positive self-esteem and success
   a. Finger painting and clay are good choices for regressed catatonic client
   b. Encourage attendance at occupational, vocational, and art therapy sessions
   c. Avoid competitive situations with paranoid—solitary activities are better

## PERSONALITY DISORDERS

A. Data Collection (see Table 4)

B. Diagnose (see Table 4)

C. Plan/Implementation (see Table 4)

●Table 4

| PERSONALITY DISORDERS | | | |
|---|---|---|---|
| TYPES | DATA | DIAGNOSE | NURSING CONSIDERATIONS |
| Paranoid | Suspiciousness<br>Hypersensitive, humorless, serious<br>Ideas of reference<br>Cold, blunted affect<br>Quick response with anger or rage | Interprets actions of others as personal threat<br>Uses projection: externalizes own feelings by projecting own desires and traits to others<br>Holds grudges | Establish trust<br>Be honest and nonintrusive<br>Low doses of phenothiazines to manage anxiety<br>Structured social situations<br>Be calm, authoritative, matter of fact |
| Schizoid | Shy and introverted; rarely has close friends<br>Little verbal interaction<br>Cold and detached | Uses intellectualization: describes emotional experiences in matter-of-fact way<br>Daydreaming may be more gratifying than real life | Same as paranoid |
| Schizotypal | Seems eccentric and odd<br>Sensitive to rejection and anger<br>Vague, stereotypical, overelaborate speech<br>Suspicious of others<br>Blunted or inappropriate affect | Similar to schizophrenia, fewer and milder psychotic episodes<br>Problems in thinking, perceiving, communicating<br>Common disorder among biological relatives of schizophrenics | Same as paranoid<br>Low-dose neuroleptics may decrease transient psychotic symptoms |
| Antisocial | Disregard for rights of others<br>Lying, cheating, stealing, promiscuous behaviors<br>Appears charming and intellectual, smooth-talking<br>Unlawful, aggressive and reckless behaviors<br>Lack of guilt, remorse, and conscience<br>Immature and irresponsible, especially in finances | Genetic predisposition<br>Correlates with substance abuse and dependency problems<br>More common in males<br>Rationalizes and denies own behaviors | Firm limit-setting<br>Confront behaviors consistently<br>Enforce consequences<br>Group therapy |
| Borderline | Seeks brief and intense relationships<br>Blames others for own problems<br>Depression, intense anger, labile mood, posttraumatic symptoms<br>Temper tantrums, physical fights<br>Impulsiveness, manipulative<br>Repetitive self-destructiveness, self-mutilation, suicidal<br>Overspending, promiscuity, compulsive overeating | 75% are women and have been sexually abused<br>Problems with identity, self image, thinking, and mood<br>Uses splitting to avoid pain and to protect self<br>Projective identification used to protect the self<br>Biological, environmental, and stress-related factors, including traumatic home environment<br>Abnormalities in serotonin systems<br>Suicidal behaviors occur when blocked, frustrated, or stressed | Help person identify and verbalize feelings and control negative behaviors<br>Use empathy<br>Behavioral contracts to decrease self-mutilation<br>Journal-writing<br>Consistent limit-setting needed<br>Supportive confrontation<br>Enforce unit rules<br>Psychopharmacology used sparingly for anxiety, psychotic states, suicidal ideation, mood swings<br>Group therapy |
| Narcissistic | Arrogant, appears indifferent to criticism while hiding anger, rage, or emptiness<br>Lacks ability to feel or demonstrate empathy<br>Sense of entitlement<br>Use others to meet their own needs<br>Displays grandiosity | Views others as superior or inferior to self<br>Shallow relationships with others<br>Feelings of others not understood or considered<br>Uses rationalization to blame others<br>Expects special treatment<br>Needs to be admired | Mirror what person sounds like, especially contradictions<br>Supportive confrontation to increase sense of self-responsibility<br>Limit-setting and consistency<br>Focus on the here and now<br>Teach that mistakes are acceptable, imperfections do not decrease worth |

*(continued)*

Table 4 (cont'd)

| PERSONALITY DISORDERS | | | |
|---|---|---|---|
| **TYPES** | **DATA** | **DIAGNOSE** | **NURSING CONSIDERATIONS** |
| **Histrionic** | Draws attention to self, thrives on being the center of attention<br>Silly, colorful, frivolous, seductive<br>Hurried, restless<br>Temper tantrums and outbursts of anger<br>Overreacts<br>Dissociation used to avoid feelings<br>Somatic complaints to avoid responsibility and support dependency | Cannot deal with feelings<br>Shallow, rapidly shifting emotions<br>Easily influenced by others | Positive reinforcement for unselfish or other-centered behaviors<br>Help clarify feelings and facilitate appropriate expression |
| **Dependent** | Dependent on others for everyday decisions<br>Passive<br>Problem initiating projects or working independently<br>Anxious or helpless when alone<br>Preoccupied with fear of being alone to care for self | Fears loss of support and approval<br>Lacks self-confidence | Emphasize decision-making to increase self-responsibility<br>Teach assertiveness<br>Assist to clarify feelings, needs, and desires |
| **Avoidant** | Timid, socially uncomfortable, withdrawn<br>Hypersensitive to criticism<br>Avoids situations where rejection is a possibility<br>Lacks self-confidence | Fears intimate relationships due to fear of ridicule<br>Believes self to be socially inept, unappealing, or inferior | Gradually confront fears<br>Discuss feelings before and after accomplishing a goal<br>Teach assertiveness<br>Increase exposure to small groups |
| **Obsessive-compulsive** | Sets high personal standards for self and others<br>Preoccupied with rules, lists, organization, details<br>Overconscientious and inflexible<br>Rigid and stubborn<br>Cold affect, may speak in monotone<br>Indecisive until all facts accumulated<br>Repetitive thoughts and actions | Difficulty expressing warmth<br>Rigid and controlling with others<br>Perfectionism interferes with task fulfillment | Explore feelings<br>Help with decision-making<br>Confront procrastination and intellectualization<br>Teach that mistakes are acceptable |

## MANIPULATIVE BEHAVIOR

**A.** Data Collection

1. Makes unreasonable requests for time, attention, and favors
2. Divides staff against each other—attempts to undermine nurse's role
3. Intimidates others
   a) Uses others' faults to own advantage, e.g., naiveté
   b) Makes others feel guilty
4. Uses seductive and disingenuous approach
   a) Makes personal approach with staff, e.g., acts more like friend than client
   b) Frequently lies and rationalizes
   c) Takes advantage of others for own gain
5. Frequently lies and rationalizes
6. May malinger or behave in helpless manner, e.g., feigns illness to avoid task

**B.** Diagnose

1. Predisposing conditions
   a. Bipolar disorder
   b. Substance abuse, alcoholism
   c. Antisocial disorders
   d. Adolescent adjustment reactions

2. Potential nursing diagnoses
   a. Social interactions, impaired
   b. Social isolation
   c. Violence: self-directed, risk for
   d. Violence: directed at others, risk for

**C.** Plan/Implementation

1. Goals
   a. Help client set limits on his behavior
   b. Help client learn to see the consequences of his behavior
   c. Help family members understand and deal with client
   d. Promote staff cooperation and consistency in caring for client

2. Use consistent undivided staff approach
   a. Clearly define expectations for client
   b. Adhere to hospital regulations
   c. Hold frequent staff conferences to avoid conflicts and increase staff communication

3. Set limits
   a. Do not allow behaviors that endanger or interfere with the rights or safety of others
   b. Carry out limit-setting, avoid threats and promises
   c. Give alternatives when possible
   d. Remain nonjudgmental
   e. Avoid arguing or allowing client to rationalize behavior
   f. Be brief in discussions

●Table 5

| NURSING CARE OF A CLIENT WHO ACTS VIOLENT | |
|---|---|
| **Problem** | **Interventions** |
| Increased agitation/anxiety | Recognize signs of impending violence, e.g., increased motor activity, pacing, or sudden stop—"calm before the storm"<br>Identify self, speak calmly but firmly, and in normal tone of voice<br>Help verbalize feelings<br>Use nonthreatening body language, e.g., arms to side, palm outward, keep distance, avoid blocking exit, avoid body contact<br>Avoid disagreeing with client or threatening client<br>Decrease stimuli—remove threatening objects or people |
| Violence | Intercede early<br>Continue nonthreatening behavior<br>If client needs to be restrained to protect self or others, get help (at least four people)<br>Move in organized, calm manner, stating that nurse wants to help and that you will not permit client to harm self or others<br>Use restraints correctly, e.g., never tie to bedside rail, check circulation frequently |

4. Be constantly alert for potential manipulation
   a. Favors, compliments
   b. Attempts to be personal
   c. Malingering, helplessness

5. Be alert for signs of destructive behavior
   a. Suicide
   b. Homicide

## VIOLENT/AGGRESSIVE BEHAVIOR

A. Data Collection

   1. Physical or verbal abuse of staff and/or other clients

   2. Overt anger and passive-aggressive behaviors

B. Diagnose

   1. Assault cycle: triggering phase, escalation phase, verbal aggression phase, crisis phase, recovery phase, postcrisis depression phase

   2. Caused by intrapersonal, familial, interpersonal, and environmental stressors

C. Plan/Implementation (see Table 5)

   1. Consider the source and the target of the anger

   2. Consider displacement of anger in delusions and hallucinations

3. Observe anger at a safe distance

4. Allow client to ventilate without violence

5. Ask client to state his/her own potential for violence

6. Contract with the client to use nonviolent methods to control anger

7. Be prepared to use seclusion if escalation with potential for violence exists

## EATING DISORDERS

**A.** Data Collection (see Table 6)

**B.** Diagnose (see Table 6)

**C.** Plan/Implementation (see Table 6)

Table 6

| EATING DISORDERS | | |
|---|---|---|
| **DISORDER** | **DATA TO COLLECT/DIAGNOSE** | **NURSING CONSIDERATIONS** |
| Anorexia nervosa | Most common in females 12-18 years old<br>Characterized by fear of obesity, dramatic weight loss, distorted body image, very structured food intake<br>Anemia, amenorrhea<br>Cathartics, diuretics, and enemas may be used for purging<br>Excessive exercise<br>Induced vomiting used for purging<br>May have cardiotoxicity secondary to use of ipecac<br>May have electrolyte imbalance | Monitor clinical status (e.g., weight, intake, vital signs)<br>Monitor hydration and electrolytes, especially potassium<br>Behavior modification may help in acute phase<br>Family therapy<br>Support efforts to take responsibility for self<br>Explore issues regarding sexuality<br>Contract with client |
| Bulimia | Characterized by all of the characteristics of anorexia and binge eating (eating increased amounts of high calorie food in a short period of time)<br>May be of normal weight or overweight<br>Tooth erosion and decay<br>GI bleeding (upper and/or lower)<br>May use vomiting, laxatives, enemas, diuretics or weight-loss medications | May be managed with antidepressants<br>Nutritional data and counseling |

## ACUTE ALCOHOL INTOXICATION

**A.** Data Collection (see Table 1)

**B.** Diagnose (see Table 1)

**C.** Plan/Implementation (see Table 1)

● Table 1

| POTENTIAL ALCOHOL INTOXICATION | | |
|---|---|---|
| **DATA** | **POTENTIAL NURSING DIAGNOSIS** | **NURSING CONSIDERATIONS** |
| Drowsiness | Acute confusion | Monitor vital signs frequently |
| Slurred speech | Risk for injury | Allow client to "sleep it off" |
| Tremors | Risk for ineffective | Protect airway from aspiration |
| Impaired thinking/memory loss | breathing pattern | Observe for need for IV glucose |
| Nystagmus | Risk for aspiration | Observe for injuries |
| Diminished reflexes | | Observe for signs of withdrawal and |
| Nausea/vomiting | | chronic alcohol dependence |
| Possible hypoglycemia | | Counsel about alcohol use |
| Increased respiration | | Potential problems of alcohol |
| Belligerence/grandiosity | | poisoning and CNS depression |
| Loss of inhibitions | | |
| Depression | | |

## ALCOHOL WITHDRAWL

**A.** Data Collection (see Table 2)

**B.** Diagnose—potential nursing diagnoses

1. Anxiety

2. Injury, risk for

3. Self-care deficit

4. Thought process, altered

**C.** Plan/Implementation (see Table 2)

Table 2

| ALCOHOL WITHDRAWAL | | |
|---|---|---|
| **WITHDRAWAL** | **DELIRIUM** | **NURSING CONSIDERATIONS** |
| Tremors | Tremors | Administer sedation as needed, |
| Easily startled | Anxiety | usually benzodiazepines |
| Insomnia | Panic | Monitor vital signs, particularly |
| Anxiety | Disorientation, confusion | pulse, BP, temperature |
| Anorexia | Hallucination | Seizure precautions |
| Alcoholic | Vomiting | Provide quiet, well-lit |
| hallucinations | Diarrhea | environment |
| | Paranoia | Orient client frequently |
| | Delusional symptoms | Don't leave hallucinating, |
| | Ideas of reference | confused client alone |
| | Suicide attempts | Administer anticonvulsants as |
| | Grand mal convulsions (especially first 48 | needed |
| | hours after drinking stopped) | Administer thiamine IV or IM as |
| | Potential coma/death | needed |
| | | Administer IV glucose as needed |
| | | 10% mortality rate |

## CHRONIC ALCOHOL DEPENDENCE

**A.** Data Collection

1. Persistent incapacitation

2. Cyclic drinking or "binges"

3. Daily drinking with increase in amount

4. Potential chronic central nervous system disorder (see Table 3)

5. Sexual relationships may be disturbed

6. Others in family may take over alcoholic's role, e.g., children
   may take parent's role, resulting in loss of childhood opportunities

7. Children often feel shame and embarrassment

8. High percentage of children develop problems with alcohol
   themselves

9. Incidence of family violence is increased with alcohol use

Table 3

| CHRONIC CNS DISORDERS ASSOCIATED WITH ALCOHOLISM | | | |
|---|---|---|---|
| | **ALCOHOLIC CHRONIC BRAIN SYNDROME (DEMENTIA)** | **WERNICKE'S SYNDROME** | **KORSAKOFF'S PSYCHOSIS** |
| **Symptoms** | Fatigue, anxiety, personality changes, depression, confusion Loss of memory of recent events Can progress to dependent, bedridden state | Confusion, diplopia, nystagmus, ataxia Disorientation, apathy | Memory disturbance with confabulation, loss of memory of recent events, learning problem Possible problem with taste and smell, loss of reality testing |
| **Nursing considerations** | Balanced diet, abstinence from alcohol | IV or IM thiamine, abstinence from alcohol | Balanced diet, thiamine, abstinence from alcohol |

**B.** Diagnose—potential nursing diagnoses

    1. Imbalanced nutrition: less than body requirements

    2. Chronic low self-esteem

    3. Social isolation

    4. Dysfunctional family processes: alcoholism

**C.** Plan/Implementation

    1. Counseling the alcoholic
       a. Identify problems related to drinking—in family relationships, work, medical, and other areas of life
       b. Help client to see/admit problem
          1) Confront denial with slow persistence
          2) Maintain relationship with client

    2. Establish control of problem drinking
       a. Concrete support to identify potentially troublesome settings that trigger drinking behavior
       b. Alcoholics Anonymous—valuable mutual support group
          1) Peers share experiences
          2) Learn to substitute contact with humans for alcohol
          3) Stresses living in the present; stop drinking one day at a time
       c. Disulfiram—drug used to maintain sobriety; based on behavioral therapy
          1) Once sufficient blood level is reached, disulfiram interacts with alcohol to provide severe reaction
          2) Symptoms of disulfiram-alcohol reaction include flushing, coughing, difficulty breathing, nausea, vomiting, pallor, anxiety
          3) Contraindicated in diabetes mellitus, atherosclerotic heart disease, cirrhosis, kidney disease, psychosis

    3. Counsel the spouse of the alcoholic
       a. Initial goal is to help spouse focus on self
       b. Explore life problems from spouse's point of view
       c. Spouse can attempt to help alcoholic once strong enough
       d. Al-Anon: self-help group of spouses and relatives
          1) Learn "loving detachment" from alcoholic
          2) Goal is to try to make one's own life better and not to blame the alcoholic
          3) Provides safe, helpful environment

    4. Counsel children of alcoholic parents
       a. Overcome denial of problem
       b. Establish trusting relationship
       c. Work with parents as well; avoid negative reactions to parents
       d. Referral to Alateen: organization for teenagers of alcoholic parent; self-help, similar to Al-Anon

## NONALCOHOLIC SUBSTANCE ABUSE

**A.** Data Collection (see Table 4)

**B.** Diagnose

1.  Drug addiction—a physiological and psychological dependence; increasing doses needed to maintain "high" (tolerance)

2.  Substance abusers have a low frustration tolerance and need for immediate gratification to escape anxiety

3.  Addiction may result from prolonged use of medication for physical or psychological pain

4.  Becomes a problem with some nurses

5.  Potential nursing diagnoses
    a.  Ineffective denial/coping
    b.  Dysfunctional family processes: substance abuse
    c.  Violence: directed toward self or others, risk for

**C.** Plan/Implementation

1.  Observe for signs and symptoms of intoxication or drug use
    a.  Examine skin for cuts, needle-marks, abscesses, or bruises
    b.  Recognize symptoms of individual drug overdose
        1)  Hypotension, decreased respirations with narcotics and sedatives
        2)  Agitation with amphetamines and hallucinogens

2.  Treat symptoms of overdose
    a.  Maintain respiration—airway when needed
    b.  IV therapy as necessary
    c.  Administer naloxone
        1)  Antagonist to narcotics—induces withdrawal, stimulates respirations
        2)  Short-acting—symptoms of respiratory depression may return; additional doses may be necessary
    d.  Gastric lavage for overdose of sedatives taken orally
    e.  Dialysis to eliminate barbiturates from system

3.  Observe for signs of withdrawal, e.g., sweating, agitation, panic, hallucinations
    a.  Identify drug type
    b.  Seizure precautions
    c.  Keep airway on hand
    d.  Detoxify gradually
        1)  Methadone or naltrexone used for long-term maintenance and acute withdrawal (narcotic)
        2)  Decreasing doses of drug substitute

4.  Treat panic from acute withdrawal and/or marked depression
    a.  Hospitalize temporarily for psychotic response
    b.  Decrease stimuli, provide calm environment

c. Protect client from self-destructive behavior

d. Stay with client to reduce anxiety, panic, and confusion

e. Assure client that hallucinations are from drugs and will subside

f. Administer medications as indicated to manage symptoms of withdrawal and panic

g. Monitor vital signs

5. Promote physical health

  a. Identify physical health needs

    1) Rest

    2) Nutrition

    3) Shelter

● Table 4

| NONALCOHOLIC SUBSTANCE ABUSE | | | |
|---|---|---|---|
| **MEDICATION/DRUG** | **SYMPTOMS OF ABUSE** | **SYMPTOMS OF WITHDRAWAL** | **NURSING CONSIDERATIONS** |
| **Barbiturates**<br>(downers, barbs, pink ladies, rainbows, yellow jackets)<br>Phenobarbital<br>Nembutal | Respiratory depression<br>Decreased BP and pulse<br>Coma, ataxia, seizures<br>Increasing nystagmus<br>Poor muscle coordination<br>Decreased mental alertness | Anxiety, insomnia<br>Tremors, delirium<br>Convulsions | Maintain airway<br>(intubate, suction)<br>Check LOC and vital signs<br>Start IV with large-gauge needle<br>Give sodium bicarbonate to promote excretion<br>Give activated charcoal, use gastric lavage<br>Hemodialysis |
| **Narcotics**<br>Morphine<br>Heroin (horse, junk, smack)<br>Codeine<br>Dilaudid<br>Meperidine<br>Methadone—<br>  for detoxification and maintenance | Marked respiratory depression<br>Hyperpyrexia<br>Seizures, ventricular dysrhythmias<br>Euphoria, then anxiety, sadness, insomnia, sexual indifference<br>Pinpoint pupils<br>Stupor leading to coma | Watery eyes, runny nose<br>Loss of appetite<br>Irritability, tremors, panic<br>Cramps, nausea<br>Chills and sweating<br>Elevated BP<br>Hallucinations, delusions | Maintain airway<br>(intubate, suction)<br>Control seizures<br>Check LOC and vital signs<br>Start IV, may be given bolus of glucose<br>Have lidocaine and defibrillator available<br>Treat for hyperthermia<br>Give naloxone to reverse respiratory depression<br>Hemodialysis |
| **Stimulants**<br>(uppers, pep pills, speed, crystal meth)<br>Cocaine (crack)<br>Amphetamine<br>Benzedrine<br>Dexedrine | Tachycardia, increased BP, tachypnea, anxiety<br>Irritability, insomnia, agitation<br>Seizures, coma, hyperpyrexia, euphoria<br>Nausea, vomiting<br>Hyperactivity, rapid speech<br>Hallucinations<br>Nasal septum perforation (cocaine) | Apathy<br>Long periods of sleep<br>Irritability<br>Depression, disorientation | Maintain airway<br>(intubate, suction)<br>Start IV<br>Use cardiac monitoring<br>Check LOC and vital signs<br>Give activated charcoal, use gastric lavage<br>Monitor for suicidal ideation<br>Keep in calm, quiet environment |
| **Cannabis derivatives**<br>(pot, weed, grass, reefer, joint, mary jane)<br>Marijuana<br>Hashish | Fatigue<br>Paranoia, psychosis<br>Euphoria, relaxed inhibitions<br>Increased appetite<br>Disoriented behavior | Insomnia, hyperactivity<br>Decreased appetite | Most effects disappear in 5-8 hr as drug wears off<br>May cause psychosis |
| **Hallucinogens**<br>LSD (acid)<br>PCP (angel dust, rocket fuel)<br>Mescaline (buttons, cactus) | Nystagmus, marked confusion, hyperactivity<br>Incoherence, hallucinations, distorted body image<br>Delirium, mania, self-injury<br>Hypertension, hyperthermia<br>Flashbacks, convulsions, coma | None | Maintain airway<br>(intubate, suction)<br>Control seizures<br>Check LOC and vital signs<br>"Talk down" client<br>Reduce sensory stimuli<br>Small doses of diazepam<br>Check for trauma, protect from self-injury |

    b. Complete physical work-up

       1) Heroin addicts need to be followed for liver and cardiac complications, sexually transmitted disease, AIDS

       2) Dental care

6. Administer methadone for maintenance when indicated

    a. Synthetic narcotic—blocks euphoric effects of narcotics

    b. Eliminates craving and withdrawal symptoms

    c. Daily urine collected to monitor for other drug abuse while on methadone

7. Implement measures for antisocial personality disorders/manipulative behaviors

    a. Structured, nonpermissive environment

    b. Milieu therapy—peer pressure to conform

    c. Set limits but remain nonjudgmental

    d. Refer to drug-free programs (Synanon, Phoenix House, Odyssey House) for confrontation and support to remain drug-free

8. Treat underlying emotional problems

    a. Individual therapy—give support and acceptance

    b. Group therapy—to learn new ways of interacting

    c. Promote use of self-help groups

9. Assist client with rehabilitation, e.g., work programs, vocational counseling, family counseling, completion of schooling

## CHILD ABUSE

**A.** Data Collection

1.  Inconsistency between type/location of injury (bruises, burns, fractures, especially chip/spiral) with the history of the incident(s)

2.  Unexplained physical or thermal injuries

3.  Withdraws or is fearful of parents

4.  Sexual abuse—genital lacerations, sexually transmitted diseases

5.  Emotional neglect, failure to thrive, distrubed sleep, change in behavior in school

**B.** Diagnose

1.  Intentional physical, emotional, and/or sexual misuse/trauma or intentional omission of basic needs (neglect), usually related to diminished/limited ability of parent(s) to cope with, provide for, and/or relate to child

2.  Those at high risk include children born prematurely and/or of low birth weight, children under 3 years of age, and children with physical and/or mental disabilities

3.  Potential nursing diagnoses
    a.  Risk for trauma
    b.  Interrupted family processes/impaired parenting

**C.** Plan/Implementation

1.  Provide for physical needs first

2.  Mandatory reporting of identified/suspected cases to appropriate agency

3.  Nonjudgmental treatment of parents; encourage expression of feelings

4.  Provide role modeling and encourage parents to be involved in care

5.  Reinforce teaching of growth and development concepts, especially safety, discipline, age-appropriate activities, and human nutrition

6.  Provide emotional support for child; play therapy (dolls, drawings, making up stories) may be more appropriate way for child to express feelings

7. Initiate protective placement and/or appropriate referrals for long-term follow-up

8. Documentation should reflect only what nurse saw or was told, not nurse's interpretation or opinion

## ELDER ABUSE

**A.** Data Collection

1. Battering, fractures, bruises

2. Over/undermedicated

3. Absence of needed dentures, glasses

4. Poor nutritional status, dehydration

5. Physical evidence of sexual abuse

6. Urine burns, excoriated skin, pressure ulcers

7. Fear, apprehension, withdrawl from usual activities

**B.** Diagnose

1. Elderly with chronic illness and depletion of financial resources who are dependent on children and grandchildren

2. Population trends of today contribute to decline in amount of people available to care for elderly

3. Potential nursing diagnoses
   a. Compromised family coping
   b. Risk for trauma
   c. Nutrition, less than body requirements

**C.** Plan/Implementation

1. Provide for safety

2. Provide for physical needs first

3. Report to appropriate agencies (state laws vary)

4. Initiate protective placement and/or appropriate referrals

5. Consider client's rights of self-determination

## SEXUAL ABUSE

**A.** Data Collection

1. Sexually abused child
   a. Disturbed growth and development
   b. Child becomes protective (parent) of others
   c. Uses defense mechanisms (e.g., denial, dissociation)
   d. Sleep and eating disturbances
   e. Depression and aggression, emotional deadening, amnesia
   f. Poor impulse control

      g.  Somatic symptoms (e.g., chronic pain, GI disturbances)

      h.  Truancy and running away

      i.  Self-destructiveness

  2.  Adult victims of childhood sexual abuse

      a.  Response is similar to delayed postraumatic stresss disorder (PTSD)

      b.  Nightmares

      c.  Unwanted, intrusive memories

      d.  Kinesthetic sensations

      e.  Flashbacks

      f.  Relationship issues, fears of intimacy and abandonment

  3.  Sexually abused adult

      a.  Uses defense mechanisms (e.g., denial, dissociation)

      b.  Relationship issues, abusive relationships, fears of intimacy and abandonment

      c.  Somatic complaints

      d.  Homicidal thoughts, violence

      e.  Hypervigilance, panic attacks, phobias/agoraphobia

      f.  Suicidal thoughts/attempts

      g.  Self-mutilation

      h.  Compulsive eating/dieting, binging/purging

**B.**  Diagnose

  1.  Victims from every sociocultural, ethnic, and economic group

  2.  Within the family (incest) and outside the family

  3.  Usually involves younger, weaker victim

  4.  Victim is usually urged and coerced, manipulated through fear

  5.  Difficult to expose abuse; common for child not to be believed

**C.**  Plan/Implementation

  1.  Establish trusting relationship

  2.  Use empathy, active support, compassion, warmth

  3.  Nonjudgmental approach

  4.  Group and individual therapy; appropriate referrals

  5.  Medications as needed (e.g., antianxiety)

  6.  Report to appropriate agencies

## DOMESTIC VIOLENCE

**A.**  Data Collection

  1.  Frequent visits to health care provider's office or emergency room for unexplained trauma

  2.  Client being cued, silenced, or threatened by an accompanying family member

3. Evidence of multiple old injuries, scars, healed fractures seen on x-ray

4. Fearful, evasive, or inconsistent replies and nonverbal behaviors such as flinching when approached or touched

**B.** Diagnose

1. Family violence is usually accompanied by brainwashing (e.g., victims blame themselves, feel unworthy, and fear that they won't be believed)

2. Long-term results of family violence are depression, suicidal ideation, low self-esteem, and impaired relationships outside the family

3. Women and children are the most common victims, but others include adolescents, men, and parents

**C.** Plan/Implementation

1. Provide privacy during initial interview to insure that the perpetrator of violence does not remain with client; make a statement, e.g., "This part of the exam is always done in private."

2. Carefully document all injuries using body maps or photographs (with consent)

3. Determine the safety of client by specific questions about weapons in the home, substance abuse, extreme jealousy

4. Develop with client a safety or escape plan

5. Refer the client to community resources such as shelters, hotlines, and support groups

PHYSIOLOGICAL
INTEGRITY 2

[PHYSIOLOGICAL ADAPTATION]

## Chapter 7

Medical Emergencies

Fluid and Electrolyte
Imbalances

Alterations in Body Systems

Cancer

## UPPER AIRWAY OBSTRUCTION

**A.** Data Collection

1. Inability to breathe or speak

2. Cyanosis

3. Collapse

4. Death can occur within 4–5 minutes

**B.** Diagnose—potential nursing diagnosis

1. Airway clearance, ineffective

**C.** Planning/Implementation

1. Heimlich maneuver

2. Five plus five if conscious
   a) Give 5 back blows between shoulder blade with heel of hand
   b) Give 5 abdominal thrusts (Heimlich maneuver)
   c) Alternate between 5 back blows and 5 thrusts until the blockage is dislodged

3. If unconscious begin CPR; remove object if visible

●Table 1

| INTUBATION | |
|---|---|
| **METHOD** | **NURSING CONSIDERATIONS** |
| Endotracheal tube— tube passed through the nose or mouth into the trachea | Auscultate and observe for bilateral breath sounds and bilateral chest excursion<br>Mark tube at level it touches mouth or nose<br>Secure with tape to stabilize<br>Encourage fluids to facilitate removal of secretions |
| Tracheostomy—surgical incision made into trachea via the throat; tube inserted through incision into the trachea | Cuff is used to prevent aspiration and to facilitate mechanical ventilation<br>Maintain cuff pressure at 14-20 mm Hg<br>Encourage fluids to facilitate removal of secretions<br>Sterile suctioning if necessary<br>Frequent oral hygiene<br>Indications for suctioning tracheostomy<br>• Noisy respirations<br>• Restlessness<br>• Increased pulse<br>• Increased respirations<br>• Presence of mucus in airway |

2. Intubation (see Table 1 and Figure 1)

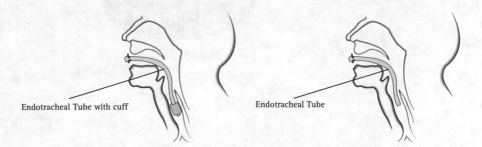

Endotracheal Tube with cuff

Endotracheal Tube

**Figure 1.   Endotracheal Tube**

3. Tracheostomy (see Table 1 and Figure 2)

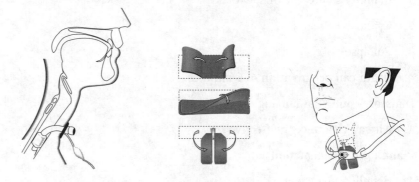

**Figure 2.   Tracheostomy Tube**

4. Suctioning

5. Mechanical ventilation

   a. Prepare client psychologically for use of ventilator

   b. Monitor client's response to the ventilator

      1) Obtain vital signs at least q 4 hours

      2) Listen to breath sounds (rales, rhonchi, wheezes, equal breath sounds, decreased or absent breath sounds)

      3) Observe for need for suctioning

      4) Respiratory monitoring—pulse oximetry

      5) Monitor ABGs

      6) Check for hypoxia (restlessness, cyanosis, anxiety, tachycardia, increased respiratory rate)

      7) Check neurologic status

      8) Check chest for bilateral expansion

   c. Provide good oral hygiene at least twice each shift

   d. Observe for need for tracheal/oral/nasal suctioning q 2 hours and perform as necessary

   e. Move endotracheal tube to opposite side of mouth q 24 hours to prevent ulcers

   f. Monitor intake and output

   g. Create alternative methods of communication with client (letter board, pencil and paper); provide access to call light

    h.  Perform and document ventilator and equipment checks—care for client first, ventilator second

        1)  Check ventilator settings as ordered by health care provider—tidal volume (TV), respiratory rate, $pO_2$ (fraction of inspired oxygen), mode of ventilation, sigh button/cycle (usually 1–3/h) (may cause lung damage from excessive pressure)

        2)  Check that alarms are set (low pressure and low exhaled volume)

        3)  Check temperature and level of water in humidification system

        4)  Check PEEP (positive end-expiratory pressure) maintained at end of expiration to open collapsed alveoli and improve oxygenation

        5)  Drain condensation from tubing away from client

        6)  Verify that tracheostomy or endotracheal cuff is inflated to ensure tidal volume

    i.  Observe for gastrointestinal distress (diarrhea, constipation, tarry stools)

    j.  Document observations/procedures in medical record

  6.  Oxygen administration

## CARDIOPULMONARY ARREST

**A.**  Data Collection

  1.  Breathless

  2.  Pulseless

  3.  Unconscious

**B.**  Diagnose

  1.  Failure to institute ventilation within 4 to 6 minutes will result in cerebral anoxia and brain damage

  2.  Purpose—to re-establish $CO_2/O_2$ exchange and adequate circulation

**C.**  Plan/Implementation

  1.  Basic Life Support

    a.  Recognition

      i.   All ages: unresponsive

      ii.  Adults: no breathing or no normal breathing (i.e., only gasping)

      iii.  Children and infants: no breathing or only gasping

      iv.  No pulse palpated within 10 seconds (HCP only)

    b.  Activate EMS system

    c.  CPR sequence:  C-A-B

    d.  Compression rate: at least 100/minute

    e.  Compression depth

      i.   Adults: at least 2 inches (5 cm)

      ii.  Children: at least ½ anterior posterior diameter or about 2 inches (5 cm)

      iii.  Infants: at least ¼ anterior posterior diameter or about 1 ½ inches (4 cm)

    f.  Chest wall recoil

      i.   Allow complete recoil between compressions

      ii.  HCPs rotate compressors every 2 minutes

    g. Compression interruptions

      i. Minimize interruptions in chest compressions

      ii. Attempt to limit interruptions to <10 seconds

    h. Airway

      i. Head tilt-chin lift

      ii. HCP suspected trauma; jaw thrust

    i. Compression-to-ventilation ratio (until advance airway placed)

      i. Adult: 30:2; 1 or 2 rescuers

      ii. Children and infants: 30:2 single rescuer; 15:2 2 HCP rescuers

    j. Ventilations when rescuer untrained or trained and not proficient: compressions only

    k. Ventilations with advanced airway (HCP)

      i. 1 breath every 6–8 seconds (8–10 breaths/minute)

      ii. Asynchronous with chest compressions

      iii. About 1 second per breath

      iv. Visible chest rise

    l. Defibrillation

      i. Attach and use AED as soon as possible

      ii. Minimize compressions before and after shock

      iii. Resume CPR beginning with compressions immediately after each shock

2. Continue CPR until one of the following occurs

    a. Victim responds

    b. Another qualified person takes over

    c. Victim is transferred to an emergency room

    d. Rescuer is physically unable to continue

**D.** Evaluation

1. Has cardiac function been re-established?

2. Has cerebral anoxia been prevented?

## CROUP SYNDROMES: ACUTE EPIGLOTTITIS, ACUTE LARYNGOTRACHEOBRONCHITIS

**A.** Data Collection

1. Barklike cough, use of accessory muscles

2. Dyspnea, inspiratory stridor, cyanosis

3. Decrease in noisy respirations may indicate decompensation

**B.** Diagnose

1. Viral—infection in the area of the larynx

2. Medical emergency due to narrowed airway in children

3. Potential nursing diagnoses

    a. Risk for suffocation

    b. Anxiety

**C.** Plan/Implementation

   1. Care at home

     a. Steamy shower

     b. Sudden exposure to cold air

     c. Sleep with cool humidified air

   2. Hospitalization required

     a. Increasing respiratory distress

     b. Hypoxia or depressed sensorium

     c. High temperature (102°F)

   3. Nursing care if hospitalized

     a. Maintain airway (keep tracheostomy set at bedside)

     b. Oxygen hood

     c. Monitor heart rate and respiration for early sign of hypoxia

     d. Oxygen with humidification

     e. IV fluids

     f. Medications: antipyretics, bronchodilators, nebulized epinephrine, steroids

     g. Position in infant seat or prop with pillow

## MYOCARDIAL INFARCTION (MI)

**A.** Data Collection

   1. Symptoms vary depending on whether pain, shock, or pulmonary edema dominates clinical picture

   2. Chest pain—severe, crushing, prolonged; unrelieved by rest or nitroglycerin; often radiating to one or both arms, jaw, neck, and back (see Figure 3); women may present with atypical symptoms (fatigue, shortness of breath)

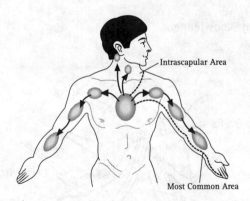

Intrascapular Area

Most Common Area

**Figure 3. Ischemic Pain Patterns**

   3. Dyspnea

   4. Nausea, vomiting, gastric discomfort, indigestion

   5. Apprehension, restless, fear of death

   6. Acute pulmonary edema, sense of suffocating

7. Cardiac arrest

8. Shock—systolic blood pressure below 80 mm Hg, gray facial color, lethargy, cold diaphoresis, peripheral cyanosis, tachycardia or bradycardia, weak pulse

9. Oliguria—urine output of less than 20 ml/hour

10. Low-grade fever—temperature rises to 100°–103°F within 24 hours and lasts 3 to 7 days

11. Dysrhythmias, heart block, asystole

12. WBC—leukocytosis within 2 days, disappears in 1 week

13. Erythrocyte sedimentation rate (ESR)—elevated

14. CK–MB—first enzyme tube to be elevated after MI; appears 3–6 hours; peaks 18–24 hours

15. LDH—appears 12–24 hours; peaks 48–72 hours; lasts 6–12 days

16. Troponin—peaks in 4–12 hours; remains elevated for up to 3 weeks

17. Myoglobin—begins to rise within 1 hour; peaks in 4 to 6 hours; returns to normal in less than 24 hours

18. Electrocardiogram—ST segment elevation, T wave inversion, Q wave formation

**B.** Diagnose

1. Formation of localized necrotic areas within the myocardium, usually following the sudden occlusion of a coronary artery and the abrupt decrease of blood and oxygen to the heart muscle

2. Causes
   a. Complete or near complete occlusion of a coronary vessel (most common)
   b. Decreased blood and oxygen supply to the heart muscle
   c. Hypertrophy of the heart muscle from CHF or hypertension
   d. Embolism to a coronary artery

3. Potential nursing diagnoses
   a. Risk for decreased cardiac output
   b. Anxiety/fear
   c. Deficient knowledge

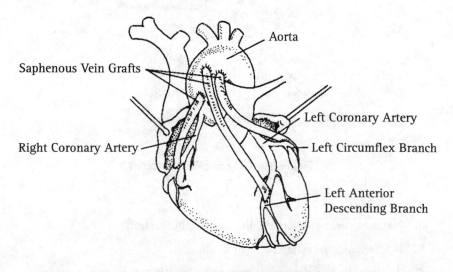

**Figure 4.   Coronary Artery and Heart**

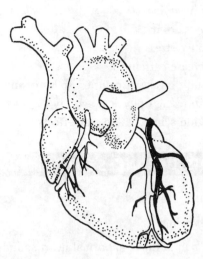

**Figure 5.  Coronary Blood Vessels**

**C.** Plan/Implementation

1. Provide thrombolytic therapy—streptokinase or tissue-type plasminogen activator (t-PA) to dissolve thrombus in coronary artery within 6 hours of onset

2. Relieve client's and family's anxiety

3. Bedrest to decrease stress on heart, allow to use bedside commode for bowel movement

4. Monitor vital signs, pain status, lung sounds, level of consciousness, ECG, oxygen saturation

5. Monitor intake and output
   a. Intake—fluid intake 2,000 ml daily; too much may precipitate CHF, and too little may result in dehydration
   b. Output—Foley catheter, if necessary; oliguria indicates inadequate renal perfusion, concentrated urine indicates dehydration

6. Carefully monitor IV infusion—vein should be kept open in case emergency IV drugs are necessary

7. Administer medications: beta blockers (e.g., Inderal), morphine sulfate for pain (reduces preload, afterload pressures, and decreases anxiety), dysrhythmics (e.g., lidocaine, verapamil), anticoagulant medications (e.g., heparin, coumadin)

8. Prevent complications
   a. Dysrhythmias
   b. Shock
   c. Congestive heart failure
   d. Rupture of heart muscle
   e. Pulmonary embolism
   f. Recurrent MI

9. Reinforce teaching
   a. Healing not complete for 6–8 weeks

    b. Modify lifestyle
       1) Stop smoking
       2) Reduce stress
       3) Decrease caffeine
       4) Modify intake of calories, sodium, and fat
    c. Maintain regular physical activity
    d. Medication schedule and side effects

## RHYTHM DISTURBANCES (DYSRHYTHMIAS)

**A.** Data Collection

    1. Dizziness, syncope

    2. Chest pain, palpitations, abnormal heart sounds

    3. Nausea, vomiting

    4. Dyspnea

    5. Abnormal pulse rate—increased, decreased, or irregular

**B.** Diagnose

    1. Caused by interruption in normal conduction process

    2. Can occur at any point in the normal conduction pathway

    3. Types of dysrhythmias

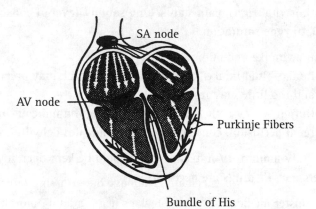

**Figure 6. Transmission of Electrical Impulses**

    a. Sinus dysrhythmias—dysrhythmias originate in the sinoatrial node and are conducted along the normal conductive pathways
       1) Tachycardia—sympathetic nervous system increases the automaticity of the SA node
         a) Heart rate is increased above 100 beats per minute
         b) Causes—pain, exercise, hypoxia, pulmonary embolism, hemorrhage, hyperthyroidism, or fever
       2) Bradycardia—parasympathetic nervous system (vagal stimulation) causes automaticity of the SA node to be depressed

a) Heart rate decreased to below 60 beats per minute

b) Causes—myocardial infarction, the Valsalva maneuver, or vomiting, arteriosclerosis in the carotid sinus area, ischemia of SA node, hypothermia, hyperkalemia, or drugs such as digitalis and propranolol

b. Atrial dysrhythmias—abnormal electrical activity that results in stimulation outside the SA node but within the atria

  1) Atrial flutter

    a) Arises from an ectopic focus in the atrial wall causing the atrium to contract 250 to 400 times per minute

    b) AV node blocks most of the impulses, thereby protecting the ventricles from receiving every impulse

    c) Some clients are unaware of this dysrhythmia, while others complain of palpitations or fainting

    d) Causes—stress, hypoxia, drugs, or disorders such as chronic heart disease, hypertension

  2) Atrial fibrillation

    a) Most common atrial dysrhythmia arising from several ectopic foci

    b) Client presents with a grossly irregular pulse rate

    c) Confusion, syncope, and dizziness may occur with severe hypoxia; pump failure may result

    d) Causes—chronic lung disease, heart failure, and rheumatic heart disease, chronic hypertension

c. Ventricular dysrhythmias—occur when one or more ectopic foci arise within the ventricles

  1) Premature ventricular contractions (PVCs)

    a) One or more ectopic foci stimulate a premature ventricular response

    b) May decrease the efficiency of the heart's pumping action

    c) Palpitations, a feeling of irregular heartbeat, or a "lump in the throat"

    d) Causes—ischemia due to a myocardial infarction, infection, mechanical damage due to pump failure, deviations in concentrations of electrolytes (e.g., potassium, calcium), nicotine, coffee, tea, alcohol, drugs such as digitalis and reserpine, psychogenic factors (stress, anxiety, fatigue), and acute or chronic lung disease

  2) Ventricular tachycardia

    a) Three or more PVCs occurring in a row

    b) Indicative of severe myocardial irritability

    c) Physical effects include chest pain, dizziness, fainting, occasional collapse

  3) Ventricular fibrillation

    a) Most serious of all dysrhythmias because of potential cardiac standstill; death will occur if not treated

    b) Several ectopic foci within the ventricles are discharged at a very rapid rate

c) Causes–acute myocardial infarction, hypertension, rheumatic or arteriosclerotic heart disturbances, or hypoxia

d) Unless blood flow is restored (by CPR) and the dysrhythmia is interrupted (by defibrillation), death will result within 90 seconds to 5 minutes

d. Heart block–delay in the conduction of impulses within the atrioventricular system

1) Complete heart block

a) AV junction blocks all impulses to the ventricles, causing the atria and ventricles to dissociate and beat independently (each with its own pacemaker establishing a rate, ventricular rate is low, 20 to 40 beats per minute)

b) Causes–congenital defects, vascular insufficiency, fibrosis of the myocardial tissue, or myocardial infarction

c) Symptoms–palpitations, dizziness, syncope, dyspnea, mental confusion, and cyanosis

d) If not treated immediately, may lead to death

4. Diagnostic tests

a. EKG (see Figure 7)

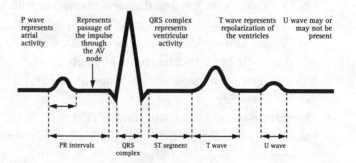

**Figure 7.  Components of an EKG**

b. ABGs

c. Holter recorder

1) 24-hour continuous EKG tracing

2) Client keeps diary of activities

d. Cardiac catheterization (see Reduction of Risk Potential)

e. Echocardiogram–noninvasive, sound waves used to examine cardiac structures

f. Stress testing–client walks on treadmill, pedals stationary bicycle, or climbs set of stairs, EKG monitored before, during, and after exercise testing

**C.** Plan/Implementation

1. Vital signs

2. Cardiac monitor identifies changes in rhythm and rate (see Figure 8)

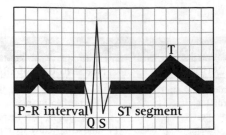

**Figure 8. Components of an EKG**

a. Determine rate
   1) If regular, count the number of R-R intervals (or number of QRS complexes) in 6 seconds, multiply by 10
b. Determine rhythm
   1) Presence or absence of P wave—SA node originated impulse
   2) Measure P-R interval—normal: 0.12–0.20 seconds (each small box = 0.04 seconds)
   3) Measure QRS duration—normal: 0.04–0.12 seconds
   4) Check P wave, QRS complex, ST segment, and T wave

Table 2

| DEFIBRILLATION VERSUS CARDIOVERSION | | |
|---|---|---|
| | **DEFIBRILLATION** | **CARDIOVERSION** |
| **Indication** | Emergency treatment of ventricular fibrillation | Elective procedure for dysrhythmias such as atrial fibrillation |
| **Action** | Completely depolarizes all myocardial cells so SA node can re-establish as pacemaker | Same |
| **Nursing considerations** | Start CPR before defibrillation<br>Plug in defibrillator and turn on<br>Turn on monitor and attach leads to client<br>Apply gel or paste to paddles (rub paddle surfaces together)<br>Select electric charge as ordered<br>Paddles placed over right sternal border and over the apex of the heart<br>Person with paddles calls "all clear"<br>Push discharge button<br>Check monitor between shocks for rhythm<br>Don't stop to check pulse after shocks, continue CPR, intubate, start IV<br>Epinephrine given 1 mg IV push every 3-5 minutes<br>Sodium bicarbonate given to treat acidosis | Informed consent<br>Diazepam IV<br>Digoxin withheld for 48 hours prior to procedure<br>Synchronizer turned on, check at the R wave<br>Oxygen discontinued<br>Observe for airway patency<br>Plug in defibrillator and turn on<br>Turn on oscilloscope and attach leads to client<br>Apply gel or paste (rub paddle surfaces together)<br>Voltage 25-360 joules<br>Paddles placed over right sternal border and over the apex of the heart<br>Person with paddles calls "all clear"<br>Push discharge button<br>Check monitor between shocks for rhythm<br>After procedure, obtain vital signs every 15 minutes for 1 hour; every 30 minutes for 2 hours; then every 4 hours |

Table 3

| PACEMAKERS | | | |
|---|---|---|---|
| **TYPES** | **ACTION** | **COMPLICATIONS** | **NURSING CONSIDERATIONS** |
| Demand (synchronous; noncompetitive) | Functions when heart rate goes below set rate | Dislodgement and migration of endocardial leads<br>Wire breakage<br>Cracking of insulation surrounding wires<br>Infection of sites surrounding either pacing wires or pulse generator<br>Interference with pacemaker function by exposure to electromagnetic fields (old microwave ovens, MRI equipment, metal detectors at airports)<br>Perforation of myocardium or right ventricle<br>Abrupt loss of pacing | Observe for infection, bleeding<br>Monitor heart rate and rhythm; for preset rate pacemakers, client's rate may vary 5 beats above or below set rate<br>Provide emotional support<br>Check pulse daily, report any sudden increase or decrease in rate<br>Carry ID card or wear identification<br>Request hand scanning at security check points at airports<br>Avoid situations involving electromagnetic fields<br>Periodically check generator<br>Take frequent rest periods at home and at work<br>Wear loose clothing over area of pacemaker<br>All electrical equipment used in vicinity of client should be properly grounded<br>Immobilize extremity if temporary electrode pacemaker is used to prevent dislodgement<br>Document model of pacemaker, date and time of insertion, location of pulse generator, stimulation threshold, pacer rate<br>Place cell phone on side opposite generator |
| Fixed rate (asynchronous; competitive) | Stimulates ventricle at preset constant rate | | |
| Temporary | Used in emergency situations (after MI with heart block, cardiac arrest with bradycardia)<br>Inserted through peripheral vein, tip of catheter is placed at apex of right ventricle | | |
| Permanent | Lead is passed into right ventricle, or right atrium and right ventricle, and generator is implanted under skin below clavicle or in abdominal wall | | |

    c.  Medications

       1)  Antiarrhythmics

       2)  Antilipid medications

  3.  Defibrillation (see Table 2)

  4.  Pacemakers—electronic apparatus used to initiate heartbeat when the SA node is seriously damaged and unable to act as a pacemaker (see Table 3)

## HEAD INJURY

A. Data Collection

1. Skull fracture—Battle's sign (ecchymosis over mastoid bone), raccoon eyes (bilateral periorbital ecchymosis), rhinorrhea, otorrhea

2. Concussion—transient mental confusion or loss of consciousness, headache, no residual neurological deficit, possible loss of memory surrounding event, long-term effects (lack of concentration, personality changes)

3. Contusion—varies from slight depression of consciousness to coma, with decorticate posturing (flexion and internal rotation of forearms and hands) or decerebrate posturing (extension of arms and legs, pronation of arms, plantar flexion, opisthotonos), indicates deeper dysfunction, generalized cerebral edema

4. Laceration—penetrating trauma with bleeding

5. Hematoma
   a. Epidural—short period of unconsciousness, followed by lucid interval with ipsilateral pupillary dilation, weakness of contralateral extremities
   b. Subdural—decreased level of consciousness, ipsilateral pupillary dilation, contralateral weakness, personality changes

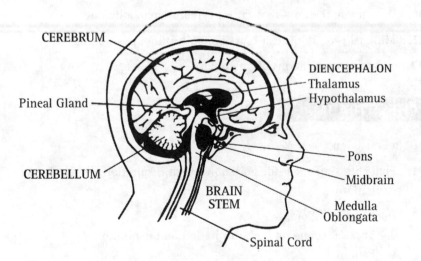

**Figure 9.  Central Nervous System**

B. Diagnose

1. Skull is a closed vault with a volume ratio of three components:  brain tissue, blood, and CSF; sudden increase in any of these can cause brain dysfunction

2. Ingestion of drugs and alcohol may delay manifestations of symptoms of damage

3. Generalized brain swelling occurs in response to injury

4. Diagnosed by x-ray, CT scan, lumbar puncture (LP), EEG, MRI

5. May be two points of impact of brain with skull
   a. Coup (direct impact)
   b. Contrecoup (rebound to skull wall opposite direct impact)

6. May cause twisting of brain stem

C. Plan/Implementation

1. Evaluate level of consciousness; check vital signs, pupil size, shape, equality, and reaction to light; check nose and ears for CSF leakage

2. Neurological data collection

3. Monitor level of consciousness, careful I and O

4. Seizure precautions, prophylactic anticonvulsants

5. Elevate the head of bed 30° to decrease intracranial pressure; monitor neurologic status after position change

6. Regulate hydration according to I and O, overhydration

7. Prevent infection if open wound

8. Manage increased intracranial pressure (ICP) and cerebral edema, administer glucocorticoids, mannitol, furosemide

9. Hypothermia—to decrease metabolic demands

10. Barbiturate therapy—to decrease cerebral metabolic rate

11. Minimal procedures (e.g., suctioning, turning, positioning)

12. Prevent complications of immobility

## CHEST TRAUMA

A. Data Collection

1. Flail chest—affected side goes down with inspiration and up during expiration

2. Open pneumothorax
   a. Sucking sound on both inspiration and expiration
   b. Pain
   c. Hyperresonance
   d. Decreased respiratory excursion
   e. Diminished/absent breath sounds on affected side
   f. Weak, rapid pulse
   g. Anxiety, diaphoresis
   h. Altered ABGs

3. Pneumothorax
   a. Dyspnea, pleuritic pain
   b. Absent or restricted movement on affected side

    c. Decreased or absent breath sounds, cyanosis

    d. Cough and fever

    e. Hypotension

**B.** Diagnose

  1. Flail chest—fracture of multiple adjacent ribs causing the chest wall to become unstable and respond paradoxically

  2. Open pneumothorax—penetrating chest wound causing the intrapleural space to be open to atmospheric pressure and resulting in collapse of lung

  3. Pneumothorax—collapse of lung due to air in the pleural space caused by surgery, disease, or trauma (see Figure 10)

    a. Spontaneous—without a known cause

    b. Tension—pressure builds up; shifting of heart and great vessels

    c. Hemothorax—blood in pleural space

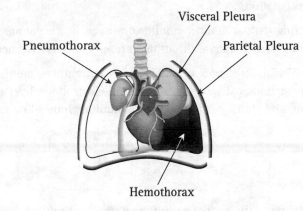

**Figure 10.  Pneumothorax and Hemothorax**

  4. Potential nursing diagnoses

    a. Ineffective breathing pattern

    b. Impaired gas exchange

    c. Anxiety

    d. Acute pain

**C.** Plan/Implementation

  1. Flail chest

    a. Monitor for shock

    b. Humidified $O_2$

    c. Pain management

    d. Monitor ABGs

    e. Encourage turning, deep breathing, and coughing

  2. Open pneumothorax

    a. Thoracentesis

    b. Chest tubes (see Reduction of Risk Potential)

## ABDOMINAL INJURIES

**A.** Data Collection

1. Penetrating—symptoms of hemorrhage

2. Blunt—abdominal pain, rigidity, distension; nausea and vomiting; shock; ecchymosis (around umbilicus—Cullen's-sign; in either flank—Turner's sign) indicative of retroperitoneal bleeding; bruits indicate renal artery injury; resonance over spleen with client on left side (Balance's sign) indicates rupture of spleen; resonance over liver indicates pathology

3. Diagnosis—x-ray, CT scan; exploratory laparotomy

**B.** Diagnose

1. Penetrating—open wound resulting in hemorrhage if major blood vessels/liver/spleen/pancreas/kidney are involved; increased risk of infection (peritonitis) from rupture of bowel

2. Blunt—usually injury to solid organs (spleen, liver, pancreas)

**C.** Plan/Implementation

1. Penetrating—NPO, NG tube, monitor drainage, bowel sounds; indwelling catheter, monitor output carefully, observe for hematuria

2. Blunt—IV with large-bore needle in upper extremities; monitor CVP; check hematological values, ABGs, serum electrolytes, liver and kidney function, and clotting studies; cardiac monitor; indwelling catheter

## SHOCK

**A.** Data Collection

1. Cool, clammy skin, cyanosis, decreased capillary refill

2. Restlessness, decreased alertness, anxiety

3. Weakness

4. Tachycardia, weak or absent pulse, decreased blood pressure

5. Metabolic acidosis

6. Oliguria, increased urine specific gravity

7. Respirations shallow, rapid

8. Increased muscle weakness

**B.** Diagnose

1. Sudden reduction of oxygen and nutrients; decreased blood volume causes a reduction in venous return, decreased cardiac output, and a decrease in arterial pressure

2. Types of shock
   a. Hypovolemic shock—loss of fluid from circulation
      1) Hemorrhagic shock (external or internal)
      2) Cutaneous shock, e.g., burns resulting in external fluid loss

       3) Diabetic ketoacidosis

       4) Gastrointestinal obstruction, e.g., vomiting and diarrhea

       5) Diabetes insipidus

       6) Excessive use of diuretics

       7) Internal sequestration, e.g., fractures, hemothorax, ascites

  b. Cardiogenic shock—decreased cardiac output

       1) Myocardial infarction

       2) Dysrhythmias

       3) Pump failure

  c. Distributive shock—inadequate vascular tone

       1) Neural-induced loss of vascular tone

          a) Anesthesia

          b) Pain

          c) Insulin shock

          d) Spinal cord injury

       2) Chemical—induced loss of vasular tone

          a) Toxic shock

          b) Anaphylaxis

          c) Capillary leak—burns, decreased serum protein levels

**C.** Plan/Implementation

1. Maintain adequate oxygenation + tissue perfusion

2. Maintain systolic BP greater than 90 mm

3. Maintain patent airway

  a. If necessary, ensure ventilation by Ambu bag or ventilator assistance

  b. Provide supplemental oxygen to maintain adequate blood $pO_2$

4. Indwelling catheter, hourly outputs

5. Monitor ABGs and treat acidosis

6. Keep warm (maintain body temperature)

7. Intravenous administration of blood or other appropriate fluids (plasma expanders, electrolyte solutions)

8. Medications

  a. Antibiotics—when shock is due to an infection (septic shock), antibiotic therapy should be instituted immediately; blood, urine, sputum, and drainage of any kind should be sent for culture and sensitivity (C and S); usually use combination of ampicillin, polymyxin, and cephalothin

  b. Medications to improve myocardial contractions and vasoconstrict

  c. Medications to maintain adequate urine output, e.g., mannitol, furosemide

  d. Medications used to restore blood pressure, adrenergics/sympathomimetics (e.g., dobutamin hydrochloride)

9. Low-dose corticosteroids for septic shock

10. Large volumes of fluids

Table 4

| GLASGOW COMA SCALE | | | | | | | | | | | | | | | | | | | | | | |
|---|---|---|---|---|---|---|---|---|---|---|---|---|---|---|---|---|---|---|---|---|---|---|
| **Eyes Open** | Spontaneously | 4 | | | | | | | | | | | | | | | | | | | | |
| | To speech | 3 | | | | | | | | | | | | | | | | | | | | |
| | To pain | 2 | | | | | | | | | | | | | | | | | | | | |
| | None | 1 | | | | | | | | | | | | | | | | | | | | |
| **Best Verbal Response** | Oriented | 5 | | | | | | | | | | | | | | | | | | | | |
| | Confused | 4 | | | | | | | | | | | | | | | | | | | | |
| | Inappropriate words | 3 | | | | | | | | | | | | | | | | | | | | |
| | Incomprehensible sounds | 2 | | | | | | | | | | | | | | | | | | | | |
| | None | 1 | | | | | | | | | | | | | | | | | | | | |
| **Best Motor Response** | Obeys commands | 6 | | | | | | | | | | | | | | | | | | | | |
| | Localizes pain | 5 | | | | | | | | | | | | | | | | | | | | |
| | Flexes to pain | 4 | | | | | | | | | | | | | | | | | | | | |
| | Flexor posture | 3 | | | | | | | | | | | | | | | | | | | | |
| | Extensor posture | 2 | | | | | | | | | | | | | | | | | | | | |
| | No response | 1 | | | | | | | | | | | | | | | | | | | | |

# INCREASED INTRACRANIAL PRESSURE

A. Data Collection

1. Altered LOC—often earliest sign

2. Glasgow coma scale (see Table 4)
   a. Level of consciousness
   b. Score of 3–8 indicates severe head trauma; score of 15 indicates client is alert and oriented

3. Confusion, restlessness (early signs)

4. Pupillary changes (early signs)

5. Vital signs changes—increased BP, decreased pulse (late changes)

B. Analysis

1. Diagnostic tests
   a. Neurological tests (e.g., lumbar puncture, EEG, myelogram)

2. Causes
   a. Cerebral edema
   b. Hemorrhage
   c. Space-occupying lesions

3. Complications
   a. Cerebral hypoxia
   b. Decreased cerebral perfusion
   c. Herniation—pupil constriction

C. Plan/Implementation

1. Monitor vital signs hourly—be alert for increased systolic pressure, widening pulse pressure and bradycardia (Cushing's triad—very late sign)

2. Monitor pupillary reactions

3. Monitor muscle strength

4. Monitor verbal response and change in level of consciousness

5. Monitor Glasgow coma scale

6. Maintain respiratory function

7. Elevate head 30–45° to promote venous drainage from brain

8. Avoid neck flexion and head rotation—support in cervical collar or neck rolls; avoid coughing, sneezing, bending

9. Reduce environmental stimuli

10. Prevent the Valsalva maneuver, teach client to exhale while turning or moving in bed

11. Administer stool softeners

12. Restrict fluids to 1,200–1,500 ml/day

13. Administer medications
    a. Osmotic diuretics—to reduce fluid volume (e.g., mannitol)
    b. Corticosteroid therapy—to reduce cerebral edema
    c. Antiseizure medications

## SEIZURES

**A.** Data Collection (see Table 5)

1. Episodes of abnormal motor, sensory, autonomic, or psychic activity due to abnormal discharge from brain cells

**B.** Analysis

1. Causes
    a. Epilepsy
    b. Fever in child
    c. Head injury
    d. Hypertension
    e. CNS infection
    f. Brain tumor or metastasis
    g. Drug withdrawal
    h. Stroke

**C.** Plan/Implementation

1. During seizure
    a. Protect from injury
    b. Raise side rails or ease client to floor
    c. Use side rails according to agency policy
    d. Loosen restrictive clothing
    e. Do not restrain
    f. Do not try to insert a bite block, padded tongue blade, or oral airway
    g. Protect nurse—client may be flailing arms

    h. Place client on side with head extended

    i. Monitor onset, duration, pattern of seizure

2. After seizure

    a. Position on side to prevent aspiration, reduce environmental stimuli

    b. Provide oxygen and suction equipment, if needed

    c. Reorient as needed

    d. Provide description of seizure in record

       1) Circumstances surrounding seizure

       2) How seizure started (location of first tremors or stiffness)

       3) Type of body movements

       4) Areas of body involved

       5) Presence of automations (involuntary motor activities, e.g., lip smacking)

       6) Incontinence

       7) Duration of each phase

       8) Unconsciousness during seizure or paralysis after seizure

       9) Actions after seizures (e.g., confusion, sleep, speech)

3. To prevent seizures

    a. Administer anticonvulsant medications (e.g., phenytoin, phenobarbital)

       1) Don't discontinue abruptly

       2) Avoid alcohol

       3) Good oral hygiene

       4) Carry medical identification

    b. Avoid seizure triggers

       1) Alcoholic beverages

       2) Stress

       3) Caffeine

       4) Fever

       5) Hyperventilation

    c. Complementary/Alternative therapies

       1) Ketogenic diet to prevent seizures

          a) Diet high in fat and low in carbohydrates mimics effects of fasting and places the body in a constant state of ketosis

          b) Suppresses many types of seizures (tonic-clonic, absence, complex partial) and is effective when other methods of seizure control fail

● Table 5

| SEIZURES | | |
|---|---|---|
| TYPE | AGE GROUP | DATA |
| **Generalized seizures**<br>Tonic-clonic | All | Aura<br>Usually starts with tonic or stiffening phase, followed by clonic or jerking phase<br>May have bowel/bladder incontinence; in postictal phase, sleeps, hard to arouse |
| Absence | Usually children | Staring spell, or staring spell with lip smacking, chewing |
| Myoclonic | Onset in children | Brief muscular contraction involving one or more limbs, trunk |
| Infantile spasms | Infants and children | Gross flexion, extension of limbs<br>Treated with ACTH |
| Atonic seizures | Infants and children | Sudden loss of muscle tone and posture control, causing child to drop to floor |
| Tonic seizures | Infants and children | Stiffening of limbs |
| **Partial seizures**<br>Seizures beginning locally | All | Jacksonian, or focal seizure, starting at one location, may spread |
| Sensory | All | Tingling, numbness of a body part; visual, olfactory, taste symptoms |
| Affective | All | Inappropriate fear, laughter, dreamy states, depersonalization |
| **Complex partial seizures**<br>Temporal lobe/psychomotor seizures | All | Aura complex<br>Most commonly involves automatism—lip-smacking, picking at clothing, dreamy states, feelings of déja vu, hallucinations; may have antisocial, violent behavior, somatosensory complaints, bizarre behavior |
| Partial seizures with secondary generalization | All | May spread from an original discharge site to other parts of the brain and become generalized |

## STROKE

A. Data Collection

1. Confusion/disorientation

2. Changes in vital signs and neurological signs

3. Change in level of consciousness, seizures

4. Aphasia

5. Hemiplegia

6. Bladder and/or bowel incontinence

7. Headache, vomiting

8. Hemianopsia—loss of half of visual field

9. Dysphagia—difficulty swallowing

10. Decreased sensation/neglect syndrome

11. Emotional lability

**B.** Diagnose

1. Abrupt onset of neurological deficits resulting from interference with blood supply to the brain

2. Causes
   a. Thrombosis
   b. Embolism
   c. Hemorrhage

3. Risk factors
   a. Advanced age
   b. Hypertension
   c. Transient ischemic attacks (TIAs)
   d. Diabetes mellitus
   e. Smoking
   f. Obesity
   g. Elevated blood lipids
   h. Oral contraceptives
   i. Atrial fibrillation

**C.** Plan/Implementation

1. Immediate care
   a. Maintain patent airway
   b. Minimize activity
   c. Keep head of bed elevated 15–30° to prevent increased intracranial pressure
   d. Maintain proper body alignment
   e. Keep side rails in upright position
   f. Administer thrombolytics within 3 hours of symptoms

2. Intermediate care and rehabilitative needs
   a. Position for good body alignment and comfort
   b. Institute measures that facilitate swallowing
      1) Allow client to sit in upright position with head flexed slightly
      2) Instruct client to use tongue actively
      3) Administer liquids slowly, avoid milk-based products
      4) Place food on unaffected side of mouth
      5) Provide semisolid foods (easiest to swallow)
      6) Instruct to swallow while eating; maintain upright position for 30–45 minutes after eating
   c. Monitor elimination patterns
   d. Provide skin care
   e. Perform passive and/or active range-of-motion exercises
   f. Orient to person, time, and place
   g. Move affected extremities slowly and gently
   h. Assist with use of supportive devices (e.g., commode, trapeze, cane)
   i. Address communication needs—face client and speak clearly and slowly; give the client time to respond; use verbal and nonverbal communication

j. Do not approach from visually impaired side

k. Encourage use of affected side

## SPINAL INJURY

A. Data Collection

1. Loss of motor and sensory function below level of injury (see Table 6)

2. Spinal shock symptoms
   a. Flaccid paralysis of skeletal muscles
   b. Complete loss of all sensation
   c. Decreased pulses, bradycardia
   d. Suppression of somatic (pain, touch, temperature) and visceral reflexes

3. Postural hypotension

Table 6

| SPINAL CORD INJURY | | |
|---|---|---|
| **LEVEL OF INJURY** | **FUNCTIONAL ABILITY** | **SELF-CARE CAPABILITY** |
| C3 and above | Inability to control muscles of breathing | Unable to care for self, life-sustaining ventilatory support essential |
| C4 | Movement of trapezius and sternocleidomastoid muscles, no upper extremity muscle function, minimal ventilatory capacity | Unable to care for self, may self-feed with powered devices (depending on respiratory function) |
| C5 | Neck movement, possible partial strength of shoulder and biceps | Can drive electric wheelchair, may be able to feed self with powered devices |
| C6 | Muscle function in C5 level; partial strength in pectoralis major | May self-propel a lightweight wheelchair, may feed self with devices, can write and care for self, can transfer from chair to bed |
| C7 | Muscle function in C6 level, no finger muscle power | Can dress lower extremities, minimal assistance needed, independence in wheelchair, can drive car with hand controls |
| C8 | Muscle function in C7 level, finger muscle power | Same as C7; in general, activities easier |
| T1-T4 | Good upper extremity muscle strength | Some independence from wheelchair, long leg braces for standing exercises |
| T5-L2 | Balance difficulties | Still requires wheelchair, limited ambulation with long-leg braces and crutches |
| L3-L5 | Trunk-pelvis muscle function intact | May use crutches or canes for ambulation |
| L5-S3 | Waddling gait | Ambulation |

4. Circulatory problems—edema

5. Alteration in normal thermoregulation

**B.** Diagnose

1. Types of spinal cord injuries
   a. Concussion without direct trauma
   b. Penetrating wound or fracture dislocation
   c. Hemorrhage
   d. Laceration—damage related to level of cord affected
   e. Compression—often dural/epidural hematoma; if pressure on the cord is not relieved early, will cause ischemia, cord necrosis, and permanent damage

2. Categories of neurological deficit
   a. Complete—no voluntary motor activity below level of injury
   b. Incomplete—some voluntary motor activity below level of injury
   c. Paraplegia-thoracic vertebral injury or lower; lower extremity involvement
   d. Tetraplegia (quadriplegia)-cervical/vertebral injury; all 4 extremities involved

3. Causes
   a. Trauma due to accidents
      1) Car accidents, falls, sports, and industrial accidents
      2) Occurs predominantly in young white males (ages 15–30)
      3) May be related to substance abuse
   b. Neoplasms

4. Diagnosis—neurological examination, x-rays, CT scan, MRI, myelography, distal rectal exam to determine extent of neurological deficit

**C.** Plan/Implementation

1. Prevention
   a. Drive within the speed limit
   b. Use seat belts in car
   c. Wear helmets when riding motorcycles and bicycles
   d. Don't drink and drive

2. Data to gather (triage)
   a. Airway, breathing, circulation (ABC)
   b. Stabilization of vital signs
   c. Head-to-toe data gathering

3. Immobilize cervical spine
   a. Skeletal traction—Gardner-Wells, Crutchfield, Vinke tongs, halo traction
   b. Surgical stabilization—reduction and stabilization by fusion, wires, and plates

4. Administer steroid therapy and antispasmodics

5. Hyperbaric oxygen therapy

6. Move client by log-rolling technique; use turning frames

7. Provide good skin care

8. Provide emotional support

9. Ensure adequate nutrition

10. Reduce aggravating factors that cause spasticity

11. Bladder and bowel training, catheterization

12. Prevent complication of autonomic hyperreflexia (dysreflexia)
    a. Usually caused by bladder or bowel distention; other causes: pain, tactile stimulation
    b. Occurs in clients with spinal cord lesions above T6 after spinal shock has subsided
    c. Symptoms—pounding headache, profuse sweating, especially of forehead, nasal congestion, piloerection (goose flesh), bradycardia, hypertension
    d. Place client in sitting position
    e. Catheterize or irrigate existing catheter to re-establish patency
    f. Check rectum for fecal mass
    g. Hydralazine may be given slowly IV

[PHYSIOLOGICAL ADAPTATION]

## FLUID VOLUME IMBALANCES

**A.** Data Collection (see Table 1)

**B.** Diagnose (see Table 1)

**C.** Plan/Implementation (see Table 1)

●Table 1

| FLUID VOLUME IMBALANCES | | |
|---|---|---|
| | **VOLUME DEFICIT** | **VOLUME OVERLOAD** |
| **Data** | Thirst (early sign)<br>Temperature increases<br>Rapid and weak pulse<br>Respirations increase<br>Poor skin turgor—skin cool, moist<br>Hypotension<br>Emaciation, weight loss<br>Dry eye sockets, mouth and mucous<br>  membranes<br>Anxiety, apprehension, exhaustion<br>Urine specific gravity >1.030<br>Decreased urine output<br>Increased hemoglobin, hematocrit,<br>  Na+, serum osmolality<br>Headache, lethargy, confusion,<br>  disorientation, weight loss | No change in temperature<br>Pulse increases slightly and is<br>  bounding<br>Respirations increase, shortness of<br>  breath, dyspnea, rales (crackles)<br>Peripheral edema—bloated<br>  appearance, weight gain<br>Hypertension<br>May have muffled heart sounds<br>Jugular vein distention<br>Urine specific gravity <1.010<br>Apprehension<br>Increased venous pressure<br>Decreased hematocrit BUN,<br>  hemoglobin, Na+, serum osmolality |
| **Diagnose** | Isotonic loss<br>Vomiting<br>Diarrhea<br>GI suction<br>Sweating<br>Decreased intake<br>Hemorrhage<br>Third space shift | Isotonic gain, increase in the<br>  interstitial compartment,<br>  intravascular compartment, or<br>  both<br>CHF<br>Renal failure<br>  Cirrhosis of the liver<br>  Excessive ingestion of sodium<br>Excessive or too rapid intravenous<br>  infusion |
| **Plan/<br>Implementation** | Force fluids<br>Provide isotonic IV fluids: lactated<br>  Ringer's or 0.9% NaCl<br>I and O, hourly outputs<br>Daily weights (1 liter fluid = 1 kg<br>  or 2.2 lb)<br>Monitor vital signs<br>Check skin turgor<br>Determine urine specific gravity | Administer diuretics<br>Restrict fluids<br>Sodium-restricted diet (average<br>  daily diet—6-15 mg Na+)<br>Daily weight<br>Auscultate breath sounds<br>Check feet/ankle/sacral region<br>  for edema<br>Semi-Fowler's position if dyspneic |

## ADH DISORDERS

A. Data Collection (see Table 2)

B. Analysis (see Table 2)

C. Plan/Implementation (see Table 2)

Table 2 •

| ADH DISORDERS | | |
| --- | --- | --- |
| | **DIABETES INSIPIDUS (Decreased ADH)** | **SIADH—SYNDROME OF INAPPROPRIATE ANTIDIURETIC HORMONE SECRETION (Increased ADH)** |
| **Data** | Excessive urine output<br>Chronic, severe dehydration<br>Excessive thirst<br>Anorexia, weight loss<br>Weakness<br>Constipation | Anorexia, nausea, vomiting<br>Lethargy<br>Headaches<br>Change in level of consciousness<br>Decreased deep tendon reflexes<br>Tachycardia<br>Increased circulating blood volume<br>Decreased urinary output |
| **Diagnose** | Head trauma<br>Brain tumor<br>Meningitis<br>Encephalitis<br>Deficiency of ADH<br>Diagnosis tests:<br>  Low urine specific gravity<br>  Urinary osmolality below plasma<br>  level<br>High serum sodium | Small cell carcinoma of lung<br>Pneumonia<br>Positive-pressure ventilation<br>Brain tumors<br>Head trauma<br>Stroke<br>Meningitis<br>Encephalitis<br>Feedback mechanism that regulates ADH<br>  does not function properly; ADH is<br>  released even when plasma<br>  hypo-osmolality is present<br>Diagnostic tests:<br>  Serum sodium decreased, plasma<br>  osmolality decreased<br>Increased urine specific gravity |
| **Nursing considerations** | Record intake and output<br>Monitor urine specific gravity, skin<br>  condition, weight, blood pressure,<br>  pulse, temperature<br>Administer Pitressin | Restrict water intake (500-600 ml/24 h)<br>Administer diuretics to promote excretion<br>  of water<br>Hypertonic saline (3% NaCl) IV<br>Administer demeclocycline<br>Weigh daily<br>I and O<br>Monitor serum Na$^+$ levels<br>Determine LOC |

## POTASSIUM IMBALANCES

A. Data Collection (see Table 3)

B. Diagnose (see Table 3)

C. Plan/Implementation (see Table 3)

D. Pharmacology (see Electrolytes and Replacement Solutions, page 521 and Electrolyte Modifiers, page 521)

●Table 3

| POTASSIUM IMBALANCES | | |
|---|---|---|
| | **HYPOKALEMIA** | **HYPERKALEMIA** |
| **Data** | <3.5 mEq/L<br>Anorexia, nausea, and vomiting<br>Muscle weakness, paresthesias<br>Dysrhythmias, increased sensitivity to digitalis | >5.0 mEq/L<br>EKG changes, dysrhythmias, cardiac arrest<br>Muscle weakness<br>Paralysis<br>Nausea<br>Diarrhea |
| **Diagnose** | Potassium—main intracellular ion; involved in cardiac rhythm, nerve transmission<br>Normal level—3.5-5.0 mEq/L<br>Causes—vomiting, gastric suction, diarrhea, diuretics and steroids, inadequate intake | Causes—renal failure, use of potassium supplements, burns, crushing injuries |
| **Plan/ Implementation** | Administration of oral potassium supplements—dilute in juice to avoid gastric irritation<br>Increase dietary intake—raisins, bananas, apricots, oranges, beans, potatoes, carrots, celery<br>IV supplements—40 mEq/L usual concentration; cannot give concentration greater than 40 mEq/L into peripheral IV or without cardiac monitor<br>Increases risk of digoxin toxicity<br>Protect from injury<br>Determine renal function prior to administration | Restrict dietary potassium and potassium-containing medications<br>Sodium polystyrene sulfonate cation exchange resin (causes diarrhea)<br>Orally—dilute to make more palatable<br>Rectally—give in conjunction with sorbitol to avoid fecal impaction<br>In emergency situation, calcium gluconate given IV, sodium bicarbonate given IV, regular insulin and dextrose<br>IV administration of regular insulin and dextrose shifts potassium into the cells<br>Peritoneal or hemodialysis<br>Diuretics |

## SODIUM IMBALANCES

A.  Data Collection (see Table 4)

B.  Diagnose (see Table 4)

C.  Plan/Implementation (see Table 4)

Table 4

| SODIUM IMBALANCES | | |
|---|---|---|
| | **HYPONATREMIA** | **HYPERNATREMIA** |
| **Data** | <135 mEq/L<br>Nausea<br>Muscle cramps<br>Increased intracranial pressure, confusion, muscular twitching, convulsions | >145 mEq/L<br>Elevated temperature<br>Weakness<br>Disorientation<br>Delusion and hallucinations<br>Thirst, dry swollen tongue, sticky mucous membranes<br>Postural hypotension with decreased ECF<br>Hypertension with normal or increased ECF<br>Tachycardia |
| **Diagnose** | Sodium—main extracellular ion; responsible for water balance<br>Normal—135-145 mEq/L<br>Causes—vomiting, diuretics, excessive administration of dextrose and water IVs, prolonged low-sodium diet, excessive water intake | Causes—hypertonic tube feedings without water supplements, diarrhea, hyperventilation, diabetes insipidus, ingestion of OTC drugs such as Alka-Seltzer, inhaling large amounts of salt water (near-drowning), inadequate water ingestion |
| **Plan/ Implementation** | Oral administration of sodium-rich foods—beef broth, tomato juice<br>IV lactated Ringer's or 0.9% NaCl<br>Water restriction (safer method)<br>I and O<br>Daily weight | IV administration of hypotonic solution—0.3% NaCl or 0.45% NaCl; 5% dextrose in water<br>Offer fluids at regular intervals<br>Decrease sodium in diet<br>Daily weight |

## CALCIUM IMBALANCES

A.  Data Collection (see Table 5)

B.  Diagnose (see Table 5)

C.  Plan/Implementation (see Table 5)

●Table 5

| CALCIUM IMBALANCES | | |
|---|---|---|
| | **HYPOCALCEMIA** | **HYPERCALCEMIA** |
| **Data** | Ionized serum calcium <4.5 mg/dL or total serum calcium <8.6 mg/dL (total serum calcium used)<br>Nervous system becomes increasingly excitable<br>Tetany<br>  Trousseau's sign—inflate BP cuff on upper arm to 20 mm Hg above systolic pressure; carpal spasms within 2-5 minutes indicate tetany<br>  Chvostek's sign—tap facial nerve 2 cm anterior to the earlobe just below the zygomatic arch; twitching of facial muscles indicates tetany<br>Seizures<br>Confusion<br>Paresthesia<br>Irritability | Ionized serum calcium >5.1 mg/L or total serum calcium >10.2 mg/dL (total serum calcium used)<br>Sedative effect on central and peripheral nervous system<br>Muscle weakness, lack of coordination<br>Constipation, abdominal pain, and distension<br>Confusion<br>Depressed or absent tendon reflexes<br>Dysrhythmias |
| **Diagnose** | Calcium—needed for blood clotting, skeletal muscle contraction<br>Normal—ionized serum calcium <4.25 mg/dL or total serum calcium <8.6 mg/dL<br>Regulated by parathyroid hormone and vitamin D, which facilitates reabsorption of calcium from bone and enhances absorption from the GI tract<br>Causes—hypoparathyroidism, pancreatitis, renal failure, steroids and loop diuretics, inadequate intake, post-thyroid surgery | Causes—malignant neoplastic diseases, hyperparathyroidism, excessive intake, immobility, excessive intake of calcium carbonate antacids |
| **Plan/ Implementation** | Orally—calcium gluconate (less concentrated) or calcium chloride; administer with orange juice to maximize absorption<br>Parenterally—calcium gluconate<br>Effect is transitory and additional doses may be necessary<br>Use caution with digitalized clients because both are cardiac depressants<br>Calcium may cause vessel irritation and should be administered through a long, stable intravenous line<br>Avoid infiltration since tissue can become necrotic and slough<br>Administer at a slow rate to avoid high serum concentrations and cardiac depression<br>Seizure precautions<br>Maintain airway because laryngeal stridor can occur<br>Maintain safety needs since confusion is often present<br>Increase dietary intake of calcium<br>Calcium supplements<br>Regular exercise<br>Administer phosphate-binding antacids, calcitriol, vitamin D | IV administration of 0.45% NaCl or 0.9% NaCl<br>Encourage fluids<br>Lasix<br>Calcitonin—decreases calcium level<br>Mobilize the client<br>Restrict dietary calcium<br>Prevent development of renal calculi<br>Increase fluid intake<br>Maintain acidic urine<br>Prevent UTI<br>Surgical intervention may be indicated in hyperparathyroidism<br>Injury prevention<br>Limit intake of calcium carbonate antacids |

## MAGNESIUM IMBALANCES

A. Data Collection (see Table 6)

B. Analysis (see Table 6)

C. Plan/Implementation (see Table 6)

Table 6

| MAGNESIUM IMBALANCES | | |
|---|---|---|
| | **HYPOMAGNESEMIA** | **HYPERMAGNESEMIA** |
| **Data Collection Findings** | <1.3 mEq/L<br>Magnesium acts as a depressant<br>Increased neuromuscular irritability<br>Tremors, tetany, seizures<br>Dysrhythmias<br>Depression, confusion<br>Dysphagia | >2.3 mEq/L<br>Depresses the CNS<br>Depresses cardiac impulse transmission<br>Hypotension<br>Facial flushing, muscle weakness<br>Absent deep tendon reflexes, paralysis<br>Shallow respirations |
| **Diagnose** | Normal—1.3-2.3 mEq/L<br>Causes—alcoholism, GI suction, diarrhea, intestinal fistulas, abuse of diuretics or laxatives<br>Usually seen with other electrolyte deficits | Causes—renal failure, excessive magnesium, administration (antacids, cathartics) |
| **Plan/ Implementation** | Increased intake of dietary Mg—green vegetables, nuts, bananas, oranges, peanut butter, chocolate<br>Parenteral administration of supplements—magnesium sulfate<br>Monitor cardiac rhythm and reflexes to detect depressive effects of magnesium<br>Keep self-inflating breathing bag, Monitor respiratory status airway and oxygen at bedside, in case of respiratory emergency<br>Calcium preparations may be given to counteract the potential danger of myocardial dysfunction that may result from magnesium intoxication secondary to rapid infusions<br>Oral—long-term maintenance with oral magnesium<br>Monitor for digitalis toxicity<br>Maintain seizure precautions<br>Provide safety measures because confusion is often present<br>Test ability to swallow before PO fluids/food because of dysphagia | Discontinue oral and IV Mg<br>Emergency<br>Support ventilation<br>IV calcium gluconate Hemodialysis<br>Monitor reflexes<br>Teach about OTC drugs containing Mg<br>Monitor cardiac rhythm; have calcium preparations available to antagonize cardiac depression |

## BURNS

**A.** Data Collection

    1. "Rule of Nines" (see Figure 1)

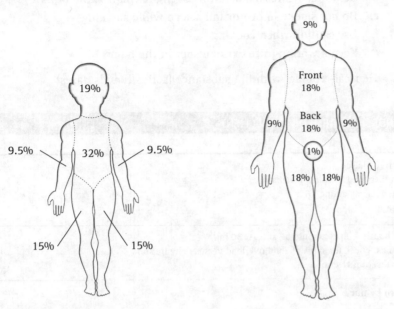

**Figure 1. Rule of Nines**

    2. Determination of intensity (see Table 7)

● Table 7

| CLASSIFICATION OF BURNS | | | | |
|---|---|---|---|---|
| **SUPERFICIAL** | **SUPERFICIAL PARTIAL-THICKNESS** | **DEEP PARTIAL-THICKNESS** | **FULL-THICKNESS** | **DEEP FULL-THICKNESS** |
| Similar to first-degree | Similar to second-degree | Similar to second-degree | Similar to third-degree | Similar to third-degree |
| Skin pink to red Painful | Skin pink to red Painful | Skin red to white Painful | Skin red, white, brown, black Pain possible | Skin black No pain |
| Epidermis Sunburn | Epidermis and dermis Scalds, flames | Epidermis and dermis Scalds, flames, tar, grease | All skin layers Prolonged contact with hot objects | All skin layers, possibly muscles and tendon Flames, electricity |
| Heals in 3 to 5 days | Heals in 2 weeks | Heals in 1 month Possible grafting | Heals in weeks to months | Heals in weeks to months Escharotomy Grafting |

**B.** Analysis (see Table 8)

    1. At risk

        a. Young children

        b. Elderly

2. Prevention
   a. Keep all matches and lighters away from children
   b. Do not leave children alone around fires
   c. Install and maintain smoke detectors
   d. Set water-heater temperature no higher than 120°F (48.9°C)
   e. Do not smoke in bed or fall asleep while smoking
   f. Use caution when cooking
   g. Keep a working fire extinguisher in the home

3. Thermal—contact with hot substance (solids/liquids/gases)

Table 8

| NURSING CARE FOR BURN CLIENT | |
|---|---|
| **GOAL** | **NURSING CONSIDERATIONS** |
| Correct fluid and electrolyte imbalance | First 24-48 h (emergent/resuscitative phase):<br>  IV fluids balanced salt solution (Lactated Ringers), plasma<br>  Rapid for first 8 h, more slowly over remaining 16 h<br>2-5 d after burn (intermediate phase):<br>  Packed RBCs<br>  Indwelling catheter to monitor hourly output; should be at least 30 ml/h<br>  Careful administration of IV fluids; check for signs of fluid overload versus dehydration<br>  Monitor blood pressure, TPR, wt, serum electrolytes |
| Promote healing | Cap, gown, mask, and gloves worn by nurse<br>Wound care at least once a day<br>Debridement (removal of nonviable tissue)—hydrotherapy is used to loosen dead tissue, 30 min maximum<br>Escharotomy (incising of leathery covering of dead tissue conducive to bacterial growth)—used to alleviate constriction, minimize infection<br>Dressing: careful sterile technique, avoid breaking blisters, wound may be covered or left exposed<br>Application of topical antibacterial agents: silver sulfadiazine—closed method; monitor for hypersensitivity, rash, itching, burning sensation in areas other than burn, decreased WBC; mafenide open method; monitor acid/base balance and renal function; remove previously applied cream; Silver nitrate—keep dressings wet with solution to avoid over concentrations; handle carefully; can leave a gray/black stain<br>Grafting: biological (human amniotic membrane, cadaver, allograft); autografting when granulation bed is clean and well vascularized<br>Tetanus prophylaxis<br>Avoid hypothermia and add humidity |
| Support nutrition | High-caloric, high-carbohydrate, high-protein diet; may require PN or tube feeding; oral nutrient supplements; vitamins B, C, and iron; $H_2$ histamine blockers and antacids to prevent stress ulcer (Curling's ulcer)<br>NG tube to prevent gastric distention, early acute gastric dilation, and paralytic ileus associated with burn shock; monitor bowel sounds |
| Control pain | Pain medication (morphine/meperidine)—given IV at first due to impaired circulation and poor absorption<br>Monitor VS frequently; analgesic 30 min before wound care |
| Prevent complications of immobility | Prevent contractures—maintain joints in neutral position of extension; shoes to prevent foot drop; splints; active and passive ROM exercises at each dressing change; turn side to side frequently; skin care to prevent breakdown<br>Stryker frame or Circ-O-Lectric bed may facilitate change of position<br>Facial exercises and position that hyperextends neck for burns of face and neck<br>Consult with physical therapist |
| Support client | Counsel client regarding change in body image<br>Encourage expression of feelings and demonstrate acceptance of client<br>Evaluate client's readiness to see scarred areas, especially facial area<br>Assist client's family to adjust to changed appearance<br>Consider recommending client for ongoing counseling<br>Support developmental needs of children, e.g., sick children need limits on behavior<br>Assist client in coping with immobilization, pain, and isolation<br>Prepare client for discharge—anticipate readmission for release of contractures/cosmetic surgery; proper use of any correctional orthopedic appliances, pressure garments (used to decrease scarring); how to change dressings |

4. Chemical—contact with strong acids or strong bases; prolonged contact with most chemicals

5. Electrical—contact with live current; internal damage may be more severe than expected from external injury

6. Radiation—exposure to high doses of radioactive material

C. Plan/Implementation

1. Emergency care—on the scene
   a. Stop the burning process
   b. Thermal—smother; stop, drop, and roll
   c. Chemical—remove clothing and flush/irrigate skin/eyes
   d. Electrical—shut off electrical current or separate person from source with a nonconducting implement
   e. Ensure airway, breathing, and circulation
   f. Immediate wound care—keep person warm and dry; wrap in clean, dry sheet/blanket

2. Nursing care (see Table 8)

3. Stages following severe burns (see Table 9)

●Table 9

| PHASES FOLLOWING SEVERE BURNS | |
|---|---|
| **EMERGENT/RESUSCITATIVE** | **INTERMEDIATE/ACUTE** |
| First 24-48 hours | Begins 36-48 hours after burn |
| Fluid loss through open wound or extravasation into deeper tissues | Decrease in peripheral edema |
| Hypovolemia | Blood volume restored |
| Renal complications possible | Diuresis if renal system unimpaired |
| $K^+$ (hyperkalemia) | $K^+$ (hypokalemia) |
| ↓ BP, ↑ Pulse | ↑ BP |

## ADRENAL DISORDERS

A. Data Collection (see Table 10)

B. Analysis (see Table 10)

1. Adrenal cortex
   a. Glucocorticoids
   b. Mineralocorticoids
   c. Androgen and estrogen

2. Adrenal medulla
   a. Norepinephrine
   b. Epinephrine

C. Plan/Implementation

   1. Addison's disease

     a. High-protein, high-carbohydrate, high-sodium, low-potassium diet

     b. Wear Medic-Alert bracelet

     c. Protect from infection

     d. Monitor for hypoglycemia, hyponatremia

     e. Assist with 24-hour urine collection for 17-hydroxycorticosteroids (refrigerate urine during collection)

     f. Administer hormonal replacement—may be lifelong

     g. Avoid factors that precipitate Addisonian crisis

       1) Physical stress

       2) Psychological stress

       3) Inadequate steroid replacement

Table 10

| ADRENAL DISORDERS | | |
|---|---|---|
| | **ADDISON'S DISEASE** | **CUSHING'S SYNDROME** |
| **Data** | Fatigue, weakness, dehydration, ↓ BP, hyperpigmentation, ↓ resistance to stress, alopecia<br>Weight loss, pathological fractures<br>Depression, lethargy, emotional liability | Fatigue, weakness, osteoporosis, muscle wasting, cramps, edema, ↑ BP, purple skin striations, hirsutism, emaciation, depression, decreased resistance to infection, moon face, buffalo hump, obesity (trunk), mood swings, masculinization in females, blood sugar imbalance |
| **Diagnose** | Hyposecretion of adrenal hormones (mineralocorticoids, glucocorticoids, androgens)<br>Pathophysiology:<br>↓ Na+ dehydration<br>↓ Blood volume + shock<br>↑ K+ metabolic acidosis + arrhythmias<br>↓ Blood sugar + insulin shock<br>Diagnostic tests:<br>CT and MRI<br>Hyperkalemia and hyponatremia<br>↓ Plasma cortisol<br>↓ Urinary 17-hydroxycorticosteroids and 17-ketosteroids<br>ACTH stimulation test<br>Treatment: hormone replacement | Hypersecretion of adrenal hormones (mineralocorticoids, glucocorticoids, androgens)<br>Pathophysiology:<br>↑ Na+ ↑ blood volume + ↑ BP<br>↓ K+ metabolic alkalosis + shock<br>↑ Blood sugar + ketoacidosis<br>Diagnostic tests:<br>Skull films<br>Blood sugar analysis<br>Hypokalemia and hypernatremia<br>Plasma cortisol level<br>Urinary 17-hydroxycorticosteroids and 17-ketosteroids<br>Treatment: hypophysectomy, adrenalectomy |

     h. Observe for clinical manifestations of Addisonian crisis

       1) Nausea and vomiting

       2) Abdominal pain

       3) Fever

       4) Extreme weakness

       5) Severe hypoglycemia and dehydration develop rapidly

       6) Blood pressure falls, leading to shock and coma; death results if not promptly treated

     i. Treatment of Addisonian crisis

       1) Monitor hydrocortisone therapy

       2) Carefully monitor IV infusion of 0.9% NaCl or $D_5W$/NaCl

       3) Administer IV glucose, glucagon

       4) Administer insulin with dextrose in normal saline; administer potassium-binding and excreting resin; sodium polystyrene sulfonate

       5) Monitor vital signs

2. Cushing's syndrome

    a. Assure the client that most physical changes are reversible with treatment

    b. High-protein, low-carbohydrate, high-potassium, low-sodium, low-calorie diet

    c. Use careful technique to prevent infection

    d. Eliminate environmental hazards for pathological fractures

    e. Observe for hyperactivity, GI bleeding, fluid volume overload

    f. Provide postadrenalectomy care

       1) Flank incision—painful to breathe, so encourage coughing and deep breathing

       2) Ensure client safety to reduce risk of fractures

       3) Monitor for shock

       4) Monitor for hypertension

       5) Administer cortisone and mineralocorticoids as ordered

    g. Anticipate slow recovery from anesthesia in obese client

    h. Anticipate slow wound healing

    i. Monitor glucose level, monitor urine output

## CHRONIC OBSTRUCTIVE PULMONARY DISEASE (COPD)

**A.** Data Collection

1. Change in skin color–cyanosis or reddish color

2. Weakness, weight loss

3. Risk factors
   a. Smoking tobacco
   b. Passive tobacco smoke
   c. Occupational exposure
   d. Air pollution, coal, gas, asbestos exposure
   e. Genetic abnormalities–alpha l-antitrypsin deficiency

4. Use of accessory muscles of breathing, dyspnea

5. Changes in posture–day and hs

6. Cough, changes in color, consistency of sputum

7. Abnormal ABGs–$PaO_2$, and $PaCO_2$

8. Adventitious breath sounds

9. Changes in sensorium, memory impairment

**B.** Diagnose

1. Most common cause of lung disease in United States

2. Group of conditions associated with obstruction of air flow entering or leaving the lungs; genetic and environmental causes–smoking and air pollution
   a. Asthma–chronic disease with episodic attacks of breathlessness
   b. Emphysema–overinflation of alveoli resulting in destruction of alveolar walls; predisposing factors: smoking, chronic infections, and environmental pollution
   c. Chronic bronchitis–inflammation of bronchi with productive cough
   d. Cystic fibrosis–hereditary dysfunction of exocrine glands causing obstruction because of flow of thick mucus
      1) Causes: sweat gland dysfunction, respiratory dysfunction, GI dysfunction
      2) Diagnostic tests
         a) Sweat test–elevated levels of sodium and chloride
         b) GI enzyme evaluation–pancreatic enzyme deficiency

3. Potential nursing diagnoses
   a. Ineffective airway clearance
   b. Imbalanced nutrition: less than body requirements
   c. Anxiety
   d. Compromised family coping
   e. Activity intolerance
   f. Deficient knowledge
   g. Social interaction, impaired
   h. Risk for infection
   i. Impaired gas exchange

**C.** Plan/Implementation

1. Determine airway clearance

2. Listen to breath sounds

3. Administer low-flow oxygen to prevent $CO_2$ narcosis for emphysema

4. Encourage fluids (6–8 glasses, 3000 ml/24 hours), provide small, frequent feedings

5. Administer medications: bronchodilators, mucolytics, corticosteroids, anticholinergics, leukotriene inhibitors, influenza, and pneumococcal vaccines

6. Metered dose inhalers (MDI)
   a. May be used with or without spacers
   b. Delivers medication directly to lungs
   c. Medications used with inhalers
      1) Beta-2 adrenergic drugs: albuterol, metaproterenol, terbutaline, salmeterol
      2) Corticosteriods: fluticasone, prednisone
      3) Cromolyn sodium and nedocromil
      4) Anticholinergics: ipratropium, tiotropium
   d. Medications should be administered so that bronchodilators are given first to open the airways, and then other medications are given
   e. Spacers attach to the MDI to hold medication in the chamber long enough for the client to inhale medication directly to the airways
   f. Reinforce teaching of proper use of MDI and spacers
   g. Caution against overuse
   h. Remind client to report decreasing effectiveness of medication and side effects
   i. Encourage client to clean equipment thoroughly
   j. Encourage client to rinse mouth thoroughly with water after steriod treatment to minimize risk of infection from oral candidiasis

7. Reinforce client teaching
   a. Breathing exercises
   b. Stop smoking
   c. Avoid hot/cold air or allergens
   d. Instructions regarding medications

e.  Avoid close contact with persons who have respiratory infections or "flu"

f.  Avoid crowds during times of the year when respiratory infections most commonly occur

g.  Maintain a high resistance with adequate rest, nourishing diet, avoidance of stress, and avoidance of exposure to temperature extremes, dampness, and drafts

h.  Practice frequent, thorough oral hygiene and handwashing

i.  Advise about prophylactic influenza vaccines

j.  Instruct to observe sputum for indications of infection

## PNEUMONIA

**A.** Data Collection

1.  Fever, chills

2.  Cough productive of rust-colored, green, whitish-yellow sputum (depending on organism)

3.  Dyspnea, pleuritic pain, accessory muscle use, upright position

4.  Tachycardia, crackles, sonorous wheezes, bronchial breath sounds

**B.** Diagnose

1.  Causes include bacteria, fungus, virus, parasite, chemical

2.  Inflammatory process that results in edema of lung tissues and extravasion of fluid into alveoli, causing hypoxia

3.  Risk factors
    a.  Community-acquired pneumonia
        1)  Older adult
        2)  Has not received pneumococcal vaccination
        3)  Has not received yearly flu vaccine
        4)  Chronic illness
        5)  Exposed to viral infection or flu
        6)  Smokes or drinks alcohol
    b.  Hospital-acquired pneumonia
        1)  Older adult
        2)  Chronic lung disease
        3)  Aspiration
        4)  Presence of endotracheal, tracheostomy, or nasogastric tube
        5)  Mechanical ventilation
        6)  Decreased level of consciousness
        7)  Immunosuppression (disease or pharmacologic etiology)

4.  Potential nursing diagnoses
    a.  Airway clearance, ineffective
    b.  Activity intolerance
    c.  Deficient knowledge
    d.  Deficient fluid volume

**C.** Plan/Implementation

1. Obtain vital signs every 4 hours

2. Cough and breathe deeply every 2 hours

3. Auscultate breath sounds

4. Incentive spirometer–5-10 breaths per hour while awake

5. Chest physiotherapy

6. Encourage fluids to 3,000 ml/24 h

7. Suction as needed

8. Oxygen therapy

9. Semi-Fowler's position/bedrest

10. Reinforce teaching about fluid intake and smoking cessation

11. Medications
    a. Mucolytics
    b. Expectorants
    c. Bronchodilators (e.g., beta-2 agonists)
    d. Antibiotics

## HEART FAILURE (HF)

**A.** Data Collection (see Table 1)

**B.** Diagnose

1. Failure of the cardiac muscle to pump sufficient blood to meet the body's metabolic needs

2. Ventricles cannot empty completely, which causes backup of circulation

3. Causes of heart failure (see Table 2)

Table 1

| HEART FAILURE | |
|---|---|
| **LEFT-SIDED FAILURE** | **RIGHT-SIDED FAILURE** |
| Dyspnea, paroxysmal nocturnal dyspnea | Dependent edema (ankle, lower extremities) |
| Orthopnea | Liver enlargement and abdominal pain |
| Pleural effusion | Anorexia, nausea, bloating |
| Cheyne-Stokes respirations | Coolness of extremities secondary to venous |
| Pulmonary edema, rales (crackles) | congestion in major organs |
| Cough with frothy, blood-tinged sputum | Anxiety, fear, depression |
| Decreased renal function—elevated BUN, albuminuria | |
| Edema, weight gain | |
| Changes in mental status (cerebral anoxia) | |
| Fatigue, muscle weakness | |

4. Potential nursing diagnoses
   a. Decreased cardiac output
   b. Activity intolerance
   c. Anxiety
   d. Deficient knowledge
   e. Impaired gas exchange
   f. Ineffective tissue perfusion (cerebral)

●Table 2

| CAUSES OF HEART FAILURE | | |
|---|---|---|
| **DISEASE** | **PATHOLOGY** | **RESULT** |
| Hypertensive disease | Vessels become narrowed; peripheral resistance increases | Cardiac muscle enlarges beyond its oxygen supply |
| Arteriosclerosis | Degenerative changes in arterial walls cause permanent narrowing of coronary arteries | Cardiac muscle enlarges beyond its oxygen supply |
| Valvular heart disease | Stenosed valves do not open freely; scarring and retraction of valve leaflets result in incomplete closure | Workload increases until heart fails |
| Rheumatic heart disease | Infection causes damage to heart valves, making them incompetent or narrowed | Incompetent valves cause blood to regurgitate backward; workload increases until heart fails |
| Ischemic heart disease | Coronary arteries are sclerosed or thrombosed | Blood supply is insufficient to nourish heart |
| Constrictive pericarditis | Inflamed pericardial sac becomes scarred and constricted, causing obstruction in blood flow | Low cardiac output and increased venous pressure Decreases filling of heart |
| Circulatory overload (IV fluid overload; sodium retention; renal shutdown) | Excessive fluid in circulatory system | Overwhelms heart's ability to pump |
| Pulmonary disease | Damage to arterioles of lungs causes vascular constriction; this increases workload of heart | Right ventricular enlargement and failure |
| Tachydysrhythmias | Decreases ventricular filling time | Decreased cardiac output |

C. Plan/Implementation
   1. Administer cardiac glycosides
      a. Digoxin—fundamental drug in the treatment of heart failure, especially when associated with low cardiac output
      b. Two categories of dosages
         1) Digitalizing or loading dose—aimed at administering the drug in divided dosages over a period of 24 hours until an "optimum" cardiac effect is reached (used infrequently)

2) Maintenance dose—client placed on this dose after digitalization; smaller in amount and designed to replace the digoxin lost by excretion while maintaining "optimal" cardiac functioning

2. Administer angiotensin-converting enzyme (ACE) inhibitors or angiotensin-receptor blockers (ARBs)—decrease afterload and improve myocardial contractility

3. Administer diuretics—thiazide diuretics, carbonic anhydrase inhibitors, aldosterone antagonists, loop diuretics

4. Administer vasodilators—decrease afterload and improve contractility

5. Administer morphine—decrease afterload

6. Administer inotropic agents—improve cardiac contractility

7. Administer Human B-type natriuretic peptides—vasodilates

8. Administer beta-adrenergic blockers—decrease myocardial oxygen demand

9. Diet
    a. Restricted sodium diet
       1) Normal intake: 6-15 g/day
       2) No table salt: 1.6-2.8 g/day
       3) No salt: 1.2-1.4 g/day
       4) Strict low-sodium diet: 0.2-1 g/day
    b. Low calorie, supplemented with vitamins—promotes weight loss, thereby reducing the workload of the heart
    c. Bland, low residue—avoids discomfort from gastric distention and heartburn
    d. Small, frequent feedings to avoid gastric distention, flatulence, and heartburn

10. Record I and O

11. Weigh daily

12. Oxygen therapy and continuous positive airway pressure (CPAP)

13. Reinforce teaching about disease process and medications

## ANGINA PECTORIS

A. Data Collection

1. Pain—may radiate down left arm; arm pain associated with stress, exertion, or anxiety

2. Relieved with rest and nitroglycerin

B. Diagnose

1. Cause—coronary atherosclerosis

2. Risk factors for coronary artery disease
    a. Nonmodifiable (client has no control)

       1) Increasing age

       2) Family history of coronary heart disease

       3) Men more likely to develop heart disease than premenopausal women

       4) Race

    b. Modifiable risk factors (client can exercise control)

       1) Elevated serum cholesterol

       2) Cigarette smoking or secondhand exposure

       3) Hypertension

       4) Diabetes mellitus

       5) Physical inactivity

       6) Obesity

       7) Depression or chronic stress

       8) Oral contraceptive use or hormone replacement therapy

       9) Substance abuse—methamphetamines or cocaine

  3. Significance—warning sign of ischemia

**C.** Plan/Implementation

  1. Health promotion

    a. No smoking

    b. Follow balanced diet that limits intake of fat and sodium

    c. Check blood pressure and cholesterol regularly

    d. Engage in regular physical activity—goal is reduction of blood pressure and pulse rate upon exertion

  2. Administer vasodilators, aspirin, glycoprotein IIIb/IIIa inhibitors, angiotension receptor blockers, calcium channel blockers

  3. Exercise program—goal is reduction of blood pressure and pulse rate upon exertion

  4. Percutaneous transluminal coronary angioplasty (PTCA)

    a. Balloon-tipped catheter inserted under fluoroscopy to the occluded coronary artery

    b. Plaque is compressed against wall to open lumen of vessel

    c. IV heparin by continuous infusion is used to prevent thrombus formation

    d. IV or intracoronary nitroglycerin or sublingual nifedipine given to prevent coronary vasospasm

    e. Monitor for complications (closure of vessel, bleeding, reaction to the dye, hypokalemia, dysrhythmias)

    f. Health care provider will prescribe nitrate, calcium channel blocker, and aspirin therapy

  5. Coronary artery bypass graft surgery (CABG)

    a. Indications—to increase blood flow to heart muscle in clients with severe angina

    b. Saphenous vein or internal mammary artery used for graft; as many as five arteries may be bypassed

    c. Preoperative

       1) Educational and psychological preparation

2) Medications discontinued—digitalis 12 hours preop, diuretics 2–3 days preop, aspirin and anitcoagulants 1 week preop

3) Medications administered—potassium chloride to maintain normal potassium level, beta blockers, calcium-channel blockers, antiarrhythmics, antihypertensives, prophylactic antibiotics 20–30 minutes before surgery

d. Postoperative

1) Receives mechanical ventilation for 6–24 hours

2) Connect chest tubes to water-seal drainage system

3) Pain relief

4) Monitor for complications—fluid and electrolyte imbalance, hypotension or hypertension, hypothermia, bleeding

5) Be alert to psychological state, disorientation, or depression

6) Provide activity as tolerated with progress as ordered, from feet dangling over side of bed, to sitting in chair, to walking in room by third day

## PERIPHERAL VASCULAR DISEASE

**A.** Data Collection (see Table 3)

**B.** Diagnose

1. Predisposing factors (see Table 3)

**C.** Plan/Implementation (see Table 3)

Table 3

| PERIPHERAL VASCULAR DISEASE | | | |
|---|---|---|---|
| TYPE | DATA | PREDISPOSING FACTORS | TREATMENT/NURSING CONSIDERATIONS |
| Arterial (arteriosclerosis, Raynaud's disease, Buerger's disease) | Dependent rubor<br>Cool, shiny skin<br>Cyanosis<br>Ulcers, gangrene<br>Impaired sensation<br>Intermittent claudication<br>Decreased peripheral pulses<br>Pallor with extremity elevation<br>Rest pain | Smoking<br>Exposure to cold<br>Emotional stress<br>Diabetes mellitus<br>High-fat diet<br>Hypertension<br>Obesity | Monitor peripheral pulses<br>Good foot care<br>Do not cross legs<br>Regular exercise<br>Stop smoking<br>Transluminal angioplasty<br>Arterial bypass<br>Endarterectomy<br>Amputation<br>Vasodilators<br>Anticoagulants<br>Antiplatelet medications |
| Venous (varicose veins, thrombophlebitis) | Cool, brown skin<br>Edema, ulcers, pain<br>Normal or decreased pulses | Immobility<br>Pregnancy<br>Hereditary<br>Obesity<br>Surgery<br>CHF<br>Injury to vein wall<br>Hypercoagulability | Monitor peripheral pulses<br>Thrombectomy<br>Avoid extremes of temperature<br>Elastic stockings, TED hose, intermittent pneumatic compression devices (IPC)<br>Anticoagulants<br>Bedrest 4-7 days<br>Elevate legs<br>Warm moist packs |

## HYPERTENSION

**A.** Data Collection

1. May be no symptoms

2. Headache, dizziness

3. Anginal pain

4. Intermittent claudication

5. Retinal hemorrhages and exudates

6. Severe occipital headaches associated with nausea, vomiting, drowsiness, giddiness, anxiety, and mental impairment

7. Polyuria, nocturia, protein and RBCs in urine, diminished ability of kidneys to concentrate urine

8. Dyspnea upon exertion—left-sided heart failure

9. Edema of the extremities—right-sided heart failure

**B.** Diagnose

1. Persistent elevation of the systolic blood pressure above 140 mm Hg and diastolic blood pressure above 90 mm Hg

2. Causes
   a. Risk factors
      1) Family history of hypertension
      2) Excessive sodium intake
      3) Excessive intake of food
      4) Physical inactivity
      5) Excessive alcohol intake
      6) Low potassium intake
      7) Age
   b. Contributing factors—history of renal or cardiovascular disease, stressful lifestyle
   c. Primary (essential or idiopathic)—constitutes 90% of all cases; may be benign (gradual onset and prolonged course) or malignant (abrupt onset and short dramatic course, which is rapidly fatal unless treated)
   d. Secondary—develops as a result of another primary disease of the cardiovascular system, renal system, adrenal glands, or neurological system

3. Complications
   a. Renal failure
   b. Cerebral vascular accident (CVA)
   c. Transient ischemic attacks (TIAs)
   d. Retinal hemorrhages

4. Potential nursing diagnoses
   a. Knowledge deficit
   b. Management of therapeutic regimen: individual, ineffective
   c. Noncompliance related to medications

C. Plan/Implementation

1. Administer medications–diuretics, calcium-channel blockers, ACE inhibitors, angiotensin receptor blockers, beta blockers, aldosterone blockers, central alpha antagonists

2. Reinforce teaching
   a. Medication side effects
   b. Dietary restriction of sodium and fat
   c. Weight control
   d. Moderate alcohol intake
   e. Increase physical activity
   f. Stop smoking
   g. Health care follow-up
   h. Change positions slowly because of possible orthostatic hypotension

## ANEMIA

A. Data Collection
1. Mild
   a. Hemoglobin 13–18 g: usually asymptomatic
   b. Symptoms usually follow strenuous exertion: palpitations, dyspnea, diaphoresis

2. Moderate
   a. Dyspnea, palpitations
   b. Diaphoresis
   c. Chronic fatigue
3. Severe
   a. Pale, exhausted all the time
   b. Severe palpitations
   c. Sensitivity to cold
   d. Loss of appetite
   e. Profound weakness
   f. Dizziness
   g. Headache
   h. Cardiac complications—CHF, angina pectoris

B. Diagnose

1. A decrease in the number of erythrocytes or a reduction in hemoglobin

C. Plan/Implementation

1. Identify cause

2. Frequent rest periods

3. Frequent turning and positioning

4. Diet high in protein, iron, vitamins

5. Small, easily digestible meals

6. Good oral hygiene

7. Monitor blood transfusions

8. Protect from sources of infection

## IRON DEFICIENCY ANEMIA

A. Data Collection

1. Fatigue

2. Decreased serum albumin, gamma globulin, and transferrin

3. Glossitis (inflammation of tongue)

4. "Spoon" fingernails (koilonychia)

5. Impaired cognition

B. Diagnose

1. Most common type

2. Causes: decreased dietary intake; malabsorption after gastric resection; blood loss due to ulcers, gastritis, GI tumors, menorrhagia (excessive menstrual bleeding); poor absorption due to high-fiber diet

C. Plan/Implementation

1. Dietary addition of iron-rich foods

2. Iron supplements IM or IV iron dextran (IV route is preferred), IM route causes pain, skin staining, and higher incidence of anaphylaxis; take oral supplements with meals if experience GI upset, then resume between meals for maximum absorption; use straw if liquids are used

3. Iron Preparations

## VITAMIN B$_{12}$ ANEMIA AND PERNICIOUS ANEMIA

**A.** Data Collection

1. Pallor

2. Fatigue

3. Weight loss

4. Sore, red tongue

5. Balance and gait disturbances

6. Paresthesias in hands and feet

**B.** Diagnose

1. Pernicious anemia: gastric mucosa fails to secrete sufficient intrinsic factor required for absorption of vitamin B$_{12}$; diagnosed by Schilling test (fast for 12 hours; given small dose of radioactive B$_{12}$ in water to drink, followed by large, nonradioactive dose IM, 24-hour urine specimen collected, measured for radioactivity)

2. Inadequate dietary intake (can occur with vegans who eat no meat or meat products)

3. Bone marrow produces fewer, larger (macrocytic) red blood cells

**C.** Plan/Implementation

1. Initial IM admistration of 25 to 100 micrograms of vitamin B$_{12}$, followed by 500 to 1,000 micrograms every 1 to 2 months or cyanocobalamin nasal spray

2. Vegetarians prevent or treat by taking vitamins or fortified soy milk

## SICKLE CELL DISEASE

**A.** Data Collection

1. Pain (may be severe)

2. Swelling of joints during crisis

3. Fever

4. Jaundice (especially of sclerae)

5. Tachycardia, cardiac murmurs

6. Hemoglobin 7–10 g/dL; sickled cells on peripheral blood smear

**B.** Diagnose

1. Severe hemolytic anemia resulting from defective hemoglobin, hemoglobin becomes sickle-shaped in presence of low oxygenation

2. Symptoms are caused by hemolysis and thrombosis

C. Plan/Implementation

1. Check joint areas for pain and swelling

2. Check for signs of infection (osteomyelitis and pneumonia common)

3. Promptly treat infection (to prevent crisis)

4. Avoid high altitudes and exposure to extreme temperatures

5. Encourage fluid intake (dehydration promotes crisis)

6. Administer folic acid daily

7. During crisis provide analgesics (PCA with morphine sulfate) and hydration (3–5 L of IV fluids/day for adults; 1600 ml/m$^2$/day for child)

8. Administer hydroxyurea; risk of leukemia and bone marrow suppression

## HEMOPHILIA

A. Data Collection

1. Spontaneous easy bruising

2. Joint pain with bleeding

3. Prolonged internal or external bleeding from mild trauma, gingival bleeding, hematuria

4. Pallor

B. Diagnose

1. Causes
   a. Sex-linked, transmitted to male by female carrier, recessive trait
   b. Factor VIII deficiency—hemophilia A—most common

2. Treatment
   a. Plasma or factor VIII cryoprecipitate
   b. Bedrest
   c. Analgesics (aspirin contraindicated)

C. Plan/Implementation

1. Observe for signs of internal bleeding

2. Analgesics for joint pain—not aspirin

3. Avoid IM injections

4. Bedrest during bleeding episodes

5. Assist with coping with chronic disease and altered lifestyle

6. Reinforce teaching to avoid contact sports; engage in activities such as golf, swimming

7. Reinforce teaching about replacement of clotting factor

●Table 4

| PITUITARY DISORDERS | | |
|---|---|---|
| | **DWARFISM (HYPOPITUITARISM)** | **ACROMEGALY** |
| **Data** | Height below normal, body proportions normal, bone/tooth development retarded, sexual maturity delayed, skin fine, features delicate | Body size enlarged, coordination poor, flat bones enlarged, sexual abnormalities, deep voice, skin thick and soft, visual field changes |
| **Diagnose** | Hyposecretion of growth hormone; occurs before maturity Etiology unclear; predisposition—pituitary tumors, idiopathic hyperplasia Treatment: hormone replacement (human growth hormone, thyroid growth hormone, testosterone) Complication: diabetes | Hypersecretion of growth hormone occurs after maturity Etiology: unclear Diagnosis: growth hormone measured in blood plasma Treatment: external irradiation of tumor, atrium-90 implant transnasally, hypophysectomy (removal of pituitary or portion of it with hormone replacement) |
| **Potential nursing diagnosis** | Self-esteem disturbance Risk for sexual dysfunction | Body image disturbance Nutrition, altered Chronic pain Risk for sexual dysfuction |
| **Plan/ Implementation** | Monitor growth and development Provide emotional support Determine body image Refer for psychological counseling as needed Monitor medications Hormone replacement therapy Thyroid hormone replacement Testosterone therapy Human chorionic gonadotropin (hCG) injections | Monitor blood sugar level Provide emotional support Provide safety due to poor coordination and vision Administer dopamine agonists; somatostatin analogs; growth hormone receptor blockers Provide care during radiation therapy Provide posthypophysectomy care: Elevate head Check neurological status and nasal drainage Monitor BP frequently Observe for hormonal deficiencies (thyroid, glucocorticoid) Observe for hypoglycemia Monitor intake and output Provide cortisone replacement before and after surgery Avoid coughing Avoid toothbrushing for 2 weeks |

## PITUITARY DISORDERS

A.  Data Collection (see Table 4)

B.  Diagnose (see Table 4)

1.  Anterior hormones—Growth, TSH, ACTH, LH, FSH

2.  Posterior hormones—oxytocin, vasopressin, ADH

C.  Plan/Implementation (see Table 4)

**CANCER**

**A.** Data Collection

1. American Cancer Society Warning Signs (CAUTION)
   a. **C**hange in bowel, bladder habits
   b. **A** sore that does not heal
   c. **U**nusual bleeding or discharge
   d. **T**hickening or a lump in the breast or elsewhere
   e. **I**ndigestion or difficulty in swallowing
   f. **O**bvious change in a wart or mole
   g. **N**agging cough or hoarseness

**B.** Diagnose

1. Risk factors
   a. Immunosuppression
   b. Advancing age
   c. Genetic predisposition

2. Causative factors
   a. Physical
      1) Radiation—excessive exposure to sunlight and radiation
      2) Chronic irritation
   b. Chemical
      1) Food additives—e.g., nitrites
      2) Industry—e.g., asbestos
      3) Pharmaceutical—e.g., stilbesterol
      4) Smoking
      5) Alcohol
   c. Genetic
   d. Viral—incorporated into cell genesis: Epstein-Barr virus, Burkitt's lymphoma
   e. Stress—cocausative factor

3. Common cancer types
   a. Caucasian
      1) Lung
      2) Breast
      3) Colorectal
      4) Prostate

        b. African American

           1) Lung

           2) Prostate

           3) Breast

           4) Colorectal

           5) Uterine

        c. Asian

           1) Breast

           2) Colorectal

           3) Prostate

           4) Lung

           5) Stomach

        d. Hispanic

           1) Prostate

           2) Breast

           3) Colorectal

           4) Lung

4. Classifications

    a. Carcinoma—epithelial tissue

    b. Sarcoma—connective tissue

    c. Lymphoma—lymphoid tissue

    d. Leukemia—blood-forming tissue (WBCs and platelets)

5. Potential nursing diagnoses

    a. Skin integrity, impaired

    b. Risk for infection

    c. Fear/death anxiety

    d. Grieving

    e. Acute/chronic pain

    f. Fatigue

**C.** Plan/Implementation

1. Cancer prevention

    a. Avoid known carcinogens

        1) Don't smoke

        2) Wear sunscreen

        3) Eliminate asbestos in buildings

    b. Modify dietary habits

        1) Avoid excessive intake of animal fat

        2) Avoid nitrates found in prepared lunch meats, sausage, and bacon

        3) Decrease intake of red meat

        4) Limit alcohol intake to one or two drinks per day

        5) Increase intake of bran, broccoli, cauliflower, brussels sprouts, cabbage, and foods high in vitamin A and C

2. Chemotherapy

3. Teletherapy (Radiotherapy)

    a. External radiation (e.g., cobalt)

        1) Leave radiology markings intact on skin

2) Avoid creams or lotions, deodorants, perfumes (only vitamin A and D ointment permitted)

3) Use lukewarm water to cleanse area

4) Observe skin for redness, cracking

5) Administer antiemetics for nausea, analgesics for pain

6) Observe skin, mucous membranes, and hair follicles for side effects

7) No hot water bottle, tape; don't expose area to cold or sunlight

8) Wear cotton clothing

  b. Brachytherapy (Internal Radiation) (e.g., cesium, radium, gold)

    1) Sealed source—mechanically positioned source of radioactive material placed in body cavity or tumor

      a) Lead container and long-handled forceps in room in event of dislodged source

      b) Save all dressings, bed linens until source is removed; then discard dressings and linens as usual

      c) Urine, feces not radioactive

      d) Do not stand close or in line with radioactive source

      e) Client on bedrest while implant in place

      f) Position of source verified by radiography

    2) Unsealed source of radiation—unsealed liquid given orally, or instilled in body cavity (e.g., $^{131}I$)

      a) All body fluids contaminated

      b) Greatest danger from body fluids during first 24–96 hours

    3) Nursing care for internal radiation

      a) Assign client to private room

      b) Place "Caution: Radioactive Material" sign on door

      c) Wear dosimeter film badge at all times when interacting with client (offers no protection but measures amount of exposure; each nurse has individual badge)

      d) Do not assign pregnant nurse to client

      e) Rotate staff caring for client

      f) Organize tasks so limited time is spent in client's room

      g) Limit visitors

      h) Encourage client to do own care

      i) Provide shield in room

      j) Use antiemetics for nausea

      k) Consider body image (e.g., alopecia)

      l) Provide comfort measures, analgesic for pain

      m) Provide good nutrition

3. Skin care

  a. Avoid use of soaps, powders, lotions

  b. Wear cotton, loose-fitting clothing

4. Mouth care

  a. Stomatitis—develops 5–14 days after chemotherapy begins

  b. Symptoms—erythema, ulcers, bleeding

  c. Oral rinses with saline or soft-bristled toothbrush

d. Avoid hot (temperature) or spicy foods

e. Topical antifungals and anesthetics

5. Hair care

a. Alopecia commonly seen, alters body image

b. Assist with wig or hair piece

c. Scarves, hats

6. Nutritional changes

a. Anorexia, nausea, and vomiting commonly seen with chemotherapy

b. Malabsorption and cachexia (wasting) common

c. Make meals appealing to senses

d. Conform diet to client preferences and nutritional needs

e. Small, frequent meals with additional supplements between meals (high-calorie, high-protein diet)

f. Encourage fluids but limit at meal times

g. Perform oral hygiene and provide relief of pain before meal time

h. TPN as needed

7. Neutropenia precautions—prevent infection among clients with immunosuppression; absolute neutrophil count less than or equal to 1000 cells/mm$^3$

a. Observe skin integrity every 8 hours; auscultate breath sounds, presence of cough, sore throat; check temperature every 4 hours, report if higher than 101° F (38° C); monitor CBC and differential daily

b. Private room when possible

c. Thorough hand hygiene before entering client's room

d. Allow no staff with cold or sore throat to care for client

e. No fresh flowers or standing water

f. Clean room daily

g. Low microbial diet; no fresh salads, unpeeled fresh fruits and vegetables

h. Deep breathe every 4 hours

i. Meticulous body hygiene

j. Inspect IV site, meticulous IV site care

8. Pain relief—three-step ladder approach

a. For mild pain—nonnarcotic meds used (acetaminophen) along with antiemetics, antidepressants, glucocorticoids

b. For moderate pain—weak narcotics (codeine) and nonnarcotics are used

c. For severe pain—strong narcotics are used (morphine)

d. Give pain meds on regularly scheduled basis (preventative approach), additional analgesics given for breakthrough pain

9. Activity level

a. Alternate rest and activity

b. Maintain normal lifestyle

10. Psychosocial issues

a. Encourage participation in self-care and decision-making

b. Provide referral to support groups, organizations

c. Hospice care

## LEUKEMIA

**A.** Data Collection

1. Ulcerations of mouth and throat

2. Pneumonia, septicemia

3. Altered leukocyte count $(15,000-500,000/mm^3)$

4. Anemia, fatigue, lethargy, hypoxia

5. Bleeding gums, ecchymosis, petechiae, retinal hemorrhages

6. Weakness, pallor, weight loss

7. Headache, disorientation, convulsions

**B.** Diagnose

1. Fatal neoplastic disease that involves the blood-forming tissues of the bone marrow, spleen, and lymph nodes; abnormal, uncontrolled, and destructive proliferation of one type of white cell and its precursors

2. Diagnostic tests
   a. Bone marrow aspiration
      1) Informed consent required
      2) Done at iliac crest and sternum
      3) Local anesthetic used
      4) Apply sterile dressing to area after procedure; apply pressure to site if bleeding
      5) Complications
         a) Osteomyelitis
         b) Bleeding
         c) Puncture of vital organs

3. Classification of the leukemias
   a. Acute leukemia—rapid onset and progresses to a fatal termination within days to months; more common among children and young adults
   b. Chronic leukemia—gradual onset with a slower, more protracted course; more common between ages 25 and 60

4. Factors associated with development
   a. Viruses
   b. Ionizing radiation
   c. Genetic predisposition
   d. Absorption of certain chemicals, e.g., benzene, pyridine, and aniline dyes

**C.** Plan/Implementation

1. Monitor for signs of bleeding, e.g., petechiae, bruising, bleeding, thrombocytopenia

2. Monitor for signs of infection, e.g., changes in vital signs, chills, neutropenia

3. Good mouth care

4. High-calorie, high-vitamin diet

5. Frequent feedings of soft, easy-to-eat food

6. Antiemetics

7. Neutropenia precautions, if necessary

8. Strict handwashing

9. Prevent skin breakdown, e.g., turning, positioning

10. Administer and monitor blood transfusions (whole blood, platelets)

11. Administer medications, treatments as ordered, and observe for side effects
    a. Chemotherapy
       1) Nausea, vomiting, diarrhea
       2) Stomatitis, alopecia, skin reactions
       3) Bone marrow depression
    b. Radiation or radioisotope therapy
    c. Bone marrow transplants

## SKIN CANCER

**A.** Data Collection

1. Basal cell carcinoma—small, waxy nodule on sun-exposed areas of body (e.g., face); may ulcerate and crust

2. Squamous cell carcinoma—rough, thick, scaly tumor seen on arms or face

3. Malignant melanoma—variegated color (brown, black mixed with gray or white) circular lesion with irregular edges seen on trunk or legs

**B.** Diagnose

1. Major risk factor—overexposure to sun

2. Basal cell carcinoma—most common type of skin cancer; rarely metastasize but commonly reoccurs

3. Squamous cell carcinoma—may metastasize to blood or lymph

4. Malignant melanoma—most lethal of skin cancers; frequently seen 20–45 years old; highest risk persons with fair complexions, blue eyes, red or blond hair, and freckles; metastases to bone, liver, spleen, CNS, lungs, lymph

5. Diagnosed by skin lesion biopsy

**C.** Plan/Implementation

1. Postop care following surgical excision

2. Promote prevention
   a. Avoid exposure to sun 10 AM to 3 PM
   b. Use sunscreen with SPF (solar protection factor) to block harmful rays (especially important for children)

    c. Reapply sunscreen after swimming or prolonged time in sun

    d. Use lip balm with sunscreen protection

    e. Wear hat when outdoors

    f. Do not use lamps or tanning booths

    g. Teach client to examine skin surfaces monthly

  3. Teach how to identify danger signs of melanoma—change in size, color, shape of mole or surrounding skin

  4. Chemotherapy for metastases

## INTRACRANIAL TUMORS

**A.** Data Collection—signs and symptoms vary depending on location

  1. Motor deficits

  2. Language disturbances

  3. Hearing difficulties, visual disturbances (occipital lobe)

  4. Dizziness, paresthesia (cerebellum)

  5. Seizures (motor cortex)

  6. Personality disturbances (frontal lobe)

  7. Papilledema

  8. Nausea and vomiting

  9. Drowsiness, changes in level of consciousness

**B.** Diagnose

  1. Types—classified according to location

    a. Supratentorial—incision usually behind hairline, surgery within the cerebral hemisphere

    b. Infratentorial—incision made at nape of neck around occipital lobe; surgery within brain stem and cerebellum

  2. Causes—unknown

  3. Medical/surgical management—intracranial surgery and radiation

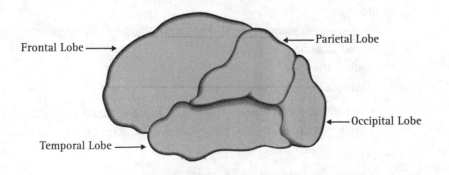

**Figure 1. Divisions of the Brain**

C. Plan/Implementation

1. Preoperative care
   a. Detailed neurological data collection for baseline data
   b. Head shave—prep site
   c. Psychological support
   d. Prepare client for postoperative course

2. Postoperative care
   a. Maintain patent airway
   b. Elevate head of bed 30–45° after supratentorial surgery
   c. Position client flat and lateral on either side after infratentorial surgery
   d. Monitor vital and neurological signs
   e. Observe for complications—respiratory difficulties, increased intracranial pressure, hyperthermia, meningitis, wound infection
   f. Administer medications—corticosteroids, osmotic diurectics, mild analgesics, anticonvulsants, antibiotics, antipyretics, antiemetics, hormone replacement as needed; no narcotics postoperatively (masks changes in LOC), use acetaminophen

## PANCREATIC TUMORS

A. Data Collection

1. Weight loss

2. Vague upper or midabdominal discomfort

3. Abnormal glucose tolerance test (hyperglycemia)

4. Jaundice, clay-colored stools, dark urine

B. Diagnose

1. Tumors may arise from any portion of the pancreas (head or tail); each has unique clinical manifestations

2. Diagnostic tests–CT, CT-guided needle biopsy, MRI

3. Risk factor–smoking, pancreatitis, exposure to enviromental toxins

C. Plan/Implementation

1. Medical
   a. High-calorie, bland, low-fat diet; small, frequent feedings
   b. Avoid alcohol
   c. Anticholinergics
   d. Antineoplastic chemotherapy

2. Surgery (Whipple procedure)—removal of head of pancreas, distal portion of common bile duct, the duodenum, and part of the stomach

3. Postop care
   a. Monitor for peritonitis and intestinal obstruction
   b. Monitor for hypotension
   c. Monitor for steatorrhea

d. Administer pancreatic enzymes

e. Monitor for diabetes mellitus

## CARCINOMA OF THE LARYNX

A. Data Collection

1. Pain radiating to the ears

2. Hoarseness, dysphagia, foul breath

3. Dyspnea

4. Enlarged cervical nodes

5. Hemoptysis

B. Diagnose

1. Diagnostic tests
   a. Laryngoscopic examination
   b. Biopsy
   c. CT, MRI
   d. X-rays

2. Causes
   a. Industrial chemicals
   b. Cigarette smoking and alcohol use
   c. Straining of the vocal cords
   d. Chronic laryngitis
   e. Family predisposition

C. Plan/Implementation

1. Caring for the client with a laryngectomy
   a. Preoperative care
      1) Explain compensatory methods of communication
      2) Referral to speech therapy
   b. Postoperative care
      1) Laryngectomy care—stoma care, suction
      2) Place in semi-Fowler's position
      3) Turn, cough, and deep breathe
      4) Nasogastric, gastrostomy, or jejunostomy feeding tube

2. Observe for postoperative complications after laryngectomy
   a. Respiratory difficulties
   b. Fistula formation
   c. Rupture of carotid artery
   d. Stenosis of trachea

3. Monitor weight, food intake, and fluid intake and output

4. Communication for total laryngectomy clients
   a. Esophageal speech
   b. Artificial larynx—commonly used mechanical device for speech

5. Radiation therapy—small, localized cancers; sore throat, increased hoarseness, dysphagia

PHYSIOLOGICAL
INTEGRITY 3

[REDUCTION OF RISK POTENTIAL]

**Chapter 8**

Sensory and Perceptual
Alterations

Alterations in Body Systems

Perioperative Care

Diagnostic Tests

Therapeutic Procedures

## IMPAIRED VISION

**A.** Data Collection

1. Redness, burning, pain in eyes

2. Edema

3. Increased lacrimation and exudate

4. Headache, squinting

5. Nausea and vomiting

6. Altered growth and development

7. Visual disturbances

8. Altered visual function tests (see Table 1)

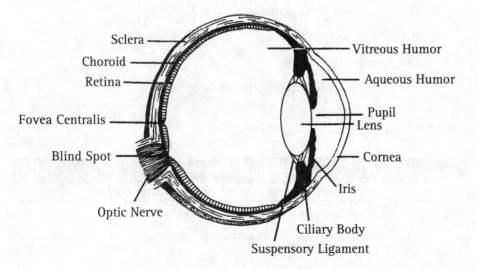

**Figure 1.  Anatomy of the Eye**

Table 1

| VISUAL FUNCTION TESTS | | |
|---|---|---|
| **TEST** | **PROCEDURE** | **CLIENT PREPARATION** |
| Tonometry— measures intraocular pressure | Cornea is anesthetized<br>Tonometer registers degree of indentation on cornea when pressure is applied<br>Pressure increased in glaucoma | Client will be recumbent<br>Remove contact lenses<br>Advise not to squint, cough, or hold breath during procedure |
| Visual fields— measurement of range of vision (perimetry) | Client is seated a measured distance from chart of concentric circles<br>Client asked to fix eyes on a point on a chart at center of circle<br>Client instructed to indicate when he/she first sees pointer; this point is recorded as a point in field of vision<br>This procedure is repeated around 360° of a circle<br>Normal visual fields for each eye are approximately a 50° angle superiorly, 90° laterally, 70° inferiorly, and 60° medially | None |
| Snellen test— test of visual acuity | Client stands 20 feet from chart of letters<br>One eye is covered at a time<br>Client reads chart to smallest letter visible<br>Test results indicate comparison of distance at which this client reads to what normal eye sees at 20 feet | None |

**B.** Diagnose

1. Disorders of accommodation (see Table 2)

2. Burns of the eye (see Table 3)

3. Eye trauma (see Table 4)

4. Eye infections/inflammation (see Table 5)

Table 2

| DISORDERS OF ACCOMMODATION | |
|---|---|
| **TYPES** | **NURSING CONSIDERATIONS** |
| Myopia (nearsightedness)—light rays refract at a point in front of the retina | Corrective lenses |
| Hyperopia (farsightedness)—light rays refract behind the retina | Corrective lenses |
| Presbyopia with aging | Commonly occurs after age 35<br>Corrective lenses |
| Astigmatism—uneven curvature of cornea causing blurring of vision | Corrective lenses |

● Table 3

| BURNS OF THE EYE | |
|---|---|
| **TYPES** | **NURSING CONSIDERATIONS** |
| **Chemical**<br>Acids, cleansers, insecticides | Eye irrigation with copious amounts of water for 15-20 minutes |
| **Radiation**<br>Sun, lightening, eclipses | Prevention—use of eye shields |
| **Thermal**<br>Hot metals, liquids, other occupational hazards | Use of goggles to protect the cornea; patching; analgesics |

● Table 4

| EYE TRAUMA | |
|---|---|
| **TYPES** | **NURSING CONSIDERATIONS** |
| Nonpenetrating—abrasions | Eye patch for 24 hours |
| Nonpenetrating—contusions | Cold compresses, analgesics |
| Penetrating—pointed or sharp objects | Cover with patch; refer to surgeon |

**C.** Plan/Implementation

1. Prevent eye injuries
   a. Provide safe toys
   b. Use eye protectors when working with chemicals, tools
   c. Use eye protectors during sports
   d. Protect eyes from ultraviolet light

● Table 5

| EYE INFECTION/INFLAMMATION | | |
|---|---|---|
| **TYPE OF INFECTION** | **CAUSE** | **NURSING CONSIDERATIONS** |
| Conjunctivitis (pinkeye) | Bacteria<br>Virus<br>Allergies | Warm, moist compresses<br>Topical antibiotics<br>Hydrocortisone ophthalmic ointment |
| Stye | *Staphylococcal* organism | Warm compresses<br>Antibiotics<br>Incision and drainage |
| Chalazion (inflammatory cyst) | Duct obstruction | Incision and drainage |
| Keratitis (inflammation of cornea) | Virus<br>Spread of systemic disease | Antibiotics<br>Hot compresses<br>Steroids, except with herpes simplex |
| Uveitis (inflammation of iris, ciliary body, choroid) | Local or systemic infection | Warm compresses<br>Dark glasses<br>Antibiotics, analgesics, sedatives |

2. Care of the blind client
    a. Enhance communication
        1) Address client by name
        2) Always introduce self
        3) State reason for being there
        4) Inform client when leaving the room

    b. Provide sense of safety and security
        1) Explain all procedures in detail
        2) Keep furniture arrangement consistent
        3) Provide hand rail
        4) Doors should never be half open
        5) Have client follow attendant when walking by lightly touching attendant's elbow (1/2 step ahead)
        6) Instruct client in use of lightweight walking stick when walking alone

    c. Foster sense of independence
        1) Provide assistance only when needed
        2) Identify food and location on plate or tray
        3) Encourage recreational and leisure time activities

3. Care of artificial eye
    a. Remove daily for cleansing
    b. Cleanse with mild detergent and water
    c. Dry and store in water or contact-lens soaking solution
    d. Remove before general surgery
    e. Insertion method
        1) Raise upper lid and slip eye beneath it
        2) Release lid
        3) Support lower lid and draw it over the lower edge of eye

    f. Removal method
        1) Draw lower lid downward
        2) Slip eye forward over lower lid and remove

4. Instill eye drops

## STRABISMUS

A. Data Collection

   1. Visible deviation of eye

   2. Diplopia

   3. Child tilts head or squints to focus

B. Diagnose

   1. Eyes do not function as a unit

   2. Imbalance of the extraocular muscles

C. Plan/Implementation

   1. Nonsurgical intervention begins no later than age 6

   2. Occlusion of unaffected eye to strengthen weaker eye

   3. Corrective lenses combined with other therapy to improve acuity

   4. Orthoptic exercises designed to strengthen eye muscles

   5. Surgery

## DETACHED RETINA

A. Data Collection

   1. Flashes of light

   2. Blurred or "sooty" vision, "floaters"

   3. Sensation of particles moving in line of vision

   4. Delineated areas of vision blank

   5. A feeling of a curtain coming up or down

   6. Loss of vision

   7. Confusion, apprehension

B. Diagnose

   1. Separation of the retina from the choroid

   2. Cause
      a. Trauma
      b. Aging process
      c. Diabetes
      d. Tumors

**C.** Plan/Implementation

1. Bedrest

2. Affected eye or both eyes may be patched to decrease movement of eye (as ordered by health care provider)

3. Specific positioning—area of detachment should be in the dependent position

4. Take precautions to avoid bumping head, moving eyes rapidly, or rapidly jerking the head

5. Surgery to reattach retina to choroid; gas or air bubble used to apply pressure to retina

6. No hair-washing for 1 week

7. Administer sedatives and tranquilizers

8. Avoid strenuous activity for 3 months

9. Care of client undergoing eye surgery
   a. Preoperative care
      1) Determine visual acuity
      2) Prepare periorbital area
      3) Orient to surroundings
      4) Preoperative teaching—prepare for postoperative course
      5) Teach postop need to avoid straining at stool, stooping
   b. Postoperative care
      1) Observe for complications—hemorrhage, sharp pain, infection
      2) Avoid sneezing, coughing, straining at stool, bending down
      3) Protect from injury; restrict activity
      4) Keep signal bell within reach
      5) Administer medications as ordered: antiemetics for nausea/vomiting, sedatives for restlessness
      6) Eye shield worn for protective purposes
      7) Discharge teaching—avoid stooping or straining at stool; use proper body mechanics

## CATARACTS

**A.** Data Collection

1. Objects appear distorted and blurred; decreased color perception

2. Annoying glare; double vision

3. Pupil changes from black to gray to milky white

**B.** Diagnose

1. Partial or total opacity of the normally transparent crystalline lens

2. Cause
   a. Congenital
   b. Trauma
   c. Aging process
   d. Associated with diabetes mellitus, intraocular surgery
   e. Drugs—steroid therapy
   f. Exposure to radioactivity

**C.** Plan/Implementation

1. Surgical management—laser surgery
   a. Extracapsular extraction—cut through the anterior capsule to expose the opaque lens material, most common procedure
   b. Intracapsular extraction—removal of entire lens and capsule; easier for health care provider to do; places client at greater risk for retinal detachment and loss of structure for intraoccular lens implant
   c. Lens implantation
   d. Observe for postoperative complications
      1) Hemorrhage indicated by sudden sharp pain
      2) Increased intraocular pressure
      3) Slipped suture(s)
      4) If lens implant—pupil should remain constricted; if aphakic (without lens) pupil remains dilated
   e. Avoid straining; no heavy lifting
   f. Bend from the knees to pick things up
   g. Instruct in installation of eye drops to affected eye, use of night shields
   h. Usually suggest to sleep on unaffected side (decreases pain and swelling when elevated)
   i. Protect eye from bright lights and water
   j. Adjustments needed in perception if aphakic
   k. Report increased pain, change in vision, increased floaters

## GLAUCOMA

A. Data Collection

1. Cloudy, blurry vision or loss of vision

2. Artificial lights appear to have rainbows or halos around them

3. Decreased peripheral vision

4. Pain, headache

5. Nausea, vomiting

B. Diagnose

1. Abnormal increase in intraocular pressure leading to visual disability and blindness; obstruction of outflow of aqueous humor

2. Types
   a. Angle-closure (closed-angle) glaucoma–sudden onset
   b. Open-angle (primary) glaucoma–blockage of aqueous humor flow

3. Causes
   a. Closed-angle glaucoma—associated with emotional disturbances, allergy, and vasomotor disturbances
   b. Open-angle glaucoma—associated with trauma, tumor, hemorrhage, and iritis

4. Potential nursing diagnosis
   a. Disturbed sensory perception

C. Plan/Implementation

1. Medications: prostaglandin agonists, adrenergic agonists, beta-adrenergic blockers, cholinergic agonists, carbonic anhydrase inhibitors

2. Surgery—laser trabeculoplasty

3. Avoid tight clothing (e.g., collars)

4. Reduce external stimuli

5. Avoid heavy lifting, straining at stool

6. Avoid use of mydriatics (e.g., Atropine)

7. Educate public to five danger signs of glaucoma
   a. Brow arching
   b. Halos around lights
   c. Blurry vision
   d. Diminished peripheral vision
   e. Headache or eye pain

## HEARING LOSS

**A.** Conductive loss

1. Data Collection
    a. Pain, fever, headache
    b. Discharge
    c. Altered growth and development
    d. Personality changes, e.g., irritability, depression, suspiciousness, withdrawal

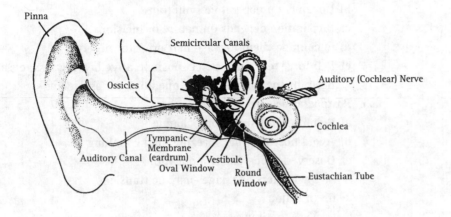

**Figure 2. Anatomy and Physiology of the Ear**

2. Analysis
    a. Disorder in auditory canal, eardrum, or ossicles
    b. Causes
        1) Infection
        2) Inflammation
        3) Foreign body
        4) Trauma
        5) Ear wax
    c. Complications—meningitis resulting from initial infection
    d. Diagnostics
        1) Audiogram—quantitative (degree of loss)
        2) Tuning fork—qualitative (type of loss)

3. Plan/Implementation
    a. Heat
    b. Antibiotics
    c. Hearing aid
    d. Ear irrigations
        1) Tilt head toward side of affected ear, gently direct stream of fluid against sides of canal
        2) After procedure, instruct client to lie on affected side to facilitate drainage
        3) Contraindicated if there is evidence of swelling or tenderness

    e. Ear drops

       1) Position the affected ear uppermost

       2) Pull outer ear upward and backward for adult (3 years of age and older)

       3) Pull outer ear downward and backward for child (under 3 years of age)

       4) Place drops so they run down the wall of ear canal

       5) Have client lie on unaffected ear to encourage absorption

    f. Surgery

       1) Preoperative care

          a) Baseline hearing determination

          b) Document preoperative symptoms

          c) Preparation depends on nature of incision

          d) Encourage client to wash hair prior to surgery

          e) Reinforce teaching—expect postoperative hearing loss; discuss need for special position of operative ear as ordered

       2) Postoperative care

          a) Reinforce dressing, don't change

          b) Avoid noseblowing, sneezing, and coughing

          c) Observe for possible complications

             i. Facial nerve damage—may be transient

             ii. Infection

             iii. Vertigo, tinnitus

          d) Do not apply any pressure if bleeding is noted—notify health care provider immediately

          e) Administer medications

          f) Provide for client safety

          g) Position on unaffected side (decreases swelling and pain of surgical site)

       3) Discharge teaching—avoid getting water in ear, flying, drafts, crowds, people with respiratory infections

**B.** Perceptive (sensorineural) loss

  1. Data Collection

    a. Pain, fever, headache

    b. Discharge

    c. Altered growth and development

    d. Personality changes (e.g., irritability, depression, suspiciousness, withdrawal)

  2. Analysis

    a. Due to disorder of the organ of Corti or the auditory nerve

    b. Causes

       1) Congenital—maternal exposure to communicable disease

       2) Infection, drug toxicity

       3) Trauma

       4) Labyrinth dysfunction—Ménière's disease

        c. Complications

            1) Vertigo

            2) Tinnitus

            3) Vomiting

    3. Plan/Implementation

        a. Care of the deaf/hard of hearing client

            1) Enhance communication

                a) Position self directly in front of client

                b) Well-lit, quiet room

                c) Get client's attention

                d) Move close to better ear, if appropriate

                e) Speak clearly and slowly; do not shout

                f) Keep hands and other objects away from mouth when speaking

                g) Have client repeat statements

                h) Use appropriate hand motions

                i) Write messages down if client able to read

        b. Surgery

## ACUTE OTITIS MEDIA

**A.** Data Collection

    1. Fever, chills

    2. Headache

    3. Ringing in ears

    4. Deafness

    5. Sharp pain

    6. Head rolling, crying, ear-tugging (child)

    7. Red, bulging tympanic membrane

**B.** Diagnose

    1. Definition–infection of middle ear

    2. Cause–pathogenic organisms (i.e., bacteria and viruses)

    3. Complications

        a. Chronic otitis media–children more susceptible because of short eustachian tube

        b. Residual deafness

        c. Perforation of tympanic membrane

        d. Cholesteatoma growth

        e. Mastoid or brain involvement

**C.** Plan/Implementation

    1. Administer medication as ordered

        a. Antibiotics–organism-specific

        b. Antihistamines for allergies (see page 498)

        c. Nasal decongestants

2. Report persistent symptoms to health care provider

3. Ventilatory tubes—inserted in eustachian tube for continuous ventilation

4. Myringotomy—tympanic membrane incision to relieve pressure and release purulent fluid; no water can be allowed to enter the ear

5. Tympanoplasty—surgical reconstruction of ossicles and tympanic membrane

6. Bedrest if temperature is elevated

7. Position on side of involved ear to promote drainage

## MÉNIÈRE'S SYNDROME

**A.** Data Collection

1. Nausea and vomiting

2. Incapacitating vertigo, tinnitus

3. Feeling of pressure/fullness in the ear

4. Fluctuating, progressive decreased hearing on involved side

5. Nystagmus, headache

**B.** Diagnose

1. Dilation of the membrane of the labyrinth

2. Recurrent attacks of vertigo with sensorineural hearing loss

3. Attacks recur several times a week; periods of remission may last several years

4. Complication—hearing loss

**C.** Plan/Implementation

1. Drug therapy
   a. Antihistamines in acute phase (epinephrine, diphenhydramine)
   b. Antiemetics (e.g., prochlorperazine)
   c. Antivertigo medications (e.g., meclizine, diazepam, metoclopramide)
   d. Diuretics (e.g., hydrochlorothiazide/triamterene)

2. Bedrest during acute phase

3. Provide protection when ambulatory

4. Low-sodium diet (2,000 mg/day); avoid caffeine, nicotine, alcohol

5. Decompression of endolymphatic sac with Teflon shunt (method of choice)

6. Total labyrinthectomy—last resort due to possible complication of Bell's palsy

7. Reinforce client education
   a. Need to slow down body movements—jerking or sudden movements may precipitate attack
   b. Need to lie down when an attack occurs
   c. If driving, pull over and stop car

8. Occupational counseling—if occupation involves operating machinery

## CRANIAL NERVE DISORDERS

**A.** Data Collection (see Table 6)

**B.** Diagnose (see Table 6)

**C.** Plan/Implementation (see Table 6)

## GUILLAIN-BARRÉ SYNDROME

**A.** Data Collection

1. Paresthesias, pain often occurring in glove-and-stocking distribution; pain

2. Motor losses symmetrical, usually beginning in lower extremities, then extend upward to include trunk, upper extremities, cranial nerves, and vasomotor function; deep tendon reflexes disappear; respiratory muscle compromise

●Table 6

| CRANIAL NERVE DISORDERS | | | |
|---|---|---|---|
| | **TRIGEMINAL NEURALGIA (TIC DOULOUREUX)** | **BELL'S PALSY (FACIAL PARALYSIS)** | **ACOUSTIC NEUROMA** |
| **Data Collection Findings** | Stabbing or burning facial pain—excruciating, unpredictable, paroxysmal<br>Twitching, grimacing of facial muscles | Inability to close eye<br>Decreased corneal reflex<br>Increased lacrimation<br>Speech difficulty<br>Loss of taste<br>Distortion of one side of face | Deafness—partial, initially<br>Twitching, grimacing of facial muscles<br>Dizziness |
| **Analysis** | Type of neuralgia involving one or more branches of the fifth cranial nerve<br>Causes—infections of sinuses, teeth, mouth, or irritation of nerve from pressure | Peripheral involvement of the seventh cranial nerve<br>Predisposing factors—vascular ischemia, viral disease, edema, inflammatory reactions | Benign tumor of the eighth cranial nerve |
| **Nursing considerations** | Identify and avoid stimuli that exacerbate the attacks<br>Administer medications—carbamazepine and analgesics<br>Treatment—Carbamazepine, alcohol injection to nerve, resection of the nerve, microvascular decompression<br>Avoid rubbing eye<br>Chew on opposite side of mouth | Protect head from cold or drafts<br>Administer analgesics<br>Assist with electric stimulation<br>Teach isometric exercises for facial muscles (blow and suck from a straw); massage, warm packs<br>Provide emotional support for altered body image<br>Prevent corneal abrasions (artificial tears)<br>Treatment—electrical stimulation, analgesics, steroid therapy, antiviral medications<br>Recovery takes 3-5 weeks | Pre- and postoperative care for posterior fossa craniotomy<br>Comfort measures—assist with turning of head and neck<br>Treatment—surgical excision of tumor |

3. Excessive or inadequate autonomic dysfunction
   a. Hypotension, tachycardia
   b. Vasomotor flushing
   c. Paralytic ileus
   d. Profuse sweating

4. Progression period—average 10 days, with duration of maximum symptoms 10 days

5. Recovery period—several months to a year; 10% residual disability

**B.** Diagnose

1. Progressive inflammatory autoimmune response occurring in peripheral nervous system, resulting in compression of nerve roots and peripheral nerves; demyelination occurs and slows or alters nerve conduction

2. Possible causes
   a. Infective, viral
   b. Autoimmune response
   c. May follow immunizations

3. Course
   a. Acute, rapidly ascending sensory and motor deficit that may stop at any level of the CNS
   b. Protracted, develops slowly, regresses slowly
   c. Prolonged course with phases of deterioration and partial remission

**C.** Plan/Implementation

1. Intervention is symptomatic

2. Steroids in acute phase

3. Plasmapheresis, IV immunoglobulins, adrenocorticotropic hormone, corticosteroids

4. Mechanical ventilation, elevate head of bed, suctioning

5. Prevent hazards of immobility

6. Maintain adequate nutrition, hydration

7. Physical therapy, range of motion

8. Pain-reducing measures

9. Eye care

10. Prevention of complications—URI, aspiration, constipation, urinary retention

11. Psychosocial support to deal with fear, anxiety, and altered body image

## MENINGITIS

**A.** Data Collection

  1. Headache, fever, photophobia

  2. Signs of meningeal irritation
     a. Nuchal rigidity—stiff neck
     b. Kernig's sign—when hip flexed to 90°, complete extension of the knee is restricted and painful
     c. Brudzinski's sign—attempts to flex the neck will produce flexion at knee and thigh
     d. Opisthotonic position—extensor rigidity with legs hyperextended and forming an arc with the trunk

  3. Changes in level of consciousness

  4. Seizures

  5. Symptoms in infants
     a. Refuse feedings, vomiting, diarrhea
     b. Bulging fontanelles
     c. Vacant stare, high-pitched cry

**B.** Diagnose

  1. Causes
     a. Infection (viral, bacterial, fungal)
     b. Neurosurgical procedures, basilar-skull fractures
     c. Otitis media, mastoiditis

**C.** Plan/Implementation

  1. IV antibiotic therapy—penicillin, cephalosporin, vancomycin

  2. Monitor ABG, arterial pressures, body weight, serum electrolytes, urine volume, specific gravity, osmolality

  3. Droplet precautions for *Haemophilus influenzae*, type b, and *Neisseria meningitidis*

  4. Prevention
     a. Vaccine 65+ years old with chronic diseases; revaccination in 5 years
     b. Hib vaccine for infants

## MIGRAINE HEADACHE

**A.** Data Collection

  1. Prodromal—depression, irritability, feeling cold, food cravings, anorexia, change in activity level, increased urination

  2. Aura—light flashes and bright spots, numbness and tingling (lips, face, hands), mild confusion, drowsiness, dizziness

  3. Headache—throbbing (often unilateral), photophobia, nausea, vomiting, 4 to 72 hours

4. Recovery—pain gradually subsides, muscle aches in neck and scalp, sleep for extended period

**B.** Diagnose

1. Episodic events or acute attacks

2. Seen more often in women before menses

3. Familial disorders due to inherited vascular response to different chemicals

4. Precipitating factors—stress, menstrual cycles, bright lights, depression, sleep deprivation, fatigue, foods containing tyramine, monosodium glutamate, nitrites, or milk products (aged cheese, processed foods)

**C.** Plan/Implementation

1. Prevention and treatment
   a. Medications
      1) Beta blockers
      2) Triptan preparations
      3) Acetaminophen and NSAIDs
      4) Topiramate
      5) Ergotamines–dihydroergotamine; take at beginning of headache
   b. Modify trigger factors

2. Implementation
   a. Avoid triggers
   b. Comfort measures
   c. Quiet dark environment
   d. Elevate head of bed 30°

3. Complementary/Alternate therapy
   a. Riboflavin (vitamin $B_2$) supplement
      1) 400 mg daily may reduce the number and duration but not the severity of the headaches
   b. Massage, meditation, relaxation techniques

## HUNTINGTON'S DISEASE

**A.** Data Collection

1. Depression and temper outbursts

2. Choreiform movements
   a. Slight to severe restlessness
   b. Facial grimacing
   c. Arm movements
   d. Irregular leg movements
   e. Twisting, turning, struggling
   f. Tongue movements
   g. Person is in constant motion by end of disease progression

3. Personality changes
   a. Irritabilty
   b. Paranoia, demanding, memory loss, decreased intellectual function
   c. Dementia
   d. Psychosis seen at end stage

**B.** Diagnose

1. Rare, familial, progressive, degenerative disease that is passed from generation to generation (dominant inheritance)

**C.** Plan/Implementation

1. Drug therapy—intended to reduce movement and subdue behavior changes
   a. Chlorodiazepoxide hydrochloride
   b. Haloperidol
   c. Chlorpromazine

2. Supportive, symptomatic

3. Genetic counseling for all family members

## ALTERATIONS IN GLUCOSE METABOLISM

**A.** Data Collection

1. Polyuria, polydipsia, polyphagia

2. Weight change

**B.** Diagnose

1. Diabetes mellitus is a genetically heterogeneous group of disorders that is characterized by glucose intolerance

2. Types (see Table 1)

●Table 1

| ALTERATIONS IN GLUCOSE METABOLISM | |
|---|---|
| **Type** | **Nursing Considerations** |
| Type 1 diabetes | Acute onset before age 30<br>Insulin-producing pancreatic beta cells destroyed by autoimmune process<br>Requires insulin injection<br>Ketosis prone |
| Type 2 diabetes | Usually older than 30 and obese<br>Decreased sensitivity to insulin (insulin resistance) or decreased insulin production<br>Ketosis rare<br>Treated with diet and exercise<br>Supplemented with oral hypoglycemic agents |
| Others:<br>Gestational diabetes<br>Impaired fasting glucose | Onset during pregnancy, second or third trimester<br>High-risk pregnancy<br>Fasting plasma glucose of 100–125 mg/dL; risk factor for future diabetes risk |

3. Risk factors for type 2 diabetes

   a. Parents or siblings with diabetes

   b. Obesity (20% or more above ideal body weight)

   c. African American, Hispanic, Native American, or Asian American

   d. Older than 45 years

   e. Previously impaired fasting glucose

   f. Hypertension

   g. HDL cholesterol levels less than or equal to 35 mg/dL; triglyceride levels greater than or equal to 250 mg/dL

   h. History of gestational diabetes or delivery of baby greater than 9 lb

4. Diagnostic tests
   a. Blood glucose monitoring—presence of sugar in the urine is a sign of diabetes and calls for an immediate blood glucose test; normal range in fasting blood is 60–110 mg/dL
   b. Urine ketones indicate that diabetic control has deteriorated, body has started to break down stored fat for energy
   c. Glycosylated hemoglobin ($HbA_{1c}$)—blood sample can be taken without fasting; normal 4–6%
   d. Special considerations—medications, illness, and stress will affect testing

**C.** Plan/Implementation

1. Nutrition management
   a. Provide all essential food constituents—lower lipid levels if elevated
   b. Achieve and maintain ideal weight
   c. Meet energy needs
   d. Achieve normal-range glucose levels
   e. Methods
      1) Food exchange—foods on list in specified amounts contain equal number of calories and grams of protein, fat, and carbohydrate (see Table 2)
      2) Carbohydrate counting
      3) Food guide pyramid
      4) Glycemic index

Table 2

| DIABETIC EXCHANGE LIST | |
|---|---|
| **EXCHANGE** | **EXAMPLE** |
| Bread/starch | 1 slice of bread<br>1/2 cup pasta |
| Vegetable | 1 cup raw leafy vegetables<br>1/2 cup cooked vegetables |
| Milk | 1 cup yogurt<br>2 oz processed cheese |
| Meat, poultry, eggs, fish | 2-3 oz cooked meat, fish, poultry<br>2 eggs |
| Fruit | 1/2 cup cooked fruit<br>1 medium apple |
| Fat | 1 tsp mayonnaise |
| Free items | Mustard, pickle, herbs |

2. Insulin management (see page 492)
   a. Insulin lowers blood glucose by facilitating uptake and the use of glucose by muscle and fat cells; decreases the release of glucose from the liver
   b. Mixing insulins—draw up regular insulin first
   c. Site selection—abdomen, posterior arms, anterior thighs, hips; rotate sites
   d. Self-injection—use disposable syringe once and discard into hard plastic container with tight-fitting top
   e. "Sick day rules"
      1) Take insulin or oral agent as ordered
      2) Check blood glucose or urine ketones every 3–4 hours
      3) Report altered levels to health care provider
      4) If unable to follow normal meal plan, substitute soft foods (soup, custard, gelatin) 6–8 times per day
      5) If vomiting, diarrhea, or fever, report to health care provider and take liquids (cola, broth, Gatorade) every 0.5–1 hour

3. Oral hypoglycemic agents—improve both tissue responsiveness to insulin and/or the ability of the pancreatic cells to secrete insulin (see page 489)

4. Self-monitoring of blood glucose (SMBG)
   a. Check client's eyesight to make sure he/she can see directions and read results
   b. Calibrate monitor as instructed by manufacturer
   c. Check expiration date on test strips
   d. If taking insulin, check 2–4 times daily
   e. If not receiving insulin, check 2–3 times per week
   f. Keep log book of results
   g. Testing should be done at peak action time of medication

5. Skin and foot care
   a. Inspect feet daily (use mirror if client is elderly or has decreased joint mobility)
   b. Wear well-fitting shoes; break in new shoes slowly (wear 1–2 hours initially with gradual increase in time)
   c. Don't walk barefoot or use heating pad on feet
   d. Cut toenails straight across without rounding corners

6. Exercise
   a. Use proper foot care
   b. Don't exercise in extreme temperatures
   c. Don't exercise when control of diabetes is poor

7. Complications
   a. Hypoglycemia (insulin reaction) (see Table 3)
   b. Hyperglycemia (diabetic ketoacidosis) (see Table 3)
   c. HHNKS (hyperglycemic hyperosmolar nonketotic syndrome; see Table 3)
   d. Diabetic retinopathy
   e. Coronary artery disease
   f. Cerebrovascular disease

Table 3

| GLUCOSE IMBALANCES | | | |
|---|---|---|---|
| | **HYPOGLYCEMIA (Insulin Reaction)** | **HYPERGLYCEMIA (Diabetic Ketoacidosis)** | **HHNKS (Hyperglycemia Hyperosmolar Nonketotic Syndrome)** |
| **Data Collection Findings** | Blood sugar less than 50–60 mg/dL Irritability, confusion, tremors, blurring of vision, coma, seizures Hypotension, tachycardia Skin cool and clammy, diaphoresis | Blood sugar 300–800 mg/dL Headache, drowsiness, weakness stupor, coma Hypotension, tachycardia Skin warm and dry, dry mucous membranes, elevated temperature Polyuria progressing to oliguria, polydipsia, polyphagia Kussmaul's respirations (rapid and deep) Fruity odor to breath | Glucose levels greater than 800 mg/dL Occurs in adults over 50 year old Occurs in Type 2 (NIDDM) diabetics Ketosis and acidosis do not occur Hypotension Dry mucous membranes, poor skin turgor Tachycardia Alteration in sense of awareness, seizures, hemiparesis |
| **Plan/ Implementation** | Liquids containing sugar if conscious; skim milk is ideal if tolerated Dextrose 50% IV if unconscious, glucagon 1 mg IM, SQ Follow with additional carbohydrate in 15 minutes Determine and treat cause Client education | Major complication is fluid volume deficit 1 L of 0.9% NaCl per hour during first 2-3 hrs followed by 0.45% NaCl 200-500 ml/h; then $D_5W$ or $D_5$ 1/2 NS Regular IV insulin 5 units/h Potassium replacement EKG q 2–4 h Check $K^+$ q 2–4 h Determine level of consciousness, urine output, temperature hourly Obtain vital signs q 15 minutes until stable Obtain CVP q 30 minutes Check blood glucose levels hourly | Normal saline or 0.45% NaCl Regular insulin Potassium as soon as urine output is satisfactory Determine and treat cause Client education Exercise regimen |
| **Cause** | Too much insulin or oral hypoglycemia agent Inadequate food Excessive physical activity | Decreased or missed insulin Illness or infection Untreated diabetes | Acute illness Medications (thiazides) Treatments (dialysis) |

## ALTERATIONS IN PROTEIN METABOLISM

A.  Data Collection (see Table 4)

B.  Diagnose—potential nursing diagnoses

　　1.  Nutrition: less than body requirements, altered

　　2.  Knowledge deficit regarding dietary restrictions

C.  Plan/Implementation (see Table 4)

●Table 4

| ALTERATIONS IN PROTEIN METABOLISM | | |
|---|---|---|
| **DISORDER** | **DATA COLLECTION FINDINGS** | **NURSING CONSIDERATIONS** |
| Phenylketonuria (PKU)–inborn error of phenylalanine utilization | High blood phenylalanine that leads to intellectual delay | Specially prepared milk substitutes for infants (Lofenalac)<br>Low-protein diet for children (no meat, dairy products, eggs, NutraSweet) |
| Gout–inborn error of purine metabolism | High uric acid level that leads to progressive joint deterioration | Low-purine diet (no fish or organ meats) |
| Celiac disease–(sprue) inborn error of wheat and rye metabolism | Intestinal malabsorption that leads to malnutrition<br>Diarrhea<br>Failure to thrive | Gluten-free diet (no wheat, oats, rye, barley) |
| Renal failure | Increased protein and albumin losses in urine that leads to protein deficiency | High-calorie, low-protein diet, as allowed by kidney function |
| Protein allergy | Diarrhea that leads to malnutrition and water loss | Change dietary protein source |

## ALTERATIONS IN FAT METABOLISM

A. Data Collection (see Table 5)

B. Diagnose–potential nursing diagnoses

   1. Nutrition: less than body requirements, altered

   2. Knowledge deficit regarding dietary restriction

C. Plan/Implementation (see Table 5)

●Table 5

| ALTERATIONS IN FAT METABOLISM | | |
|---|---|---|
| **DISORDER** | **DATA COLLECTION FINDINGS** | **NURSING CONSIDERATIONS** |
| Hepatobiliary disease | Decreased bile leads to fat malabsorption | Low-fat, high-protein diet<br>Vitamins |
| Cystic fibrosis | Absence of pancreatic enzymes leads to malabsorption of fat (and fat-soluble vitamins), weight loss<br>Infection and lung disease lead to increased need for calories and protein | Pancreatic enzyme replacement (cotazym pancreas) before or with meals<br>High-protein diet<br>High-calorie diet in advanced stages |
| Atherosclerosis (thickening and hardening of the arteries) | Associated with high blood cholesterol and triglyceride levels<br>Risk factors–diet, high blood pressure, diabetes, stress, sedentary lifestyle, and smoking | Low-saturated fat diet<br>Cholesterol-lowering agents given before meals |

## INFECTIONS OF THE GI TRACT

**A.** Data Collection

    1. Headache

    2. Abdominal discomfort, anorexia

    3. Watery diarrhea, nausea, vomiting

    4. Low-grade fever

**B.** Diagnose

    1. Acute illness caused by ingested food contaminated by toxins or parasites

    2. Types (see Table 6)

Table 6

| COMMON INFECTIONS OF THE GASTROINTESTINAL TRACT | | |
|---|---|---|
| **PARASITE OR BACTERIUM** | **SOURCE** | **NURSING CONSIDERATIONS** |
| Enterotoxigenic *E. coli* | Undercooked beef | Causes rapid, severe dehydration, cook beef until meat no longer pink and juices run clear |
| *Salmonella* | Poultry, eggs | Causes gastroenteritis, systemic infection |
| *Campylobacter* | Poultry, beef, pork | Cook and store food at appropriate temperatures |
| *Giardia lamblia* | Protozoan, contaminated water | Treated with metronidazole, good personal hygiene |
| *Shigella* | Fecal contamination | Affects pediatric population, antimicrobial therapy |

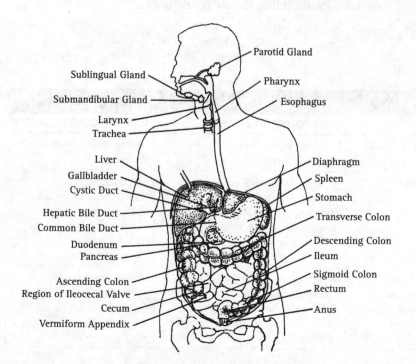

**Figure 1. The Digestive System**

**C.** Plan/Implementation

    1. Prevention

        a. Good sanitation

        b. Good hygiene measures, e.g., handwashing

        c. Proper food preparation, e.g., thorough cooking; heat canned foods 10–20 minutes and inspect cans for gas bubbles

    2. Nursing considerations

        a. Maintain fluid and electrolytes

        b. Monitor vital signs

        c. Medications: antibiotics, antispasmodics, antiemetics

        d. Teach importance of good handwashing and cleaning of utensils when preparing food

## HIATAL HERNIA

**A.** Data Collection

    1. Heartburn

    2. Regurgitation

    3. Dyspepsia

**B.** Diagnose

    1. Opening in diaphragm through which the esophagus passes becomes enlarged, part of the upper stomach comes up into the lower portion of the thorax

**C.** Plan/Implementation

    1. Administer medications

        a. $H_2$ receptor blockers (e.g., cemetadine, ranitidine)

        b. Antacids (e.g., aluminum hydroxide, magnesium hydroxide)

        c. Cytoprotective agents (e.g., sucralfate)

        d. Proton pump inhibitors (pantoprazole)

    2. Surgery to tighten cardiac sphincter (fundoplication)

    3. Small, frequent feedings

    4. Do not lie down for at least 1 hour after meals; elevate head of bed 4–8 inches when sleeping

    5. Do not eat before going to bed to prevent reflux of food

## PYLORIC STENOSIS

**A.** Data Collection

    1. Vomiting (projectile in infants)

    2. Epigastric fullness

    3. Irritability (in infants)

4. Infant always hungry

5. Infant fails to gain weight

6. Palpable olive-shaped tumor in epigastrium (infants)

7. Peristaltic waves

**B.** Diagnose

1. In adults, narrowing or obstruction of the pyloric sphincter caused by scarring from healing ulcers; in infants, obstruction caused by hypertrophy and hyperplasia of pylorus

2. Inflammation and edema can reduce the size of the opening until there is complete obstruction

3. Infants usually don't show symptoms until the second to fourth week after birth; then regurgitation develops into projectile vomiting; most frequently seen in male, white, full-term infants

4. Obstruction in adults usually caused by peptic ulcer

5. Surgical intervention
   a. Pyloromyotomy (infants)—incision through circular muscles of the pylorus
   b. Vagotomy and antrectomy—removal of gastrin-secreting portion of the stomach and severing of vagus nerves
   c. Vagotomy and pyloroplasty or gastroenterostomy—establishes gastric drainage, involves severing of vagus nerves

**C.** Plan/Implementation

1. Preoperative
   a. Prevent regurgitation and vomiting
      1) IV fluids
      2) Check skin turgor, fontanelles, urinary output
      3) Measure vomitus
      4) Correct fluid and electrolyte abnormalities—alkalosis, hypokalemia
      5) Gastric decompression with NG tube
      6) Monitor for complications—alkalosis, hypokalemia, dehydration, and shock
      7) Support parents
         a) Allow verbalization of parents' anxieties
         b) Instruct parents on expected progress and behavior

2. Postoperative
   a. Keep incision site clean and dry
   b. Provide parenteral fluids at ordered rate
   c. Monitor warmth
   d. Small, frequent feedings of glucose water or electrolyte solution 4–6 hours postoperatively
   e. If clear fluids retained start formula 24 hours postop
   f. Reinforce teaching parents to fold diaper so it doesn't touch incision

## GASTRITIS

**A.** Data Collection

  1. Uncomfortable feeling in abdomen

  2. Headache

  3. Anorexia, nausea, vomiting (possibly bloody)

  4. Hiccupping

**B.** Diagnose

  1. Inflammation of stomach that may be acute or chronic

**C.** Plan/Implementation

  1. NPO slowly progressing to bland diet

  2. Antacids often relieve pain

  3. Referral to appropriate agency if alcohol abuse is verified

## ULCER

**A.** Data Collection (see Table 7)

**B.** Diagnose

  1. Excavation formed in the mucosal wall, caused by erosion that may extend to muscle layers or through the muscle to the peritoneum (see Figure 1)

  2. *H. pylori* frequently present

  3. Familial tendency

●Table 7

| DUODENAL VERSUS GASTRIC ULCER | | |
|---|---|---|
| | **CHRONIC DUODENAL ULCER** | **CHRONIC GASTRIC ULCER** |
| Age | 30-60 years | 50 years and older |
| Sex | Male-female ratio: 3:1 | Male-female ratio: 1:1 |
| Risk factors | Blood group type O, COPD, chronic renal failure, alcohol, smoking, cirrhosis, stress | Gastritis, alcohol, smoking, NSAIDs, stress |
| Gastric secretion | Hypersecretion | Normal to hyposecretion |
| Pain | 2-3 hours after meal; nighttime, often in early sleeping hours<br>Food intake relieves pain | ½ to one hour after meal or when fasting<br>Relieved by vomiting<br>Ingestion of food does not help |
| Vomiting | Rare | Frequent |
| Hemorrhage | Less likely | More likely |
| Malignancy | Rare | Occasionally |

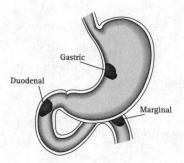

**Figure 2. Sites for Ulcers**

**C.** Plan/Implementation

1. Avoid oversecretion and hypermotility in the gastrointestinal tract

2. Dietary modification
   a. Eat 3 meals per day; small frequent feedings not necessary if taking antacids or histamine blocker
   b. Avoid extremes in temperature
   c. Avoid coffee, alcohol, and caffeinated beverages
   d. Avoid milk and cream

3. Reduce stress

4. Stop smoking—inhibits ulcer repair

5. Medications
   a. Antacids (e.g., magnesium and aluminum hydroxide); administer 1 hour before or after meals
   b. Histamine receptor site antagonist (e.g., cimetidine, ranitidine); take with meals
   c. Anticholinergics (e.g., propantheline); give 30 minutes before meals
   d. Cytoprotective agents (e.g., sucralfate); give 1 hour before meals
   e. Proton pump inhibitors (e.g., omeprazole)

6. Surgical intervention (see Figure 2)
   a. Diagnostic workup—upper-GI series, endoscopy, CAT scan
   b. Gastrectomy—removal of stomach and attachment to upper portion of duodenum
   c. Vagotomy—cutting the vagus nerve (decreases HCl secretion)
   d. Billroth I—partial removal (distal one-third to one-half) of stomach, anastomosis with duodenum
   e. Billroth II—removal of distal segment of stomach and antrum, anastomosis with jejunum

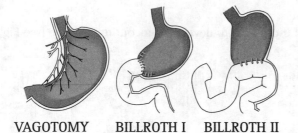

VAGOTOMY    BILLROTH I    BILLROTH II

**Figure 3.  Common Surgeries for Ulcers**

7. Postoperative
   a. Gather vital signs
   b. Inspect dressings
   c. Provide gastric decompression as ordered
   d. Vitamin $B_{12}$ via parenteral route (required for life); iron supplements
   e. Encourage deep breathing
   f. Observe for peristalsis
      1) Levin tube—single-lumen tube at low suction
      2) Salem sump—double-lumen for drainage
         a) Prevent irritation to nostril
         b) Lubricate tube around nares with water-soluble jelly
         c) Control excessive nasal secretions
         d) Observe nasogastric drainage for volume and blood
      3) Listen for bowel sounds
      4) Record passage of flatus or stool

   g. Preventive measures for "dumping syndrome" (rapid passage of food to stomach causing diaphoresis, diarrhea, hypotension)
      1) Restrict fluids with meals, drink 1 hour ac or 1 hour pc
      2) Eat in semi-recumbent position
      3) Lie down 20–30 minutes after eating
      4) Eat smaller, frequent meals
      5) Low carbohydrates and fiber diet
      6) Antispasmotics

## ESOPHAGEAL ATRESIA AND TRACHEOESOPHAGEAL FISTULA

A. Data Collection

1. Excessive saliva, drooling

2. Stomach distention

3. Choking, coughing, sneezing

4. Cyanosis

**B.** Diagnose

1. Failure of esophagus to develop as a continuous tube (see Figure 4)

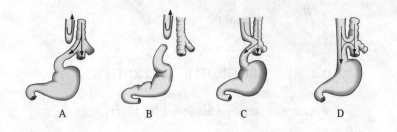

**Figure 4. Tracheosophageal Fistula**

2. Often occurs with anomalies of heart or the genitourinary or musculoskeletal system

**C.** Plan/Implementation

1. Surgical repair
   a. Preoperative
      1) Position supine of prone with head of bed elevated on incline plane at least 30 degrees
      2) IV fluids and antibiotics through umbilical artery catheter
      3) Maintain patent airway
   b. Postoperative
      1) Care for incision site—observe for inflammation
      2) Prevent pulmonary complications—suction and position
      3) IV fluids and antibiotics
      4) TPN until gastrostomy or oral feedings tolerated

## CROHN'S DISEASE (REGIONAL ENTERITIS, ILEITIS, OR ENTEROCOLITIS) ULCERATIVE COLITIS

**A.** Data Collection (see Table 8)

**B.** Diagnose

1. Crohn's disease—inflammatory condition of any area of large or small intestine, usually ileum and ascending colon

2. Ulcerative colitis—inflammatory condition of the colon characterized by eroded areas of the mucous membrane and tissues beneath it

**C.** Plan/Implementation

1. Diet—high-protein, high-calorie, low-fat, and fiber; PN used for bowel rest

2. Medications—analgesics, anticholinergics, antibiotics, corticosteroids to reduce inflammation, immune modulators, salicylate-containing compounds

3. Maintain fluid, electrolyte balance; provide PN if bowel rest is needed

4. Ileostomy

● Table 8

| CROHN'S DISEASE VERSUS ULCERATIVE COLITIS | | |
|---|---|---|
| | **CROHN'S DISEASE REGIONAL ENTERITIS** | **ULCERATIVE COLITIS** |
| **Data** | | |
| Usual age of onset | 20–30 and 50–80 years | Young adult to middle age (30-50) |
| Fatty stool (steatorrhea) | Frequent | Absent |
| Malignancy results | Rare | 10–15% |
| Rectal bleeding | Occasional: mucus, pus, fat in stool | Common; blood, pus, mucus in stool |
| Abdominal pain | After meals | Predefecation |
| Diarrhea | Diarrhea rare; 5–6 unformed stools per day | 10-20 liquid stools per day; often bloody |
| Nutritional deficit, weight loss, anemia, dehydration | Common | Common |
| Fever | Present | Present |
| Anal abscess | Common | Common |
| Fistula and anorectal fissure fistula | Common | Rare |
| **Diagnose** | | |
| Level of involvement | Ileum, right colon | Rectum, left colon |
| Inflammation | Noncontinuous segment | Continuous segment |
| Course of disease | Prolonged, variable Complications–bowel abscess, fistula formation, intestinal obstruction | Remissions and relapses Complications–hemorrhage, abscess formation, arthritis, uveitis |
| **Nursing considerations** | High-protein, high-calorie, low-fat, and low-fiber diet May require PN to rest bowel Analgesics, anticholinergics, sulfonamides (Gantrisin), corticosteriods, antidiarrheals, and antiperistaltics Maintain fluid/electrolyte balance Monitor electrolytes Promote rest, relieve anxiety Ileostomy in severe cases | |

## APPENDICITIS

A. Data Collection

1. Periumbilical abdominal pain shifts to right lower quadrant at McBurney's point (located between umbilicus and the right iliac crest)

2. Anorexia, nausea, vomiting

3. Localized tenderness

4. Muscle guarding

5. Low-grade fever

B. Diagnose

1. Highest incidence 11–30 years of age

2. Differential CBC count; WBC 15,000 to 20,000 cells/mm$^3$

C. Plan/Implementation

1. No heating pads, enemas, or laxatives preop

2. Maintain NPO status until blood laboratory reports received, IV fluids to prevent dehydration

3. No analgesics until cause of pain is determined

4. Ice bag to abdomen to alleviate pain

5. Observe for signs and symptoms of peritonitis

6. Surgical removal of appendix (appendectomy)
   a. Normal postop care
   b. Fowler's position to relieve abdominal pain and ease breathing

7. Sudden cessation of pain–perforation emergency

8. Antibiotic therapy

## DIVERTICULAR DISEASE

A. Data Collection

1. Cramping pain in left lower quadrant of abdomen relieved by passage of stool or flatus

2. Fever, increased WBC

3. Constipation alternating with diarrhea

B. Diagnose

1. Infection, inflammation, or obstruction of diverticula (sacs or pouches in the intestinal wall) cause the client to become symptomatic

2. Associated with deficiency in dietary fiber

C. Plan/Implementation

1. Uncomplicated
   a. Antispasmodics, anticholinergic (e.g., dicyclomine)
   b. Bulk laxatives
   c. High-fiber diet
   d. Increase fluids

2. Acute
   a. Bedrest
   b. NPO progressing to oral fluids to semi-solids
   c. IV fluids
   d. NG tube
   e. Antibiotics
   f. Surgery–drain abscess, resect obstruction

## PERITONITIS

A. Data Collection

1. Abdominal pain, possibly severe

2. Abdominal rigidity and distension, rebound tenderness

3. Nausea, vomiting

4. Ascites

5. Increased temperature, leukocytosis

6. Paralytic ileus

7. Symptoms may be masked in elderly persons or those receiving corticosteroids

**B.** Diagnose

1. Inflammation of part or all of the parietal and visceral surfaces of the abdominal cavity

2. Causes
   a. Ruptured appendix, ectopic pregnancy
   b. Perforated ulcer, bowel, or bladder
   c. Traumatic injury
   d. Blood-borne organisms

**C.** Plan/Implementation

1. Preoperative care
   a. Monitor vital signs, I and O
   b. Antibiotics and IV fluids
   c. Gastric decompression; monitor NG drainage
   d. NPO
   e. Reestablish fluid/electrolyte balance, monitor serum electrolytes
   f. Analgesics

2. Postoperative care
   a. NPO
   b. NG tube
   c. Semi-Fowler's position
   d. IV fluids with electrolyte replacement
   e. Antibiotics
   f. PN

## HIRSCHSPRUNG'S DISEASE

**A.** Data Collection

1. Newborn—failure to pass meconium, refusal to suck, abdominal distention

2. Child—failure to gain weight, delayed growth, constipation alternating with diarrhea

**B.** Diagnose

1. A ganglionic disease of the intestinal tract; inadequate motility causes mechanical obstruction of intestine

2. Diagnostic tests—radiographic contrast studies

**C.** Plan/Implementation

1. Help parents adjust to congenital defect in child

2. Foster infant/parent bonding

3. Prepare for surgery
   a. Enemas
   b. Low-fiber, high-calorie, high-protein diet
   c. TPN if needed
   d. Oral antibiotics
   e. Measure abdominal girth at level of umbilicus

4. Postoperative care
   a. Monitor fluid and electrolytes
   b. Maintain nutrition
   c. Let parents know colostomy is usually temporary, closed when child is 17–22 lb

## INTUSSUSCEPTION

**A.** Data Collection

1. Colicky abdominal pain

2. Causes child to scream and draw knees to abdomen

3. Vomiting

4. Currant jellylike stools containing blood and mucus

5. Tender, distended abdomen

6. May have palpable sausage-shaped mass in the upper right quadrant of the abdomen

7. Usual client is 3 months to 3 years old

**B.** Diagnose

1. Telescoping of one portion of the bowel into another (usually the ileum into the cecum and colon)

2. Results in intestinal obstruction, and blocked blood and lymph circulation

3. Diagnosis can often be made based on findings alone

**C.** Plan/Implementation

1. Non-surgical intervention
   a. Water-soluble contrast medium or air pressure to "push" the telescoped portion out
   b. Postprocedural care
      1) Monitor vital signs
      2) Auscultate bowel sounds
      3) Observe for passage of water-soluble contrast medium
      4) Encourage parental rooming-in

2. Surgical intervention
   a. Manually reducing the telescoped portion of the bowel
   b. Removal of any damaged bowel portions

3. Preparation for surgery
   a. NPO
   b. CBC and urinalysis
   c. Sedation
   d. Correct hypovolemia and electrolyte imbalances
   e. Treat peritonitis, if present
   f. Nasogastric suctioning (decompression) may be needed
   g. Consent form signed

4. Postoperative care
   a. Monitor vital signs
   b. Inspect sutures and dressing
   c. Auscultate for return of bowel sounds
   d. Administer pain medications and antibiotics as ordered
   e. Progress diet with return of bowel sounds

## ABDOMINAL HERNIAS

**A.** Data Collection

1. Lump at site of hernia may disappear in reclining position and reappear on standing/coughing/lifting

2. Strangulated hernia—severe abdominal pain, nausea and vomiting, distention, intestinal obstruction

**B.** Diagnose

1. Protrusion of an organ through the wall of the cavity in which it is normally contained

2. Types
   a. Inguinal—protrusion of intestine through abdominal ring into inguinal canal
   b. Femoral—protrusion of intestine into femoral canal
   c. Umbilical—protrusion of intestine through umbilical ring
   d. Ventral or incisional—protrusion through site of an old surgical incision
   e. Reducible—the protruding structure can be replaced by manipulation into the abdominal cavity
   f. Irreducible or incarcerated—the protruding structure cannot be replaced by manipulation
   g. Strangulated—blood supply to the intestines is obstructed (emergency situation)

**C.** Plan/Implementation

1. Preoperative care for herniorrhaphy
   a. Observe respiratory system for potential causes of increased intra-abdominal pressure—may cause interference with postop healing
   b. Surgery is postponed until respiratory conditions are controlled
   c. Truss—pad placed under hernia, held in place with belt

2. Postoperative care
   a. Relieve urinary retention
   b. Turning and deep breathing, but avoid coughing
   c. Provide scrotal support
   d. Provide ice packs for swollen scrotum
   e. Advise no pulling, pushing, heavy lifting for 6–8 weeks
   f. Inform client that sexual function is not affected
   g. Instruct client that ecchymosis will fade in a few days

## MECKEL'S DIVERTICULUM

**A.** Data Collection

1. Symptoms seen by 2 years of age

2. Painless rectal bleeding, abdominal pain

3. Hematochezia (currant jelly–like stool)

4. Signs and symptoms of appendicitis if diverticulum becomes inflamed from infection

**B.** Diagnose

1. A congenital sac or pouch in the ileum

2. Contains gastric or pancreatic tissue that secretes acid

3. Most common GI malformation

**C.** Plan/Implementation

1. Preoperative care
   a. IV fluids
   b. Observe for rectal bleeding
   c. Bedrest

2. Postoperative care
   a. Surgical (if symptomatic)—removal of the diverticulum
   b. Prevent infection
   c. Maintain nutrition

## INTESTINAL OBSTRUCTION

**A.** Data Collection

1. Nausea, vomiting

2. High-pitched bowel sounds above area of obstruction, decreased or absent bowel sounds below area of obstruction

3. Abdominal pain and distention, pain often described as "colicky"

4. Obstipation (absence of stool and gas)

**B.** Diagnose

1. Mechanical obstruction—physical blockage of lumen of intestines, usually seen in the small intestine
   a. Hernia
   b. Tumors
   c. Adhesions
   d. Strictures due to radiation or congenital
   e. Intussusception (telescoping of bowel within itself)
   f. Volvulus (twisting of bowel)

2. Nonmechanical obstruction—no mechanical blockage, absence of peristalsis
   a. Abdominal trauma/surgery
   b. Spinal injuries
   c. Peritonitis, acute appendicitis
   d. Wound dehiscence (breakdown)

**C.** Plan/Implementation

1. Intestinal decompression
   a. Insertion of a plastic or rubber tube into the stomach or intestine via the nose or mouth; the purpose may be diagnostic, preventive, or therapeutic; fluid or air may be removed
   b. Tubes
      1) Salem sump or Levin tubes (nasogastric)
      2) Miller-Abbott (intestinal)
      3) Cantor (intestinal)

2. NPO

3. Fluid/electrolyte replacement; monitor I and O and electrolyte levels

4. Assist with ADL

5. Good oral and skin care

6. Fowler's position to facilitate breathing

7. Bowel surgery
   a. Purpose—removal of diseased portion of bowel; creation of an outlet for passage of stool when there is an obstruction or need for "bowel rest"
   b. Types of surgeries
      1) Exploratory laparotomy; possible adhesion removal
      2) Resection and anastomosis—diseased portion of bowel is removed and remaining ends are joined together
      3) Abdominal perineal resection—abdominal incision through which the proximal end of the sigmoid colon is exteriorized through a permanent colostomy; the distal end of the sigmoid colon, rectum, and anus are removed through the perineal route
      4) Intestinal ostomies

## INTESTINAL OSTOMIES FOR FECAL DIVERSION

**A.** Data Collection

1. Cancer of colon or rectum

2. Diverticulitis

3. Intestinal obstruction

**B.** Diagnose

1. Ostomy is opening into colon to allow passage of intestinal contents

2. Stoma is opening on abdomen where intestine is sutured to skin surface

3. Types (see Figure 5)

4. Common intestinal ostomies (see Table 9)

5. Continent ileal reservoir (Koch pouch)—surgical creation of pouch of small intestine acts as an internal reservoir for fecal discharge, nipple value as outlet

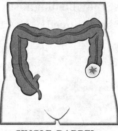 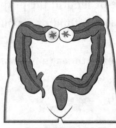 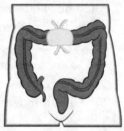

SINGLE-BARREL (usually permanent)   DOUBLE-BARREL (usually temporary)   LOOP (can be temporary or permanent)

**Figure 5.  Types of Colostomies**

**C.** Plan/Implementation

1. Preoperative care
   a. Psychological support and explanations
   b. Diet—high calorie, high protein, high carbohydrates, low-residue week before; NPO after midnight
   c. Intubation prior to surgery—NG or intestinal
   d. Activity—assist PRN, client will be weakened from extensive preparation procedures
   e. Elimination—laxatives, enemas evening before and morning of surgery
   f. Have enterostomal clinician see client for optimum placement of stoma
   g. Medications: antibiotics (e.g., erythromycin) day before surgery
   h. Monitor for fluid/electrolyte imbalance

2. Postoperative care
   a. NG or intestinal decompression until peristalsis returns; maintain NPO status

b. Clear liquids progressing to solid, low-residue diet for first 6–8 weeks

c. Monitor I and O and fluid/electrolyte balance

d. Observe and record condition of stoma

    1) First few days appears beefy-red and swollen

    2) Gradually, swelling recedes and color is pink or red

    3) Notify RN or health care provider immediately if stoma is dark blue, "blackish," or purple—indicates insufficient blood supply

e. Observe and record description of any drainage from stoma

    1) Usually just mucus or serosanguineous for first 1–2 days

    2) Begins to function 3–6 days postop

f. Promote positive adjustment to ostomy

    1) Encourage client to look at stoma

    2) Encourage early participation in ostomy care

    3) Reinforce positive aspects of colostomy

● Table 9

| COMMON INTESTINAL OSTOMIES FOR FECAL DIVERSION | | | |
|---|---|---|---|
| | **ILEOSTOMY** | **TRANSVERSE COLOSTOMY** | **DESCENDING OR SIGMOID COLOSTOMY** |
| **Part of intestine involved** | End of ileum, rest of large intestine removed | Transverse colon (usually temporary) | Descending or sigmoid colon (usually permanent) |
| **Ostomy returns** | Liquid, semiliquid, soft | Soft to fairly firm; softer toward ileum | Descending—fairly firm stool; sigmoid—solid stool |
| **Odor** | Slightly odorous | Very foul-smelling | Usually foul-smelling |
| **Drainage** | Highly corrosive because of enzymes | Irritating | Less irritating |
| **Appliance** | Open-ended pouch worn at all times (fecal material drained, then appliance reclosed) | Pouch worn continually | Varies; with regular irrigation, sometimes no appliance is worn; if firm stool, many use closed pouch; if liquid, open-ended pouch |
| **Nursing considerations** | If continent ileal reservoir (Koch pouch) made in surgery, no appliance worn; contents removed q 4–6 hours via catheter Usually on low-residue diet; no meats, corn, nuts | Usually single-loop colostomy; inflamed bowel segment brought through abdominal wall; incision closed; opening made by cautery (painless) in loop for fecal drainage Diet usually not restricted after first 6 weeks | Typical for colon cancers Reinforce dressing postop Diet usually not restricted after first 6 weeks |

3. Skin care
   a. Effect on skin depends on composition, quantity, consistency of drainage, medications, location of stoma, frequency in removal of appliance adhesive

   b. Principles of skin protection (see Figure 6)
      1) Pouch opening $\frac{1}{8}$ inch larger than stoma
      2) Use skin barrier under all tapes (water, paste, powder)
      3) Use skin barrier to protect skin immediately surrounding the stoma
      4) Cleanse skin gently and pat dry; do not rub
      5) Pouch applied by passing adhesive area to skin for 30 seconds
      6) Change appliance immediately when seal breaks or when $\frac{1}{3}$ or $\frac{1}{4}$ full

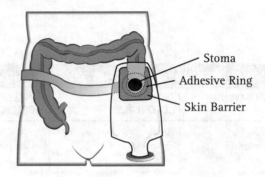

Stoma
Adhesive Ring
Skin Barrier

**Figure 6.  Colostomy Appliance**

4. Colostomy irrigations
   a. Purpose—to stimulate emptying of colon of gas, mucus, feces at scheduled times to avoid need for appliance
   b. Usually begins 5–7 days postop
   c. When possible, should be sitting upright on toilet for procedure
   d. Performed after a meal, same time each day
   e. 500–1,500 ml of lukewarm water used for solution
   f. Special irrigating sleeve and cone are used
   g. Insert catheter 8 cm (3 inches)
   h. Hang irrigating container at shoulder height (18–20 inches above stoma)
   i. Clamp tubing if client complains of cramps; allow client to rest before resuming procedure
   j. Water flows in over 5–10 minutes
   k. Allow 10–15 minutes for most of return
   l. Leave sleeve in place while client moves around for 30–45 minutes
   m. Clean with soap and water, pat dry

5. Care of continent ileal reservoir (Koch pouch)
   a. Postop—catheter inserted and attached to drainage bag, q3h instill 10–20 ml NS into pouch, drain by gravity, kept in place 2 weeks

  b. To drain—lubricate catheter, insert 5 cm (2 inches), drain into toilet,
     wash and dry stoma

  c. If resistance, inject 20 ml air or water using syringe through catheter

## CIRRHOSIS

**A.** Data Collection

  1. Digestive disturbances
     a. Indigestion, dyspepsia
     b. Flatulence, constipation, diarrhea
     c. Anorexia, weight loss
     d. Nausea and vomiting

  2. Circulatory
     a. Esophageal varices, hematemesis, hemorrhage
     b. Ascites
     c. Hemorrhoids
     d. Increased bleeding tendencies, anemia
     e. Edema in extremities
     f. Spider angiomas

  3. Biliary
     a. Jaundice, pruritus
     b. Dark urine, clay-colored stools
     c. Increased abdominal girth

  4. Compensated
     a. Vascular spiders
     b. Ankle edema
     c. Indigestion
     d. Flatulence
     e. Abdominal pain
     f. Enlarged liver

  5. Decompensated
     a. Ascites
     b. Jaundice
     c. Weight loss
     d. Purpura
     e. Epistaxis

**B.** Diagnose

  1. Replacement with normal liver tissue with widespread fibrosis and
     nodule formation
     a. Alcoholic cirrhosis—due to alcoholism and poor nutrition
     b. Biliary cirrhosis—result of chronic biliary obstruction and infection
     c. Postnecrotic cirrhosis—result of previous viral hepatitis

  2. Complications
     a. Portal hypertension with esophageal varices due to elevated pressure
        throughout entire portal venous system

1) Dilated tortuous veins usually found in the submucosa of the lower esophagus

2) Hemorrhage from rupture leading cause of death in clients with cirrhosis

    b. Peripheral edema and ascites

1) Ascites—accumulation of serous fluid in peritoneal and abdominal cavity

2) Associated with dehydration and hypokalemia

    c. Hepatic encephalopathy (coma)

1) Occurs with liver disease

2) Results from accumulation of ammonia and other toxic metabolites in the blood

3) Change in level of consciousness

4) Symptoms of impending coma—disorientation to time, place, person, asterixis (flapping tremor of hand when arm extended and hand help upward [dorsiflexed])

5) Jaundice

    d. Hepatorenal syndrome

1) Functional renal failure

2) Azotemia, ascites

**C.** Plan/Implementation

1. Shunts to relieve portal hypertension

2. Provide appropriate nutrition

    a. Early stages—high-protein, high-carbohydrate diet, supplemented with vitamin B complex

    b. Advanced stages—fiber, protein, fat, and sodium restrictions, high-calorie diet, protein foods of high biologic value

    c. Small, frequent feedings

    d. Fluid restriction

    e. Avoid alcohol

3. Administer blood products

4. Observe vital signs for shock

5. Monitor abdominal girth

6. Maintain skin integrity

    a. Avoid strong soaps

    b. Alleviate dry, itching skin

    c. Frequent position changes

7. Observe degree of jaundice

8. Promote rest

9. Promote adequate respiratory function

10. Reduce exposure to infection

11. Promote safety
    a. Electric razor
    b. Soft-bristle toothbrush
    c. Pressure to site after venipuncture

12. Reduce ascites
    a. Sodium, fluid restrictions
    b. Diuretics

13. Treatment of bleeding esophageal varices
    a. Balloon tamponade—Sengstaken-Blakemore tube (see Figure 7), Minnesota tube
       1) Gastric inflation balloon—inflated with 100–200 ml air
       2) Gastric aspiration—connect to suction
       3) Esophageal inflation balloon—pressure on esophageal and gastric balloons 25–40 mm Hg, measured by manometer q 24 h
       4) Esophageal aspiration
       5) Tubing irrigated hourly
       6) Deflate balloons sequentially, esophageal balloon first
       7) Complications—necrosis of nose, stomach mucosa, or esophagus; asphyxiation
    b. Endoscopic sclerotherapy—injection of sclerosing agent into the esophagus, causes varices to become fibrotic
    c. Administration of vasopressin or propranolol IV or interarterial temporarily lowers portal pressure by constriction of splenic artery, IV octreotide (Sandostatin)
    d. Room-temperature saline lavage
    e. Esophageal banding therapy—modified endoscope with rubber band passed into esophagus, varices are banded
    f. Transjugular intrahepatic postsystemic shunting (TIPS)
    g. Surgical bypass

14. Treatment of hepatic encephalopathy
    a. Administer medications: lactulose, Neomycin
    b. Bedrest

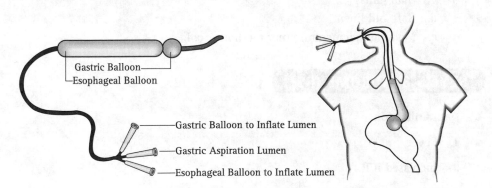

Gastric Balloon
Esophageal Balloon

Gastric Balloon to Inflate Lumen

Gastric Aspiration Lumen

Esophageal Balloon to Inflate Lumen

**Figure 7. Sengstaken–Blakemore Tube**

## JAUNDICE

**A.** Data Collection

1. Yellowish or greenish-yellow discoloration of skin and sclerae due to elevated bilirubin concentration in the blood

2. Dark-colored urine, clay-colored stools

3. Pruritus

**B.** Diagnose

1. Hemolytic—caused by destruction of great number of blood cells, leads to a high concentration of bilirubin that exceeds the liver's ability to excrete it
   a. Hemolytic transfusion reactions
   b. Hemolytic anemia
   c. Sickle-cell crisis

2. Intrahepatic—due to obstructed flow of bile through liver or biliary duct system
   a. Cirrhosis
   b. Hepatitis

3. Extrahepatic
   a. Cholelithiasis
   b. Tumors
   c. Side effect of medications–phenothiazines, antithyroids, sulfonamides, tricyclic antidepressants, androgens, estrogens

**C.** Plan/Implementation

1. Treat underlying cause

2. Relief of pruritus
   a. Medications: antihistamines
   b. Baking soda or alpha Keri baths
   c. Keep nails trimmed and clean; teach to rub with knuckles rather than nails
   d. Soft, old linen
   e. Moderate temperature (not too hot or cold)

## REYE'S SYNDROME (RS)

**A.** Data Collection

1. Fever

2. Increased ICP

3. Decreased level of consciousness, coma

4. Decreased hepatic function

5. Diagnosed by liver biopsy

**B.** Diagnose

1. Acute metabolic encephalopathy of childhood that causes hepatic dysfunction

2. Causes
   a. Link between use of aspirin with viral illness
   b. Associated with viruses, especially URI, gastroenteritis

**C.** Plan/Implementation

1. Neurological checks

2. Maintain hydration and electrolytes with IV

3. Endotracheal tube and ventilator may be needed

4. Promote family support

5. Monitor CVP or Swan-Ganz catheter

## CHOLECYSTITIS, CHOLELITHIASIS

**A.** Data Collection

1. Intolerance to fatty foods

2. Indigestion

3. Nausea, vomiting, flatulence, eructation

4. Severe pain in upper right quadrant of abdomen radiating to back and right shoulder (biliary colic)

5. Elevated temperature

6. Leukocytosis

7. Diaphoresis

8. Dark urine, clay-colored stools

**B.** Diagnose

1. Cholecystitis—inflammation of gallbladder

2. Cholelithiasis—presence of stones in gallbladder

3. Risk factors
   a. Obesity
   b. Sedentary lifestyle
   c. Women, especially multiparous
   d. Highest incidence 40+ years
   e. Pregnancy
   f. Familial tendency
   g. Hypothyroidism
   h. Increased serum cholesterol

**C.** Plan/Implementation

1. Rest

2. IV fluids

3. NG suction

4. Analgesics

5. Antibiotics

6. Low-fat liquids—powdered supplements high in protein, carbohydrates stirred into skim milk

7. Avoid fried foods, pork, cheese, alcohol

8. Laparoscopic laser cholecystectomy—removal of gallbladder by a laser through a laparoscope; laparoscope is attached to video camera and procedure is viewed through monitor; four small puncture holes made in abdomen

   a. Preoperative care
      1) NPO on day prior to outpatient (ambulatory) procedure
   b. Postoperative care
      1) Monitor for bleeding
      2) Resume normal activity in 1 week
      3) May need to be on low-fat diet for several weeks

9. Traditional cholecystectomy—removal of gallbladder through a high abdominal incision
   a. Preoperative care
      1) Nutritional supplements of glucose and protein hydrolysates to aid in would healing and prevent liver damage, if needed
      2) NG tube insertion before surgery
   b. Postoperative care
      1) Medicate for pain
      2) Monitor T tube, if present—inserted to ensure drainage of bile from common bile duct until edema in area diminishes
      3) Maintain in semi-Fowler's position
      4) Observe for jaundice—yellow sclerae, stool that does not slowly progress from light to dark color after removal of T tube
      5) Low-fat, high-carbohydrate, high-protein diet

## PANCREATITIS

A. Data Collection

1. Abdominal pain, nausea, vomiting 24–48 hours after heavy meal or alcohol ingestion; pain relief with position change

2. Hypotension

3. Acute renal failure

4. Grey-blue discoloration in flank and around umbilicus

B. Diagnose

1. Acute pancreatitis (acute inflammation of the pancreas) is brought about by digestion of the organ by the enzymes it produces, principally trypsin

2. Chronic pancreatitis—progressive chronic fibrosis and inflammation of the pancreas, with obstruction of its ducts and destruction of its secreting cells

3. History
   a. Alcoholism
   b. Bacterial or viral infection
   c. Trauma
   d. Complication of mumps

4. Medications—thiazide diuretics, corticosteroids, oral contraceptives

C. Plan/Implementation

1. NPO, gastric decompression

2. Medications: antibiotics, opioids (meperidine avoided because of toxicity), histamine-blockers, proton pump inhibitors

3. Maintain fluid/electrolyte imbalance

4. Respiratory care—ABG, humidified oxygen, intubation, and ventilation

5. Cough and deep breathe q2h

6. Semi-Fowler's position or other position of comfort

7. Monitor for shock and hyperglycemia

8. TPN

9. Long-term treatment includes avoidance of alcohol and caffeine; low-fat, bland diet; small, frequent meals

## SYSTEMIC LUPUS ERYTHEMATOSUS (SLE)

A. Data Collection

1. Musculoskeletal problems
   a. Polyarthralgia, arthritis, joint swelling
   b. Polymyositis—inflammation of skeletal muscle

2. Dermatological problems
   a. Butterfly rash across bridge of nose and cheeks—characteristic facial sign
   b. Papular rash; erythematous, purpuric lesions
   c. Oral ulcers
   d. Alopecia

3. Cardiopulmonary problems
   a. Pericarditis
   b. Pleural effusion

4. Renal problems
   a. Hematuria
   b. Proteinuria
   c. May end in renal failure

5. CNS problems
   a. Changes in behavior
   b. Psychosis

6. Vascular and lymphatic problems
   a. Papular, erythematous and purpuric lesions on fingertips, toes, forearms and hands
   b. Lymphadenopathy
   c. Raynaud's phenomenon–pain and color changes during exposure to cold

**B.** Diagnose

1. Chronic, systemic inflammatory disease of connective tissue that involves skin, joints, serous membranes, kidneys, hematologic system, CNS

2. Exaggerated production of autoantibodies

3. Diagnostic tests–rheumatoid factor (RF), antinuclear antibody (ANA), decreased C3 and C4 complement levels, increased immunoglobulin levels, increased anti-DNA levels, increased C-reactive protein levels

4. Potential nursing diagnosis
   a. Impaired skin integrity
   b. Body image disturbance

**C.** Plan/Implementation

1. Monitor for exacerbations–fever

2. Relieve pain and discomfort, NSAID therapy, acetaminophen

3. Antimalarial (e.g., hydroxychloroquine)

4. Protect skin from ultraviolet rays and sunlight because of photosensitivity, scaly and itchy rash

5. Corticosteroids for exacerbations

6. Immunosuppressive medications (e.g., cyclophosphamide, azathioprine)

7. Gamma globulins

8. Plasmapheresis

9. Education and support

## DERMATOLOGICAL DISORDERS

A. Data Collection (see Table 10)

Table 10

| SELECTED SKIN DISORDERS | | |
|---|---|---|
| **Disorder** | **Data** | **Nursing Considerations** |
| Impetigo | Reddish macule becomes honey-colored Crusted vesicle, then crust; pruritus<br>Caused by *Staphylococcus, Streptococcus* | Skin isolation: careful handwashing; cover draining lesions; discourage touching lesions<br>Antibiotics—may be topical ointment and/or PO<br>Loosen scabs with Burow's solution compresses; remove gently<br>Restraints if necessary; mitts for infants to prevent secondary infection<br>Monitor for acute glomerulonephritis (complication of untreated impetigo) |
| Herpes simplex type I | Pruritic vesicular groupings on nose, lips, and oral mucous membranes<br>Chronically recurrent | Spread by direct contact, handwashing; bland, soft foods; mouth rinses with tetracycline-based preparations; avoid direct contact; administer antivirals (acyclovir, famciclovir and valacyclovir) |
| Herpes zoster | Vesicular eruption along nerve distribution<br>Pain, tenderness, and pruritus over affected region<br>Primarily seen on face, thorax, trunk | Caused by reactivation of chickenpox virus (varicella)<br>Analgesics; compresses, antivirals<br>Systemic corticosteroids to diminish severity<br>Prevent spread—contagious to anyone who has not had chickenpox or who is immunosuppressed<br>Antivirals: Famciclovir, valacyclovir |
| Scabies | Minute, reddened, itchy lesions<br>Linear burrowing of a mite at finger webs, wrists, elbows, ankles, penis | Reduce itching—topical antipruritic (calamine lotion/topical steroids), permethrin 5% cream or crotamiton 10%<br>Institute skin precautions to prevent spread<br>Scabicide—lindane or crotamiton lotion; apply lotion (not on face) to cool, dry skin (not after hot shower because of potential for increased absorption); leave lindane on for 8-12 hours, then shower off; crotamiton may be applied at bedtime for 2 or more consecutive nights; treat all family members (infants upon recommendation of health care provider)<br>Repeat in 10 days for eggs<br>Launder all clothing and linen after above treatment<br>The rash and itching may last for 2-3 weeks even though the mite has been destroyed; treat with antipruritic |
| Pediculosis (lice) | Scalp: white eggs (nits) on hair shafts, with itchy scalp<br>Body: macules and papules<br>Pubis: red macules | OTC pyrethrin, permethrin 1%, lindane<br>Kills both lice and nits with one application<br>May suggest to repeat in 7 d—depends on severity |
| Tinea | Pedis (athlete's foot)—vesicular eruptions in interdigital webs<br>Capitis (ringworm)—breakage and loss of hair; scaly circumscribed red patches on scalp that spread in circular pattern; fluoresces green with Wood's lamp<br>Corporis (ringworm of body)—rings of red scaly areas that spread with central clearing | Antifungal—topical ointment, creams, lotions; PO griseofulvin for resistant cases or if fingernails/toenails are involved; other topical antifungals include butenafine, ciclopirox, econazole, ketoconazole, miconazole, terbinafine<br>Keep areas dry and clean<br>Frequent shampoos |

*(continued)*

● Table 10 (cont'd)

| SELECTED SKIN DISORDERS | | |
|---|---|---|
| **Disorder** | **Data** | **Nursing Considerations** |
| Psoriasis | Chronic recurrent thick, itchy, erythematous papules/plaques covered with silvery white scales with symmetrical distribution Commonly on the scalp, knees, sacrum, elbows, and behind ears Elevated sedimentation rate with negative rheumatoid factor | Topical administration of coal-tar preparations—protect from direct sunlight for 24 h Steroids followed by warm, moist dressings with occlusive outer wrapping (enhances penetration) Tar preparations—may stain skin Antimetabolites (e.g., methotrexate)—check liver function studies Ultraviolet light (wear goggles to protect eyes) Anthralin preparations—apply only to affected areas using tongue blade or gloves Counseling to support/enhance self-image/self-esteem Important for nurse to touch client to demonstrate acceptance |
| Acne vulgaris | Comedones (blackheads/whiteheads), papules, pustules, cysts occurring most often on the face, neck, shoulders, and back | Good hygiene and nutrition PO tetracycline (advise sunscreen with SPF of 15; avoid sun exposure) Antibacterial agents—azelaic acid, clindamycin, erythromycin Isotretinoin—risk of elevated LFTs, dry skin and fetal damage Drying preparations—Benoxyl/vitamin A may cause redness and peeling early in treatment and photosensitivity Ultraviolet light and surgery Monitor for secondary infection Emotional support Accutane (contraindicated with pregnancy) |
| Eczema (Atropic dermatitis) | Children: rough, dry, erythematous skin lesions that progress to weeping and crusting; distributed on the cheeks, scalp, and extensor surfaces in infants and on flexor surfaces in children Adults: hard, dry, flaking, scaling on face, upper chest, and antecubital and popliteal fossa | Onset usually in infancy around 2-3 mo; often outgrown by 2-3 y May be precursor of adult asthma or hay fever Elimination from diet of common offenders, especially milk, eggs, wheat, citrus fruits, and tomatoes Eliminate clothing that is irritating (rough/wool) or that promotes sweating; cotton clothing is best Avoid soap and prolonged or hot baths/showers, which tend to be drying; may use warm colloid baths Lotions to affected areas Keep fingernails short and clean; arm restraints/mittens may be necessary Topical steroids Antihistamines |

B. Diagnose—potential nursing diagnoses

1. Impaired tissue integrity

2. Acute or chronic pain

3. Risk for infection

4. Impaired social interaction

## PREOPERATIVE CARE

**A.** Data Collection (see Table 1)

**B.** Plan/Implementation

    1. Teaching (see Tables 2 and 3)

        a. Age-appropriate

            1) Toddler—simple directions

● Table 1

| FEARS OF SURGERY AT DIFFERENT DEVELOPMENTAL STAGES | | |
|---|---|---|
| **AGE GROUP** | **SPECIFIC FEARS** | **NURSING CONSIDERATIONS** |
| Toddler | Separation | Teach parents to expect regression, e.g., in toilet training and difficult separations |
| Preschooler | Mutilation | Allow child to play with models of equipment<br>Encourage expression of feelings, e.g., anger |
| School-ager | Loss of control | Explain procedures in simple terms<br>Allow choices when possible |
| Adolescent | Loss of independence, being different from peers, e.g., alterations in body image | Involve adolescent in procedures and therapies<br>Expect resistance<br>Express understanding of concerns<br>Point out strengths |

            2) Preschool and school-aged—allow to play with equipment

            3) Adolescent—expect resistance

        b. Family-oriented—have parents reinforce teaching

    2. Promote safe environment for hospitalized child

        a. Prevent or minimize the effects of separation on the child

            1) Encourage parental involvement in child's care, especially through rooming-in facilities

            2) Assign the same nurse to care for the child

            3) Provide objects that recreate familiar surroundings (e.g., toys from home)

Table 2

| AGE-APPROPRIATE PREPARATION FOR HEALTH-CARE PROCEDURES | | |
|---|---|---|
| **Age** | **Special Needs** | **Typical Fears** |
| Newborn | Include parents<br>Mummy restraint | Loud noises<br>Sudden movements |
| 6-12 month | Model desired behavior | Strangers, heights |
| Toddler | Simple explanations<br>Use distractions<br>Allow choices | Separation from parents<br>Animals, strangers<br>Change in environments |
| Preschooler | Encourage understanding by playing<br>  with puppets, dolls<br>Demonstrate equipment<br>Talk at child's eye level | Separation from parents<br>Ghosts<br>Scary people |
| School-ager | Allow questions<br>Explain why<br>Allow to handle equipment | Dark, injury<br>Being alone<br>Death |
| Adolescent | Explain long-term benefit<br>Accept regression<br>Provide privacy | Social incompetence<br>War, accidents<br>Death |

3. Preparation for surgery
   a. Preoperative checklist
      1) Informed consent
      2) Lab tests, chest x-ray, EKG
      3) Skin prep
      4) Bowel prep
      5) IVs
      6) NPO
      7) Preop meds, sedation, antibiotics
      8) Removal of dentures, jewelry, nail polish
      9) Nutrition—may need TPN or tube feedings preoperatively

4. Complementary/Alternative Therapies
   a. Supplements should not be taken near the time of surgery, may interact with anesthesia, may affect coagulation parameters
      1) Echinacea
      2) Garlic
      3) Ginkgo
      4) Ginseng
      5) Kava
      6) St. John's wart
   b. Eliminate all dietary supplements (other than multivitamins) at least 2 to 3 weeks before surgery
   c. May resume the supplements if health care provider advises

d.  What to expect postoperatively
1) Discuss postoperative procedures—deep breathing, leg exercises, moving in bed, incentive spirometer (sustained maximal inspiration device), equipment to expect postoperatively
2) Explain importance of reporting pain or discomfort after surgery
3) Explain what will be done to relieve pain, e.g., changing position, medication
4) Provide for growth and development needs of children

## INTRAOPERATIVE CARE

Table 3

| ANESTHESIA | | |
|---|---|---|
| **MEDICATION** | **SIDE EFFECTS** | **NURSING CONSIDERATIONS** |
| General anesthesia via inhalation (Halothane) | Respiratory depression, circulatory depression<br>Delirium during induction and recovery<br>Nausea and vomiting, aspiration during induction, myocardial depression, hepatic toxicity | Check history of sensitization<br>Maintain airway<br>Protect and orient client<br>Monitor vital signs, labs<br>Prevent aspiration postop by elevating head of bed, turning head to side (unless contraindicated) |
| Nitrous oxide | Hypotension, postop nausea and vomiting | Monitor vital signs<br>Adequate oxygenation is essential, especially during emergence |
| IV thiopental sodium | Respiratory depression, low BP, laryngospasm<br>Poor muscle relaxation, hypotension, irritating to skin and subcutaneous tissue | Monitor vital signs, especially airway, breathing<br>Straps for operative table, proper positioning<br>Protect IV site, check for placement periodically |
| Spinal anesthesia Saddle | Hypotension, headache | Monitor vital signs<br>Encourage oral fluids |
| Conduction blocks Epidural Caudal | Hypotension, respiratory depression | Headache prevented<br>Monitor vital signs |
| Local anesthesia | Excitability, toxic reactions such as respiratory difficulties, vasoconstriction if substance contains epinephrine | Monitor client<br>Do not use local anesthesia with epinephrine on fingers (circulation is less optimal) |
| Conscious sedation (diazepam, midazolam) | Respiratory depression, apnea, hypotension, bradycardia | Never leave the client alone<br>Constantly monitor airway, level of consciousness, pulse oximetry, ECG<br>Vital signs every 15–30 minutes<br>Observe client's ability to maintain patent airway and respond to verbal commands |

## POSTOPERATIVE CARE

**A.** Data Collection

1. Anesthesia, immobility, and surgery can affect any system in the body

**B.** Diagnose

1. Neuropsychosocial
   a. Stimulate client postanesthesia
   b. Monitor level of consciousness

2. Cardiovascular
   a. Monitor vital signs q 15 min × 4, q 30 min × 2, q 1 hour × 2, then as needed
   b. Monitor I and O
   c. Check potassium level

3. Respiratory
   a. Check breath sounds
   b. Turn, cough, and deep breathe (unless contraindicated, e.g., brain, spinal, eye surgery)
   c. Determine pain level—use verbal or visual scale, offer pain medication
   d. Reinforce how to use incentive spirometer—hold mouthpiece in mouth, exhale normally, seal lips and inhale slowly and deeply, keep balls or cylinder elevated 20 seconds, exhale and repeat
   e. Encourage use of client-controlled analgesia (PCA)
   f. Get out of bed as soon as possible

4. Gastrointestinal
   a. Check bowel sounds in 4 quadrants for 5 minutes (high-pitched tympany is abnormal)
   b. Keep NPO until bowel sounds are present
   c. Provide good mouth care while NPO
   d. Provide antiemetics for nausea and vomiting
   e. Check abdomen for distention
   f. Check for passage of flatus and stool

5. Genitourinary
   a. Monitor I and O
   b. Encourage to void
   c. Notify RN or health care provider if unable to void within 8 hours
   d. Catheterize if needed

6. Extremities
   a. Check pulses
   b. Observe color, edema, temperature
   c. Inform client not to cross legs
   d. Keep knee gatch flat
   e. Prohibit use of pillows behind knee
   f. Apply antiembolic stockings (TED hose) before getting out of bed
   g. Pneumatic compression devices (Venodynes)
   h. Monitor for pain, swelling, and warmth in the distal extremity

7. Wounds
   a. Dressing
      1) Document amount and character of drainage
      2) Health care provider changes first postop dressing
      3) Use aseptic technique
      4) Note presence of drains
   b. Incision
      1) Observe site (e.g,. edematous, inflamed, excoriated)
      2) Observe drainage (e.g., serous, serosanguineous, purulent)
      3) Note type of sutures
      4) Note if edges of wound are well approximated
      5) Anticipate infection 3–5 days postop
      6) Change dressing frequently to prevent skin breakdown around site and minimize bacterial growth

8. Drains—prevent fluids from accumulating in tissues

9. GI tubes—check placement
   a. Upper GI tubes—used for gastric decompression
   b. Lower GI tubes—used to decompress bowel

10. Potential complications (see Table 4)

Table 4

| POTENTIAL COMPLICATIONS OF SURGERY | | |
|---|---|---|
| **COMPLICATION** | **DATA COLLECTION FINDINGS** | **NURSING CONSIDERATIONS** |
| Hemorrhage | Decreased BP, increased pulse<br>Cold, clammy skin | Replace blood volume<br>Monitor vital signs |
| Shock | Decreased BP, increased pulse<br>Cold, clammy skin | Treat cause<br>Oxygen<br>IV fluids |
| Atelectasis and pneumonia | Dyspnea, cyanosis, cough<br>Tachycardia<br>Elevated temperature<br>Pain on affected side | Experienced second day postop<br>Suctioning<br>Postural drainage<br>Antibiotics<br>Cough and turn |
| Embolism | Dyspnea, pain, hemoptysis<br>Restlessness<br>ABG—low $O_2$, high $CO_2$ | Experienced second day postop<br>Oxygen<br>Anticoagulants (heparin)<br>IV fluids |
| Deep vein thrombosis | Positive ultrasound | Experienced 6-14 days up to 1 year later<br>Anticoagulant therapy |
| Paralytic ileus | Absent bowel sounds, no flatus or stool | Nasogastric suction<br>IV fluids<br>Decompression tubes |
| Infection of wound | Elevated WBC and temperature<br>Positive cultures | Experienced 3-5 days postop<br>Antibiotics, aseptic technique<br>Good nutrition |
| Dehiscence | Disruption of surgical incision or wound | Experienced 5-6 days postop<br>Low Fowler's position, no coughing<br>NPO<br>Notify health care provider |
| Evisceration | Protrusion of wound contents | Experienced 5-6 days postop<br>Low Fowler's position, no coughing<br>NPO<br>Cover viscera with sterile saline dressing or wax paper (if at home)<br>Notify health care provider |
| Urinary retention | Unable to void after surgery<br>Bladder distension | Experienced 8-12 hours postop<br>Catheterize as needed |
| Urinary infection | Foul-smelling urine<br>Elevated WBC | Experienced 5-8 days postop<br>Antibiotics<br>Force fluids |
| Psychosis | Inappropriate affect | Therapeutic communication<br>Medication |

## BLOOD TESTS

Table 1

| LABORATORY TESTS | | |
|---|---|---|
| **TEST** | **PURPOSE/PREPARATION** | **NORMAL VALUES** |
| Red blood cell count (RBC), erythrocytes | Determines actual number of cells in relation to volume | Adult man—4.6-6.2 million/mm$^3$<br>Adult woman—4.2-5.4 million/mm$^3$<br>Child—3.2-5.2 million/mm$^3$ |
| White blood cell count (WBC), leukocytes | Establishes amount and maturity of white blood cell elements | Adult—5,000-10,000/mm$^3$<br>Child—5,000-13,000/mm$^3$ |
| Hemoglobin | Determines the amount of hemoglobin/100 mL of blood | Man—13-18 g/dL<br>Woman—12-16 g/dL<br>Child (3-12 years)—11-12.5 gm/dL |
| Hematocrit | Measures percentage of red blood cells per fluid volume of blood | Man—42-52%<br>Woman—35-47%<br>Child (3-12 years)—35-45% |
| Bleeding time | Measures duration of bleeding after standardized skin incision<br>Used for preoperative screening | 1.5–9.5 minutes |
| Partial thromboplastin time (PTT) | Monitors effectiveness of heparin therapy<br>Detects coagulation disorders | Lower limit of normal: 20-25 sec<br>Upper limit of normal: 32-39 sec |
| Platelet count (thrombocyte count) | Used to diagnose hemorrhagic diseases, thrombocytopenia | 150,000-450,000/mm$^3$ |
| Prothrombin time (PT) | Monitors effectiveness of Coumadin therapy<br>Detects coagulation disorders | 9.5-12.0 seconds |
| International normalized ratio (INR) | Monitors effectiveness of anticoagulation therapy | 1.0<br>2–3 for therapy in atrial fibrillation, deep venous thrombosis, and pulmonary embolism<br>2.5–3.5 for therapy in prosthetic heart valves |
| Sedimentation rate (ESR) | Speed at which RBCs settle in well-mixed venous blood<br>Indicates inflammation | Man <50 yrs: <15 mm/h<br>Man >50 yrs: <20 mm/h<br>Woman <50 yrs: <25 mm/h<br>Woman >50 yrs: <30 mm/h |

*(continued)*

Table 1 (cont'd)

| LABORATORY TESTS | | |
|---|---|---|
| **TEST** | **PURPOSE/PREPARATION** | **NORMAL VALUES** |
| Glucose tolerance test (GTT) | Measures ability of body to secrete insulin in response to hyperglycemia | Fasting—60-110 mg/dL<br>1 hour—190 mg/dL<br>2 hours—140 mg/dL<br>3 hours—125 mg/dL |
| Total cholesterol | Evaluates tendency for athlerosclerosis<br>Overnight fast | 150–200 mg/dL |
| Low-density lipoproteins (LDL) | Determines whether elevated cholesterol levels are caused by increased LDL or HDL<br>Fast for 12-14 hours | <160 mg/dL if no CAD and <2 risk factors<br><130 mg/dL if no CAD and 2 or more risk factors<br><100 mg/dL if CAD present |
| High-density lipoproteins (HDL) | Same as for LDLs, above | Men 35–70 mg/dL,<br>women 35–85 mg/dL |
| Creatinine (CR) | Test of renal function<br>NPO 8 hours<br>List medications client is taking on lab slip | Adult—0.7-1.4 mg/dL<br>Child—0.4-1.2 mg/dl<br>Infant—0.3-0.6 mg/dL |
| Alkaline phosphatase | Evaluates liver and bone function<br>NPO 8-12 hours<br>List medications client is taking on lab slip | Adult—50-120 units/L<br>Infant and adolescent up to 104 FU/L |
| Creatine kinase (CK) nerve | Used to diagnose acute MI<br>Detected in blood in 3-5 hours | MM bands present: skeletal muscle damage<br>MB bands present: cardiac muscle damage |
| Serum albumin | Used to detect protein malnutrition | 3.5-5.5 g/dL |
| BUN | Evaluate renal function | Values affected by protein intake, tissue breakdown, fluid volume changes<br>10-20 mg/dL |
| Triglycerides | Detect risk for atherosclerosis | 100–200 mg/dL |

## ARTERIAL TESTS

Table 2

| ARTERIAL DIAGNOSTIC TESTS | | | |
|---|---|---|---|
| **TEST** | **PURPOSE** | **PREPARATION/TESTING** | **POST-TEST NURSING CARE** |
| Angiography (arteriography) | Indicates abnormalities of blood flow due to arterial obstruction or narrowing | Contrast dye is injected into the arteries and x-ray films are taken of the vascular tree | Disadvantages include potential allergic reactions to radiopaque dye, potential irritation, or thrombosis of the injection site |
| Exercise tests for intermittent claudication | Claudication with exercise indicates inability of damaged arteries to increase the blood flow needed for increased tissue oxygenation | Client exercises until pain occurs; the length of time between start of exercise and the onset of pain is recorded | None |

## VENOUS TESTS

Table 3

| VENOUS DIAGNOSTIC TESTS | | | |
|---|---|---|---|
| **TEST** | **PURPOSE** | **PREPARATION/TESTING** | **POST-TEST NURSING CARE** |
| Ultrasonic flow detection— Doppler studies | Indicates obstruction in blood flow in extremities | Electronic stethoscope that detects sound of blood flow | None |

## RESPIRATORY/CARDIAC TESTS

Table 4

| RESPIRATORY/CARDIAC TESTS | | | |
|---|---|---|---|
| **TEST** | **PURPOSE** | **PREPARATION/TESTING** | **POST–TEST NURSING CARE** |
| Pulmonary function | Detects impaired pulmonary function<br>Follows the course of pulmonary disease and evaluates treatment responses | Explain purpose<br>No smoking 4 hours before test<br>May withhold bronchodilator medications<br>Asked to breathe into machine | Observe for dyspnea |
| Arterial blood gases (ABGs) | Measurements of tissue oxygenation, carbon dioxide removal, and acid-base balance<br>$pO_2$–partial pressure oxygen<br>$pCO_2$–partial pressure carbon dioxide<br>Evaluates clients being mechanically ventilated or with cardiovascular disease | Perform Allen test–checks collateral circulation<br>Arterial blood is obtained in heparinized syringe<br>Unclotted blood is necessary<br>Air bubbles cannot be present in specimen<br>Results (see Table 5) | Apply pressure to site for 5 minutes to prevent hematoma (15 minutes if client is receiving anticoagulants)<br>Send specimen on ice and occlude needle to avoid air in syringe<br>Note on lab slip if client was breathing room air or oxygen (document liters)<br>Check arm for swelling, discoloration, pain, numbness, tingling |
| Sputum analysis | Identify cause of pulmonary infection<br>Identify abnormal lung cells | Encourage fluid intake night before test<br>Instruct client to rinse mouth with water<br>Do not brush teeth, eat, or use mouthwash before test<br>Use sterile container<br>Ultrasonic/heated nebulizer treatment 10-15 minutes prior aids in collection<br>Teach client how to expectorate<br>Collect early in the AM if possible | None |
| Bronchoscopy | Allows visualization of larynx, trachea, and mainstem bronchi<br>Possible to obtain tissue biopsy, apply medication, aspirate secretions for laboratory examination, aspirate a mucus plug causing airway obstruction, or remove aspirated foreign objects | Explain procedure<br>Maintain NPO for 6 hours before test<br>Inspect mouth for infection<br>Administer premedication–Valium, Versed, Demerol, atropine<br>Remove dentures<br>Prepare client for sore throat after procedure | Sit or lie on side, remain NPO until gag reflex returns<br>Observe for respiratory difficulties |
| Thoracentesis | Aspiration of fluid or air from pleural space<br>To obtain specimen for analysis, relieve lung compression, obtain lung tissue for biopsy, or instill medications into pleural space | Explain procedure<br>Take vital signs<br>Shave area around needle insertion site<br>Position client sitting with arms on pillows on over-bed table or lying on side in bed<br>Expect stinging sensation with injection of local anesthetic and feeling of pressure when needle inserted<br>No more than 1,000 ml fluid removed at one time | Auscultate breath sounds frequently<br>Monitor vital signs frequently<br>Check for leakage of fluid, location of puncture site, client tolerance<br>Sterile dressing after procedure |

*(continued)*

Table 4 (cont'd)

| RESPIRATORY/CARDIAC TESTS | | | |
|---|---|---|---|
| **TEST** | **PURPOSE** | **PREPARATION/TESTING** | **POST-TEST NURSING CARE** |
| Chest x-ray | To identify abnormalities such as foreign bodies, fluid, infiltrates, tumors | Explain procedure<br>Remove all jewelry from neck and chest<br>Female clients of childbearing age wear a lead apron | None |
| Lung biopsy | Removal of lung tissue for culture or cytology | Explain procedure<br>Administer premedication—sedatives or analgesics<br>Have client hold breath in midexpiration<br>Performed with fluoroscopic monitoring<br>Position client as for thoracentesis | Monitor vital signs and breath sounds every 4 hours for 24 hours<br>Report signs of respiratory distress<br>Chest x-ray taken after procedure to check for complication of pneumothorax<br>Sterile dressing applied after procedure |
| Computed tomography (CT) | Provides three-dimensional assessment of the lungs and thorax | Noninvasive | If dye, note reaction |
| Magnetic resonance imaging (MRI) | Provides detailed pictures of body structures | Explain procedure<br>Ask the client about claustrophobia<br>Remove all metal jewelry and metal objects<br>Ask if client has metal implanted in body (pacemaker, clips) | None |
| Pulse oximetry | Measures oxygen saturation through the skin | Clean site using cotton ball with soap and water, then alcohol<br>Dry skin | Rotate site every 4 hours to prevent skin irritation |
| Stress test | Determine cardiovascular response to increased workload stairs<br>EKG monitored before, during, and after exercise testing | Client walks on treadmill, pedals stationary bicycle, or climbs set of | None |
| Ultrasound echocardiogram | Noninvasive sound waves used to determine cardiac structures | None | None |
| Cardiac catheterization | Usually used with angiography<br>Introduction of catheter into chambers of heart to evaluate ventricular function and obtain chamber pressures | NPO 8-12 hours<br>Signed permit<br>Empty bladder<br>Check pulse<br>Explain that client may experience feeling of heat, palpitations, desire to cough when dye injected | Monitor vital signs q 15 min for 2 hours, then q 30 min for 1 hour, then q 1 hour for 3 hours<br>Check pulses, sensation, bleeding at insertion site q 30 min for 3 hours, then q 1 hour for 3 hours<br>Bedrest 6-8 hours with insertion site extremity straight |

Table 5

| ARTERIAL BLOOD GASES (ABG) | | | |
|---|---|---|---|
| **VALUE** | **NORMAL** | **ACIDOSIS** | **ALKALOSIS** |
| pH | 7.35-7.45 | Below 7.35 | Above 7.45 |
| $PaO_2$ | 85-95 mm Hg | | |
| $SaO_2$ | 95-99% | | |
| $PaCO_2$ | 35-45 mm Hg | Respiratory >45 mm Hg | Respiratory <35 mm Hg |
| $HCO_3$ | 22-26 mEq/L | Metabolic <22 mEq/L | Metabolic >26 mEq/L |

## NEUROLOGICAL TESTS

● Table 6

| NEUROLOGICAL TESTS | | | |
|---|---|---|---|
| **TEST** | **PURPOSE** | **PREPARATION/TESTING** | **POST–TEST NURSING CARE** |
| Cerebral angiography | Indentifies aneurysms, vascular malformations, narrowed vessels | Informed consent<br>Explain procedure:<br>  Lie flat; dye injection into femoral artery by needle/catheter; fluoroscopy and radiologic films taken after injection<br>Well hydrated<br>Preprocedure sedation<br>Skin prep, chosen site shaved<br>Mark peripheral pulses<br>May experience feeling of warmth and metallic taste when dye injected | Neurological data gathering every 15-30 minutes until vital signs are stable<br>Keep flat in bed 12-14 hours<br>Check puncture site every hour<br>Immobilize site for 6-8 hours<br>Observe distal pulses, color, and temperature<br>Observe symptons of complications, allergic response to dye, puncture site hematoma<br>Force fluids, accurate intake and output |
| Lumbar puncture (LP) | Insertion of needle into subarachnoid space to obtain specimen, relieve pressure, inject dye or medications | Explain procedure<br>Informed consent<br>Procedure done at bedside or in treatment room<br>Positioned in lateral recumbent fetal position at edge of bed | Neurological data gathering every 15-30 minutes until stable<br>Position flat for several hours<br>Encourage PO fluid to 3,000 mL<br>Oral analgesics for headache<br>Observe sterile dressing at insertion site for bleeding or drainage |
| Electroencephalogram (EEG) | Records electrical activity of brain | Explain procedure<br>Procedure done by technician in a quiet room<br>Painless<br>Tranquilizer and stimulant medications withheld for 24-48 hours pre-EEG<br>Stimulants such as caffeine, cola, and tea, cigarettes withheld for 24 hours pre-EEG<br>May be asked to hyperventilate 3-4 minutes and watch bright, flashing light<br>Meals not withheld<br>Kept awake night before test | Help client remove paste from hair<br>Administer prescribed medication withheld before EEG<br>Observe for seizure activity in seizure-prone clients |
| Echoencephalography | Evaluates brain structure through sound waves | Explain procedure—hand-held transducer used to record sound waves | None |
| CT (computed tomography) | Detects hemorrhage, infarction, abscesses, tumors | Written consent<br>Explain procedure<br>Painless<br>Immobile during exam<br>If contrast dye used, may experience flushed, warm face, and metallic taste during injection | Observe for allergic responses to contrast dye, e.g., rash, pruritus, urticaria<br>Encourage PO fluids |
| Myelogram | Visualizes spinal column and subarachnoid space | Informed consent<br>Explain procedure<br>NPO for 4-6 hours before test<br>Obtain allergy history<br>Phenothiazines, CNS depressants, and stimulants withheld for 48 h prior to test<br>Table will be moved to various positions during test | Neurologic data gathering every 2-4 hours<br>When metrizamide water-soluble dye used, head should be raised 30-45° for 3 hours<br>Oral analgesics for headache<br>Encourage PO fluids<br>Observe for distended bladder<br>Inspect injection site |
| PET (positron emission tomography) | Used to assess metabolic and physiological function of brain; diagnose stroke, brain tumor, epilepsy, Parkinson's disease, head injury | Client inhales or is injected with radioactive substance, then is scanned<br>Tell client may experience dizziness, headache<br>Teach relaxation exercises | None |

## LIVER FUNCTION TESTS

Table 7

| LIVER FUNCTION TESTS | | | |
|---|---|---|---|
| **TEST** | **PURPOSE** | **PREPARATION/TESTING** | **POST–TEST NURSING CARE** |
| Pigment studies | Parameters of hepatic ability to conjugate and excrete bilirubin<br>Abnormal in liver and gall bladder disorders, e.g., with jaundice<br>Direct bilirubin increases in obstruction | Fast 4 h<br>Normal<br>  Serum bilirubin, direct 0-0.3 mg/dL<br>  Serum bilirubin, total 0-0.9 mg/dL<br>  Urine bilirubin, total 0 | Over 70% of the parenchyma of the liver may be damaged before liver function tests become abnormal |
| Protein studies<br>  Serum albumin | Proteins are produced by the liver<br>Levels may diminish in hepatic disease<br>Severely decreased serum albumin results in generalized edema | Normal<br>3.5-5.5 g/dL | None |
| Coagulation studies<br>  Prothrombin time (PT)<br>  Partial thromboplastin time (PTT) | May be prolonged in hepatic disease<br>In liver disease, PTT prolonged due to lack of vitamin K | Normal<br>  PT 9.5-12.0 seconds<br>  PTT<br>Lower limit of normal 20-25 seconds; upper limit of normal 32-39 seconds | Put specimen in ice<br>Apply pressure to site for 5 min (15 min if on anticoagulants) |
| Liver enzymes | With damaged liver cells, enzymes are released into bloodstream | Normal<br>  AST 10-40 units (male)<br>  ALT 10-40 units (male)<br>  LDH 90-176 units/L | None |
| Blood amomia<br>  (arterial) | Liver converts ammonia to urea<br>With liver disease, ammonia levels rise | Normal<br>  15–45 mcg/dL | None |
| Abdominal x-ray | To determine gross liver size | None | None |
| Liver scan | To demonstrate size, shape of liver, visualize scar tissue, cysts, or tumors; use radiopaque dye | None | Question client about seafood (iodine) allergy before radiopaque dye administration; anaphylaxis common, aqueous-based dye available for hypersensitive individuals<br>Resume diet |
| Cholecystogram and cholangiography | For gallbladder and bile duct visualization; radiopaque material injected directly into biliary tree | Fat-free dinner evening before exam<br>Ingestion of dye in tablet form (Telepaque tablets—check history of allergies to iodine) evening before<br>NPO after dye ingestion<br>X-rays followed by ingestion of high-fat meal followed by further x-rays | Question client about seafood (iodine) allergy |
| Celiac axis arteriography | For liver and pancreas visualization; uses contrast media of organic iodine | None | Question client about seafood (iodine) allergy prior to radiopaque dye administration; anaphylaxis common |

Table 7 (cont'd)

| LIVER FUNCTION TESTS | | | |
|---|---|---|---|
| **TEST** | **PURPOSE** | **PREPARATION/TESTING** | **POST–TEST NURSING CARE** |
| Splenoportogram (splenic portal venography) | To determine adequacy of portal blood flow; uses contrast media of organic iodine | None | Question client about seafood (iodine) allergy prior to radiopaque dye administration; anaphylaxis common |
| Liver biopsy | Sampling of tissue by needle aspiration | Administer vitamin K IM to decrease chance of hemorrhage<br>NPO morning of exam (6 h)<br>Sedative administration just before exam<br>Teach client that he will be asked to hold his breath for 5-10 seconds<br>Performed at bedside, supine position, lateral with upper arms elevated | Position on right side for 2–3 h with pillow under costal margin<br>Frequent vital signs to detect hemorrhage and shock; check clotting time, platelets, hematocrit<br>Expect mild local pain and mild pain radiating to right shoulder<br>Report complaints of severe abdominal pain immediately—may be indication of perforation of bile duct and peritonitis<br>Avoid heavy lifting for 1 week |
| Bilirubin | Detect presence of bilirubin due to hemolytic or liver disease | Total bilirubin 0.3–1.0 mg/dL<br>Direct (conjugated) bilirubin 0.1–0.4 mg/dL<br>Indirect (unconjugated) bilirubin 0.1–0.4 mg/dL | None |

## GASTROINTESTINAL TESTS

Table 8

| GASTROINTESTINAL DIAGNOSTIC TESTS | | | |
|---|---|---|---|
| **TEST** | **PURPOSE** | **PREPARATION/TESTING** | **POST–TEST NURSING CARE** |
| Stomach/esophagus endoscopy | Visualization of esophagus and/or stomach by means of a lighted, flexible fiberoptic tube introduced through the mouth to the stomach to determine presence of ulcerations, tumors, or to obtain tissue or fluid samples | Verify that informed consent from client has been obtained<br>Maintain NPO before procedure (at least 8 h)<br>Teach client about numbness in throat due to local anesthetic applied to posterior pharynx by spray or gargle | Maintain NPO until gag reflex returns<br>Observe for vomiting of blood, respiratory distress<br>Inform client to expect sore throat for 3 to 4 days after procedure |
| Sigmoidoscopy/ Proctoscopy | Direct visualization of the sigmoid colon, rectum, and anal canal | Laxative night before exam and enema or suppository morning of procedure<br>NPO at midnight | Allow client to rest<br>Observe for hemorrhage, perforation<br>Encourage fluids |
| Colonoscopy | Direct visualization of the colon; used as a diagnostic aid; removes foreign bodies, polyps, or tissue for biopsy | Clear liquid diet 24-72 h before exam (per health care provider order)<br>Cathartic in evening for 2 days prior to exam<br>Enema on morning of exam<br>Golytely lavage solution to cleanse bowel; clear liquid diet noon day before test | Allow to rest<br>Observe for passage of blood and abdominal pain, signs of perforation, hemorrhage, or respiratory distress<br>Follow-up x-rays<br>Resume diet |

*(continued)*

Table 8 (cont'd)

| GASTROINTESTINAL DIAGNOSTIC TESTS | | | |
|---|---|---|---|
| **TEST** | **PURPOSE** | **PREPARATION/TESTING** | **POST–TEST NURSING CARE** |
| Ammonia | Detect liver disorders | Normal 15–45 mcg/dL<br>Avoid smoking before test | None |
| Amylase | Diagnose pancreatitis and acute cholecystitis | Normal 6-160 Somogyi U/dL<br>Restrict food 1-2 hours before test<br>Avoid opiates 2 hours before test | None |
| Lipase | Diagnose acute and chronic pancreatitis, biliary obstruction, hepatitis, cirrhosis | Normal <200m/ l<br>NPO 8-12 hrs before test<br>Avoid opiates 24 hrs prior to test | None |
| Gastric aspirate | Aspiration of gastric contents to evaluate for presence of abnormal constituents such as blood, abnormal bacteria, abnormal pH, or malignant cells | NPO before test<br>NG tube passed, stomach contents aspirated and sent for evaluation<br>Histamine is sometimes used to stimulate hydrochloric acid secretion<br>pH—measures acid/alkaline range; (4.5-7.5); normal gastric pH less than 4; generally overly acidic environment can lead to ulcerative activity<br>Guaiac—tests for presence of blood; normally, blood absent | Encourage fluids |
| Upper GI series<br>Barium swallow | Ingestion of barium sulfate to determine patency and size of esophagus, size and condition of gastric walls, patency of pyloric valve, and rate of passage to small bowel | Maintain NPO after midnight<br>Inform client that stool will be light-colored after procedure | Encourage fluids<br>Laxatives to prevent constipation<br>Stool will be white from barium |
| Lower GI series<br>Barium enema | Instillation of barium (radiopaque substance) into colon via rectum for fluoroscopy x-rays to view tumors, polyps, strictures, ulcerations, inflammation, or obstructions of colon | Low-residue diet for 1–2 days<br>Clear liquid diet and laxative evening before test; cleansing enemas until clear morning of test | Cleansing enemas after exam to remove barium and prevent impaction<br>X-rays may be repeated after all barium is expelled |
| Paracentesis | Needle aspiration of fluid in abdominal cavity used for diagnostic examination of ascitic fluid and treatment of massive ascites resistant to other therapies | Done at bedside—client in semi-Fowler's position or sitting upright on edge of bed<br>Empty bladder prior to procedure to avoid accidental perforation | Check vital signs frequently for shock and/or infection<br>Report elevated temperature and/or abdominal pain to health care provider<br>Observe for sign of hypovolemic shock |

# REPRODUCTIVE TESTS

●Table 9

| REPRODUCTIVE TESTS AND PROCEDURES | | | |
|---|---|---|---|
| TEST | PURPOSE | PREPARATION/TESTING | POST–TEST NURSING CARE |
| Culdoscopy | Visualization of ovaries, fallopian tubes, uterus via lighted tube inserted into vagina and through cul-de-sac | Local anesthetic and/or light sedation<br>Knee-chest position during procedure | Position on abdomen after procedure<br>Observe for vaginal bleeding<br>Avoid douching and intercourse for 2 weeks |
| Colposcopy | Similar to pelvic exam | Performed between menstrual periods<br>Takes 20 minutes<br>Lithotomy position<br>Cervix is washed with dilute acetic acid | None |
| Laparoscopy | Visualization of pelvic cavity through an incision beneath the umbilicus to view structures | Carbon dioxide introduced to enhance visualization<br>General anesthesia<br>Foley catheter inserted for bladder decompression | Out of bed after procedure<br>Regular diet |
| Cultures and smears | Samples of tissues are taken to identify infectious processes or identify abnormal cells | No anesthetic needed<br>Chlamydia smear needs media preparation by laboratory | None |
| Cervical biopsy | Sample tissue taken to identify unusual cells | No anesthesia used<br>May have cramping sensation | Provide written instructions<br>Restrictions on intercourse, douching, and swimming for 3 days |

# URINARY SYSTEM TESTS

●Table 10

| URINARY SYSTEM DIAGNOSTIC TESTS | | | |
|---|---|---|---|
| TEST | PURPOSE | PREPARATION/TESTING | POST–TEST NURSING CARE |
| Urinalysis | Detect kidney abnormalities | Advise client to save first AM specimen<br>Overnight specimen is more concentrated<br>pH 4.5-8<br>Specific gravity 1.010-1.030 | None |
| Urine culture and sensitivity | Identify bacteria in urine | Cleanse external meatus with povidone-iodine or soap and water before test<br>Obtain midstream specimen<br>Normal—less than 100,000 colonies/mL | None |
| Cystometrogram | Test of muscle tone | Prepare client for Foley catheter<br>Instillation of saline may cause feeling of pressure in bladder during test | Advise client to report any post-test symptoms |
| Creatinine clearance | Evaluate renal function | 24-hour urine collection<br>Blood drawn for creatinine level at end of urine collection<br>Normal—1.42-2.08 mL/s (male) | None |

*(continued)*

Table 10 (cont'd)

| URINARY SYSTEM DIAGNOSTIC TESTS | | | |
|---|---|---|---|
| **TEST** | **PURPOSE** | **PREPARATION/TESTING** | **POST–TEST NURSING CARE** |
| BUN | Evaluate renal function | Values affected by protein intake, tissue breakdown, fluid volume changes 10-20 mg/dL | None |
| Cystoscopy | Direct visualization by cystoscope of bladder and urethra | Bowel preparation Teach client to deep-breathe to decrease discomfort NPO if general anesthesia used | Monitor character and volume of urine Check for abdominal distention, urinary frequency, fever Urine usually pink-tinged Abdominal or pelvic pain indicates trauma Provide antimicrobial prophylaxis |
| Cystourethrogram | X-ray study of bladder and urethra | Explain procedure to client: catheter inserted into urethra, radiopaque dye injected, client voids, x-rays taken during voiding | Advise client to report any symptoms |
| Intravenous pyelogram | Provides x-ray visualization of kidneys, ureters, and bladder | Bowel preparation NPO after midnight Check allergies to shellfish or iodine, chocolate, eggs, milk Burning or complaints of salty taste may occur during injection of radiopaque dye into vein X-rays are taken at intervals after dye injection | Postprocedure x-rays usually done Client should be alert to signs of dye reaction: edema, itching, wheezing, dyspnea |
| Renal scan | Evaluation of kidneys | Radioactive isotope injected IV Radioactivity measured by radioactivity counter Fluids forced before procedure | None |
| Ultrasound | Images of renal structures obtained by sound waves | Noninvasive procedure No preparation required Full bladder required | None |
| Kidney biopsy | Kidney tissue obtained by needle aspiration for pathological evaluation | NPO 6–8 hours X-ray taken prior to procedure Skin is marked to indicate lower pole of kidney (fewer blood vessels) Position: prone and bent at diaphragm Client instructed to hold breath during needle insertion | Pressure applied to site for 20 min Keep on affected side for 30–60 min Pressure dressing applied Check vital signs q 15–15 min for 1 h Client kept flat in bed Bedrest for 6–8 hours Intake 3,000/day Observe for hematuria and site bleeding |
| Schilling test | Diagnoses vitamin $B_{12}$ deficiency (pernicious anemia) | Radioactive vitamin $B_{12}$ is administered to the client Low value excreted in urine indicates pernicious anemia, (normal is >10% of dose excreted in 24 hours) | Vitamin $B_{12}$ (cyancobalamin injection for life) |

## CHEST PHYSIOTHERAPY

**A.** Breathing exercises

1. Diaphragmatic or abdominal breathing
   a. Client positioned on back with knees bent
   b. Place hands on abdomen

2. Pursed lip breathing
   a. Breathe in through nose
   b. Purse lips and breathe out through mouth
   c. Exhalation should be twice as long as inspiration

**B.** Coughing techniques

1. Instruct client to lean slightly forward and take three slow, deep breaths though the nose, exhaling slowly through slightly parted or pursed lips

2. Client should then take another deep breath and cough several times during expiration

3. Client must be encouraged to cough from deep within the chest and avoid nonproductive coughing that wastes energy

**C.** Postural drainage—uses gravity to facilitate removal of bronchial secretions

1. Client is placed in a variety of positions to facilitate drainage into larger airways

2. Five positions used—head down, prone, right and left lateral, upright

3. Stay in each position 10–15 minutes

4. Breathe in slowly through nose; breathe out through pursed lips

5. Performed 2–4 times daily before meals and at hs

6. Secretions may be removed by coughing or suctioning

**D.** Percussion and vibration—usually performed during postural drainage to augment the effect of gravity drainage

1. Percussion—rhythmic striking of chest wall with cupped hands over areas where secretions are retained

2. Vibration—hand and arm muscles of person doing vibration are tensed, and a vibrating pressure is applied to the chest as the client exhales

3. Place towel over area

4. Percussion alternated with vibration, 5 min in each position

E. Incentive spirometer—used to maximize respiration and mobilize secretions

1. Client must inhale deeply and hold breath for 3–5 seconds to achieve effective lung expansion

2. Client must form seal around mouthpiece with lips

3. Sitting in semi-Fowler's position

4. Do 10 breaths/h while awake

## SUCTIONING

A. Procedure

1. Wear protective eyewear

2. Hyperoxygenate before, during, and after suctioning—100% oxygen for 3 minutes or 3 deep breaths

3. Explain procedure to client (potentially frightening procedure)

4. Semi-Fowler's position

5. Lubricate catheter with sterile saline and insert without applying suction

6. Advance catheter as far as possible or until client coughs; do not apply suction

7. Withdraw catheter 1–2 cm, apply suction and withdraw catheter with a rotating motion for no more than 10 seconds; wall suction set between 80–120 mm Hg

8. Repeat procedure after client has rested

9. Hyperoxygenate for 1–5 minutes after suctioning endotracheal tube or tracheostomy tube suctioned, then mouth is suctioned; provide mouth care

B. Complications

1. Hypoxia

2. Bronchospasm

3. Vagal stimulation

4. Tissue trauma

5. Cardiac dysrhythmias

6. Infection

## TRACHEOSTOMY CARE

**A.** Procedure

1. Perform every 8 hours and as needed

2. Explain procedure

3. Hyperoxygenate or deep breathe

4. Suction tracheostomy tube

5. Remove old dressings

6. Open sterile tracheostomy care kit

7. Put on sterile gloves

8. Remove inner cannula (permanent or disposable)

9. Clean with hydrogen peroxide if permanent inner cannula

10. Rinse with sterile water, dry

11. Reinsert into outer cannula

12. Clean stoma site with hydrogen peroxide and sterile water, then dry

13. Change ties or velcro tracheostomy tube holders as needed; old ties must remain in place until new ties are secured; tie on side of neck, allowing 2 fingers to be inserted under tie

14. Apply new sterile dressing; do not cut gauze pads

15. Document site of tracheostomy, type/quantity of secretions, client tolerance of procedure

16. Purpose of cuff—prevents aspiration of fluids; inflated during continuous mechanical ventilation, during and after eating, during and 1 hour after a tube feeding, when client is unable to handle oral secretions, when client may aspirate; check cuff pressure q 8 hours, maintain at less than 25 cm/$H_2O$

**B.** Complications

1. Airway obstruction

2. Trachial necrosis

3. Infection

## OXYGEN THERAPY

Table 1

| OXYGEN ADMINISTRATION | | |
|---|---|---|
| **METHOD** | **OXYGEN DELIVERED** | **NURSING CONSIDERATIONS** |
| Nasal cannula or prongs | 23–42% at 1–6 L/min | Determine patency of nostril<br>Apply water-soluble jelly to nostrils every 3-4 hours<br>Perform good mouth care |
| Face mask | 40–60% at 6–8 L/min (oxygen flow minimum 5 L) | Remove mask every 1-2 hours<br>Wash, dry, apply lotion to skin<br>Emotional support to decrease feeling of claustrophobia |
| Partial rebreather mask | 50–75% at 8–11 L/min | Adjust oxygen flow to keep reservoir bag two-thirds full during inspiration |
| Nonrebreather mask | 80–100% at 12 L/min | Adjust oxygen flow to keep bag two-thirds full |
| Venturi mask | 24–55% at 4–10 L/min | Provides high humidity and fixed concentrations<br>Keep tubing free of kinks |
| Tracheostomy collar or T-piece | 30–100% at 8–10 L/min | Observe for fine mist<br>Empty condensation from tubing<br>Keep water container full |
| Oxygen hood | 30–100% at 8–10 L/min | Used for infants and young children<br>Provides cooled humid air<br>Check $O_2$ concentration with $O_2$ analyzer every 4 hours<br>Refill humidity jar with sterile distilled water<br>Clean humidity jar daily<br>Cover client with light blanket and towel or cap for head<br>Change linen frequently<br>Monitor client's temperature frequently |

| HAZARDS OF OXYGEN ADMINISTRATION | | ● Table 2 |
|---|---|---|

| COMPLICATION | NURSING CONSIDERATIONS |
|---|---|
| Infection | Change masks, tubing, mouthpieces daily |
| Drying and irritation of mucosa | Administer humidified oxygen |
| Respiratory depression ($CO_2$ narcosis) | Monitor respiratory rates frequently<br>Alternate between breathing room air and $O_2$ at prescribed intervals<br>Administer mixed $O_2$ (air and $O_2$) rather than pure $O_2$<br>Administer minimal concentrations necessary<br>Periodically inflate the lungs fully |
| Oxygen toxicity | Premature infants exposed to excessive amounts of $O_2$ for prolonged periods may develop retinopathy of prematurity (ROP); may result in irreversible blindness from vasoconstriction of the retinal blood vessels<br>Lungs of clients on respirators (children and adults) are most susceptible to pulmonary damage<br>Pulmonary damage includes atelectasis, exudation of protein fluid into alveoli, damage to and proliferation of pulmonary capillaries, and interstitial hemorrhage<br>Early symptoms include cough, nasal congestion, sore throat, reduced vital capacity, and substernal discomfort |
| Combustion | Be sure electrical plugs and equipment are properly grounded<br>Enforce no-smoking rules<br>Do not use oils on the client or on $O_2$ equipment |

## MONITOR CHEST TUBES

A. Intrapleural drainage system with one or more chest catheters held in pleural space by suture to chest wall, attached to drainage system

B. Nursing care (see Figures 1 and 2)

  1. Encourage the client to change position frequently

  2. The drainage system must be maintained below the level of insertion, without kinks in tubing

  3. Observe for fluctuations of fluid in water-seal chamber; stops fluctuating when:

    a. Lung re-expands

    b. Tubing is obstructed

    c. Loop hangs below rest of tubing

    d. Suction is not working

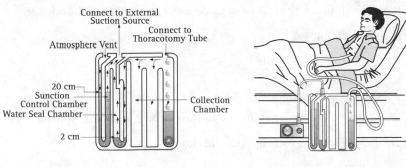

**Figure 1.  Chest Tubes**          **Figure 2.  Pleur–evac**

B. Complications

1. Observe for constant bubbling in the water-seal chamber; this indicates air leak in the drainage system; report to the RN or health care provider

2. If the chest tube becomes dislodged, apply pressure over the insertion site with a dressing that is tented on one side to allow for the escape of air; report to the RN or health care provider

3. If the tube becomes disconnected from the drainage system, cut the contaminated tip off of the tubing, insert a sterile connector, and reattach to the drainage system; otherwise immerse the end of the chest tube in 2 cm of sterile water until the system can be re-established; report to the RN or health care provider.

## EAR PROCEDURES

A. Ear irrigations

1. Tilt head toward side of affected ear, gently direct stream of fluid against sides of canal

2. After procedure, instruct client to lie on affected side to facilitate drainage

3. Contraindicated if there is evidence of swelling or tenderness

B. Ear drops

1. Position the affected ear uppermost

2. Pull outer ear upward and backward for adult

3. Pull outer ear downward and backward for child

4. Place drops so they run down the wall of ear canal

5. Have client lie on unaffected ear to encourage absorption

## EYE PROCEDURES

A. Eye irrigation

1. Tilt head back and toward the side of affected area

2. Allow irrigating fluid to flow from the inner to the outer canthus

3. Use a small bulb syringe or eye dropper to dispense fluid

4. Place small basin close to head to collect excess fluid and drainage

B. Eyedrop instillation

1. Equipment must be sterile
   a. Wash hands, before instillation
   b. Do not allow dropper to touch eye
   c. Do not allow drops from eye to flow across nose into opposite eye

2. Tilt head back and look up; pull lid down

3. Place drops into center of lower conjunctival sac
   a. Instruct client not to squeeze eye
   b. Teach client to blink between drops

4. To prevent systemic absorption, press the inner canthus near the bridge of the nose for 1–2 minutes

## NASOGASTRIC TUBES

**A.** Types

1. Levin—single-lumen stomach tube used to remove stomach contents or provide tube feeding

2. Salem sump—double-lumen stomach tube; most frequently used tube for decompression with suction

3. Sengstaken-Blakemore—triple-lumen gastric tube with inflatable esophagus balloon, stomach ballon, gastric suction lumen used for treatment of bleeding esophageal varices

4. Keofeed/Dobhoff—soft silicone rubber, medium-length tube used for long-term feedings; placement verified by x-ray; takes 24 hours to pass from stomach into intestines; lay on right side to facilitate passage

**B.** Insertion of Levin/Salem sump

1. Measure distance from tip of nose to earlobe plus distance from earlobe to bottom of xiphoid process

2. Mark distance on tube with tape and lubricate end of tube with water-soluble jelly

3. Insert tube through the nose to the stomach

4. Offer sips of water and advance the tube gently; bend the head forward (closes the epiglottis, closing the trachea)

5. Observe for respiratory distress, an indication that tube is misplaced in the lungs; if in correctly, secure tube with hypoallergenic tape

**C.** Verify placement of tube initially and before administering feeding

1. X-ray is only sure way to verify placement

2. Aspirate gastric contents

3. Observe color—gastric aspirate usually cloudy and green but may also be off-white, tan, bloody, or brown

4. Measure pH of aspirate
   a. Gastric—usually less than or equal to 4
   b. Intestinal—usually greater than 4
   c. Respiratory—usually greater than 5.5

**D.** Nursing care of Levin/Salem pump

1. Check residual before intermittent feeding and q 4 hours with continuous feeding; hold feeding if more than 100 ml

2. Instill 15–30 mL saline or water according to agency policy
   a. Before and after each dose of medications and each tube feeding
   b. After checking residuals and pH
   c. Every 4–6 hours with continuous feedings
   d. When feeding is discontinued

3. Control rate of feeding—use enteral pump or count drops in gravity administration

4. Administer fluid at room temperature

5. Change bag every 24–72 hours

6. Elevate head of bed 30° while feeding is running and for 30 min after feeding

7. Check patency every 4 h; document drainage

8. Measure I and O

9. Good mouth care, lubricate tube around nares with water-soluble jelly

10. Hang the amount of fluid that will be infused in 4 hours

E. Irrigation of Levin/Salem sump

   1. Verify placement of tube

   2. Insert 30–50 ml syringe filled with normal saline into tube, inject slowly

   3. If resistance felt, check to see if tube is kinked, have client change position

   4. Pull back on plunger or bulb to withdraw solution; if irrigating solution not removed, record as input

   5. Repeat if needed

F. Removal of Levin/Salem sump

   1. Clamp tube, remove tape

   2. Instruct client to exhale and remove tube with smooth, continuous pull

## SURGICAL DRAINS

| SURGICAL DRAINS | | | Table 3 |
|---|---|---|---|
| **TYPE** | **DESCRIPTION** | **NURSING CONSIDERATIONS** | |
| Penrose | Simple latex drain | Note location<br>Usually not sutured in place, but layered in gauze dressing<br>Expect drainage on dressing | |
| T tube | Used after gallbladder surgery<br>Placed in common bile duct to allow passage of bile | Monitor drainage<br>Fasten tubing to dressings<br>Keep below waist<br>May clamp for 1 hour before and after each meal<br>May be discharged with T tube in place<br>Remove 7–14 days<br>Teach client about care | |
| Jackson-Pratt | Portable wound self-suction device with reservoir | Monitor amount and character of drainage<br>Notify health care provider if it suddenly increases or becomes bright red | |
| Hemovac | Larger portable wound self-suction device with reservoir<br>Used after mastectomy | Monitor and record amount and character of drainage<br>Notify health care provider if it suddenly increases or becomes bright red<br>Empty when full or every 8 h<br>Remove plug (maintain sterility), empty contents, place on flat surface, cleanse opening and plug with alcohol sponge, compress evacuator completely to remove air, replace plug, check system for operation | |

## ENEMAS

A.  Types

1.  Oil retention—softens feces

2.  Soapsuds—irritates colon, causing reflux evacuation

3.  Tap water—softens feces, stimulating evacuation, volume expander

B.  Procedure—installation of solution into rectum and sigmoid colon; promote defecation by stimulating peristalsis

1.  Explain procedure to client

2.  Position in Sims' position with right knee flexed

3.  Use tepid solution

4.  Hold irrigation set at 12–18 inches for high enema, 3 inches for low enema

5.  Insert tube no more than 3–4 inches for adult, 2–3 inches for child, 1–1.5 inches for infant

6. Ask client to retain solution for 5–10 minutes

7. Do not administer in presence of abdominal pain, nausea, vomiting, or suspected appendicitis

## URINARY CATHETERS

A. Types of catheters (see Table 4)

B. Procedure for catheterization

1. Female
   a. Explain procedure to client
   b. Assemble equipment
   c. Client should be placed in dorsal recumbent position or in Sims' position
   d. Drape client with sterile drapes using sterile technique
   e. Apply sterile gloves
   f. Lubricate catheter tip and place in sterile catheter tray
   g. Separate labia with thumb and forefinger and wipe from the meatus toward the rectum with sterile povidone-iodine swab and discard swab
   h. Insert catheter 2 to 3 inches into the urethra
   i. Insert catheter an additional inch after urine begins to flow to ensure balloon portion of catheter is in the bladder
   j. Inflate balloon
   k. Gently apply traction to the catheter
   l. Tape drainage tubing to client's thigh

2. Male
   a. If uncircumcised, retract the foreskin to expose urinary meatus
   b. Cleanse glans and meatus with sterile povidone-iodine swabs in circular motion
   c. Hold penis perpendicular to the body; insert catheter into urethra 6–7 inches
   d. Replace the foreskin

Table 4

| URINARY CATHETERS | | |
|---|---|---|
| **TYPE** | **CHARACTERISTICS** | **COMMENTS** |
| Whistle-tip | Straight | For blood clot removal |
| Coude | Curved | For BPH to avoid prostate trauma |
| Robinson | Hollow–2 openings | For intermittent catheterizations |
| Filiform | Stiff | For urethral strictures |
| Foley | Double lumen with inflatable balloon toward tip | Indwelling for urinary drainage |
| Pezzer | Mushroom tip, otherwise like a Foley | Indwelling for urinary drainage |
| Malecot | Wing-shaped tip | Used as nephrostomy tube—anchored in renal pelvis through flank incision |
| Suprapubic | Placed in bladder via abdominal incision Dressing over site | Used in conjunction with urethral drainage |

  e. Inflate balloon

  f. Gently apply traction to the catheter until resistance is felt, indicating the catheter is at the base of the bladder

  g. Tape drainage tubing to client's thigh

**C.** Principles of drainage system care

 1. Catheter should not be disconnected from drainage system, except to perform ordered irrigations

 2. Urine samples should be obtained from drainage port with a small-bore needle using sterile technique; clamp tubing below port

 3. Drainage bags should not be elevated above level of cavity being drained (to prevent reflux)

 4. Avoid kinks in tubing

 5. Avoid removing more than 700 ml at one time; if more urine in bladder clamp after 700 ml, wait 15–30 min, then continue

 6. Coil excess tubing on bed

**D.** Catheter irrigation

 1. Purpose—prevent obstruction of flow and catheter or remove buildup of sediment in long-term use

 2. Procedure—urethral catheter irrigation

  a. Closed urethral catheter irrigation

   1) Draw solution into syringe using sterile technique

   2) Clamp catheter below injection port

   3) Cleanse port with antiseptic swab

   4) Insert needle into injection port at 30° angle

   5) Slowly inject fluid

   6) Withdraw needle

   7) Remove clamp

   8) Solution drains into the bad

  b. Open urethral catheter irrigation

   1) Use sterile technique

   2) Cleanse around catheter; disconnect tubing

   3) Gently instill 30 ml of solution

   4) Allow fluid to drain by gravity into sterile basin

   5) If solution is easily instilled but does not return, have client turn to side; if still doesn't return, depress the syringe bulb to provide gentle suction

   6) Disinfect ends of catheter tubing and reconnect

**E.** Nursing care

 1. Use aseptic technique on insertion

 2. Do not disturb integrity of closed drainage system

 3. Check for kinks

 4. Perineal care with soap and water 2–3 times daily, then apply antimicrobial ointment to insertion site

5. Keep urine collection bag below the level of the urinary bladder

6. Secure to leg to prevent traction

7. Monitor I and O; minimum urinary drainage catheter output should be 30 ml/h

8. Monitor for signs and symptoms of infection (foul-smelling urine with pus, blood, or mucus streaks)

9. Adhere to special precautions for type of catheter used
   a. Ureterostomy tube—never irrigate
   b. Straight catheter—do not remove more than 1,000 ml at one time
   c. Nephrostomy tube—never clamp

10. Clamp indwelling catheters intermittently prior to removal

F. Intermittent self-catheterization

1. Used to treat neurogenic bladder caused by spinal cord injury, multiple sclerosis (MS), brain injury
   a. Caused by meurologic condictions: spinal cord injury, multiple sclerosis (MS), brain injury

2. Preparation
   a. Gather equipment
      1) Straight or curved-tip 12 or 14 Fr Tiemann catheter (most common for male clients)
      2) Clean container or plastic bag
      3) Water-soluble lubricant
      4) Washcloth with soap and water
      5) Container for urine
   b. Wash hands
   c. Wash catheter with warm water and soap, rinse, and dry completely

3. Insertion
   a. Clear perineum with soap and water
   b. Lubricate catheter with water-soluble lubricant
   c. Locate catheter insertion point
      1) Female: combination visualization and palpation
      2) Male: visualize penile meatus
   d. Insert catheter slowly until urine returns, the advance 1/2–1 inch
   e. Press down with abdominal muscles to promote complete emptying
   f. Once bladder is drained, remove gently
   g. Immediately rinse catheter with cool tap water to remove residue, dry thoroughly
   h. Wash hands

4. Reinforce client teaching
   a. Should be done every 6–8 hours
   b. Should be performed a consistent times daily
   c. Uses clean technique, not sterile technique
   d. Removes 350–400 ml each time
   e. Performed in a comfortable postition, sitting or standing

f.   Use catheter for 2–4 weeks and then discard
g.   Store catheter in sandwich-sized bag or clean container
h.   Never store catheter wet or in antiseptic solution
i.   Should drink 250 ml at 2-hour intervels or up to 2 L at regular intervals

PHYSIOLOGICAL
INTEGRITY 4

[PHARMACOLOGICAL AND PARENTERAL THERAPIES]

**Chapter 9**

Blood Component Therapy

Intravenous Therapy

Medications

Side Effects of Medications

PHYSIOLOGICAL
INTEGRITY 4

UNIT 1  **BLOOD COMPONENT THERAPY**

[PHARMACOLOGICAL AND PARENTERAL THERAPIES]

## MONITORING ADMINISTRATION OF BLOOD AND BLOOD PRODUCTS

●Table 1

| BLOOD COMPONENTS | | |
|---|---|---|
| **PRODUCT** | **ADVERSE REACTIONS** | **NURSING CONSIDERATIONS** |
| Packed red blood cells | Reactions less common than with whole blood | Companion solution–0.9% NaCl<br>Monitor client during transfusion<br>Give over 2-4 h |

●Table 2

| BLOOD GROUP COMPATIBILITY | | |
|---|---|---|
| **BLOOD GROUP** | **CAN ACT AS DONOR** | **CAN RECEIVE BLOOD FROM** |
| O | O, A, B, AB | O |
| A | A, AB | O, A |
| B | B, AB | O, B |
| AB | AB | O, A, B, AB |

**A.** Stay with client for first 15–30 minutes after blood starts into the client

**B.** Recheck vital signs 15 minutes after infusion started

**C.** Take vital signs every hour until completed, then hourly for 3 hours

**D.** For elderly check vital signs every 15 minutes throughout transfusion

**E.** Ask client to report itching or flank pain over kidneys

**F.** If transfusion reaction suspected
    a. Stop blood or blood product and report to RN
    b. Restart normal saline
    c. Save blood container and tubing and return to blood bank
    d. Collect urine sample and send to lab for hemoglobin determination
    e. Monitor voiding for hematuria

**B.** Autologous transfusion

1. Preoperative donation collected 4–6 weeks before surgery

2. Iron supplements may be ordered

3. Benefits
   a. Prevention of viral infection from donated blood
   b. Used for clients with history of transfusion reactions
   c. Rare blood type

4. Contraindications
   a. Acute infection
   b. Chronic disease
   c. Hemoglobin <11 g/L, hematocrit <33%
   d. Cerebrovascular disease
   e. Cardiovascular disease

● Table 3

| BLOOD TRANSFUSION REACTIONS | | | |
|---|---|---|---|
| **TYPE OF REACTION** | **CAUSE** | **SYMPTOMS** | **NURSING CONSIDERATIONS** |
| Allergic reaction Hypersensitivity | Hypersensitivity to antibodies in donor's blood | Occurs immediately or within 24 hours Mild–urticaria, itching, flushing Anaphylaxis– hypotension, dyspnea, decreased oxygen saturation, flushing | Prevention–premedicate with antihistamines Stop the blood Restart the 0.9% NaCl Notify the health care provider Supportive care: Benadryl, oxygen, corticosteroids |
| Acute intravascular hemolytic reaction | Incompatibility | Occurs within minutes to 24 hours Chills, nausea, vomiting, pain in lower back, hypotension, increase in pulse rate, decrease in urinary output, hematuria | Stop the blood Supportive care: oxygen, Benadryl, airway management |
| Febrile nonhemolytic reaction (most common) | Antibodies to donor platelets or leukocytes | Occurs in minutes to hours Fever, chills, nausea, headache, flushing, tachycardia, palpitations | Stop the blood Supportive care Antipyretics (avoid aspirin in thrombocytopenic clients) Seen with clients after multiple transfusions |
| Sepsis | Bacterial contamination of transfused component | Occurs within minutes to <24 hours Tachycardia, hypotension, high fever, chills, circulatory shock | Stop the blood Obtain blood culture Antibiotics, IV fluids, vasopressors, steroids |
| Circulatory overload | Large volume over short time | Occurs within minutes to hours–dyspnea, crackles, increased respiratory rate, tachycardia | Monitor clients at high-risk (elderly, heart disease, children) Slow or discontinue transfusion |

## PARENTERAL FLUIDS

**A.** Definition of terms

1.  Tonicity—concentration of a substance dissolved in water

2.  Isotonic fluids—same concentration as body fluids

3.  Hypertonic solution—solute concentration greater than that of body fluids

4.  Hypotonic solution—solute concentration less than that of body fluids

5.  ECF—extracellular fluid

6.  Intake refers to all possible avenues of intake, e.g., oral fluids, food, IV fluids, gavage feedings, irrigations

7.  Output refers to all possible avenues of output, e.g., insensible losses, urine, diarrhea, vomitus, sweat, blood, and any drainage

**B.** Types (see Table 1)

●Table 1

| INTRAVENOUS FLUIDS | | |
|---|---|---|
| **TYPE OF FLUID** | **IV FLUID** | **NURSING CONSIDERATIONS FOR IVs** |
| Isotonic | 0.9% NaCl<br>Lactated Ringer's<br>5% dextrose in water<br>  (is isotonic but becomes<br>  hypotonic when glucose<br>  metabolized) | Main purpose—to maintain or restore fluid and<br>  electrolyte balance<br>Secondary purpose—to provide a route for<br>  medication, nutrition, and blood components<br>Type, amount, and sterility of fluid must be<br>  carefully checked<br>Macrodrip—delivers 10, 12, or 15 drops per |
| Hypotonic | 0.45% NaCl | milliliter; should be used if rapid<br>  administration is needed<br>Microdrip—deliver 60 drops per milliliter; should<br>  be used when fluid volume needs to be smaller<br>  or more controlled, e.g., clients with<br>  compromised renal or cardiac status, clients<br>  on "keep-open" rates, pediatric clients<br>Maintain sterile technique |
| Hypertonic | 10-15% dextrose in water<br>3% NaCl<br>Sodium bicarbonate 5% | Monitor rate of flow<br>Observe for infiltration—cool skin, swelling, pain<br>Observe for phlebitis—redness, pain, heat, swelling<br>Change tubing every 72 hours, change<br>  bottle every 24 hours |

**C.** Administration

1. Calculate IV flow rate (see Table 2)

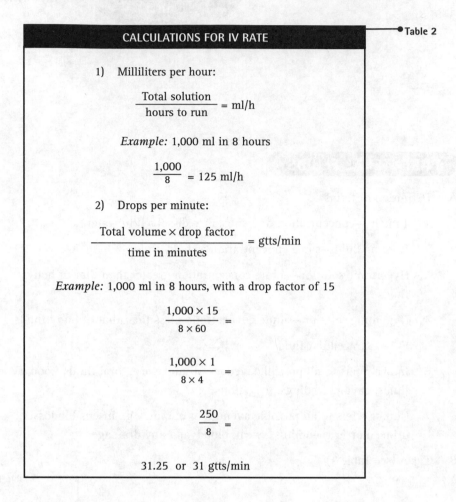

### CALCULATIONS FOR IV RATE                                    ● Table 2

1) Milliliters per hour:

$$\frac{\text{Total solution}}{\text{hours to run}} = \text{ml/h}$$

*Example:* 1,000 ml in 8 hours

$$\frac{1,000}{8} = 125 \text{ ml/h}$$

2) Drops per minute:

$$\frac{\text{Total volume} \times \text{drop factor}}{\text{time in minutes}} = \text{gtts/min}$$

*Example:* 1,000 ml in 8 hours, with a drop factor of 15

$$\frac{1,000 \times 15}{8 \times 60} =$$

$$\frac{1,000 \times 1}{8 \times 4} =$$

$$\frac{250}{8} =$$

31.25  or  31 gtts/min

2. Nursing care
   a. Change continuous use standard tubing every 96 hours, unless contaminated
   b. Change intermittent-use tubing every 24 hours, unless contaminated
   c. Change fluid container every 24 hours

## MONITOR PERIPHERAL IV

**A.** Complications

1. Circulatory overload
   a. Observe for:
      1) Crackles
      2) Dyspnea

        3) Confusion

        4) Seizures

    b. Nursing care

        1) Notify RN

        2) Collect VS

        3) Elevate HOB

2. Infiltration (extravasation if tissue-damaging medication is used)
    a. Observe for:
        1) Edema
        2) Pain
        3) Coolness in area
        4) Significant decrease in flow rate
    b. Nursing care
        1) Discontinue IV
        2) Apply warm compresses to infiltrated site
        3) Apply sterile dressing
        4) Elevate arm

3. Phlebitis
    a. Observe for:
        1) Reddened, warm area around insertion site or on path of vein
        2) Tenderness
        3) Swelling
    b. Nursing care
        1) Discontinue IV
        2) Apply warm, moist compresses

4. Thrombophlebitis
    a. Observe for:
        1) Pain
        2) Swelling
        3) Redness and warmth around insertion site or along path of vein
        4) Fever
        5) Leukocytosis
    b. Nursing care
        1) Discontinue IV
        2) Apply warm compress
        3) Elevate the extremity

5. Hematoma
    a. Observe for:
        1) Ecchymosis
        2) Immediate swelling at site
        3) Leakage of blood at site
    b. Nursing care
        1) Discontinue IV
        2) Apply pressure with sterile dressing

        3) Apply cool compresses (or ice bag) intermittenly for 24 h to site, followed by warm compresses

6. Clotting
    a. Observe for:
        1) Decreased IV flow rate
        2) Back flow of blood into IV tubing
    b. Nursing care
        1) Discontinue IV

## PHARMACOLOGY CALCULATIONS

### Equivalents

1oz = 30 mL

1 oz = 2 tablespoons (T or Tbsp)

1 cup = 8 oz

1 cup = 240 ml

1 pint = 2 cups

1 pint = 480 ml

1 quart = 2 pints

1 tsp = 60 gtt (drops)

1 tsp = 5 ml

1 T = 3 teaspoons (tsp)

1 gt (drop) = 1 minim

grains (gr) $\times$ 60 = milligrams (mg)

mg $\div$ 60 = gr

grams $\times$ 15 = grains

grains $\div$ 15 = grams

### Metric Conversions

1000 milligrams (mg) = 1 gram

1000 milliliters (ml) = 1 L

1000 micrograms (mcg) = 1 mg

### Converting from one unit to another

Larger to smaller:  multiply

grams to mg = grams $\times$ 1000

Small to larger:  divide

milligrams to grams = mg $\div$ 1000

### Pediatric dosage formulas

$$\frac{\text{Child's age in months}}{150 \text{ months}} \times \text{usual adult dose} = \text{child's dose}$$

$$\frac{\text{Child's weight in pounds}}{150 \text{ pounds}} \times \text{usual adult dose} = \text{child's dose}$$

$$\frac{\text{Child's body surface area (m}^2)}{1.73 \text{ m}^2} \times \text{usual adult dose} = \text{child's dose}$$

| AGENTS USED TO TREAT SHOCK, CARDIAC ARREST, AND ANAPHYLAXIS | | |
|---|---|---|
| **MEDICATION** | **SIDE EFFECTS** | **NURSING CONSIDERATIONS** |
| Norepinephrine | Headache<br>Palpitations<br>Nervousness<br>Epigastric distress<br>Angina, hypertension<br>  tissue necrosis with<br>  extravasation | Vasoconstrictor to increase blood pressure and<br>  cardiac output<br>Reflex bradycardia may occur with rise in BP<br>Client should be attended at all times<br>Monitor urinary output<br>Infuse with dextrose solution, not saline<br>Monitor blood pressure<br>Protect from light |
| Dopamine | Increased ocular pressure<br>Ectopic beats<br>Nausea<br>Tachycardia, chest pain,<br>  dysrhythmias | Low-dose–dilates renal and coronary arteries<br>High-dose–vasoconstrictor, increases<br>  myocardial oxygen consumption<br>Headache is an early symptom of drug excess<br>Monitor blood pressure, peripheral<br>  pulses, urinary output<br>Use infusion pump |
| Epinephrine | Nervousness<br>Restlessness<br>Dizziness<br>Local necrosis of skin | Stimulates alpha and beta adrenergic receptors<br>Monitor BP<br>Carefully aspirate syringe before IM and<br>subcutaneous doses;<br>  inadvertent IV administration can be harmful<br>Always check strength:<br>  1:100 only for inhalation, 1:1,000 for<br>  parenteral administration (SC or IM)<br>Ensure adequate hydration |
| Isoproterenol | Headache<br>Palpitations<br>Tachycardia<br>Changes in BP<br>Angina, bronchial asthma | Stimulates beta 1 and beta 2 adrenergic<br>receptors<br>Used for heart block, ventricular<br>  arrhythmias, and bradycardia<br>Bronchodilator used for asthma and<br>bronchospasms<br>Don't give at hs–interrupts sleep patterns<br>Monitor BP, pulse |
| Phenylephrine | Palpations<br>Tachycardia<br>Hypertension<br>Dysrhythmia<br>Angina<br>Tissue necrosis with<br>  extravasation | Potent alpha 1 agonist<br>Used to treat hypotension |
| Dobutamine<br>hydrochloride | Hypertension<br>PVCs<br>Asthmatic episodes<br>Headache | Stimulates beta 1 receptors<br>Incompatible with alkaline solutions<br>  (sodium bicarbonate)<br>Administer through central venous catheter or<br>large peripheral vein using an infusion pump<br>Don't infuse through line with other meds<br>(incompatible)<br>Monitor EKG, BP, I and O, serum potassium |

*(continued)*

## AGENTS USED TO TREAT SHOCK, CARDIAC ARREST, AND ANAPHYLAXIS (cont'd)

| MEDICATION | SIDE EFFECTS | NURSING CONSIDERATIONS |
|---|---|---|
| Milrinone | Dysrhythmia<br>Thrombocytopenia<br>Jaundice | Positive inotropic agent<br>Smooth muscle relaxant used to treat<br> severe heart failure |
| Sodium<br> nitroprusside | Hypotension | Dilates cardiac veins and arteries<br>Decreases preload and afterload<br>Increases myocardial perfusion |
| Diphenhydramine<br>HCl | Drowsiness<br>Confusion<br>Insomnia<br>Headache<br>Vertigo<br>Photosensitivity | Blocks effects of histamine on<br> bronchioles, GI tract, and blood vessels |
| **Actions** | Varies with med | |
| **Indications** | Hypovolemic shock<br>Cardiac arrest<br>Anaphylaxis | |
| **Side effects** | Serious rebound effect may occur<br>Balance between underdosing and overdosing | |
| **Nursing<br> considerations** | Monitor vital signs<br> Measure urine output<br>Observe for extravasation<br>Observe extremities for color and perfusion | |

| ANTIANXIETY AGENTS | | |
|---|---|---|
| **MEDICATION** | **SIDE EFFECTS** | **NURSING CONSIDERATIONS** |
| **Benzodiazepine Derivatives** | | |
| Chlordiazepoxide Diazepam | Lethargy, hangover Respiratory depression Hypotension | CNS depressant Use–anxiety, sedation, alcohol withdrawal, seizures May result in toxic build-up in the elderly Potential for physiological addiction/overdose Can develop tolerance and cross-tolerance Cigarette smoking increases clearance of drug Alcohol increases CNS depression |
| Alprazolam Clonazepam Lorazepam Oxazepam | Drowsiness, light-headedness, hypotension, hepatic dysfunction Increased salivation Orthostatic hypotension Memory impairment and confusion | CNS depressant Safer for elderly Don't combine with alcohol or other depressants Check renal and hepatic function Don't discontinue abruptly (true for all antianxiety agents) Teach addictive potential |
| Midazolam | Retrograde amnesia Euphoria Hypotension Dysrhythmia Cardiac arrest Respiratory depression | CNS depressant Use–preoperative sedation, conscious sedation for endoscopic procedures and diagnostic tests |
| **Nonbenzodiazepine Antianxiety Agents** | | |
| Buspirone | Light-headedness Confusion Hypotension, palpitations | Little sedation Requires more than or equal to 3 weeks to be effective Cannot be given as a PRN medication Particularly useful for generalized anxiety disorder (GAD) No abuse potential Used for clients with previous addiction Avoid alcohol and grapefruit juice Monitor for worsening depression or suicidal tendencies |
| Hydroxyzine | Drowsiness, ataxia Leukopenia, hypotension | Produces no dependence, tolerance, or intoxication Can be used for anxiety relief for indefinite periods |

*(continued)*

| ANTIANXIETY AGENTS (cont'd) | | |
|---|---|---|
| **MEDICATION** | **SIDE EFFECTS** | **NURSING CONSIDERATIONS** |
| Herbals | | |
| Kava | Impaired thinking, judgment, motor reflexes, vision, decreased plasma proteins, thrombocytopenia, leukocytopenia, dyspnea, and pulmonary hypertension | Similar activity to benzodiazepines<br>Suppresses emotional excitability and produces mild euphoria<br>Do not take with CNS depressants<br>Should not be taken by women who are pregnant or lactating or by children under the age of 12 |
| Melatonin | Sedation, confusion, headache, and tachycardia | Influences sleep-wake cycles (levels are high during sleep)<br>Used for prevention and treatment of "jet lag" and insomnia<br>Use cautiously if given with benzodiazepines and CNS depressants<br>Contraindicated in hepatic insufficiency, history of cerebrovascular disease, depression, and neurologic disorders |
| **Action** | Affects neurotransmitters | |
| **Indications** | Anxiety disorders, insomnia, petit mal seizures, panic attacks, acute manic episodes | |
| **Side effects** | Sedation<br>Depression, confusion<br>Anger, hostility<br>Headache<br>Dry mouth, constipation<br>Bradycardia<br>Elevations in LDH, AST, ALT<br>Urinary retention | |
| **Nursing considerations** | Monitor liver function<br>Monitor for therapeutic blood levels<br>Avoid alcohol<br>Caution when performing tasks requiring alertness (e.g., driving car)<br>Benzodiazepines are also used as muscles relaxants, sedatives, hypnotics, anticonvulsants | |

| ANTACID MEDICATIONS | | |
|---|---|---|
| **MEDICATION** | **SIDE EFFECTS** | **NURSING CONSIDERATIONS** |
| Aluminum hydroxide gel Calcium carbonate Aluminum hydroxide and magnesium trisilicate | Constipation that may lead to impaction, phosphate depletion<br><br>Aluminum and magnesium | Monitor bowel pattern Compounds contains sodium; check if client is on sodium-restricted diet<br><br>antacid compounds interfere with tetracycline absorption Encourage fluids Monitor for signs of phosphate deficiency—malaise, weakness, tremors, bone pain Shake well Careful use advised for kidney dysfunction |
| Magnesium hydroxide | Excessive dose can produce nausea, vomiting, and diarrhea | Store at room temperature with tight lid to prevent absorption of $CO_2$ Prolonged and frequent use of cathartic dose can lead to dependence Administer with caution to clients with renal disease |
| Aluminum hydroxide and magnesium hydroxide | Slight laxative effect | Encourage fluid intake Administer with caution to clients with renal disease |
| **Action** | Neutralizes gastric acids; raises gastric pH; inactivates pepsin | |
| **Indications** | Peptic ulcer Indigestion Reflex esophagitis Prevent stress ulcers | |
| **Side effects** | Constipation, diarrhea Acid rebound between doses Metabolic acidosis | |
| **Nursing considerations** | Use medications with sodium content cautiously for clients with cardiac and renal disease Absorption of tetracyclines, quinolones, phenothiazides, iron preparations, isoniazid reduced when given with antacids Effectiveness of oral contraceptives and salicylates may decrease when given with antacids | |

| ANTIDYSRHYTHMICS | | |
|---|---|---|
| **MEDICATION** | **SIDE EFFECTS** | **NURSING CONSIDERATIONS** |
| **Class IA Type Drugs**<br><br>Procainamide<br>Quinidine | Hypotension<br>Heart failure | Monitor blood pressure<br>Monitor for widening of the PR, QRS or QT intervals<br>Toxic side effects have limited use |
| **Class IB Drugs**<br><br>Lidocaine | CNS: slurred speech, confusion, drowsiness, confusion, seizures<br>Hypotension and bradycardia | Monitor for CNS side effects<br>Monitor BP and heart rate and cardiac rhythm |
| **Class II Drugs**<br><br>Propanolol<br>Esmolol hydrochloride<br>Sotalol hydrochloride | Bradycardia and hypotension<br>Bronchospasm<br>Increase in heart failure<br>Fatigue and sleep disturbances | Monitor apical heart rate, cardiac rhythm and blood pressure<br>Observe for shortness of breath and wheezing<br>Observe for fatigue, sleep disturbances<br>Observe apical heart rate for 1 minute before administration |
| **Class III Drugs**<br><br>Amiodarone hydrochloride | Hypotension<br>Bradycardia and atrioventricular block<br>Muscle weakness, tremors<br>Photosensitivity and photophobia<br>Liver toxicity | Continuous monitoring of cardiac rhythm during IV administration<br>Monitor QT interval during IV administration<br>Monitor heart rate, blood pressure during initiation of therapy<br>Instruct client to wear sunglasses and sunscreen |
| **Class IV Drugs**<br><br>Verapamil<br>Diltiazem hydrochloride | Bradycardia<br>Hypotension<br>Dizziness and orthostatic hypotension<br>Heart failure | Monitor apical heart rate and blood pressure<br>Instruct clients about orthostatic precautions<br>Instruct clients to report signs of heart failure to health care provider |

## ANTIBIOTICS/ANTI-INFECTIVES: AMINOGLYCOSIDES

| | |
|---|---|
| Examples | Gentamicin<br>Neomycin<br>Streptomycin<br>Tobramycin<br>Amikacin |
| Actions | Bacteriocidal<br>Inhibits protein synthesis in many Gram-negative bacteria |
| Indications | Treatment of severe systemic infections of CNS, respiratory, GI, urinary tract, bone, skin, soft tissues, acute pelvic inflammatory disease (PID), tuberculosis (streptomycin) |
| Side effects | Ototoxicity, Nephrotoxicity<br>Anorexia, nausea, vomiting, diarrhea |
| Nursing considerations | Check eighth cranial nerve function (hearing)<br>Check renal function (BUN, creatinine)<br>Usually prescribed for 7–10 days<br>Encourage fluids<br>Small, frequent meals |

## ANTIBIOTICS/ANTI-INFECTIVES: CEPHALOSPORINS

| | |
|---|---|
| Example | Multiple preparations:<br>1st generation example: cephalexin<br>2nd generation example: cefaclor cefoxitin<br>3rd generation example: ceftriaxone<br>4th generation example: cefepime |
| Actions | Bacteriocidal<br>Inhibits synthesis of bacterial cell wall |
| Indications | Pharyngitis<br>Tonsillitis<br>Otitis media<br>Upper and lower respiratory tract infections<br>Dermatological infections<br>Gonorrhea<br>Septicemia<br>Meningitis<br>Perioperative prophylaxis<br>Urinary tract infections |
| Side effects | Abdominal pain, nausea, vomiting, diarrhea<br>Increased risk bleeding<br>Hypoprothrombinemia<br>Rash<br>Superinfections<br>Thrombophlebitis (IV), abscess formation (IM, IV) |
| Nursing considerations | Take with food<br>Administer liquid form to children, don't crush tablets<br>Have vitamin K available for hypoprothrombinemia<br>Avoid alcohol while taking medication and for 3 days after finishing course of medication<br>Cross allergy with penicillins (cephalosporins should not be given to clients with a severe penicillin allergy)<br>Monitor renal and hepatic function<br>Monitor for Thrombophlebitis |

## ANTIBIOTICS/ANTI-INFECTIVES: FLUOROQUINOLONES

| Examples | Ciprofloxacin, Levofloxacin |
|---|---|
| Actions | Broad spectrum bactericidal; interferes with DNA replication in Gram-negative bacteria |
| Indications | Treatment of infection caused *by E. coli* and other bacteria, chronic bacterial prostatitis, acute sinusitis, postexposure inhalation anthrax |
| Side effects | Headache<br>Nausea<br>Diarrhea<br>Elevated BUN, AST, ALT, serum creatinine, alkaline phosphatase<br>Decreased WBC and hematocrit<br>Rash<br>Photosensitivity<br>Achilles tendon rupture |
| Nursing considerations | Culture and sensitivity before starting therapy<br>Take 1 h before or 2 h after meals with glass of water<br>Encourage fluids<br>If needed administer antacids 2 h after medication<br>Take full course of therapy |

## ANTIBIOTICS/ANTI-INFECTIVES: GLYCOPEPTIDES

| Example | Vancomycin |
|---|---|
| Action | Bacteriocidal<br>Binds to bacterial cell wall, stopping its synthesis |
| Indications | Treatment of resistant staph infections, pseudomembranous enterocolitis due to *C. difficile* infection |
| Side effects | Thrombophlebitis<br>Abscess formation<br>Nephrotoxicity<br>Ototoxicity |
| Nursing considerations | Monitor renal function and hearing<br>Poor absorption orally; administer IV: peak 5 minutes, duration 12–24 hours<br>Avoid extravasation during therapy; it may cause necrosis<br>Give antihistamine if "red man syndrome": decreased blood pressure, flushing of face and neck<br>Contact health care provider if signs of superinfection: sore throat, fever, fatigue |

## ANTIBIOTICS/ANTI-INFECTIVES: LINCOSAMIDES

| Example | Clindamycin HCl Phosphate |
|---|---|
| Action | Both bacteriostatic and bactericidal, it suppresses protein synthesis by preventing peptide bond formation |
| Indications | Staph, strep, and other infections |
| Side effects | Diarrhea<br>Rash<br>Liver toxicity |
| Nursing considerations | Administer oral med with a full glass of water to prevent esophageal ulcers<br>Monitor for persistent vomiting, diarrhea, fever, or abdominal pain and cramping, superinfectious |

CH. 9
**PHYSIOLOGICAL INTEGRITY 4**
PHARMACOLOGICAL AND
PARENTERAL THERAPIES

| ANTIBIOTICS/ANTIINFECTIVES: MACROLIDES | |
|---|---|
| **Examples** | Erythromycin<br>Azithromycin |
| **Actions** | Bacteriostatic; bactericidal; binds to cell membrane and causes changes in protein function |
| **Indications** | Acute infections<br>Acne and skin infections<br>Upper respiratory tract infections<br>Prophylaxis before dental procedures for clients allergic to PCN with valvular heart disease |
| **Side effects** | Abdominal cramps, diarrhea<br>Confusion, uncontrollable emotions<br>Hepatotoxicity<br>Superinfections |
| **Nursing considerations** | Take oral med 1 h before or 2-3 h after meals with full glass of water<br>Take around the clock to maximize effectiveness<br>Monitor live function<br>Take full course of therapy |

| ANTIBIOTICS/ANTI-INFECTIVES: PENICILLINS | |
|---|---|
| **Examples** | Amoxicillin<br>Ampicillin<br>Methicillin<br>Nafcillin<br>Penicillin G<br>Penicillin V |
| **Actions** | Bactericidal; inhibit synthesis of cell wall of sensitive organisms |
| **Indications** | Effective against gram positive organisms<br>Moderate to severe infections<br>Syphilis<br>Gonococcal infections<br>Lyme disease |
| **Side effects** | Glossitis, stomatitis<br>Gastritis<br>Diarrhea<br>Superinfections<br>Hypersensitivity reactions |
| **Nursing considerations** | Culture and sensitivity before treatment<br>Monitor serum electrolytes and cardiac status if given IV<br>Monitor and rotate injection sites<br>Good mouth care<br>Yogurt or buttermilk if diarrhea develops<br>Instruct client to take missed drugs as soon as possible; do not double dose |

## ANTIBIOTICS/ANTI-INFECTIVES: SULFONAMIDES

| | |
|---|---|
| **Example** | Sulfisoxazole<br>Sulfasalazine<br>Trimethoprim/Sulfamethoxazole |
| **Actions** | Bacteriostatic; competitively antagonize paraminobenzoic acid, essential component of folic acid synthesis, causing cell death |
| **Indications** | Ulcerative colitis, Crohn's disease<br>Otitis media<br>Conjunctivitis<br>Meningitis<br>Toxoplasmosis<br>UTIs<br>Rheumatoid arthritis |
| **Side effects** | Peripheral neuropathy<br>Crystalluria, proteinuria<br>Photosensitivity<br>GI upset<br>Stomatitis<br>Hypersensitivity reaction |
| **Nursing considerations** | Culture and sensitivity before therapy<br>Take on an empty stomach with a full glass of water<br>Take around the clock<br>Encourage fluid intake (8 glasses of water/day)<br>Protect from exposure to light (sunscreen, protective clothing)<br>Good mouth care |

## ANTIBIOTICS/ANTIINFECTIVES: TETRACYCLINES

| | |
|---|---|
| **Examples** | Doxycycline<br>Minocycline<br>Tetracycline HCl |
| **Actions** | Bacteriostatic; inhibits protein synthesis of susceptible bacteria |
| **Indications** | Treatment of syphilis, chlamydia, gonorrhea, malaria prophylaxis, chronic periodontitis, acne; treatment of anthrax (Vibramycin); as part of combination therapy to eliminate *H. pylori* infections; drug of choice for stage 1 Lyme disease (tetracycline HCl) |
| **Side effects** | Discoloration and inadequate calcification of primary teeth of fetus if taken during pregnancy<br>Glossitis<br>Dysphagia<br>Diarrhea<br>Phototoxic reactions<br>Rash<br>Superinfections |
| **Nursing considerations** | Take 1 h before or 2-3 h after meals<br>Do not take with antacids, milk, iron preparations (give 3 h after medication)<br>Note expiration date (becomes highly nephrotoxic)<br>Protect from sunlight<br>Monitor renal function<br>Topical applications may stain clothing<br>Use contraceptive method in addition to oral contraceptives |

| ANTIBIOTIC MEDICATIONS OVERVIEW | | |
|---|---|---|
| **MEDICATION** | **SIDE EFFECTS** | **NURSING CONSIDERATIONS** |
| **Penicillins**<br>Amoxicillin<br>Ampicillin<br>Pericillin | Skin rashes, diarrhea<br>Allergic reactions<br>Renal, hepatic, hematological<br>  abnormalities<br>Nausea, vomiting | Obtain C and S before first dose<br>Take careful history of penicillin reaction<br>Observe for 20 minutes post IM injection<br>Give 1-2 h ac or 2-3 h pc to reduce gastric acid destruction of drug<br>Monitor for loose, foul-smelling stool and change in tongue<br>Teach to continue medication for entire time prescribed, even if<br>  symptoms resolve<br>Check for hypersensitivity to other drugs, especially cephalosporins |
| **Sulfonamides**<br>Sulfisoxazole | Headache,<br>GI disturbances<br>Allergic rash<br>Urinary crystallization | Monitor I and O, force fluids<br>Maintain alkaline urine<br>Bicarbonate may be indicated to elevate pH<br>Avoid vitamin C, which acidifies urine |
| Sulfasalazine | Nausea, vomiting<br>Skin eruption<br>Agranulocytosis | Advise client to avoid exposure to sunlight<br>Maintain fluid intake at 3,000 ml/day to avoid crystal formation |
| Trimethoprim/<br>  Sulfamethoxazole | Hypersensitivity reaction<br>Blood dyscrasias<br>Rash | Obtain C and S before first dose<br>IV solution must be given slowly over 60-90 minutes<br>Never administer IM<br>Encourage fluids to 3,000/day |
| **Tetracylines**<br>(Tetracycline, Panmycin) | Photosensitivity<br>GI upset, renal, hepatic, hematological<br>  abnormalities<br>Dental discoloration of<br>  deciduous ("baby") teeth,<br>  enamel hypoplasia | Give between meals<br>If GI symptoms occur, administer with food EXCEPT milk products or<br>  other foods high in calcium (interferes with absorption)<br>Observe for change in bowel habits, perineal rash, black "hairy" tongue<br>Good oral hygiene<br>Avoid during tooth and early development periods (fourth month<br>  prenatal to 8 years of age)<br>Monitor I and O<br>Caution client to avoid sun exposure<br>Decomposes to toxic substance with age and exposure to light |
| Doxycycline | Photosensitivity | Check client's tongue for *Monilia* infection |
| **Aminogylcosides**<br>Gentamicin | Ototoxicity cranial nerve VIII<br>Nephrotoxicity | Check creatinine and BUN<br>Check peak—2 h after med given<br>Check trough—at time of dose/prior to med<br>Monitor for symptoms of bacterial overgrowth, photosensitivity<br>Teach to immediately report tinnitus, vertigo, nystagmus, ataxia<br>Monitor I and O<br>Audiograms if given long-term |
| Neomycin sulfate | Hypersensitivity reactions | Ophthalmic—remove infective exudate around eyes before<br>  administration of ointment |

*(continued)*

| ANTIBIOTIC MEDICATIONS OVERVIEW (cont'd) | | |
|---|---|---|
| **MEDICATION** | **SIDE EFFECTS** | **NURSING CONSIDERATIONS** |
| **Fluoroquinolones**<br>Ciprofloxacin | Seizures<br>GI upset<br>Rash | Contraindicated in children less than 18 years of age<br>Give 2 hours pc or 2 hours before an antacid or iron preparation<br>Avoid caffeine<br>Encourage fluids |
| **Macrolides**<br>Azithromycin<br>Erythromycin | Pain at injection site<br>Nausea, diarrhea | Can be used in clients with compromised renal<br>  function because excretion is primarily through the bile |
| **Cephalosporins**<br>(Ceclor, Ancef, Suprax,<br>Keflex, Rocephin,<br>Cefoxitin) | Diarrhea, nausea<br>Dizziness, abdominal pain<br>Eosinophilia, superinfections<br>Allergic reactions | Can cause false-positive Coombs' test (which will<br>  complicate transfusion cross-matching procedure)<br>Cross-sensitivity with penicillins<br>Take careful history of penicillin reactions |
| **Glycopeptides**<br>Vancomycin | Liver damage | Poor absorption orally, but IV peak 5 minutes, duration 12–24 hours<br>Avoid extravasation during therapy—may cause necrosis<br>Give antihistamine if "red man syndrome": decreased blood pressure,<br>  flushing of face and neck<br>Contact health care provider if signs of superinfection: sore throat,<br>  fever, fatigue |
| **Lincosamides**<br>Clindamycin HCl phosphate | Nausea<br>Vaginitis<br>Colitis may occur 2–9 days or<br>  several weeks after starting meds | Administer oral med with a full glass of water to prevent<br>  esophageal ulcers<br>Monitor for persistent vomiting, diarrhea, fever, or abdominal pain<br>  and cramping |

| TOPICAL ANTIBACTERIALS | | |
|---|---|---|
| **MEDICATION** | **SIDE EFFECTS** | **NURSING CONSIDERATIONS** |
| Bacitracin ointment | Nephrotoxicity<br>Ototoxicity | Overgrowth of nonsusceptible organisms can<br>  occur |
| Neosporin cream | Nephrotoxicity<br>Ototoxicity | Allergic dermatitis may occur |
| Povidone-iodine solution | Irritation | Don't use around eyes<br>May stain skin<br>Don't use full-strength on mucous membranes |
| Silver sulfadiazine cream | Neutropenia<br>Burning | Use cautiously if sensitive to sulfonamides |
| Tolna flake cream | Irritation | Use small amount of medication<br>Use medication for duration prescribed |
| Nystatin cream | Contact dermatitis | Do not use occlusive dressings |

| GENITOURINARY MEDICATIONS | | |
|---|---|---|
| **MEDICATION** | **SIDE EFFECTS** | **NURSING CONSIDERATIONS** |
| Nitrofurantoin | Diarrhea<br>Nausea, vomiting<br>Asthma attacks | Anti-infective<br>Check CBC<br>Give with food or milk<br>Avoid acidic foods (cranberry juice, prunes, plums) which increase drug action<br>Check I and O<br>Monitor pulmonary status |
| Phenazopyridine | Headache<br>Vertigo | Urinary tract analgesic, spasmolytic<br>Inform client that urine will be bright orange<br>Take with meals |
| **Anticholinergics**<br>Oxybutynin<br>Hyoscyamine<br>Propantheline<br>Darifenacin<br>Solifenacin<br>Tolterodine | Drowsiness<br>Blurred vision<br>Dry mouth<br>Constipation<br>Urinary retention | Used to reduce bladder spasms and treat urinary incontinence<br>Increase fluids and fiber in diet<br>Oxybutynin–older adults require higher dose and have greater incidence of side effects |
| **Anti–impotence**<br>Sildenafil<br>Vardenafil<br>Tadalafil | Headache<br>Flushing<br>Hypotension<br>Priapism | Treatment of erectile dysfunction<br>Take 1 hour before sexual activity<br>Never use with nitrates–could have fatal hypotension<br>Do not take with alpha blockers, e.g., doxazosin (Cardura)–risk of hypotension<br>Do not drink grapefruit juice |
| **Testosterone inhibitors**<br>Finasteride | Decreased libido<br>Impotence<br>Breast tenderness | Treatment of benign prostatic hyperplasia (BPH) by Proscar; male hair loss by Propecia<br>Pregnant women should avoid contact with crushed drug or client's semen–may adversely affect male fetus |

| ANTICHOLINERGIC MEDICATIONS | | |
|---|---|---|
| **MEDICATION** | **SIDE EFFECTS** | **NURSING CONSIDERATIONS** |
| Propantheline bromide | Decreased gastric motility<br>Decreased effect of vagus nerve | Used for urinary incontinence and peptic ulcer disease<br>Give 30 minutes ac<br>Give hs dose at least 2 h after last meal<br>Monitor vital signs, I and O |
| Belladonna | Dry mouth, vertigo | Action peaks in 2 hours |
| Atropine sulfate | Tachycardia<br>Headache, blurred vision<br>Insomnia, dry mouth<br>Dizziness<br>Urinary retention<br>Angina, mydriasis | Used for bradycardia<br>When given PO give 30 minutes before meals<br>Check for history of glaucoma, asthma, hypertension<br>Monitor I and 0, orientation<br>When given in nonemergency situations make certain client voids before taking drug<br>Educate client to expect dry mouth, increased respiration and heart rate<br>Client should avoid heat (perspiration is decreased)<br>Antidote-physostigmine salicylate |
| Iproproprium<br>Tiotropium<br>Iprotropium plus albuterol | Dry mouth<br>Irritation of pharynx | Used for bronchospasm and long-term treatment of asthma<br>Iproproprium administered as aerosol or in nebulizer<br>Tiotropium administered in powder form by HandiHaler |
| Benztropine<br>Trihexyphenydil | Urinary retention<br>Blurred vision<br>Dry mouth<br>Constipation | Used for Parkinson's Disease<br>Increase fluids, bulk foods and exercise<br>Taper before discontinuation<br>Orthostatic hypotension precautions |
| Scopolamine | Urinary retention<br>Blurred vision<br>Dry mouth<br>Constipation<br>Confusion and sedation | Used for motion sickness<br>Contraindicated in acute angle glaucoma |
| **Actions** | Competes with acetylcholine at receptor sites in autonomic nervous system; causes relaxation of ciliary muscles (cycloplegia) and dilation of pupil (mydriasis); causes bronchodilation and decreases bronchial secretions; decreases mobility and GI secretions | |
| **Indications** | Atropine—bradycardia, mydriasis for ophthalmic exam, preoperatively to dry secretions<br>Scopolamine—motion sickness, vertigo, mydriasis for ophthalmic exam, preoperative to dry secretions | |
| **Side effects** | Blurred vision<br>Dry mouth<br>Urinary retention<br>Changes in heart rate | |
| **Nursing considerations** | Monitor for urinary retention<br>Contraindicated for clients with glaucoma | |

| ANTICOAGULANT MEDICATIONS | | |
|---|---|---|
| **MEDICATION** | **SIDE EFFECTS** | **NURSING CONSIDERATIONS** |
| Heparin | Can produce hemorrhage from any body site (10%)<br>Tissue irritation/pain at injection site<br>Anemia<br>Thrombocytopenia<br>Fever | Monitor therapeutic partial thromboplastin time (PTT) at 1.5–2.5 times the control without signs of hemorrhage<br>Lower limit of normal 20–25 sec; upper limit of normal 32–39 sec<br>For IV administration: use infusion pump, peak 5 minutes, duration 2–6 hours<br>For injection: give deep SQ; never IM (danger of hematoma), onset 20–60 minutes, duration 8–12 hours<br>Antidote: protamine sulfate within 30 minutes<br>Can be allergenic |
| Enoxaparin low-molecular weight heparin | Same as heparin | Less allergenic than heparin<br>Must be given deep SQ, never IV or IM<br>Does not require lab test monitoring |
| Warfarin | Hemorrhage<br>Diarrhea<br>Rash<br>Fever | Monitor therapeutic prothombin time (PT) at 1.5–2.5 times the control, or monitor international normalized ratio (INR)<br>Normal PT 9.5–12 sec; normal INR 2.0–3.5<br>Onset: 12–24 hours, peak 1.5–3 days, duration: 3–5 days<br>Antidotes: vitamin K, whole blood, plasma<br>Teach measures to avoid venous stasis<br>Emphasize importance of regular lab testing<br>Client should avoid foods high in vitamin K: many green vegetables, pork, rice, yogurt, cheeses, fish, milk |
| **Action** | Heparin blocks conversion of fibrinogen to fibrin<br>Coumadin interferes with liver synthesis of vitamin K–dependent clotting factors | |
| **Indications** | For heparin: prophylaxis and treatment of thromboembolic disorders; in very low doses (10–100 units) to maintain patency of IV catheters (heparin flush)<br>For coumadin: management of pulmonary emboli, venous thromboembolism, MI, atrial dysrhythmias, post cardiac valve replacement<br>For Persantine: as an adjunct to coumadin in postop cardiac valve replacement, as an adjunct to aspirin to reduce the risk of repeat stroke or TIAs | |
| **Side effects** | Nausea<br>Alopecia<br>Urticaria<br>Hemorrhage<br>Bleeding/heparin-induced thrombocytopetria (HIT) | |
| **Nursing considerations** | Check for signs of hemorrhage: bleeding gums, nosebleed, unusual bleeding, black/tarry stools, hematuria, fall in hematocrit or blood pressure, guaiac-positive stools<br>Client should avoid IM injections, ASA-containing products, and NSAIDs<br>Client should wear medical information tag<br>Instruct client to use soft toothbrush, electric razor, to report bleeding gums, petechiae or bruising, epistaxis, black tarry stools<br>Monitor platelet counts and signs and symptoms of thrombosis during heparin therapy; if HIT suspected, heparin discontinued and non-heparin anticoagulant (lepirudin) given | |
| **Herbal interactions** | Garlic, ginger, ginkgo may increase bleeding when taken with warfarin (Coumadin)<br>Large doses of anise may interfere with anticoagulants<br>Ginseng and alfalfa my decrease anticoagulant activity<br>Black haw increases action of anticoagulant<br>Chamomile may interfere with anticoagulants | |
| **Vitamin interaction** | Vitamin C may slightly prolong PT<br>Vitamin E will increase warfarin's effect | |

## ANTICONVULSANT MEDICATIONS

| MEDICATION | SIDE EFFECTS | NURSING CONSIDERATIONS |
|---|---|---|
| Clonazepam | Drowsiness<br>Dizziness<br>Confusion<br>Respiratory depression | Benzodiazepine<br>Do not discontinue suddenly<br>Avoid activities that require alertness |
| Diazepam | Drowsiness, ataxia<br>Hypotension<br>Tachycardia<br>Respiratory depression | IV push doses shouldn't exceed 2 mg/minute<br>Monitor vital signs–resuscitation equipment available if given IV<br>Alcohol increases CNS depression<br>After long-term use, withdrawal leads to symptoms such as vomiting, sweating, cramps, tremors, and possibly convulsions |
| Fosphenytoin | Drowsiness<br>Dizziness<br>Confusion<br>Leukopenia<br>Anemia | Used for tonic–clonic seizures, status epilepticus<br>Highly protein-bound<br>Contact health care provider if rash develops |
| Levetiracetam | Dizziness<br>Suicidal ideation | Avoid alcohol<br>Avoid driving and activities that require alertness |
| Phenytoin sodium | Drowsiness, ataxia<br>Nystagmus<br>Blurred vision<br>Hirsutism<br>Lethargy<br>GI upset<br>Gingival hypertrophy | Give oral medication with at least 1/2 glass of water, or with meals to minimize GI irritation<br>Inform client that red-brown or pink discoloration of sweat and urine may occur<br>IV administration may lead to cardiac arrest–have resuscitation equipment at hand<br>Never mix with any other drug or dextrose IV<br>Instruct in oral hygiene<br>Increase vitamin D intake and exposure to sunlight may be necessary with long-term use<br>Alcohol increases serum levels<br>Increased risk toxicity older adults |
| Phenobarbital | Drowsiness, rash<br>GI upset<br>Initially constricts pupils<br>Respiratory depression<br>Ataxia | Monitor vital signs–resuscitation equipment should be available if given IV<br>Drowsiness diminishes after initial weeks of therapy<br>Don't take alcohol or perform hazardous activities<br>Nystagmus may indicate early toxicity<br>Sudden discontinuation may lead to withdrawal<br>Tolerance and dependence result from long-term use<br>Folic acid supplements are indicated for long-term use<br>Decreased cognitive function older adults |
| Primidone | Drowsiness<br>Ataxia, diplopia<br>Nausea and vomiting | Don't discontinue use abruptly<br>Full therapeutic response may take 2 weeks<br>Shake liquid suspension well<br>Take with food if experiencing GI distress<br>Decreased cognitive function older adults |
| Magnesium sulfate | Flushing<br>Sweating<br>Extreme thirst<br>Hypotension<br>Sedation, confusion | Monitor intake and output<br>Before each dose, knee jerks should be tested<br>Vital signs should be monitored often during parenteral administration<br>Used for pregnancy-induced hypertension |
| Valproic acid | Sedation<br>Tremor, ataxia<br>Nausea, vomiting<br>Prolonged bleeding time | Agent of choice in many seizure disorders of young children<br>Do not take with carbonated beverage<br>Take with food<br>Monitor platelets, bleeding time, and liver function tests |

*(continued)*

| ANTICONVULSANT MEDICATIONS (cont'd) | | |
|---|---|---|
| **MEDICATION** | **SIDE EFFECTS** | **NURSING CONSIDERATIONS** |
| Carbamazepine | Myelosuppression<br>Dizziness, drowsiness<br>Ataxia<br>Diplopia, rash | Monitor intake and output<br>Supervise ambulation<br>Monitor CBC<br>Take with meals<br>Wear protective clothing due to photosensitivity<br>Multiple drug interactions |
| Ethosuximide | GI symptoms<br>Drowsiness<br>Ataxia, dizziness | Monitor for behavioral changes<br>Monitor weight weekly |
| Gabapentin | Increased appetite<br>Ataxia<br>Irritability<br>Dizziness<br>Fatigue | Monitor weight and behavioral changes.<br>Can also be used to treat postherpetic neuralgia |
| Lamotrigine | Diplopia<br>Headaches<br>Dizziness<br>Drowsiness<br>Ataxia<br>Nausea, vomiting<br>Life-threatening rash when<br>  given with valproic acid | Take divided doses with meals or just<br>  afterward to decrease adverse effects |
| Topiramate | Ataxia<br>Confusion<br>Dizziness<br>Fatigue<br>Vision problems | Adjunct therapy for intractable partial seizures<br>Increased risk for renal calculi<br>Stop drug immediately if eye problems—could<br>  lead to permanent damage |
| **Action** | Decreases flow of calcium and sodium across neuronal membranes | |
| **Indications** | Partial seizures: Luminal, Mysoline, Tegretol, Neurontin, Lamictal<br>Generalized tonic-clonic seizures: Luminal, Mysoline, Tegretol<br>Absence seizures: Zarontin<br>Status epilepticus: Valium, Ativan, Dilantin | |
| **Side effects** | Cardiovascular depression<br>Respiratory depression<br>Agranulocytosis<br>Aplastic anemia | |
| **Nursing considerations** | Tolerance develops with long-term use<br>Don't discontinue abruptly<br>Caution with use of medications that lower seizure threshold (MAO inhibitors)<br>Barbiturates and benzodiazepines also used as anticonvulsants<br>Increased risk adverse reactions older adults | |

## ANTIDEPRESSANTS: MONOAMINE OXIDASE (MAO) INHIBITORS

| | |
|---|---|
| Examples | Phenelzine sulfate, isocarboxazid, tranylcypromine |
| Actions | Interferes with monoamine oxidase, allowing for increased concentration of neurotransmitters (epinephrine, norepinephrine, serotonin) in synaptic space, causing stabilization of mood |
| Indications | Depression<br>Chronic pain syndromes |
| Side effects | Hypertensive crisis when taken with foods containing tyramine (aged cheese, bologna, pepperoni, salami, figs, bananas, raisins, beer, Chianti red wine) or OTC meds containing ephedrine, pseudoephedrine<br>Photosensitivity<br>Weight gain<br>Sexual dysfunction<br>Orthostatic hypotension |
| Nursing considerations | Not first-line drugs for depression<br>Should not be taken with SSRIs<br>Administer antihypertensive medications with caution<br>Avoid use of other CNS depressants, including alcohol<br>Discontinue 10 days before general anesthesia<br>Medications lower seizure threshold<br>Monitor for urinary retention |

## ANTIDEPRESSANTS: SELECTIVE REUPTAKE INHIBITORS

| | |
|---|---|
| Example | SSRIs: Fluoxetine, Paroxetine, Sertraline hydrochloride<br>SNRIs: Citalopram, Venlafaxine, Duloxetine |
| Actions | Inhibits CNS neuronal uptake of serotonin; acts as stimulant counteracting depression and increasing motivation |
| Indications | Depression<br>Obsessive-compulsive disorders<br>Obesity<br>Bulimia |
| Side effects | Headache, dizziness<br>Nervousness<br>Insomnia, drowsiness<br>Anxiety<br>Tremor<br>Dry mouth<br>GI upset<br>Taste changes<br>Sweating<br>Rash<br>URI<br>Painful menstruation<br>Sexual dysfunction<br>Weight gain |
| Nursing considerations | Take in AM<br>Takes 4 weeks for full effect<br>Monitor weight<br>Good mouth care<br>Do not administer with MAOIs–risk of serotonin syndrome<br>Monitor for thrombocytopenia, leukopenia, and anemia |

| ANTIDEPRESSANTS: TRICYCLICS | |
|---|---|
| Examples | Amitriptyline <br> Imipramine |
| Actions | Inhibits presynaptic reuptake of neurotransmitters norepinephrine and serotonin; anticholinergic action at CNS and peripheral receptors |
| Indications | Depression <br> Obstructive sleep apnea |
| Side effects | Sedation <br> Anticholinergic effects (dry mouth, blurred vision) <br> Confusion (especially in elderly) <br> Photosensitivity <br> Disturbed concentration <br> Orthostatic hypotension <br> Bone marrow depression <br> Urinary retention |
| Nursing considerations | Therapeutic effect in 1–3 weeks; maximum response in 6–9 weeks <br> May be administered in daily dose at night to promote sleep and decrease side effects during the day <br> Orthostatic hypotension precautions <br> Instruct client that side effects will decrease over time <br> Sugarless lozenges for dry mouth <br> Do not abruptly stop taking medication (headache, vertigo, nightmares, malaise, weight change) <br> Avoid alcohol, sleep-inducing drugs, OTC drugs <br> Avoid exposure to sunlight, wear sunscreen <br> Older adults: strong anticholinergic and sedation effects |

| ANTIDEPRESSANTS: HETEROCYCLICS | |
|---|---|
| Examples | Bupropion <br> Trazodone |
| Actions | Does not inhibit MAO; has some anticholinergic and sedative effects; alters effects of serotonin on CNS |
| Indications | Treatment of depression and smoking cessation |
| Side effects | Dry mouth <br> Nausea <br> Bupropion–insomnia and agitation <br> Trazodone–sedation, orthostatic hypotension |
| Nursing considerations | May require gradual reduction before stopping <br> Avoid use with alcohol, other CNS depressants for up to 1 week after end of therapy |

| ANTIDEPRESSANT MEDICATIONS OVERVIEW | | |
|---|---|---|
| **MEDICATION** | **SIDE EFFECTS** | **NURSING CONSIDERATIONS** |
| **Monoamine oxidase inhibitors (MAOIs)** Isocarboxazid Tranylcypromine sulfate Phenelzine sulfate | Postural hypotension If foods with tyramine ingested, can have hypertensive crisis: headache, sweating, palpitations, stiff neck, intracranial hemorrhage Potentiates alcohol and other medications | Inhibits monoamine oxidase enzyme, preventing destruction of norepinephrine, epinephrine, and serotonin Avoid foods with tyramine—aged cheese, liver, yogurt, herring, yeast, beer, wine, sour cream, pickled products Avoid caffeine, antihistamines, amphetamines Takes 3-4 weeks to work Avoid tricyclics until 3 weeks after stopping MAO inhibitors Monitor vital signs Sunblock required |
| **Tricyclics** Amitriptyline hydrochloride Imipramine Desipramine hydrochloride Doxepin Nortriptyline | Sedation/drowsiness, especially with Elavil Blurred vision, dry mouth, diaphoresis Postural hypotension, palpitations Nausea, vomiting Constipation, urinary retention Increased appetite | Increases brain amine levels Suicide risk high after 10-14 days because of increased energy Monitor vital signs Sunblock required Increase fluid intake Take dose at bedtime (sedative effect) Use sugarless candy or gum for dry mouth Delay of 2-6 weeks before noticeable effects |
| **Selective reuptake inhibitors** **SSRIs** Fluoxetine Paroxetine Sertraline hydrochloride **SNRIs** Citalopram Venlafaxine | Palpitations, bradycardia Nausea, vomiting, diarrhea or constipation, increased or constipation, increased or decreased appetite Urinary retention Nervousness, insomnia | Decreases neuronal uptake of serotonin Take in AM to avoid insomnia Takes at least 4 weeks to work Can potentiate effect of digoxin, coumadin, and Valium Used for anorexia |
| **Heterocyclics** Bupropion Trazodone | Dry mouth Nausea | May require gradual reduction before stopping Avoid use with alcohol, other CNS depressants for up to 1 week after end of therapy |
| **Herbals** St. John's Wort | Dizziness, hypertension, allergic skin reaction, phototoxicity | Avoid use of St. John's wort and MAOI within 2 weeks of each other Do not use alcohol Contraindicated in pregnancy Avoid exposure to sun and use sunscreen Discontinue 1 to 2 weeks before surgery |
| **Herbal interactions** | St. John's wort—interacts with SSRIs; do not take within 2 weeks of MAOI Ginseng may potentiate MAOIs Avoid Ma huang or ephedra with MAOIs Kava kava should not be combined with benzodiazepines or opioids due to increased sedation Increase use of Brewer's yeast with MAOIs can increase blood pressure | |

| ANTIDIABETIC AGENTS/INSULIN | | | | | |
|---|---|---|---|---|---|
| **INSULIN TYPES** | **ONSET OF ACTION** | **PEAK ACTION** | **DURATION OF ACTION** | **TIME OF ADVERSE REACTION** | **CHARACTERISTICS** |
| **Rapid-acting**<br>Lispro<br>Aspart<br>Glulisine | 15–30 min<br>10–20 min<br>10–15 min | 1 h<br>40–50 min<br>1–1.5 h | 3 h<br>4–6 h<br>3–5 h | Midmorning:<br>trembling, weakness | Client should eat within 5–15 min after injection; also used in insulin pumps |
| **Short-acting**<br>Regular | 30–60 min | 2–3 h | 4–6 h | Midmorning, midafternoon: weakness, fatigue | Clear solution; given 20–30 min before meal; can be alone or with other insulins |
| **Intermediate-acting**<br>Isophane<br>Insulin determir | 2–4 h | 6–12 h<br>12–24 h | 16–20 h<br>varies | Early evening: weakness, fatigue | White and cloudy solution; can be given after meals |
| **Very long-acting**<br>Glargine | 1 h | Continuous (no peak) | 24 h | | Maintains blood glucose levels regardless of meals; cannot be mixed with other insulins; given at bedtime |
| **Action** | Reduces blood glucose levels by increasing glucose transport across cell membranes; enhances conversion of glucose to glycogen | | | | |
| **Indications** | Type 1 diabetes; type 2 diabetes not responding to oral hypoglycemic agents; gestational diabetes not responding to diet | | | | |
| **Side effects** | Hypoglycemia | | | | |
| **Nursing considerations** | Teach client to rotate sites to prevent lipohypertrophy, fibrofatty masses at injection sites; do not inject into these masses<br>Only regular insulin can be given IV; all can be given SQ | | | | |
| **Herbal interactions** | Bee pollen, ginkgo biloba, glucosamine may increase blood glucose<br>Basil, bay leaf, chromium, echinacea, garlic, ginseng may decrease blood glucose | | | | |

| ANTIDIABETIC MEDICATIONS: ORAL HYPOGLYCEMIC AGENTS | | |
| --- | --- | --- |
| **MEDICATION** | **SIDE EFFECTS** | **NURSING CONSIDERATIONS** |
| **Sulfonylureas**<br>Glimepiride<br>Glipizide<br>Glyburide | GI symptoms and dermatologic reactions | Only used if some pancreas beta-cell function<br>Stimulates release of insulin from pancreas<br>Many drugs can potentiate or interfere with actions<br>Take with food if GI upset occurs |
| **Biguanides**<br>Metformin | Nausea<br>Diarrhea<br>Abdominal discomfort | No effect on pancreatic beta cells; decreases glucose production by liver<br>Not given if renal impairment<br>Can cause lactic acidosis<br>Avoid alcohol<br>Do not give with alpha-glucodiase inhibitors |
| **Alpha glucosidase inhibitors**<br>Acarbose<br>Miglitol | Abdominal discomfort<br>Diarrhea<br>Flatulence | Delays digestion of carbohydrates<br>Must be taken immediately before a meal<br>Can be taken alone or with other agents |
| **Thiazolidinediones**<br>Rosiglitazone<br>Pioglitazone | Infection<br>Headache<br>Pain<br>Rare cases of liver failure | Decreases insulin resistance and inhibits gluconeogenesis<br>Regularly scheduled liver-function studies<br>Can cause resumption of ovulation in perimenopause |
| **Meglitinides**<br>Repaglinide | Hypoglycemia<br>GI disturbances<br>URIs<br>Back pain<br>Headache | Increases pancreatic insulin release<br>Medication should not be taken if meal skipped |
| **Gliptins**<br>Sitagliptin | Upper respiratory infections<br>Hypoglycemia | Enhances action of incretin hormones |
| **Incretin mimetics**<br>Exanatide | GI upset<br>Hypoglycemia<br>Pancreatitis | Interacts with many medications<br>Administer 1 hour before meals |
| **Indications** | Type 2 diabetes | |
| **Nursing considerations** | Monitor serum glucose levels<br>Avoid alcohol<br>Teaching for disease: dietary control, symptoms of hypoglycemia and hyperglycemia<br>Good skin care | |
| **Herbal interactions** | Bee pollen, ginkgo biloba, glucosamine may increase blood glucose<br>Basil, bay leaf, chromium, echinacea, garlic, ginseng may decrease blood glucose | |

| MEDICATIONS THAT REVERSE HYPOGLYCEMIA | | |
|---|---|---|
| **MEDICATION** | **SIDE EFFECTS** | **NURSING CONSIDERATIONS** |
| Glucagon | Nausea, vomiting | Given SQ or IM, onset is 8–10 min with duration of 12–27 min<br>Should be part of emergency supplies for diabetics<br>May repeat in 15 min if needed |
| **Action** | Hormone produced by alpha cells of the pancreas to simulate the liver to change glycogen to glucose | |
| **Indications** | Acute management of severe hypoglycemia | |
| **Side effects** | Hypotension<br>Bronchospasm<br>Dizziness | |
| **Nursing considerations** | May repeat in 15 minutes if needed<br>IV glucose must be given if client fails to respond<br>Arouse clients from coma as quickly as possible and give carbohydrates orally to prevent secondary hypoglycemic reactions | |

| ANTIDIARRHEAL MEDICATIONS | | |
|---|---|---|
| **MEDICATION** | **SIDE EFFECTS** | **NURSING CONSIDERATIONS** |
| Bismuth subsalicylate | Darkening of stools and tongue<br>Constipation | Give 2 h before or 3 h after other meds to prevent impaired absorption<br>Encourage fluids<br>Take after each loose stool until diarrhea controlled<br>Notify health care provider if diarrhea not controlled in 48 h<br>Absorbs irritants and soothes intestinal muscle<br>Do not administer for more than 2 days in presence of fever or in clients less than 3 years of age<br>Monitor for salicylate toxicity<br>Use cautiously if already taking aspirin<br>Avoid use before x-rays (is radiopaque) |
| Diphenoxylate hydrochloride and atropine sulfate | Sedation<br>Dizziness<br>Tachycardia<br>Dry mouth<br>Paralytic ileus | Onset 45-60 min<br>Monitor fluid and electrolytes<br>Increases intestinal tone and decreases peristalsis<br>May potentiate action of barbiturates, depressants |
| Ioperamide | Drowsiness<br>Constipation | Monitor children closely for CNS effects |
| Opium alkaloids | Narcotic dependence, nausea | Acts on smooth muscle to increase tone<br>Administer with glass of water<br>Discontinue as soon as stools are controlled |
| **Action** | Absorbs water, gas, toxins, irritants, and nutrients in bowel; slows peristalsis; increases tone of smooth muscles and sphincters | |
| **Indications** | Diarrhea | |
| **Side effects** | Constipation, fecal impaction<br>Anticholinergic effects | |
| **Nursing considerations** | Not used with abdominal pain of unknown origin<br>Monitor for urinary retention | |

| ANTIEMETIC MEDICATIONS | | |
|---|---|---|
| **MEDICATION** | **SIDE EFFECTS** | **NURSING CONSIDERATIONS** |
| Trimethobenzamide HCl | Drowsiness<br>Headache | Give IM deep into upper outer quadrant of gluteal muscle to reduce pain and irritation |
| Prochlorperazine dimaleate | Drowsiness<br>Orthostatic hypotension<br>Diplopia, photosensitivity | Check CBC and liver function with prolonged use<br>Wear protective clothing when exposed to sunlight |
| Ondansetron | Headache, sedation<br>Diarrhea, constipation<br>Transient elevations in liver enzymes | New class of antiemetics—serotonin receptor antagonist<br>Administer 30 min prior to chemotherapy |
| Thiethylperazine maleate | Transient leukopenia<br>Extrapyramidal symptoms<br>Orthostatic hypotension<br>Blurred vision, photosensitivity<br>Dry mouth<br>Constipation, urine retention | Give deep IM<br>Stay in bed for 1 h after receiving drug<br>Wear protective clothing when exposed to sunlight |
| Metoclopramide | Restlessness, anxiety, drowsiness<br>Extrapyramidal symptoms<br>Dystonic reactions | Monitor BP<br>Avoid activities requiring mental alertness<br>Take before meals<br>Used with tube feeding to decrease residual and risk of aspiration<br>Administer 30 min prior to chemotherapy |
| Meclizine | Drowsiness, dry mouth<br>Blurred vision<br>Excitation, restlessness | Contraindicated with glaucoma<br>Avoid activities requiring mental alertness |
| Dimenhydrinate | Drowsiness<br>Palpitations, hypotension<br>Blurred vision | Avoid activities requiring mental alertness |
| Promethazine | Drowsiness<br>Dizziness<br>Constipation<br>Urinary retention<br>Dry mouth | If used for motion sickness, take $\frac{1}{2}$ to 1 hour before traveling; avoid activities requiring alertness; avoid alcohol, other CNS depressants |
| Droperidol | Seizures<br>Arrhythmias<br>Hypotension<br>Tachycardia | Often used either IV or IM in ambulatory care settings; observe for extrapyramidal symptoms (dystonia, extended neck, flexed arms, tremor, restlessness, hyperactivity, anxiety), which can be reversed with anticholinergics |

*(continued)*

## ANTIEMETIC MEDICATIONS (*cont'd*)

| MEDICATION | SIDE EFFECTS |
|---|---|
| Action | Blocks effect of dopamine in chemoreceptor trigger zone; increases GI motility |
| Indications | Nausea and vomiting caused by surgery, chemotherapy, radiation sickness, uremia |
| Side effects | Drowsiness, sedation<br>Anticholinergic effects |
| Nursing considerations | When used for viral infections may cause Reye's syndrome in clients less than 21 years old<br>Phenothiazine medications are also used as antiemetics |
| Herbals | Ginger—used to treat minor heartburn, nausea, vomiting; may increase risk of bleeding if take with anticoagulants, antiplatelets, thrombolytic medication; instruct to stop medication if easily bruised or other signs of bleeding noted, report to health care provider; not approved for morning sickness during pregnancy |

## ANTIFUNGAL MEDICATIONS

| MEDICATION | SIDE EFFECTS | NURSING CONSIDERATIONS |
|---|---|---|
| Amphotericin B | IV: nicknamed "amphoterrible"<br>GI upset<br>Hypokalemia-induced muscle pain<br>CNS disturbances in vision, hearing<br>Peripheral neuritis<br>Seizures<br>Hematological, renal, cardiac, hepatic abnormalities<br>Skin irritation and thrombosis if IV infiltrates | Refrigerate medication and protect from sunlight<br>Monitor vital signs; report febrile reaction or any change in function, especially nervous system dysfunction<br>Check for hypokalemia<br>Meticulous care and observation of injection site |
| Nystatin | Mild GI distress<br>Hypersensitivity | Discontinue if redness, swelling, irritation occurs<br>Instruct client in good oral, vaginal, skin hygiene |
| Flucanozal | Nausea, vomiting<br>Diarrhea<br>Elevated liver enzymes | Drug excreted unchanged by kidneys; dosage reduced if creatine clearance is altered due to renal failure<br>Administer after hemodialysis |
| Metronidazole | Headaches, vaginitis, nausea, flu-like symptoms (systemic use) | Reduce dosage hepatic disease<br>Monitor CBC, LFTs, cultures<br>Give tablet with food or milk |
| **Action** | Impairs cell membrane of fungus, causing increased permeability | |
| **Indications** | Systemic fungal infections (e.g., candidiasis, oral thrush, histoplasmosis) | |
| **Side effects** | Hepatotoxicity<br>Thrombocytopenia<br>Leukopenia<br>Pruritus | |
| **Nursing considerations** | Administer with food to decrease GI upset<br>Small, frequent meals<br>Check hepatic function<br>Teach client to take full course of medication, may be prescribed for prolonged period | |

| ANTIGOUT MEDICATIONS | | |
|---|---|---|
| **MEDICATION** | **SIDE EFFECTS** | **NURSING CONSIDERATIONS** |
| Colchicine | GI upset<br>Agranulocytosis<br>Peripheral neuritis | Analgesic, anti-inflammatory<br>Give with meals<br>Check CBC, I and O<br>For acute gout in combination<br>  with NSAIDs |
| Probenecid | Nausea, constipation<br>Skin rash | For chronic gout<br>Reduces uric acid<br>Check BUN, renal function tests<br>Encourage fluids<br>Give with milk, food, antacids<br>Alkaline urine helps prevent renal<br>  stones |
| Allopurinol | GI upset<br>Headache, dizziness, drowsiness | Blocks formation of uric acid<br>Encourage fluids<br>Check I and O<br>Check CBC and renal function<br>  tests<br>Give with meals<br>Alkaline urine helps prevent renal<br>  stones<br>Avoid ASA because it inactivates<br>  drug |
| **Action** | Decreases production and reabsorption of uric acid | |
| **Indications** | Gout<br>Uric acid stone formation | |
| **Side effects** | Aplastic anemia<br>Agranulocytosis<br>Renal calculi<br>GI irritation | |
| **Nursing<br>  considerations** | Monitor for renal calculi | |

| ANTIHISTAMINE MEDICATIONS | | |
|---|---|---|
| **MEDICATION** | **SIDE EFFECTS** | **NURSING CONSIDERATIONS** |
| Chlorpheniramine maleate | Drowsiness, dry mouth | Most effective if taken before onset of symptoms |
| Diphenhydramine HCl | Drowsiness<br>Nausea, dry mouth<br>Photosensitivity | Don't combine with alcoholic beverages<br>Give with food<br>Use sunscreen<br>Older adults: greater risk of confusion and sedation |
| Promethazine HCl | Agranulocytosis<br>Drowsiness, dry mouth<br>Photosensitivity | Give with food<br>Use sunscreen |
| Loratadine<br>Cetirizine<br>Fexofenadine | Drowsiness | Reduce dose or give every other day for clients with renal or hepatic dysfunction |
| **Action** | Blocks the effects of histamine at peripheral $H_1$ receptor sites; anticholinergic, antipruritic effects | |
| **Indications** | Allergic rhinitis<br>Allergic reactions<br>Chronic idiopathic urticaria | |
| **Side effects** | Depression<br>Nightmares<br>Sedation<br>Dry mouth<br>GI upset<br>Bronchospasm<br>Alopecia | |
| **Nursing considerations** | Administer with food<br>Good mouth care, sugarless lozenges for dry mouth<br>Good skin care<br>Use caution when performing tasks requiring alertness (e.g., driving car)<br>Avoid alcohol | |

| ANTILIPEMIC AGENTS | | |
|---|---|---|
| **MEDICATION** | **SIDE EFFECTS** | **NURSING CONSIDERATIONS** |
| **Bile acid sequestrants** Cholestyramine Colestipol HMG-COA reductase inhibitors Folic acid derivatives Nicotinic acid | Constipation Rash Fat-soluble vitamin deficiency Abdominal pain and bloating | Increases loss of bile acid in feces; decreases cholesterol Sprinkle powder on noncarbonated beverage or wet food, let stand 2 min, then stir slowly Administer 1 h before or 4–6 h after other meds to avoid blocking absorption Instruct client to report constipation immediately |
| **HMG-CoA reductase inhibitors (statins)** Lovostatin Pravastatin Simvastatin Atorvastatin Fluvastatin Rosuvastatin | Myopathy Increased liver enyme levels | Decreases LDL cholesterol levels; causes peripheral vasodilation Take with food; absorption is reduced by 30% on an empty stomach; avoid alcohol Contact health care provider if unexplained muscle pain, especially with fever or malaise Take at night Give with caution with liver function |
| **Nicotinic acid** Niacin | Flushing Hyperglycemia Gout Upper GI distress Liver damage | Decreases total cholesterol, LDL, triglycerides, increases HDL Flushing will occur several hours after med is taken, will decrease over 2 wk Also used for pellagra and peripheral vascular disease Avoid alcohol |
| **Folic acid derivatives** Fenofibrate Gemfibrozil | Abdominal pain Increased risk gallbladder disease Myalgia and swollen joints | Decreases total cholesterol, VLDL, and triglycerides Administer before meals Instruct clients to notify health care provider if muscle pain occurs |
| **Action** | Inhibits cholesterol and triglyceride synthesis; decreases serum cholesterol and LDLs | |
| **Indications** | Elevated total and LDL cholesterol Primary hypercholesterolemia Reduce incidence of cardiovascular disease | |
| **Side effects** | Varies with medication | |
| **Nursing considerations** | Medication should be used with dietary measures, physical activity, and cessation of tobacco use Lipids should be monitored every 6 wk until normal, then every 4–6 mo | |
| **Herbals used to lower cholesterol** | Flax or flax seed—decreases the absorption of other medications Garlic—increases the effects of anticoagulants; increases the hypoglycemic effects of insulin Green tea—produces a stimulant effect with the tea contains caffeine Soy | |

| ANTIHYPERTENSIVES: ACE INHIBITORS (ANGIOTENSIN–CONVERTING ENZYME) | | |
|---|---|---|
| **Example** | Captopril | Fosinopril |
| | Enalapril | Quinapril |
| | Lisinopril | Ramipril |
| | Benazepril | |
| **Actions** | Blocks ACE in lungs from converting angiotensin I to angiotensin II (powerful vasoconstrictor); causes decreased BP, decreased aldosterone secretion, sodium and fluid loss | |
| **Indications** | Hypertension CHF | |
| **Side effects** | Gastric irritation, peptic ulcer, orthostatic hypotension Tachycardia Myocardial infarction Proteinuria Rash, pruritis Persistent dry nonproductive cough Peripheral edema | |
| **Nursing considerations** | Decreased absorption if taken with food—give 1 h ac or 2 h pc Small, frequent meals Frequent mouth care Change position slowly Can be used with thiazide diuretics | |

| ANTIHYPERTENSIVES: BETA-ADRENERGIC BLOCKERS | | |
|---|---|---|
| **Examples** | Atenolol | Acebutolol |
| | Nadolol | Carvedilol |
| | Propranolol | Pindolol |
| | Metoprolol | |
| **Actions** | Blocks beta-adrenergic receptors in heart; decreases excitability of heart; reduces cardiac workload and oxygen consumption; decreases release of renin; lowers blood pressure by reducing CNS stimuli | |
| **Indications** | Hypertension (used with diuretics) Angina Supraventricular tachycardia Prevent recurrent MI Migraine headache (propranolol) Stage fright (propranolol) Heart failure | |
| **Side effects** | Gastric pain Bradycardia/tachycardia Acute severe heart failure Cardiac dysrhythmias Impotence Decreased exercise tolerance Nightmares, depression Dizziness Bronchospasm (nonselective beta blockers) | |
| **Nursing considerations** | Do not discontinue abruptly, taper gradually over 2 weeks Take with meals Provide rest periods For diabetic clients, blocks normal signs of hypoglycemia (sweating, tachycardia); monitor blood glucose Medications have antianginal and antiarrhythmic actions | |

| ANTIHYPERTENSIVES: CALCIUM-CHANNEL BLOCKERS | |
|---|---|
| Examples | Nifedipine<br>Verapamil<br>Diltiazem<br>Amlodipine<br>Felodipine |
| Actions | Inhibits movement of calcium ions across membrane of cardiac and arterial muscle cells; results in slowed impulse conduction, depression of myocardial contractility, dilation of coronary arteries; decreases cardiac workload and energy consumption, increases oxygenation of myocardial cells |
| Indications | Angina<br>Hypertension<br>Dysrhythmias<br>Interstitial cystitis<br>Migraines |
| Side effects | Dizziness<br>Headache<br>Nervousness<br>Peripheral edema<br>Angina<br>Bradycardia<br>AV block<br>Flushing, rash<br>Impotence |
| Nursing considerations | Monitor vital signs<br>Do not chew or divide sustained-release tablets<br>Medications also have antianginal actions<br>Contraindicated in heart block<br>Contact health care provider if blood pressure less than 90/60<br>Instruct client to avoid grapefruit juice (verapamil)<br>Monitor for signs of heart failure |

| ANTIHYPERTENSIVES: ANGIOTENSIN II RECEPTOR ANTAGONISTS<br>(ACE RECEPTOR BLOCKERS/ARBS) | |
|---|---|
| Examples | Candesartan<br>Eprosartan<br>Irbesartan<br>Losartan<br>Valsartan |
| Indications | Hypertension<br>Heart failure<br>Diabetic nephropathy<br>Myocardial infarction<br>Stroke prevention |
| Side effects | Angioedema<br>Renal failure<br>Orthostatic hypotension |
| Nursing considerations | Instruct client about position changes<br>Monitor for edema<br>Instruct client to notify health care provider if edema occurs |

| ANTIHYPERTENSIVES: ALPHA–1 ADRENERGIC BLOCKERS | |
|---|---|
| **Examples** | Doxazosin<br>Prazosin<br>Terazosin |
| **Actions** | Selective blockade of alpha-1 adrenergic receptors in peripheral blood vessels |
| **Indications** | Hypertension<br>Benign prostatic hypertrophy<br>Pheochromocytoma<br>Raynaud's disease |
| **Side effects** | Orthostatic hypotension<br>Reflex tachycardia<br>Nasal congestion<br>Impotence |
| **Nursing considerations** | Administer first dose at bedtime to avoid fainting<br>Change positions slowly to prevent orthostatic hypotension<br>Monitor BP, weight, BUN/creatinine, edema |

| ANTIHYPERTENSIVES: DIRECT–ACTING VASODILATORS | |
|---|---|
| **Examples** | Hydralazine<br>Minoxidil |
| **Actions** | Relaxes smooth muscle of blood vessels, lowering peripheral resistance |
| **Indications** | Hypertension |
| **Side effects** | Same as centrally acting alpha adrenergics |
| **Nursing consideratons** | Same as centrally acting alpha adrenergics |

| ANTIHYPERTENSIVE MEDICATIONS OVERVIEW | | |
|---|---|---|
| **MEDICATION** | **SIDE EFFECTS** | **NURSING CONSIDERATIONS** |
| Methyldopa | Drowsiness, dizziness, bradycardia, hemolytic anemia, fever, orthostatic hypotension | Monitor CBC<br>Monitor liver function<br>Take at hs to minimize daytime drowsiness<br>Change position slowly |
| Clonidine | Drowsiness, dizziness<br>Dry mouth, headache<br>Dermatitis<br>Severe rebound hypertension | Don't discontinue abruptly<br>Apply patch to nonhairy area<br>  (upper outer arm, anterior chest) |
| Atenolol | Bradycardia<br>Hypotension<br>Bronchospasm | Once-a-day dose increases compliance<br>Check apical pulse; if <60 bpm hold drug and<br>  call health care provider<br>Don't discontinue abruptly<br>Masks signs of shock and hypoglycemia |
| Metoprolol | Bradycardia, hypotension, heart failure, depression | Give with meals<br>Teach client to check pulse before each dose;<br>  take apical pulse before administration<br>Withhold if pulse <60 bpm |
| Nadolol | Bradycardia, hypotension, heart failure | Teach client to check pulse before each dose;<br>  check apical pulse before administering<br>Withhold if pulse <60 bpm<br>Don't discontinue abruptly |
| Hydralazine | Headache, palpitations, edema, tachycardia, lupus erythematosus-like syndrome | Give with meals<br>Observe mental status<br>Check for weight gain, edema |
| Minoxidil | Tachycardia, angina pectoris, edema, increase in body hair | Teach client to check pulse; check apical<br>  pulse before administration<br>Monitor I and O, weight |
| Captopril<br>Enalapril<br>Lisinopril | Dizziness<br>Orthostatic hypotension | Report swelling of face, lightheadedness<br>ACE-inhibitor medication |
| Propranolol | Weakness<br>Hypotension<br>Bronchospasm<br>Bradycardia<br>Depression | Beta blocker: blocks sympathetic<br>  impulses to heart<br>Client takes pulse at home before each dose<br>Dosage should be reduced gradually before<br>  discontinued |
| Nifedipine<br>Verapamil<br>Diltiazem | Hypotension<br>Dizziness<br>GI distress<br>Liver dysfunction<br>Jitteriness | Calcium-channel blocker: reduces workload<br>  of left ventricle<br>Coronary vasodilator; monitor blood pressure<br>  during dosage adjustments<br>Assist with ambulation at start of therapy |
| **Herbal interaction** | Ma-huang (ephedra) decreases effect of antihypertensive drugs<br>Black cohosh increases hypotensive effects of antihypertensives<br>Goldenseal counteracts effects of antihypertensives | |

| MEDICATIONS FOR BIPOLAR DISORDER | | |
|---|---|---|
| **MEDICATION** | **SIDE EFFECTS** | **NURSING CONSIDERATIONS** |
| Lithium | Dizziness<br>Headache<br>Impaired vision<br>Fine hand tremors<br>Reversible leukocytosis | Use for control of manic episodes in the syndrome of manic-depressive psychosis; mood stabilizer<br>Blood levels must be monitored frequently<br>GI symptoms can be reduced if taken with meals<br>Therapeutic effects preceded by lag of 1-2 weeks<br>Signs of intoxication—vomiting, diarrhea, drowsiness, muscular weakness, ataxia<br>Dosage is usually halved during depressive stages of illness<br>Normal blood target level = 1-1.5 mEq/L<br>Check serum levels 2-3 times weekly when started and monthly while on maintenance; serum levels should be drawn in AM prior to dose<br>Should have fluid intake of 2,500-3,000 ml/day and adequate salt intake |
| Carbamazepine | Dizziness, vertigo<br>Drowiness<br>Ataxia<br>CHF<br>Aplastic anemia, thrombocytopenia | Mood stablizer used with bipolar disorder<br>Traditionally used for seizures and trigeminal neuralgia<br>Obtain baseline urinalysis, BUN, liver function tests, CBC<br>Shake oral suspension well before measuring dose<br>When giving by NG tube, mix with equal volume of water, 0.9% NaCl or $D_5$ W, then flush with 100 ml after dose<br>Take with food<br>Drowsiness usually disappears in 3-4 days |
| Divalproex sodium | Sedation<br>Pancreatitis<br>Indigestion<br>Thrombocytopenia<br>Toxic hepatitis | Mood stablizers used with bipolar disorder<br>Traditionally used for seizures<br>Monitor liver function tests, platelet count before starting med and periodically after med<br>Teach client symptoms of liver dysfunction (e.g., malaise, fever, lethargy)<br>Monitor blood levels<br>Take with food or milk<br>Avoid hazardous activities |
| **Action** | Reduces amount of catecholamines released into synapse and increases reuptake of norepinephrine and serotonin from synaptic space; competes with $Na^+$ and $K^+$ transport in nerve and muscle cells | |
| **Indications** | Manic episodes | |
| **Side effects** | GI upset<br>Tremors<br>Polydipsia, polyuria | |
| **Nursing considerations** | Monitor serum levels carefully<br>Severe toxicity: exaggerated reflexes, seizures, coma, death | |

| ANTINEOPLASTIC AGENTS: ALKYLATING AGENTS | |
|---|---|
| Examples | Busulfan<br>Chlorambucil<br>Cisplatin platinol-AQ<br>Cyclophosphamide |
| Actions | Interferes with rapidly reproducing cell DNA |
| Indications | Leukemia<br>Multiple myeloma |
| Side effects | Bone marrow suppression<br>Nausea, vomiting<br>Stomatitis<br>Alopecia<br>Gonadal suppression<br>Renal toxicity (cisplatin)<br>Ototoxicity |
| Nursing considerations | Used with other chemotherapeutic agents<br>Check hematopoietic function weekly<br>Encourage fluids (10-12 glasses/day) |

| ANTINEOPLASTIC AGENTS: ANTIMETABOLITES | |
|---|---|
| Examples | Cytarabine<br>Fluorouracil<br>Pemetrexed<br>Mercaptopurine<br>Methotrexate |
| Actions | Closely resembles normal metabolites, "counterfeits" fool cells; cell division halted |
| Indications | Acute lymphatic leukemia<br>Rheumatoid arthritis<br>Psoriasis<br>Cancer of colon, breast, stomach, pancreas<br>Sickle cell anemia |
| Side effects | Nausea, vomiting<br>Diarrhea<br>Stomatitis and oral ulceration<br>Hepatic dysfunction<br>Bone marrow suppression<br>Renal dysfunction<br>Alopecia |
| Nursing considerations | Monitor hematopoietic function<br>Good mouth care<br>Small frequent feedings<br>Counsel about body image changes (alopecia); provide wig<br>Good skin care<br>Photosensitivity precautions<br>Infection control precautions |

| ANTINEOPLASTIC AGENTS: ANTITUMOR ANTIBIOTICS | |
|---|---|
| Examples | Bleomycin<br>Dactinomycin<br>Doxorubicin |
| Actions | Interferes with DNA and RNA synthesis |
| Indications | Hodgkin's disease<br>Non-Hodgkin's lymphoma<br>Leukemia<br>Many cancers |
| Side effects | Bone marrow depression<br>Nausea, vomiting<br>Alopecia<br>Stomatitis<br>Heart failure<br>Septic shock |
| Nursing considerations | Monitor closely for septicemic reactions<br>Monitor for manifestations of extravasation at injection site (severe pain or burning that lasts minutes to hours, redness after injection is completed, ulceration after 48 hours) |

| ANTINEOPLASTIC AGENTS: HORMONAL AGENTS | |
|---|---|
| Examples | Tamoxifen<br>Testosterone<br>Leuprolide<br>Testolactone |
| Actions | Tamoxifen–antiestrogen (competes with estrogen to bind at estrogen receptor sites on malignant cells)<br>Leuprolide–progestin (causes tumor cell regression by unknown mechanism)<br>Testolactone–androgen (used for palliation in advanced breast cancer) |
| Indications | Breast cancer |
| Side effects | Hypercalcemia<br>Jaundice<br>Increased appetite<br>Masculinization or feminization<br>Sodium and fluid retention<br>Nausea, vomiting<br>Hot flashes<br>Vaginal dryness |
| Nursing considerations | Same as antitumor antibiotics |

| ANTINEOPLASTIC AGENTS: VINCA ALKALOIDS | |
|---|---|
| **Examples** | Vinblastine<br>Vincristine |
| **Actions** | Interferes with cell division |
| **Indications** | Hodgkin's disease<br>Lymphoma<br>Cancers |
| **Side effects** | Bone marrow suppression (mild with VCR)<br>Neuropathies (VCR)<br>Stomatitis |
| **Nursing considerations** | Same as antitumor antibiotics |

| ANTINEOPLASTIC AGENTS: TOPOISOMERASE | |
|---|---|
| **Examples** | Irinotecan<br>Topotecan |
| **Actions** | Binds to enzyme that breaks the DNA strands |
| **Indications** | Ovary, lung, colon, and rectal cancers |
| **Side effects** | Bone marrow suppression<br>Diarrhea<br>Nausea, vomiting<br>Hepatotoxicity |

| ANTINEOPLASTIC AGENTS OVERVIEW | | |
|---|---|---|
| **MEDICATION** | **SIDE EFFECTS** | **NURSING CONSIDERATIONS** |
| **Alkylating Agents**<br>Busulfan | Bone marrow depression | Check CBC (applies to all drugs in this table)<br>Most chemotherapy causes stomatitis and requires extra fluids to flush system |
| Chlorambucil | Nausea, vomiting, bone marrow depression, sterility | Monitor for infection<br>Avoid IM injections when platelet count is low to minimize bleeding |
| Cyclophosphamide | Alopecia, bone marrow depression, hemorrhagic cystitis, dermatitis, hyperkalemia, hypoglycemia, amenorrhea | Report hematuria, force fluids<br>Monitor for infection<br>Give antiemetics |
| **Antimetabolites**<br>Fluorouracil | Nausea, stomatitis, GI ulceration, diarrhea, bone marrow depression, liver dysfunction, alopecia | Monitor for infection<br>Avoid extravasation |
| Methotrexate | Oral and GI ulceration, liver damage, bone marrow depression, stomatitis, alopecia, bloody diarrhea, fatigue | Good mouth care, avoid alcohol<br>Monitor hepatic and renal function tests |
| Mercaptopurine | Liver damage, bone marrow depression, infection, alopecia, abdominal bleeding | Check liver function tests |

*(continued)*

| ANTINEOPLASTIC AGENTS OVERVIEW (cont'd) | | |
|---|---|---|
| Cytarabine | Hematologic abnormalities, nausea, vomiting, rash, weight loss | Force fluids<br>Good oral hygiene |
| Hydroxyurea | Bone marrow depression, GI symptoms, rash | Teach client to report toxic GI symptoms promptly |
| **Antibiotic Antineoplastics**<br>Doxorubicin | Red urine, nausea, vomiting, stomatitis, alopecia, cardiotoxicity, blisters, bone marrow depression | Check EKG, avoid IV infiltration<br>Monitor vital signs closely<br>Good mouth care |
| Bleomycin | Nausea, vomiting, alopecia, edema of hands, pulmonary fibrosis, fever, bone marrow depression | Observe for pulmonary complications, treat fever with acetaminophen<br>Check breath sounds frequently |
| Dactinomycin | Nausea, bone marrow depression | Give antiemetic before administration |
| **Vinca Alkaloids**<br>Vinblastine | Nausea, vomiting, stomatitis, alopecia, loss of reflexes, bone marrow depression | Avoid IV infiltration and extravasation<br>Give antiemetic before administration<br>Acute bronchospasm can occur if given IV<br>Zyloprim given to increase excretion and decrease buildup of urates (uric acid) |
| Vincristine | Peripheral neuritis, loss of reflexes, bone marrow depression, alopecia, GI symptoms | Avoid IV infiltration and extravasation<br>Check reflexes, motor and sensory function<br>Allopurinol given to increase excretion and decrease buildup of urates (uric acid) |
| **Hormonal Agents**<br>Tamoxifen | Transient fall in WBC or platelets<br>Hypercalcemia, bone pain | Check CBC<br>Monitor serum calcium<br>Nonsteroidal antiestrogen |

| ANTINEOPLASTIC AGENTS: NURSING IMPLICATIONS FOR SIDE EFFECTS | |
|---|---|
| Bone marrow suppression | Monitor bleeding: bleeding gums, bruising, petechiae, guaiac stools, urine and emesis<br>Avoid IM injections and rectal temperatures<br>Apply pressure to venipuncture sites |
| Nausea, vomiting | Monitor intake and output ratios, appetite and nutritional intake<br>Prophylactic antiemetics may be used<br>Smaller, more frequent meals |
| Altered immunologic response | Prevent infection by handwashing<br>Timely reporting of alterations in vital signs or symptoms indicating possible infection |
| Impaired oral mucous membrane; stomatis | Oral hygiene measures |
| Fatigue | Encourage rest and discuss measures to conserve energy<br>Use relaxation techniques, mental imagery |

| ANTIPARKINSON MEDICATIONS | | |
|---|---|---|
| **MEDICATION** | **SIDE EFFECTS** | **NURSING CONSIDERATIONS** |
| Trihexyphenidyl | Dry mouth<br>Blurred vision<br>Constipation, urinary hesitancy<br>Decreased mental acuity, difficulty concentrating, confusion, hallucination | Acts by blocking acetylcholine at cerebral synaptic sites<br>Intraocular pressure should be monitored<br>Supervise ambulation<br>Causes nausea if given before meals<br>Suck on hard candy for dry mouth |
| Benztropine mesylate | Drowsiness, nausea, vomiting<br>Atropine-like effects—blurred vision, mydriasis<br>Antihistaminic effects—sedation, dizziness | Acts by lessening cholinergic effect of dopamine deficiency<br>Suppresses tremor of Parkinsonism<br>Most side effects are reversed by changes in dosage<br>Additional drowsiness can occur with other CNS depressants |
| Levodopa | Nausea and vomiting, anorexia<br>Postural hypotension<br>Mental changes: confusion, agitation, mood alterations<br>Cardiac arrhythmias<br>Twitching | Precursor of dopamine<br>Thought to restore dopamine levels in extrapyramidal centers<br>Administered in large prolonged doses<br>Contraindicated in glaucoma, hemolytic anemia<br>Give with food<br>Monitor for postural hypotension<br>Avoid OTC meds and foods that contain vitamin $B_6$ (pyridoxine); reverses effects |
| Bromocriptine mesylate | Dizziness, headache, hypotension<br>Tinnitus<br>Nausea, abdominal cramps<br>Pleural effusion<br>Orthostatic hypotension | Give with meals<br>May lead to early postpartum conception<br>Monitor cardiac, hepatic, renal, hematopoietic function |
| Carbidopa–Levodopa | Hemolytic anemia<br>Dystonic movements, ataxia<br>Orthostatic hypotension<br>Dysrhythmias<br>GI upset, dry mouth | Stimulates dopamine receptors<br>Don't use with MAO inhibitors<br>Advise to change positions slowly<br>Take with food |
| Amantadine | CNS disturbances, hyperexcitability<br>Insomnia, vertigo, ataxia<br>Slurred speech, convulsions | Enhances effect of L-Dopa<br>Contraindicated in epilepsy, arteriosclerosis<br>Antiviral |
| **Action** | Levodopa—precursor to dopamine that is converted to dopamine in the brain<br>Bromocriptine—stimulates postsynaptic dopamine receptors | |
| **Indications** | Parkinson's disease | |
| **Side effects** | Dizziness<br>Ataxia<br>Confusion<br>Psychosis<br>Hemolytic anemia | |
| **Nursing considerations** | Monitor for urinary retention<br>Large doses of pyridoxine (vitamin $B_6$) decrease or reverse effects of medication<br>Avoid use of other CNS depressants (alcohol, narcotics, sedatives)<br>Anticholinergics, dopamine agonists, MAO inhibitors, catechol-*O*-methyltransferase (COMT) inhibitors, and antidepressants may also be used | |

| ANTIPLATELET AGENTS | | |
|---|---|---|
| **MEDICATION** | **SIDE EFFECTS** | **NURSING CONSIDERATIONS** |
| Adenosine diphosphate receptor antagonists Ticlodipine Copidrogel | Thrombocytopenic purpura GI upset | Prevents platelet aggregation Higher risk of hemorrhage with ticlopidine |
| Dipyridamole Dipyridamole plus aspirin | Headache Dizziness EKG changes Hypertension, hypotension | Administer 1 h ac or with meals Monitor BP Check for signs of bleeding |
| Glycoprotein IIb and IIIa receptor antagonists Eptifibatide Abciximab | GI, retroperitoneal, and urogenital bleeding | Does not increase risk of fatal hemorrhage or hemorrhagic stroke |
| Salicylates (Aspirin) | Short-term use—GI bleeding, heartburn, occasional nausea Prolonged high dosage—salicylism: metabolic acidosis, respiratory alkalosis, dehydration, fluid and electrolyte imbalance, tinnitus | Observe for bleeding gums, bloody or black stools, bruises Give with milk, water, or food, or use enteric-coated tablets (Ecotrin) to minimize gastric distress Contraindications—GI disorders, severe anemia, vitamin K deficiency Anti-inflammatory, analgesic, antipyretic |
| **Action** | Interferes with platelet aggregation | |
| **Indications** | Venous thrombosis Pulmonary embolism CVA and acute coronary prevention Post-cardiac surgery; post-percutaneous coronary interventions Acute coronary syndrome | |
| **Side effects** | Hemorrhage, bleeding Thrombocytopenia Hematuria Hemoptysis | |
| **Nursing considerations** | Teach client to check for signs of bleeding Inform health care provider or dentist before procedures Older adults at higher risk for ototoxicity Instruct client to contact health care provider before taking any over-the-counter medications Instruct client to avoid gingko, garlic and ginger herbal preparations | |
| **Gerontologic considerations** | Dipyridamole causes orthostatic hypotention in older adults Ticlopidine–greater risk of toxicity with older adults | |

| ANTIPSYCHOTIC MEDICATIONS | | |
|---|---|---|
| **MEDICATION** | **SIDE EFFECTS** | **NURSING CONSIDERATIONS** |
| **High potency (traditional)**<br><br>Haloperidol<br>Haloperidol decanoate<br>Fluphenazine<br>Fluphenazine decanoate | Low sedative effect<br>Low incidence of hypotension<br>High incidence of extrapyramidal side effects | Used in large doses for assaultive clients<br>Used with elderly (risk of falling reduced)<br>Decanoate: long-acting form given every 2–4 wk; IM into deep muscle Z-track |
| **Medium potency (traditional)**<br><br>Perphenazine | Orthostatic hypotension<br>Dry mouth<br>Constipation | Can help control severe vomiting<br>Medication is available PO, IM, and IV |
| **Low potency (traditional)**<br><br>Chlorpromazine | High sedative effect<br>High incidence of hypotension<br>Irreversible retinitis pigmentosus at 800 mg/day | Educate client about increased sensitivity to sun (as with other phenothiazines)<br>No tolerance or potential for abuse |
| **Atypical**<br><br>Risperidone | Moderate orthostatic hypotension<br>Moderate sedation<br>Significant weight gain<br>Doses over 6 mg can cause tardive dyskinesia | Chosen as first-line antipsychotic due to mild EPS and very low anticholinergic side effects |
| Quetiapine | Moderate orthostatic hypotension<br>Moderate sedation<br>Very low risk of tardive dyskinesia and neuroleptic malignant syndrome | Chosen as first-line antipsychotic due to mild EPS and very low anticholinergic side effects |
| Ziprasidone | ECG changes—QT prolongation | Effective with depressive symptoms of schizophrenia<br>Low propensity for weight gain |
| **Action** | Blocks dopamine receptors in basal ganglia of brain, inhibiting transmission of nerve impulses | |
| **Indications** | Acute and chronic psychosis | |
| **Side effects** | Akathisia (motor restlessness)<br>Dyskinesia (abnormal voluntary movements)<br>Dystonias (abnormal muscle tone producing spasms of tongue, face, neck)<br>Parkinson syndrome (shuffling gait, rigid muscles, excessive salivation, tremors, mask-like face, motor retardation)<br>Tardive dyskinesia (involuntary movements of mouth, tongue, trunk, extremities; chewing motions, sucking, tongue thrusting)<br>Photosensitivity<br>Orthostatic hypotension<br>Neuroleptic malignant syndrome | |
| **Nursing considerations** | Lowers seizure threshold<br>May slow growth rate in children<br>Monitor for urinary retention and decreased GI motility<br>Avoid alcohol<br>May cause hypotension if taken with antihypertensives, nitrates<br>Phenothiazines also used | |

| SIDE EFFECTS: ANTIPSYCHOTIC MEDICATIONS | | |
|---|---|---|
| **MEDICATION** | **SIDE EFFECTS** | **NURSING CONSIDERATIONS** |
| Extrapyramidal | Pseudoparkinsonism<br>Dystonia (muscle spasm)<br>Acute dystonic reaction<br>Early signs: tightening of jaw,<br>  stiff neck, swollen tongue<br>Late signs: swollen airway,<br>  oculogyric crisis<br>Akathisia (inability to sit or<br>  stand still, foot tap, pace)<br>Tardive dyskinesia (abnormal,<br>  involuntary movements);<br>  may be irreversible | Pharmacologic management of Parkinsonian<br>  side effects: benztropine trihexyphenidyl<br>Recognize early symptoms of acute dystonic<br>  reaction<br>Notify health care provider for IM<br>  diphenhydramine protocol |
| Anticholinergic | Blurred vision<br>Dry mouth<br>Nasal congestion<br>Constipation<br>Acute urinary retention | Educate client that some anticholinergic<br>  side effects often diminish over time<br>Maintain adequate fluid intake and monitor<br>I and O |
| Sedative | Sleepiness<br>Possible danger if driving or<br>  operating machinery | Monitor sedative effects and maintain client<br>  safety |
| Hypotensive | Orthostatic hypotension is<br>  common | Frequent monitoring of BP and advise client to<br>  rise slowly |
| Other | Phototoxicity | Educate client regarding need for sunscreen |
| Neuroleptic<br>malignant<br>syndrome | Rigidity<br>Fever<br>Sweating<br>Autonomic dysfunction<br>  (dysrhythmias,fluctuations<br>  in BP)<br>Confusion<br>Seizures, coma | Immediately withdraw antipsychotics<br>Control hyperthermia<br>Hydration<br>Dantroline (muscle relaxant) used for rigidity<br>  and severe reactions<br>Bromocriptine (dopamine receptor antogonist)<br>  used for CNS toxicity and mild reactions |
| Atropine<br>psychosis | Skin hot to touch without<br>  fever–"red as a beet"<br>  (flushed face)<br>Dehydration–"dry as a bone"<br>Altered mental status–"mad<br>  as a hatter" | Reduce or discontinue medication<br>Hydration<br>Stay with client while confused, for safety |

| DEGREE OF SIDE EFFECTS FOR SELECTED ANTIPSYCHOTICS | |
|---|---|
| **Action** | Blocks postsynaptic dopamine receptors in brain |
| **Indications** | Psychotic disorders<br>Severe nausea and vomiting |
| **Side effects** | Drowsiness<br>Pseudoparkinsonism<br>Dystonia<br>Akathisia<br>Tardive dyskinesia<br>Neuroleptic malignant syndrome<br>Dysrhythmias<br>Photophobia<br>Blurred vision<br>Photosensitivity<br>Lactation<br>Discolors urine pink to red-brown |
| **Nursing considerations** | May cause false-positive pregnancy tests<br>Dilute oral concentrate with water, saline, 7-Up, homogenized milk, carbonated orange drink, fruit juices (pineapple, orange, apricot, prune, V-8, tomato, grapefruit); use 60 ml for each 5 ml of medication<br>Do not mix with beverages that contain caffeine (coffee, tea, cola) or apple juice; incompatible<br>Monitor vital signs<br>Takes 4-6 weeks to achieve steady plasma levels<br>Monitor bowel function<br>Monitor elderly for dehydration (sedation and decreased thirst sensation)<br>Avoid activities requiring mental alertness<br>Avoid exposure to sun<br>Maintain fluid intake<br>May have anticholinergic and antihistamine actions |

| DEGREE OF SIDE EFFECTS FOR SELECTED ANTIPSYCHOTICS | | | | |
|---|---|---|---|---|
| **MEDICATION** | **EXTRAPYRAMIDAL** | **ANTICHOLINERGIC** | **SEDATIVE** | **HYPOTENSIVE** |
| Chlorpromazine | ↑ | ↑↑ | ↑↑↑ | ↑↑↑ |
| Thioridazine | ↑ | ↑↑↑ | ↑↑↑ | ↑↑ |
| Trifluoperazine | ↑↑↑ | ↑ | ↑ | ↑ |
| Fluphenazine | ↑↑↑ | ↑ | ↑ | ↑ |
| Perphenazine | ↑↑↑ | ↑ | ↑↑ | ↑ |
| Haloperidol | ↑↑↑ | ↑ | ↑ | ↑ |
| Thiothixene | ↑↑ | ↑ | ↑ | ↑↑ |
| KEY:   ↑ mild;   ↑↑ moderate;   ↑↑↑ severe | | | | |

## ANTIPYRETIC MEDICATIONS

| MEDICATION | SIDE EFFECTS | NURSING CONSIDERATIONS |
|---|---|---|
| Acetaminophen | Overdosage may be fatal<br>GI side effects are not common | Do not exceed recommended dose |
| Salicylates (Aspirin) | Short-term use—GI bleeding, heartburn, occasional nausea<br>Prolonged high dosage—salicylism: metabolic acidosis, respiratory alkalosis, dehydration, fluid and electrolyte imbalance, tinnitus | Observe for bleeding gums, bloody or black stools, bruises<br>Give with milk, water, or food, or use enteric-coated tablets to minimize gastric distress<br>Contraindications—GI disorders, severe anemia, vitamin K deficiency<br>Anti-inflammatory, analgesic, antipyretic |
| Action | Antiprostaglandin activity in hypothalamus reduces fever; causes peripheral vasodilation; anti-inflammatory actions | |
| Indications | Fever | |
| Side effects | GI irritation<br>Occult bleeding<br>Tinnitus<br>Dizziness<br>Confusion<br>Liver dysfunction (acetaminophen) | |
| Nursing considerations | Aspirin contraindicated for client less than 21 years old due to risk of Reye's syndrome<br>Aspirin contraindicated for clients with bleeding disorders due to anticlotting activity<br>NSAIDS are also used for fever | |

## ANTITHYROID MEDICATIONS

| MEDICATION | SIDE EFFECTS | NURSING CONSIDERATIONS |
|---|---|---|
| Methimazole Propylthiouracil (PTU) | Leukopenia, fever<br>Rash, sore throat<br>Jaundice | Inhibits synthesis of thyroid hormone by thyroid gland<br>Check CBC and hepatic function<br>Give with meals<br>Report fever, sore throat to health care provider |
| Lugol's iodine solution Potassium iodide | Nausea, vomiting, metallic taste<br>Rash | Iodine preparation<br>Used 2 weeks prior to surgery; decreases vascularity, decreases hormone release<br>Only effective for a short period<br>Give after meals<br>Dilute in water, milk, or fruit juice<br>Stains teeth<br>Give through straw |
| Radioactive iodine ($^{131}$I) | Feeling of fullness in neck<br>Metallic taste<br>Leukemia | Destroys thyroid tissue<br>Contraindicated for women of childbearing age<br>Fast overnight before administration<br>Urine, saliva, vomit radioactive 3 days<br>Use full radiation precautions<br>Encourage fluids |

*(continued)*

| ANTITHYROID AGENTS/IODINES (cont'd) | |
|---|---|
| **Action** | Antithyroid agents—inhibits oxidation of iodine<br>Iodines—reduces vascularity of thyroid gland; increases amount of inactive (bound) hormone; inhibits release of thyroid hormones into circulation |
| **Indications** | Hyperthyroidism<br>Thyrotoxic crisis |
| **Side effects** | Nausea, vomiting<br>Diarrhea<br>Rashes<br>Thrombocytopenia<br>Leukopenia |
| **Nursing considerations** | Changes in vital signs or weight and appearance may indicate adverse reactions, which should lead to evaluation of continued medication use |

| THYROID REPLACEMENT MEDICATIONS | | |
|---|---|---|
| **MEDICATION** | **SIDE EFFECTS** | **NURSING CONSIDERATIONS** |
| Levothyroxine | Nervousness, tremors<br>Insomnia<br>Tachycardia, palpitations<br>Dysrhythmias, angina | Tell client to report chest pain, palpitations, sweating, nervousness, shortness of breath to health care provider |
| Liothyronine sodium | Excessive dosages produce symptoms of hyperthyroidism | Take at same time each day<br>Take in AM<br>Monitor pulse and BP |
| **Action** | Increases metabolic rate of body | |
| **Indications** | Hypothyroidism | |
| **Side effects** | Nervousness<br>Tachycardia<br>Weight loss | |
| **Nursing considerations** | Obtain history of client's medications<br>Enhances action of oral anticoagulants, antidepressants<br>Decreases action of insulin, digitalis<br>Obtain baseline vital signs<br>Monitor weight<br>Avoid OTC drugs | |

| ANTITUBERCULAR AGENTS | | |
|---|---|---|
| **MEDICATION** | **SIDE EFFECTS** | **NURSING CONSIDERATIONS** |
| **First–line agents** | | |
| Isoniazid | Hepatitis<br>Peripheral neuritis<br>Rash<br>Fever | Pyridoxine (B$_6$): 10–50 mg as prophylaxis for neuritis; 50-100 mg as treatment<br>Teach signs of hepatitis<br>Check liver function tests<br>Alcohol increases risk of hepatic complications<br>Therapeutic effects can be expected after 2–3 weeks of therapy<br>Monitor for resolution of symptoms (fever, night sweats, weight loss); hypotension (orthostatic) may occur initially, then resolve; caution client to change position slowly<br>Give before meals<br>Do not combine with phenytoin, causes phenytoin toxicity |
| Ethambutol | Optic neuritis | Use cautiously with renal disease<br>Check visual acuity |
| Rifampin | Hepatitis<br>Fever | Orange urine, tears, saliva<br>Check liver function tests<br>Can take with food |
| Streptomycin | Nephrotoxicity<br>VIII nerve damage | Check creatinine and BUN<br>Audiograms if given long-term |
| **Second–line agents** | | |
| Para-amino-salicyclic acid | GI disturbances<br>Hepatotoxicity | Check for ongoing GI side effects |
| Pyrazinamide | Hyperuricemia<br>Anemia<br>Anorexia | Check liver function tests, uric acid, and hematopoietic studies |
| **Action** | Inhibits cell wall and protein synthesis of *Mycobacterium tuberculosis* | |
| **Indications** | Tuberculosis<br>INH–used to prevent disease in person exposed to organism | |
| **Side effects** | Hepatitis<br>Optic neuritis<br>Seizures<br>Peripheral neuritis | |
| **Nursing considerations** | Used in combination (2 medications or more)<br>Monitor for liver damage and hepatitis<br>With active TB, the client should cover mouth and nose when coughing, confine used tissues to plastic bags, and wear a mask with crowds until three sputum cultures are negative (no longer infectious)<br>In inclient settings, client is placed under airborne precautions and workers wear a N95 or high-efficiency particulate air (HEPA) respirator until the client is no longer infectious | |

| ANTITUSSIVE/EXPECTORANT MEDICATIONS | | |
|---|---|---|
| **MEDICATION** | **SIDE EFFECTS** | **NURSING CONSIDERATIONS** |
| Dextromethorphan hydrobromide | Drowsiness<br>Dizziness | Antitussive<br>Onset occurs within 30 min, lasts 3-6 h<br>Monitor cough type and frequency |
| Guaifenesin | Dizziness<br>Headache<br>Nausea, vomiting | Expectorant<br>Monitor cough type and frequency<br>Take with glass of water |
| **Action** | Antitussives—suppresses cough reflex by inhibiting cough center in medulla<br>Expectorants—decreases viscosity of bronchial secretions | |
| **Indications** | Coughs due to URI<br>COPD | |
| **Side effects** | Respiratory depression<br>Hypotension<br>Bradycardia<br>Anticholinergic effects<br>Photosensitivity | |
| **Nursing considerations** | Elderly clients may need reduced dosages<br>Avoid alcohol | |

| ANTIVIRALS | | |
| --- | --- | --- |
| MEDICATION | SIDE EFFECTS | NURSING CONSIDERATIONS |
| Acyclovir | Headaches, dizziness<br>Seizures<br>Diarrhea | Used for herpes simplex and herpes zoster<br>Given PO, IV, topically<br>Does not prevent transmission of disease<br>Slows progression of symptoms<br>Encourage fluids<br>Check liver and renal function tests |
| Ribavarin | Worsening of pulmonary status, bacterial pneumonia<br>Hypotension, cardiac arrest | Used for severe lower respiratory tract infections in infants and children<br>Must use special aerosol-generating device for administration<br>Can precipitate<br>Contraindicated in females who may become pregnant during treatment |
| Zidovudine | Anemia<br>Headache<br>Anorexia, diarrhea, nausea, GI pain<br>Paresthesias, dizziness<br>Insomnia<br>Agranulocytosis | Used for HIV infection<br>Teach clients to strictly comply with dosage schedule |
| Zalcitabine | Oral ulcers<br>Peripheral neuropathy, headache<br>Vomiting, diarrhea<br>CHF, cardiomyopathy | Used in combination with zidovudine for advanced HIV |
| Didanosine | Headache<br>Rhinitis, cough<br>Diarrhea, nausea, vomiting<br>Pancreatitis, granulocytopenia<br>Peripheral neuropathy<br>Seizures<br>Hemorrhage | Used for HIV infection<br>Monitor liver and renal function studies<br>Note baseline vital signs and weight<br>Take on empty stomach<br>Chew or crush tablets |
| Famciclovir | Fatigue, fever<br>Nausea, vomiting, diarrhea, constipation<br>Headache, sinusitis | Used for acute herpes zoster (shingles)<br>Obtain baseline CBC and renal function studies<br>Remind clients they are contagious when lesions are open and draining |
| Ganciclovir | Fever<br>Rash<br>Leukemia<br>Seizures<br>GI hemorrhage<br>MI, stroke | Used for retinitis caused by cytomegalovirus<br>Check level of consciousness<br>Monitor CBC, I and O<br>Report any dizziness, confusions, seizures immediately<br>Need regular eye exams |
| Amantadine<br>Rimantadine | Dizziness<br>Nervousness<br>Insomnia<br>Orthostatic hypotension | Used for prophylaxis and treatment of influenza A<br>Orthostatic hypotension precautions<br>Instruct clients to avoid hazardous activities |
| Oseltamivir<br>Zanamivir | Nausea, vomiting<br>Cough and throat irritation | Used for the treatment of Types A and B influenza<br>Best effect if given within 2 days of infection<br>Instruct clients that medication will reduce flu-symptom duration |

*(continued)*

| ANTIVIRALS (cont'd) | |
|---|---|
| **Action** | Inhibits DNA or RNA replication in virus |
| **Indications** | Recurrent HSV 1 and 2 in immunocompromised clients<br>Encephalitis<br>Herpes zoster<br>HIV infections |
| **Side effects** | Vertigo<br>Depression<br>Headache<br>Hematuria |
| **Nursing considerations** | Encourage fluids<br>Small, frequent feedings<br>Good skin care<br>Wear glove when applying topically<br>Not a cure, but relieves symptoms |

| MEDICATIONS USED FOR ATTENTION-DEFICIT HYPERACTIVITY DISORDER | | |
|---|---|---|
| **MEDICATION** | **SIDE EFFECTS** | **NURSING CONSIDERATIONS** |
| Methylphenidate | Nervousness, palpitations<br>Insomnia<br>Tachycardia<br>Weight loss, growth suppression | May precipitate Tourette's syndrome<br>Monitor CBC, platelet count<br>Has paradoxical calming effect in ADD<br>Monitor height/weight in children<br>Monitor BP<br>Avoid drinks with caffeine<br>Give at least 6 h before bedtime<br>Give pc |
| Dextroamphetamine sulfate | Insomnia<br>Tachycardia, palpitations | Controlled substance<br>May alter insulin needs<br>Give in AM to prevent insomnia<br>Don't use with MAO inhibitor (possible hypertensive crisis) |
| **Action** | Increases level of catecholamines in cerebral cortex and reticular activating system | |
| **Indications** | Attention-deficit hyperactivity disorder (ADHD)<br>Narcolepsy | |
| **Side effects** | Restlessness<br>Insomnia<br>Tremors<br>Tachycardia<br>Seizures | |
| **Nursing considerations** | Monitor growth rate in children | |

## BRONCHODILATORS/LEUKOTRIENE-RECEPTOR BLOCKERS

| MEDICATION | SIDE EFFECTS | NURSING CONSIDERATIONS |
|---|---|---|
| Aminophylline | Nervousness<br>Nausea<br>Dizziness<br>Tachycardia<br>Seizures | IM injection causes intense pain<br>Coffee, tea, cola increase risk of adverse reactions<br>Monitor blood levels<br>IV–incompatible with multiple medications |
| Terbutaline sulfate | Nervousness, tremor<br>Headache<br>Tachycardia<br>Palpitations<br>Fatigue | Short-acting beta agonist most useful when about to enter environment or begin activity likely to induce asthma attack<br>Pulse and blood pressure should be checked before each dose |
| Ipratropium bromide<br>Tiotropium | Nervousness<br>Tremor<br>Dry mouth<br>Palpitations | Cholinergic antagonist<br>Don't mix in nebulizer with cromolyn sodium<br>Not for acute treatment<br>Teach use of metered dose inhaler: inhale, hold breath, exhale slowly |
| Albuterol | Tremors<br>Headache<br>Hyperactivity<br>Tachycardia | Short-acting beta agonist most useful when about to enter environment or begin activity likely to induce asthma attack<br>Monitor for toxicity if using tablets and aerosol<br>Teach how to correctly use inhaler |
| Epinephrine | Cerebral hemorrhage<br>Hypertension<br>Tachycardia | When administered IV monitor BP, heart rate, EKG<br>If used with steroid inhaler, use bronchodilator first, then wait 5 minutes before using steroid inhaler (opens airway for maximum effectiveness) |
| Salmeterol | Headache<br>Pharyngitis<br>Nervousness<br>Tremors | Dry powder preparation<br>Not for acute bronchospasm or exacerbations |
| Montelukast sodium<br>Zafirlukast<br>Zileuton | Headache<br>GI distress | Used for prophylactic and maintenance therapy of asthma<br>Liver tests may be monitored<br>Interacts with theophylline |

## BONE-RESORPTION INHIBITORS (BISPHOSPHONATES)

| MEDICATION | SIDE EFFECTS | NURSING CONSIDERATIONS |
|---|---|---|
| Alendronate<br>Risedronate<br>Ibandronate | Esophagitis<br>Arthralgia<br>Nausea, diarrhea | Prevention and treatment of postmenopausal osteoporosis, Paget's disease, glucocorticoid-induced osteoporosis<br>Instruct clients to take medication in the morning with 6–8 ounces of water before eating and to remain in upright position for 30 minutes<br>Bone density tests may be monitored |

| BRONCHODILATORS/XANTHINES/RESPIRATORY MEDICATIONS | | |
|---|---|---|
| **MEDICATION** | **SIDE EFFECTS** | **NURSING CONSIDERATIONS** |
| Acetylcysteine | Bronchospasm<br>Nausea<br>Vomiting | Mucolytic<br>Administered by nebulization into face mask or mouthpiece<br>Bronchospasm most likely to occur in asthmatics<br>Open vials should be refrigerated and used within 90 hours<br>Clients should clear airway by coughing prior to aerosol |
| Cromolyn sodium | Dizziness<br>Throat irritation | Mast cell stabilizer that prevents mast cell membranes from opening when an allergen binds to IgE<br>Used only for prevention of asthma attacks, not for acute treatment |
| Salmeterol | Headache | Long-acting beta agonist meant to decrease reliance on and abuse of short-acting beta agonists |
| Montelukast | Headache<br>Dizziness | Leukotriene antagonist that blocks the receptor<br>Do not abruptly substitute for oral or inhaled steroids<br>Reduce dose if hepatic damage |
| **Action** | Varies with medication | |
| **Indications** | Bronchial asthma<br>Bronchospasm of COPD<br>Chronic bronchitis<br>Emphysema | |
| **Side effects** | Seizures<br>Dysrhythmias, tachycardia<br>Pulmonary edema<br>Tremors<br>Anticholinergic effects | |
| **Nursing considerations** | May aggravate diabetes because they cause hyperglycemia<br>Monitor BP | |

| CARBONIC ANHYDRASE INHIBITORS | | |
|---|---|---|
| **MEDICATION** | **SIDE EFFECTS** | **NURSING CONSIDERATIONS** |
| Acetazolamide | Lethargy, depression<br>Anorexia, weakness<br>Decreased K$^+$ level, confusion | Used for glaucoma<br>Note client's mental status before repeating dose |
| **Action** | Decreases production of aqueous humor in ciliary body | |
| **Indications** | Open-angle glaucoma | |
| **Side effects** | Blurred vision<br>Lacrimation<br>Pulmonary edema | |
| **Nursing considerations** | Monitor client for systemic effects | |

| CARDIAC GLYCOSIDES | | |
|---|---|---|
| **MEDICATION** | **SIDE EFFECTS** | **NURSING CONSIDERATIONS** |
| Digoxin | Anorexia<br>Nausea<br>Bradycardia<br>Visual disturbances<br>Confusion<br>Abdominal pain | Administer with caution to elderly or clients with renal insufficiency<br>Monitor renal function and electrolytes<br>Instruct clients to eat high-potassium foods<br>Take apical pulse for 1 full minute before administering<br>Notify health care provider if AP <60 (adult), <90-110 (infants and young children), <70 (older children)<br>Digitalizing dose (rarely used) (oral)–0.5 to 0.75 mg po, then 0.25 mg po every 6–8 hrs to a total dose of 1–1.5 mg<br>Digitalizing dose (rarely used) (IV)–0.25 to 0.5 mg IV, then 0.25 mg IV to a total dose of 1.0 mg<br>Digoxin immune fab (Digibind)–used for treatment of life-threatening toxicity<br>Maintenance dose 0.125-0.5 mg IV or PO (average is 0.25 mg)<br>Teach client to check pulse rate and discuss side effects<br>Low K+ increases risk of digitalis toxicity<br>Serum therapeutic blood levels 0.5–2 nanograms/mL<br>Toxic blood levels ≥ 2 nanograms/mL |
| **Action** | Increases force of myocardial contraction and slows heart rate by stimulating the vagus nerve and blocking the AV node | |
| **Indications** | Heart failure, Dysrhythmias | |
| **Side effects** | Tachycardia, bradycardia, heart block<br>Anorexia, nausea, vomiting<br>Halos around dark objects, blurred vision, halo vision<br>Dysrhythmias, heart block | |
| **Nursing considerations** | Instruct client to eat high potassium foods<br>Monitor for digitalis toxicity<br>Risk of digitalis toxicity increases if client is hypokalemic | |
| **Herbal interactions** | Licorice can potentiate action of digoxin by promoting potassium loss<br>Hawthorn may increase effects of digoxin<br>Ginseng may falsely elevate digoxin levels<br>Ma-huang (ephedra) increases risk of digitalis toxicity | |

| CYTOPROTECTIVE AGENTS | | |
|---|---|---|
| **MEDICATION** | **SIDE EFFECTS** | **NURSING CONSIDERATIONS** |
| Sucralfate | Constipation<br>Dizziness | Take medication 1 hour ac<br>Should not be taken with<br>   antacids or H₂ blockers |
| **Action** | Adheres to and protects ulcer's surface by forming a barrier | |
| **Indications** | Duodenal ulcer | |
| **Side effects** | Constipation<br>Vertigo<br>Flatulence | |
| **Nursing<br>  considerations** | Action lasts up to 6 h<br>Give 2 h before or after most medications to prevent decreased absorption | |

| DIURETICS | | |
|---|---|---|
| **MEDICATION** | **SIDE EFFECTS** | **NURSING CONSIDERATIONS** |
| **Thiazide diuretics**<br>Hydrochlorothiazide<br>Chlorothiazide | Hypokalemia<br>Hyperglycemia<br>Blurred vision<br>Loss of Na⁺<br>Dry mouth<br>Hypotension | Monitor electrolytes, especially potassium<br>I and O<br>Monitor BUN and creatinine<br>Don't give at hs<br>Weigh client daily<br>Encourage potassium-containing foods |
| **Potassium<br>  sparing**<br>  Spironlactone | Hyperkalemia<br>Hyponatremia<br>Hepatic and renal damage<br>Tinnitus<br>Rash | Used with other diuretics<br>Give with meals<br>Avoid salt substitutes<br>  containing potassium<br>Monitor I and O |
| **Loop diuretics**<br>  Furosemide<br>  Ethacrynic acid | Hypotension<br>Hypokalemia<br>Hyperglycemia<br>GI upset<br>Weakness | Monitor BP, pulse rate, I and O<br>Monitor potassium<br>Give IV dose over 1-2 minutes  diuresis<br>  in 5-10 min<br>After PO dose diuresis in about 30 min<br>Weigh client daily<br>Don't give at hs<br>Encourage potassium-containing foods |
| Ethacrynic acid<br>Bumetamide | Potassium depletion<br>Electrolyte imbalance<br>Hypovolemia<br>Ototoxicity | Supervise ambulation<br>Monitor blood pressure and pulse<br>Observe for signs of electrolyte imbalance |
| **Osmotic diuretic**<br>  Mannitol | Dry mouth<br>  Thirst | I and O must be measured<br>Monitor vital signs<br>Monitor for electrolyte imbalance |
| **Other**<br>  Chlorthalidone | Dizziness<br>Aplastic anemia<br>Orthostatic hypotension | Acts like a thiazide diuretic<br>Acts in 2-3 h, peak 2-6 h, lasts 2-3 days<br>Administer in AM<br>Monitor output, weight, BP, electrolytes<br>Increase K* in diet<br>Monitor glucose levels in diabetic clients<br>Change position slowly |

*(Continued)*

| DIURETICS (cont'd) | |
|---|---|
| Action | Thiazides—inhibits reabsorption of sodium and chloride in distal renal tubule<br>Loop—inhibits reabsorption of sodium and chloride in loop of Henle and distal renal tubules<br>Potassium-sparing—blocks effect of aldosterone on renal tubules, causing loss of sodium and water and retention of potassium<br>Osmotic—pulls fluid from tissues due to hypertonic effect |
| Indications | Heart failure<br>Hypertension<br>Renal diseases<br>Diabetes insipidus<br>Reduction of osteoporosis in postmenopausal women |
| Side effects | Dizziness, vertigo<br>Dry mouth<br>Orthostatic hypotension<br>Leukopenia<br>Polyuria, nocturia<br>Photosensitivity<br>Impotence<br>Hypokalemia (except for potassium-sparing)<br>Hyponatremia |
| Nursing considerations | Take with food or milk<br>Take in AM<br>Monitor weight and electrolytes<br>Protect skin from the sun<br>Diet high in potassium for loop and thiazide diuretics<br>Limit potassium intake for potassium-sparing diuretics<br>Used as first-line drugs for hypertension |
| Herbal interactions | Licorice can promote potassium loss, causing hypokalemia<br>Aloe can decrease serum potassium level, causing hypokalemia<br>Gingko may increase blood pressure when taken with thiazide diuretics |

| ELECTROLYTES AND REPLACEMENT SOLUTIONS | | |
|---|---|---|
| **MEDICATION** | **SIDE EFFECTS** | **NURSING CONSIDERATIONS** |
| Calcium carbonate Calcium chloride | Dysrhythmias Constipation | Foods containing oxalic acid (rhubarb, spinach), phytic acid (bran, whole cereals), and phosphorus (milk, dairy products) interfere with absorption Monitor EKG Take 1-1.5 h pc if GI upset occurs |
| Magnesium chloride (Slow Mag) | Weak or absent deep tendon reflexes Hypotension Respiratory paralysis | Respirations should be greater than 16/min before medication given IV Test knee-jerk and patellar reflexes before each dose Monitor I and O |
| Potassium chloride Potassium gluconate (Kaon Liquid) | Dysrhythmias, cardiac arrest Adominal pain Respiratory paralysis | Monitor EKG and serum electrolytes Take with or after meals with full glass of water or fruit juice |
| Sodium chloride | Pulmonary edema | Monitor serum electrolytes |

| ELECTROLYTES/ELECTROLYTE MODIFIERS | |
|---|---|
| **Action** | Alkalinizing agents—release bicarbonate ions in stomach and secrete bicarbonate ions in kidneys Calcium salts—provide calcium for bones, teeth, nerve transmission, muscle contraction, normal blood coagulation, cell membrane strength Hypocalcemic agents—decrease blood levels of calcium Hypophosphatemic agents—bind phosphates in GI tract lowering blood levels; neutralize gastric acid, inactivate pepsin Magnesium salts—provide magnesium for nerve conduction and muscle activity and activate enzyme reactions in carbohydrate metabolism Phosphates—provide body with phosphorus needed for bone, muscle tissue, metabolism of carbohydrates, fats, proteins, and normal CNS function Potassium exchange resins—exchange $Na^+$ for $K^+$ in intestines, lowering $K^+$ levels Potassium salts—provide potassium needed for cell growth and normal functioning of cardiac, skeletal, and smooth muscle Replacement solution—provide water and $Na^+$ to maintain acid-base and water balance, maintain osmotic pressure Urinary acidifiers—secrete $H^+$ ions in kidneys, making urine acidic Urinary alkalinizers—convert to sodium bicarbonate, making the urine alkaline |
| **Indications** | Fluid and electrolyte imbalances Renal calculi Peptic ulcers Osteoporosis Metabolic acidosis or alkalosis |
| **Side effects** | See individual medications |
| **Nursing considerations** | Monitor clients with CHF, hypertension, renal disease |

| IRON PREPARATION | | |
|---|---|---|
| **MEDICATION** | **SIDE EFFECTS** | **NURSING CONSIDERATIONS** |
| Ferrous sulfate | Nausea<br>Constipation<br>Black stools | Food decreases absorption but may be necessary to reduce GI effects<br>Monitor Hgb, Hct<br>Dilute liquid preparations in juice, but not milk or antacids<br>Use straw for liquid to avoid staining teeth |
| Iron dextran | Nausea<br>Constipation<br>Black stools | IM injections cause pain and skin staining; use the Z-track technique to put med deep into buttock; IV administration is preferred |
| **Action** | Iron salts increase availability of iron for hemoglobin | |
| **Indications** | Iron-deficiency anemia | |
| **Side effects** | Constipation, diarrhea<br>Dark stools<br>Tooth enamel stains<br>Seizures<br>Flushing, hypotension<br>Tachycardia | |
| **Nursing considerations** | Take iron salts on empty stomach (absorption is reduced by one-third when taken with food)<br>Absorption of iron decreased when administered with tetracyclines, antacids, coffee, tea, milk, eggs (bind to iron)<br>Concurrent use of iron decreases effectiveness of tetracyclines and quinolone antibiotics<br>Vitamin C increases absorption of iron salts<br>Vitamin E delays therapeutic responses to iron salts | |

| MINERALS | | |
|---|---|---|
| **MEDICATION** | **SIDE EFFECTS** | **NURSING CONSIDERATIONS** |
| Calcium | Cardiac dysrhythmias<br>Constipation<br>Hypercalcemia<br>Renal calculi | Give 1 h before meals<br>Give 1/3 dose at bedtime<br>Monitor for urinary stones |
| Vitamin D | Seizures<br>Impaired renal function<br>Hypercalcemia<br>Renal calculi | Treatment of vitamin D deficiency, rickets, psoriasis, rheumatoid arthritis<br>Check electrolytes<br>Restrict use of antacids containing Mg |
| Sodium fluoride | Bad taste<br>Staining of teeth<br>Nausea, vomiting | Observe for synovitis |
| Potassium | Nausea, vomiting<br>Cramps, diarrhea | Prevention and treatment of hypokalemia<br>Report hyperkalemia: lethargy, confusion, fainting, decreased urine output<br>Report continued hypocalcemia: fatigue, weakness, polyuria, polydipsia, cardiac changes |

| EYE MEDICATIONS | | |
|---|---|---|
| **MEDICATION** | **SIDE EFFECTS** | **NURSING CONSIDERATIONS** |
| Methylcellulose | Eye irritation if excess is allowed to dry on eyelids | Lubricant<br>Use eyewash to rinse eyelids of "sandy" sensation felt after administration |
| Polyvinyl alcohol | Blurred vision<br>Burning | Artificial tears<br>Applied to contact lenses before insertion |
| Tetrahydrozoline | Cardiac irregularities<br>Pupillary dilation, increased intraocular pressure<br>Transient stinging | Used for ocular congestion, irritation, allergic conditions<br>Rebound congestion may occur with frequent or prolonged use<br>Apply light pressure on lacrimal sac for 1 min instillation |
| Timolol maleate<br>Levobunolol | Eye irritation<br>Hypotension | Beta-blocking agent<br>Reduces intraocular pressure in management of glaucoma<br>Apply light pressure on lacrimal sac for 1 min following instillation<br>Monitor BP and pulse |
| Proparacaine HCl<br>Tetracaine HCl,<br>cocaine | Corneal abrasion | Topical anesthetic<br>Remind client not to touch or rub eyes while anesthetized<br>Patch the eye to prevent corneal abrasion |
| Prednisolone acetate | Corneal abrasion | Topical steroid<br>Steroid use predisposes client to local infection |
| Gentamicin<br>Tobramycin | Eye irritation; itching, redness | Anti-infective agent<br>Clean exudate from eyes before use |
| Idoxuridine | Eye irritation<br>Itching lids | Topical antiviral agent<br>Educate client about possible side effects |
| Dipivefrin HCl | Increase in heart rate and blood pressure | Adrenergic<br>Monitor vital signs because of systemic absorption |
| Flurbiprofen | Platelet aggregation disorder | Nonsteroidal anti-inflammatory agents<br>Monitor client for eye hemorrhage<br>Client should not continue wearing contact lens |
| **Nursing considerations** | Place pressure on tear ducts for one minute<br>Wash hands before and after installation<br>Do not touch tip of dropper to eye or body | |

| GLUCOCORTICOIDS | | |
|---|---|---|
| **MEDICATION** | **SIDE EFFECTS** | **NURSING CONSIDERATIONS** |
| Cortisone acetate<br>Hydrocortisone<br>Dexamethasone<br>Methylprednisolone<br>Prednisone<br>Beclomethasone<br>Betamethasone<br>Budesonide | Increases susceptibility to infection<br>May mask symptoms of infection<br>Edema, changes in appetite<br>Euphoria, insomnia<br>Delayed wound healing<br>Hypokalemia, hypocalcemia<br>Hyperglycemia<br>Osteoporosis, fractures<br>Peptic ulcer, gastric hemorrhage<br>Psychosis | Prevents/suppresses cell-mediated immune reactors<br>Used for adrenal insufficiency<br>Overdosage produces Cushing's syndrome<br>Abrupt withdrawal of drug may cause headache, nausea and vomiting, and papilledema (Addisonian crisis)<br>Give single dose before 9 AM<br>Give multiple doses at evenly spaced intervals<br>Infection may produce few symptoms due to anti-inflammatory action<br>Stress (surgery, illness, psychic) may lead to increased need for steroids<br>Nightmares are often the first indication of the onset of steroid psychosis<br>Check weight, BP, electrolytes, I and O, weight<br>Used cautiously with history of TB (may reactivate disease)<br>May decrease effects of oral hypoglycemics, insulin, diuretics, K+ supplements<br>Note data: children for growth retardation<br>Protect from pathological fractures<br>Administer with antacids<br>Do not stop abruptly<br>Methylprednisolone also used for arthritis, asthma, allergic reactions, cerebral edema<br>Dexamethasone also used for allergic disorders, cerebral edema, asthma attack, shock |
| **Action** | Stimulates formation of glucose (gluconeogenesis) and decreases use of glucose by body cells; increases formation and storage of fat in muscle tissue; alters normal immune response | |
| **Indications** | Addison's disease, Crohn's disease, COPD, lupus erythematosus, leukemias, lymphomas, myelomas, head trauma, tumors to prevent/treat cerebral edema | |
| **Side effects** | Psychoses, depression, weight gain, hypokalemia, hypocalcemia, stunted growth in children, petechiae, buffalo hump | |
| **Nursing considerations** | Monitor fluid and electrolyte balance<br>Don't discontinue abruptly<br>Monitor for signs of infection | |
| **Herbal interactions** | Cascara, senna, celery seed, juniper may decrease serum potassium; when taken with corticosteroids may increase hypoglycemia<br>Ginseng taken with corticosteroids may cause insomnia<br>Echinacea may counteract effects of corticosteroids<br>Licorice potentiates effect of corticosteroids | |

| MINERALOCORTICOIDS | | |
|---|---|---|
| **MEDICATION** | **SIDE EFFECTS** | **NURSING CONSIDERATIONS** |
| Fludrocortisone acetate | Hypertension, edema due to sodium retention<br>Muscle weakness and dysrhythmia due to hypokalemia | Give PO dose with food<br>Check BP, electrolytes, I and 0, weight<br>Give low-sodium, high-protein, high-potassium diet<br>May decrease effects of oral hypoglycemics, insulin, diuretics, K+ supplements |
| **Action** | Increases sodium reabsorption, potassium and hydrogen excretion in the distal convoluted tubules of the nephron | |
| **Indications** | Adrenal insufficiency | |
| **Side effects** | Sodium and water retention<br>Hypokalemia | |
| **Nursing considerations** | Monitor BP and serum electrolytes<br>Daily weight, report sudden weight gain to health care provider<br>Used with cortisone or hydrocortisone in adrenal insufficiency | |

| HEAVY METAL ANTAGONISTS | | |
|---|---|---|
| **MEDICATION** | **SIDE EFFECTS** | **NURSING CONSIDERATIONS** |
| Deferoxamine mesylate | Pain and induration at injection site<br>Urticaria<br>Hypotension<br>Generalized erythema | Used for acute iron intoxication, chronic iron overload |
| Dimercaprol | Hypertension<br>Tachycardia<br>Nausea, vomiting<br>Headache | Used for treatment of arsenic, gold, and mercury poisoning; acute lead poisoning when used with edetate calcium disodium<br>Administered as initial dose because of its improved efficiency in removing lead from brain tissue |
| Edetate calcium disodium | | Used for acute and chronic lead poisoning, lead encephalopathy<br>Renal tubular necrosis<br>Multiple deep IM doses or IV<br>Very painful—local anesthetic procaine is injected with the drug (drawn into syringe last, after which the syringe is maintained with needle held slightly down so that it is administered first); rotate sites; provide emotional support and play therapy as outlet for frustration<br>Ensure adequate hydration and monitor I and O and kidney function—$CaNa_2EDTA$ and lead are toxic to kidneys<br>Seizure precautions—initial rapid mobilization of lead may cause an increase in brain lead levels, exacerbating symptoms |
| **Action** | Forms stable complexes with metals | |
| **Indications** | Poisoning (gold, arsenic)<br>Acute lead encephalopathy | |
| **Side effects** | Tachycardia<br>Burning sensation in lips, mouth, throat<br>Abdominal pain | |
| **Nursing considerations** | Monitor I and O, BUN, EKG<br>Encourage fluids | |

| IMMUNOMODULATORS | |
|---|---|
| **MEDICATION** | **SIDE EFFECTS** |
| Beta interferons | "Flu-like" symptoms<br>Liver dysfunction<br>Bone marrow depression<br>Injection site reactions<br>Photosensitivity<br>Central nervous system infection (natalizumab) |
| Interferon beta-1a<br>Interferon beta-1a<br>Interferon beta-1b | |
| Glatiramer acetate<br>Natalizumab | |
| **Action** | Modify the immune response<br>Decrease the movement of leukocytes into the central<br>   nervous system neurons |
| **Indications** | Multiple sclerosis |
| **Side effects** | "Flu-like" symptoms<br>Liver dysfunction<br>Bone marrow depression<br>Injection site reactions<br>Photosensitivity<br>Central nervous system infection (natalizumab) |
| **Nursing considerations** | Monitor liver function tests<br>Monitor complete blood count<br>Subcutaneous injection: rotate injection sites, apply ice, and<br>   then use warm compresses, analgesics for discomfort<br>Photosensitivity precautions |

| IMMUNOSUPPRESSANTS | | |
|---|---|---|
| **MEDICATION** | **SIDE EFFECTS** | **NURSING CONSIDERATIONS** |
| Cyclosporine | Nephrotoxicity<br>Headache<br>Seizures<br>Hypertension<br>Gingival hyperplasia<br>Leukopenia<br>Thrombocytopenia<br>Infections<br>Tremor | Take once daily in AM<br>Measure dosage carefully in oral syringe<br>Mix with whole milk, chocolate milk, fruit juice<br>Always used with adrenal corticosteroids<br>Monitor BUN, serum creatinine, liver function<br>   tests<br>To prevent thrush, swish and swallow<br>   nystatin QID<br>Use mechanical contraceptives, not oral<br>   contraceptives |
| **Action** | Prevents production of T cells and their response to interleukin-2; recognizes<br>   antigens foreign to body | |
| **Indications** | Prevent rejection for transplanted organs | |
| **Side effects** | Nausea, vomiting<br>Diarrhea<br>Hepatotoxicity<br>Nephrotoxicity<br>Infection<br>Myocardial fibrosis | |
| **Nursing considerations** | Monitor carefully for infections | |

| LAXATIVES AND STOOL SOFTENERS | | |
|---|---|---|
| **MEDICATION** | **SIDE EFFECTS** | **NURSING CONSIDERATIONS** |
| Cascara | Anorexia, nausea, abdominal cramps, hypokalemia, calcium deficiency | Avoid exposure to sunlight<br>Should be taken with full glass of water<br>Relieves constipation and softens stool in about 8 hours |
| Bisacodyl | Mild cramps, rash, nausea, diarrhea | Stimulant<br>Tablets should not be taken with milk or antacids (causes dissolution of enteric coating and loss of cathartic action)<br>Can cause gastric irritation<br>Effects in 6-12 hours |
| Phenolphthalein | Urticaria, rash, electrolyte imbalance<br>Allergic reactions, skin eruption | Caution clients against prolonged use<br>Will turn alkaline urine a pink-red color |
| Mineral oil | Pruritus ani, anorexia, nausea | Lubricant<br>Administer in upright position<br>Prolonged use can cause fat-soluble vitamin malabsorption |
| Docusate | Few side effects<br>Abdominal cramps | Stool softener<br>Contraindicated in atonic bowel, nausea, vomiting, GI pain<br>Effects in 1-3 days |
| Magnesium hydroxide | Hypermagnesemia, dehydration | Saline agent<br>Na+ salts can exacerbate heart failure |
| Psyllium hydrophilic mucilloid | Obstruction of GI tract | Take with a full glass of water; do not take dry<br>Report abdominal distention or unusual amount of flatulence |
| Polyethylene glycol and electrolytes | Nausea and bloating | Large-volume product—allow time to consume it safely |
| **Action** | Bulk-forming—absorbs water into stool mass, making stool bulky, thus stimulating peristalsis<br>Lubricants—coat surface of stool and soften fecal mass, allowing for easier passage<br>Osmotic agents and saline laxatives—draw water from plasma by osmosis, increasing bulk of fecal mass, thus promoting peristalsis<br>Stimulants—stimulate peristalsis when they come in contact with intestinal mucosa<br>Stool softeners—soften fecal mass | |
| **Indications** | Constipation<br>Preparation for procedures or surgery | |
| **Side effects** | Diarrhea<br>Dependence | |
| **Nursing considerations** | Contraindicated for clients with abdominal pain, nausea and vomiting, fever (acute abdomen)<br>Chronic use may cause hypokalemia | |

## MIOTIC EYE MEDICATIONS

| MEDICATION | SIDE EFFECTS | NURSING CONSIDERATIONS |
|---|---|---|
| Pilocarpine | Painful eye muscle spasm, blurred or poor vision in dim lights<br>Photophobia, cataracts, or floaters | Teach to apply pressure on lacrimal sac for 1 min following instillation<br>Used for glaucoma<br>Caution client to avoid sunlight and night driving |
| Carachol | Headache<br>If absorbed systemically, can cause sweating, abdominal cramps, and decreased blood pressure | Cholinergic (ophthalmic)<br>Similar to acetylcholine in action<br>Produces pupillary miosis during ocular surgery |
| **Action** | Causes contraction of sphincter muscles of iris, resulting in miosis | |
| **Indications** | Pupillary miosis in ocular surgery<br>Primary open-angle glaucoma | |
| **Side effects** | Headache<br>Hypotension<br>Bronchoconstriction | |
| **Nursing considerations** | Teach how to instill eye drops correctly<br>Apply light pressure on lacrimal sac for 1 minute after medication instilled<br>Avoid hazardous activities until temporary blurring disappears<br>Transient brow pain and myopia are common initially, disappear within 10-14 days | |

## DISEASE-MODIFYING ANTIRHEUMATIC DRUGS (DMARDS)

| MEDICATION | SIDE EFFECTS |
|---|---|
| **Nonbiologic DMARDs**<br>Methotrexate<br>Hydroxychloroquine sulfate<br>Sulfasalazine<br>Cyclosporine | |
| **Biologic DMARDs**<br>Entanercept<br>Infliximab<br>Adalimumab<br>Anakinra<br>Rituximab<br>Abatacept | |
| **Action** | Non-biologic DMARDs:<br>Interfere with immune system<br>Indirect and nonspecific effect<br><br>Biologic DMARDs:<br>Interfere with immune system (tumor necrosis factor, interleukins, T- or B-cell lymphocytes) |
| **Indications** | Rheumatoid arthritis<br>Psoriasis<br>Inflammatory bowel disease |
| **Side effects** | Stomatitis<br>Liver toxicity<br>Bleeding<br>Anemia<br>Infections<br>Hypersensitivity<br>Kidney failure |
| **Nursing considerations** | Precautions: infections, bleeding disorders<br>Monitor liver function tests<br>Monitor BUN and creatinine<br>Monitor for signs of infection<br>Monitor response to medication<br>Teach client about risk of live vaccines<br>Teach client to avoid alcohol<br>Teach client about risk of infection |

| MUSCULOSKELETAL MEDICATIONS | | |
|---|---|---|
| **MEDICATION** | **SIDE EFFECTS** | **NURSING CONSIDERATIONS** |
| Edrophonium | Seizures<br>Hypotension<br>Diarrhea<br>Bronchospasm<br>Respiratory paralysis | Diagnostic test for myasthenia gravis<br>Increased muscular strength within<br>  30-60 seconds confirms diagnosis,<br>  lasts 4-5 minutes<br>Monitor respirations closely<br>Have atropine 0.5 mg injection available |
| Neostigmine | Nausea, vomiting<br>Abdominal cramps<br>Respiratory depression<br>Bronchoconstriction<br>Hypotension<br>Bradycardia | Monitor vital signs frequently<br>Have atropine injection available<br>Observe for improvement in strength,<br>  vision, ptosis 45 min after each dose<br>Schedule dose before periods of fatigue<br>  (e.g., ac)<br>Take with milk or food<br>Potentiates action of morphine<br>Diagnostic test for myasthenia gravis |
| Pyridostigmine<br>  bromide | Seizures<br>Bradycardia<br>Hypotension<br>Bronchoconstriction | Monitor vital signs frequently<br>Have atropine injection available<br>Take extended-release tablets same time<br>  each day at least 6 h apart<br>Drug of choice for myasthenia gravis to<br>  improve muscle strength |
| Alendronate sodium | Vitamin D deficiency<br>Osteomalacia | Prevents and treats osteoporosis<br>Longer-lasting treatment for Paget's<br>  disease<br>Take in A.M. at least 30 min before other<br>  medication, food, water, or other liquids<br>Should sit up for 30 min after taking<br>  medication<br>Use sunscreen and wear protective<br>  clothing |
| Glucosamine | Nausea, heartburn, diarrhea | Antirheumatic<br>Contraindicated with shellfish allergy,<br>  pregnancy, and lactation<br>May worsen glycemic control<br>Must be taken on regular basis to be<br>  effective |
| **Action** | Inhibits destruction of acetylcholine released from parasympathetic and<br>  somatic efferent nerves | |
| **Indications** | Myasthenia gravis<br>Postoperative and postpartum functional urinary retention | |
| **Side effects** | Bronchoconstriction<br>Diarrhea<br>Respiratory paralysis<br>Muscle cramps | |
| **Nursing<br>  considerations** | Give with milk or food<br>Administer exactly as ordered and on time<br>Doses vary with client's activity level<br>Monitor vital signs, especially respirations | |

| MYDRIATIC AND CYCLOPEGIC EYE MEDICATIONS | | |
|---|---|---|
| **MEDICATION** | **SIDE EFFECTS** | **NURSING CONSIDERATIONS** |
| Atropine sulfate | Blurred vision, photophobia<br>Flushing, tachycardia<br>Dry mouth | Contraindicated with narrow-angle glaucoma<br>Suck on hard candy for dry mouth |
| Cyclopentolate | Photophobia, blurred vision<br>Seizures<br>Tachycardia | Contraindicated in narrow-angle glaucoma<br>Burns when instilled |
| **Action** | Anticholinergic action leaves the pupil under unopposed adrenergic influence, causing it to dilate | |
| **Indications** | Diagnostic procedures<br>Acute iritis, uveitis | |
| **Side effects** | Headache<br>Tachycardia<br>Blurred vision<br>Photophobia<br>Dry mouth | |
| **Nursing considerations** | Mydriatics cause pupil dilation; cycloplegics paralyze the iris sphincter<br>Watch for signs of glaucoma (increased intraocular pressure, headache, progressive blurring of vision)<br>Apply light pressure on lacrimal sac for 1 minute after instilling medication<br>Avoid hazardous activities until blurring of vision subsides<br>Wear dark glasses | |

| NARCOTICS (OPIOID ANALGESICS) | | |
|---|---|---|
| **MEDICATION** | **SIDE EFFECTS** | **NURSING CONSIDERATIONS** |
| Morphine sulfate | Dizziness, weakness<br>Sedation or paradoxic excitement<br>Nausea, flushing, and sweating<br>Respiratory depression, decreased cough reflex<br>Constipation, miosis, hypotension | Give in smallest effective dose<br>Observe for development of dependence<br>Encourage respiratory exercises<br>Use cautiously to prevent respiratory depression<br>Monitor vital signs<br>Monitor I and O, bowel patterns<br>Used for cardiac clients—reduces preload and afterload pressures, decreasing cardiac workload |
| Codeine | Same as morphine<br>High dose may cause restlessness and excitement<br>Constipation | Less potent and less dependence potential compared with morphine |
| Methadone | Same as morphine | Observe for dependence, respiratory depression<br>Encourage fluids and high-bulk foods |
| Propoxyphene | Restlessness, tremors<br>Mild euphoria | Observe for dependence in prolonged users<br>Use cautiously with CNS depressants, alcohol, and tranquilizers because of potentiating effect<br>Older adults: adverse reactions similar to narcotics |
| Merperidine | Frequent dizziness, occasional tremors<br>Uncoordinated muscular movements<br>Constipation, urinary retention<br>Bradycardia | Observe for dependence<br>Give repeated doses intramuscularly<br>Local irritation if given subcutaneously<br>Avoid giving to older adults and those with renal disease<br>Prolonged half-life of a metabolite accumulates with repeated doses and can lead to life-threatening seizures<br>Older adults: increased risk of toxicity; tremors and seizures |
| Hydromorphone | Sedation, hypotension<br>Urine retention | Keep narcotic antagonist (naloxone) available<br>Monitor bowel function |
| Oxycodone and aspirin<br>Oxycodone and acetaminophen | Lightheadedness, dizziness, sedation, nausea<br>Constipation, pruritus<br>Increased risk bleeding (oxycodone and aspirin) | Administer with milk after meals<br>Commonly prescribed as oxycodone and asprin, an acetaminophen and oxycodone combination |
| Hydrocodone/Acetaminophen | Confusion<br>Sedation<br>Hypotension<br>Constipation | Use with extreme caution with MAO inhibitors<br>Additive CNS depression with alcohol, antihistamines, and sedative/hypnotics |
| **Action** | Produces analgesia, euphoria, sedation; acts on CNS receptor cells | |
| **Indications** | Moderate-to-severe pain<br>Chronic pain<br>Preoperative medication | |
| **Side effects** | Dizziness<br>Sedation<br>Respiratory depression<br>Cardiac arrest<br>Hypotension | |
| **Nursing considerations** | Provide narcotic antagonist if needed<br>Turn, cough, deep breathe<br>Safety precautions (side rails, assist when walking)<br>Avoid alcohol, antihistamines, sedative, tranquilizers, OTC drugs<br>Avoid activities requiring mental alertness | |

| NITRATES/ANTIANGINALS | | |
|---|---|---|
| **MEDICATION** | **SIDE EFFECTS** | **NURSING CONSIDERATIONS** |
| Nitroglycerin | Flushing<br>Hypotension<br>Headache<br>Tachycardia<br>Dizziness<br>Blurred vision | Renew supply every 3 months<br>Avoid alcoholic beverages<br>Sublingual dose may be repeated every 5 minutes for 3<br>  doses<br>Protect drug from light<br>Should wet tablet with saliva and place under tongue |
| Isosorbide | Headache<br>Orthostatic<br>  hypotension | Change position slowly<br>Take between meals<br>Don't discontinue abruptly |
| **Action** | Relaxes vascular smooth muscle; decreases venous return; decreases arterial<br>  blood pressure; reduces myocardial oxygen consumption | |
| **Indications** | Angina<br>Perioperative hypertension<br>CHF associated with MI<br>Raynaud's disease (topical) | |
| **Side effects** | Hypotension<br>Tachycardia<br>Headache<br>Dizziness<br>Syncope<br>Rash | |
| **Nursing<br>  considerations** | Take sublingual tablets under tongue or in buccal pouch; may sting<br>Check expiration date on bottle<br>Discard unused med after 6 months<br>Take sustained-release tablets with water, don't chew them<br>Administer topically over 6  6 inch area using applicator, cover with plastic<br>  wrap, rotate sites<br>Administer transdermal to skin free of hair; do not apply to distal extremities;<br>  remove before defibrillation or cardioversion<br>Administer transmucosal tablets between lip and gum above the incisors or<br>  between cheek and gum; do not swallow or chew<br>Administer translingual spray into oral mucosa; do not inhale<br>Withdraw medication gradually over 4-6 wks<br>Provide rest periods<br>Teach to take medication when chest pain anticipated<br>May take q 5 min  3 doses<br>Beta-adrenergic blockers and calcium-channel blockers also used for angina | |

| NONSTEROIDAL ANTI-INFLAMMATORY (NSAIDs) | | |
|---|---|---|
| **MEDICATION** | **SIDE EFFECTS** | **NURSING CONSIDERATIONS** |
| Ibuprofen | GI upset—nausea, vomiting, diarrhea, constipation<br>Skin eruption, dizziness, headache, fluid retention | Use cautiously with aspirin allergy<br>Give with milk |
| Indomethacin | Peptic ulcer, ulcerative colitis<br>Headache, dizziness<br>Bone marrow depression | Observe for bleeding tendencies<br>Monitor I and O |
| Naproxen | Headache, dizziness, epigastric distress | Administer with food<br>Optimal therapeutic response is seen after 2 weeks of treatment<br>Use cautiously in client with history of aspirin allergy |
| Celecoxib | Fatigue<br>Anxiety, depression, nervousness<br>Nausea, vomiting, anorexia<br>Dry mouth, constipation | COX-2 inhibitor<br>Increasing doses do not appear to increase effectiveness<br>Do not take if allergic to sulfonamides, ASA, or NSAIDs |
| Ketorolac | Peptic ulcer disease<br><br>GI bleeding, prolonged bleeding<br>Renal impairment | Dosage is decreased in clients over 65 years or with impaired renal function<br>Duration of treatment is less than 5 days |
| **Actions** | NSAIDs inhibit prostaglandins<br>COX-2 inhibitors block the enzyme responsible for inflammation without blocking the COX-1 enzyme<br>ASA has antiplatelet activity | |
| **Indications** | Pain, fever, arthritis, dysmenorrhea<br>ASA: transient ischemic attacks, prophylaxis of MI, ischemic stroke, angina<br>Ibuprofen: gout, dental pain, musculoskeletal disorders | |
| **Side effects** | Headache<br>Eye changes<br>Dizziness<br>Somnolence<br>GI disturbances<br>Constipation<br>Bleeding<br>Rash | |
| **Nursing considerations** | Take with food or after meals<br>Periodic ophthalmologic exam<br>Monitor liver and renal function<br>Avoid OTC drugs; may contain similar medications<br>Also have analgesic and antipyretic actions<br>Post-op clients with adequate pain relief have fewer complications and a shorter recovery<br>Pain is the fifth vital sign and needs to be noted with others | |

| MEDICATIONS FOR PAGET'S DISEASE | | |
|---|---|---|
| **MEDICATION** | **SIDE EFFECTS** | **NURSING CONSIDERATIONS** |
| Calcitonin | Nausea, vomiting, flushing of face<br>Increased urinary frequency | Retards bone resorption<br>Decreases release of calcium from bone<br>Relieves pain<br>Observe for symptoms of tetany<br>Give at hs |
| Etidronate disodium | Diarrhea | Prevents rapid bone turnover<br>Don't give with food, milk, or antacids (reduces absorption)<br>Monitor renal function |
| Mithramycin | GI upset<br>Bone marrow depression<br>Facial flushing | Cytotoxic<br>Antibiotic<br>Monitor BUN, liver, and renal function tests, platelet count and PT<br>Check for signs of infection or bleeding |
| **Action** | Inhibits osteocytic activity | |
| **Indications** | Paget's disease | |
| **Side effects** | Decreased serum calcium<br>Facial flushing | |
| **Nursing considerations** | Monitor serum calcium levels<br>Facial flushing and warmth last 1 h | |

| THROMBOLYTIC MEDICATIONS | | |
|---|---|---|
| **MEDICATION** | **SIDE EFFECTS** | **NURSING CONSIDERATIONS (SPECIFIC)** |
| Reteplase<br>Alteplase<br>Tissue plasminogen activator | Bleeding | Tissue plasminogen activator is a naturally occurring enzyme<br>Low allergenic risk but high cost |
| Anistreplase<br>Streptokinase | Bleeding | Because streptokinase is made from a bacterium, client can have an allergic reaction. Not used if client had recent *Streptococcus* infection or received Streptase in past year |
| **Action** | Reteplase and Alteplase break down plasminogen into plasmin, which dissolves the fibrin network of a clot<br>Anistreplase and Streptokinase bind with plasminogen to form a complex that digests fibrin | |
| **Indications** | MIs within the first 6 hours after symptoms, limited arterial thrombosis, thrombotic strokes, occluded shunts | |
| **Nursing considerations (general)** | Check for signs of bleeding; minimize number of punctures for inserting IVs; avoid IM injections; apply pressure at least twice as long as usual after any puncture | |

| MEDICATIONS FOR ULCERS | | |
|---|---|---|
| **MEDICATION** | **SIDE EFFECTS** | **NURSING CONSIDERATIONS** |
| **H2-antagonists**<br>Cimetidine<br>Ranitidine<br>Famotidine<br>Nizatidine | Diarrhea<br>Confusion and dizziness<br>  (esp. in elderly with<br>  large doses)<br>Headache | Bedtime dose suppresses nocturnal acid<br>  production<br>Compliance may increase with single-dose<br>  regimen<br>Avoid antacids within 1 hour of dose<br>Dysrhythmias<br>Cimetidine–greater incidence of confusion and<br>  agitation with older adults |
| **Antisecretory agents**<br>Omeprazole<br>Lansoprazole<br>Rabeprazole<br>Esomeprazole<br>Pantoprazole | Dizziness<br>Diarrhea | Bedtime dose suppresses nocturnal acid<br>  production<br>Do not crush sustained-release capsule;<br>  contents may be sprinkled on food or instilled<br>  with fluid in NG tube |
| **Prostaglandin**<br>  **analogs**<br>Misoprostol | Abdominal pain<br>Diarrhea (13%)<br>Miscarriage | Notify health care provider if diarrhea more than<br>  1 week or severe abdominal pain or black,<br>  tarry stools |
| **Nursing**<br>  **considerations** | Other medications may be prescribed, included antacids (time administration<br>  to avoid canceling med effect) and antimicrobials to eradicate *H. pylori*<br>  infections<br>Client should avoid smoking, alcohol, ASA, and caffeine, all of which<br>  increase stomach acid | |

| VITAMINS | | |
|---|---|---|
| **MEDICATION** | **SIDE EFFECTS** | **NURSING CONSIDERATIONS** |
| Cyanocobalamin<br>(Vitamin $B_{12}$) | Anaphylaxis<br>Urticaria | Treatment of vitamin $B_{12}$ deficiency,<br>  pernicious anemia, hemorrhage,<br>  renal and hepatic diseases<br>Monitor reticulocyte count, iron, and folate<br>  levels<br>Don't mix with other solutions in syringe<br>Monitor $K^+$ levels<br>Clients with pernicious anemia need monthly<br>  injections |
| Folic acid | Bronchospasm<br>Malaise | Treatment of anemia, liver disease,<br>  alcoholism, intestinal obstruction, pregnancy<br>Don't mix with other meds in syringe |
| **Action** | Coenzymes that speed up metabolic processes | |
| **Indications** | Vitamin deficiencies | |
| **Side effects** | Some vitamins are toxic at high levels | |
| **Nursing**<br>  **considerations** | Avoid exceeding RDA (recommended daily allowance) | |

| WOMEN'S HEALTH MEDICATIONS | | |
|---|---|---|
| **MEDICATION** | **SIDE EFFECTS** | **NURSING CONSIDERATIONS** |
| **Contraceptives, systemic**<br><br>Example: Ethinyl Estradiol/norgestrel | Headache<br>Dizziness<br>Nausea<br>Breakthrough bleeding, spotting | Used to prevent pregnancy<br>Use condoms against sexually transmitted diseases<br>Take pill at same time every day<br>No smoking |
| **Contraceptives, systemic**<br><br>Levonorgestrel | Breakthrough bleeding, spotting | Prevention of pregnancy for 5 years as a contraceptive implant; emergency contraceptive in oral form when given within 72 hours of unprotected intercourse |
| **Estrogens**<br><br>Estradiol<br>Estrogens conjugated | Nausea<br>Gynecomastia<br>Contact lens intolerance | Treatment of menopausal symptoms, some cancers<br>Prevention of osteoporosis<br>Client should contact health care provider if breast lumps, vaginal bleeding, edema, jaundice, dark urine, clay-colored stools, dyspnea, blurred vision, numbness or stiffness in leg, chest pain |
| **Progestins**<br>Medroxyprogestrone acetate | Nausea<br>Contact lens intolerance | Management of abnormal uterine bleeding; prevent endometrial changes of estrogen replacement therapy, some cancers |
| **Actions** | Female hormones | |
| **Indications** | Contraceptives<br>Treatment of menopausal symptoms<br>Prevention of osteoporosis | |
| **Side effects** | Nausea<br>Breakthrough bleeding<br>Headache | |
| **Nursing considerations** | Client should know when to take medication and what to do for skipped doses<br>Client should know when to contact prescribing health care provider | |
| **Herbal** | Black cohosh—relieves hot flashes; may increase hypotensive effect of antihypertensives; do not take for more than 6 months | |

CH. 9

**PHYSIOLOGICAL INTEGRITY 4**
PHARMACOLOGICAL AND
PARENTERAL THERAPIES

| MEN'S HEALTH MEDICATIONS | | |
|---|---|---|
| **MEDICATION** | **SIDE EFFECTS** | **NURSING CONSIDERATIONS** |
| Alpha₁-adrenergic blockers<br>  Terazosin | Dizziness<br>Headache<br>Weakness<br>Nasal congestion<br>Orthostatic hypotension | Used to decrease urinary urgency, hesitancy, nocturia in prostatic hyperplasia<br>Caution to change position slowly<br>Avoid alcohol, CNS depressant, hot showers due to orthostatic hypotension<br>Requires titration<br>Administer at bedtime due to risk orthostatic hypotension<br>Effects may not be noted for 4 weeks |
|   Tamsulosin | Dizziness<br>Headache | Used to decrease urinary urgency, hesitancy, nocturia in prostatic hyperplasia<br>Caution to change position slowly<br>Administer 30 min. after same meal each day |
| 5-alpha-reductase inhibitor<br>  Finasteride | Decreased libido<br>Impotence | Used to treat benign prostatic hyperplasia by slowing prostatic growth<br>May decrease serum PSA levels<br>6-12 months therapy required to determine if medication effective<br>May cause harm to male fetus. Pregnant women should not be exposed to semen of partner taking finasteride or they should not handle crushed medication<br>Monitor liver function tests |
|   Dutasteride | Decreased libido<br>Impotence | Used to treat benign prostatic hyperplasia by slowing prostatic growth<br>May cause harm to male fetus. Pregnant women should not be exposed to semen of partner taking finasteride or they should not handle crushed medication<br>Monitor liver function |
| Anti-impotence agents<br>  Sildenafil<br>  Vardenafil<br>  Tadalafil | Headache<br>Flushing<br>Dyspepsia<br>Nasal congestion<br>Mild visual disturbance | Enhances blood flow to the corpus cavernosum to ensure erection to allow sexual intercourse<br>Should not take with nitrates in any form due to dramatic decrease in blood pressure<br>Usually taken 1 hour before sexual activity (sildenafil, vardenafil)<br>Tadalafil has longer duration of action (up to 36 hours)<br>Should not take more than one time per day<br>Notify health care provider if erection lasts longer than 4 hours |
| Saw palmetto | Urinary antiseptic used to treat PBH; may cause false-negative PSA test result | |

542

| HERBAL SUPPLEMENTS | | |
|---|---|---|
| **SUPPLEMENT** | **SIDE EFFECTS/ CONTRAINDICATIONS** | **NURSING CONSIDERATIONS** |
| **Immune System** | | |
| Echinacea<br><br>Immunostimulant, anti-inflammatory, antiviral, antibacterial<br><br>Used to prevent and treat colds, flu, wound healing, urinary tract infections | Immune suppression, tingling sensation and/or unpleasant taste on tongue, nausea, vomiting, allergic reactions | Decreases effectiveness of immunosuppressants<br><br>Contraindicated in autoimmune diseases<br><br>Avoid if allergic to ragweed, members of daisy family of plants |
| Garlic<br><br>Antimicrobial, antilipidemic, antithrombotic, antitumor, anti-inflammatory<br><br>Used to reduce cholesterol, prevent atherosclerosis, cancer, stroke, and MI; decrease blood pressure prevent and treat colds and flu | Flatulence, heartburn, halitosis, irritation of mouth, esophagus, stomach, allergic reaction<br><br>Contraindicated with peptic ulcer, reflux | May potentiate anticoagulant and antiplatelets, antihyperlipidemics, antihypertensives, antidiabetic agents, and herbs with these effects<br><br>May decrease efficacy of cyclosporine, hormonal contraceptives<br><br>Avoid if allergic to members of the lily family of plants |
| Ginseng<br><br>Stimulant and tonic to immune and nervous systems<br><br>Used to increase stamina, as aphrodisiac, adjunct chemotherapy and radiation therapy | Headache, insomnia, nervousness, palpitations, excitation, diarrhea, vaginal bleeding<br><br>May cause headache, tremors, irritability, manic episodes if combined with MAOIs or caffeine | May falsely elevate digoxin levels; observe for signs usually associated with high digoxin levels<br><br>May antagonize Coumadin<br><br>Potentiates antidiabetic agents, steroids, estrogens<br><br>Caution with cardiovascular disease, hypotension, hypertension, steroid therapy |
| **Female Reproductive System** | | |
| Evening Primrose Oil<br><br>Anti-inflammatory, sedative, astringent<br><br>Used for premenstrual and menopausal problems, rheumatoid arthritis, elevated serum cholesterol, hypertension, eczema, diabetic neuropathy | Headache, rash, nausea, seizures, inflammation<br><br>Contraindicated for clients with epilepsy, schizophrenia | May potentiate antiplatelet and anticoagulant meds<br><br>Increases risk for seizures when taken with phenothiazines, antidepressants |

*(continued)*

| HERBAL SUPPLEMENTS (cont'd) | | |
|---|---|---|
| **SUPPLEMENT** | **SIDE EFFECTS/ CONTRAINDICATIONS** | **NURSING CONSIDERATIONS** |
| **Musculoskeletal System** | | |
| Chondroitin<br><br>Collagen synthesis<br><br>Used for arthritis for cartilage synthesis (with glucosamine) | Dyspepsia, nausea | May potentiate effects of anticoagulants |
| Glucosamine<br><br>Collagen synthesis<br><br>Used for arthritis for cartilage synthesis (with chondroitin) | Dyspepsia, nausea | May impede insulin secretion or increase resistance |
| **Neurological System** | | |
| Capsicum/Cayenne Pepper<br><br>Analgesia, improves blood circulation<br><br>Used for arthritis, bowel disorders, nerve pain, PAD, chronic laryngitis, personal self-defense spray | GI discomfort, burning pain in eyes, nose, mouth, blepharospasm and swelling in eyes, skin tissue irritation, cough, bronchospasm<br><br>Avoid if allergic to ragweed or to chili pepper | May decrease effectiveness of antihypertensives, increases risk of cough with ACE inhibitors<br><br>May potentiate antiplatelet and anticoagulant meds and herbs<br><br>May cause hypertensive crisis with MAOIs<br><br>Increases theophylline absorption |
| Feverfew<br><br>Analgesic, antipyretic<br><br>Used for migraine prophylaxis, fever, menstrual problems, arthritis | Mouth ulcers, heartburn, indigestion, dizziness, tachycardia, allergic reactions | Potentiates antiplatelet and anticoagulant meds<br><br>Do not stop abruptly—causes moderate to severe pain with joint and muscle stiffness<br><br>Caution if allergic to daisy family of plants |

*(continued)*

| HERBAL SUPPLEMENTS (cont'd) | | |
|---|---|---|
| **SUPPLEMENT** | **SIDE EFFECTS/ CONTRAINDICATIONS** | **NURSING CONSIDERATIONS** |
| **Gastrointestinal System** | | |
| Flaxseed<br><br>Laxative, anticholesteremic<br><br>Used for constipation, decrease cholesterol, prevent atherosclerosis, colon disorders | Diarrhea, flatulence, nausea<br><br>Contraindicated if client has strictures or acute GI inflammation | May decrease absorption of oral meds—do not take within 2 hrs<br><br>Immature flax seeds can be very toxic<br><br>Increase fluids to minimize flatulence |
| Ginger<br><br>Antiemetic, antioxidant, digestive aid, anti-inflammatory<br><br>Used for nausea, vomiting, indigestion, gas, lack of appetite | Minor heartburn, dermatitis<br><br>Contraindicated with gallstones | May potentiate antiplatelet and anticoagulant meds, antidiabetic meds, herbs that increase bleeding times |
| Licorice<br><br>Demulcent (soothes), expectorant, anti-inflammatory<br><br>Used for coughs, colds, stomach pains, ulcers | Hypokalemia, headache, edema, lethargy, hypertension, heart failure (with overdose), cardiac arrest<br><br>Contraindicated in renal or liver disease, heart disease, hypertension; caution with hormonal contraceptives | Decreases effect of spironolactone<br><br>Avoid use with digoxin, loop diuretics, corticosteroids |
| **Genitourinary System** | | |
| Saw Palmetto<br><br>Mild diuretic, urinary antiseptic<br><br>Used for BPH, increasing sexual vigor, cystitis | Constipation, diarrhea, nausea, decreased libido, back pain | May interact with hormonal meds such as HRT and oral contraceptives<br><br>May cause a false negative PSA test result |

*(continued)*

| HERBAL SUPPLEMENTS (cont'd) | | |
|---|---|---|
| **SUPPLEMENT** | **SIDE EFFECTS/ CONTRAINDICATIONS** | **NURSING CONSIDERATIONS** |
| **Psychiatric** | | |
| Chamomile Sedative/hypnotic, anti-inflammatory, antispasmodic, anti-infective Used for stress, anxiety, insomnia, GI disorders | Allergic reactions, contact dermatitis, vomiting, depression | May potentiate sedatives and anticoagulants Avoid if allergic to ragweed, members of daisy family of plants |
| Kava Anti-anxiety, sedative/ hypnotic, muscle relaxant Used for anxiety, insomnia, seizure disorders | Hepatotoxicity, psychological dependence, mild euphoria, fatigue, sedation, suicidal thoughts, visual problems, scaly skin reaction Contraindicated in Parkinson's, history of stroke, endogenous depression | May potentiate sedative effects of other sedating meds (benzodiazepines, barbiturates), anticonvulsants, and herbs (chamomile, valerian) |
| Melatonin Hormone from pineal gland Used for insomnia, jet lag | Headache, confusion, sedation, tachycardia | Potentiates CNS depressants May decrease effectiveness of immunosuppressants, Procardia |
| St. John's Wort Antidepressant, sedative effects, antiviral, antimicrobial Used for mild to moderate depression, sleep disorders, skin and wound healing | Photosensitivity, fatigue, allergic reactions, dry mouth, dizziness, restlessness, nausea Contraindicated for major depression, transplant recipients, clients taking SSRIs (increases risk of serotonin syndrome), MAOIs (increases risk of hypertensive crisis), hormonal contraceptives | Usually decreases effectiveness of (igoxin, antineoplastics, antiviral AIDS drugs, anti-rejection drugs, theophylline, Coumadin, hormonal contraceptives May potentiate drugs and herbs with sedative effects Should avoid tyramine in diet, OTC meds |
| Valerian Sedative/hypnotic, antispasmodic Used for insomnia, restlessness, anxiety | Headache, blurred vision, nausea, excitability Contraindicated in liver disease may be hepatotoxic | May potentiate other CNS depressant meds, antihistamines, and sedating herbs |

*(continued)*

| HERBAL SUPPLEMENTS (cont'd) | | |
|---|---|---|
| **SUPPLEMENT** | **SIDE EFFECTS/ CONTRAINDICATIONS** | **NURSING CONSIDERATIONS** |
| **Cardiovascular System** | | |
| Gingko<br><br>Enhances cerebral and peripheral blood circulation; antidepressive<br><br>Used for dementia, short-term memory loss, vertigo, PADs, depression, sexual dysfunction (including from SSRIs) | Headache, GI upset, contact dermatitis, dizziness | May potentiate antiplatelet and anticoagulant meds, ASA, NSAIDS, and herbs, which increase bleeding time<br><br>May potentiate MAOIs<br><br>May decrease effectiveness of anticonvulsants |
| Hawthorn<br><br>Antianginal, antiarrhythmic, vasodilator, antihypertensive, antilipidemic<br><br>Used for mild to moderate heart failure, hypertension, cholesterol reduction | Nausea, fatigue, sweating | May potentiate or interfere with wide range of cardiovascular meds used for CHF, angina, arrhythmias, hypertension, vasodilation<br><br>Potentiates digoxin<br><br>Potentiates CNS depressants<br><br>Avoid if allergic to members of the rose family of plants |
| **Respiratory System** | | |
| Eucalyptus<br><br>Decongestant, anti-inflammatory, antimicrobial, antifungal<br><br>Used for coughs, bronchitis, nasal congestion, sore muscles, wounds | Nausea, vomiting, epigastric burning, dizziness, muscle weakness, seizures<br><br>Contraindicated with liver disease, inflammation of intestinal tract | Potentiates antidiabetic meds and possibly other herbs that cause hypoglycemia<br><br>May increase metabolism of any drugs metabolized in liver |

| DRUG INTERACTIONS WITH GRAPEFRUIT JUICE (INCREASED SERUM DRUG LEVELS) | |
|---|---|
| Calcium channel blockers: amlodipine, diltiazem, felodipine, nicardipine, nifedipine, nimodipine, nisoldipine, verapamil | |
| Caffeine | Cabamazepine<br><br>Buspirone<br><br>Midazolam |
| SSRIs: fluoxetine, fluvoxamine, sertraline | Sildenafil<br><br>Statins<br><br>Praziquantel<br><br>Dextromethorphan<br><br>Sirolimus<br><br>Tacrolimus |

## MEDICATION CLASSIFICATIONS

Agents Used to Treat Shock, Cardiac
Arrest, and Anaphylaxis  472–473
Norepinephrine
Dopamine
Epinephrine
Isoproterenol hydrochloride
Phenylephrine
Dobutamine

Antianxiety Agents  474–475
Chlordiazepoxide hydrochloride
Diazepam
Alprazolam
Clonazepam
Lorazepam
Oxazepam
Buspirone
Hydroxyzine hydrochloride

Antacid Medications  476
Aluminum hydroxide
Calcium carbonate
Magnesium hydroxide
Aluminum/magnesium hydroxide

Antidysrhythmics  477
Class IA Drugs
Class IB Drugs
Class II Drugs
Class III Drugs
Class IV Drugs

Antibiotics/Anti-infectives  478–483
Aminoglycosides
  Gentamicin
  Neomycin
  Streptomycin
  Tobramycin
  Amikacin
Cephalosporins
  Cefaclor
  Cefazolin
  Cephalexin
  Ceftriaxone
Fluoroquinolones
  Ciprofloxacin
  Levofloxacin
Glycopeptides
  Vancomycin
Lycosamides
  Clindamycin
Macrolides
  Erythromycin
  Azithromycin

Penicillins
  Amoxicillin
  Ampicillin
  Methicillin
  Nafcillin
  Penicillin G
  Penicillin V
Sulfonamides
  Sulfisoxazole
  Sulfasalazine
  Trimethoprim/sulfamethoxazole
Tetracyclines
  Doxycycline
  Tetracycline

Topical Antibacterials  483
Bacitracin ointment
Neosporin cream
Povidone-iodine
Silver sulfadiazine cream
Tolnaftate
Nystatin cream

Genitourinary Medications  484
Nitrofuranton microcrystals
Phenazopyridine
Anticholinergics
  Oxybutynin chloride
  Hyoscyamine
  Propantheline
Anti-impotence
  Sildenafil
Testosterone inhibitors
  Finasteride

Anticholinergic Medications  485
Propantheline
Belladonna
Atropine sulfate

Anticoagulant Medications  486
Heparin
Enoxaparin sodium
Warfarin

Anticonvulsant Medications  487–488
Diazepam
Phenytoin
Phenobarbitol
Primidone
Magnesium sulfate
Valproic acid
Carbamazepine
Ethosuximide
Gabapentin
Lamotrigine
Topiramate

**Antidepressants   489–491**
MAO Inhibitors
  Phenelzine
SSRIs
  Fluoxetine
  Sertraline
SNRIs
  Venlafaxine
  Duloxetine
Tricyclics
  Amitriptyline
  Imipramine
Heterocyclics
  Bupropion HCl
  Trazodone HCl

**Antidiabetic Agents/Insulin   492–493**
Rapid-Acting
  Lispro
  Aspart
Short-Acting
  Humalog R
  Novolin R
  Iletin II Regular
Intermediate-Acting
  NPH
Very Long-Acting
  Lantus
Sulfonylureas
  Glimepiride
  Glipizide
  Glyburide
Biguanides
  Metformin
Alpha Glucoside Inhibitors
  Acarbose
Thiazolidinediones
  Rosiglitazone
Meglitinides
  Repaglinide

**Medications that Reverse
Hyperglycemia   494**
Glucagon

**Antidiarrheal Medications   494**
Bismuth subsalicylate
Diphenoxylate hydrochloride/atropine
sulfate
Loperamide
Opium alkaloids

**Antiemetic Medications   495–496**
Trimethobenzamide hydrochloride
Prochlorperazine dimaleate
Ondansetron
Thiethylperazine
Metoclopramide
Meclizine
Dimenhydrinate
Promethazine
Droperidol

**Antifungal Medications   496**
Amphotericin
Nystatin
Flucanozal

**Antigout Medications   497**
Colchicine
Probenecid
Allopurinol

**Antihistamine Medications   498**
Chlorpheniramine maleate
Diphenhydramine HCl
Promethazine HCl
Loratadine
Cetirozine
Fexofenadine

**Antilipemic Agents   499**
Cholestyramine
Colestipol
HMG-CoA Reductase Inhibitors
  Lovostatin
  Pravastatin
  Simvastatin
Nicotinic acid
  Niacin

**Antihypertensives   500–503**
Captopril
Enalapril
Lisinopril
Atenolol
Propranolol
Nifedipine
Verapamil
Diltiazem
Clonidine
Methyldopa
Hydralazine
Minoxidil

**Medications for Bipolar Disorder
504**
Lithium
Carbamazepine
Divalproex

**Antiparkinson Medications   510**
Trihexyphenidyl
Benztropine
Bromocriptine
Carbidopa/levodopa
Amantadine hydrochloride

**Antiplatelet Agents   511**
Aspirin
Dipyridamole
Clopidogrel

**Antipsychotic Medications   512–514**
Haloperidol
Fluphenazine
Perphenazine
Chlorpromazine
Risperidone
Quetiapine
Ziprasidone

**Antipyretic Medications   515**
Acetaminophen
Aspirin, ASA

**Antithyroid Medications   515–516**
Methimazole
Propylthiouracil (PTU)
Potassium iodide
Radioactive iodine, [131]I

**Thyroid Replacement Medications   516**
Levothyroxine
Liothyronine sodium

**Antitubercular Agents   518**
Isoniazid
Ethambutol
Rifampin
Streptomycin
Para-amino salicylic acid (PAS)
Pyrazinamide (PZA)

**Antitussive/Expectorant Medications   513**
Dextromethorphan
Guaifenesin

**Antivirals   519–520**
Acyclovir
Ribavarin
Zidovudine
Zalcitabine
Didanosine
Famciclovir
Ganciclovir

**Medications Used for Attention-Deficit Hyperactivity Disorder   520**
Methylphenidate
Dextroamphetamine

**Bone-Resorption Inhibitors   521**
Alendronic acid
Risedronic acid
Ibandronic acid

**Bronchodilators   521**
Aminophylline
Terbutaline
Ipratropium bromide
Albuterol
Epinephrine
Acetylcysteine
Cromolyn sodium
Salmeterol
Montelukast

**Carbonic Anhydrase Inhibitors   522**
Acetazolamide

**Cardiac Glycosides   523**
Digoxin

**Cytoprotective Agents   524**
Sucralfate

**Diuretics   524–525**
Hydrochlorothiazide
Chlorothiazide
Spirnlactone
Furosemide
Ethacrynic acid
Bumetanide
Mannitol
Hygroton

**Electrolyte and Replacement Solutions   526**
Calcium carbonate
Calcium chloride
MgCl, Slow mag
Potassium chloride
Kaon Liquid

**Iron Preparations   527**
$FeSO_4$, Feosol
Iron dextran

**Minerals   527**
Calcium
Vitamin D
Sodium fluoride
Potassium

**Eye Medications   528**
Artificial tears
Tetrahydrozoline
Timolol maleate

Levobunolol
Proparacaine hydrochloride
ophthalmic
Tetracaine topical
Prednisone ophthalmic
Gentamicin
Tobramyacin ophthalmic
Idoxurine
Dipivefrin
Flurbiprofen

## Glucocorticoids   529
Cortisone acetate
Hydrocortisone sodium
Dexamethasone
Methylprednisolone
Prednisone

## Mineralocorticoids   530
Fludrocortisone

## Heavy Metal Antagonists   531
Desferal mesylate
BAL in Oil
EDTA

## Immunomodulators   532

## Immunosuppressants   532
Cyclosporine

## Laxatives and Stool Softeners   533
Cascara
Bisacodyl
Phenolphthalein
Mineral oil
Docusate
Magnesium hydroxide
Psyllium
PEG electrolyte solution

## Miotic Eye Medications   534
Pilocarpine
Carbachol

## Disease-Modifying Antirheumatic Drugs (DMARDs)   534

## Musculoskeletal Medications   535
Edrophonium
Neostigmine
Pyridostigmine
Alendronic acid
Glucosamine

## Mydriatic and Cycloplegic Eye Medications   536
Atropine sulfate
Cyclopentolate hydrochloride

## Narcotics (Opioid Analgesics)   537
Morphine sulfate

Codeine
Methadone
Merperidine
Hydromorphone hydrochloride
Oxycodone/aspirin
Hydrocodone/acetaminophen

## Nitrates/Antianginals   538
Nitroglycerin
Isosorbide

## Nonsteroidal Anti-inflammatories (NSAIDs)   539
Ibuprofen
Indomethacin
Naproxen
Celecoxib
Ketorolac

## Medications for Paget's Disease   540
Calcimar
EHDP
Pilcamycin

## Thrombolytic Medications   540
Reteplase
Alteplase
Tissue plasminogen activator
Anistreplase
Streptokinase

## Medications for Ulcers   541
Cimetidine
Ranitidine
Sucralfate
Omeprazole
Lansoprazole
Rabeprazole
Misoprostol

## Vitamins   541
Vitamin $B_{12}$
Folic acid

## Women's Health Medications   542
Ethinyl estradiol
Ethinyl estradiol/norgestrel
Estradiol
Conjugated estrogens
Medroxyprogesterone acetate

## Men's Health Medications   543
Terazosin
Tamsulosin
Finasteride
Dutasteride
Sildenafil citrate
Vardenafil

## Herbal Supplements   544–548

**Volume Equivalents**

| | |
|---|---|
| 1 fluid ounce | = 2 tablespoons |
| 1 tablespoon | = 15 milliliters |
| | = 3 teaspoons |
| 1 teaspoon | = 5 milliliters |
| 1 cup | = 240 milliters |
| | = 8 fluid ounces |

**Mass Equivalents**
1 kilogram = 2.2 pounds

**Temperature Conversion**

(Celsius degrees $\frac{9}{5}$) + 32 = Fahrenheit degrees

(Fahrenheit degrees – 32) $\frac{5}{9}$ = Celsius degrees

**Common Conversions**

| | | |
|---|---|---|
| 1 gr | = | 60 mg |
| 1 tsp | = | 5 mL |
| 1 tbsp | = | 15 mL |
| 1 oz | = | 30 mL |
| 1 kg | = | 2.2 lbs |
| F | = | $C\frac{9}{5} + 32$ |
| C | = | $F - 32 \times \frac{5}{9}$ |

## ANAPHYLAXIS

**A.** Data Collection

　1.　Hives, rash

　2.　Difficulty breathing

　3.　Decreased BP, increased pulse, increased respirations

　4.　Dilated pupils

　5.　Diaphoresis

　6.　"Panicked" feeling

**B.** Nursing considerations

　1.　Epinephrine 0.3 ml of 1:1,000 solution IM

　2.　Massage site to speed absorption

　3.　May repeat dose in 15–20 min

　4.　Wear Medic-Alert identification

　5.　Carry emergency epinephrine

## DELAYED ALLERGIC REACTION

**A.** Data Collection

　1.　Rash, hives

　2.　Swollen joints

**B.** Nursing considerations

　1.　Discontinue medication

　2.　Notify health care provider

　3.　Skin care

　4.　Comfort measures

　5.　Antihistamines, topical

　6.　Corticosteriods

## DERMATOLOGICAL REACTIONS

**A.** Data Collection

1. Hives, rashes, lesions

2. Exfoliative dermatitis (rash, fever, enlarged lymph nodes, enlarged liver)

3. Erythema multiform excidativum (Stevens-Johnson syndrome—dark red papules that don't itch or hurt)

**B.** Nursing considerations

1. Frequent skin care

2. Avoid rubbing, tight clothing, harsh soaps, perfumed lotions

3. Antihistamines

4. Topical corticosteroids

## STOMATITIS

**A.** Data Collection

1. Swollen gums (gingivitis)

2. Swollen, red tongue (glossitis)

3. Difficulty swallowing

4. Bad breath

5. Pain in mouth and throat

**B.** Nursing considerations

1. Frequent mouth care with nonirritating (nonalcoholic) solution

2. Frequent, small feedings

3. Antifungal meds

4. Local anesthetics

## SUPERINFECTIONS

**A.** Data Collection

1. Fever

2. Diarrhea

3. Black hairy tongue

4. Glossitis

5. Mucous membrane lesions

6. Vaginal itching and discharge

**B.** Nursing considerations

1. Frequent mouth care

2. Good skin care

3. Small, frequent feedings

4. Antifungal meds

## BONE MARROW DEPRESSION

**A.** Data Collection

1. Fever

2. Chills

3. Sore throat

4. Weakness

5. Back pain

6. Dark urine

7. Anemia (low Hct)

8. Thrombocytopenia (low platelet count)

9. Leukopenia (low WBC)

**B.** Nursing considerations

1. Monitor CBC

2. Rest

3. Protection from infections

4. Avoid activities that may cause injury

## LIVER IMPAIRMENT

**A.** Data Collection

1. Fever

2. Malaise

3. Nausea, vomiting

4. Jaundice

5. Light stools, dark urine

6. Abdominal pain

7. Elevated AST, ALT

8. Elevated bilirubin

9. Altered PTT

**B.** Nursing considerations

1. Small, frequent feedings

2. Good skin care

3. Comfort measures

4. Cool environment

5. Rest

## RENAL IMPAIRMENT

**A.** Data Collection

1. Elevated BUN, creatinine

2. Decreased Hct

3. Altered electrolytes ($K^+$, $Na^+$)

4. Fatigue

5. Edema

6. Irritability

7. Skin care

**B.** Nursing considerations

1. Diet and fluid restrictions

2. Good skin care

3. Electrolyte replacement

4. Rest

5. Dialysis

## OCULAR IMPAIRMENT

**A.** Data Collection

1. Blurred vision

2. Color vision changes

3. Blindness

**B.** Nursing considerations

1. Monitor vision carefully

2. Monitor lighting and exposure to light

## AUDITORY IMPAIRMENT

**A.** Data Collection

1. Dizziness

2. Ringing in ears

3. Loss of balance

4. Loss of hearing

**B.** Nursing considerations

1. Monitor hearing ability

2. Safety measures to prevent injury (falls)

## CNS IMPAIRMENT

**A.** Data Collection

1. Confusion, delirium

2. Insomnia

3. Drowsiness

4. Hallucinations

**B.** Nursing considerations

1. Safety measures to prevent injury

2. Avoid activities that require alertness (driving a car)

3. Orient to surroundings

## ANTICHOLINERGIC EFFECTS

**A.** Data Collection

1. Dry mouth

2. Altered taste perception

3. Dysphagia

4. Heartburn

5. Urinary retention

6. Impotence

7. Blurred vision

8. Nasal congestion

**B.** Nursing considerations

1. Sugarless lozenges

2. Good mouth care

3. Void before taking medication

4. Safety measures for vision changes

## PARKINSON–LIKE EFFECTS

**A.** Data Collection

1. Akinesia

2. Tremors

3. Drooling

4. Changes in gait

5. Rigidity

6. Akathisia (extreme restlessness)

7. Dyskinesia (spasms)

**B.** Nursing considerations

1. Anticholinergic meds

2. Antiparkinson meds

3. Safety measures for gait changes

# INDEX

## A

AA (Alcoholics Anonymous), 309

Abbreviations, nursing practice, 555–564

ABCDs, in disaster planning, 87

Abdomen
  injuries to, 334
  in newborn, 144
  in physical, 181
  x-ray of, 444

Abdominal breathing, 449

Abdominal hernias, 417–418

Abdominal respirations, 175

Abducens nerve (CN VI), 179

Abduction, 185

ABGs (arterial blood gases), 441, 442

Abortion
  obstetric classification for, 112
  spontaneous, classification of, 127–128

Abruptio placentae, 131–132

Absence seizures, 339

Abuse
  child, 313
  elder, 314
  substance. *See* Substance abuse

Accelerations, in fetal heart rate, 119

Accident prevention, 84–86

Accidental poisoning. *See* Poisoning

Accommodation, disorders of, 384

Accountability
  defined, 56
  legal issues and, 51

ACE inhibitors, 500

Acetaminophen (Tylenol) poisoning, 82

*N*-Acetylcysteine (Mucomyst), for acetaminophen poisoning, 82

Acne vulgaris, 432

Acoustic nerve (CN VIII), 179

Acoustic neuroma, 395

Acquired immune deficiency syndrome. *See* AIDS

Acromegaly, 370

Activated charcoal, in accidental poisoning, 81
  aspirin poisoning, 81

Active immunity, 162

Activities, age-appropriate
  for preschool children, 99
  for school-age children, 100

Activity therapy, 274

Acute kidney disorders, 264, 265

Acute leukemia, 375

Acute otitis media, 393–394

Acute pancreatitis, 429

Adaptive devices, 191–192

ADD (attention deficit disorder), 110

Addisonian crisis, 354–355

Addison's disease, 354

Adduction, 185

ADH (antidiuretic hormone) disorders, 346

ADHD (attention-deficit hyperactivity disorder), medications for, 520, 551

Adolescence
  accident prevention measures in, 86
  fear of surgery in, 433
  food pyramid RDIs in, 238
  growth and development in, 101–102
  health screening in, 160
  health-care procedures in, preparation for, 434

immunization schedule in, 164, 165, 167–168

potential problems in, 101

Adrenal disorders, 353–355

Adrenalin (epinephrine), 472

Adulthood. *See also* Elderly

accident prevention measures in, 85

CPR administration in, 321–322

domestic violence and, 315–316

elder abuse, 314

growth and development in, 103–108

20 to 35 yrs., 104

35 to 65 yrs., 104

65 yrs. and above, 105–108

health screening in, 161

immunization schedule in, 166, 167–168

normal vital signs in, 175

nutrition in, 247

respiration in, 175

sexual abuse in, 315

Advanced directives, 49

Adventitious breath sounds, 178

Advocacy, 50–51

AFP. *See* Alpha-fetal protein (AFP) test

Aggressive behavior, 304–305

learning disabilities and, 110

nursing care of client exhibiting, 304

AIDS, 75, 77–79

fetal development and, 118

HIV screening and, 160

opportunistic infections in, 75, 77

Air hunger, 175

Airborne precautions, in infection control, 70

Airway obstruction, 319–321

Albumin, serum, 440, 444

Alcohol

acute intoxication, 307

chronic dependence on, 308–309

withdrawal from, 307–308

Alcoholic chronic brain syndrome, 308

Alcoholics Anonymous (AA), 309

Aldomet (methyldopa), 503

Alkaline phosphatase, 440

Allergens

common forms, 170

response to, 169–170

Allergic reaction, to blood transfusion, 466

Allergy

atopic, 171–172

to latex, 171

to protein, 405

Alpha-1 adrenergic blockers, 502

Alpha-adrenergics, centrally acting, 502

Alpha-fetal protein (AFP) test, 116

in spina bifida diagnosis, 204

Alprazolam (Xanax), 474

ALS (amyotrophic lateral sclerosis), 210–211

Alternative therapy. *See* Complementary and alternative therapy

Alzheimer's disease, 229–231

Aminoglycosides, 478, 482

Ammonia, blood, 444

Amniocentesis, 116

in spina bifida diagnosis, 204

Amputation, 225–226

Amyotrophic lateral sclerosis (ALS), 210–211

ANA Code of Ethics, 64–65

Analgesia/analgesics, 215

for cancer clients, 373

client-controlled. *See* Client controlled analgesia (PCA)

Anaphylaxis, 170, 554

medications for, 472–473, 549

Anemia, 366–367

hemolytic, in newborn, 147, 148

iron deficiency, 367

pernicious, 368

vitamin $B_{12}$, 368

Anesthesia, forms of, 435

Anger, in depression, 283

Angina pectoris, 362–364

antianginal agents for, 533

Angiography, 440

celiac axis arteriography, 444

cerebral, 443

Angiotensin-converting (ACE) inhibitors, 500
Angle of Louis, 180
Angle-closure glaucoma, 390
Anorexia nervosa, 305
Antabuse (disulfiram) therapy, for alcoholism, 309
Antacids, 476, 549
Anthrax, 88
Antianginals, 538
Antianxiety agents, 474–475, 549
Antiarrhythmics, 330, 477
Antibiotics/antiinfectives, 478–483, 549. *See also* Topical antibacterials
  aminoglycosides, 482
  cephalosporins, 478, 483
  fluoroquinolones, 479, 483
  glycopeptides, 479, 483
  lincosamides, 479, 483
  macrolides, 480, 483
  penicillins, 480, 482
  sulfonamides, 481, 482
  tetracyclines, 481, 482
Anticholinergic effects, of medication, 558
Anticholinergics, 485, 549
Anticoagulants, 486, 549
Anticonvulsants, 487–488, 549–550
Antidepressants, 284, 489–491, 550
  heterocyclics, 490, 491, 550
  monoamine oxidase inhibitors, 489, 491, 550
  selective serotonin reuptake inhibitors, 489, 491, 550
  tricyclics, 490, 491, 550
Antidiabetics, 492–493, 550
  oral hypoglycemic agents, 493
Antidiarrheals, 494, 550
Antidiuretic hormone (ADH) disorders, 346
Antidysrhythmics, 330, 477, 549
Antiembolic stockings, postoperative, 436
Antiemetics, 495–496, 550
Antifungals, 496, 550
Antigen/antibody response, 162

Antigout medications, 497, 550
Antihistamines, 498, 550
Antihypertensives, 500–503, 550
Anti-impotence medications, 484
Antiinfectives. *See* Antibiotics/antiinfectives
Antilipemics, 330, 499, 550
Antimanic agents, 504
Antiparkinson agents, 510, 551
Antiplatelet agents, 511, 551
Antipsychotics, 512, 551
Antipyretic agents, 515, 551
Antisocial personality disorder, 301
  in drug abusers, 312
Antithyroid agents, 515–516, 551
Antitubercular agents, 517, 551
Antitussive agents, 518, 551
Antivirals, 519–520, 551
Antrectomy, in pyloric stenosis, 408
Anxiety, 274–277
  in depression, 283
  effects, 274–275
  levels, 275
  medications for, 474–475
  nursing interventions in, 276
Anxiety disorders, 277
Anxiolytics
  herbal, 475
  pharmaceutical, 474, 549
Apgar score, in newborn, 142
Apnea, 175
Appendectomy, 414
Appendicitis, 413–414
Apresoline (hydralazine), 503
Arrhythmias. *See* Dysrhythmias
Arterial blood gases (ABGs), 441, 442
Arterial diagnostic tests, 440
Arteriography. *See* Angiography
Arteriosclerosis, as heart failure cause, 361
Arthrocentesis, 199
Arthroscopy, 199
Artificial eye, care of, 386
Ascorbic acid, function and sources, 237
Aspirin poisoning, 81–82
Assault, defined, 51

Assistive devices, 189–192

Asthma, 357

Astigmatism, 384

Atarax (hydroxyzine), 474

Atelectasis, as postoperative
    complication, 438

Atenolol (Tenormin), 503

Atherosclerosis, 405

Ativan (lorazepam), 474

Atonic seizures, 339

Atopic allergy, 171–172

Atopic dermatitis, 432

Atresia, esophageal, 411–412

Atrial dysrhythmias, 327

Atrial fibrillation, 327

Atrial flutter, 327

Atrioventricular pacemaker, 330

Attachment, mother-baby, in
    postpartum period, 124

Attention deficit disorder (ADD), 110

Attention-deficit hyperactivity disorder
    (ADHD), medication for, 520, 551

Attitude, fetal parts, 120

Auditory impairment, 557–558

Auscultation, 174

Autologous blood transfusion, 466

Automated peritoneal dialysis, 267

Autonomic hyperreflexia, in spinal
    cord injury, 343

Autonomy, 64

Autosomal defects, 115

Avoidant personality disorder, 302

Axillae, 181

**B**

Babinski's sign, 145

Backache, in pregnancy, 114

Balanced suspension traction, 221

Balance's sign, 334

Balloon tamponade, for esophageal
    varices, 425

Ballottement, 173

Barbiturate abuse, 311

Barium swallow/barium enema, 445

Barrier (standard) precautions, 67, 69

Basal body temperature method
    (contraception), 155

Basal cell carcinoma, 376

Battery, defined, 51

Battle's sign, 331

Bedwetting, 255

Behavioral decision making, 58

Behavioral therapy/modification, 274

Beliefs, 64

Bell's palsy, 395

Benadryl (diphenhydramine HCl), 472

Beneficence, 64

Benign prostatic hyperplasia (BPH),
    158, 261–262

Benzodiazepine derivatives, as
    anxiolytic, 474

Beta-adrenergic blockers, 500

Bile acid sequestrants, 499, 550

Bilevel positive airway pressure
    (BIPAP), 229

Bill of Rights, 48–49

Billroth I/Billroth II procedures,
    410, 411

Biological therapy, 274

Biopsy
  cervical, 446
  liver, 444
  lung, 442
  renal, 447

Bioterrorism, 88–89

BIPAP (bilevel positive airway
    pressure), 229

Bipolar disorder, 295–297
  medications for, 504, 550

Birth control. *See* Contraception

Birthmarks, 143

Bladder exstrophy, 256

Bladder retraining/training, 254

Bleeding time, 439

Blind client, care of, 386

Blood ammonia, 444

Blood components, 465

Blood gases, arterial (ABGs), 441,
    442

Blood group compatibility, 465

Blood pressure screening, 161
  measurement errors, 162
  in physical, 176

Blood tests, 439–440

Blood transfusion
  autologous, 466
  reactions to, 465, 466
Blunt trauma. *See* Nonpenetrating
  (blunt) trauma
Body fluids/secretions, infection
  control and, 69
Body temperature
  basal method (contraception), 155
  normal, 176
Bonding, mother-baby, in postpartum
  period, 124
Bone marrow aspiration, in leukemia
  diagnosis, 375
Bone marrow depression, 556
Borderline personality disorder, 301
Boredom, in immobile clients, 188
Botulism, 88
Bowel elimination, 255
Bowel sounds, 181
Bowel surgery, in intestinal
  obstruction, 419
BPH (benign prostatic
  hypertrophy), 158
Brachytherapy, for cancer, 373
Bradycardia, 326–327
  in fetus, 119
Brain
  central nervous system anatomy
    and, 331
  divisions of, 377
Brain attack. *See* Stroke
Breast
  cancer, 157
  in physical, 181
  soreness in pregnancy, 114
Breast feeding
  for newborn, 146
  principles and potential problems, 125
Breast milk
  expression, 125
  jaundice in newborn, 147
Breast self-exam (BSE), 153, 161
Breath sounds, 178
Breathing
  abdominal, 449
  diaphragmatic, 449

Bronchitis, chronic, 357
Bronchodilators, 521
Bronchophony, 178
Bronchoscopy, 441
Brudzinski's sign, in meningitis, 397
BSE (breast self-exam), 153, 161
Bubonic plague, 88
Buck's traction, 220
Buerger's disease, 364
Bulimia, 305
BUN, 440
  in urinary system evaluation, 447
Burnout, 289
Burns, 351–353
  classification, 351
  to eye, 385
  nursing care of client with, 352
  prevention, 352
  severe, phases following, 353
Bursitis, 201
Buspirone (BuSpar), 474

**C**

CABG (coronary artery bypass graft)
  surgery, in angina pectoris,
  363–364
Calan (verapamil), 503
Calcium
  function and sources, 237
  imbalances, 348–349
Calcium channel blockers, 501
Caloric requirements, 236
*Campylobacter* infection,
  gastrointestinal, 406
Cancer, 371–374. *See also individual*
  *types of cancer*
  blood, 375–376
  breast, 157
  cervical, 157
  common types, by race/ethnicity,
    371–272
  endometrial, 158
  intracranial tumors, 377–378
  laryngeal, 379
  ovarian, 158
  pancreatic tumors, 378–379
  prostate, 158

screening tests for, 161
skin, 376–377
warning signs, 371
*Candida albicans* infection
in AIDS clients, 75
female reproductive tract, 157
Canes, 190
Cannabis derivatives, abuse of, 311
CAPD (continuous ambulatory
peritoneal dialysis), 267
Captopril (Capoten), 503
Caput succedaneum, 143
Carbohydrates, 236
Carbon dioxide ($CO_2$) narcosis, as
oxygen therapy hazard, 453
Carbonic anhydrase inhibitors, 522, 551
Cardiac arrest, medications for, 472–
473, 549
Cardiac catheterization, 442
Cardiac disease, in pregnant woman,
133–134
nutritional requirements, 248
Cardiac glycosides, for heart failure,
361–362, 523, 551
Cardiac tests, 441–442
Cardiac workload, changes in
immobile clients, 188
Cardiogenic shock, 335
Cardiopulmonary arrest, 321–322
Cardiopulmonary resuscitation (CPR),
321–322
Cardiovascular system
anatomy, 324, 325
changes in late adulthood, 106
effects of anxiety on, 274
herbal supplements, 548
postoperative care and, 436
Cardioversion, 329
Cardizem (diltiazem), 503
Care
continuity, 52–54
coordinated, 52–54
critical pathways in, 53
managed, 52
Care environment
coordination of care in, 52–54
documentation requirements in, 59–64

ethical issues in, 64–66
legal issues related to, 51–53
nurse/client relationship in, 47
responsibility and authority in,
delegating, 54–56
restraints use in, 50
rights of client in, 48–49
safety issues in. *See* Infection
control; Poisoning; *individual
diseases, agents and pathogens*
staffing issues in, 57
Care teams, 57
Carrier screening, for cystic
fibrosis, 160
Case management/manager, 53–54
Casting
for club foot (talipes equinovarus),
198
for developmental dysplasia
of hip, 196
for fractures, 222
Catapres (clonidine), 503
Cataracts, 389
Catatonic schizophrenia, 298
Catheters/catheterization
cardiac, 442
urinary, 458–461
Caudal block, for surgery, 435
CAUTION mnemonic (cancer warning
signs), 371
Celiac axis arteriography, 444
Celiac disease, 405
Central nervous system (CNS)
anatomy, 331
medications side effects and, 558
in newborn, 141
Central sleep apnea, 229
Centrally acting alpha-adrenergics, 502
Cephalhematoma, 143
Cephalosporins, 478, 483
Cerebral angiography, 443
Cerebral palsy, 207–208
Cerebrovascular accident. *See* Stroke
Cervical biopsy, 446
Cervical cancer, 157
Cervical mucus method
(contraception), 155

Cervical traction (skull tongs), 221
Cervix, changes during labor, 118
Cesarean delivery, 137–138
Chadwick's sign, 112, 113
Chain of command, 57
Chalazion, 385
Change of shift report, 62–64
Charting, incident reports and, 61
Chelation
  in accidental poisoning, 81
  for lead toxicity (plumbism), 83
Chemical burns, 353
  to eye, 385
Chemical dependency
  acute alcohol intoxication, 307
  chronic alcohol dependence, 308–309
  nonalcoholic substance abuse,
    310–312
Chemical hazards, 84
Chemical restraint, 50
Chemotherapy, for tuberculosis, 72
Chest
  in newborn, 144
  physiotherapy, 449–450
Chest pain. See also Angina pectoris
  patterns in myocardial infarction, 323
Chest trauma, 332–333
Chest tubes, monitoring, 453–454
Chest x-ray, 442
Cheyne-Stokes respiration, 175
Chickenpox (varicella), 68
  airborne precautions for, 70
  fetal development and, 118
  immunization schedules, 163–166, 168
Child abuse, 313
  sexual, 314
Child development
  in adolescence, 101–102
  age-appropriate toys and. See Toys,
    age-appropriate
  in Down syndrome, 109–110
  factors influencing, 93
  in fetal alcohol syndrome, 109
  in infancy, 96–97
  intellectual delay and, 108–109
  learning disabilities and, 110
  in preschool children, 99
  in school-age children, 100–101

stages of, fear of surgery and, 433
  in toddlerhood, 98
Childbearing. See also Neonate
  maternal complications, 127–140
  normal, 111–126
Childhood
  communicable diseases of, 68
  lead toxicity in, 83
  poisoning prevention in, 79–81
Children
  food pyramid RDIs, 238
  medication dosage formulas, 471
Chinese, food types preferred by, 243
Chlamydia infection, 76
Chlordiazepoxide (Librium), 474
Cholangiography, 444
Cholecystectomy
  laparoscopic laser, 428
  traditional, 428
Cholecystitis, 427–428
Cholecystography, 444
Cholelithiasis, 427–428
Cholesterol
  herbals lowering, 240, 499
  screening in screening for, 160
  total, 440
Choreiform movements, 398
Chorionic villus sampling, 116
Chromosomal alterations, fetal
    development and, 115
Chronic, 357
Chronic alcohol dependence, 308–309
Chronic leukemia, 375
Chronic obstructive pulmonary disease
    (COPD), 357–359
Chronic pancreatitis, 429
Chronic renal failure, 265
Chvostek's sign
  in Graves' disease, 233
  in hypocalcemia, 349
  in hypoparathyroidism, 234
Circulatory overload, 345
  in blood transfusion, 466
  as heart failure cause, 361
Circumcision
  in newborn, 141
  in newborn care, 146

Cirrhosis, 423–425

Claudication, intermittent, exercise tests for, 440

Clear liquid diet, 241

Cleft lip and palate, 149–151

Client advocacy, 50–51

Client conditions, documenting changes in, 60

Clonazepam (Klonopin), 474

Clonidine (Catapres), 503

Clostridium difficile, contact precautions for, 70–71

Clotting, 469

Club foot (talipes equinovarus), 198–199

CMV. See Cytomegalovirus (CMV) infection

CN. See Cranial nerves (CN)

CNS. See Central nervous system (CNS)

Coagulation studies, 444

Code of Ethics, ANA, 64–65

Cognitive/mental functioning changes in depression, 282 effects of anxiety on, 275

Coitus interruptus, 156

Cold stress, in newborn, 151

Collaborative practice team, 52

Colonoscopy, 445

Colostomy, 420–423 appliance, 422 irrigations, 422

Colostrum, 146

Colposcopy, 446

Combustion, as oxygen therapy hazard, 453

Communicable diseases childhood, 68 in infection diagnosis, 67

Community-acquired pneumonia, risk factors, 359

Compartment syndrome, 218

Compensation (ego defense mechanism), 276

Complaints, handling, 65–66

Complementary and alternative therapy. See also Herbal supplements for Alzheimer's disease, 231

for anxiety, 475

for depression, 284, 491

for emesis, 476

for lowering cholesterol, 499

for migraine headaches, 398

nutrition for elderly, 247

nutritional supplements, 240

for pain relief, 215

in preoperative care, 434

for prostatic hypertrophy, 262

for seizures, 338

Complete abortion, 127

Complete heart block, 328

Complete spinal cord injury, 342

Complex partial seizures, 339

Computed tomography (CT) in neurological testing, 443 in respiratory/cardiac testing, 442

Concussion, 331

Condoms, male and female, 155

Conduction blocks, for surgery, 435

Condylomata acuminata, 76

Confidentiality, 48, 64

Congenital hip dislocation, 195–197

Congenital malformations, urinary tract, 256

Conjunctivitis, 385

Conscious sedation, for surgery, 435

Constipation in immobile clients, 188 in pregnancy, 114

Constrictive pericarditis, as heart failure cause, 361

Contact precautions, in infection control, 70

Continent ileal reservoir (Koch pouch), 420 care, 422–423 in ileostomy, 421

Continuity of care, 52–54

Continuous ambulatory peritoneal dialysis (CAPD), 267

Continuous peritoneal dialysis, 267

Continuous positive airway pressure (CPAP), 229

Continuous quality improvement (CQI), 52 in case management, 54

Contraception, 154
   methods, 155–156
Contraction stress test (CST), 117
Contractions, in labor
   characteristics, 122
   effect on fetal heart rate, 119–120
   phases, 121
Contractures
   changes in immobile clients, 188
   preventing in burn clients, 352
Contusions, 217
   in head injury, 331
Conversion hysteria, 277
Coombs test, 148
Coordinated care, 52–54
COPD (chronic obstructive pulmonary
      disease), 357–359
Corgard (nadolol), 503
Cornea, inflammation of, 385
Coronary arteries, in heart
      anatomy, 324
Coronary artery, bypass graft surgery,
      in angina pectoris, 363–364
Coude urinary catheter, 458
Cough, 176
Coughing techniques, 449
Counseling
   in alcoholism, 309
   techniques, 291
CPAP (continuous positive airway
      pressure), 229
CPR (cardiopulmonary resuscitation),
      321–322
CQI (continuous quality
      improvement), 52
CR (creatinine), 440
Cranial nerves (CN)
   disorders, 395
   observation of, 179
Creatine kinase (CK), 440
Creatinine (CR), 440
Creatinine clearance, 446
Crises intervention, 278–280
Critical thinking, 58
Crohn's disease, 412–413
Croup syndromes, 322–323
Croupette, 452
Crutch walking, 189–190

Cryptococcus neoformans infection, in
      AIDS clients, 77
CST (contraction stress test), 117
CT. See Computed tomography (CT)
Culdoscopy, 446
Cullen's sign, 334
Cultural food patterns, 242–243
Cultural norms, 64
   support systems and, 290
Cultures, in infection evaluation, 67
   in reproductive tests, 446
   urine, 446
Cushing's syndrome, 354, 355
Cutaneous anthrax, 88
Cutaneous ureterostomy, 263
CVA (cerebrovascular accident).
      See Stroke
Cyanocobalamin (B$_{12}$), function and
      sources, 237
Cyanosis, 176
Cycloplegic eye medications, 536, 552
Cyst
   inflammatory, of eye, 385
   ovarian, 158
Cystic fibrosis, 116, 357–358, 405
   screening for, 160
Cystitis, 258–259
Cystometrogram, 446
Cystoscopy, in urinary system
      evaluation, 447
Cystostomy, suprapubic, 262
Cystourethrogram, in urinary system
      evaluation, 447
Cytomegalovirus (CMV) infection
   in AIDS clients, 77
   fetal development and, 118
Cytoprotective agents, 524, 551

D
DDH (developmental dysplasia of the
      hip), 195–197
Deaf client, care of, 393
Debridement, 352
Decelerations, in fetal heart rate, 119–120
Decision making, 58–59
Decubitus ulcer, in immobile
      clients, 188
Deep tendon reflexes (DTRs), 181
Defibrillation, 329

Dehiscence, as postoperative complication, 438
Dehydration, 345
Delayed union, of fracture, 218
Delegation, 54–56
    defined, 54
    guidelines for, 54
    hierarchy in, 56
    how to achieve, 55
    ineffective, 56
    levels, 55–56
    obstacles to, 56
    rights, 56
    steps for, 54–55
Delivery
    care of newborn and, 123–124
    by Cesarean section, 137–138
    factors affecting, 120–122
    precipitous (preterm), 138
Delusions, in schizophrenia, 297
Demand pacemaker, 330
Dementia, 308
Denial (ego defense mechanism), 275
Denver II developmental screening test, 93–94, 160
Dependent personality disorder, 302
Depression, 281–285
    in immobile clients, 188
    in postpartum period, 126, 140
    psychodynamics of, 282
    types, 282
Dermatitis, atopic, 432
Dermatological disorders, 431–432
Dermatological reactions, 555
Descending colostomy, 421
Detached retina, 387–388
Development, and growth
    in adulthood, 103–108. See also Adulthood, growth and development in
    in children/adolescents. See Child development
    fetal. See Fetal development
Developmental dysplasia of the hip (DDH), 195–197
Diabetes
    gestational, 132–133, 401
    in pregnant woman, 132–133

type 1, 401
type 2, 401
Diabetes insipidus, 346
Diabetic exchange list, 402
Diabetic ketoacidosis, 404
Diagnostic testing
    arterial tests, 440
    blood tests, 439–440
    gastrointestinal, 445
    liver function, 444
    neurological, 443
    reproductive, 446
    respiratory/cardiac, 441–442
    urinary system, 446–447
    venous, 440
Dialysis, 266–267
Diaphragm (contraceptive device), 155
Diaphragmatic breathing, 449
Diaphragmatic excursion, in thoracic, 178
Diazepam (Valium), 474
Diets. See also Nutrition
    supplements in, use guidelines, 240
    therapeutic, 241
Digestive system, anatomy of, 406. See also Gastrointestinal (GI) tract
Digitalis (digoxin), for heart failure, 361–362
Diltiazem (Cardizem), 503
Diphenhydramine HCl (Benadryl), 472
Diphtheria, 68
    tetanus, pertussis (DTaP) vaccine, 164, 169
    vaccination schedules, 163–167
Direct-acting vasodilators, 502
Disaster planning, 87
    bioterrorism, 88–89
Discomfort(s)
    in labor, monitoring, 123
    of pregnancy, 114
Disease-Modifying Antirheumatic Drugs (DMARDs), 534
Dislocations, joint, 217
Disorganized schizophrenia, 298
Displacement (ego defense mechanism), 275

Disseminated zoster (shingles)
  airborne precautions for, 70
  fetal development and, 118
  vaccination against, 166
Dissociation (ego defense
    mechanism), 277
Distributive shock, 335
Disulfiram (Antabuse) therapy, for
    alcoholism, 309
Diuretics, 524–525, 551
Diverticular disease, 414
Dizziness, in pregnancy, 114
Dobutrex (dubutamine
    hydrochloride), 472
Documentation
  change in client conditions, 60
  change of shift report, 62–64
  incident report, 60–61
  purpose and characteristics, 59–60
  terminology used for, 572–576
Domestic violence, 315–316
Dopamine (Intropin), 472
Doppler studies, in venous diagnostic
    tests, 440
Dorsiflexion, 185
Double-barrel colostomy, 420
Down syndrome (trisomy 21),
    109–110, 115
DPT vaccine, administration
    schedule, 163
Drainage system care, principles of, 459
Drains. See Surgical drains
Droplet precautions, in infection
    control, 70
Drug abuse, 310–312
DTaP (diphtheria, tetanus, pertussis)
    vaccine, 163
  in child, nursing considerations, 169
DTRs (deep tendon reflexes), 181
Dubutamine hydrochloride
    (Dobutrex), 472
Dumping syndrome, preventive
    measures for, 411
Duodenal ulcer, 409
  site of, 410
Durable power of attorney, 49
Dwarfism, 370

Dying client, 279
Dyspnea, 175
Dysreflexia, in spinal cord injury, 343
Dysrhythmias, 326–330
  medical management, 330, 477

E
Ear
  anatomy and physiology, 391
  infections, 393–394
  irrigations, 391–392, 453
  in newborn, 144
  in adult, 177
Ear drops, instillation technique,
    392, 454
Early adulthood
  food pyramid RDIs in, 238
  growth and development in, 103
  immunization schedules in, 166,
    167–168
  potential nursing diagnoses in, 103
Eating disorders, 305
Echocardiography, 442
Eclampsia, 129, 130
ECT. See Electroconvulsive therapy (ECT)
Ectopic pregnancy, 128–129
Eczema, 432
EDC (estimated date of confinement), 112
EEG (electroencephalography), 443
Ego defense mechanisms, 275–277
Egophony, 178
EKG (electrocardiography),
    components of, 328, 329
Elderly, 85
  abuse of, 314
  food pyramid RDIs in, 238
  health screening in, 161
  nutrition in, 247
  rest and sleep disturbances in,
    228–229
  system changes in, 106–107
Electrical burns, 353
Electrical impulse transmission, in
    heart, 326
Electrocardiography (EKG),
    components of, 328, 329

Electroconvulsive therapy (ECT), 284
   nursing considerations for, 285
Electroencephalography (EEG), 443
Electrolyte imbalances
   in adrenal disorders, 353–355
   calcium, 348–349
   magnesium, 350
   potassium, 347
   sodium, 348
Electrolyte modifiers, 526
Electrolyte replacement solutions,
      526, 551
ELISA (enzyme-linked immunosorbent
      assay), in AIDS diagnosis, 77
Embolism
   coronary artery, 324
   as postoperative complication, 438
Emphysema, 357
Enalapril (Vasotec), 503
Encephalopathy, hepatic, as cirrhosis
      complication, 424
Endocrine system, changes in late
      adulthood, 107
Endometrial cancer, 158
Endometriosis, 158
Endoscopic sclerotherapy, for
      esophageal varices, 424
Endoscopy, stomach/esophagus, 445
Endotracheal intubation, 319, 320
Enemas, 457–458
Engorgement, lactation and, 125
Enteral nutrition, 248, 455–456
   complications, 249
   conditions requiring, 249
Enterocolitis, 412–413
Enterotoxigenic E. coli infection,
      gastrointestinal, 406
Enuresis, 255
Environmental control, in infection
      control, 69
Enzyme studies, hepatic, 444
Enzyme-linked immunosorbent assay
      (ELISA), in AIDS diagnosis, 77
Epidural block, for surgery, 435
Epidural hematoma, in head injury,
      331
Epiglottitis, 322–323

Epinephrine (Adrenalin), 472
Episiotomy, in postpartum period, 124,
      126
Epispadias, 182, 256
Erb's point, 180
Ergonomic hazards, 84
Erikson's developmental tasks, 94
Erythematous skin color, 143
Erythrocyte sedimentation rate
      (ESR), 439
   in infection, 67
Escharotomy, 352
Escherichia coli infection,
      gastrointestinal, 406
Esophageal atresia, 411–412
Esophageal varices, as cirrhosis
      complication, 423–424
   treatment of, 425
ESR. See Erythrocyte sedimentation
      rate (ESR)
ESR (sedimentation rate), 439
Estimated date of confinement (EDC), 112
Ethical reasoning process, 65
Ethical standards, in nurse/client
      relationship, 47
Ethics, 64–66
Eversion, 185
Evisceration, as postoperative
      complication, 438
Exchange list, diabetic, 402
Exchange transfusion, for hemolytic
      anemia in newborn, 148
Exercise
   tests for intermittent
      claudication, 440
   therapeutic, for immobile
      clients, 187
Expectorants, 518, 551
Experimentation, in problem
      solving, 59
Expression of breast milk, 125
Extension, 185
External radiation therapy, for
      cancer, 372–373
Extracorporeal shock wave
      lithotripsy, 258

Extremities
  in newborn, 144
  postoperative care of, 436
Eye
  anatomy, 383
  artificial, care of, 386
  burns to, 385
  infections, 385
  inflammation, 385
  irrigation, 454
  in newborn, 144
  in physical, 177
  protection against infection, 69
  trauma to, 385
Eye medications, 528, 552
  eyedrop instillation technique,
    454–455

**F**

Face, in newborn, 144
Face mask, for oxygen
    administration, 452
Face shield, 69
Face-to-face change-of-shift
    report, 63
Facial nerve (CN VII), 179
Facial paralysis, 395
False imprisonment, 51
False labor, 122
Family therapy, 274
  in schizophrenia, 300
  situational role changes and, 287
Fat emboli, as fracture
    complication, 218
Fat metabolism, alterations in, 405
Fats, 236
Fat-soluble vitamins, 236
Fear(s)
  in depression, 283
  of health-care procedures, 434
  of surgery, 433
Febrile reaction, to blood
    transfusion, 466
Fecal diversion, for intestinal
    ostomies, 420–423
Femoral hernia, 417
Fertilization, 113
Fetal alcohol syndrome, 109

Fetal development
  diagnostic testing and, 115–118
  genetic considerations, 116–117
  maternal considerations, 116–117
Fetal heart rate (FHR), 113
  accelerations, in, 119
  effect of contractions on, 119–120
  fetal distress and, 122
  monitoring during labor, 119–120
  non-stress test and, 117
Fetal movement (FM), 113
Fetus
  development, 115–118
  distress in, monitoring for, 122
  monitoring, 119
  position and orientation, 120–121
FHR. *See* Fetal heart rate (FHR)
Fibrocystic changes, in breast tissue, 157
Fibroids, uterine, 157
Fidelity, 64
Filiform urinary catheter, 458
Fistula, tracheoesophageal, 411–412
Fixed rate pacemaker, 330
Flail chest, 332, 333
Flexion, 185
Fluid replacement solutions, 526
Fluid requirements, 236
Fluid volume imbalances, 345
  in burn clients, 252, 353
Fluoride, function and sources, 237
Fluoroquinolones, 479, 483
FM (fetal movement), 113
Foley urinary catheter, 458
Folic acid
  derivatives, 499
  function and sources, 237
Fontanelles, 143
Food groups (food pyramid), 238, 239
Formula feeding
  full-term infant, 245
  newborn, 146
Fractures, 218–222
  complications, 218
  hip, 223–224
  skull, 331
  types, 219
French Americans, food types
    preferred by, 243

Full liquid diet, 241

Full-term infants, nutrition for, 244–245

## G

Galactosemia, screening for, 160

Games, age-appropriate, for school-age children, 100

Gastrectomy, in ulcer management, 410

Gastric aspirate, 445

Gastric lavage, in accidental poisoning, 81

  aspirin (salicylate) poisoning, 81

Gastric ulcer, 409

  sites, 410

Gastritis, 409

Gastrointestinal (GI) tract

  anatomy, 406

  changes in late adulthood, 107

  effects of anxiety on, 274

  herbal supplements, 546

  infections, 406–407

  postoperative care and, 436

  tests, 445

Gastrointestinal tubes, 455–456

  postoperative care, 437

GDM. *See* Gestational diabetes (GDM)

General anesthesia, 435

Generalized seizures, 339

Genital herpes, 76

Genitalia, in physical, 182

Genitourinary system

  herbal supplements, 546

  medications for, 484, 549

  in newborn, 144

  postoperative care and, 436

German measles. *See* Rubella (German measles)

Gestational diabetes (GDM), 132–133, 401

  risk factors, 133

Gestational trophoblastic disease, 135

GI. *See* Gastrointestinal (GI) tract

*Giardia lamblia* infection, gastrointestinal, 406

Glasgow coma scale, 336

Glaucoma, 390

Glomerulonephritis, 260–261

Glossopharyngeal nerve (CN IX), 179

Gloves, 69

Glucocorticoids, 529, 552

Glucose metabolism, alterations in, 401–404

Glucose tolerance test (GTT), 439

  in pregnant woman, 132, 133

Glycopeptides, 479, 483

Glycosylated hemoglobin testing, in pregnant woman, 132, 133

Gonorrhea, 76

  in pregnant woman, 135

Good Samaritan laws, 51

Gout, 200, 405

  risk factor for, 199

Gowns, 69

Grafting, 352

Grand mal seizures, 339

Graves' disease, 232, 233

Gravida (obstetric classification), 112

Greeks, food types preferred by, 243

Grieving client, 279

Group B beta-hemolytic streptococcus, fetal development and, 118

Group therapy, 274

  schizophrenia and, 300

Growth, and development

  in adulthood. *See* Adulthood, growth and development in

  in children. *See* Child development

  factors influencing, 93

  fetal. *See* Fetal development

GTT. *See* Glucose tolerance test (GTT)

Guillain-Barré syndrome, 395–396

## H

Habitual abortion, 127

*Haemophilus influenzae* type B (Hib) conjugate vaccine, administration schedules, 163, 165

HAI. *See* Hospital-acquired infections (HAI)

Hair

  care in cancer clients, 373

  in physical, 176

Hallucinations, in schizophrenia, 297

Hallucinogens, abuse of, 311

Halo jacket, 222

Halothane, as general anesthesia, 435

Handwashing, 69

Hard of hearing client, care of, 393

HAV. *See* Hepatitis A

Hazardous materials, 84

Hazards
   fetal development and, 117–118
   management goals, 84
   materials, 84
   types, 83–84

HBV. *See* Hepatitis B

HCV (Hepatitis C), 73

HDL (high-density lipoproteins), 440

HDV (Hepatitis D), 73

Head
   in newborn, 143–144
   in physical, 177

Head injury, 331–332

Health
   maintaining, in child growth and
      development, 93–95
   promoting, 159
   religious and spiritual influences on,
      292–293

Health screening, 160–161

Hearing, changes in late adulthood,
   106

Hearing loss, 391–393
   conductive, 391–392
   perceptive (sensorineural), 392–393

Heart. *See also* Cardiac *entries*
   coronary arteries and, 324
   electrical impulse transmission in,
      326

Heart block, 328

Heart failure (HF), 360–362
   causes, 361
   left-sided, 360
   right-sided, 360

Heart sounds, in physical, 180

Heartburn, in pregnancy, 114

Heat regulation, in newborn, 141

Heavy metal antagonists, 531, 552

Hegar's sign, 113

Heimlich maneuver, 319

Hematocrit, 439

Hematoma, 469
   in head injury, 331

Hemodialysis, 266

Hemoglobin, 439

Hemolytic disease (anemia), of
   newborn, 147, 148

Hemolytic jaundice, 426

Hemolytic reaction, acute, to blood
   transfusion, 466

Hemophilia, 369

Hemorrhage
   as postoperative complication, 438
   postpartum, 139

Hemorrhoids
   in physical, 182
   in pregnancy, 114

Hemothorax, 333

Hemovac drain, 457

HepA vaccine, administration
   schedules, 163–166

Hepatic encephalopathy, as cirrhosis
   complication, 424
   treatment, 425

Hepatitis, 72–74
   classifications, 73

Hepatitis A, 73
   fetal development and, 118
   immunization schedules, 163–166,
      168

Hepatitis B, 73
   fetal development and, 118
   HepB vaccine in child, nursing
      considerations for, 169
   immunization schedules,
      163–166, 168

Hepatitis C, 73

Hepatitis D, 73

Hepatobiliary disease, 405

Hepatorenal syndrome, as cirrhosis
   complication, 424

HepB vaccine
   in child, nursing considerations for,
      169
   immunization schedules, 163–166,
      168

Herbal interactions
   with anticoagulants, 486
   with antidepressant
      medications, 491

with antidiabetics, 492, 493
with antihypertensives, 503
with cardiac glycosides, 523
with diuretics, 525
with glucocorticoids, 529
Herbal supplements, 544–548
  for anxiety, 475
  for depression, 491
  for emesis, 476
  guidelines for, 240
  for lowering cholesterol, 240, 499
  for men's health, 543
  for women's health, 542
Hernia
  abdominal, 417–418
  hiatal, 407
Herniated intervertebral disk, 193–194
  surgical procedures for, 193
Herpes simplex, 431
  contact precautions for, 70–71
  fetal development and, 118
  as sexually transmitted disease, 76
Herpes zoster, 431. *See also*
    Disseminated zoster (shingles)
  vaccine for, 166
Heterocyclics, 490, 491, 550
HF. *See* Heart failure (HF)
HHNKS (hyperglycemia hyperosmolar
    nonketotic syndrome), 404
Hiatal hernia, 407
Hib *(Haemophilus influenzae* type B)
    conjugate vaccine, 163, 165
Hierarchy
  in care teams, 57
  in delegation, 56
High-density lipoproteins (HDL), 440
Highly sensitive C-reactive protein
    (hsCRP), in infection
    evaluation, 67
High-protein diet, 241
High-roughage, high-fiber diet, 241
Hip
  congenital dislocation, 195–197
  developmental dysplasia, 193–197
  fracture, 223–224
  replacement, 223, 224
Hip spica cast, 196

Hirschsprung's disease, 415–416
Hispanics, food types preferred by, 242
Histamine (H2-receptor blockers), 170
Histrionic personality disorder, 302
HIV (human immunodeficiency virus),
    screening for, 160. *See also* AIDS
HMG-CoA reductase inhibitors,
    499, 550
Homicide, potential for, 282
Hormone injections (contraception), 155
Hospital-acquired infections (HAI), 67
  pneumonia risk factors, 359
Hospitalized clients, rest and sleep
    disturbances in, 227–228
Hoyer lift, 191
HPV (human papillomavirus) vaccine,
    administration schedules,
    164–166, 168
$H_2$-receptor antagonists, in ulcer
    treatment, 541
hsCRP (highly sensitive C-reactive
    protein), in infection
    evaluation, 67
Human immunodeficiency virus (HIV),
    screening for, 160
Human papillomavirus (HPV) vaccine,
    administration schedules,
    164–166, 168
Huntington's chorea, 398–399
Hydatidiform mole, 135
Hydralazine (Apresoline), 503
Hydrocephalus, 205–206
Hydroxyzine (Vistaril; Atarax), 474
Hyperbilirubinemia, 147
Hypercalcemia, 188, 349
Hyperextension, 185
Hyperglycemia, 404
  in pregnancy. *See* Gestational
    diabetes (GDM)
Hyperglycemia hyperosmolar
    nonketotic syndrome
    (HHNKS), 404
Hyperkalemia, 347
Hyperkinesis, learning
    disabilities and, 110
Hypermagnesemia, 350
Hypernatremia, 348

Hyperopia, 384

Hyperparathyroidism, 234

Hyperpnea, 175

Hypersensitivity, 170
  to blood transfusion, 170

Hypertension, 365–366
  causes, 365
  complications, 365
  medications for, 500–503, 550

Hypertensive disease, as heart failure cause, 361

Hyperthyroidism, 232, 233

Hypertonic intravenous fluids, 467

Hyperventilation, 175

Hypocalcemia, 349

Hypoglossal nerve (CN XII), 179

Hypoglycemia, 404
  medications reversing, 494, 550
  in newborn, 148–149

Hypoglycemic agents, oral, 493

Hypokalemia, 347

Hypomagnesemia, 350

Hyponatremia, 348

Hypoparathyroidism, 234

Hypopituitarism, 370

Hypospadias, 182, 256

Hypothyroidism, 160, 232, 233

Hypotonic intravenous fluids, 467

Hypoventilation, 175

Hypovolemic shock, 334–335

## I

IFA (immunofluorescence assay), in AIDS diagnosis, 77

Ileal conduit, for urinary diversion, 263

Ileitis, 412–413

Ileostomy, 421

Immobility, 187
  complications, 188
  therapeutic exercises for, 187
  therapeutic positions for, 189

Immune system, herbal supplements for, 544

Immunity, 162–169

Immunizations, 162–169
  contraindications to, 162
  recommended schedules, 163–166

Immunofluorescence assay (IFA), in AIDS diagnosis, 77

Immunomodulators, 532

Immunosuppressants, 532, 552

Impaired fasting glucose, 401

Impaired vision, 383–386

Impetigo, 431

Implantation
  ectopic pregnancy and, 128–129
  fertilized ovum, 114

Implants, subdermal (contraceptive), 155

Inactivated poliovirus (IPV) vaccine
  administration schedules, 163–165, 168
  in child, nursing considerations, 169

Incarcerated (irreducible) hernia, 417

Incentive spirometer, 450

Incident reports, 60–61
  situations requiring, 61

Incisional (ventral) hernia, 417

Incomplete abortion, 127

Incomplete spinal cord injury, 342

Incontinence, urinary, in postpartum period, 126

Indecisiveness, in depression, 283

Inderal (propranolol), 503

Individual (psychoanalytical) therapy, 274

Inevitable abortion, 127

Infancy
  accident prevention measures in, 85
  CPR administration in, 321–322
  growth and development in, 95–96
  health screening in, 160
  health-care procedures in, preparation for, 434
  immunization schedule in, 163, 165
  normal vital signs in, 175
  nutritional requirements in, 243–245
  potential problems in, 96
  seizures (spasms) in, 339

Infantile spasms, 339

Infarction, myocardial, 323–326

Infection control
  standard (barrier) precautions, 67, 69
  transmission-based precautions, 70–71

Infection(s), 67
   antibiotics/antiinfectives for,
      478–483
   blood transfusion and, 466
   childhood, 68
   ear, 393–394
   eye, 385
   GI tract, 406
   as hazards to fetal development,
      117–118
   as oxygen therapy hazard, 453
   as postoperative complication, 438
   in postpartum period, 139–140
   superinfections, 555–556
Infertility, 157
Inflammation
   corneal, 385
   eye, 385
   in infection diagnosis, 67
Influenza immunization schedules,
      163–167
Informed consent, 48–49
   for use of restraints, 50
Infratentorial tumors, 377
Inguinal hernia, 417
INH (isoniazid) prophylaxis, for
      tuberculosis, 72
Inhalation anthrax, 88
Inhalational anesthesia, 435
Inhalers, for COPD clients, 358
Inspection (visual examination),
      172–172
Insulin, 492, 550
   management in diabetic clients, 403
   reaction to, 404
Integumentary system, changes in late
      adulthood, 106
Intellectual delay, 108–109
   classification of, 108
Intermittent claudication, exercise
      tests for, 440
Intermittent peritoneal dialysis, 267
Intermittent self-catheterization,
      urinary, 460–461
Internal fixation, of fracture, 219
Internal radiation therapy, for cancer,
      373

Intestinal obstruction, 418–419
Intestinal ostomies, for fecal diversion,
      420–423
Intoxication
   alcoholic, 307–309
   nonalcoholic, 310–312
Intracranial pressure, increased
   as medical emergency, 336–337
   in spina bifida, 205
Intracranial tumors, 377–378
Intraocular pressure
   glaucoma and, 390
   measurement of, 384
Intraoperative care, 435
Intrauterine device (IUD), 155
Intravenous anesthesia, 435
Intravenous fluids, 467
   flow rate calculations, 468
   monitoring, 468–469
Intravenous pyelogram, in urinary
      system evaluation, 447
Introjection (ego defense mechanism),
      276
Intropin (dopamine), 472
Intubation
   for enteral nutrition. See Enteral
      nutrition
   postoperative care, 437
   in upper airway obstruction, 319
Intussusception, 416–417
Invasion of privacy, 51
Inversion, 185
Iodine(s), 515–516
   function and sources, 237
Ipecac, syrup of, 80
IPV (inactivated poliovirus) vaccine.
      See Inactivated poliovirus (IPV)
      vaccine
Iron, function and sources, 237
Iron deficiency anemia, 367
Iron preparations, 527, 551
Irreducible (incarcerated) hernia, 417
Irrigations
   colostomy, 422
   ear, 391–392, 454
   eye, 454
   urinary catheters, 459

Ischemic heart disease, as heart failure cause, 361
Isolation, of tubercular clients, 72
Isometric exercises, 187
Isoniazid (INH) prophylaxis, for tuberculosis, 72
Isoproterenol (Isuprel), 472
Isotonic intravenous fluids, 467
Isuprel (isoproterenol), 472
Italians, food types preferred by, 243
IUD (intrauterine device), 155

**J**

Jackson-Pratt drain, 457
Japanese, food types preferred by, 243
Jaundice, 426
   in newborn, causes of, 147
Joint dislocations, 217
Joint disorders, 199–200
Joint movements, 185
JRA (juvenile rheumatoid arthritis), 200
Justice, 64
Juvenile rheumatoid arthritis (JRA), 200

**K**

Kaposi's sarcoma, 77
Kava, for anxiety, 475
Kegel exercises, 126, 254
Keofeed/Dobhoff tube, 455
Keratitis, 385
Kernig's sign, in meningitis, 397
Ketoacidosis, diabetic, 404
Ketogenic diet, for seizures, 338
Kidney. *See also* Renal *entries*
   anatomy, 257
   biopsy, in urinary system evaluation, 447
Klinefelter's syndrome, 115
Klonopin (clonazepam), 474
Knee replacement, 224
Koch pouch. *See* Continent ileal reservoir (Koch pouch)
Korsakoff's psychosis, 308
Kussmaul's respirations, 175
Kyphosis, 185, 197

**L**

Labor, 118–124
   factors affecting, 120–122
   fetal monitoring during, 119–120
   fourth stage, 124
   induction, 136–137
   onset, 118
   postpartum period and, 124–125
   precipitous (preterm), 136
   stages, 122, 123, 124
   true *vs.* false, 122
Laboratory blood tests, 439–440
Laceration, in head injury, 331
Lactation
   nutrition during, 247–248
   prevention methods, 124
   principles, 125
   problems associated with, 125
Laminectomy, 193
Lanugo, 143
Laparoscopic laser cholecystectomy, 428
Laparoscopy, 446
Laryngectomy, 379
Laryngotracheobronchitis, 322–323
Larynx, carcinoma of, 379
Late adulthood. *See also* Elderly
   growth and development in, 105–108
   immunization schedules in, 166, 167–168
Latex allergy, 171
Laxatives, 533, 552
LDL (low-density lipoproteins), 440
Lead toxicity (plumbism), 82–83
   screening for, 160
Learning disabilities, 110
Leg cramps, in pregnancy, 114
Legal issues, 51
Leukemia, 375–376
Levin tube, 455–456
Levophed (norepinephrine), 472
Librium (chlordiazepoxide), 474
Lice (pediculosis), 431
Licensed practical or vocational nurses (LPN/LVNs), 57
Lie, of fetus, 120
Lift (Hoyer), 191

Lightening, at onset of labor, 114

Lightheadedness, in pregnancy, 114

Lincosamides, 479, 483

Linea nigra, 112

Lipoproteins
  high-density, 440
  low-density, 440

Liquid diets, 241

Lisinopril (Zestril; Prinivil), 503

Liver. *See also* Hepatic *entries*
  biopsy, 444
  encephalopathy. *See* Hepatic
    encephalopathy, as cirrhosis
    complication
  function tests, 444
  impairment, 556–557
  infection. *See* Hepatitis
  scan, 444

Living will, 49

Local anesthesia, 435

Logan bar, 150

Loop colostomy, 420

Lopressor (metoprolol), 503

Lorazepam (Ativan), 474

Lordosis, lumbar spine, 185

Lou Gehrig's disease, 210–211

Low phenylalanine diet, 241

Low-density lipoproteins (LDL), 440

Lower GI series, 445

Lower limb amputation, prosthesis
    fitting after
  delayed, 225, 226
  immediate, 225, 226
  postoperative care, 226

Low-fat, cholesterol-restricted diet, 241

Low-residue diet, 241

LP (lumbar puncture), 443

LPN/LVNs (licensed practical or
    vocational nurses), 57

Lumbar lordosis, 185

Lumbar puncture (LP), 443

Lung
  biopsy, 442
  disease, as heart failure cause, 361
  function tests, 441
  in physical, 178

Lyme disease, 74–75

## M

Macrolides, 480, 483

Magnesium imbalances, 350

Magnetic resonance imaging
    (MRI), 442

Malecot urinary catheter, 458

Malignant melanoma, 376

Malpractice, 51

Malunion, of fracture, 218

Mammography, 153, 161

Managed care, 52

Manipulative behavior, 303–304
  in bipolar disorder, 296
  in drug abusers, 312

Mantoux test (PPD), 71

MAO (monoamine oxidase) inhibitors,
    489, 491, 550

"Mask of pregnancy," 112

Masks, 69

Maslow hierarchy of needs, 271–272

Mass casualties, triage for, 87

Mastitis, 157

Maternal cardiac disease, 133–134

Maternal diabetes, 132–133
  nutritional requirements, 248
  risk factors, 133

McBurney's point, in appendicitis, 413

MCV4 (meningococcal conjugate
    vaccine), administration
    schedule, 163–164, 166

MD (muscular dystrophy), 207–208

MDI (metered dose inhalers), 358

Measles. *See* Rubeola (measles)

Measles, mumps, rubella (MMR)
    vaccine
  in child, nursing considerations
    for, 169
  immunization schedules, 163–167

Measurements at term, in newborn,
    142

Mechanical restraint, 50

Mechanical ventilation, 320–321

Meckel's diverticulum, 418

Meconium, 144

Medical emergencies
  abdominal injuries, 334
  cardiopulmonary arrest, 321–322

chest trauma, 332–333

croup syndromes, 322–323

head injury, 331–332

increased intracranial pressure, 336–337

myocardial infarction, 323–326

rhythm disturbances, 326–330

seizures, 337–339

shock, 334–336

spinal cord injury, 341–343

stroke (brain attack), 339–341

upper airway obstruction, 319–321

Medications. *See* Herbal supplements; Pharmacological therapy

Melanoma, 376

Melatonin, for anxiety, 475

Ménière's syndrome, 394–395

Meningitis, 397

droplet precautions for, 70

Meningocele, in spina bifida, 204

Meningococcal conjugate vaccine (MCV4), administration schedule, 163–164, 166

Menopause, 154

Mental health

concepts, 271–274

herbal supplements promoting, 547

Mental illness treatment modalities, 274

Metabolism, inborn errors of, 115

Metered dose inhalers (MDI), 358

Methadone, 312

Methyldopa (Aldomet), 503

Metoprolol (Lopressor), 503

MI (myocardial infarction), 323–326

Midazolam. *See* Versed (midazolam)

Middle adulthood

food pyramid RDIs in, 238

growth and development in, 104

immunization schedules in, 166, 167–168

potential nursing diagnoses in, 104

Migraine headache, 397–398

Milia, 143

Milieu therapy, 274

Milrinone (Primacor), 472

Mineralocorticoids, 530, 552

Minerals, 237, 527, 551

Minors, informed consent and, 48–49

Minoxidil, 503

Miotic eye medications, 534, 552

Missed abortion, 127

Mixed sleep apnea, 229

MMR vaccine. *See* Measles, mumps, rubella (MMR) vaccine

Mobility, 185–187

conditions limiting, 193–210

promoting in amputee, 225

Mongolian spots, 143

Monoamine oxidase (MAO) inhibitors, 489, 491

Mononucleosis, 68

Morning sickness, 113, 114

Moro reflex, 145

Motor neuron disease, 210–211

Mouth

care in cancer clients, 372–373

in newborn, 144

in physical, 177–178

MRI (magnetic resonance imaging), 442

MRSAs (multidrug-resistant organisms), 71

MS (multiple sclerosis), 208–210

Mucomyst (*N*-Acetylcysteine), for acetaminophen poisoning, 82

Mucosal drying/irritation, as oxygen therapy hazard, 453

Multidrug-resistant organisms (MRSAs), 71

Multiple puncture test, 71

Multiple sclerosis (MS), 208–210

Mumps, 68

droplet precautions for, 70

immunization schedules, 163–167

live attenuated vaccine in child, nursing considerations for, 169

Murmurs, in heart sound, 180

Muscular dystrophy (MD), 207–208

Musculoskeletal system

changes in late adulthood, 107

effects of anxiety on, 275

herbal supplements, 545

medications for, 535, 552

in physical, 181–182

trauma to, 217–226

Muslims, dietary laws, 242
Myasthenia gravis, 208–210
Mydriatic eye medications, 536, 552
Myelography, 443
Myelomeningocele, in spina bifida, 204
Myocardial infarction (MI), 323–326
Myoclonic seizures, 339
Myomas, uterine, 157
Myopia, 384
Myringotomy, 394
Myxedema, 232–233

**N**

Nadolol (Corgard), 503
Nägele's rule, 112
Nails, in physical, 176–177
Naloxone (Narcan), for drug overdose, 310
NAPs (nursing assistive personnel), 53, 57
Narcissistic personality disorder, 302
Narcotic-addicted infants, 149
Narcotics, 537, 552
  abuse, 311
Nasal cannula, for oxygen administration, 452
Nasogastric tubes, 455–456
Native Americans, significance of food for, 242
Natural family planning, 155
Nausea and vomiting, in pregnancy, 113, 114
Neck, in physical, 178
Needs, Maslow hierarchy of, 271–272
Negligence, 51
Neonatal abstinence syndrome, 149
Neonate
  accident prevention measures for, 84–85
  physical, 141–146
  complications in, 147–151
  health screening in, 160
  health-care procedures in, preparation for, 434
  immediate care of, 123–124
  immunization schedule in, 163

narcotic-addicted, 149
  normal vital signs in, 175
  respiration/perfusion, 175
Neo-Synephrine (phenylephrine), 472
Nephrectomy, 258
Nephrolithotomy, 258
  percutaneous, 258
Nephrons, 260
  infection of, 259–260
  in kidney anatomy, 257
Nephrostomy, 258, 263
Nerve impulse transmission disorders, 208–210
Neural tube defects, 204–205
Neuralgia, trigeminal, 395
Neurectomy, for pain relief, 215
Neurological deficit, categories in spinal cord injury, 342
Neurological system
  changes in late adulthood, 106
  herbal supplements, 545
  in physical, 181–182
Neurological tests, 443
Neuroma, acoustic, 395
Neuromuscular disorders, 207–208
Neuron, anatomy and physiology of, 207
Neuropsychosocial system, postoperative care and, 436
Neutropenia precautions, for cancer clients, 373
Nevi, in newborn, 143
Newborn. *See* Neonate
Niacin (nicotinic acid), function and sources, 237
Nicotinic acid (niacin), 499, 550
  function and sources, 237
Nifedipine (Procardia), 503
Nipples
  postpartum care, lactation and, 125
  stimulation, fetal response to, 117
Nitrates, 538
Nitrogen balance, changes in immobile clients, 188
Nitropress (sodium nitroprusside), 472
Nitrous oxide, for anesthesia, 435

Nonalcoholic substance abuse, 310–312

Nonbenzodiazepine anxiolytic agents, 474

Nonmaleficence, 65

Nonpenetrating (blunt) trauma
abdominal, 334
to eye, 385

Nonrebreather mask, for oxygen administration, 452

Nonsteroidal anti-inflammatory drugs (NSAIDs), 539

Non-stress test (NST), 117

Nonunion, of fracture, 218

Norepinephrine (Levophed), 472

Norplant, 155

Nose, in physical, 177

NSAIDs (nonsteroidal anti-inflammatory drugs), 539

NST (non-stress test), 117

Nuchal rigidity, in meningitis, 397

Nurse Practice Acts, 51, 53

Nurse/client relationship, aspects of, 47

Nursing
abbreviations used in, 560–569
ethical principles, 65

Nursing assistants, 53

Nursing mothers, lactation principles and, 125
nutrition for, 247–248

Nutrient requirements, 236

Nutrition, 235–240
adequate, physical signs of, 235
in adolescence, 246
in adults and elderly, 247
in bipolar disorder, 297
for burn clients, 352
for cancer clients, 373
in cirrhosis, 424
cultural food patterns, 242–243
in depression, 282
in diabetic clients, 402
enteral, 248–249
for full-term infants, 244–245
in heart failure clients, 362
in newborn, 141
in other ages, 176
during pregnancy and lactation, 247–248
for premature infants, 243–244
for preschool and school-age children, 246
therapeutic diets, 241
for toddlers, 245
total parenteral, 249–252

Nystagmus, 177

O

Obsessive compulsive disorder (OCD), 277, 302

Obstetric classification, of pregnancy, 112

Obstruction
intestinal, 418–419
upper airway, 319–321

Obstructive jaundice, 426

Obstructive sleep apnea, 229

OCD (obsessive compulsive disorder), 277

Ocular impairment, 557

Oculomotor nerve (CN III), 179

Olfactory nerve (CN I), 179

Omnibus Budget Reconciliation Act, 50

Open pneumothorax, 332, 333

Open-angle glaucoma, 390

Opioid analgesics. See Narcotics

Opisthotonic position, in meningitis, 397

Opportunistic infections, in AIDS clients, 75, 77

Optic nerve (CN II), 179

Optimizing decision making, 58

Oral contraceptives, 155

Oral hypoglycemic agents, 403, 493

Orchitis, 158

Organ transplantation, kidney, 267–268

Organizational hierarchy, 57

Orthodox jews, dietary laws, 242

Orthostatic hypotension, 188

Osteoarthritis, 200
risk factors for, 199

Osteomalacia, 203
Osteomyelitis, 202–203
Osteoporosis, 188, 201–202
Otitis media, acute, 393–394
Ovarian cancer, 158
Ovarian cyst, 158
Oxazepam (Serax), 474
Oxygen tent, 452
Oxygen therapy
   administration methods, 452
   hazards, 453
Oxygen toxicity, 453
Oxytocin
   fetal response to, 117
   inducing labor with, 137

## P

t-PA (tissue-type plasminogen
      activator), in myocardial
      infarction, 325
Pacemakers, 330
Packed red cells (blood product), 465
Paget's disease, 200
   medications for, 540
Pain, 213–215
   ischemic patterns, in myocardial
      infarction, 323
   phantom, 225
   potential responses to, 213
Pain relief
   in burn clients, 352
   in cancer clients, 373
   methods, 215
   client-controlled. See Client
      controlled analgesia (PCA)
Palmar grasp, 144
Palpation, in physical, 173
Pancreatic tumors, 378–379
Pancreatitis, 428–429
Pap smear, 161
Para (obstetric classification), 112
Paracentesis, 445
Paralysis, facial, 395
Paralytic ileus, as postoperative
      complication, 438
Paranoid personality disorder, 301
Paranoid schizophrenia, 298
Paraplegia, 342

Parathyroid disorders, 234
Parenteral fluids, 467–468
Parenteral nutrition, 249–252
Parenting, with newborn, 141
Parkinson-like effects, of
      medication, 559
Parkinson's disease, 208–210
Partial rebreather mask, for oxygen
      administration, 452
Partial seizures, 339
Partial thromboplastin time (PTT),
      439, 444
Passive immunity, 162
Pathologic jaundice, in newborn,
      147, 148
Client Bill of Rights, 48–49
Client controlled analgesia (PCA), 215
   postoperative, 436
   in sickle-cell disease, 369
Client placement, for infection
      control, 69
Pavlik harness, 196
PCA. See Client controlled analgesia
      (PCA)
PCC (Poison Control Center), 80
PCV (pneumococcal vaccine),
      administration schedule, 163–167
Pectoriloquy, whispered, 178
Pediculosis, 431
   contact precautions for, 70–71
Pelvic inflammatory disease (PID), 157
Penetrating trauma
   abdominal, 334
   to eye, 385
Penicillins, 480, 482
Penis, care in newborn, 146
Penrose drain, 457
Pentothal, as intravenous
      anesthesia, 435
Perceptual deficits, learning disabilities
      and, 110
Percussion
   chest, 449
   in physical, 173–174
Percutaneous nephrolithotomy, 258
Percutaneous transluminal coronary
      angioplasty (PTCA), for angina
      pectoris, 363

Percutaneous ureterolithotomy, 258

Pericarditis, constrictive, as heart failure cause, 361

Periodic breathing, 176

Peripheral arterial disease (PAD), 364

Peripheral IV, monitoring, 468–469

Peripheral vascular system, in physical, 180–181

Peritoneal dialysis, 266
  types, 267

Peritonitis, 414–415

Pernicious anemia, 368

Personal Protective Equipment, 69

Personality disorders, 301–302

Personnel, 57

Pertussis (Whooping cough), 68
  immunization schedules, 163–167

PET (positron emission tomography), 443

Petit mal seizures, 339

Pezzer urinary catheter, 458

Phantom pain, 225

Pharmacological therapy. *See also individually named drugs*
  classifications, 549–552. *See also individual classes of drugs, e.g.* Antianxiety medications
  equivalents and dosage formulas, 471
  for shock, cardiac arrest and anaphylaxis, 472–473
  terminology related to, 568–569

Pharynx, in physical, 177–178

Phenylephrine (Neo-Synephrine), 472

Phenylketonuria (PKU), 116, 160, 405

Phlebitis, 469

Phobia, 277

Phosphorus, function and sources, 237

Phototherapy
  for depression, 284
  for hemolytic anemia in newborn, 148

Physical, performance of, 172–182

Physiologic jaundice, in newborn, 147

PID (pelvic inflammatory disease), 157

Pigment studies, 444

PIH (pregnancy-induced hypertension), 129–130

Pinkeye (conjunctivitis), 385

Pinna, in physical examination, 177

Pituitary disorders, 370

PKU (phenylketonuria), 116, 160, 405

Placenta
  in early pregnancy, 114
  premature separation, 131–132

Placenta previa, 130–131

Plague
  bubonic, 88
  pneumonic, 89

Plantar flexion, 185

Plantar grasp, 145

Platelet count, 439

Play, in child development, 93

Play therapy, 274
  for abused child, 313

Pleural friction rub, in breath sound, 178

Pleur-evac tube, 453

Plumbism (lead toxicity), 82–83
  screening for, 160

PMI (point of maximal impulse), 180

PN. *See* Parenteral nutrition

Pneumococcal vaccine (PCV), administration schedule, 163–167

*Pneumocystis jiroveci* infection, in AIDS clients, 75

Pneumonia, 359–360
  droplet precautions for, 70
  as postoperative complication, 438

Pneumonic plague, 89

Pneumothorax, 332–333

Point of maximal impulse (PMI), 180

Poison Control Center (PCC), 80

Poisoning
  aspirin (salicylate), 81–82
  inducing vomiting, contraindications for, 80
  preventing in children, 79–80
  recognizing signs and management of, 80
  recurrence prevention, 81
  Tylenol (acetaminophen), 82

Poliovirus vaccine. *See* Inactivated poliovirus (IPV) vaccine

Port wine stain, 143
Position(s)
    fetal, 120–121
    therapeutic, for immobile clients,
        187, 189
Positive-supporting reflex, 145
Positron emission tomography
    (PET), 443
Postoperative care, 436–438
    lower limb amputation, 226
"Postpartum blues," 126
Postpartum period
    depression in, 126, 140
    hemorrhage in, 139
    immediate, care in, 124–125
    infection in, 139–140
    lactation in, establishing, 125
Post-traumatic stress disorder (PTSD),
    280–281
Postural drainage, 449
Posture, in newborn, 142
Potassium
    function and sources, 237
    imbalances, 347
Power of attorney, durable, 49
PPD (purified protein derivative)
    test, 71
Precipitous delivery, 138
Precipitous labor, 136
Preeclampsia, 129, 130
Pregnancy
    danger signs in, 118
    discomforts, 114
    ectopic, 128–129
    and estimated date of
        confinement, 112
    fetus, 113
    findings in, 112–113
    nutrition during, 247–248
    obstetric classification, 112
    verifying, 113
Pregnancy-induced hypertension
    (PIH), 129–130
Premature infants, nutrition for,
    243–244
Premature ventricular contractions
    (PVCs), 327

Preoperative care, 433–435
Preoperative checklist, 434
Presbyopia, 384
Preschool children
    accident prevention measures
        for, 85
    fear of surgery in, 433
    growth and development in, 99
    health-care procedures in,
        preparation for, 434
    immunization schedules, 163, 165
    nutrient intake for, 246
    potential problems in, 99
    vaccination in, nursing
        considerations, 169
Prescriptive decision making, 58
Presentation, of fetus, 120
Preterm (precipitous) delivery, 138
Preterm (precipitous) labor, 136
Primacor (milrinone), 472
Prinivil (lisinopril), 503
Prioritizing, in disaster planning, 87
Privacy, 48
    invasion of, 51
Problem solving, 59
Procardia (nifedipine), 503
Proctoscopy, 445
Professionalism, 47
Projection (ego defense mechanism),
    275
Prolapse
    umbilical cord, during labor, 119, 124
    uterine, 157
Pronation, 185
Prophylactic medications/supplements,
    for newborn, 145
Propranolol (Inderal), 503
Prostate cancer, 158
Prostatectomy, 262
Prostate-specific antigen (PSA), 261
Prostatic hypertrophy, 158, 261–262
Prostatitis, 158
Prosthesis fitting, after lower limb
    amputation
    delayed, 225, 226
    immediate, 225, 226
    postoperative care, 226
Protein allergy, 405

Protein metabolism, alterations in, 404–405

Protein studies, 444

Proteins, 236

Prothrombin time (PT), 439, 444

PSA (prostate-specific antigen), 261

Psoriasis, 432

Psychiatric health, herbal supplements for, 547

Psychoanalytical (individual) therapy, 274

Psychomotor seizures, 339

Psychophysiologic hazards, 84

Psychosis, as postoperative complication, 438

Psychosocial behavior
adapting, counseling techniques for, 291
anxiety and, 275
religious and spiritual influences, 292–293
schizophrenia and, 300

PT (prothrombin time), 439, 444

PTCA (percutaneous transluminal coronary angioplasty), for angina pectoris, 363

Ptosis, 177

PTSD (post-traumatic stress disorder), 280–281

PTT (partial thromboplastin time), 439, 444

Puberty, changes in, 102

Puerto Ricans, food types preferred by, 242

Pulmonary disease, as heart failure cause, 361

Pulmonary function tests, 441

Pulse oximetry, 442

Pulses, in physical, 180–181

Pupillary reflex, 144

Pupils, in physical, 177

Purposeful inaction, in problem solving, 59

Pursed lip breathing, 449

PAD (peripheral arterial disease), 364

PVCs (premature ventricular contractions), 327

Pyelolithotomy, 258

Pyelonephritis, 259–260

Pyloric stenosis, 407–408

Pyloromyotomy, in pyloric stenosis, 408

Pyloroplasty, in pyloric stenosis, 408

Pyridoxine ($B_6$), function and sources, 237

## Q

Quadriplegia, 342

Quality assurance (QA), 52

## R

Radiation burns, 353
to eye, 385

Radioimmunoprecipitation assay (RIPA), in AIDS diagnosis, 77

Radiotherapy, for cancer
external, 372–373
internal, 373

Rales (crackles), in breath sound, 178

Range of motion exercises, 187

Range of vision, measurement of, 384

Rape trauma, 279

Raynaud's disease, 364

RBC (red blood cell) count, 439

RDI (recommended daily intake), 238

Reaction formation (ego defense mechanism), 276

Reasoning process, ethical, 65

Rebreather mask, partial, for oxygen administration, 452

Recommended daily intake (RDI), 238

Red blood cell (RBC) count, 439

Reducible hernia, 417

Reduction of fracture, 219

Reflexes, in newborn, 141, 144–145

Refusal of treatment, 49

Regional enteritis, 412–413

Registered nurses (RNs), 57

Regression
as ego defense mechanism, 277
in schizophrenia, 300

Religion
influence on diet, 242
influence on health, 292–293

Renal anatomy, 257

Renal calculi, 256–257

Renal diet, 241

Renal failure, 264–268, 405

acute, 264, 265

chronic, 265

dialysis for, 266–267

renal transplant in, 267–268

Renal impairment, 557

Renal scan, in urinary system evaluation, 447

Renal transplant, in renal failure, 267–268

Reports

incident, 60–61

shift change, 60–63

Repression (ego defense mechanism), 276

Reproduction, 153–154

Reproductive system

changes in late adulthood, 107

herbal supplements, 544

problems, 154, 157–158

self-care screening, 161

Reproductive tests, 446

Residual schizophrenia, 298

Respiration/perfusion

in newborn, 141, 142, 175

patterns of, 175–176

in physical, 175

Respiratory depression, as oxygen therapy hazard, 453

Respiratory secretions, stasis in immobile clients, 188

Respiratory syncytial virus (RSV), contact precautions for, 70–71

Respiratory system

changes in late adulthood, 106

herbal supplements, 548

medications for, 522

postoperative care and, 436

Respiratory tests, 441–442

Responsibility, defined, 56

Rest disturbances

in Alzheimer's disease, 229–231

in elderly clients, 228–229

in hospitalized clients, 227–228

Restraints, 50

Retina, detached, 387–388

Retrograde ureteroscopy, 258

Reye's syndrome (RS), 68, 426–427

Rheumatic heart disease, as heart failure cause, 361

Rheumatoid arthritis, 200

risk factors for, 199

Rho(D) immune globulin (IGIM) administration

in ectopic pregnancy, 129

hydatidiform mole and, 135

in postpartum period, 124

Rhonchi, in breath sound, 178

Rhythm (cardiac) disturbances, 326–330

Rhythm method, 155

Riboflavin ($B_2$), function and sources, 237

Rinne test, 177

RIPA (radioimmunoprecipitation assay), in AIDS diagnosis, 77

Risk management/manager, 52

incident report and, 61

RNs (registered nurses), 57

Robinson urinary catheter, 458

Role changes, 287–288

ROM (rupture of membranes), 118–119

Rooting reflex, 144

Rotation, 185

Rotavirus immunization schedules, 163, 165

RS (Reye's syndrome), 68, 426–427

RSV (respiratory syncytial virus), contact precautions for, 70–71

Rubella (German measles), 68

immunization schedules, 163–166, 168

live attenuated vaccine in child, nursing considerations for, 169

Rubeola (measles), 68

airborne precautions for, 70

immunization schedules, 163–167

MMR vaccine in child, nursing considerations for, 169

Rule of Nines, 351

Rupture of membranes (ROM), 118–119

Russell's traction, 221

RV (retrovirus vaccine), 165

# S

S2 "dubb" sound, 180

S1 "lubb" sound, 180

Safety hazards, 84

Salem sump, 455–456

Salicylate poisoning, 81–82

*Salmonella* infection,
  gastrointestinal, 406

Satisficing decision making, 58

Scabies, 431

  contact precautions for, 70–71

Scarlet fever, 68

Schilling test, 368

  in urinary system evaluation, 447

Schizoid personality disorder, 302

Schizophrenia, 297–300

  types, 298

Schizotypal personality disorder, 302

School-age child

  accident prevention measures for,
    85–86

  CPR administration in, 321–322

  fear of surgery in, 433

  growth and development in,
    100–101

  health screening in, 160

  health-care procedures in,
    preparation for, 434

  immunization schedules, 164, 165

  normal vital signs in, 175

  nutrient intake for, 246

  potential problems in, 100

  vaccination in, nursing
    considerations for, 164, 165

Sclerotherapy, endoscopic, for
  esophageal varices, 424

Scoliosis, 185, 197–198

Sedimentation rate. *See* Erythrocyte
  sedimentation rate (ESR)

Seizures, 337–339

Selective reuptake inhibitors 489, 491,
  550

Self-catheterization, intermittent
  urinary, 460–461

Self-destructive behavior

  in depression, 282

  suicide and, 286

Self-determination Act, 49

Self-esteem

  in depression, 283

  schizophrenia and, 300

Sengstaken-Blakemore tube, 455

  for esophageal varices, 425

Sensory input, changes in immobile
  clients, 188

Sequence, for incident reports, 61

Serax (oxazepam), 474

Serum albumin, 440, 444

Sexual abuse, 314–315

Sexual activity, in postpartum
  period, 126

Sexuality, 111

Sexually transmitted diseases (STDs),
  75, 76. *See also* AIDS; *individual
  diseases*

  in pregnant woman, 134–135

Shift change report, 62–64

*Shigella,* in GI tract infection, 406

Shingles. *See* Disseminated zoster
  (shingles)

Shock, 334–335

  medications for, 472–473, 549

  in myocardial infarction, 323

  as postoperative complication, 438

Shunts, in hydrocephalus, 205, 206

SIADH (syndrome of inappropriate
  antidiuretic hormone), 346

Sickle cell disease, 115, 368–369

  nutritional requirements in
    pregnancy, 248

SIDS (sudden infant death
  syndrome), 290

Sigmoid colostomy, 421

Sigmoidoscopy, 445

Single-barrel colostomy, 420

Sinus dysrhythmias, 326

Sinuses, in physical, 177

Situational crises, 279

Situational role changes, 287–288

Skeletal traction, 220

  in spinal cord injury, 342

Skin

  care in cancer clients, 372

  changes in late adulthood, 106

changes in pregnancy, 112
in newborn, 142
in physical, 176
Skin cancer, 376–377
Skin testing, for tuberculosis, 71
Skin traction, 220
Skull fracture, 331
Skull tongs (cervical traction), 221
SLE (systemic lupus erythematosus),
    429–430
Sleep apnea syndrome, 229
Sleep disturbances
    in Alzheimer's disease, 229–231
    in elderly, 228–229
    in hospitalized clients, 227–228
    sleep apnea syndrome, 229
Sliding board, 191
Smallpox, 89
    immunization, 167
Smears, in reproductive tests, 446
Smell, changes in late adulthood, 106
Snellen test, 384
Social networks, support systems
    and, 290
Social withdrawal, in depression, 283
Sodium
    function and sources, 237
    imbalances, 348
    restriction in diet, 241
Sodium nitroprusside (Nitropress), 472
Solid foods, introducing infant to, 245
Southeast Asians, food types preferred
    by, 243
Spermicides, 155
Spica cast, 196
Spina bifida, 204–205
Spina bifida occulta, 204
Spinal accessory nerve (CN XI), 179
Spinal cord injury, 341–343
    level, functional/self-care capability
        and, 341
    neurological deficit categories in, 342
    types, 342
Spirituality, influence on health,
    292–293
Splenic portal venography, 444
Splenoportogram, 444

Splinting, of fracture, 219
Spontaneous abortion, classification
    of, 127–128
Sprains, 217
Sprue, 405
Sputum analysis, 441
Squamous cell carcinoma, 376
SSRIs (selective reuptake inhibitors),
    489, 491, 550
Standard (barrier) precautions, 67, 69
Staphylococcus aureus infection, 67
Statins, 499
Station, of fetus, 121
STDs. See Sexually transmitted
    diseases (STDs)
Stenting, urinary tract, 258
Stepping reflex, 145
Sterilization (contraception), 156
Stimulants abuse, 311
Stomatitis, 555
Stool, in newborn, 144
Stool softeners, 533, 552
"Stork bites," 143
Strabismus, 177, 387
Strangulated hernia, 417
Strawberry mark, 143
Streptococcus, group B
        beta-hemolytic, fetal
        development and, 118
Streptococcus pharyngitis, droplet
    precautions for, 70
Stress, 288–289
Stress testing, 328, 442
Stroke, 339–341
    as hypertension complication, 365
    immediate care and rehabilitative
        needs, 340–341
Stye, 385
Subdermal implants (contraceptive),
    155
Subdural hematoma, in head injury,
    331
Sublimation (ego defense
    mechanism), 277
Substance abuse
    alcoholic, 307–309
    nonalcoholic, 310–312

Substitution (ego defense mechanism), 276
Sucking chest wound, 332, 333
Sucking reflex, 144
Suctioning, 450
Sudden infant death syndrome (SIDS), 290
Suicide, 285–287
  impending, behavioral clues for, 285
  potential for, 282
Sulfonamides, 481, 482
Superinfections, 555–556
Supination, 185
Support systems, 290
Suppression (ego defense mechanism), 277
Suprapubic cystostomy, 262
Suprapubic urinary catheter, 458
Supratentorial tumors, 377
Surgery
  fears at different developmental stages, 433
  intraoperative care, 435
  postoperative care, 436–438
  postoperative expectations, 435
  potential complications, 438
  preoperative care, 433–435
  preoperative checklist for, 434
Surgical drains
  care principles, 459
  in postoperative care, 437
  types, 457
Survival needs, in schizophrenia, 298
Suspiciousness, in schizophrenic client, 297
  nursing care, 300
Symbolization (ego defense mechanism), 276
Sympathectomy, for pain relief, 215
Syndrome of inappropriate antidiuretic hormone (SIADH), 346
Syphilis, 76
  fetal development and, 118
  in pregnant woman, 134
Syrup of Ipecac, 80
Systemic lupus erythematosus (SLE), 429–430

T
T tube, 457
Tachycardia
  in fetus, 119
  ventricular, 327
Tachydysrhythmias, as heart failure cause, 361
Tactile fremitus, 178
Talipes equinovarus (club foot), 198–199
Taped change-of-shift report, 63
Tarasoff Act, 51
Taste, changes in late adulthood, 106
Tay-Sachs' disease, 115, 116
TD. See Tetanus/diphtheria (TD) booster
Tdap (tetanus, diphtheria, pertussis) vaccine, administration schedules, 164–167
TED hose, postoperative, 436
Teletherapy, for cancer, 272–373
Temporal lobe seizures, 339
Tenormin (atenolol), 503
TENS (transcutaneous electrical nerve stimulation), 215
Term
  measurements at, in newborn, 142
  as obstetric classification, 112
Testicular self-exam, 154, 161
Testing. See Diagnostic testing
Testosterone inhibitors, 484
Tetanus
  diphtheria, pertussis (Tdap) vaccine, administration schedules, 164–167
  immunization schedules, 163–167
Tetanus/diphtheria (TD) booster, 166
  in child, nursing considerations for, 169
Tetany, in Graves' disease, 233
Tetracyclines, 481, 482
Tetraplegia, 342
Therapeutic communication, 273
  response types in, 272
  responses to avoid in, 273
  in schizophrenia, 299

Therapeutic diets, 241

Therapeutic exercises, for immobile clients, 187

Therapeutic nature, of nurse/client relationship, 47

Therapeutic positions, for immobile clients, 189

Thermal burns, 352
to eye, 385

Thiamine (B$_1$), function and sources, 237

Thomas splint, 221

Thoracentesis, 441

Thoracolumbosacral orthotic (TLSO) brace, 198

Thorax, in physical, 178

Threatened abortion, 127

Thrombocyte (platelet) count, 439

Thrombolytic therapy
medications, 540
in myocardial infarction, 325

Thrombophlebitis, 364, 469

Thrombus formation, 188
changes in immobile clients, 188

Thyroid disorders, 231–233
medications for, 515–516, 551

Thyroid replacement agents, 516, 551

Thyroid storm, in Graves' disease, 233

TIA (transient ischemic attack), as hypertension complication, 365

Tilt table, 189

Tine test, 71

Tinea, 431

Tissue-type plasminogen activator (t-PA), in myocardial infarction, 325

TLSO (thoracolumbosacral orthotic) brace, 198

TNA (Total Nutrient Admixture), 250

Toddlerhood
accident prevention measures in, 85
in child growth and development, 98
fear of surgery in, 433
health-care procedures in, preparation for, 434
immunization schedule in, 163
nutritional requirements in, 245–246
potential problems in, 98

Toilet training, 254

Tonic neck, in newborn, 145

Tonic seizures, 339

Tonic-clonic seizures, 339

Tonometry, 384

Tonsillitis, 68

Topical antibacterials, 483, 549
for burn wounds, 352

TORCH test series, 117

Total cholesterol, 440

Total Nutrient Admixture (TNA), 250
administration methods, 250
complications of, 249–251
solutions for, 250

Toxic hepatitis, 73

Toxic shock syndrome (TSS), 157

Toxoplasmosis, fetal development and, 117

Toys, age-appropriate
for infants, 97
for preschool children, 99
for school-age children, 100
for toddlers, 98

T-piece, for oxygen administration, 452

Tracheobronchitis, 322–323

Tracheoesophageal fistula, 411–412

Tracheostomy, 319, 320
care, 451
in Grave's disease, 233
for sleep apnea syndrome, 229

Tracheostomy collar, for oxygen administration, 452

Traction, 220–222

Transcutaneous electrical nerve stimulation (TENS), 215

Transient ischemic attack (TIA), as hypertension complication, 365

Transmission-based precautions, in infection control, 70–71

Transplantation, kidney, 267–268

Transport, infection control and, 69

Transurethral prostatectomy (TURP), 262

Transverse colostomy, 421

Trauma
   abdominal, 334
   to chest, 332–333
   to eye, 385
   to head, 331–332
   musculoskeletal, 217–226
   and post-traumatic stress disorder,
      280–281
   rape, 279
   spinal cord, 341–343
Triage, in disaster planning, 87
Trial and error, in problem
     solving, 59
Tricyclic antidepressants,
     490, 491, 550
Trigeminal nerve (CN V), 179
Trigeminal neuralgia, 395
Trisomy 21 (Down syndrome),
     109–110, 115
Trochlear nerve (CN IV), 179
Trousseau's sign
   in Graves' disease, 233
   in hypocalcemia, 349
   in hypoparathyroidism, 234
True labor, 122
Trunk, in newborn, 144
TSS (toxic shock syndrome), 157
Tubal ligation, 156
Tube feeding. *See* Enteral nutrition
Tuberculosis, 71–72
   airborne precautions for, 70
   testing in child, nursing
     considerations for, 169
Turner's sign, 334
Turner's syndrome, 115
TURP (transurethral prostatectomy),
     262
Tylenol (acetaminophen)
     poisoning, 82
Tympanoplasty, 394

**U**

UGI (upper GI series), 445
Ulcerative colitis, 412–413
Ulcers, 409–411
   decubitus, in immobile clients, 188
   duodenal, 409, 410
   gastric, 409, 410
   medications for, 541, 552
   sites for, 410
   surgical procedures for, 410–411
Ultrasonography, 117
   echocardiography, 442
   in urinary system evaluation, 447
   in venous diagnostic tests, 440
Umbilical cord
   care, 146
   in newborn, 144
   prolapse during labor, 119, 124
Umbilical hernia, 417
Undifferentiated schizophrenia, 298
Undoing (ego defense mechanism), 276
Upper airway obstruction, 319–321
Upper GI series (UGI), 445
Ureteral calculi, 256–257
Ureterolithotomy, 258
   percutaneous, 258
Ureteroscopy, retrograde, 258
Ureterosigmoidostomy, 263
Ureterostomy, cutaneous, 263
Urinalysis, 446
Urinary bladder, exstrophy, 256
Urinary catheters, 458–461
Urinary diversions, 263
Urinary elimination, 253–255
Urinary frequency, in pregnancy, 114
Urinary incontinence, in postpartum
     period, 126
Urinary retention, as postoperative
     complication, 438
Urinary stasis, in immobile clients, 188
Urinary tract, 253
   changes in late adulthood, 107
   common surgeries of, 258
   congenital malformations of, 256
   tests, 446
Urinary tract infection (UTI)
   fetal development and, 117
   as postoperative complication, 438
Uterine fibroids, 157
Uterus, displacement/prolapse, 157
UTI. *See* Urinary tract infection (UTI)
Uveitis, 385

# V

Vaccination, 162–169
  immunization schedules, 163–166
Vaccinia immunization, 167
Vaginitis
  atrophic, 157
  simple, 157
Vagotomy
  in pyloric stenosis, 408
  in ulcer management, 410, 411
Vagus nerve (CN X), 179
Valium (diazepam), 474
  for conscious sedation, 435
Values, 64
Valvular heart disease, as heart failure
    cause, 361
Vancomycin-resistant organisms,
    contact precautions for, 70–71
Variances, 53
  reporting of, 57
Varicella (chickenpox), 68
  airborne precautions for, 70
  fetal development and, 118
  immunization schedules, 163–166, 168
Varicose veins, 364
Vasectomy, 156
Vasodilators, direct-acting, 502
Vasotec (enalapril), 503
Vegetarian diet, 238–239
Venography, splenic portal, 444
Venous diagnostic tests, 440
Venous thromboembolism (VTE), as
    postoperative complication, 438
Ventral (incisional) hernia, 417
Ventricular atrial shunt, in
    hydrocephalus, 206
Ventricular drainage, in
    hydrocephalus, 206
Ventricular dysrhythmias, 327–328
Ventricular fibrillation, 327–328
Ventricular tachycardia, 327
Ventriculoperitoneal shunt, in
    hydrocephalus, 205, 206
Venturi mask, for oxygen
    administration, 452
Veracity, 64
Verapamil (Calan), 503
Vernix caseosa, 143

Versed (midazolam), 474
  for conscious sedation, 435
Vertigo, in pregnancy, 114
Vibration, of chest, 449–450
Violent behavior, 304–305
  nursing care of client exhibiting, 304
Vision
  changes in late adulthood, 106
  impaired, 383–386
Vistaril (hydroxyzine), 474
Visual acuity, test of, 384
Visual fields, 384
Visual function tests, 384
Vital signs
  in newborn, 142
  in physical, 175–176
Vitamin $B_{12}$ anemia, 368
Vitamins, 236, 541, 552
  fat-soluble, 236
  water-soluble, 237
Vocal resonance, 178
Volume deficit, 345
Volume overload, 345
Vomiting
  inducing in accidental
    poisoning, 80–82
  in pregnancy, 113, 114

# W

Walkers, 190
Water-soluble vitamins, 237
WBC. *See* White blood cell (WBC)
  count
Weber test, 177
Wellness programs, 159
Wernicke's syndrome, 308
Wheezes, in breath sound, 178
Whipple procedure, 378
Whispered pectoriloquy, 178
Whistle-tip urinary catheter, 458
White blood cell (WBC) count, 439
  in infection, 67
Whooping cough (Pertussis), 68
Withdrawal
  from alcohol, 307–308
  from nonalcoholic substances,
    310–311
Women's health medications, 542, 552

Wounds
  infected, as postoperative
    complication, 438
  postoperative care of, 437

## X

Xanax (alprazolam), 474
Xanthines, 522
X-rays
  abdominal, 444
  chest, 442
Xylocaine, as local anesthesia, 435

## Y

Young adulthood
  food pyramid RDIs in, 238
  growth and development in, 103
  immunization schedules in, 166,
    167–168
  potential nursing diagnoses in,
    103

## Z

Zestril (lisinopril), 503
Zoster vaccine, 166